# THE PRESENT

# STATE

## OF THE

## Ottoman Empire.

Containing the MAXIMS of the

## TURKISH POLITIE,

The moſt material Points of the

## MAHOMETAN RELIGION,

Their SECTS and HERESIES, their CONVENTS and
RELIGIOUS VOTARIES.

### THEIR

## MILITARY DISCIPLINE,

With an exact Computation of their

## FORCES both by LAND and SEA.

Illuſtrated with divers Pieces of Sculpture, repreſenting the variety of
Habits amongſt the *Turks*.

---

## IN THREE BOOKS.

By *PAUL RYCAUT* Eſq;

Secretary to his Excellency the Earl of *Winchilſea*, Embaſſador Extraordinary for his Majeſty *Charles* the Second, *&c.* to *Sultan Mahomet
Han* the Fourth, Emperour of the *Turks*.

---

*LONDON*,

Printed for *John Starkey* and *Henry Brome*, at the *Mitre* between the
*Middle-Temple-Gate* and *Temple-Bar* in *Fleet-ſtreet*, and the
*Star* in *Little-Britain*. 1668.

MEDIEVAL AND RENAISSANCE
TEXTS AND STUDIES

VOLUME 500

SIR PAUL RYCAUT

# The Present State of the Ottoman Empire

*Sixth Edition, 1686*

*Edited with an Introduction by*

John Anthony Butler

ARIZONA CENTER FOR MEDIEVAL

ACMRS

AND RENAISSANCE STUDIES

Tempe, Arizona
2017

Published by ACMRS (Arizona Center for Medieval and Renaissance Studies)
Tempe, Arizona
© 2017 Arizona Board of Regents for Arizona State University.
All Rights Reserved.


**Library of Congress Cataloging-in-Publication Data**

*This publication has been submitted to the Library of Congress for cataloging.*
*The catalog record was not available at the time of printing.*

∞
This book is made to last. It is set in Adobe Caslon Pro,
smyth-sewn and printed on acid-free paper to library specifications.
*Printed in the United States of America*

*This book is dedicated to Michael and Eileen (Sue) Hoskins
in gratitude for those wonderful times in
Salisbury, Stonehenge, and Old Sarum,
and to the memory of the Hon. Helen and Professor Frank Goldby,
my surrogate grandparents.*

# TABLE OF CONTENTS

# *Introduction*
# THE LIFE AND TIMES OF SIR PAUL RYCAUT

## Early Life and Careeer

Paul Ricaut,[1] whose name in Dutch means "rich wood," was born in 1628 or 1629,[2] the tenth and youngest son of a family of thirteen children[3] which had originated in the Spanish Netherlands. His grandfather Andreas was a nobleman from the Duchy of Brabant, now part of Belgium. His father, Peter Ricaut, was a Huguenot merchant and banker born in Antwerp around 1578, who had been in England since 1600. His mother was Mary, the daughter of Rogier van der Colge (sometimes rendered as "Vercolge" or even "Vercolcia"), a merchant

---

[1] Anderson notes that the name is pronounced "Rye-court," and that it was spelled "Ricaut" until 1667 (Sonia P. Anderson, *An English Consul, in Turkey: Paul Ricaut at Smyrna 1667–78* [Oxford: Oxford University Press, 1989], 19). However, there is a Court of Chancery document concerning Rycaut's personal estate which calls him "Sir Paul Richaut (alias Sir Paul Rycaut)," which may indicate how his name was pronounced by some people in 1708 (PRO C6/3541/63). Linda Darling states that "We [Americans] say *Ree-co*, but Rycaut apparently pronounced his name *Rye-coat*" (Linda Darling, "Ottoman Politics through British Eyes," *Journal of World History* [1994]: 71). The spelling "Ricaut" will be used until the biographical account reaches the year 1667. Much of the information on the Ricaut family here presented is taken from Sonia P. Anderson, "Sir Paul Rycaut, F. R. S. (1629–1700): his Family and Writings," *Huguenot Society Proceedings* 21, 5 (1970): 464–491. My thanks to the Huguenot Society for supplying me with a copy.

[2] Ricaut's date of birth is disputed. The *Dictionary of National Biography* gives it as "autumn, 1628" (Vol. 50, 39), whilst Anderson gives "between 17ᵗʰ November and 23 December 1629." We know that Paul was baptised on 23 December, 1629. Thomas Wright and James Rose, for example, state that "the date of his birth is not known" (*A New General Biographical Dictionary* [Oxford: Oxford University Press, 1857], 11, 67).

[3] For Paul's sister Mary, see below; an unmarried sister, Petra, is recorded as having been buried in the Allington parish church on 8 October, 1654 (Charles Henry Fielding, *Memories of Malling and its Valley* [West Malling, UK, 1893]. http://www.ebooksread. com. 10). However, she is not mentioned in Sonia Anderson's article on Rycaut's family, and may be from a different part of the family. Siblings were Peter (b. and d. 1611), Sara (1634–1635), Mary (1612–1683), Peter (1615–1685), Andrew (b. 1617), John (b. 1619/20), James (1621–1695), Samuel (b. 1623/24), Philip (b. 1626), Thomas (1628–1690) and Anne (1632–1665).

from Courtrai or Kortrijk in West Flanders, who had lived in London since the 1570s, and his wife Anna van Asse or Aase. Rogier van der Colge died in 1597. Peter's mother, Emerantia Garcia Gonzalez or Gonsala, had been Spanish, which may account for some modern historians believing that his "sympathies lay with the Spanish."[4] By 1633 Peter Ricaut was making a great deal of money through the handling of government loans and contracts with clients who included the kings of England and Spain, and in that year he purchased the old Carmelite priory at Aylesford in Kent. Known as The Friars, this beautiful thirteenth-century building in which Paul Ricaut was born had passed, on Henry VIII's dissolution of the monasteries, to Sir Thomas Wyatt of Allington (1503–1542), the poet. By the 1590s The Friars, having gone through the hands of several owners, had come into the possession of Sir William Sedley of Aylesford, Bt. (1558–1618), from whose son Sir John (1597–1638) Peter Ricaut bought it in 1633.[5] It would become the main home of the Ricaut family for nearly twenty-five years. Soon afterwards Peter Ricaut bought another old estate, Owley Manor (also known as Owley House) in Wittersham, Kent, which had been in existence since the fourteenth century and could also boast a Wyatt connection. Situated on the Isle of Oxney, now part of Romney Marsh, it had once been owned by Sir Thomas Wyatt "the Younger" (1521–1554), the poet's unfortunate son, who in 1554 had raised a failed rebellion against Mary I and as a result lost both his head and property.

In 1641 Peter Ricaut was knighted by Charles I for his generous services to the crown, although some questions have been asked about the nature of those services, and there is evidence that some of Sir Peter's business ventures were less than completely above board. In the 1620s and 1630s, for example, he had acted as a "broker and leaser for ships on behalf of Genoese principals and their intermediaries," and had been instrumental in finding ways to get around naval blockades and a Parliamentary ban on English ships carrying contraband grain in the Levant.[6] His social success seemed assured, however, when his eldest son

---

[4] Toby Osborne, *Dynasty and Diplomacy in the Court of Savoy: Political Culture and the Thirty Years War* (Cambridge: Cambridge University Press, 2002), 211. For example, Peter Ricaut also remitted 10,000 crowns in that year (1633) to the rather shady Piedmontese diplomat Cesare Alessandro Scaglia (Osborne, *Dynasty and Diplomacy* 211), employed by the Duke of Savoy, but who was also working for Philip IV until about 1636.

[5] William Sedley was created the first baronet by James I in 1611. Perhaps the best-known member of this family was the wit, poet, translator, dramatist and MP Sir Charles Sedley (1639–1701), the fifth baronet. It is curious how the homes of the Ricaut family both have literary associations.

[6] For further details, see A. Hamilton, A. H. de Groot, A. H, M. van den Boogert, eds., *Friends and Rivals in the East: Studies in Anglo-Dutch Relations from the Seventeenth to Nineteenth Centuries.*( Leiden: Brill, 2000), esp. 47–53, and Anderson, Sonia P., "Sir Paul Rycaut," 463–64.

Peter married Barbara, daughter of Sir Thomas Smythe (1599–1635), first viscount Strangford of Ostenhanger or Westenhanger in the Irish peerage,[7] and his eldest daughter Mary married a baronet, Sir John Mayney[8] of Linton in Kent. A year or two earlier Peter had sat for a portrait by Vandyke,[9] and now it looked as if the family had truly arrived. Unfortunately the Civil War intervened, and when his eldest son Peter signed the Kentish Petition (1642), a strong statement of support for the prerogatives of the king, the elder Ricaut found himself under arrest as well and his estate confiscated by order of Parliament. The Friars then became the headquarters of the Parliamentary Committee for Kent. Sir Peter, after his release from the Tower of London, found himself summoned to attend this Committee on more than one occasion, and was fined one-twentieth of his income.

Together with some of his family, the harried Sir Peter left for the Continent, and until 1647 he remained there, after which he returned to England and compounded for his estate. It was restored to him minus his library, but that, too, was formally impounded in 1650, after which Sir Peter was accused by the Parliamentary government of treasonous correspondence with Royalist agents.

---

[7] The Smythes, who had a predilection for the name Thomas, can be a confusing family. Ostenhanger, now known as Westenhanger, is not in Ireland but in south-eastern Kent near Ashford. The castle of that name there was actually owned by another branch of the Smythe family, having been purchased by Thomas "Customer" Smythe (c. 1522–1591), the famous collector of customs revenues for London and father of Sir Thomas Smythe (c. 1558–1625), the first Governor of the East India Company. The viscountcy of Strangford, which is in county Down, Ireland, was bestowed on the other Sir Thomas Smythe in 1628; he had married Barbara, daughter of Sir Robert Sidney, earl of Leicester (1563–1626), brother of the poet Sir Philip Sidney, and it was their daughter whom Peter Ricaut married.

[8] Sir John Mayney or Maney (c. 1608–1676), a scion of an old Kentish family, was created a baronet by Charles I in 1641. He was an ardent Royalist and served the king loyally throughout the Civil War, and in fact ended up, like Sir Peter Ricaut, completely ruined financially and dependent on family for his sustenance. It was Sir John who sold Owley Manor in Wittersham to Sir Peter. The family's condition was so bad that they never recovered from it, and Sir John's son Sir Anthony Mayney, whom Burke calls an "unfortunate gentleman," a dissolute spendthrift whom Rycaut was constantly helping with money, died of starvation in 1706 after frittering away his inheritance from his uncle. Burke states that he "died of actual want, his brother, broken down by indigence, having previously, in 1694, committed suicide" (Sir John Burke, *A Genealogical and Heraldic History of the Extinct and Dormant Baronetcies of England* [London: Scott Webster and Geary, 1838], 349). The Linton baronetcy became extinct after Sir Anthony's death.

[9] There is a painting of "Sir Peter Ricaut standing on a Terrace" (*Courtauld List* 1982, 227) in Kedleston Hall, Derbyshire, later the seat of the Curzon family, although it is not listed as being by Vandyck (Christopher Wright, *British and Irish Paintings in Public Collections* [New Haven: Yale University Press, 2006], 314).

When he died on 22 February 1653, he was effectively ruined.[10] As Sonia Anderson notes, "Sir Peter's principal legacy to his sons consisted of bad debts owing to him which Parliament had been unable to reach" ("Sir Paul Rycaut," 468). In spite of the efforts of Paul Ricaut, his brother Peter and his mother to raise money to pay the debts incurred by Sir Peter, Lady Mary was finally obliged to sell The Friars to Sir John Banks,[11] a wealthy naval contractor and merchant, in 1657. The transaction, which took over a year to complete, proved somewhat troublesome, and Paul had to make peace between Banks and Peter Ricaut, a man whom Anderson describes as "quarrelsome" (*English Consul,* 24). He was, perhaps, simply more reluctant than Paul or his mother to part with the family estate. In a strange twist of fate, the priory ended up going back to the Carmelites in 1949; now restored, it can be appreciated for the fine building it is, and one can see why the Ricauts seem to have been so attached to it.

In spite of the adversity of his family and resultant setbacks, young Paul finished school[12] and began to attend Trinity College, Cambridge, at which he matriculated in 1646.[13] In 1647 he was elected to a scholarship and received his BA in 1650, after which, as so many young men of his class did, he proceeded to study the law at Gray's Inn (1651–1652). Along with the other Inns of Court, Gray's was not so much a training-ground for budding lawyers but a finishing-school for aspiring young gentlemen like Paul Ricaut, and he never did become a lawyer. However, his father's mounting debts resulted in Paul being sent to Spain, together with his elder brother Peter, to collect a debt owing to Sir Peter from count Gondomar, Spain's former ambassador to England (1613–1622), who had, together with other Spanish grandees, borrowed several large sums of money from Sir Peter Ricaut in 1621 in order to buy weapons to equip a ship. However,

---

[10] Sir Peter Ricaut was formally declared "ruined" in March 1649 (*Calendar of Proceedings of Committee for Advance of Money* 134, cited in *DNB* 50, 41).

[11] Sir John Banks (1627–1699) was a merchant who had made his fortune in Eastern and African trade. Created a baronet by Charles II, he went on to become Governor of the East India Company (1673–1674) and was five times an MP. In 1668 he was elected a member of the Royal Society.

[12] One of his schoolmates was the future Sir Peter Wyche (1628–c. 1699), whose father, another Sir Peter Wyche (1593–1643) had been ambassador to the Ottoman Empire from 1627 to 1641. The elder Wyche had provided lodgings in Constantinople for the oriental scholar Edward Pococke, several times cited by Ricaut in his book. Pococke served as a temporary chaplain in the English embassy. The younger Wyche was ambassador to Russia and Poland (1669–1670) and became a Fellow of the Royal Society in 1663.

[13] There is no entry, however, for a Paul Ricaut or Rycaut in the *Alumni Cantabrigienses*; instead, the Venns seem to have misread the name (or it was simply misprinted), which is rendered as "Ricant or Rycant" (J. Venn and J. A. Venn, *Alumni Cantabrigienses* [Cambridge: Cambridge University Press, 1922–53], Volume 3, 503). Paul's brothers Samuel and Thomas also attended Trinity College; the former graduated MA in 1641, and the latter was listed as a pensioner in 1646.

"an attempt to impound Gondomar's securities in Spain," Anderson tells us, "was frustrated by Philip IV" and other measures taken to collect this debt also failed ("Sir Paul Rycaut," 468). The king later changed his mind and attempted to assist in the collection of this and other Spanish debts, but no one paid any attention; apparently Philip could hinder the payment of a debt but was powerless to enforce its payment, and Sir Peter had to chalk up the loss to experience.

Paul took the opportunity of being in Spain to enrol at the University of Alcalá de Henares, otherwise known as the College of San Ildefonso, founded in 1499 by Cardinal Francisco Ximénes de Cisneros, the religious reformer and Regent of Spain. The university is a few kilometres northeast of Madrid and is still, as it was in Ricaut's time, well-known for its specialisation in Spanish literature. One wonders whether the young Englishman had to subject himself to the *gran nevada* (big snowfall), a rather interesting, if unsanitary, hazing ordeal reserved for new students. It involved the student proceeding, dressed in a black gown, to an open area known as the "Patio of Philosophers," where he would be welcomed by a mob of older students who would then spit on him until the robe turned white! Here Ricaut learned enough Spanish to translate Part 1 of Baltasar Gracián's *El Criticón* (1651), apparently as an exercise.[14] It is a lengthy novel about Critilo, a shipwrecked man of a philosophical bent who meets a "natural man" on an island (shades of *The Tempest*) and develops a pessimistic and ironic outlook on life as they converse and compare world views before embarking together on a voyage to the Isle of Immortality. Ricaut duly followed this up with translations of parts 2 and 3 (1653–1657).[15] He would later return to his love of Spanish writing, this time translating Garcilaso de la Vega's *Royal Commentaries of Peru in two Parts* (1688).[16] This book was a pioneering work of pre-Hispanic

---

[14] See María Antonia Garcés, "The Translator Translated: Inca Garcilaso and English Imperial Expansion," in *Travel and Translation in the Early Modern Period*, ed. Carmine di Biase (Amsterdam: Rodopi, 2006), 203–29, esp. 214ff.

[15] Baltasar Gracián y Morales (1601–1658), a Jesuit, was a leading exponent of the *conceptismo* style of writing, which emphasized simple vocabulary and directness but combined it with wit, metaphor, and word play, somewhat like English "metaphysical" poetry. His other works included *Wit and the Art of Inventiveness* (1648), which was a treatise on aesthetics and literature, *The Art of Worldly Wisdom* (1647; tr. Joseph Jacobs [London: Macmillan, 1904]) and *El discreto* (1646), a book on manners and the art of being a gentleman. Gracián was prone to getting into trouble with his superiors; he once preached a sermon in which he included a "letter" sent from hell by the devil himself. The full text of Rycaut's translation of *El Criticón* may be read online at http://www.erbzine. com/mag18/critick.htm. The translation was not published until 1681, after Rycaut rediscovered it when clearing out some old papers.

[16] Garcilaso de la Vega (1539–1616), also known as Gomez Suarez de Figueroa, the Spanish *mestizo* historian, was surnamed El Inca, so as not to be confused with the poet of the same name (1501–1536); he was the son of a Spanish nobleman and an Inca mother who came from the royal family. For details, see Ian Campbell Ross, "Ottomans, Incas,

Inca history gathered from oral sources, including his own relatives by marriage, written by a man who had his foot in both camps. "Rycaut's text," María Antonia Garcés comments, "is far more readable today than any of its successors and the merits of his translation are beginning to be recognized once more" (Di Biase, *Travel and Translation*, 219).

Whilst Paul was in Spain pursuing his literary and scholarly interests, Oliver Cromwell, now Lord Protector of England, suddenly became very helpful to the Ricaut family by intervening in 1654 with an attempt to collect Gondomar's debt from the current Spanish ambassador to England, Alonso de Cárdenas, who had succeeded Gondomar in 1638. Cromwell wrote a personal letter to Cárdenas, who had had a long relationship with Parliament,[17] on the family's behalf, and, incredibly enough, may also have given to the Ricauts letters of marque, a government licence which authorized them to become privateers. In his letter, Cromwell wrote that "all fit endeavours" had been "diligently used for attaining of satisfaction" of the debt, mentioning "two journeys made purposely in this behalf to the court of Spain, by the eldest son [Peter] of the said Sir Peter (at 1000 *l* sterling charge)." The Protector went on to note "the fruitlessness of our own mediation by our said letters," and demanded that "reprisal be granted to the said sons and executors against the king of Spain and his subjects for satisfaction of the said debt together with the damages and expenses sustained."[18] Unfortunately, war with Spain then broke out, and Paul, abandoning his intellectual pursuits in Spain, joined the navy, serving for a short time under Cromwell's most distinguished commander, Admiral Robert Blake. His one taste of action (he watched rather than participated) came when his brother Philip,[19] who had been captain

---

and Irish Literature: Reading Rycaut," *Eighteenth Century Ireland* 22 (2007): 11–27. The book, usually known as the *Royal Commentaries of the Incas and General History of Peru*, is available in a modern translation by Harold Livermore (Austin: University of Texas Press, 1987), with which Garcés, comparing it to Rycaut's, is not impressed (Di Biase, *Travel and Translation*, 219).

[17] For details, see A. J. Loomie, "Alonso de Cárdenas and the Long Parliament 1640–1648," *English Historical Review* (1982): 289–307.

[18] Thomas Birch, ed., *A Collection of the State Papers of John Thurloe, Esq., Secretary First to the Council of State, and afterwards to the Two Protectors, Oliver and Richard Cromwell* (London: Printed for the Executor of F. Gyles, 1742), 3, 75. The *DNB* entry for Ricaut (50, 39) mistakenly says that the family did not receive any help from Cromwell. Sonia Anderson not only thinks otherwise but adds the privateering story as well, and Cromwell's letter seems quite unequivocal (*English Consul*, 24). Did Ricaut join Blake's expedition against the Tunisians just to help his brother, or were there further family motives? In any case, Anderson notes that "at least one of the Protector's letters to Cardenas was drafted by Paul Rycaut" ("Paul Rycaut," 470 and n. 24), which certainly suggests that Ricaut was well-acquainted with Cromwell.

[19] Philip Ricaut is probably the person of that name who was assaulted by Philip Herbert, seventh Earl of Pembroke (1652–1683), in 1678. "Without any provocation,"

of a merchant ship carrying a cargo of currants, found his ship captured by Tunisians, or, more accurately, taken over by Barbary pirates, whose actions had apparently been condoned by the Bey of Tunis, Hamuda Pasha. Blake was sent (1654) to retaliate by attacking Tunisian ships and bombarding Ghar al-Milh, then known by its Portuguese name of Porto Farina; he completely destroyed the heavily fortified town and burnt nine Tunisian ships, but after a few years the Tunisians rebuilt the place and it once again became a pirate haven, Maltese and even English pirates now joining the local gangs based there.

## Diplomatic Apprenticeship

Paul Ricaut's sympathies, in spite of his seemingly good relationship with the Protector, nonetheless always remained firmly royalist, and he appears to have met secretly (1658) with the exiled Charles II in Antwerp (Anderson, *English Consul*, 24). In the same year he was appointed private secretary to Sir Heneage Finch, earl of Winchilsea (1628–1689). Winchilsea became Charles II's first ambassador to the Ottoman Empire in 1660, and had been recommended by the king himself for the post to the Levant Company. The Company had been trading in the area since its inception under Elizabeth I in 1580 and was responsible for providing English ambassadors to the Ottoman Empire; from the outset the purpose of English-Ottoman contact had been trade and nothing else. In its structure the Levant Company hierarchy consisted of a governor and sub-governor based in London and responsible to the king himself, then a board of twelve directors, also in London. On the spot were the three consuls, each with a vice-consul, in charge of factories at Istanbul, Aleppo (the headquarters), and Smyrna, and under them came a small army of secretaries, factors, treasurers, agents and interpreters. Charles II was seeking to increase the Levant Company's influence, to which end, upon his accession, he granted it a renewed royal charter, allowing it to make its own laws and even further expand the possibilities for trade with the Ottoman Empire. These new powers gave the Company additional influence at the Sultan's court; it could now, for example, have its members

---

the earl "struck the said Philip Ricaut such a blow upon the eye as almost knocked him down, and then fell upon him with such violence that he almost stifled him with his gripe in the dust, and likewise his lordship drew his sword, and was in danger of killing him, had he not slipt into the house and the door being shut upon him." Pembroke, a notorious brawler, murderer (of at least two people) and drunkard who was later imprisoned in the Tower and convicted of murder (he was promptly pardoned by Charles II), had to pay Ricaut £2000 and was bound over to keep the peace for a year (George L. Craik, ed., *English Causes Célèbres or, Reports of Remarkable Trials* [London: Charles Knight, 1880], 1, 227–29). A more complete account of Pembroke's trial may also be found in Sir John Bernard Burke, ed., *The Patrician* (London: E. Churton, 1848), 5, 151ff.

elect the English consuls at Smyrna and Constantinople. The Levant Company was finally disbanded in 1823.

Winchilsea also took with him a secretary who could act as chancellor or "cancellier," a kind of senior accountant of the factory in Constantinople, and also deputise for the ambassador when the occasion arose, duties which called for a higher-level employee than a mere private secretary. The first candidate for the position, which Ricaut also applied for, had been Robert Bargrave,[20] an experienced traveller and cousin to Sir Edward Dering,[21] another Kentishman who had earlier recommended Ricaut for the junior post. The senior job went, in the end, to Bargrave. However, there is little doubt that Ricaut and his family, in spite of their various adversities, had friends in the right places who did not forget them, and the interconnections between all these people would make for some interesting reading in a full biography of Ricaut.

Winchilsea turned out to be a man of character and ability, although Francesco Giavarina, the Venetian ambassador to Charles II's court, reported in 1660 that he was "a young man full of idle talk, informed about many things but not very steady."[22] In the same year, apparently due to his friendship with the former Parliamentary general George Monck, who had been instrumental in engineering the restoration of Charles II, he was appointed simultaneously Governor of Dover Castle, Lord Warden of the Cinque Ports, and Lord Lieutenant of Kent. Winchilsea married four times and fathered at least fifteen children; whilst in Turkey he was said to have "had many women," for whom "he built little houses," and when he returned from the ambassadorship, Charles II said to him jokingly "My Lord, you have not only built a town, but peopled it, too." The earl wittily replied "Oh, Sir, I was your representative." In any case, Winchilsea, the first nobleman to hold the post, in the end proved an excellent choice for ambassador. As Wood puts it, "his flippant exterior concealed both the ambition and the ability to exploit the opportunities thus presented" (*Levant Company,*

---

[20]  Robert Bargrave (1628–1661), son of John Bargrave, Dean of Canterbury, was a merchant who worked for the Levant Company. He travelled extensively in Europe, visiting Spain, Italy, Germany and the court of Queen Elizabeth of Bohemia in Heidelberg, where he met many English exiles. He also travelled to Turkey, and made a long journey home through Bulgaria and other countries of Eastern Europe. His *Travel Diary* has been edited by Michael G. Brennan (London: Hakluyt Society, 1999).

[21]  Sir Edward Dering, second baronet (1623–1684) was the MP for Lismore in Ireland (1662), East Retford (1678) and Hythe (1679, 1681). He served as Commissioner of the Treasury from 1679 to 1684. His *Parliamentary Diary 1670–73* has been edited by Maurice Bond (New Haven: Yale University Press, 1940). His wife Mary was a composer.

[22]  *Calendar of State Papers, Venetian Series 1639–1661*, 168, cited in Alfred C. Wood, *History of the Levant Company* (Abingdon, UK: Frank Cass [1935], 1964), 96.

96), although Roger North[23] rather cattily commented that because Winchilsea had "a goodly person and mustachios, with a world full of talk and that all (as his way was) of mighty wonders" (*Lives* III, 37, cited in Wood, *Levant Company*, 96), he was able to secure the friendship of Grand Vizier, Fazil Ahmet Köprülü. And North was correct—Winchilsea did have an interest in "mighty wonders;" in 1669, for example, on a visit to the Sicilian port of Catania on his way back from Constantinople, he witnessed a spectacular eruption of Mount Aetna that moved him to venture into print, writing a short but vivid account of the disaster which was erroneously said to have killed twenty-seven thousand people.[24] Winchilsea, whilst he might have been a polished courtier, womaniser and raconteur, was also, it turned out, a good judge of character and a man who appreciated able subordinates, as his treatment of Paul Ricaut demonstrates. In other words, he was very much like the king who employed him. Samuel Pepys remarked in 1669 that Winchilsea was a man who could speak with "admirable eloquence" whilst pleading a cause he sincerely believed in.[25]

Once he took up his position, Ricaut seems to have decided that he would record his experiences and "set down in a blank book," as he tells in the address to the reader in his *History of the Turkish Empire 1623–1677*, "what occurred in that Empire either as to civil or military affairs, with what casualties and changes befell our trade." His purpose for writing that book, he went on rather sententiously, although, as it turned out, quite presciently, was that it "might serve for examples and precedents to future ages." Accordingly, on 20 December 1660 he embarked

---

[23] Roger North (1651–1734), son of the politician Dudley, fourth baron North, trained as a lawyer, but his interests and fame as a writer lay elsewhere. He was an expert in the theory of music, a bibliophile, and biographer. His *Lives of the Norths* was published shortly after his death with an autobiography, and his treatise *The Musical Grammarian* (1728) is available in a modern edition. North's *Lives* has been republished by Kessinger Reprints (2007) from Augustus Jessop's Bohn Standard Library edition of 1890. North's brother, another Sir Dudley (1641–1691), was a successful merchant, pioneer economist and former treasurer of the Levant Company in Constantinople who wrote the *Discourses upon Trade* (1691), which was published anonymously.

[24] Contemporary reports do not support this claim; many villages were destroyed and Catania was covered with lava, but apparently, there were few, if any, human casualties. Winchilsea related that "all the elements seemed at this time to make war upon us, and to conspire together for the punishment of the inhabitants," and he described the cataclysm in great detail, not forgetting to include an account of looting, "the land everywhere infested with thieves." He concluded that "the dreadful inundation from Monte Gibello. . .destroyed many castles and towns, with an infinite loss and utter ruin to the inhabitants" (Earl of Winchilsea, *A True and Exact Relation of the Late Prodigious Earthquake and Eruption of Mount Aetna or Monte Gibello; As it came in a Letter Written to His Majesty from Naples* [London, 1669], n. p. n.).

[25] Samuel Pepys, *Diary*, 21 April, 1669. http://www.pepysdiary.com/encyclopedia/766, n.p.n.

with two ships belonging to the Levant Company and a pinnace lent to the expedition by the king's brother James, duke of York (the future James II), who was then Lord High Admiral. One of these, a warship supplied by Charles II and named *Plymouth*, ran into problems with one of its masts, and they had to stop at Lisbon until the damage was repaired, after which they proceeded to Algiers, where they entered into some fruitless negotiations with the Ottoman *dey*, [26] Ismail Pasha, about ending the forced searches of foreign ships and the removal of foreign passengers and goods by the authorities. The ships sailed on to Smyrna (modern day Izmir), from which they departed on 6 January; leaving behind the seriously-ill Bargrave, who died shortly thereafter. It was at this point that Ricaut was elevated to the senior position, endorsed by Winchilsea himself.

It may be useful to give some idea of what Constantinople and the Ottoman court were like when Ricaut took up residence, as there must have been considerable culture shock when he and Winchilsea first arrived in the "city of the world's desire," so different from and much larger even than cosmopolitan London must have been in 1660. Modern readers of the accounts of European diplomats and travellers surely wonder at how well people like Ricaut coped with what must have seemed such an alien environment, possibly one fraught with unlooked-for dangers, governed in a radically different way, dominated by a non-Christian religion, and full of the pitfalls involved in dealing with completely strange customs and mores.

As Winchilsea and Ricaut entered the city, there would have been many sights which caught their eye and evoked wonder in them. The New Imperial Palace, better-known as the Topkapi, was the Sultan's principal residence; it had been built by Mehmet II between 1459 and 1478, and takes its name from the Turkish words for "cannon gate." [27] It contained the private apartments of the Sultan and many government offices, including the Imperial Divan with its gold-encrusted walls, which was where officials and ambassadors met with the Grand Vizier. At one time the Sultan had also sat there in person, but by Ricaut's time he was concealed behind a curtain, so that those in the room often did not know whether he was listening to them or not. There was also a throne-room, built in the European style by Süleyman the Magnificent; Philip Mansel cites a seventeenth-century palace inventory indicating that the throne was "decorated with five cushions, six 'skirts' and fifteen bolsters, sewn with emeralds, rubies

---

[26] Dey was the title given to the Ottoman governors of Tripoli, Tunis and Algiers. The dey was appointed for life by prominent citizens from the religious, military and merchant communities. Deys, who were pretty much autonomous, were often paid protection money by Barbary pirates, which is what sometimes made negotiating with them a rather difficult proposition. The title is not to be confused with *beys*, who were under the command of the dey.

[27] Philip Mansel, *Constantinople: City of the World's Desire, 1453–1924* (London: John Murray, 1995), 57.

and pearls, and, like the mats on the floor, drenched in gold thread" (*Constantinople*, 63).

All this magnificence contributed to the remoteness and almost hieratic nature of the Sultan, which must have been a marked contrast for Ricaut to the rather informal court of Charles II. "In the Ottoman world view," Mansel states, "other monarchs owed their crowns. . .to their overlord the Sultan. Only he was Emperor" (*Constantinople*, 62). Everything within the palace reflected the absolute power of the Sultan, whose word meant life or death to every one of his subjects; even Louis XIV could only have dreamed of such power. People at the court dressed magnificently in different-coloured kaftans, and there was often music accompanying the various ceremonies of the court, music which Ricaut must, at first, have found strange and discordant. He would also have marvelled at the wonderful mosques: the Fatih mosque where Mehmet II "the Conqueror" was buried; the Süleymaniye, whose beauty lay in the "elegant spaces beneath its dome, in the opening-out of its side domes, in the proportion of its walls and empty spaces;"[28] the Sultan Ahmet; and the various imperial kiosks. Perhaps, as he gazed at Hagia Sofia, he wistfully recollected that this great Turkish city had been the capital of the Byzantine Empire and the mosque had once reflected the glory not of the conqueror Mehmet II but of Justinian. Rarely, if ever, did westerners refer to the city as "Istanbul," for to them it was always the lost city of Christendom, Constantinople.[29] Ricaut would have noticed the continual presence of the Janissaries in what must have seemed to him their outlandishly garish uniforms, and perhaps seen the Sultan passing in procession through the streets followed by all the officials of the Sultan's court in their different costumes, each observing correct order and decorum as they paraded along in stately dignity. The sound of an Ottoman military band marching through the streets must have seemed to him a mere cacophony. What he made of the muezzin's call or the whirling dervishes he does not say, and all the time the ordinary life of cosmopolitan Constantinople teemed around him with its alien sights, smells, and sounds. For a man as sanguine and even-keeled as Ricaut seemed to have been, the prospect of spending extended time in this environment must nevertheless have seemed rather daunting. It is regrettable that in the end he chose not to record his first impressions, and that he decided, when he came to write his book, that he would concentrate upon more practical matters.[30]

---

[28] Orhan Pamuk, *Istanbul: Memories and the City*, trans. Maureen Freely (New York: Vintage Books, 2006), 255.

[29] The name "Istanbul" is the usual form since the Turkish republic was established in 1924. In Ottoman times the usual form was "Constantiniyya" or "Dar-al-Saadat," which is translated as "Gate of Felicity," and which gave rise to the term "Sublime Porte" used by Europeans to refer to the city.

[30] It would be curious if Rycaut did not know of such works as Pierre Gilles's *De topographia Constantinopoleos et de illius antiquitatibus* (1562), which gave details and

Things appeared to go well for Winchilsea's embassy at first. On 26 February they were received in audience by Sultan Mehmet IV[31] and the venerable Grand Vizier Mehmet Köprülü, whom Evliya Celebi had described as "not like other Grand Viziers. . .he knows the ways of the world."[32] A supremely able and ruthless old man, Mehmet would soon pass from the scene (October 1661) and be succeeded by his equally competent son Fazil Ahmet, whom Winchilsea and Rycaut met at Adrianople in December 1661, and whose "prudence, firmness, wisdom and discretion" had made a great impression on foreigners, particularly on the Venetian ambassador (Mansel, *Constantinople*, 142). Winchilsea renewed the so-called "capitulations" with the Turks in 1662, which permitted English traders to live and work in the Ottoman Empire, and was also able, no doubt by flourishing his "mustachios" at the Grand Vizier, to negotiate a treaty with Algiers through the agency of Ahmet Köprülü, which gave the English, at least in theory, some protection against the depredations of the Algerians and their Ottoman masters. It was here, also, that Ricaut achieved a literary coup, namely the publication of the first English printed work in Turkey, the *Capitulations and Articles of Peace* (1661), which was produced in Constantinople by a prominent Jewish publisher, Abraham ben Jedediah Gabbai (Anderson, *English Consul*, 30).[33]

---

illustrations of many famous buildings in Constantinople, and would have appealed to Rycaut's antiquarian bent. Gilles, or Petrus Gyllius (1490–1555) was there from 1547 to 1551 as an agent for François I, who wanted to acquire ancient manuscripts. This work, which was not available in English until 1729, is available in a newly translated version by Kimberley Byrd (New York: Italica Press, 2009). There was also Melchior Lorck's posthumous *Wolgerissene und geschnittene Figuren* (1619); Lorck (1526-after 1583), a Danish artist, had accompanied Busbecq on his mission and produced an impressive book of drawings as well as a large panoramic view of the city. For details of both Gilles and Lorck, see Amanda Wunder, "Western Travelers and Eastern Antiquities," *Journal of Early Modern History* 7 (2010): 89–119.

[31] James Mather, drawing on various sources, describes the scene vividly; there was Ricaut bringing up the rear of the ambassador's delegation, "clutching the ambassador's letters of credential made up in a purse of cloth of gold," and the ambassador himself, escorted by "two Chief Porters of the Gate carrying long silver staves," who "took Winchilsea under each arm and carried him forward" to the silent Sultan, who sat motionless on his throne and never addressed a single world to the foreigners during the entire audience (*Pashas, Traders and Travellers in the Islamic World* [New Haven: Yale University Press, 2011], 133).

[32] Robert Dankoff, ed., *The Intimate Life of an Ottoman Statesman: Melek Ahmed Pasha, as Portrayed in Evliya Celebi's Book of Travels* (Albany: SUNY Press, 1991), 204.

[33] This short (twenty-eight pages) work is now available in a modern reprint (New York: Kessinger Reprints, 2010). Abraham ben Jedediah Gabbai was originally from Leghorn (Livorno), where his father, Jedediah ben Isaac (d. 1671) had run a printing establishment since 1650. The family set up in Florence and then went to Smyrna, where Abraham, sent there by his father, directed the business from 1659 to 1680, after which he moved to Salonika. For further details on the Gabbais see, for example, Marvin J.

Ricaut also began to learn Turkish at this time, which enabled him to assume some of the duties of the head dragoman, Georgio Draperio or de Draperiis,[34] one of which was that of interpreter.

Winchilsea then appointed Ricaut to be his steward in the place of Richard Knevett or Knyvett, whom he had sent home with the dispatches of the treaties, and the two men developed a relationship that went, at least on the earl's part, beyond mere professional courtesy. "I have found him so modest, discreet, able, temperate and faithful to me in all I have entrusted him," Winchilsea wrote on 11 January 1662/3 to his cousin Sir Heneage Finch (later earl of Nottingham) "that I have removed him from my steward's table to my own, and use him more like a friend than a servant." He added, tellingly, "and yet I find his temper, modesty and carriage towards me the same as when he stood at a more remote distance" (Finch MSS, *Letter Book 2*, 329; cited in Anderson, *English Consul*, 32–33). Ricaut, it appears, knew his place and was content to stay in it rather than take advantage of Winchilsea's friendship; this modesty was a characteristic that would stand him in good stead throughout his life. In 1665 Ricaut was joined in Constantinople by his nephew James, for whom he had secured a position, presumably with Winchilsea's help, as acting "canceller."[35]

Ricaut did not spend all his time with Winchilsea in Constantinople. In 1663 he was sent on a fact-finding mission to what was then known as the Barbary States, comprising Tunisia, Tripolitania, Algeria, and Morocco. These regions, a hotbed of pirates and marauders of various sorts, sometimes aided and abetted, as we have seen, by local or Ottoman authorities, were a constant thorn

---

Heller, "Jedediah ben Isaac Gabbai and the First Decade of Hebrew Printing in Livorno," http://www.sefarad.org/publication. The Gabbais remained in Turkey, where they later became one of the three wealthiest Jewish banking families in Istanbul, which led to the execution of the head of their family in 1827 (Finkel, *Osman's Dream*, 438).

[34] In the end, in addition to Spanish, Ricaut "understood perfectly the Greek both ancient and modern, the Turkish, Latin, Italian and French languages" (*Biographica Britannica* [London, printed for W. Innys, 1760], 5, 3501). Draperio, from a Genoese family which had for centuries traded in the Ottoman Empire, was apparently unreliable in his duties (Anderson, *English Consul*, 31). A man of this name was also prior of the community in Pera, but whether they are one and the same the editor is unsure.

[35] James Ricaut (1643–1705) served in Constantinople until 1667 and subsequently (see below) joined his uncle in Smyrna. In 1695 he was appointed cancellier by the Levant Company. He was the son of Ricaut's brother James (1621–1695). For details, see David Wilson, *List of British Consular Officials in the Ottoman Empire and its Territories from the Sixteenth Century to about 1860*. http://www.levantineheritage.com, 8–9. James seems to have been a reasonably good chancellor, but his private life was rather different; he was, in 1676, "found in a Polish widow's house in a compromising situation with two Turkish women (a capital offence), and had to be smuggled away to Constantinople" (Anderson, *English Consul*, 99). James also borrowed a lot of money from people which he did not pay back, but his uncle still watched out for his interests and lent James a considerable sum.

in the side of European shipping. Piracy sometimes escalated into real war, particularly from the 1630s onwards, and treaties were continuously being made and broken. In 1675, for example, Sir John Narborough[36] managed to negotiate a peace with the dey of Tripoli, Ibrahim Misrli-oglu, through what would later be termed "gunboat diplomacy," but there was no lasting result until 1682, when most of the Barbary States had either been defeated in battle or signed treaties. Two years later, Rycaut was in Hungary on diplomatic business, and then back to England, where Charles II presented him with a service medal. Afterwards he was sent on another mission, this time to the Balkans, and for some months in 1666 he was in England once again.

Using the material he had collected during his time in Constantinople with Winchilsea, Ricaut finished the first draft of the book which would bring him real fame as a writer, *The Present State of the Ottoman Empire, containing the Maxims of the Turkish Polity, the most material points of the Mahometan Religion, their Sects and Heresies, their Convents and Religious Votaries. Their Military Discipline, with an Exact Composition of their Forces both by Sea and Land.* When he returned to England in 1666 he engaged John Starkey and Henry Brome[37] as his publishers, and the book duly appeared in a folio edition the same December. However, because of the Great Fire of London earlier in September of that year, only a few copies were available, and they were expensive; when Samuel Pepys wanted to buy one, he complained "I did agree for Rycaut's late history of the Turkish Polity, which costs me 55s, whereas it was sold plain before the fire for 8s."[38] However, Pepys goes on to say that "I have bought it finely bound and truly coloured,

---

[36] Rear-Admiral Sir John Narborough (c. 1640–1688) had a distinguished career in the Dutch wars during the reign of Charles II. After serving in Tunisia and Algeria successfully combatting Barbary pirates, he was appointed Commissioner of the Royal Navy in 1680.

[37] John Starkey was a publisher and bookseller of republican leanings who numbered John Milton amongst his clients, as well as Richard Baxter, the Puritan divine, and John Harrington, author of *Oceana.* Starkey also published translations of Tasso and Corneille. As Laura Knoppers points out, Starkey also had an interest in books about the East, publishing Procopius's *Secret History* and other works similar to Rycaut's. In any case, the staunchly royalist Rycaut did not choose Starkey for the same reasons as Milton had. For details see Laura L. Knoppers, ed., *The Complete Works of John Milton.* Volume II: *The 1671 Poems, Paradise Regain'd and Samson Agonistes* (Oxford: Oxford University Press, 2008), xxiv–xlii or Mary Knights, "John Starkey and Ideological Networks in Late Seventeenth-Century England," *Media History* II (2005), 127–45. For Henry Brome, Starkey's colleague and younger brother of the royalist poet and dramatist Alexander Brome (1620–1666), see Nicholas von Maltzahn, "Henry Brome (d. 1681)," *ODNB* 7, 68–70. The 1686 edition was printed by Charles Brome (d. after 1711), Henry's son, who had succeeded his mother Joanna in the business after her death in 1684.

[38] It is interesting to note that Pepys uses the spelling "Rycaut" before Ricaut himself adopted it.

all the figures, of which there was but six books done so."[39] Pepys was a great fan of Rycaut's books; he went on "to acquire first editions of all Rycaut's subsequent publications" (Anderson, *English Consul,* 43). Because of the scarcity of this volume, of which only twenty-two copies survived the fire, this first edition is often forgotten, and many scholars assume that the 1668 edition, published when Ricaut was already out of the country again, is in fact the first (Anderson, *English Consul,* 43).

On December 12, 1666, Ricaut was elected a Fellow of the Royal Society on the strength of his book on the Ottoman Empire; this honour enabled him to meet, correspond and converse with some of the finest minds in the kingdom. Samuel Pepys had been admitted in 1665, but we do not know how well he and Ricaut were acquainted, although it is hard to imagine that they would not have met through the Society. What likely appealed to the latitudinarian Ricaut about membership was not so much the prestige gained by being able to write FRS after his name, but the whole concept of the founders that the Royal Society remain "opposed to the claims of party interest, whether political and religious," that it be free from "the limits set by provincialism and nationalism," and that it "sought the co-operation of Europe and the civilised world at large."[40] Amongst the fellows Ricaut certainly would have encountered, through the agency of Thomas Smith,[41] the Levant Company's chaplain in Constantinople, was the chemist Robert Boyle,[42] who had been a Fellow since the inception of the Royal Society in 1663. Boyle, who was a member of the Levant Company, was also friendly with

---

[39] Robert Latham, ed., *The Shorter Pepys* (Berkeley: University of California Press, 1985), 753.

[40] Margery Purver, *The Royal Society: Concept and Creation* (London: Routledge and Kegan Paul, 1967), 238.

[41] Thomas Smith (1630–1710) had come to Turkey in 1668 as chaplain to Sir Daniel Harvey, Winchilsea's successor in Constantinople, who died there in 1672. He was deeply interested in the controversies between the various branches of the Orthodox churches, and hoped that they would reconcile their differences. Smith would go on to become vice-president of Magdalen College, Oxford, a post from which he was dismissed by James II, but reinstated in 1689 after the Glorious Revolution. He resigned his position and became a retired scholar, having always had an antiquarian bent. His *Remarks upon the Manners, Religion and Government of the Turks, together with a Survey of the Seven Churches of Asia, as they now lye in their Ruines, and a brief Description of Constantinople* was published in 1678.

[42] The Hon. Robert Boyle (1627–1691), a son of the earl of Cork, was perhaps the most eminent English chemist, natural philosopher and inventor of his times. Boyle was elected to the Royal Society in 1663. He was also a keen theologian, although he was never ordained and seems to have felt that religious speculation was somehow more objective coming from a layman. Boyle was a director of the East India Company and fervently supported missionary work. He wrote *Some Considerations about the Reconcileableness of Reason and Religion* (1675) and many other works on religious subjects, including

the earl of Winchilsea's cousin Sir John Finch,[43] who himself would become English ambassador to the Ottoman court in 1672. Boyle, Smith and Ricaut were all interested in the history and workings of the Greek and Armenian Churches, an intellectual pastime which would lead to Ricaut's publishing *The Present State of the Greek and Armenian Churches, Anno Christi 1678* (1679).[44] The friendship with Boyle also led to Ricaut's volunteering his services, when he returned to Turkey in 1667, to answer some "inquiries for Turkey" and keep his eyes and ears open for any information which might prove useful to the government.[45]

## Rycaut in Smyrna[46]

In 1668, shortly after Winchilsea had left his post and had been succeeded by Sir Daniel Harvey, Paul Ricaut, whom we must now call Rycaut,[47] received his first diplomatic appointment in his own right when the Levant Company made him consul at Smyrna after the sudden death, in the previous year, of the incumbent,

---

atheism. His *Works* have been recently edited by M. Hunter and E. B. Davis (14 volumes; London: Pickering and Chatto, 1999–2000).

[43] Sir John Finch (1626–1682) was Winchilsea's nephew and cousin to Sir Daniel Harvey. He had an interesting career, studying philosophy under the Cambridge Platonist Henry More together with his half-sister Anne (later Duchess of Conway), herself a philosopher, whose *Principles of the Most Ancient and Modern Philosophy* was posthumously published in 1690. He then graduated from the University of Padua with a medical degree (1666), which he never put to use. Finch lectured at Christ's College, Cambridge, and became a Fellow of the Royal Society in 1663, along with his inseparable friend and fellow doctor Sir Thomas Baines (1622–1681), who would accompany him to Turkey and die there. Like Smith and Ricaut,.Finch was interested in theology, and his correspondence contains references to many conversations with Orthodox patriarchs. Finch returned to England with Baines's body, and died soon afterwards. For details, see Archibald Malloch, "Sir John Finch and Sir Thomas Baines," *History of Medicine* (March, 1916): 155–58.

[44] For details of Rycaut's relationship with Smith, see Hélène Pignot, "A Trip to the Origins of Christianity: Sir Paul Rycaut's and Thomas Smith's accounts of the Greek Church in the seventeenth century," *Studies in Travel Writing* 13 (2009): 193–205.

[45] The information here is taken from Charles G. D. Littleton, "Ancient Languages and New Science: the Levant in the Intellectual Life of Robert Boyle," in A. Hamilton, M. van der Boogert, Bart Westerweel, eds. *The Republic of Letters and the Levant* (Leiden: Brill, 2005), esp. 163–65.

[46] Much of the information given here may be found in Sonia P. Anderson, *An English Consul in Turkey*. This account is intended simply as an outline of Rycaut's life in Smyrna, and readers who want more are directed to Anderson's thoroughly researched and readable account.

[47] The spelling of Rycaut's name on the title pages of the various editions remains "Ricaut."

William Cave. Rycaut was lucky to be able to take this post, "the prize among [the Levant consulships],"[48] as he had been suffering from the plague, which is what probably had killed his predecessor, but he was hard at work a very short time after his recovery. It was a position Rycaut would occupy for the next eleven years. Cave's term of office had followed some instability and a fast turnover of the post. In 1660 Anthony Bokenham had left after less than a year in office, followed in very rapid succession by Richard Baker, who was "superseded and went into hiding," and two further incumbents, Anthony Isaacson and Samuel Taylor, neither of whom was confirmed in office. During the Civil War period, too, the Smyrna consulship had been unstable; the appointment of Spencer Bretton in 1649, for example, had been disputed by both royalists and Parliamentarians, and after a seven-year hiatus his successor was only an acting consul, Joseph Edwards, in 1658. In 1650, the Levant Company was noting the "sad factions and divisions among yourselves" in a letter to the consuls at Smyrna and Aleppo (*CSP Domestic Series* [1650], IX, 42). When a full-time consul was finally appointed in March 1659 during the protectorate of Richard Cromwell, it was in the person of an experienced diplomat named William Prideaux, a former envoy to Russia who had also been employed by the East India Company as ambassador to China. However, Prideaux died in office the next year (Wilson, *Consular Officials*, 14),[49] which at least made it easier for the restored government of Charles II to appoint a successor without dispute.

In 1668 the second edition of Rycaut's book on the Ottoman Empire was published, and the following year he was granted the sum of two thousand dollars for the two years he had already served. His nephew James, who had also been in Constantinople, joined Rycaut in Smyrna, again as a cancellier for the Levant Company, where he would remain until well after his uncle had departed. The English factory at Smyrna, which had boasted its own consul since 1611, was a successful and profitable venture for the Levant Company, and Rycaut appears to have thrived there. Thomas Smith described Smyrna as "one of the most flourishing cities of the lesser Asia, both for its great trade and the number of its inhabitants." Smyrna was also a place where Greek influence was still felt, the Greeks having inhabited the area from about the third millennium B.C.E. until 1330, when the city was taken by the beys of Aydin, rulers of Anatolia since 1307. After a short spell of occupation by Timur's forces in 1402, which temporarily displaced

---

[48] Geoff Berridge, *British Diplomacy in Turkey 1583 to the Present Day: A Study of the Evolution of the Resident Embassy* (Leiden: Martinus Nijhoff, 2009), 77.

[49] Anthony Bokenham (1616–1704) had served as Bendysh's secretary before becoming consul. He was a fellow of Pembroke College, Cambridge, and ended his long life as Rector of Helmingham. Spencer Bretton (d. 1659) had entertained Isaac Barrow in Smyrna, and when he died Barrow wrote a Latin elegy for him. For Bretton, see *CSP Domestic Series* (1650), IX, 42–43. For Prideaux, see Timothy Venning, "William Prideaux 1604/5–1660," *ODNB* Index No.101066273.

the beys, Smyrna was returned by Timur to the rulers of Aydin, who kept it as a semi-independent state until 1425, after which it came under direct Ottoman control. It remained, however, an international city; Smith tells us that its people included "Franks, Jews and Armenians as well as Greeks and Turks."[50] George Sandys had been less kind when he saw it some sixty years earlier, lamenting that Smyrna, once known for its churches, was now "violated by Mahometans, her beauty is turned to deformity, her knowledge into barbarism, her religion into impiety" (*Travels*, 12).

By Rycaut's time the English population of Smyrna had grown considerably; in 1635 they had asked for a chaplain to be sent out to them and in 1674, during Rycaut's term of office, we find two fellow travellers, the pioneering French archaeologist Jacques Spon (1647–1685), whose specialty was Greek monuments, and the English botanist, traveller, and antiquarian Sir George Wheeler (1650–1723), being entertained in Smyrna "by a large English colony."[51] Thomas Smith noted that the English merchants were very interested in Greek antiquities, relating that those "English gentlemen who live in Smyrna, out of a pious zeal and a justly commendable curiosity" (*Remarks*, 206) would take the six-hour journey from Smyrna every autumn to visit the ruins of Ephesus, which he described as "being reduced to an inconsiderable number of poor cottages, wholly inhabited by Turks" (*Remarks*, 256). Thus Rycaut was able to continue having contacts with some of the leading intellectuals of his time even in Smyrna, which, together with his Royal Society connections and circle of friends in England, would give him credibility as an authority on matters Turkish and Oriental and help publicise his book amongst the circles of the learned. Rycaut was using his time, connections and ability to make himself agreeable to interact with people who mattered, men whose friendships might prove both enjoyable personally and useful to him in his career.

---

[50] Thomas Smith, *Remarks upon the Manners, Religion and Government of the Turks* (London: EEBO Reprints, 2011), 265.

[51] George Jeffery, "The Levant Company in Smyrna," *Notes and Queries* 11 (1915), 61. There were several other visitors to Smyrna around this time and earlier in the century who were noted travellers and antiquarians. They included the merchant Edmund Prideaux (1644–1728), elder brother of the oriental scholar Humphrey, who wrote an influential work, *The True Nature of Imposture, fully displayed in the Life of Mahomet* (1697), the French jeweller and traveller Jean-Baptiste Tavernier (1605–1689), who was there on his way to Persia in 1630 and the Dutch artist Cornelis de Bruyn (1652–1726), who was there in 1682 as a guest of the Dutch merchant community, and whose *Voyage to the Levant* was translated into English two years after Rycaut's death (1702). A later visitor to Smyrna with an antiquarian bent was Aubrey de la Mottraye (c. 1674–1743), a French Protestant based in England (he received a pension from George I) whose book on his travels (1721) was illustrated by none other than William Hogarth. For further details, see Hyde Clarke, "History of the British Colony at Smyrna. Presented to the British Library by the author, 1862," http://www.charnaud.co.uk/note.

Smyrna also provided Rycaut with an ideal environment for indulging in his archaeological and antiquarian interests, and it was at this time that he made the acquaintance of Lord Henry Howard,[52] "with whom he established a warm relationship," and for whom Rycaut provided "rarities from Asia."[53] It would likely have been Howard who nominated Rycaut for membership in the Royal Society, of which he and his brother Charles were very generous patrons and supporters. We find Rycaut reporting to Howard from Smyrna that "antiquities and paintings are very rarely to be found in the Eastern parts of the world," blaming their scarcity, as Sandys and others before him, such as Busbecq and the artist Melchior Lorck, on the "barbarism of the Turks" (Peck, *Consuming Splendor*, 330–31).

There had been a great deal of rivalry between the English and French in the Levant, particularly during the period from 1583 to 1612, which, according to Arthur Horniker, "involved claims to jurisdiction over Christian nations which were not officially represented at the Porte and over their merchants trading in the ports and territories of the Ottoman Empire,"[54] and capitulations had been signed between the Turks and French as early as 1536. This made the English relative latecomers to trading in the area, and in these early days they traded under the flag of France until 1583, when a formal treaty with the Ottoman Empire made William Harborne England's first ambassador and "placed English merchants on a footing of complete equality with the French with regard to privileges in the Levant trade" (Horniker, "Rivalry," 290). The Levant Company, formed from a merger of the Venice and Turkey Companies (1592), then began to operate independently, and its factories were now in formal rivalry with those of France.

The English Consul, at Smyrna could not himself indulge in trading, and whilst he owed his employment to the Levant Company he, like the other consuls, also dealt directly with the ambassador. Rycaut's friendship with Winchilsea obviously stood him in good stead, and it certainly did him no harm that the latter's successors in the ambassadorship were both Finch relatives. The consul also needed some kind of written authority from the host country, as Anderson

---

[52] Lord Henry Howard (1628–1684), who later became the sixth duke of Norfolk (1677) was a politician, diplomat and, from 1666, a Fellow of the Royal Society. In 1669 Charles II appointed him ambassador to Morocco. Howard, though himself not a learned man, was very generous to the Royal Society, donating it space after the Great Fire of 1666 and turning over his considerable library, which he did not use much, to it. His later years were marred by depression and drinking problems after the death of his wife. Howard published *A Relation of the Journey of the Right Honourable Lord Henry Howard to Vienna, and thence to Constantinople* (1671).

[53] Linda Levy Peck, *Consuming Splendor: Society and Culture in Seventeenth Century England* (Cambridge: Cambridge University Press, 2005), 330. For further details of Howard's (and his brother Charles's) relationship with the Royal Society, see 326–37.

[54] Arthur Horniker, "Anglo-French Rivalry in the Levant from 1583 to 1612," *Journal of Modern History* 18, 4 (1946): 289.

notes, "until it arrived, [the consul] was powerless unless his predecessor could vouch for him before the cadi" (*English Consul,* 95). The document was known as the *beràt,* and in Rycaut's case it proved somewhat difficult to obtain because William Cave was dead and could not support the application. In the end, it was procured by one of Rycaut's friends, the physician and imperial dragoman Antonio della Torre. The beràt, "as well as being a simple grant, [may] also be a notification of regulations concerning the requirements of service consequent of that grant,"[55] which meant that Rycaut could not begin his duties until it arrived and clarified exactly what those were. The consul had a fair amount of power over his countrymen, whom he could fine or imprison for legal infractions, and he enjoyed a measure of diplomatic immunity which was supposedly guaranteed by the Ottoman authorities. The Levant Company, however, had to be involved in the consul's disciplinary decisions, and it could dismiss him at any time.

There were also other foreign representatives in Smyrna, particularly Venetians, who had a long-standing trade relationship with the Levant area, the recently-arrived (1666) Genoese, Dutch, who had traded under the English aegis until 1612, and, of course, the French. All of these had consuls on the spot in Smyrna, with whom Rycaut would have had to form some sort of working relationship, and were all, of course, like Rycaut, responsible either directly or indirectly to their ambassadors at the Ottoman court as well as to the trading companies of their respective countries. Some consuls were impeded in their work by uncooperative ambassadors and meddling company officials who could make their lives very difficult, just as Sir Sackville Crowe and Sir John Eyre had apparently done for the English merchants.

The colourful Venetian consul deserves a special mention here. He was the remarkable Francesco Lupazzoli, an extremely tough old gentleman who had been born in 1587 and held the position of consul from 1669, although there were only a few Venetians left trading in Smyrna because the Ottomans kept raising the levies on their goods. He got along badly with the French consul, Henri Dupuy, but persevered in his "sinecure" (Goodwin, *Lords of the Horizons,* 217) until he was forced to retire temporarily in 1682, when Venice and the Ottoman Empire renewed formal hostilities. Incredibly, Lupazzoli returned to his duties in 1699 at the age of 112, surviving until 1702. "He never touched wine, brandy, coffee or sherbet," his son Bartolommeo, who was a priest stationed in Smyrna, recorded by way of explaining his father's longevity, and "he did not take snuff or tobacco." He married five times, as well as leaving, so it was said, about a hundred illegitimate children (Cited in Anderson, *English Consul,* 52 and n. 9), an improbable number which Jason Goodwin reduces to a more manageable twenty-four, although confirming that Lupazzoli sired the last one at ninety-five (*Lords of the Horizons,* 217 and note.).

---

[55] Nedjet Gök, "An Introduction to the *beràt* in Ottoman Diplomatics," *Bulgarian Historical Review* (2001): 141–50, here 141.

England had fewer factors in Smyrna than did France, but, as the Italian traveller Cornelio Magni[56] noted in 1672, "what they lack in quantity they make up for in quality" (cited in Anderson, *English Consul,* 66). Anderson estimates that there were about a hundred consular employees in Smyrna when Rycaut arrived there in 1667. Magni's reference to lack of quality amongst the French officials likely alluded to the hapless Henri Dupuy, who had run into marital troubles after getting engaged to a beautiful and intelligent young Greek widow. Dupuy's father forced him to return to France and marry someone more suitable, whilst one of the English merchants in Smyrna successfully courted the lady and married her. Dupuy, whose family had held the consulship for years, was replaced by Antoine Fouquier, and three years later by Louis Chambon, who quarrelled with his nominal superior the French ambassador Vantelet.[57] The Dupuy saga, however, was not over, and Henri came back as consul yet again (1683), remaining for a further two years until he was bought out.

The Genoese, with whom Rycaut's father had dealt, were relative latecomers, whose first consul, Count Giovanni Luca Durazzo, had arrived in 1665 as a tourist, but who then persuaded his government to allow him to conduct trade negotiations, which he did so successfully that the Ottomans granted him very generous capitulations, in return for which Durazzo received an official appointment as Genoese resident in Constantinople. Ottavio Doria succeeded as vice-consul in Smyrna; however, the Genoese only remained in the Levant until 1683, and their relations with other countries, particularly with France (whose officials did not recognise them) and England, were not good. In 1671 Doria resigned, and his designated successor managed to accidently shoot himself soon after arriving in Smyrna. The comic opera was not yet over, as Doria stayed on, "but on account of his debts was repudiated by the Genoese government" (Anderson, *English Consul,* 53), and the next Genoese consul lasted only until his death in 1674. A replacement duly showed up the next year, but after a quarrel with the Ottoman authorities over the landing of goods, left in a huff, only to have his ship impounded by the Turks when it docked in Constantinople harbour. The last Genoese resident was compelled to sneak away from his post disguised as a friar.[58]

---

[56] Cornelio Magni (1638–1692), born in Parma, travelled to the Levant in 1671, returning to Italy in 1674 after visiting the Balkans, Syria, Palestine, Cyprus, and Greece. He published an account of his experiences in two volumes, *Quanto di più curioso e vago hà potuto raccorre C. M. nel primo biennio da esso consumato in viaggi, e di more per la Turchia* (1679, 1692). Magni supplied a wealth of information about Ottoman political, economic and religious matters.

[57] For Rycaut's account of Vantelet and his "barbarous usage" by the Turks, see 131, n. 17. His successor, the marquis de Nointel, was, however, able to renew the capitulations with the Ottomans in 1672.

[58] For further details, see Thomas Allison Kirk, *Genoa and the Sea: Policy and Power in an Early Modern Maritime Republic 1559–1684* (Baltimore: Johns Hopkins University

The Dutch, at least initially, did rather better than the Genoese. After they received their official recognition in 1612, Dutch merchants had prospered, but the consuls were engaged in bureaucratic struggles with their superiors in Amsterdam and with other people who believed they had the right to interfere. One such person was the strait-laced evangelical chaplain Thomas Coenen, "a frustrated preacher for a reluctant and non-devout community of Dutch merchants,"[59] whom Rycaut would consult when he came to write about the pseudo-messiah Sabbatai Sevi. He quarrelled with the consul Gerard Smits, who took office in 1662, and when that official left, Coenen also found himself on the outs with Justinus Colyer, who took up the consular post in 1668. Like the Genoese, the Dutch seem to have suffered from the unpredictability of fortune and the elements; Smits's original successor, Jakob van Dam, "the most splendid and hospitable" (Hamilton et al., *Friends and Rivals*, 18) of the Dutch consuls, had narrowly escaped from an earthquake in Ragusa as he made his way out to the Levant, but the new resident, travelling at the same time, had not been so lucky. Van Dam, who had been the Dutch consul in Smyrna for twenty years (1668–1688),[60] had hoped to be made resident himself, but the post went to Colyer instead, and for a while the two men did not get along. Colyer, an able and conscientious administrator, liked a good party with plenty of drinking and merrymaking, which offended Coenen but did not faze Rycaut, who seems to have enjoyed his congenial company and respected him. Indeed, Rycaut was called upon to patch up relations between van Dam and Colyer, and was on good terms with all of them, perhaps because of his Brabant ancestry and his fluency in Dutch. When Colyer was called to Constantinople by van Dam to settle matters he was attacked by bandits on the way, but seems not to have suspected the resident of arranging the ambush (he did not), and their relationship actually improved after that, van Dam remaining in Smyrna until his return to the Netherlands in 1688.

At about the same time, Rycaut also became, as Charles Littleton states, "a celebrated member of the Republic of Letters" (Hamilton et al., *Republic of Letters*, 164), a widely dispersed and informal group of international scholars, amateur and professional, who corresponded with each other, often in Latin, on scientific and philosophical matters. The French were particularly active in this endeavour; it was Pierre Bayle, the philosopher and compiler of the well-known *Historical and Critical Dictionary*, who may well have coined the phrase "Republic of Letters" in the *Nouvelles de la Républiques des Lettres* (1664), and they introduced the first genuinely academic journal, the *Journal des Sçavants*, which

---

Press, 2005).

[59] Michael Schwartz, "Kabbalah: Sabbatai Sevi and his Contemporaries," Part 1, http://www.blogcritics.org.

[60] For further information on the background, see Ismail Hakki Kadi, *Ottoman and Dutch Merchants in the Eighteenth Century: Competition and Cooperation in Ankara, Izmir and Amsterdam* (Leiden: Brill, 2012).

appeared in 1665 under the editorship of Denis de Sallo, sieur de la Coudraye, an eminent Parisian lawyer. There was no formal membership list or specific meeting place for this group; scholars conducted their business mostly through letters, which led to the coining of the term "man of letters" to denote intellectuals who wrote to each other on a variety of subjects. In England, many members of the Royal Society, including Sir Isaac Newton and Robert Hooke, were also affiliated with the Republic of Letters, and Rycaut himself was an active member. It also, as Carol Pal has demonstrated, it also included a number of eminent women in its membership. In England, James I's daughter Queen Elizabeth of Bohemia and the educator Bathsua Makin were perhaps the best known.[61]

It was in Smyrna that Rycaut became interested in the strange career of a Jewish impostor, Sabbatai Sevi, who had established what we might term a cult in Smyrna. A former Hasidic rabbi, Sevi came to believe in 1648 that he was the Messiah, and between this declaration and his imprisonment in 1666 by order of Mehmet IV, he managed, with help from another self-declared prophet, Nathan of Gaza,[62] to build up a large following in Cairo, Jerusalem and Salonica. In Smyrna, where he settled in 1665, he became so influential that he was able to depose the local rabbi, Aharon Lapapa, who was not convinced of his claims. Even after he was forced to convert to Islam, possibly by the Sultan himself,[63] Sevi continued his proselytising and attracted even more followers, to whom he appeared as a pious Muslim. Finally, after years of successful imposture, Mehmet IV's toleration wore thin, especially when Sevi's message included the Sultan's possible deposition; Sevi was put in prison and then exiled to a city in what is now Montenegro. After his death his followers remained and even expanded their numbers. Known as the *Donme*, they "still form another distinct

---

[61] For the surprisingly prominent role of women intellectuals in the Republic of Letters see Carol Pal, *The Republic of Women: Rethinking the Republic of Letters in the Seventeenth Century* (Cambridge: Cambridge University Press, 2012).

[62] Nathan of Gaza (1643–1680) was a German Jew born in Jerusalem as Nathan ben Elisha ha-Levi. After studying the Kabbalah he began to have visions and decided that Sabbatai Sevi was the Messiah. Nathan, who was based in Gaza (which he declared a holy city), acted as a kind of publicist for Sevi, although they seem to have eventually parted company when in 1665 Sevi left for Turkey and Nathan travelled to Africa, Europe and India promoting the Messiah's cause. Nathan was also approached by Thomas Coenen for information, but does not seem to have been very forthcoming.

[63] For details of Mehmet IV and Sabbatai Sevi, see David Baer, *Honored by the Glory of Islam: Conversion and Conquest in the Ottoman Empire* (Oxford: Oxford University Press, 2007), 121–39. Mehmet was assisted in the conversion by the ubiquitous Vani Effendi, who "interrogated" Sevi as the Sultan watched from a window; apparently Sevi converted when the Sultan told him that he might be put to death if he persisted in his "nonsense." The account, given by Abdi Pasha, also noted that "from the exalted graciousness of the Chosroes-like Sultan a salaried position at the Middle Gate valued at 150 *akçe* was deemed proper for him" (*Honored*, 128).

community in the Istanbul mosaic. . .the smallest group awaits the return of Sabbatai Sevi as the Messiah" (Mansel, *Constantinople*, 142).

With encouragement from Howard, who seems to have been equally fascinated with this impostor, Rycaut decided to write an account of Sevi, which was included in a work entitled *History of the Three late famous Impostors, viz. Padre Ottomano, Mahomed Bei and Sabatai Sevi* (1669),[64] but he did not put his name on it, probably because, as Sonia Anderson postulates, "many of his Jewish acquaintances at Smyrna still believed in Sabbatai's divine mission, in spite of his conversion to Islam" ("Sir Paul Rycaut," 475), and he did not wish to offend their sensibilities. The subject-matter of this book illustrates Rycaut's relationship with the many Jewish people he met during his time at Smyrna, although his acquaintance with them went back at least as far as 1655, when he had heard Oliver Cromwell speaking eloquently in favour of Jewish resettlement in England. "His is the principal surviving account of Cromwell's speech in favour of their admission," Anderson noted (*English Consul*, 24). The agreement was ratified by Charles II in 1670 after representatives from the Jewish community successfully petitioned the king to relieve them from the provisions of the Conventicle Act, which made it illegal for more than five people to assemble for religious purposes unless they belonged to the Church of England. Rycaut would have known all about this because "one of [his] brothers saw this as an opportunity for levying hush-money on the Jews by threats to prosecute them under the act" (Anderson, *English Consul*, 211). In fact, Charles's action was financially-motivated, too, "as the price of obtaining supplies which would not be granted on any other terms."[65] For the Jews, it must have looked like one step forward, two steps back.

The essay on Sevi, "written by an English person of quality there resident, soon after the affair happened," was edited safely in England by the eminent

---

[64] Padre Ottomano was allegedly the son of the mad Sultan Ibrahim (1640–48); in 1644, together with his mother Zafira, he was captured by the Knights of Malta when they boarded a large Turkish ship. For details, see Thomas Freller and Dolores Campoy, *Padre Ottomano and Malta: A Story of the 1001 Nights.* (Valletta: Midsea Books, 2006). Muhammad Bey, a Wallachian captured by the Turks in 1651, claimed to be Prince Ioannes Michael Cigala, a direct descendant of Süleyman the Magnificent. See *Celebrated Claimants from Perkin Warbeck to Arthur Orton* (London: Chatto and Windus, 1874; Teddington: Echo Library, 2006), 34–37. John Evelyn credited one "Signor Cisij, a Persian gentleman," with having written the sections on Padre Ottomano and Muhammad Bey (*Claimants*, 35), and an entry in his diary for 29 September 1668 reads "I had much discourse with Signor Pietro Cisij, a Persian gentleman, about the affairs of Turkey, to my great satisfaction" (William Braye, ed., *The Diary of John Evelyn* [New York: M. Walter Dunne, 1901], 2, 44). This may be the same person as Giovanni Jacopo Cesii, described elsewhere as "a Persian merchant of high repute throughout the Levant. . .descended from a noble Roman family" (*Claimants*, 36).

[65] H. S. Q. Henriques, *The Jews and English Law* (Clark, NJ: Law Book Exchange Reprints, 2006), 135.

diarist and founding member of the Royal Society, John Evelyn, under whose name it was printed, together with a dedication to Lord Arlington, also the dedicatee of Rycaut's *Present State of the Ottoman Empire*. Michael Heyd writes that Evelyn "obtained the manuscript from Rycaut through the mediation of Lord Henry Howard."[66] Rycaut's primary source for his information, as he was back in England during the critical period of the events, was Thomas Coenen, now author of his own book on the subject, *Vain Expectations of the Jews as Revealed in the Figure of Sabbatai Sevi* (1669). Gershom Scholem states that Rycaut "gathered his information (orally and in writing) from Coenen," and goes on to say that "his dependence on Coenen is apparent even in his misunderstandings of the latter." Heyd notes that Rycaut followed Coenen, whom Scholem called "one of the shrewdest observers" (*Sabbatai Sevi*, 372) of Sevi, in labelling Sabbatai Sevi as demonically inspired, although he evidently did not share Coenen's anti-Semitism and did not attempt to link Sevi's beliefs to Catholicism, which was another subtext in Coenen's book.[67] Scholem also believes that after Rycaut "sent his own report in 1668 to friends in England, it was pirated by Evelyn."[68] However, Sonia Anderson's speculation about Evelyn's assumed authorship makes more sense, as does the likely involvement of Howard; Rycaut had to live in Smyrna and he had Jewish friends. Furthermore, the "English person of quality there resident" was not John Evelyn, whose travels were limited to a "grand tour" of Italy in his youth, but Paul Rycaut, who eventually declared in writing soon after he got back to England that it had been "an issue of my pen" (*Turkish History*, 200), a point that Scholem appears to have overlooked, as did Sir Geoffrey Keynes in his biography of John Evelyn (Anderson, *English Consul*, 214, n. 15). All in all, Rycaut's interest in antiquities and strange religious people was certainly an excellent way to stave off any feelings of isolation or boredom with the routine of his job he may have felt in Smyrna. He was certainly lucky to have been a person with outside interests, and in some ways Smyrna must have been an ideal place for him. He was more independent there than he had been in Constantinople, and the combination of classical, Turkish, Jewish, and Christian cultures must have been exciting for him.

[66] Michael Heyd, "The Jewish Quaker," in Allison P. Coudert and Jeffrey Shoulson, ed., *Hebraica Veritas? Christian Hebraists and the Study of Judaism in Early Modern Europe* (Philadelphia: University of Pennsylvania Press, 2004), 243.

[67] For a full treatment of Coenen, see Yosef Kaplan, "Thomas Coenen in Smyrna: Reflections of a Dutch Calvinist on the Sabbatean Awakening of the Levantine Jews," introduction to the Hebrew edition of Thomas Coenen, *Vain Expectation of the Jews as Revealed in the Figure of Sabbatai Zevi* (Jerusalem: Ben-Zion Dinur Trust for Research in Jewish History, 1998), 22–108.

[68] Gershom Scholem, *Sabbatai Sevi: The Mystical Messiah, 1626–1676*, trans. R. J. Zvi Werblowsky (Princeton, NJ: Princeton University Press, 1973), 432 n. 235.

The Sabbatai Sevi book serves both as an illustration of Rycaut's lively curiosity and of his involvement with the Jewish community in Smyrna. Eliezer Bashan tells us that the Jews had a "part in local and international trade [in Smyrna] from the beginning of the seventeenth century," and that they often functioned "as intermediaries for Europeans arriving there."[69] Rycaut probably met such distinguished Jewish intellectuals as Chaim Benveniste (1603–1673), a renowned rabbinical scholar and exegete, and of course rabbi Aharon Lapapa (c. 1590–1674), who were known to have contacts with the Levant Company. It was Lapapa, as we have seen, who had opposed and subsequently excommunicated Sabbatai Sevi, for which the latter managed to have him deposed. Mordechai Sevi, Sabbatai's father, "who first followed the mean trade of a poulterer,"[70] not only acted as a broker, but also, as Rycaut himself mentioned, "served an Englishman in Smyrna" (Bashan, "Contacts," 56). Bashan further relates an occasion in 1671 when the head office of the Levant Company wrote to Rycaut about "a complaint you make, of an Order of the Jewish Synagogue, That no Jew should bear Testimony against another before the Turkish justice." The Company was worried that Rycaut's objection might jeopardise the payment of "debts standing out to the English," and they want him to take "peculiar care" that the situation is handled properly (Bashan, "Contacts" 56). Indeed, "the slow and bad payment of those Debts," the Company wrote to Rycaut on March 11, 1671, "should deter the factory from trusting those whom they have found so unfaithfull" (Bashan, "Contacts," 71). Rycaut needed to steer carefully in these situations, and it is a tribute to him that relations between the Jews and the English remained cordial during his ten-year term in Smyrna

Meanwhile in Constantinople, Winchilsea's cousin and successor Sir Daniel Harvey, a merchant and nephew of the celebrated Dr. William Harvey, was destined only to survive until 1672, succumbing at age forty to a fever whilst still in office. However, he was accompanied in Constantinople by two people whom Rycaut would have found congenial, namely his secretary, the poet and dramatist Sir George Etherege,[71] and, perhaps more importantly for Rycaut, his chaplain

---

[69] Eliezer Bashan, "Contacts between Jews in Smyrna and the Levant Company of London in the Seventeenth and Eighteenth Centuries," *Jewish Historical Review* 29: 53–73, here 54.

[70] Henry Hart Milman, *The History of the Jews from the Earliest Period down to Modern Times* (New York: W. J. Middleton, 1875), 3, 369.

[71] Sir George Etherege (c. 1636–1691/92) is perhaps best-known for having written *The Man of Mode* (1676), the quintessential Restoration comedy of manners, which is still enjoyed today, and for his association with the scandalous circle of John Wilmot, earl of Rochester. However, after the success of the play, which was his last one, Etherege became a diplomat, subsequently serving as resident minister to the Imperial court at Regensburg (1685). Unlike most of Rycaut's acquaintances, Etherege remained loyal to James II, and accompanied the king into exile at the court of Louis XIV.

Thomas Smith, with whom, as we have seen above, Rycaut shared an antiquarian's interest in Greek and Coptic churches in the Ottoman Empire. Etherege and Smith were with Harvey when he stopped in Smyrna to change ships, and it appears that Smith encouraged Rycaut to publish his own book on the subject. G. J. Toomer remarks, however, that Smith "was privately critical of it when Rycaut finally published his book in 1679,"[72] likely because he had issued his own book on the subject three years earlier.

Harvey was followed as ambassador by his relative Sir John Finch, the nephew of Rycaut's former employer, whose tenure was not a happy one; indeed, Finch himself had written in 1667 that "I doe perfectly abhor the thoughts of going to Constantinople," a sentiment which was, according to G. F. Abbott, "prophetic."[73] As it turned out, Finch was singularly ill-equipped to deal with either Ahmet Köprülü or Kara Mustafa, and his embassy, which lasted until 1681, was one long series of misfortunes. Finch arrived in the company of his lifelong friend and personal physician Sir Thomas Baines, who remained in Constantinople until his death in September 1681, an event which deeply affected Finch and likely hastened his own demise soon after he returned to England in 1682, having personally overseen the embalming of Baines's body and sailed home with it.[74] From the beginning of his embassy to the end Finch encountered problems; he had to deal with the issue of Barbary pirates, the renewal of the capitulations which had not been reviewed since 1662, quarrels between the Greek and Latin churches and the difficulties of Ottoman diplomacy, with which he was not familiar. It took him several months to set up his first audience with Mehmet IV, and even then he had to find a way to get the Sultan's attention amidst preparations for a gigantic festival in Edirne which Mehmet wished to stage to celebrate the marriage of his daughter and the circumcision of his sons. Finch had set out to impress the Sultan with a large retinue, but discovered that the Turks had not prepared sufficient accommodation for it; they were all put up in substandard inns and accorded little formal notice. After Finch had been led to believe that the capitulations had been approved and renewed, he was told that neither Mehmet IV nor the Grand Vizier had even had time to read them, let alone

---

[72] G. J. Toomer, *Eastern Wisedome and Learning: The Study of Arabic in Seventeenth-Century England.* (Oxford: Oxford University Press, 1996), 246. Toomer is citing a letter of Smith's (MS Smith 55, fol. 153) quoted by Anderson.

[73] G. F. Abbott, *Under the Turk in Constantinople: A Record of Sir John Finch's Embassy 1674–1681* (London: Macmillan, 1920), 5.

[74] The nature of the relationship between Baines and Finch has given rise to a great deal of speculation, but what is interesting about Baines is that he was invited to discuss religion with Mehmet IV's favourite cleric, Vani Effendi; the conversation was recorded by John Covel. For details, see James Mather, *Pashas*, 183–86.

approve them, and he simply had to wait until approval came.[75] This ill-omened beginning to Finch's term set the pattern.

In 1677, Rycaut received a visit in Smyrna from his old friend and employer, the earl of Winchilsea, who arrived in the company of Peter Ricaut (the other members of the family had kept the old spelling) and informed him that Finch's position as ambassador was being reconsidered by the king. Peter Ricaut now had the post of secretary to Winchilsea, and the earl apparently felt that Paul Rycaut might wish to become ambassador in Constantinople, even though he himself had been thinking about re-applying for the post (Anderson, *English Consul*, 249). Rycaut then resigned his consulate, and the Levant Company selected as his successor William Raye, who had once been a factor in Smyrna but had returned to England in 1670 for a number of years. Like Rycaut, Raye was an avid antiquarian.[76]

Rycaut set sail from Smyrna in April 1677, after which he travelled for a while in Italy and France, arriving back in England by December of the same year. He was rewarded for his services to the Levant Company with a cash grant and a position as a "Company assistant," which gave him an executive rank in the day-to-day running of the Company's affairs, put him on numerous committees, and "served Rycaut's turn by placing him frequently in the Company's eye" (Anderson, *English Consul*, 251). It was on this visit that Rycaut finally met Robert Boyle (Hamilton, *Republic of Letters*, 164), with whom he had been corresponding whilst he was in Smyrna. Now Rycaut had to find himself new employment, which, given the politics of the times, was not going to be an easy task, and would take a great deal of perseverance, persistence, and the cultivation of the appropriate people for patronage. However, given his excellent record as a consul and the high regard in which he was held, Rycaut likely felt reasonably optimistic about his chances.

## Later Life and Career

Once he was firmly ensconced again in England, Rycaut commissioned Sir Peter Lely, Principal Painter-in-Ordinary to the king, to paint his portrait, perhaps recalling his father's signal that he had "arrived" by having his portrait painted by Vandyke, for Lely was not only the premier portraitist of the age, but one of the most expensive as well. This is the familiar portrait, now in the National Portrait Gallery, that we find reproduced as an engraving by Robert White in the various editions of Rycaut's *History of the Turks*, which was published the

---

[75] For further details, see Gerald MacLean and Nabil Matar, *Britain and the Islamic World 1558–1713* (Oxford: Oxford University Press, 2011), 201ff.

[76] William Raye held the Smyrna consulate from 1677 to 1703. After he retired to England, he presented the Bodleian Library with six hundred ancient Greek coins, for which gift he received an honorary degree from Oxford University.

same year (1677) and would continue to be published up to 1699. The East was in his blood, and it seems that Rycaut could not easily get away from its pull; accordingly, when Sir John Finch was finally recalled by Charles II in 1681, Rycaut apparently felt that he might have a chance to succeed him, but decided to try for deputy governor of the Levant Company instead, thinking that this position would give him a better chance at the real prize. As it happened, Rycaut got neither post, the ostensible reason being that Charles II "did not think fit to send out as ambassador any person who had formerly resided in Turkey under a lesser character" (Cited in Abbott, *Under the Turk*, 213). The post went to James Brydges, baron Chandos (1642–1714), another friend of Rycaut's "who wrote to him at great length from Turkey lamenting his own situation," but nevertheless offering "to procure material for any further histories which his correspondent might have in mind" (Anderson, *English Consul*, 255). Chandos, whose waxed "mustachios" were even more formidable than Winchilsea's, stayed in Constantinople, constantly complaining about his unhappy lot, until 1687. His misery, however, did not stop Chandos from making a fair amount of money on the side from various private dealings whilst he was in Turkey.

Rycaut may have been disappointed with the results of his job applications, but he certainly did not give up his interests in Levant Company business or indeed in the affairs of the east. In 1682 he was contacted by Sir Leoline Jenkins, Charles II's secretary of state, who asked him whether he would go on a secret mission to Algiers. Rycaut was to sort out the problem of the seizure of English (and French) ships and their crews by the Algerians during a conflict which had been going on since 1677, as well as continuing fruitless negotiations with Algerian authorities concerning the fate of the imprisoned sailors. Over the years the dey of Algiers, Ismail Pasha, who had been in office since 1659, had procrastinated about the return of both ships and captives; "promises in abundance were obtained," Joseph Allen relates, "but. . .were never respected, unless their fulfilment was occasionally enforced by the guns of a man-of-war."[77] Rycaut's task, as outlined by Jenkins, was to represent himself as a government agent especially appointed to negotiate for the freeing of prisoners, bribe the right people, including Ismail Pasha, with various presents or money, and try to patch up any grievances the Algerians might have had against the English. However, Rycaut never got to Algiers, because a few days before he was due to leave a peace was negotiated by Admiral Arthur Herbert (later earl of Torrington), who courteously, but somewhat tardily, informed him that he was no longer needed. In a mildly ironic twist, the one Ricaut who did go to Algiers was Peter's son Philip, who was given the post of consul-general in 1683, only to be recalled in 1685. Paul Rycaut also failed to secure a post as English ambassador to Sweden in the same year, after which he seems to have spent his time enjoying his wide circle of

---

[77] Joseph Allen, *Battles of the British Navy, from A.D. 1000 to 1840* (London: A. H. Baily, 1842), 1, 75.

friends, antiquarianism and writing his *Life of Numa Pompilius*. Rycaut's friends at the time included Sir Thomas Browne, author of *Religio medici* and the poet laureate John Dryden, as well as Oliver Cromwell's erstwhile son-in-law Thomas Belasyse, viscount Fauconberg, who was now, of course, a reconciled royalist. It was Dryden's publisher who invited Rycaut to contribute to the new translation of Plutarch's *Lives* directly from the Greek which was being issued under the poet's editorship, resulting in the *Life of Numa*. That Dryden could attest to Rycaut's Greek language skills is high praise indeed.

In 1685, shortly after the death of Charles II, Rycaut was appointed secretary to Henry Hyde, earl of Clarendon, recently made Lord Lieutenant of Ireland by James II, and was knighted the same year. This seems to have ushered in one of the happiest periods of Rycaut's life, as he was accompanied to Ireland by his nephew Philip, and, perhaps more significantly, by his brother John's widow, Grace. Rycaut and Grace moved in together, with Grace ostensibly taking on the role of "housekeeper," as there was a law forbidding marriage with one's deceased sibling's spouse. This arrangement would last until Grace's death in 1697, which Rycaut saw as "the greatest affliction of his life" (Anderson, *English Consul,* 266). We have little information about Grace Ricaut, and even Anderson does not know her maiden name. Rycaut's brother Thomas, slightly older than Paul, was still practicing as a lawyer in Dublin, but would end up a ruined man after the Glorious Revolution and died two years later (1691). For the first (and last) time in his life, Rycaut was surrounded by the closest equivalent to a real family he would ever have.

When James II succeeded, his agenda as king was to restore, as far as he was able to, the rights and privileges of the Catholic church. To this end, James needed to find ministers sympathetic to his cause, which proved rather more difficult than he thought it would. Clarendon and his brother Laurence, earl of Rochester, had been close to James for many years. As Duke of York James had married their sister Anne (d. 1671), and when he took power he appointed Rochester Lord Lieutenant of Ireland, a post he declined, although he did agree to become Lord Treasurer. Clarendon, meanwhile, received the position of Lord Privy Seal, and it was left to him to accept the offer of the Lord Lieutenancy of Ireland. James attempted personally to convert Rochester to Catholicism, but did not succeed, although it appears that Rochester maintained a broad-minded attitude throughout his term of office. When it became evident that he would never convert, James reluctantly dismissed him in 1687, and Clarendon lost the Privy Seal in the same year. It appeared, then, that Rycaut had, at least at first, attached himself to the right people, as the Hyde brothers were very much, at least for a time, in James's favour. However, both would end up supporting the replacement of James II as king with William of Orange in 1688, as did Rycaut, who was, after all, "a cavalier of the old stamp" (Anderson, *English Consul,* 268), and Winchilsea, who nonetheless chivalrously helped his old master escape capture before joining with William.

Clarendon, and by extension Rycaut, was not going to have an easy time in Ireland. His first, and major, clash was with the commander of the English forces in Ireland, the earl of Tyrconnel, a strong proponent of James II's pro-Catholic policies and *de facto* the most powerful man in Ireland; he was also, as Anderson notes, "a shameless and resourceful adventurer intent on the viceroyalty" (*English Consul,* 266). Tyrconnel was on leave in England for the first few months of Clarendon's administration, but Clarendon's respite would not last long. As James intended to allow Catholics the right to serve as administrators and jurists or to join the army, Clarendon, who was, according to Bishop Burnet, "a friendly, good-natured man, naturally sincere and punctual to tediousness," found himself in the position of having to carry out the king's directives whilst at the same time not offending the Protestants and his own religious views. He had, in the end, little choice, and after warning the established clergy not to antagonise Catholics, he tried to advise James not to proceed too far and too fast with his programme, advice which largely fell on deaf ears. Upon Lord Tyrconnel's return to Ireland in 1686 and more active interference with his administration, Clarendon found his position becoming increasingly untenable, and in January 1687 he was recalled by James II and replaced as Lord Lieutenant by Tyrconnel. One of the victims of this political storm was Paul Rycaut, who found himself charged with extortion by Catholics egged on by Tyrconnel, and of being unreasonably severe in carrying out some of his duties which involved subordinates. James II, for his part, appears to have tacitly approved of these unwarranted manoeuvres against his officials, and did nothing to rectify the situation. Clarendon, who himself had successfully warded off an onslaught of Tyrconnel's slanders, sprang to his secretary's defence, and succeeded in getting all charges against Rycaut dropped. The two men had become friends in much the same way that Winchilsea had taken to Rycaut, and Clarendon had been grateful for his support.

The next year, perhaps to return the favour for Clarendon's acting on his behalf in Ireland, Rycaut helped reconcile the earl with George Savile, earl of Halifax and author of the well-known political treatise *The Character of a Trimmer* (1688), a work advocating compromise in politics, and now the most powerful man in the political opposition to James II. Clarendon tells us that "Sir Paul Rycaut desired me to be at his house tomorrow in the evening; that my lord Halifax would meet me there." It appeared that Clarendon, who had formerly been Queen Catherine of Braganza's private secretary, had fallen out with the queen in the matter of some money owed him for his services, and there was a rumour abroad that he wished to take the queen to court. Furthermore, Clarendon had noticed that Halifax, a former close friend, had not, like other "persons of quality," paid him a visit "upon my coming to town out of Ireland," which, he wrote, he "looked upon as declining any acquaintance with me," and felt that this apparent snub must have been connected with the gossip about legal action against the queen. Rycaut brought the two men together at dinner and reconciled them, after which Halifax promised that he would speak to Queen Catherine and "do. . .all the good offices in his power to the queen dowager." Some time later Clarendon met Rycaut again, but was told that Halifax, in spite of carrying out his promise to intercede, had not made any headway with the queen, and so the matter passed.[78] The two men were reconciled personally after a second meeting, but Clarendon remained uncompensated.

Rycaut's friendship with Halifax also speaks volumes about his own politics. The latter had been the person who actually offered the English crown to William and Mary in 1688, and he represented a particular brand of compromise which perfectly suited Rycaut. Halifax had served the Stuarts loyally, but never as a catspaw. He lost his position on Charles II's privy council due to a serious disagreement with the king, but three years later in 1679 he was reappointed, and a few years after that the king made him Lord Privy Seal. Halifax, who had spoken eloquently against the Exclusion Bill, which had sought to abrogate the Duke of York's right to the succession, was rewarded for his loyalty to James II by dismissal. Like Rycaut, however, he did not move against James until he saw that the king's Catholic policies were divisive and dangerous, at which point he joined the opposition. Halifax's short book, *The Character of a Trimmer*, defended what some people today might call fence-sitting, arguing that the middle way is always the best way, avoiding extremes and keeping politics balanced, fair and reasonable. "In no other English work," Witherspoon and Warnke wrote, "have the counsels of independence, reasonableness, moderation and compromise been so persuasively set forth."[79] Rycaut might well have agreed with Halifax when the latter wrote, "Our Trimmer adoreth the goddess Truth, though in all ages she hath been scurvily used, as well as those that worshipped her. . .our climate is a Trimmer between that part of the world where men are roasted, the other where they are frozen" (*Prose and Poetry*, 692). In his own way Rycaut, too, was a trimmer, and for most of his life steered quite skilfully between the fire and the ice.

In April 1688 Rycaut published his continuation of Bartolommeo Platina's *Lives of the Popes* (1479), using an anonymous English translation of 1651, which he brought up to date from its conclusion in the year 1471 and which appeared in the same year as Halifax's *Trimmer*. This work, which had been controversial in its time, was notable as the first papal history to have been written by a humanist rather than simply by an annalist or chronicler, and became essential reading for anyone interested in the history of the sixteenth-century papacy. Platina, who had been arrested and tortured by order of pope Paul II, had dared to criticise popes whom he thought had behaved badly; he urged the papacy to mend its ways and set an appropriate moral example. It was this aspect of Platina's

[78] Henry Hyde, Earl of Clarendon. *The State Letters of Henry, Earl of Clarendon, Lord Lieutenant of Ireland*, ed., John Douglas (Oxford: Oxford University Press, 1763), 2, 17, 21.

[79] Alexander Witherspoon and Frank Warnke, eds. *Seventeenth Century Prose and Poetry*. 2nd ed, (1929, repr. San Diego: Harcourt, Brace, Jovanovich, 1982), 667.

book which had appealed to Protestants, and Rycaut's edition came out precisely during the time James II was considering the restoration of the Catholic faith in England. As with other books by Rycaut, the timing seems to have been either serendipitous or intentional, especially when one considers the updating process. Platina's book ostensibly placed the papacy under scrutiny, but Rycaut simply extended that scrutiny to drive home the point that the Church of Rome was a corrupt, power-hungry entity that England would do best to keep at arm's length. What was more, he did not dedicate the work to James II, which would most certainly have made him look like a toady. Perhaps he hoped that the king might eventually reconcile himself with the Church of England instead of veering off towards the outstretched arms of Rome or Louis XIV. In the introduction Rycaut pointedly alludes to the time when "it shall please the King of Kings to translate [James II] from a fading to an immortal crown," hoping that "there will never want one of his royal line to sit upon the throne and defend his loyal people against all the encroachments and usurpations of foreign jurisdiction" (cited in Anderson, *English Consul*, 265). What leaps out from the page here is the indirect allusion to Charles I's speech on the scaffold, when the king stated "I go from a corruptible to an incorruptible crown, where no disturbance can be, no disturbance in the world," and the fact that James II's only son would soon be born (10 June 1688), only to become the "Old Pretender" rather than his father's successor. The allusion to "encroachments and usurpations of foreign jurisdiction," too, would not have been lost on Rycaut's readers.

Shortly after his recall to England, Rycaut also finished his translation of Garcilaso de la Vega's *Royal Commentaries of Peru*, which he had been asked to do before he took up the position in Ireland. The publisher of this book was Christopher Wilkinson "at the Black Boy in Fleet Street," whose eclectic list of titles included John Chamberlayne's *Natural History of Coffee, Tea, Chocolate and Tobacco* (1682) as well as works on history and antiquarianism. Wilkinson, who was active from about 1669 to 1693, was a printer and bookseller who sold art prints as well as books, and was also "one of the most important publishers in London."[80] He had asked Rycaut to translate the book because it had been popular both in its original Spanish and in a French translation, but due to his sudden relocation to Ireland and the time-consuming work there Rycaut had not been able to do much more than send Wilkinson a few chapters from time to time, which were printed in instalments. This had been a huge project for Rycaut, as Garcilaso's book ran to over a thousand pages, but he did it, and the book duly appeared as an expensive folio edition which Rycaut dedicated, this time, to James II.

---

[80] Henry Plomer, *A Dictionary of the Printers and Booksellers who were at work in England, Scotland and Ireland, 1668–1725* (Oxford: Oxford University Press, 1922), 315.

The next year saw Rycaut in his last official post, that of Resident at Hamburg,[81] the first English diplomat to be officially accredited to that city, recommended by Halifax as successor to Sir Peter Wyche the younger, with whom he had gone to school so many years before and who had also been a candidate for the Smyrna consulship in 1667 and 1677 (Anderson, *English Consul,* 271). Wyche had been acting informally as English representative in Hamburg for a number of years. The Hanseatic city of Hamburg had established a trading office in London as far back as 1281, and the cloth trade between the two cities had been flourishing since 1567. There was even a Hamburg Company there, which from time to time attempted to monopolise the cloth-trade. English residents in Hamburg even had their own church, with which Rycaut seems to have become increasingly involved, probably due to the efforts of his private chaplain, Lionel Gatford (d. 1715), who was appointed in 1690 and later became chaplain to the Hamburg factory. Rycaut had always had a strong tolerant bent in his religious beliefs, and on his return to England after his sojourn in Smyrna he had cultivated the friendship of several high-ranking latitudinarian churchmen such as Henry Compton, the Bishop of London, as well as Edward Stillingfleet, the Bishop of Worcester, and three men who were all, in Rycaut's lifetime, to serve as successive archbishops of Canterbury, William Sancroft (1678–1690), John Tillotson (1691–1694) and Thomas Tenison (1694–1715). It was Tenison, for example, who argued that "no man's mind may be forced, for it is beyond the reach of human power," a sentiment that would have certainly appealed to Rycaut.[82] Another significant and potentially useful friendship was established around this time with William Blathwayt (c. 1649–1717), who was secretary at war from 1683 to 1692, and with whom Rycaut carried on a considerable correspondence during his Hamburg years.[83] Blathwayt, who collected Dutch old master paintings, was a great promoter of trade in North America and the Caribbean, and also held the position of secretary to the Privy Council's Trade and Foreign Plantations Committee. A man described by Lisa Jardine as "William and Mary's imperial fixer. . .whose successful career was based on the way he could make things happen,"[84] Blathwayt, who was never raised to the peerage nor even given a knighthood, was nevertheless one of the most powerful civil servants in

---

[81] For further details of Rycaut's career in Hamburg, see Anderson, *English Consul,* 271–85. As this period of his life is beyond the scope of the present book, it does not seem germane to repeat the information here.

[82] Thomas Tenison, *An Argument for Union* (1683), cited in John Marshall, *John Locke, Toleration, and Early Enlightenment Culture* (Cambridge: Cambridge University Press, 2006), 468.

[83] "Letters to William Blathwayt, 1692–1699," Princeton University Library Manuscripts Division, Department of Rare Books and Special Collections.

[84] Lisa Jardine, "The Original Artful Dodger," BBC "Point of View," http://news.bbc.co.uk/go/pr/fr (2007). The term "Imperial fixer" comes from Stephen Saunders

England, with a finger in many pies, which enabled him to amass a huge fortune and live in the grand style on his estate at Dyrham Park in Gloucestershire.

In Hamburg Rycaut, as usual, pursued other interests apart from his work, and his one publication in the *Philosophical Transactions* of the Royal Society was a short paper on "the small creatures called sable-mice,"[85] which are the rather attractive little brown creatures with shiny pink noses now known as lemmings, although Rycaut takes the "innumerable multitudes" of them in Lapland rather seriously. Rycaut had this paper, which included "a delightful pen and wash illustration" (Anderson, *English Consul*, 275) delivered to the Royal Society by his friend John Ellis,[86] the under-secretary of state, whom he had befriended whilst he had been in Ireland, where Ellis, a man described as "industrious and obliging, if not of much ability,"[87] had been secretary to the Commissioners of Ireland. More significantly, Rycaut had also put the finishing touches to his updated *Turkish History*, this time with a dedication to William III, which would be published soon after his return to England in 1700. His publishers decided that it would be a good idea to combine Rycaut's two Turkish books with that of Knolles in a two-volume abridgment, and had accordingly engaged John Savage[88] to carry out the work, which was then sent to Rycaut for approval. As far

Webb, "William Blathwayt, Imperial Fixer: Muddling Through to Empire, 1689–1717," *William and Mary Quarterly* (1969): 373–415.

[85] "A Relation of the Small Creatures Called Sable-Mice, which Have Lately Come in Troops into Lapland, about Thorne, and Other Places Adjacent to the Mountains, in Innumerable Multitudes. Communicated from Sir Paul Rycaut, F. R. S. to Mr. Ellis, and from him to the R. S.," *Philosophical Transactions of the Royal Society* 21 (1699): 110–12.

[86] John Ellis (c. 1643–1738) lived a long and rather interesting life. He served as secretary to several generations of the Butler family, who were the earls of Ormonde and Ossory in the Irish peerage, and was also one of the numerous lovers of Barbara Castlemaine (later Duchess of Cleveland), Charles II's best-known mistress after Nell Gwynne. He was appointed under-secretary in 1695 and held the post for ten years. He went on to become MP for Harwich (1702–1710) and Comptroller of the Mint (1701–1710). Ellis's letters were edited and published by a descendent, George Agar-Ellis, FRS (later earl of Dover) as the *Ellis Correspondence* (London: H. Colburn, 1829).

[87] E. M. Thompson, ed., *Letters of Humphrey Prideaux to John Ellis 1674–1722* (London: Camden Society, 1875), viii. Prideaux (1628–1674) was archdeacon of Suffolk and a distinguished orientalist. He wrote a *Life of Mahomet* (1697) and a *History of the Jews* (1717), and would surely have been known to Rycaut through Ellis.

[88] Anderson unfairly calls Savage a "competent hack writer" (*English Consul*, 283), which he was most certainly not. Dr. John Savage (1673–1747) was rector of Bygrave and was known amongst his contemporaries as "the Aristippus of his age" (Alexander Chalmers, *Biographical Dictionary* [London, 1761] 27, 186). He had, amongst other literary undertakings, translated works by the French dramatist Paul Scarron. Perhaps this soubriquet was why Rycaut, the reader of Guez de Balzac, approved of Savage's efforts. Savage, likely through his acquaintance with Rycaut, was also interested in Graciàn, and translated his *Oràculo manual y arte de prudencia* (1702).

as his abridgment methods were concerned, Savage tells us in his preface that
his objectives lay in "weeding out the superfluous embellishments. . ., cutting
off excrescencies, and avoiding unnecessary digressions," and he seems to have
done a reasonable job. When the definitive French translation of Rycaut's work
appeared in 1709 in six parts, the sixth part was "an expanded translation of Savage's version of *The Present State*" (Anderson, *English Consul*, 285). Unfortunately
Rycaut, who had liked Savage's work and had agreed to write a preface to the
book, died of a sudden stroke (16 November 1700) before he could complete it.
He was buried at Aylesford near his parents in the ancient Norman church of St.
Peter and St. Paul, where his monument may still be seen today.

Sir Paul Rycaut never married, and we know next to nothing about any personal relationships with women that he might have had, apart from that with
Grace Ricaut, and even about that, as we have seen, there was virtual silence.
His family consisted of nieces and nephews whom he often helped and supported when they needed it, but his real joy appears to have been in his friends, who
were numerous and included all ranks and sorts of people. Rycaut's preference, if
it could be called that, was for scholars, antiquarians, and intellectuals, categories into which most of the people he knew fell. Anderson tells us that Rycaut
did not smoke, but that he enjoyed a good table. His executor was Francis De-
laet, Rycaut's cousin by marriage, and some of his relatives, including the pov-
erty-stricken Sir Anthony Mayney, received legacies, as did his brother Peter's
widow Barbara and several others. Rycaut left Sir Peter Lely's portrait of himself
to Sir William Fermor, later baron Leominster (1648–1711), a Member of Parliament and a great collector of art and antiquities. Leominster lived at Easton
Neston Manor in Northamptonshire, a custom-built house designed by Nicholas
Hawksmoor, who had been recommended by Sir Christopher Wren. According
to Anderson, Leominster, who had been his next-door neighbour in London after his return from Smyrna, was "Rycaut's dearest friend" (*English Consul*, 260),
although he and Rycaut had not seen much of each other since Leominster had
gone into the country become absorbed in the building and setting-up of his
house. "I am a great lover of solitude," Rycaut had written to Lord Clarendon in
1690, "yet methinks the society of 2 or 3 good friends is necessary" (cited in Anderson, *English Consul*, 272). Let that be his epitaph.

## England and the Ottoman Empire I: Reality

Essentially there were two Ottoman Empires where England was concerned.
The first was the political reality of diplomats, statesmen and soldiers, and the
second was a realm of the imagination, a construction of poets, dramatists, and
theologians, most of whom had never set foot within its borders. Later on we

could add artists to this list, but the proper age of "orientalist"[89] art was still around the corner in Rycaut's time, although there were notable pioneering artists such as Melchior Lorck, who depicted the wonders of the Ottoman Empire. Travel writers, at least those who were not diplomats, might be said to fall somewhere in between these two ways of looking at Turkey, depending on what their motives for writing might have been. Many misunderstandings developed, but these were to be expected when for both Europeans and Ottomans the territory was, at first, so unfamiliar, and on both sides stereotyping had already developed before any real contact of a formal nature had been made. The two cultures, Christian and Islamic, had been viewing each other with a mixture of suspicion, awe, fear, curiosity, and respect since the time of the Crusades, and, in the case of the Ottoman Empire, since its foundation by Osman I in 1299. As for Sir Paul Rycaut, his lifetime coincided with an expanding literary interest in things oriental; as we shall see, there was a great vogue for "Turk" plays, particularly from the 1660s to the 1690s, and a renewed interest in travel books and Turkish histories, all of which likely had their impact on Rycaut's written output. In his case, however, what he said was tempered by the reality of his personal experiences in Smyrna and Constantinople. It also displayed, as M. Fatih Çalişir points out, "a multidimensional and relatively impartial approach,"[90] and Rycaut was "an openminded observer."[91] Rycaut's book was certainly a useful "reality check" for those who wished to know more about the Ottoman Empire, but its author's assumptions and speculations were sometimes coloured by the same stereotypes and generalisations about Turkey which could be found in the "Turk" plays, many of which had been formed by generations of misunderstanding and misinterpretation of Islam and Ottoman civilisation.

The Ottoman Empire as a political entity had been a subject of English interest for a considerable length of time before Rycaut came on the scene with *The Present State of the Ottoman Empire.* In fact, it is reasonable to ask here why it was Rycaut's book, rather than someone else's, which eventually became the authority on the subject. After all, much of the information set out by Rycaut was derived, as we shall see, from earlier writers such as Ogier de Busbecq, Richard Knolles, George Sandys, Ottavio Bon and others. Why was it, then, that later

---

[89] In this context the term "orientalist" or "orientalism" is to be taken simply as a word for people interested in the culture, languages and history of what we might term the "East," that is, attempting, in the context of their times, to *understand* these things, not bring them under European control. It has nothing to do with the views of Edward Said in his books *Orientalism* or *Culture and Imperialism*, with which the editor fervently disagrees.

[90] M. Fatih Çalişir, "Decline of a 'Myth:' Perspectives on the Ottoman 'Decline,'" *Tarih Okulu Dergisi (Journal of the History School)* 9 (2011), 47.

[91] Phyllis S. Lachs, *The Diplomatic Corps under Charles II and James II.* (Piscataway: Rutgers University Press, 1966), 144.

writers on the Ottoman Empire invariably mentioned, paraphrased and even copied lengthy passages from this particular English work? The answer partly lies in the timeliness of Rycaut's publication of his book in 1666, because in that period the Ottoman Empire was becoming more significant to both English trade and diplomacy, and because it was already apparent, at least to those who bothered looking, that Sultan Mehmet IV, together with his Köprülü viziers, had a new design for Ottoman expansion in Europe and a possible renewal of hostilities with the Holy Roman Empire. Within a few years of the publication of Rycaut's book, the Sultan's armies had captured Crete, forced part of Ukraine to accept Ottoman overlordship, fought wars against Poland, Lithuania, and Russia, and by 1683 were once again at the gates of Vienna. The fortunes of war for the Ottomans ebbed and flowed until 1699, the year before Rycaut's death, when peace was finally made between the Turks and the various European powers. The Ottoman Empire was, to put it simply, a threatening presence whether it was at peace or at war with Europe, and there was a need to get to know it and understand it. The second reason for the book's popularity was, in all likelihood, its conciseness and the easy authority with which it was written, and, of course, as Phyllis Lachs suggested, "no doubt its rich collection of anecdotes about people at the Turkish court contributed to its success" (*Diplomatic Corps*, 146). In any case, its list of readers is impressive, John Locke, Pepys, Montesquieu, Leibniz, Racine, and Sir William Temple[92] being numbered amongst contemporaries, as well as several dramatists looking for interesting material.[93] Later readers of Rycaut included Thomas Jefferson and Lord Byron. By the time the final edition came out in 1686 the Ottomans were, if not exactly on the run, certainly pulling back; they lost most of their territory in Hungary, and over the next few years they would experience decisive defeats by Christian powers, but they were by no means finished as a world power.

---

[92] Sir William Temple (1628–1699) was a diplomat and essayist, best-known for his witty and informative correspondence with his fiancée Dorothy Osborne. He negotiated the marriage between William of Orange and Charles II's niece Mary, but he preferred living in retirement to political office, refusing the post of secretary of state. He travelled extensively in Europe (although not in Turkey) as a diplomat, but he retired because of the government's anti-Dutch policy, and wrote his *Observations on the United Provinces* (1687). Temple employed Jonathan Swift as his secretary from 1688.

[93] Anderson adds the names of the German physician Martin Vogel, who used Rycaut's book as a source for information about "eastern narcotics," and went as far as to contact the Royal Society for Rycaut's address, and Kelemen Mikes (1690–1761), a Hungarian politician and essayist who had lived in Turkey for decades and used the book to find information for a series of imaginary letters about Turkey which became a best-seller in the eighteenth century. Finally, the historian and composer Prince Dimitrie Cantemir (1673–1723) lifted large chunks of Rycaut's book for inclusion in his treatise on Islam, published in 1722 (*English Consul*, 45–46) and his *History of the Growth and Decay of the Ottoman Empire* published posthumously (1734).

There is, of course, the other side of the coin, namely that Rycaut was trying to raise himself up further than the relative backwater of Smyrna and the consulship there, perhaps hoping he might be made Winchilsea's successor, or perhaps Sir John Finch's. Abbott, indulging in some amateur physiognomy with an engraving of Lely's portrait of Rycaut, states that Rycaut had "a refined face that combines the irritability of the scholar with the keenness of a place-hunter," suggesting that he was, like so many others, an office-seeker who needed a patron. He further guesses from this likeness that Rycaut's appearance "does not extend to a sense of humour," and concludes that it was this lack which condemned Rycaut to his comparatively humble place in the pecking-order of late Stuart power politics. "Charles II," Abbott declared, "had little use for men who could not laugh" (*Under the Turk*, 53). It might have been that Rycaut had little to laugh about, given the precarious state of his family finances and his realisation that in order to succeed he would have had to go against what was essentially his honest and upright nature. Furthermore, Rycaut's humour was dry and ironic rather than slapstick; for example, in a letter he called the Danes "great huffs," who "will hector and brave it whilst they have an advantage," and he wryly forgave an impolite Austrian count because "he is an Austrian, who are commonly proud and stiff in their behaviour" (cited in Anderson, *English Consul*, 244). In any case, it would appear that Winchilsea, if not Arlington, had seen Rycaut as more of a friend than a mere place hunter; Abbott's judgment is rather severe, given the political dynamic of the time, where just about everyone was a place hunter. More than half a century century after John Donne's speaker in "The Canonization" had advised his friend to "get thee a place / Observe his Honour, or his Grace / Or the king's real, or his stamp'd face," things had not changed that much, and Rycaut needed a career.

As Daniel Goffman tells us, some sort of formal connections between the Ottoman Empire and Europe had started with Venice and other Italian city-states. In 1453, for example, shortly before launching his attack on the Byzantine Empire, Mehmet II had granted certain privileges and protection to the Genoese community in Pera, which had been followed up by agreements concluded with Florence and Venice (Aksan and Goffman, *Early Modern Ottomans*, 68–69). In 1536 a treaty, known as the "capitulations," was signed between Süleyman the Magnificent and François I of France's representative Jean de La Forêt,[94] which

---

[94] Jean de La Forêt (d. 1537) was the first official French ambassador to the Ottoman Empire, taking up his post in 1533. In 1530, however, Antonio Rincon, a Spanish-born diplomat working for the French, had been sent there as an envoy, and when the ambassador unexpectedly died, Rincon succeeded to the position, which had become official in 1536 after the signing of the capitulations. For an interesting analysis of the 1535 treaty see Anthony Piccirillo, *"A Vile, Infamous, Diabolical Treaty:" The Franco-Ottoman Alliance of Francis I and the Eclipse of the Christendom Ideal*, (Senior honors thesis, Georgetown University, 2009). Piccirillo argues that "the most important result of the alliance

gave the French the advantage of having an almost exclusive presence and influence at the Sultan's court, although the *ahidname* (charter) given to them was, as Daniel Goffman suggests, "perhaps never ratified."[95] As Lord Kinross tells us, however, whether ratified or not, these capitulations were "the stronger through being on a bilateral, not a unilateral basis, thus not revocable, as others, at the Sultan's will."[96] The French certainly took advantage of their friendly relations with the Ottomans; Gabriel de Luetz, baron d'Aramon, the French ambassador from 1546 until his death in 1553, actually accompanied Süleyman on his campaign against the Persians and served as an unofficial adviser to the Sultan.[97] When Selim II succeeded Süleyman (1566), the new French ambassador, Guillaume de Grandchamp de Grandrye, who served from 1566 to 1571, proposed to the Sultan that he allow France to send its Protestant community to settle in Moldavia, and topped this plan (which he mendaciously said had originated with king Charles IX) by suggesting that he himself be appointed *voivode* or governor! These events demonstrate just how important the French presence at the Ottoman court was, even though Grandchamp ran into serious problems when the Ottomans seized French ships and goods because Charles IX was not repaying a large debt he owed to the money-lender Joseph Nasi, a Portuguese Jew who was an Ottoman citizen. Nonetheless, the capitulations were renewed in 1569, and again under Henri III a few years later. He signalled their importance to France by sending a higher-ranking diplomat than was usual to the Ottoman court which "confirmed. . .the precedence of the French above other ambassadors" (Kinross, *Ottoman Centuries*, 321).

This hegemonic agreement did not sit well with some other European powers, and England, in a state of on-and-off hostility with Spain, began to think of the Ottoman Sultan, with his antipathy towards the Hapsburgs, as a possible ally. The English did not seem troubled when the Ottomans suffered their catastrophic defeat at the battle of Lepanto (1572), and kept up their hopes that the

---

was not to be found in its political, diplomatic or economic consequences, but rather in shifting the ideological paradigm of the time" (7). Accompanying La Forêt to Instanbul was Guillaume Postel (1510–1581), the eminent linguist, who also served as a diplomat. Rycaut may well have been familiar with Postel's *De la république des Turcs* (1560) and in his description of Islam he could have used Postel's *Alcorani seu legis Mahometi et evengelistarum concordiae liber* (1543), in which Postel, fairly objectively for his times, compares the Bible and Qu'ran.

[95] Virginia Aksan and David Goffman, eds., *The Early Modern Ottomans: Remapping the Empire* (Cambridge: Cambridge University Press, 2007), 68.

[96] Lord John Patrick Kinross, *The Ottoman Centuries: The Rise and Fall of the Turkish Empire* (1977; Reprint, New York: Perennial Books, 2002), 320.

[97] De Luetz left a record of his experiences in the Ottoman Empire in the shape of a book written by his secretary Jean Chesneau, *Le voyage de Monsieur d'Aramon dans le Levant* (1547). De Luetz was accompanied by, amongst others, Guillaume Postel (see above) and the traveller André Thévet.

Turks might still be brought on side and indeed, perhaps, pressured a little. Accordingly, Elizabeth I decided to alter the equation by demanding that English merchants be allowed to operate under their own flag instead of that of France, and in 1575 two men were sent, under the auspices of London merchants, to the court of Murad III to seek a trade agreement independent of any with the French. It worked; in 1578 William Harborne, who worked for the merchant Sir Edward Osborne, became, after a few blips and bumps in the arrangements, the first official English ambassador to the Ottoman Empire, and in 1583 "formal diplomatic relations between England and Turkey began. . ., when Sultan Murad III granted to Queen Elizabeth a treaty of peace and friendship, which enlivened and regularized the intercourse between their respective subjects."[98] The tone of the Ottoman reply was exalted but polite; "Make it known to your men and the rest of your merchants and traders that they can come to the God-guarded realms of the Padishah," Grand Vizier Siyavuş Pasha wrote to Queen Elizabeth, requesting her further, "Do not be deficient in friendship."[99] By that time, as noted above, the Levant Company, for which the English ambassador was now formally an agent, had also been established, but the delay in getting a formal treaty had been simply a matter of the Turks not being quite sure of Harborne's official status, which Elizabeth had remedied by formally appointing him as her ambassador (Kinross, *Ottoman Centuries*, 325). As well, there were numerous protests from the French ambassador. Harborne's "calm pertinacity," as Kinross called it, had obviously worked well (*Ottoman Centuries*, 327).

Both French and Venetians had been extremely unhappy about any new arrangements with England; the French ambassador, Jacques de Germigny, a man of "excitable temperament" (Kinross, *Ottoman Centuries*, 327) who had been in Constantinople since 1579, at one point going so far as to launch a formal protest at a banquet given by the Sultan to Harborne and his embassy.[100] He even threatened to sever relations with the Turks and then tried to bribe the Grand Vizier, Koca Sinan Pasha, who bluntly told him that "there was no occasion for such a row," and went on to explain that Turkey "was open to all who desired peace" (Kinross, *Ottoman Centuries*, 326). However, the French and other Europeans at the Ottoman court assumed that the English were cultivating such a close

[98] Arthur Leon Horniker, "William Harborne and the Beginning of Anglo-Turkish Diplomatic and Commercial Relations," *Journal of Modern History* 14, No. 3 (1942), 289.
[99] PRO *State Papers* 102/61/5, cited in Bernard Lewis, ed., *A Middle East Mosaic: Fragments of Life, Letters and History* (New York: Modern Library, 2001), 138.
[100] Germigny had managed previously to get Murad III to revoke the agreements, and Harborne had been forced to return to England in 1580. Elizabeth I decided to send an official embassy and Murad reinstated the treaty, at which point the squabbling began all over again. For details, see Horniker, "William Harborne," 299–303, and a fuller treatment in Susan Skilliter, *William Harborne and the Trade in Turkey, 1578–82* (London: British Academy, 1977).

relationship with the Turks that they were passing on vital information to them, and, as Horniker notes, they did have some reason to be dubious of English motives. He cites a letter from Murad III to Elizabeth I in which the Sultan tells the Queen that he would have loved to help her attack Spain (with which he had made a treaty in 1580), but he was too busy fighting the Persians to be of any assistance (Horniker, "William Harborne," 306). What Murad actually meant by this diplomatic evasion was that he was really not very interested in getting his country embroiled in war for the sake of any Christian powers.

When Germigny finished his term of office in Constantinople (1585) he was replaced by Jacques Savary de Lancosme, who proved just as intractable as far as Harborne was concerned. As well as quarrels with the English, de Lancosme managed to annoy the Imperial ambassador at the Ottoman court by going into the church reserved by the Ottomans for the use of foreigners and "usurping the place of honour" that was reserved for the Imperial ambassador. The new Grand Vizier, Hadim Pasha, then closed the church, remarking that it would not be opened again unless "M. de Lancosme ceased to play the fool" (Kinross, *Ottoman Centuries*, 327). None of this nonsense fazed the unflappable Harborne, whose position, of course, was improved by the immature antics of his rivals. He must have chuckled to himself when he heard that de Lancosme, as a member of the Catholic League, had refused to recognise the legitimacy of the Protestant Henri IV's accession in 1589 and found himself clapped in gaol by the Ottoman authorities. Harborne himself left Constantinople just before the defeat of the Spanish armada in 1588; apparently everyone there had believed that the English would be defeated, but they changed their minds after English privateers appeared in Turkish waters and started raiding European shipping, and the English victory over Spain must have alerted the Ottoman authorities to the potential power of this small and relatively insignificant Christian country.

The back-and-forth negotiations, promises, capitulations and squabbles between English and other ambassadors continued after Murad III's death (1595) into the next reign, that of Mehmet III (1595–1603), and in 1599 Elizabeth I decided to take a personal hand in things by sending the new Sultan, a cultured man who had nonetheless slaughtered nineteen of his own brothers and half-brothers to ensure his safe tenure on the throne, an entire boatload of gifts. As Lord Kinross tells us, Mehmet III received "woollen goods, which disquieted the Venetians as a possible threat to their own trade" and "a self-playing organ" designed and presented to the Sultan in person at the Pearl Pavilion by its inventor Thomas Dallam,[101] which produced, amongst other mechanical special

---

[101] Thomas Dallam (c. 1570–1614) also built the original organ for the chapel of King's College, Cambridge. There is little of Dallam's work left, due to vandalism during the Civil War. Dallam's diary has been edited by J. T. Bent (London: Hakluyt Society, 1893), and more information on the instrument may be found in Stanley Mayes, *An Organ for the Sultan* (New York: Putnam, 1956). Dallam may have been the first Englishman

effects, "a bush full of artificial blackbirds and thrushes, which sang and shook their wings at the end of the music." Mehmet was also "impressed especially by the well-armed English naval vessel, the *Hector*, which had brought Dallam and his organ" (Kinross, *Ottoman Centuries*, 328). The organ was such a hit with the Sultan that Dallam was told "that if I would stay the Grand Signior would give me two wives, either two of his Concubines or else two virgins of the best I could choose myself, in city or country" (cited in Lewis, *Middle East Mosaic*, 141). To get himself out of this situation, Dallam had to lie and pretend that he had a wife and children back in England. Unfortunately, Mehmet III's enthusiasm was not shared by his son Ahmet I, who ordered the destruction of Dallam's organ on the grounds that it was some kind of diabolical heathen invention, thus anticipating by some decades the smashing-up of other Dallam organs during the Civil War in England at the hands of zealous puritans.[102]

During the whole of Mehmet III's reign the Turks were, on and off again, engaged in fighting the Hapsburgs and Hungarians; at one time (1596) the English ambassador, Sir Edward Barton,[103] "was taken on the campaign by Mehmet to accompany the Habsburg ambassador to the Sultan and ensure that he and his suite were safely conveyed back to their own territory."[104] This incident would appear to show that by now the English had gained a degree of respect and recognition in Ottoman ruling circles and were being seen as trustworthy intermediaries as well as trading partners. It also paid off, certainly for the Turks, to keep at least one significant Christian power on side, and it could not have hurt England to have the Holy Roman Empire engaged with the Ottomans, yet at

---

to see the inner court of the harem; he was shown there by a rather nervous Turkish host, where he peered through a grate in the wall and observed some women, "and verrie prettie ones in deede" as he wrote. He only tore himself away when his companion "stamped with his foote to make me give over looking," and, he says, "I was verrie loth to dow, for that sighte did please me wondrous well" (cited in Bernard Lewis, *Istanbul and the Civilization of the Ottoman Empire* [Norman: University of Oklahoma Press, 1963], 76–77).

[102] Gerald MacLean, *The Rise of Oriental Travel: English Visitors to the Ottoman Empire 1580–1720* (London: Palgrave Macmillan, 2004), 5.

[103] Sir Edward Barton (c. 1533–1598) had been in Constantinople since 1578, when he had been employed by the Levant Company. He succeeded William Harborne as English ambassador in 1588, and seems to have gained the trust and affection of the Turks by his thorough command of their language and cultural sensitivity. Barton impressed the Turks by appearing at court "apparelled in a suit of cloth of silver, with an upper gown of cloth of gold, accompanied with 7 gentlemen in costly suits of satin" (cited in Bernard Lewis, *Istanbul*, 73). In 1598 the plague broke out in Istanbul, and Barton left the city for Heybeliada Island, just off the coast near the capital, to avoid it, but failed to do so, dying in office and being buried there before being transferred to the English cemetery in Istanbul.

[104] Caroline Finkel, *Osman's Dream,: The History of the Ottoman Empire 1300–1923* (New York: Basic Books, 2005), 175.

the same time also trusting English motives in assisting their ambassador to get home in one piece.

In spite of what appeared to be a successful relationship between England and the Ottoman Empire at the end of the sixteenth century, the French were still a power to be reckoned with, and they had not yet finished attempting to cause trouble between the English and their Turkish hosts. Furthermore, the Dutch United Provinces now added themselves to the equation, which might have made things worse for England if the Dutch had not been beholden to English assistance in their struggle for independence from Spain. As it turned out, the French refused to recognise the United Provinces as a sovereign country, and insisted they were still part of Spain. What was more, if the English had thought Lancosme was bad, he was nothing in comparison with his successor Savary de Brèves,[105] a man who spoke both Arabic and Turkish and was deeply-versed in Turkish culture as well as being intimately acquainted with the ins and outs of Ottoman-French diplomacy. Barton's successor Henry Lello,[106] the man who had organised Dallam's presentation of the organ to Mehmet III, was not happy with de Brèves, and complained bitterly of the Frenchman with his "great bribes" and "receiving now the Pope's pay," sparing, Lello went on, "nothing to hinder all my designs" (cited by Kinross, *Ottoman Centuries*, 329). The animosity between French and English culminated with what had been a harmless snowball-fight between embassy personnel degenerating into an all-out and rather childish brawl involving both the distinguished representatives of the European powers and their suites. "Several were badly wounded," the astonished Venetian ambassador wrote to his government, "and had not night fallen, worse would have happened, for the Ambassadors themselves began to take part" (cited by Kinross, *Ottoman Centuries*, 329). In the end, de Brèves did exactly what he had wanted to do from the outset, which was to make sure that the English did

---

[105] François Savary, comte de Brèves (1560–1627) was a cousin of Lancosme, but, unlike him, did support Henri IV's claims and was in the king's favour. His extensive knowledge of Turkish culture and his command of languages made him a formidable diplomatic rival to the English; he actively encouraged the Turks to commence hostilities against Spain, and of course pulled off a great diplomatic coup with the eventual renewal of the capitiulations. He was also a pioneering orientalist and established an Arabic printing-press in Paris. He later served as ambassador to the Pope and finally to Tunisia in 1608. He wrote a *Relation de ses voyages* which was published posthumously (1628).

[106] Sir Henry Lello of Clunton (c. 1558–1630), whose family was of Italian descent, went to Istanbul as an attaché to Barton, and succeeded him as ambassador in 1598, serving until 1606. He does not seem to have been as effective an ambassador as either Barton or Harborne, and was certainly no match for the sophisticated and experienced de Brèves. However, upon his return to England, Lello was knighted by James I and went on to become Warden of the Fleet Prison and Keeper of the Palace of Westminster. For details, see Orhan Burian, ed., *The Report of Lello, third English Ambassador to the Sublime Porte* (Ankara: Türk Tarih Kurumu Basimevi, 1952).

not get their capitulations renewed. Although at first he failed when the Ottomans renewed them in 1601, a move which also put the Dutch under protection from the English flag, he prevailed three years later (May 1604), when Mehmet III's son Ahmet I granted France its capitulations at the expense of the English and Venetians. De Brèves was also able to discuss with the new Sultan joint action against Barbary pirates and even "a possible pilgrimage to Jerusalem."[107] The Dutch received their own separate trade capitulations in 1612, when Cornelis Haga[108] became the first official ambassador of the United Provinces in Constantinople, and from then on were able to operate freely and profitably on their own.

When Ahmet I succeeded his father in 1603, he inherited a war with the Hapsburgs that was going reasonably well for the Ottoman Empire, as they had regained most of their territory in Hungary and strengthened their position is other areas such as Bosnia. However, the war had taken a toll on the Ottoman treasury, and it is likely that when hostilities ceased in 1606 the Turks were as relieved as their Christian enemies. A treaty was signed between the two powers at a place called Sitva Torok on November 11. The emperor no longer had to pay tribute to the Sultan in order to have his title to Hungary recognised, and the latter's candidate for the ruler of Transylvania was finally approved in 1613.[109] At about the same time, Ahmet had to turn his attention to Persia, which was now ruled by Shah Abbas I, a man who would set about making his country once more a force to be reckoned with and, from time to time, the scourge of Ottoman security. It was the relationship between the Safavids and the Ottomans which the European powers, including England, would now have to reckon with, and they would have to decide whether it might be possible to play one side off against the other to their own advantage. Much would come to depend on how ambassadors conducted themselves at the Sultan's court if there were also to be some contact between England and Persia. The scene was set, from this

---

[107] Bernard Lewis, *The Muslim Discovery of Europe* (New York: W. W. Norton, 2001), 163.

[108] Cornelis Haga (1578–1654) was trained as a lawyer at the University of Leiden, and served his first diplomatic post in Sweden. In 1612 he was sent to Istanbul, where he stayed as ambassador until 1639, establishing many consular posts in the Ottoman Empire during his term of office. As well, Haga encouraged the Dutch merchants' introduction of tobacco into the Ottoman capital "in the face of vigorous but vain opposition by the Mufti. The Ottoman Turks took to it with such relish that within half a century the pipe was seen almost as their national emblem" (Kinross 329). Upon his return to Holland Haga continued his distinguished political career, rising in 1645 to President of the High Council. See further *A true declaration of the arrival of Cornelius Haga (with others that accompanied him) ambassador for the General States of the United Netherlands, at the great city of Constantinople, faithfully translated out of the Dutch copy* (1613), in *Harleian Miscellany* vol. 3 (London: Dutton, 1809), 215–24.

[109] Stanford J. Shaw, *History of the Ottoman Empire and Modern Turkey* (Cambridge: Cambridge University Press, 1976), 1. 188.

point on, for a new player in the eastern power game to begin manoeuvering for a place in the sun. Of course, the Hapsburgs were by no means written off as enemies to the Ottomans, and in spite of the Thirty Years War (1618–1648) intervening, Hapsburg-Ottoman hostilities would break out again in 1663 and lasting until the Turks were turned back at the gates of Vienna thirteen years later. The French, meanwhile, kept up their relations with the Ottomans, and by 1673 Louis XIV had managed to get the capitulations renewed; the co-operation of the Turks was ensured by the fact that along with his diplomats the French king had sent a large fleet into the Dardanelles. By the time that the Ottomans were practically banging on the gates of Vienna, Louis had cemented his relationship with them to the point of not offering any assistance to the Austrians, and indeed attempting to prevent Jan III Sobieski of Poland from lifting the siege of the city, which he did in 1683.

Henry Lello was succeeded as English ambassador by Sir Thomas Glover, who had actually been born and raised in Istanbul by his English father and Polish mother. Glover was fluent in Turkish, Greek, Polish, and Italian, and had served as secretary to Sir Edward Barton, Harborne's successor. His success as ambassador was assured by his background and experience, as well his linguistic ability, and under his leadership England was well-represented. Alfred Wood noted his "assertive and flamboyant" personality, and states that Glover, like Barton before him, "appeared before the Sultan with a brave array of gold lace and jewels, and bore himself with a haughty courage which never failed him" (*Levant Company*, 82). Glover hosted the poet and traveller George Sandys when he came to Constantinople in 1610–1611. His relatively short term of office gave way to the nearly decade-long tenure[110] of Sir Paul Pindar (1565–1650), a vastly successful London merchant who, like Glover, had served his diplomatic apprenticeship as a secretary, this time to Henry Lello (1597–1607), and had also been consul at Aleppo. He was accompanied to Constantinople by his brother Ralph, and there is extant a dual portrait by an anonymous artist in 1614 of the two men as they appeared during Sir Paul's time at the Ottoman court.[111] Pindar's most helpful asset at the Ottoman court was likely his friendship with Mehmet III's

---

[110] Pindar's tenure of office was from 1611 to 1620, but he seems to have been recalled to England in 1616 (*CSP Domestic Series 1611–1618*, 408) and was there again in 1620, the year in which he was knighted by James I. His house, on Bishopsgate Street, was famous for its architecture; the front part of it may be seen in the Victoria and Albert Museum, London. Henry Neville Maugham (1868–1904), brother of Somerset Maugham, wrote a play entitled *Sir Paul Pindar* (1899), and there is a London pub named for him.

[111] The National Portrait Gallery description states that the portrait may not be the original 1614 one, but a copy by Thomas Trotter (c. 1750–1803), who specialized in making engravings from earlier paintings. It was engraved by W. T. Fry in 1794 and published by J. Simco (NPG D27227).

powerful mother, Safiye Sultan,[112] a woman of Venetian descent whose influence over her son was considerable. He was "eventually. . . to be one of the richest men in England," although, as Godfrey Goodwin states, "he lost some of this wealth because of his generous loans to the House of Stuart,"[113] but did not, unlike the unfortunate Sir Peter Rycaut, go bankrupt over it. Pindar was a generous and philanthropic man in other ways. A story is told, for example, of how he petitioned for and succeeded in getting a young man known as "Running" Jack reprieved from execution, after which he fed and raised him as if he were his own son.[114] He also donated "almost £10,000" to "establish the east end and repair the south transept" of Old St. Paul's Cathedral in London.[115]

Pindar's term as ambassador covered the last years of the reign of Ahmet I, the first reign of Mustafa I and the first year of Osman II's. Ahmet I, described by Kinross as "capricious and deficient in judgment," a man who "did little on his

---

[112] Safiye Sultan (c. 1550–1619), born Sofia Baffo, was one of the most powerful women in early modern Ottoman history. Together with her aunt Nur Banu, who was also her mother-in-law, she exercised a great deal of influence on the government of the Ottoman Empire during her term as Valide Sultana (1595–1603). Her outlook, as may have been expected, was pro-Venetian, but she also corresponded with Queen Elizabeth I, who sent her the gift of a carriage. Her dates of birth and death are uncertain — the latter is sometimes given as 1605.

[113] Ottavio Bon, *The Sultan's Seraglio* (London: Saqi Books, 1996), 14–15. When Pindar came to Constantinople, he was accompanied by Robert Withers (d. c. 1640), who would translate, edit and add passages to Ottavio Bon's account, and whose version of Bon's book was one of two English versions made of *The Sultan's Seraglio*. Bon, who of course knew Pindar, served as Venetian ambassador to the Ottoman court from 1604 to 1607. It was published by Samuel Purchas in 1625. Rycaut made some use of the work in his discussion of the Seraglio and of the various court officers. Another version was edited by the Oxford mathematician John Greaves (1653), who wrote in his preface that the book "was freely presented to me at Constantinople," and that he "altered. . .but a little in the dress." Greaves wrote that he did not know at the time that Withers was the author (Robert Withers, *A Description of the Grand Signour's Seraglio or Turkish Emperours Court*, ed. John Greaves. London, 1653), A2-A3.

[114] See *The Parliaments censure to the Jesuites and fryers. Being examined upon Wednesday by a committee in the Court of Wards. With their confessions at the same time, also those 18 that were suspected to adjoyn with the Irish rebels, with a pilgrim, and four more Irish souldiers. Likewise a relation of him that killed Sir Henrie Paget, and many other fellons. With the names of every particular one. Also the censure of the sessions house to 13 condemned prisoners, 6 men and 7 women, one man being cal'd by the name of Running Jack, was repriev'd by Sir Paul Pindar, April 23. Whereunto is annexed, more exceeding true and joyfull news from Ireland, describing a great and bloudy battel fought in the Neweries, April the 18, 1642.* Imprinted at London for H. Blunon, 1642. Curiously, Blunon also published in the same year *King Charles his Letter to the Great Turke, the High and Mighty Emperor Sultan Morat Han.*

[115] For details, see Marion Roberts, *Dugdale and Hollar: History Illustrated* (Cranbury, NJ: Associated University Presses, 2002), 80–81.

own initiative" (*Ottoman Centuries,* 290), had not fulfilled his original promise. He was noted, however, for *not* slaughtering his relatives when he came to the throne and for having tried to ban tobacco; he was also responsible for a number of beautiful buildings being erected in the capital, notably the famous Blue Mosque and his own tomb. Early in the reign George Sandys thought that "his aspect was as haughty as his empire was large," but had also seen Ahmet as "of no bloody disposition, nor otherwise notoriously vicious." He noted at the same time, however, that the Sultan was nonetheless "an unrelenting punisher of offences. . .having caused eight of his pages, at my being there, to be thrown into the sea for sodomy (an ordinary crime, if esteemed a crime, in that Nation) in the night time."[116] Caroline Finkel nevertheless dubs Ahmet "the sedentary Sultan," but was also a little kinder; Ahmet's "uncomfortable experiences," she writes, "inclining him to favour conciliation rather than confrontation" (*Osman's Dream,* 185). The Ottoman historian Na'ima, writing some years after the reign, flatteringly characterised Ahmet as "the protector and encourager of the learned and the lovers of concord," and went on to praise him as "the friend and support of the neglected, infirm and poor."[117] Rycaut himself, who was not present at the time, noted in his continuation of Knolles that Ahmet was "by nature proud and ambitious, though not so cruel as many of his predecessors," although he continued disapprovingly that he was "much given to sensuality and pleasure, for the gratifying of which he kept three thousand concubines and virgins in a Seraglio, being the fairest daughters of the Christians."[118]

The Sultan died at the early age of twenty-seven in 1617, at which point the trouble started; Ahmet's strange brother "Deli" (crazy) Mustafa was hauled out of his confinement in the Seraglio, where, according to Rycaut, he had spent his time studying the Qur'an, and proclaimed Sultan Mustafa I. He had been locked up there for fourteen years, but the excuse was given that Ahmet's sons were said to be too young, and poor Mustafa, "considered soft in the head," a man

---

[116] George Sandys, *Sandys Travels, Containing a History of the Original and Present State of the Turkish Empire. . .*(La Vergne, TN: Nabu Reprints, 2012), 57. The poet and translator George Sandys (1577–1644) was a seasoned traveller; he traversed Egypt and the Holy Land and visited Constantinople (1610–1615). A few years later he went to America under the auspices of the Virginia Company, of which he was the Colonial Treasurer, where he remained for ten years (1621–1631). Sandys translated Ovid's *Metamorphoses* (1621–1626) and part of Vergil's *Aeneid,* as well as venturing into theological territory with a translation of Hugo Grotius's *Christ's Passion* (1641) and what was perhaps his most famous religious work, the *Paraphrases upon the Psalms and Hymns dispersed through the Old and New Testaments* (1641).

[117] Mustafa Na'ima, *Annals of the Turkish Empire from 1591 to 1659,* trans. Charles Fraser (London: Oriental Translation Fund, 1832), 1, 455. Na'ima (1655–1716) was an Ottoman bureaucrat who, according to Baki Tezcan, became the "first official chronicler" (Aksan and Goffman, eds., *The Early Modern Ottomans,* 189) of the Empire.

[118] Sir Paul Rycaut, *The Turkish History* (London: Isaac Cleave, 1701), 2, 52.

described by the contemporary Ottoman historian Ibrahim Peçevi as "filling his pockets with gold and silver coins, tossing them out of boats and otherwise distributing them to any indigent he happened upon" (Finkel, *Osman's Dream*, 197), ascended the throne. He also indulged in childish antics such as pulling off his ministers' turbans and tugging their beards,[119] and Na'ima recorded a story about Mustafa feeding goldfish in the ponds of the palace gardens with gold coins (*Annals* 1, 455). Sir Thomas Roe, then ambassador, commented that some people thought Mustafa had special links with the divine; he reported that the Sultan had "visions and angelic superstitions" and was, "in plain terms, between a madman and a fool" (cited in Kinross, *Ottoman Centuries*, 291). Rycaut noted that Mustafa, once established on the throne, "behaved himself so cruelly. . .that he was hated of all men" and that he was especially nasty to the French (*Turkish History*, 2, 52). Given the probable state of affairs, not to mention that of the exchequer should Mustafa I remain for long on the throne, the Janissaries decided that he needed to go, and he was packed off back to the Seraglio for safe keeping. It was not, however, to be the last people heard of Sultan Mustafa I.

In 1619 Sir Paul Pindar's term of office ended; he returned home the following year and was briefly succeeded as ambassador by Sir John Eyre, appointed "under pressure from the Duke of Buckingham" (Abbott, *Under the Turk*, 10).[120] He immediately ran into trouble with the Levant Company through his high-handedness and, what was worse, his misappropriation of Company funds to the tune of some £3000 (Eyre claimed that his salary was in arrears), which led to immediate calls for his replacement. On 9 July 1621, James I wrote personally to Osman II in an elaborately-illuminated letter announcing the recall of Eyre and the appointment of Sir Thomas Roe, who had been English ambassador to the court of the Mughal Emperor Jahangir (1613–1618). In the interim James nominated a senior agent, John Chapman, as his deputy until Roe arrived in Constantinople, after which time Chapman served as Roe's secretary. "And because we

---

[119] Ebru Boyar and Kate Fleet, *A Social History of Ottoman Istanbul* (Cambridge: Cambridge University Press, 2009), 42.

[120] Sir John Eyre (1580–1639) was an MP and diplomat who had served in Spain (1609). He attempted to orchestrate the murder of Sir Edward Herbert (later Lord Herbert of Chirbury) in 1610, believing that Herbert was having an affair with his wife. On his way home from Turkey Eyre narrowly escaped being captured by pirates and lost all his possessions. He later fell on hard times and died in relative poverty. His friendship with Buckingham saved him from the consequences of his aggressive actions.

George Villiers, first duke of Buckingham (1592–1628) was the hated favourite of James I and Charles I, a man who charmed himself into a position of great power and influence, and whom some historians now think was more than just a favourite to James I and more than a friend to Louis XIII's wife, Anne of Austria. Buckingham was assassinated by a disgruntled petitioner, an event which caused great rejoicing in London and great distress to Charles I. The verdict on Buckingham from modern historians is mixed, but W. L.'s innuendo is clear enough.

doe well conceave how necessary it is for the supporting of our subjects which doe trade and remaine within your Dominions," James wrote to the Sultan, he wanted to send someone of "quality and discretion, through whose interposition and industry our people might not only bee. . .releeved in their juste and reasonable occasions."[121] Soon after he arrived in December 1621, Roe noted in a letter to Sir George Calvert (later Baron Baltimore), James's secretary of state, that the "displacing of Sir John Eyre" had been carried out to "the great content of the nation." He later elaborated to Calvert that "I shall be unwilling to add any thing to the many complaynts that I heare are sent against him, nor is it my duty to prejudge," and he further observed, "I must witness a truth: he hath fully and temperately obeyed, so that, for his remorse, submission, and receipt of mee, I have no cause to accuse him." Still later, Roe told Calvert "I am not his judge, I will not be his accuser: there are enough prepared for that office. He hath taken mony by force, and pretends it was his right; for which he had no other way" (*Negotiations*, 11, 14, 15).

Sir Thomas Roe (c. 1581–1644) was an experienced courtier and a consummate diplomat; during his time in Delhi he had cultivated the friendship of the Emperor with gifts and with his special capacity for entering into the culture of the Mughal court, which under Jahangir involved a great deal of entertaining, hard drinking and an ability to converse intelligently about artistic matters and religion. Roe was also an astute observer of other cultures, and he kept detailed records of his experiences in both Delhi and Constantinople, which he put into two books covering the time he spent in each. The first was the *True and Faithful Relation of what hath lately happened in Constantinople concerning the Death of Sultan Osman* (1622), and the second has already been mentioned. Roe supplemented his account with many letters and dispatches which may still be read with interest today, giving a detailed picture of the life of a seventeenth-century diplomat and a vivid portrayal of the people as well as the intrigues and setbacks which beset anyone who represented a foreign country in these two powerful states. Rycaut no doubt knew the earlier of these works, which describes the first assassination of a reigning Ottoman Sultan, and which contributed to the generally negative attitude English readers would come to have of the workings of the Ottoman court, where the young and reputedly reform-minded Osman II was done to death by Janissary factions and conspirators fearful of losing their grip on power and wealth, a dire warning to any sovereign who found himself in a similar position.

Roe's term of office coincided with a turbulent period in Ottoman history. Reversing their decision about the youthfulness of Ahmet I's sons, the senior

---

[121] James I to Osman II, 9 July 1621. Christie's Lot 321, Sale 6348. http:// www. christies.com/lotfinder/lot/james-vi-and-i-king-of-scotland-1837964-details.aspx? intobjectid=1837964. The complete letter may be found printed in the *Proceedings of the Society of Antiquaries* (December 1887).

statesmen of the empire had set up as Sultan in the place of *deli* Mustafa, the eldest son, Osman II, who was fourteen at the time (1618). This, at least from their standpoint, proved a mistake; it seemed that young Osman had a mind of his own and that he saw himself not just as a potential military genius like Süleyman the Magnificent, but as a great reformer and possible moderniser of the Ottoman state. In order to prove his claims as the former, Osman decided to start a war with Poland; as Lord Kinross notes, "a pretext for this could be found in recurrent frontier disputes over slave and cattle thefts between the Sultan's vassals, the Crimean Tatars, and the Cossacks of the Ukraine, who were held to be subjects of the Poles" (*Ottoman Centuries*, 291). In fact, it was more likely that Osman II initiated the hostilities because king Zygmunt III had supported with a Polish army a Moldavian ruler whom the Turks had deposed, but in any case Osman wished to flex his military muscles, and in the same year (1618) the Thirty Years War rather conveniently broke out in Europe, which might have led the Sultan or his advisers to consider what weakening effect this might have on the Ottoman Empire's chief adversaries. Yet, in spite of the fact that James I's son-in-law Frederick, the Protestant Elector Palatine and King of Bohemia, had been the immediate cause of the outbreak of the Thirty Years War when he accepted the throne of Bohemia over the protests of the Holy Roman Emperor, England was never directly involved in the conflict, although various English volunteers and adventurers were. James I did his best to maintain some semblance of neutrality, and indeed was acutely aware that Frederick had done the wrong thing in accepting the Bohemian throne. In a sense this left England in a fairly strong position, as wars cost money and James was always woefully short of that commodity. It also left England free to make alliances elsewhere, and the Ottoman court was one place where influence might be established. It was during the 1620s, too, that England began to turn its attention to Persia, the inveterate foe of the Ottomans, and in 1622, the same year which saw the murder of Osman II, an English force assisted Emamqoli Khan, Abbas I's general, to expel the Portuguese from the port of Hormuz. Two years later Shah Abbas sent the English adventurer Sir Robert Sherley to the court of James I as his envoy and in 1627 Sir Dodmore Cotton led a formal embassy to the Persian court.

Osman II, in spite of his youth, apparently saw himself as a warrior-Sultan, and decided to lead the Ottoman armies himself, to which end he ordered the death of his brother Mehmet, fearing that he might make a bid for the throne in Osman's absence. The army had already been mobilised when war had started in Europe, and in 1621 all-out conflict broke out, which some blamed on Cossack raids "across the Black Sea" (Finkel, *Osman's Dream*, 198). The campaign began in May, but Osman's unenthusiastic troops were unable to secure any victories and found themselves bogged down in front of the town of Khotin, which was defended by a powerful Polish-Lithuanian army. The Sultan was compelled to reconsider his plans and make peace, and by January of the next year Osman II was back home performing serious damage control by celebrating a victory which had never happened. Osman then decided it was time for him to make his pilgrimage to Mecca, but Esad Effendi, the influential Sheykh ul-Islam, together with the Grand Vizier Dilaver Pasha, attempted to persuade him to stay in the capital. Osman categorically refused and prepared to leave. On 18 May 1622 a mutiny broke out amongst the Janissaries, who had long been disaffected by their Sultan's conduct and the desultory nature of the campaign, and they demanded that Osman execute the Grand Vizier and some others, which he refused to do. "Meanwhile," Finkel relates, "palace staff sympathetic to the uprising opened the gates to the troops" (*Osman's Dream*, 200), and started to demand the whereabouts of crazy Mustafa, who had apparently taken refuge in the harem. When Mustafa was found, they dragged him out "by a rope"[122] and saluted him as Sultan once again; the unfortunate Dilaver Pasha, however, who had tried to flee, was immediately attacked, caught and cut to pieces by the infuriated crowd. Meanwhile, Mustafa himself wandered distractedly around calling for his nephew and asking him to come back and take the throne again.[123] To cut a long story short—these actions were the beginning of the end for Osman II, who was eventually hunted down and murdered, the first Ottoman Sultan to suffer such a fate.[124] He would not, however, be the last. Meanwhile Sir Thomas Roe remained at the Ottoman court and wrote a detailed account of the events culminating in the Sultan's death. Because Osman's murder was the first Turkish regicide, Roe believed it to be, mistakenly, as it turned out, "a fatal sign, I think, of [the Turks'] declination" (cited in Kinross, *Ottoman Centuries*, 295). Roe was writing the Ottoman Empire off rather prematurely, as events would certainly

---

[122] Jason Goodwin, *Lords of the Horizons: A History of the Ottoman Empire* (New York: Henry Holt, 1999), 171.

[123] Colin Imber, *The Ottoman Empire 1300–1650: The Structure of Power* (New York: Palgrave Macmillan, 2009), 99.

[124] Scholars and contemporaries are ambiguous about the nature of Osman II's death. Caroline Finkel, for example, writes merely that "Osman was taken on a market barrow to the fortress of Yedikule and there strangled" (*Osman's Dream*, 201). Sir Thomas Roe recorded that the Sultan was taken to the prison of the Seven Towers, where, during a vigorous struggle, "a strong knave struck him on the head with a battle-axe and the rest, leaping upon him, strangled him without much ado" (Roe, cited in Kinross, *Ottoman Centuries*, 294). However, Evliya Celebi, the seventeenth-century Turkish traveller, gives a different version; according to him, Kara Davut Pasha, the new Grand Vizier, killed him "by compression of his testicles," and Jason Goodwin goes on to say that this was "a mode of execution reserved by custom to the Ottoman Sultans," (cited in *Lords of the Horizons*, 170), a rather odd thing to imply since Osman II was the first victim of regicide. The unwitting source for some of this misinformation was probably François-Charles Pouqueville (1770–1838), a French traveller, diplomat, doctor, and archaeologist, whose *Travels through the Morea and several parts of the Ottoman Empire* (1806) contains an account of Osman's murder (113–14). Pouqueville spent three years in the Ottoman Empire (1798–1801) as a hostage and then a prisoner of the Sultan.

prove. However, Mustafa's second reign, like his first, was mercifully short; he was packed off back to his confinement in 1623, where he survived until 1639, one of the most pitiful figures in Ottoman history until Murad V was deposed and confined for his alleged insanity in 1876 and remained locked up until his death twenty-seven years later.

Mustafa was replaced by the eleven-year-old Prince Murad, another son of Sultan Ahmet, who, as Murad IV, would reign until 1640, proving himself not simply a man of tremendous physical strength, but also an active, warlike, ruthless and efficient ruler when he reached his majority in the 1630s. Lord Kinross went so far as to call Murad IV "an Ottoman Nero" (*Ottoman Centuries*, 301), probably not merely because Murad composed music and wrote poetry, both of which were of considerable artistic quality, but because of what Rycaut called his "most cruel and implacable disposition." Jason Goodwin's judgment that Murad was "the last Sultan to rule, rather than merely reign, for a century and a half" (*Lords of the Horizons*, 171) reflects Rycaut's own verdict that Murad IV was "certainly the most absolute prince who ever swayed the Ottoman Empire." However, Rycaut also went on to call him a man "of no religion, a great dissembler, ready, active and revengeful" (*Turkish History* 2, 93–94). Murad IV, who seems to have had somewhat stricter moral standards than his subjects, or was perhaps simply a "micro-manager," moved swiftly to close coffee-houses and re-institute Ahmet I's non-smoking policy, for which he was lavishly praised by the historian Ibrahim Peçevi, who wrote in 1635 "May Almighty God add increase to the life and might and justice and equity of our sovereign lord. . .who has closed all the coffee-houses. . .and who has commanded that smoking be totally forbidden" (cited in Lewis, *A Middle East Mosaic*, 395). To enforce his orders, Murad, it is said, personally patrolled the streets of Constantinople and apprehended lawbreakers, who were usually executed; he also tried to ban the drinking of wine, although he himself was a formidable drinker and may have died from the effects of over-indulgence.

Meanwhile, Roe was succeeded as ambassador by Sir Peter Wyche, "a very honest, plain man,"[125] father of Paul Rycaut's schoolmate, whose wife Jane distinguished herself as being the first Englishwoman to visit the Seraglio, a fact reported by the pioneering cultural anthropologist John Bulwer, who noted that the ladies had been very curious about Lady Wyche's farthingale, a kind of hoop skirt which was worn underneath one's dress to support its voluminous folds. It was during Wyche's term of office that a terrible fire ravaged Constantinople (1633) and consumed thousands of houses.[126] Apart from his successful attempt

---

[125] Cited in Arthur Collins, *The English Baronetage* (London, 1741), 4, 221.

[126] John Bulwer, *Anthropometamorphosis* (London, 1653), 54. John Bulwer (1606–1656) was a distinguished doctor and natural philosopher who wrote several books on subjects such as gestures, lip reading, and sign-language. The honour of being the first European *man* to get into the women's part of the Seraglio (Thomas Dallam only saw it

to secure from Murad IV a reduction of the duty on English cloth, Wyche played host to two distinguished orientalists, Edward Pococke (1604–1691) and John Greaves,[127] both of whom "met with a kind reception" from him at the embassy.[128] Wyche also lodged Pococke in his own house and made him temporary chaplain to the English embassy. Pococke, who is mentioned twice in Rycaut's book, was the newly-appointed Professor of Arabic at Oxford, a chair which had been established as part of Archbishop Laud's efforts to modernise and reform university education. He had been abroad before, having served as chaplain to the English factor at Aleppo in 1630, and soon after taking up his academic post he was again on the move to Turkey, this time in the company of John Greaves, the recently-appointed Professor of Geometry at Gresham's College in London. Greaves, like Pococke, owed his career to Laud, although neither of them was excessively high church in his religious outlook, and it speaks volumes for the much-maligned Laud that his genuine interest in promoting learning, particularly about the East, included appointing men who did not necessarily follow his political line. Both Greaves and Pococke were asked to collect manuscripts and other interesting articles for Laud, and it seems that Greaves, in particular, was quite unscrupulous, at least by today's standards, in his assiduity. Greaves apparently persuaded one of the sipahis (cavalrymen or knights) of the Sultan to steal a copy of Ptolemy's *Almagest* from the library at the Seraglio; "this theft," Godfrey Goodwin informs us, "was not regarded as dishonourable at the time, but rather an act of rescue" (Bon, *Seraglio*, 16). As for Wyche himself, he seems to have been highly-regarded by Murad IV; even allowing for what the English considered oriental hyperbole, it must have gratified him to be referred to by the Sultan himself in a letter to Charles I as "the esteemed and famous lord and your trusty Sir Peter Wyche, whose end be happy."[129]

---

through a fence) probably goes to Domenico Gerosolimitano (c. 1552–1621), who was formerly Rabbi Samuel Vivas. After a career as a rabbi and a doctor in Cairo, he became physician to Murad III, which is probably why he was able to gain entry into a section of the palace forbidden to all but the Sultan and eunuchs. In 1593 he converted to Christianity and worked for the Inquisition in Mantua as a censor of Jewish books. Bernard Lewis believes that "his account, still [1963] unpublished, may underlie many of the descriptions by seventeenth-century European writers" (*Istanbul*, 66). See also Thomas Dallam's account.

[127] John Greaves (1602–1652) may perhaps be considered the earliest Egyptologist. His *Pyramidographia* (1646), which was part travel book and part scientific treatise, contained a great deal of information, mathematical calculations, and speculation on the pyramids of Giza. Greaves was probably the first to suggest that they could have been royal tombs.

[128] John Ward, *Lives of the Professors of Gresham College* (London, 1740), 138.

[129] Thomas Nabbes, *Continuation of Knolles's History of the Turks, printed as an appendix to the said history, as collected out of the despatches of Sir Peter Wyche* [London, 1638]) , 10; cited in Collins, *Baronetage* 4, 221. Nabbes (1605–1641) was a fairly well-known drama-

The next English ambassador was Sir Sackville Crowe (c. 1611–1683), a former Treasurer of the Navy whose tenure of office from the outset was a complete and utter disaster, not least for the ambassador himself, whose appointment by Charles I was not approved of by the Levant Company. "W. L.," who wrote an account of Crowe's successor Sir Thomas Bendish or Bendysh, described him scornfully as "a quondam[130] servant, and favourite, to George Duke of Buckingham," and went on to speak of Crowe's "injurious oppressions" of Levant merchants by means of a forged letter from Charles I to Sultan Ibrahim, who had come to the throne in 1640 at the sudden death of Murad IV, who was only twenty-nine.[131] Whether W. L.'s accusation of forgery was true or not, Crowe seems to have spent a great deal of his time quarrelling with the Levant Company, which eventually succeeded in procuring his recall in disgrace; he travelled back to England as a prisoner and was immediately thrown into the Tower of London, where he languished until 1652. Six years later Crowe succeeded in getting the Levant Company to drop all charges against him, but he nevertheless ended his days in the Fleet Prison, a broken and dishonoured old man.

On the other side of the coin, however, Alfred Wood states that Crowe "managed the affairs of the merchants with ability and resolution" (*Levant Company*, 89), and that his royalist sympathies when the Civil War broke out during his tenure in Constantinople were largely to blame for his differences with the Levant Company. Apparently Crowe had been channelling money and property from traders into the royalist cause;[132] this action certainly must have contributed to his detention and eventual imprisonment after his return to England, and did him little good in 1647. After Bendysh's arrival, however, Crowe stubbornly clung on to what he considered his legal authority from the king and refused to leave his post. With assistance from Sir Henry Hyde, the English Consul, in the Morea, a prominent if financially shady royalist merchant whose father had been attorney-general to James I's queen, he gained the support of the French, Austrians and Venetians, who did not recognise the new Commonwealth government in England. In 1650, the exiled Charles II actually "appointed" Hyde as his representative in Constantinople; Bendysh, meanwhile, had the backing of Isaac Pennington, a Parliament supporter and Governor of the Levant Company since 1644, who sat on the government committee approving his appointment,

---

tist who specialised in plays with a moral message, although he also wrote comedies. He is perhaps best-remembered for his historical play *Hannibal and Scipio* (1637). In spite of his interest in the Ottomans, Nabbes does not appear to have written any "Turk" plays.

[130] Former.

[131] W. L., *Newes from Turkie, or A true relation of the passages of the Right Honourable Sir Thomas Bendish, Baronet, Lord Ambassador, with the Grand Seigneur at Constantinople, his entertainment and reception* (London, 1648), A3.

[132] James Mather, *Pashas: Traders and Travellers in the Islamic World* (New Haven, CT: Yale University Press, 2011), 123.

a body which also included Oliver Cromwell as one of its members. The quarrel between the three men eventually led to tragedy, particularly for the rather incautious Hyde, who ended up on the scaffold for his royalist sympathies,[133] having been arrested by Bendysh and shipped back to England. It probably left the Ottomans wondering about the way the English seemed to conduct their affairs, although the crisis involving the deposition and murder of Sultan Ibrahim was taking place at precisely the same time. It was Bendysh who played host to the mathematician and theologian Isaac Barrow when he visited Constantinople in 1655 after he had been expelled from his fellowship at Cambridge by the Protectoral authorities.[134]

The anonymous W. L., moreover, was obviously a Company or Parliamentary man, and he heaped lavish praise on Crowe's successor for taking care of the Company's business in what he considered a more appropriate manner. Sir Thomas Bendysh, appointed by the House of Lords to clean up the mess left by Crowe (when Crowe was finally winkled out of his position and forcibly sent home), was, according to Fissel and Goffman, "a clever negotiator and a pragmatist" ("Viewing," 421). He had, they went on, "proven his ability to strike bargains with the Ottomans and stimulate commerce," and, according to W. L., "live[d] amongst the Turks, in great estimation and honour, equal if not superior to any former ambassador" (*Newes from Turkie*, A4). As for Crowe, he did not leave quietly; "Sir *Sackvile Crow* was to us a roaring lion," an official wrote; he "threatens nothing but Ruine and destruction, and since my Lord [Bendysh] came, told some of us, he would be as *Sampson*, if they forced him hence he would pull the house upon them." Eventually Crowe was "by two Chouzes [*chiauses*] without further help led into a Boat, and carryed where he never intended" (*Newes from Turkie*, 24), with Hyde as his fellow passenger.

During this time (1640–1648) the Ottoman Empire was ruled by Sultan Ibrahim, who at best might be termed eccentric and at worst described as a complete madman. Murad IV, on his deathbed due to excessive drinking, had originally commanded that Ibrahim, his one surviving brother, whom he had kept locked away for the entire reign, be eliminated. The Valide Sultana had ensured that Murad's orders were not carried out, and, thanks to her motherly concern,

---

[133] For an account of the whole rather sad affair, see M. C. Fissel and Daniel Goffman, "Viewing the Scaffold from Istanbul: The Bendysh-Hyde Affair, 1647–51," *Albion* 22 (1990), 421–48. This is an excellent retelling and analysis of the whole episode, which will not be rehearsed in full here.

[134] Isaac Barrow (1630–1677) was a pioneer in the field of calculus as well as being a distinguished theologian. He travelled in Europe and the Ottoman Empire for nearly four years, returning to England in 1659. He subsequently became the first Lucasian Professor at Cambridge and was also appointed Regius Professor of Greek at the Restoration. He was also Master of Trinity College and Gresham Professor of Geometry. He was elected a Fellow of the Royal Society in 1663.

the Empire fell into the hands of a man who was "an irresponsible voluptuary, fitful in temper, unscrupulous in character, and avaricious in spirit" (Kinross, *Ottoman Centuries*, 313). Ibrahim was, like Mustafa before him, immediately dubbed *deli* (crazy), and set about to live up to this appellation; for example, he decided that as his favourite perfume was amber, he would impose a tax on this substance, which could be paid either in money or in kind, which meant giving a great deal of amber to him as a "gift." He also seems to have had a fur fetish, particularly a passion for sable, levying a tax on this material as well and apparently planning to cover the floors and even the ceilings of the Seraglio with fur. "Heavy furs covered the walls and ceilings of the Topkapi Palace," Stanford Shaw tells us; what was more, "rich furs were given to important officials as they went to their posts, and they were expected to provide more furs and gifts in return' (*History of the Ottoman Empire* 1, 202). Ibrahim also loved fat women, and sent envoys all over his empire to procure the fattest girls they could find for his harem.

These actions in themselves may have seemed frivolous or harmless insofar as the actual government of the Empire was affected, but Ibrahim did not stop there; he executed several Grand Viziers and at one point may have threatened to drown all the women in his harem, which had reached in number nearly three hundred persons all told. More seriously, at least from Ibrahim's point of view, "several of his concubines and daughters formed their own political factions" (Shaw, *History of the Ottoman Empire* 1, 202),[135] which may have been the reason he might have contemplated this cruel and drastic solution in the first place. Ibrahim was, in the end, simply another name on the list of deficient Sultans whose weaknesses signalled to some observers the beginning of a decline in Ottoman power and prestige on the world stage, although, as in 1914, it would have been foolish simply to have written the empire off at this stage. It must be noted, however, that for the first years of the new reign Murad IV's last Grand Vizier, Kara Mustafa Pasha, "continued Murat's reforming policies, stemming inflation by increasing the gold and silver content of the coinage and reducing government extravagances" (Shaw, *History of the Ottoman Empire* 1, 201). One of the "extravagances" reduced, however, was the salaries of many Janissaries and Sipahis, a move which would later come back to haunt the administration. Ibrahim had Kara Mustafa executed in 1644.

---

[135] Jason Goodwin, for example, believes that Ibrahim did, in fact, carry out his threat. "He had all the women in his harem sewn alive into sacks and thrown into the Bosphorus," Goodwin writes, and also states that one of the women "floated free" and was rescued by a foreign ship, ending up in Paris, where she "caused a sensation" (*Lords of the Horizons*, 211–12). Since Turhan Hadice (see below), Mehmet IV's mother, and Khadija Muazzez (d. 1687), mother of Ahmed II, were also concubines of Ibrahim's and outlived him, he either missed a couple, or the whole story is apocryphal, as some historians claim.

By 1648 the Ottomans were getting tired of Ibrahim's excesses, and a plot was hatched to dispose of him as quickly as possible. The army was engaged with fighting in the Crimea against the Cossacks, and soon war broke out in Crete after Maltese pirates seized a Turkish ship that was ferrying pilgrims to Mecca. Sultan Ibrahim reacted with uncontrolled rage to this attack, which to his mind was being initiated by Christian powers against Muslims, and he ordered that all unbelievers, by which he meant Christians, should be killed wherever they could be found in the entire Ottoman Empire. However, calmer heads prevailed and foreign ambassadors found themselves placed under house arrest instead, whilst Ibrahim punished the Levant Company and other businesses by ordering them to close down. Furthermore, "when it was pointed out to him that the Order of Malta was composed almost entirely of Frenchman" (Kinross, *Ottoman Centuries*, 315) the Sultan even contemplated attacking France, but was persuaded to attack Crete instead, as it was known that the Maltese ships had stopped there to pick up supplies. Unfortunately Crete was a Venetian colony, and the Ottoman Empire was supposed to be observing a peace treaty with Venice. However, that did not stop Ibrahim from ordering an attack on Canea, a town in the west of Crete, followed up with another one on Candia, the main city of the island. This last action would cost the Ottomans dearly; they found themselves stuck in front of that city for twenty years as the Venetians instituted a blockade and stoutly resisted them. As Stanford Shaw remarks, however, "that both sides were able to carry on so long indicates that despite elements of decline both still had considerable wealth at their command" (*History of the Ottoman Empire* 1, 202).

Ibrahim dug himself deeper and deeper into trouble; his capricious cruelty and unpredictable actions were bad enough, but now he had precipitated a needless and lengthy war with Venice which would alienate the Janissaries, the Sipahis and even the Grand Mufti, who was eventually persuaded to issue a *fetva* deposing Ibrahim and replacing him with Prince Mehmet, Ibrahim's seven-year-old son by his wife Turhan Hadice. However, they needed the consent of the Valide Sultana, whose power was still very considerable and who was known to disapprove of Ibrahim's misrule. The old lady herself, after initially going through some soul-searching (Ibrahim was, after all, her son) and token resistance, assented to the deposition when it was broached by the Grand Vizier Sofu Mehmet Pasha and the mufti, although "in the company of statesmen," as Caroline Finkel tells us, "convention required that she appear to resist them" (*Osman's Dream*, 235). At first, after an initial outburst, it looked as if Ibrahim would go quietly; in any case, it would appear that murdering another Sultan was not on the minds of those who moved against him—yet. Most unfortunately for Ibrahim, his deposition and confinement in the Seraglio was immediately followed by an uprising by some of the Sipahis who were still loyal to him, and at that point the Grand Mufti, the Grand Vizier and other high officials decided the ultimate act must take place after all. Ibrahim was at first confined in the "Cage" (*Kafes*) which was the place in the Topkapi Seraglio where unwanted heirs were detained, often indefinitely or until the end of their lives, and then strangled as he sat in his room reading the Qur'an. Some accounts, however, state that Ibrahim "became madder and caused so much disturbance" that strangling had become necessary.[136] Appropriately enough, *deli* Ibrahim was buried in the same tomb as his uncle *deli* Mustafa.

English relations with the Ottoman court continued to be somewhat scrappy during Ibrahim's reign; when Bendysh arrived there in 1647 he seems, by his own accout, to have run into problems not just with Ottoman authorities but with the French and Venetian ambassadors as well. If W. L. is to be believed, these difficulties were largely due to the conduct of Sir Sackville Crowe rather than that of Bendysh himself, but the latter surmounted them by adopting the same tone with Turkish officials as Glover had before him. In one letter occasioned by procrastination from Ottoman officials he told the Grand Vizier "I am the first Ambassadour from England that ever presented Letters from the King, and a present to the Vizeere, that were returned with such dishonour as my selfe from you." Bendysh went on in even stronger words: "It becomes not mee, neither came I hither to plead my own rights," he wrote, "having Letters from so great and powerfull a King, as the King of England" (*Newes from Turkie*, 13). His persistence in using language like this probably did not help him when he later quarrelled with the religious authorities, which led to a personal beating from the Grand Mufti and a term of imprisonment. In spite of his royalist sympathies, Sir Thomas continued on as ambassador all through the Commonwealth and both Protectorates, but when Winchilsea was sent to replace him in 1660 he suddenly reacted as if he were another Sir Sackville Crowe, digging in his heels and refusing to leave Turkey until late 1661. A few years later, back in England and still feeling ill-treated, he published an eight-page *Remonstrance, or Manifest* in which he sought to "inform the world. . .of the services he hath done them [the Levant Company] and this nation, there; which by their carriage towards him, many of them seem to have forgotten" (*Remonstrance* [London, 1665], title page).

We have now come down to the time when the earl of Winchilsea arrived at the Ottoman court in the company of Paul Rycaut. The new Sultan, Mehmet IV, was, as Sir Thomas Roe recorded, "a very swarthy man, his face shining and pretty full eye, black and sparkling. . .He hath a great deal of Majesty in his countenance, and terror, too, when he pleased to put it on."[137] He would remain on the throne until his own peaceful deposition thirty-nine years later in 1687, the longest-reigning of all the Ottoman Sultans. There have been few detailed studies in English of the era of Mehmet IV; emphasis has been placed by historians on the fact that as he indulged in a great deal of hunting (he was styled *Avçi*,

---

[136] Jane Taylor, *Imperial Istanbul* (London: I. B. Tauris, 1998), 61.

[137] Sir Thomas Roe, *Negotiations in his Embassy to the Ottoman Porte from the year 1621 to 1628* (London: Samuel Richardson, 1749), 3. Cited in Mansel, *Constantinople* 138.

"the hunter"), this Sultan did not play a very active role in affairs of state. As Lord Kinross tells us, Mehmet IV's "hunting exploits were immortalized in poetry like the military exploits of his more illustrious forebears," and further that "he would write accounts of them in his own hand" (*Ottoman Centuries*, 334). However, the Victorian scholar Sir Edward Creasy, whose overseas experience was actually in Ceylon and who unfortunately did not give his sources, wrote that Mehmet IV "was never indifferent to literary pursuits, and he showed an hereditary fondness for the society of learned men." He went on to say that Mehmet encouraged historians in particular; "he loved to see them at court," Creasy wrote, and "he corrected their work with his own pen."[138]

There are some contemporary glimpses, too. In 1657, for example, Charles X of Sweden sent an embassy under Claes Brorson Rålamb to the Sultan which was very well-documented, and included a remarkable series of illustrations depicting the young Sultan and his court progressing through the city. Rålamb also provided a detailed account of what he observed, yet he says very little about Mehmet IV himself, who by the time the Swedes arrived was only seventeen years old and just coming of age, a time, Rålamb wrote, "when all Turkish emperors are obliged to make their first journey to Adrianople, which was their first residency in Europe."[139] Rålamb was mistaken about the reason for the procession—Mehmet was probably on his way to Edirne to hunt, not participating in some esoteric rite of passage—but he says nothing about the Sultan's character here or anywhere else, and it would appear from this account that the Sultan was little better than a decorative cipher.

We also have another account, written by a decidedly odd character, the determined and courageous Quaker traveller Mary Fisher (1623–1698), who set out for Constantinople in 1657, the same year as Rålamb, to convert Mehmet IV and his court to Christianity. She took ship to Smyrna, where the English

---

[138] Sir Edward Creasy, *History of the Ottoman Empire from the Beginning of their Empire to the Present Time* (London: Richard Bentley, 1877), 2, 70. The historian who found the most favour at Mehmet IV's court was Al-Rahman Abdi Pasha (d. 1692), "usually described, though whether correctly is open to some doubt, as the first officially-appointed historiographer" (N. K. Singh and A. Samiuddin, eds., *Encyclopaedic Historiography of the Muslim World* [Delhi: Global Vision Publishing House, 2004], 3, 815). Abdi, who is Creasy's source, was Imperial Private Secretary (1669), and he did write the annals of the reign, the *Ta'rikh-i Weka'i* (1685). Creasy notes a story in which Abdi told the Sultan, who had just come back from hunting and had asked him what he had been writing that day, that nothing memorable had happened, upon which Mehmet "playfully" stabbed him with a hunting-spear and told him that now he did have something to write about (Creasy, *History* 2, 70). Creasy's source for the story is von Hammer, who apparently was citing Abdi himself. The historian went on to become successively Governor of Bosnia, Basra, Egypt, Rumelia, and Crete.

[139] Karin Ådahl, ed., *The Sultan's Procession* (Istanbul: Swedish Research Institute, 2006), 84.

Consul, horrified that a woman should be travelling alone, put her on a Venetian ship with instructions to take her back where she came from. Fisher was not deterred by this setback; when the Venetians stopped in at a Greek port she simply jumped ship and made her way to Constantinople anyway, where she somehow persuaded the Grand Vizier to present her to the Sultan. Amazingly, she was not only able to get an audience but deliver her message, too. "He was very noble unto me," she wrote of Mehmet IV, "and so were all about him," concluding rather astonishingly that "[the Turks] are more near Truth than many nations."[140] Whilst paying the Muslim Turks that compliment, Fisher no doubt had in mind the dreadful treatment she had received two years earlier from the Christian puritans of New England, who had imprisoned her, strip-searched her (likely to see whether she had witches' marks on her body), flogged her, and even added insult to injury by burning her books.[141] The Turks, on the other hand, probably thought that Mary Fisher was quite mad, which gave her a special link, in their eyes, with the divine.

The case of Mary Fisher gives us indirect insight into the sultanate of Mehmet IV, especially in the light of a recent re-examination of his reign by the historian Marc David Baer. Drawing on Ottoman sources, which he explains for the first time in English, Baer concentrates on Mehmet's reputation for effecting personal conversions to Islam, especially after he had come under the influence of Mehmet Vani Effendi, "the enemy of innovators and the beloved of those that believe in the oneness of God."[142] Mehmet likely showed courtesy and toleration towards Fisher because he saw something of himself in her even though she would have been classed as an unbeliever; she was fervent for Christian converts, and for her part must have recognised a fellow zealot for a faith that was, in many aspects, not that much different from what she considered to be the "truth."

These references are really just tantalising tidbits of information, but all they tell us in the end is that Mehmet IV was fond of hunting, appreciated literature and was kind to eccentric Quakers. We know also, of course, that later on he took personal charge of his army in the war against the Hapsburgs, but even then he handed over the command to his generals and resumed his hunting whilst they

---

[140] Cited in *Quaker Faith and Practice: the Book of Christian Discipline* (London: Society of Friends, 2008), 19.27.

[141] For further details, see, for example, Bernadette Andrea, *Women and Islam in Early Modern English Literature* (Cambridge: Cambridge University Press, 2009), particularly chapter 3, "Early Quaker Women, the Missionary Position and Mediterraneanism."

[142] Nihadi, *Tarih-i Nihadi*, fol. 191b, cited in Marc David Baer, *Honored by the Glory of Islam: Conversion and Conquest in Ottoman Europe* (Oxford: Oxford University Press, 2008), 111. Baer makes his case for Mehmet IV very convincingly, clearly demonstrating that this Sultan was not the effete, lazy, and ineffectual ruler that historians have made him out to be.

pressed on to the very gates of Vienna and catastrophic defeat. A. N. Kurat, for example, indicates that the two Köprülü viziers, who followed the Sultan's mother in effectively running the Ottoman Empire, were the dominant forces in the realm, and that Mehmet himself seems to have been, for the most part, a Sultan on the sidelines.[143] Marc Baer commented that "In the eye of writers during the first decade of Mehmet IV's reign, the ruler wilted into the background, overshadowed by his powerful mother" (*Honored*, 61). After that, as Lord Kinross states, "Sultan Mehmet, heeding the counsel of reforming elements, left the government of his empire implicitly in [Mehmet] Köprülü's hands and later in those of his son Ahmet, who succeeded him" (*Ottoman Centuries*, 332). Does this verdict, which seems to be that of most historians, really conform to the actual facts of Mehmet IV's rule?

This is not, in the end, the whole picture of the era; indeed, the concentration of modern historians on Mehmet's passion for hunting seems more a reflection of the prejudices of their own times than of what people actually felt in the seventeenth century. As Baer points out, "[Mehmet IV] is damned, when mentioned at all, for his 'addiction to the hunt,' which acquired 'a pathological nature.'" Hunting, as we know, has long been the pastime of kings; James I was renowned for it, and the depredations which Edward VII and his son George V inflicted on the partridge, pheasant, and woodcock populations of the English countryside are well-known. The current Prince of Wales has frequently come under hostile scrutiny for his love of fox hunting. In Mehmet's time, however, "prowess in hunting demonstrated courage in facing death and magnanimity in either sparing a great animal or distributing the rewards of the hunt" (Baer, *Honored*, 180); it had nothing to do with sitting safely behind bushes with loaders or in a trench whilst beaters whipped the game birds up into the sky, from which the "hunters" picked them off. It had to do with the serious demonstration of the ruler's manhood. "If a Sultan aimed to demonstrate his martial skill and practice for war," Baer tells us, "the struggle between man and beast was the best arena" (*Honored*, 180). A Sultan needed to show that he was worthy of the appellation *ghazi*, which meant "warrior for the faith against the infidels" (*Honored*, 11), and hunting was a stage on the way to accomplishing that goal. What was more important, as Mehmet IV hunted he travelled quite far, and would naturally come across non-Muslims as he did so, or if he stopped for refreshment, the activity afforded him an opportunity to also "hunt" for potential converts.

Rycaut himself missed these points, comparing Mehmet with Nimrod and claiming that the people around the Sultan found his hunting not just "tedious to the court," but also "troublesome and expensive to the whole country." He described hunting as a form of "oppression" which actually killed off some of the

---

[143] A. N. Kurat, "The Ottoman Empire under Mehmet IV," in *New Cambridge Modern History*, ed. F. L. Carsten, vol. 5 (Cambridge: Cambridge University Press, 1961), 500–17.

Sultan's followers, who were unused to the hardships and the cold nights, not to mention the exercise, and there is no reason to doubt him. It was, Baer tells us, this view of Mehmet IV which eventually prevailed, even in the Ottoman Empire, just a generation after the Sultan's death, and Rycaut was, perhaps, one of the earliest writers to misrepresent all that the Sultan stood for, based solely on a cultural misunderstanding of the symbolic role of hunting. Marc Baer, on the other hand, sees Mehmet as "demonstrating real personal leadership, piety, military prowess and male virtue in an era when the Sultan was expected to be a ceremonial figure of little significance" (*Honored*, 251). Yet Rycaut wrote of "the absolute and unlimited power of this prince," the idea that "his mouth is the law itself," and that he can "alter and annul the most settled and fixed rules, at least to waive and dispense with them when they are an obstacle to his government." His subjects are taught, he tells us, that "obedience to the emperor" is "a principle of religion rather than of state," but observes a little later in the same chapter that "the decay of Turkish discipline" was started "in the time of Sultan Ibrahim, when women governed, and now in this present age of Sultan Mehmet, whose counsels are given chiefly by his mother, negros, eunuchs and some handsome young *mosayp* or favourite." Rycaut wants, it seems, to have it both ways: on the one hand Mehmet IV is an absolute monarch whose very word is law, yet what he says is merely whatever is put into his mouth by the people around him, and as a consequence "discipline" is under threat. If Mehmet was really a "sedentary" Sultan, the fact was certainly lost on the religious scholars at the end of his reign. Baer states that by 1686 they "desired a sedentary Sultan in Istanbul" (*Honored*, 233), and that when this was not forthcoming, they moved to depose him, with help from the administration and from the military. There is some irony in this; Ottoman successes against the Hapsburgs had been, to say the least, questionable, with the failed siege of Vienna as the straw which broke the camel's back; however, by that time Mehmet had virtually withdrawn from the scene of the conflict. From then on the Sultan was requested to remain behind in the capital and refrain from taking part in any more military ventures.

We know further that Mehmet IV was temperate in a court where many people seem to have drunk too much. Caroline Finkel cites Dr. John Covel, who was in Turkey during the 1670's, as stating that "all at court drank, except for the Sultan and the two Mustafa Pashas" (*Osman's Dream*, 278).[144] Both Murad IV and Ibrahim had been exceedingly heavy drinkers. It could also be said

---

[144] John Covel (1638–1722) first went to Istanbul as a chaplain to the Levant Company in 1670, but soon he seems to have been practically running the English embassy. Having returned to England in 1677, he resumed his academic and clerical career; he served as Master of Christ's College, Cambridge (1688–1722), and became a pioneer in the scientific study of fossils. Theodore Bent published Covel's account of his sojourn and travels in the Ottoman Empire (London: Hakluyt Society, 1893) and J-P Grélois has recently re-edited it with a French introduction (Paris: Réalités Byzantines, 1998).

that Mehmet was humane, as his brother Süleyman, born in 1642, was allowed to live quietly in relative obscurity until 1687, when a *fetva* was issued deposing Mehmet and Süleyman found himself elevated to the supreme power. The deposed Sultan made a dignified exit. "If your desire is to remove me from the throne," Mehmet replied resignedly to the Grand Vizier's report, "then I desire that my son Mustafa, may he be entrusted to God, passes to my place. . .after this, if you resolve to do me harm, I take refuge in God from evil" (Silhadar Findikili Mehmet Ağa, *Silahdar Tarihi* 2:291, cited in Baer, *Honored*, 236). However, Süleyman II repaid his brother by allowing him to remain alive; Mehmet was placed nominally under house arrest in the Topkapi Palace, but actually died in Edirne (1693), suggesting that his confinement was not that strict, although his wish that his son Mustafa succeed him was set aside for the time being. Mustafa II eventually succeeded in 1695, reigning only until 1703.

Thus it was that during Rycaut's time in Turkey the power appeared, particularly to outsiders like Rycaut, behind the throne rather than actually on it, although it would not be fair, as we have seen, to say that Mehmet IV never exerted his powers, especially as he grew to maturity. Furthermore, he was not entirely uninformed about politics or diplomacy; in 1653, for example, he appointed an ambassador to India, and was later reported by Mustafa Na'ima as recommending that "a learned and able man be appointed as ambassador, for ambassadors are the honour of kings" (cited in Lewis, *Middle East Mosaic*, 141), which may or may not be a genuine example of youthful wisdom. Rycaut gives an account of the deposition and death of Sultan Ibrahim and the elevation of Mehmet IV to the throne as a child, and he also spends a fair amount of time discussing the rule of the rival Sultanas which followed, but even he has little to say about Mehmet IV as a person, even though it is certainly likely that he had met the Sultan more than once. During the minority of Murad IV, Ibrahim's mother Kösem Sultan had been virtual regent, and she was still very much alive and active when Mehmet IV succeeded to the throne. His mother, Turhan Hadice, was rather young to take the reins of power into her own hands, and the men who had deposed Ibrahim felt that it would not do to share power with a woman who was only in her twenties. What they did was interesting; the position of "Queen Mother" was now settled on Kösem Sultan rather than the younger woman, which they hoped would help to settle the factionalism which had descended on the court during the reign of Ibrahim. In any case, the plan did not work, even with a pliant Grand Vizier, for rebellions broke out in various parts of the empire and viziers came and went with alarming rapidity, some lasting barely a few months.

The two women, moreover, did not get along with each other. A revolt broke out amongst tradesmen and merchants in Constantinople (1651), who were furious with the debasement of the coinage, corruption had emptied the treasury, and the Janissaries were even more restless than usual. Kösem Sultan had an enemy in the powerful Sheikh ul-Islam, Karaçelebizade Abdül Aziz Effendi, who now found himself the unwilling target of a request from the merchants to head up a delegation to intercede with the Sultan. He did not wish to risk getting involved, and prevaricated; when they insisted, he tried to run away, but was caught and forced to assent to their demands. When the Sultan heard, he decided he would give the Sheikh ul-Islam a hearing, but before he could get to it Kösem Sultan arrived and confronted Abdül Aziz Effendi, who, after being questioned about his business, managed to persuade the Queen Mother that the Grand Vizier Melek Ahmet Pasha be dismissed. Mehmet IV, after speaking with her, agreed, "and ordered [the Grand Vizier] to write a memorandum designed to bring to an end the unrest" (Finkel, *Osman's Dream*, 241), but the populace wanted one from the Sultan himself, not his vizier. After the people, supported by the Janissaries, demanded the Grand Vizier's ousting, Kösem Sultan thought she could find a replacement in Kara Çavuş Mustafa, the commander of the Janissaries. He refused the job if it meant that he had to come to the Topkapi to receive the seals of office, and Siyavuş Pasha found himself catapulted into the position instead.

The end of the story was the murder of Kösem Sultan, told in great detail by Rycaut. This was followed by the dismissal of the Sheikh ul-Islam and the unfurling of the sacred standard of the Prophet, an act which rallied the people of Constantinople against the Janissaries and brought Turhan Hadice's faction to power. As Rycaut gives the ensuing events accurately and graphically in book 1, chapter 4, we need not recapitulate them any further here.

## Travellers, Historians and Rycaut's Sources: A Mosaic of Views

The Ottoman Empire, along with Persia and other eastern powers, signified for sixteenth and early seventeenth century readers in England at once a place of exotic mystery and of terrifying power. It was seen by Englishmen through a veil of "prejudice against Islam, fear of a powerful enemy, the lure of eastern trade, and a fair amount of ignorance and hearsay," as Linda Darling succinctly puts it ("Ottoman Politics," 73). No one quite knew how it operated, but what they did know was that it was Muslim and "decadent," that its rulers were cruel people with hundreds of wives and concubines, and that they wished to extend their domination over the world. Richard Knolles, whose work will be discussed below, believed that the Ottomans had an "ardent and infinite desire of sovereignty."[145] Such beliefs were, as is well-known, reflected in travellers' accounts, histories, and all manner of literature from serious drama to broadside ballads.[146] Rycaut

---

[145] Richard Knolles, Epistle to *The Generall Historie of the Turkes* (London, 1603), n.p.n.
[146] Scholars have tended to concentrate on drama rather than other literature, but for those who did not attend theatrical performances there were always popular ballads,

was likely a theatre-goer as well as a reader of history and travel-writing, and would not have failed to have become thoroughly conversant with what dramatists and travellers said and believed about the Ottoman Empire. We will discuss here some of the named influences on his book, but also show how far Rycaut's interpretation of what he saw in Turkey reflected what others already thought or supposed, and thus suggest possibilities for the origin of some of his own ideas and conclusions.

We begin with Richard Knolles (c. 1545–1610), whose *Generall Historie of the Turkes* (1603) was one of the most influential books in English on the subject, although it was not quite the earliest.[147] Knolles, a Fellow of Lincoln College, Oxford, was a schoolmaster of an institution established in 1563 at Sandwich, Kent, by Sir Roger Manwood, an eminent barrister and jurist, who, together with his son Sir Peter, became patrons and encouragers of Knolles's historiographical ambitions. Knolles seems to have led a fairly quiet life in Kent, teaching, writing his fourteen-hundred-page book on the Ottoman Empire and translating Jean Bodin's *Six livres de la république*. He never travelled to Turkey, or indeed to anywhere else outside England that we know about. Knolles dedicated the first edition of his work to James I; its publication coincided with that king's accession to the English throne. Also, James was known to be hostile to the Turks, having in his youth celebrated the 1572 victory at Lepanto with a poem written in 1591, in which he calls them "faithless" and puts them in league with Satan.[148] Knolles's book went into another printing during its author's lifetime (1610) as well as a third, posthumous edition in 1621. Further editions appeared in 1638, 1679, and 1699 (a very much abridged edition), which indicates how popular Knolles's work was. Rycaut himself would undertake a continuation of Knolles's work, taking

broadsides, and pamphlets. For details see Katie S. Sisneros, *Fearing the "Turban'd Turk:" Socio-Economic Access to Genre and the "Turke" of Early Modern English Drama and Broadside Ballads* (Unpublished Masters Thesis, University of Nebraska, 2010).

[147] Peter Ashton had translated Paolo Giovio's *Turcicarum rerum commentarius* in 1546; Ralph Carr's *The Mahometane or Turkish Historie* (1600), a work in three books, does not seem to have had the same impact on readers as Knolles and is not mentioned by Rycaut. It does, however, contain extensive passages translated from French and Italian historians. There were earlier European works available to Rycaut, too, which included Giovanantonio Menavino's *Delle legge, religione et vita de' Turchi* (1548), Georgius de Hungaria's *Tractatus de moribus, condicionibus et nequicia Turcorum* (written about 1460, printed 1576), Thomas Newton's *History of the Saracens. . .drawn out of Augustine Curio and other sundry good authors* (1575) and René Lusinge, sieur des Alymes's *The beginning, continuance and decay of estates, wherein are handled many notable questions concerning the establishment of empires and monarchies* (1606), translated by Sir John Finnett, a work which extensively discusses the Ottoman state and government. The translator was James I's master of ceremonies.

[148] For details of this poem, see Robert Appelbaum, "War and Peace in the *Lepanto* of James VI and I," *Modern Philology*, Vol. 97 (2000): 333–63.

Turkish history down to the year 1679, and adding his own book to it as a kind of appendix (1687–1700), thus piggy-backing on a well-respected text to gain fame for his own efforts.

Rycaut was not the only one; a continuation based on the papers of Sir Peter Wyche was issued by Thomas Nabbes in 1638, as we have mentioned previously. Knolles's book, which Matthew Dimmock calls "authoritative and antagonistic,"[149] was widely read, and in the next century would be commended for its style by, amongst others, Samuel Johnson in *The Rambler*, although he thought that few people would be interested in the subject matter in spite of the quality of Knolles's writing. "None of our writers can, in my opinion," Johnson declared, "justly contest the superiority of Knolles," but he goes on to dismiss the "remoteness and barbarity" of the Ottoman Empire and deplores the fact that Knolles employed "his genius upon a foreign and uninteresting subject."[150] A later admirer of Knolles was George Saintsbury, who noted that "he [Knolles] has his obscure and complicated matter perfectly in hand," that he possessed "very considerable narrative power," and was "a great craftsman, if not exactly a great artist."[151] Some years before Alexander Chalmers, paraphrasing Johnson's earlier judgment, had praised Knolles for his "pure, nervous, elevated and clear" style, although he also noted that the book was "obscured by time and sometimes vitiated by false wit."[152] Orhan Burian, a Turkish scholar, commented succinctly that Knolles "writes with hatred," but at the same time "seems fascinated by the possibilities of his subject,"[153] and Filiz Turhan characterises Knolles's "tone" as one "of admiration and contempt," which she believes "anticipates the tone of many subsequent writings."[154] This attitude, which we may label "the fascination of the abomination," was completely typical of so many European writers that it has become almost a cliché and certainly a commonplace.

The purpose of Knolles's book was not, of course, to present his readers with a strictly objective history of the Turks and their empire. Knolles was writing for Christian readers, specifically English ones, who wanted information about what seemed to them a very potent menace to their religion and their way of life if its expansion were to continue and if the European powers were unable to stop its

[149] Matthew Dimmock, *New Turkes: Dramatizing Islam and the Ottomans in Early Modern England* (Aldershot, UK: Ashgate Books, 2005), 201.
[150] Samuel Johnson, *The Rambler*, 122 (May 18, 1751). http://www.readbookonline.net/readOnline/28579/.
[151] Cited in Henry Craik, ed., *English Prose* (New York: Macmillan, 1916), 209.
[152] Alexander Chalmers, *General Biographical Dictionary* [London, 1812–17] (New York: Kessinger Reprints, 2004), 19, 405.
[153] Orhan Burian, "A Dramatist of Turkish History and his Source: Goffe in the Light of Knolles," *Journal of the Royal Central Asian Society* (1953), 266.
[154] Filiz Turhan, *The Other Empire: British Romantic Writings about the Ottoman Empire* (London: Routledge, 2003), 11–12.

spread. He might even have hoped that his book would contribute, in some small way, to an informed debate on the subject of putting together a coalition of western powers against the Ottoman Empire. Knolles was hardly alone in this desire; he himself had drawn on a massive compendium of sources, which included the German historian and legal scholar Hans Löwenklau (Leunclavius), the exiled Albanian priest Marin Barleti (Barletius), the French chronicler Jacques Fontaine (Fontanus), and the Italian historian Paolo Giovio (Jovius) as well as contemporary travellers such as Ogier de Busbecq and Nicolas Nicolay.[155] The primary source for Knolles's book, however, was Jean-Jacques Boissard's *Vitae et icones sultanorum Turcicorum* (1597); indeed, Orhan Burian, whilst acknowledging the value of Knolles's work as a synthesis, believed that the latter was "mainly relying on Boissard" ("Dramatist," 266). Boissard (1528–1602), who was probably better-known as a writer of Latin poetry and an antiquarian than he was as either a traveller or an orientalist, had certainly never been on any journey further east than Greece and Italy. Knolles, as Bernard Lewis puts it, "was expressing the common feelings of Europe when he spoke of the Turkish Empire as 'the present terror of the world'" (*Muslim Discovery*, 32). He also demonstrated the prurience that would appear again and again in plays and fiction about the Turks from his own time through John Brooks's potboiler *The Lustful Turk: Lascivious Scenes from a Harem* (1828) down to T. E. Lawrence's account of the predatory Turkish officer in his quasi-autobiographical *Seven Pillars of Wisdom* (1922). Knolles commented that Turks "are for the most part all Sodomites" (*General History*, 962),

---

[155] Some of these are discussed in Sila Senlen, "Richard Knolles's *The Generall Historie of the Turkes* as a Reflection of Christian Historiography," http://dergiler.ankara.edu. tr/dergiler/19/23/140.pdf. Further information on this subject may also be found in Donald Lach, *Asia in the Making of Europe* (University of Chicago Press, 1977), 2, 228ff. The authoritative work on Knolles is V. J. Parry's posthumously-published *Richard Knolles's History of the Turks*, ed. Salih Ozbaran (Istanbul: The Economic and Social Foundation of Turkey, 2003). Löwenklau (1533–1593) wrote the *Pandects of Turkish History* (1588) and *Annales sultanorum Othmanidarum* (1596). Barleti (c. 1450–1513), who fled his native city Shkodër in 1478 after enduring two Ottoman sieges, went to Italy; his *Chronicorum Turcicorum* was printed in 1578. Jacques Fontaine or Fonteyn, a native of Bruges, was the author of *De bello Rhodio libri III* (1524), in which he gives a blow-by-blow description of Süleyman the Magnificent's siege of that city in 1522. Paolo Giovio (1483–1552) was the author of *Historiarum sui temporis* (1551–1552). In Volume 2 of that work, amongst other things, he discusses a plan for having the Portuguese conquer the spice routes in order to weaken the Turks, whom he believes wish to overrun Europe. He is very worried about the power of Süleyman the Magnificent. Nicolas Nicolay (1517–1583) was a French soldier and geographer; in 1551 he was sent by Henri II to accompany Gabriel de Luetz (see above) in his embassy to Süleyman the Magnificent, and his *Quatre premiers livres de navigations* (1568) were the result. This work was translated into English by Thomas Washington as *The Navigations, Peregrinations and Voyages made unto Turkie by M. Nicolas Nicolay* (1585).

which of course made them an even greater menace to Christianity. The sexual immorality of Turks was, as we have seen above, well-documented in the imagination of several English dramatists, many of whom took their moral compass as well as their "facts" from historians like Knolles and his sources rather than from what was actually the case.

Knolles's attitude towards the Turks, their religion, and their society was typical not only of its own day, but of many years to come; Gerald Maclean notes, for example, that when the Protestant minister William Biddulph travelled in the Ottoman Empire some years later (1600–1612), his experiences, which he recorded in *Travels of Certain Englishmen* (1609), far from broadening his mind, "reinforced prejudices he had brought with him" (MacLean, *Oriental Travel*, 96), most likely planted by reading Knolles. Biddulph, MacLean tells us, had "little or no interest in [Turkish] social, cultural or political life" (*Oriental Travel*, 101) and indeed seems to have believed that too much interest in these things could somehow threaten Protestant religious stability. The English ambassador Henry Lello had warned Thomas Dallam that he must be very careful when he presented his mechanical organ to Mehmet III, because the Sultan was "the grand enemy of all Christians,"[156] and there was no telling what he might do.

The sexual misconceptions of the Turks continued apace as well, and not just in plays. As early as 1586, for example, we find the Welsh minister and historian Meredith Hanmer, a contemporary of Knolles, inveighing against "Mahometical Sodomites"[157] in a sermon preached after some Turkish galley-slaves were liberated from the Spaniards by Sir Francis Drake. Rycaut himself spoke of "the libidinous flames of depraved nature" which he found typical of Turks, but, at least according to Nabil Matar's way of looking at it, he "invoked the theory of 'Platonick love' to explain homosexuality among the Turks." This was linked, of course, with Castiglione's idea of Neoplatonic love in *The Courtier*, which was "a relationship of harmonious nonsexual male friendship" (*Turks*, 121), that could be found found expressed by Shakespeare in his sonnets and in many personal letters of the time. "It will not be from our purpose," Rycaut explained, "to acquaint the reader that the doctrine of Platonic love hath found disciples in the schools of the Turks." This put the Turks in the same category as Castiglione's urbane and polished courtiers, that is, in the tradition of Socrates, Alcibiades, and the other participants in Plato's *Symposium* rather than as sex-crazed sodomites. It all makes Rycaut look a little confused, as in the same paragraph he refers to "the deformity of their depraved inclinations." The women, too, "die

---

[156] Thomas Dallam, *The Diary of Master Thomas Dallam*, in *Early Voyages and Travels in the Levant*, ed. J. T. Bent (London: Hakluyt Society, 1893), 1, 65.

[157] Meredith Hanmer, *The Baptising of a Turke* (London, 1586), 4. Hanmer (1543–1604) spent most of his career in Ireland, where he became chancellor of St. Canice, Kilkenny. After Drake freed the slaves, they were given passage back to Turkey, but one of them "defected" and converted to Christianity.

with amorous affections one to the other." Were the Turks really like Hanmer's "Sodomites," or were they just engaging in a sophisticated variation of male or female bonding? Rycaut seems rather wavering on this point, allowing prudery and stereotyping to get in the way of objectivity, whilst at the same time trying to explain it all away in terms of classical archetypes.

Biddulph and other writers (including Rycaut, to a different extent) had used the Ottoman experience to advocate reforms in England; it was almost as if English writers were afraid that their country would somehow become like the way they saw the Ottoman Empire, a seething hotbed of corruption, sexual deviance, immorality, unspeakable cruelty, and decidedly the wrong religious beliefs. For Rycaut, who as a young man had experienced the instability of the Civil War and had welcomed the Restoration, there were certainly lessons to be learned from reading the accounts of those who had ventured before him, actually or imaginatively, into the belly of the Ottoman beast. The prejudiced view of Islam taken by many Western writers is far too well-known to rehearse here in detail, but a few examples may give an idea of it. More than a century and a half after Martin Luther had declared that "the spirit or soul of Antichrist is the Pope, his flesh or body the Turk" (Luther, *Table-talk*, cited in Lewis, *Mosaic*, 13), Rycaut's friend Thomas Smith decried Islam as "a religion. . .made up of folly and imposture and gross absurdities," which, he went on to state, "has nothing to recommend itself to the choice of any sober and wise man." Furthermore, Smith continued, Islam had "no subtle, no grave discourses of learning or reason, not so much as an argument that looks like probable" (*Remarks*, 27). George Sandys, whilst giving a reasonably fair account of its practices, nonetheless reiterated Christian prejudice by calling Islam an "irreligious religion" (*Travels*, 46) and concluding that "neither it came from God (save as a scourge by permission) neither can bring them to God that follow it" (47). For Rycaut himself, whilst he accepts some of the standard anti-Islamic prejudices, it is possible that in his detailed discussion of the numerous Islamic sects (which, incidentally, was copied almost *verbatim* by Smith), he might be suggesting that if observers believed that the Ottoman state was in decline and that Islam was a false religion, they might think how much sectarian divisions had contributed to the disorder in a state and perhaps reflect on the fragmentation of religion during the Civil War years, not to mention the continuous strife between Catholics and Protestants in Europe. If Islam had been a united religion, would the Ottoman Empire have become even more powerful?

This having been said, Rycaut also had the benefit of less prejudiced accounts, such as the *Turkish Letters* of the Hapsburg ambassador Ogier Ghiselin de Busbecq, whom he, like Knolles before him, quotes on more than one occasion. As Amanda Wunder observes, "the genre of the published letter permitted a degree of informality, honesty, and spontaneity rarely found in a composed book" ("Western Travelers," 96), and this is certainly true with Busbecq. He resided in Constantinople for the better part of eight years (1554–1562), and his letters, written from Constantinople to Nicholas Michault, a colleague in the

Hapsburg diplomatic service, reveal that he was a most tolerant and broad-minded, not to mention patient man. Busbecq does not waste time dilating on the subjects we have discussed above; he is much more interested in court intrigues and studying the various kinds of flowers and shrubs that he found in Turkey as well as taking the trouble to find out how ordinary people in the countryside lived. Indeed, his main claim to fame in some circles may well be his introduction of tulips to Europe. Like Rycaut, Busbecq was interested in the Turkish military as well as in religion, and conveyed what information he could about it back to his master in Vienna, which seems to have been a *sine qua non* of travel accounts from the Ottoman Empire, and comprises the whole of the third part of Rycaut's book. Busbecq took pains to show what sort of prejudices, presuppositions and fears the Turks had about their Christian neighbours and erstwhile adversaries. He gave a balanced account of the court of Süleyman the Magnificent, and evidently genuinely admired the now ageing Sultan, whom he saw and spoke to on several occasions. In the fourth letter, for example, Busbecq states that he wants to "tell you of an act of kindness on the part of the Emperor," and goes on to relate how he reminded Süleyman of some money that was owed him and for which he had forgotten to ask for the correct amount. The Sultan, "with his usual generosity," ordered the money to be paid at once, and never questioned the amount. "If I ever allow myself to forget so generous an act of kindness," Busbecq wrote with commendable hyperbole, "I shall regard myself as no longer worthy to live upon this earth" (*Turkish Letters*, 130). Busbecq was also very concerned about the lack of readiness he saw on the part of Christian powers in Europe to combat possible Turkish expansion. "The defeat of the Christians at sea," he wrote uneasily, "made me very anxious lest the Turks should become more arrogant" (*Turkish Letters*, 122).

Besides Busbecq, there were also some English writers who exhibited more broad-mindedness than Knolles or Hanmer, and whom Rycaut could have read. The essayist Francis Osborne, for example, although he had never travelled to Turkey, nevertheless wrote in his *Political Reflections on the Government of Turkey* (1656) that the Sultan (Mehmet IV) is not "lycorish after the choice of the Issue of Kings for his own bed," but finds "the same content in the embraces of a subject or a slave," because such "modesty," Osborne reasoned, "acquits him from the danger of having a Spie in his Bosome, or a coequall in his counsels," and "renders the Government less factious" (Cited in Lewis, *Middle East Mosaic*, 197).[158] Sir Henry Blount's *Voyage into the Levant* (1636) was unique for its time

---

[158] Francis Osborne (1593–1659), a former Master of the Horse to William Herbert, earl of Pembroke, was a Parliamentary supporter during the Civil War. He is probably best-known for his very popular *Advice to his Son* (1656–1658), in which, amongst other things, he supplies advice on travelling. The book was attacked for its misogynistic outlook by writers even at the time. Osborne also wrote *Traditional Memoirs of the Reign of Q. Elizabeth and K. James* (1658), an anecdotal history.

in that the author decided that the best way to experience the Ottoman Empire
was to steer clear of his own countrymen, suspend his preconceived notions or
prejudices, and even adopt local clothing. "Hee who would behold these times
in their greatest glory," Blount states at the beginning of his lively and interesting account, "could not find a better Scene than Turkey," and he writes further of
"weaning his mind from a former habit of opinion," an action which he expresses
by the odd metaphor "putting off the old man."[159]

Another source whom Rycaut likely drew upon was Michel Baudier (c.
1589–1645), court historiographer to Louis XIII and the author of three works
on the Ottoman Empire, which he himself had never visited. They were the
*Inventarie général de l'histoire des Turcs* (1619), *Histoire général de la réligion des
Turcs, avec la vie de leur prophète Mahomet* (1626) and *Histoire general du sérail et
de la cour du grand Turc* (1635), the last of which was also available to Rycaut in
an English translation by Edward Grimeston,[160] issued in the same year. How
accurate Baudier's information was may be a moot point, but his claims are certainly confident. "I approach unto the proudest of all other princes," he states in
his introduction; "yea, so near as I dive into his secrets, visit his person, discover
his most hidden affections and relate his most particular loves." Baudier claims
that the seraglio is "where the secret of all these things is carefully shut up," and
promises to discuss Turkish manners, customs, government and court-system.[161]
Appended to the volume is Baudier's much shorter *History of the Court of the King
of China*, which he based on conversations with a Jesuit who had been there; it
is likely, then, that Baudier used the same approach with his Turkish book. On
Grimeston's second title page we find that the book also offers "an image of the
Ottoman greatness, a table of human passions, and the examples of the incon-
stant prosperities of the court," indicating that Baudier and his translator had a
moral purpose in writing this book.

Baudier concentrates on describing in intimate detail the Ottoman court
and its workings, the seraglio being the focus of the second book, in which he

---

[159] Sir Henry Blount, *Voyage into the Levant* (London, 1636; repr. New York: General Books Reprints, 2010), 8. Blount (1602–1682) was in the Levant for a relatively short
time (1634–1635), but his book went into eight editions and was expanded to cover other
places he had visited at the same time. He fought for Charles I in the Civil War, but in
1655 sat as a member of Cromwell's trade commission. His entry in Chalmers's *General
Biographical Dictionary* characterises his travel writing as exhibiting "more of the philosopher than the traveller" (3, 422), and credits Blount with a number of other works,
including a satire.

[160] Edward Grimeston (d. 1640), serjeant-at-arms to the speaker of Parliament, was
one of the most prolific and distinguished translators of his time. He is perhaps best-
known for his version of Louis Turquet de Mayerne's *History of Spain* (1612), as well as,
amongst others, histories of France and the Netherlands.

[161] Michel Baudier, *The History of the Imperiall Estate of the Grand Seigneurs*, trans.
Edward Grimeston (London, 1635; repr. La Vergne, TN: Nabu Reprints, 2011), 2–3.

includes a chapter entitled "Of the loves of the great ladies of the Turk's court and of their violent affections among themselves," indicating the usual prurient European fascination with same-sex relationships as they were imagined. Baudier writes of "a foolish womanish lover," who goes to take a bath with other women, "and burns with a flame which [she] is not able to quench," after which she "attempts to do that (although in vain) which I must here conceal." Of course, for Baudier, this lust may be blamed on "Mahometan ignorance" (*Imperial Estate*, 167). Rycaut perhaps had this in mind when he wrote of Turkish harem women's "lasciviousness and wanton carriage," and how they "die with amorous affections one to the other," for such things are not mentioned in, for example, Busbecq. Nabil Matar notes that Rycaut and Baudier both see "sexual repression" as causing these relationships as well as women's frustration with their husbands preferring boys.[162] In other matters, Baudier does not spend much time discussing religion or military matters, but concentrates on the structure of the Sultan's court, the functions of its various officers and the day-to-day life of the Sultan himself, concluding with a detailed description of the burial-ceremony of the Sultans. Baudier took pains to show how all the pomp, power, and majesty of the Ottoman Sultan is nonetheless reduced to dust, as is that of the Chinese emperor in the second part of his book. "For a lesson to sovereign monarchs," Baudier proclaims lugubriously, is "that in their stately thrones the crown and the royal mantle cover only a pile of earth inanimated and a heap of living dust" (*Imperial Estate*, 248).

Other books which might have been helpful to Rycaut included Cornelio Magni's *La relazione del seraglio del Gran Signore e della parti più di esso, distesa dà Alberto Bobovio Leopolitana* (1682) and Guillaume-Joseph Grelot's *Rélation nouvelle d'un voyage de Constantinople* (1680). Magni's book, like Busbecq's, is epistolary in nature and is doubly useful because it contains an account by Woyciech Bobowski of the seraglio and other "*parti più recondite.*" It is even possible that Rycaut may have met Magni through Bobowski. Grelot, whose book was translated into English by Milton's nephew John Phillips (1683), was an artist as well as a traveller; his lavishly illustrated book records travels he undertook in the 1660s and, interestingly, seems to suggest that Louis XIV, to whom Grelot dedicated the work, should think about attacking Constantinople. "I am in hopes," Grelot wrote in his preface, "that Your Majesty. . .will permit me to give you a prospect of those places which you know how to subdue."[163] If Rycaut had read this, he would have been somewhat alarmed, although it is unlikely that he would have seen the French as being able to carry out such an undertaking as Grelot was, perhaps hyperbolically, suggesting. However, Grelot was persuaded

---

[162] Nabil Matar, *Turks, Moors and Englishmen in the Age of Discovery* (New York: Columbia University Press, 1999), 123.

[163] Cited in Michèle L. Longino, "Imagining the Turk in Seventeenth Century France: Grelot's Version," 2000, http://www.duke.edu/~michelel/projects/visions, 2.

that the Turks were, in general, "fair, forgiving, kind, generous, clean and modest people," although he, like many other writers, blamed their apparent indiffer-
ence to their past and its culture on their "natural stupidity."[164]

A rather different view was expressed by an English contemporary of Rycaut's, Henry Marsh, who in his *New Survey of the Turkish Empire* (1663, first
edition 1633), had gone as far as advocating a full-scale crusade directed at the
Ottoman Empire. It was Marsh's book, according to Bridget Orr, that was "the
most intemperate and hostile account of the Ottomans in this period,"[165] and it
concentrated principally on the way Marsh had seen, as he put it, the "afflictions
of captives and Christians under the Turkish tribute."[166] Yet even Marsh could
not refrain from praising the Ottoman Empire's "majestical and august form and
feature," which he described as "perfect. . .in this beautiful and fair proportion."[167]
Rycaut could have found more conventional prejudice against Islam expressed in
the third volume of Fynes Moryson's *Itinerary*, published in 1617,[168] although
Moryson's geographical and cultural observations are often judicious and accu-
rately-expressed, and he, too, had actually spent time in Turkey. For Moryson,

[164] Asli Çirakman, *From the "Terror of the World" to the "Sick Man of Europe:" European Images of the Ottoman Empire and Society from the Sixteenth Century to the Nineteenth*
(Bern: Peter Lang, 2005), 189.

[165] Bridget Orr, *Empire on the English Stage 1660–1714* (Cambridge: Cambridge
University Press, 2001), 63. Not much seems to be known about the author, whom Orr
inexplicably calls "John Marsh," but he dedicated the book to Sir Andrew Riccard (1604–
1672), who was successively governor of the East India Company and of the Turkey
Company. We do know that Marsh spent thirteen years in the Ottoman Empire and that
he knew Arabic. See also Barbara Shapiro, *Political Communication and Political Culture
in England 1558–1688* (Stanford, CA: Stanford University Press, 2012), 65.

[166] Cited in Glenn Sanders, "'A plain Turkish Tyranny:' Images of the Turk in Anti-
Puritan Polemic," in *Puritanism and its Discontents*, ed. Laura Lunger Knoppers (Newark:
University of Delaware Press, 2003), 164. Sanders describes one of Marsh's illustrations:
"Four slaves appear yoked to the plow, Christians beaten by Turkish plowmen. The stee-
ple on the building in the background suggests a church, but now it is a mosque, crescent
atop the steeple and muezzin in the minaret" (*Puritanism*, 172).

[167] Cited in Anna Suranyi, *The Genius of the English Nation: Travel Writing and National Identity in Early Modern England* (Cranbury, NJ: Associated University Presses,
2008), 58.

[168] Fynes Moryson (1566–1630) was an MP and gentleman-traveller whose eastern
journeys took place from 1593 to 1597. The full title of his book, which he wrote in Latin
and translated into English, was *An Itinerary Containing his Ten Years Travel through the
Twelve Dominions of Germany, Bohemia, Switzerland, Netherland, Denmark, Poland, Italy,
Turkey, France, Scotland and Ireland*. Three volumes appeared in his lifetime, and a fourth
was published in 1903. Moryson had some problems with his unwieldy manuscript when
it came to publishing it; Andrew Hadfield remarks that "presumably the problem was
deciding exactly what to do with his material" (*Literature, Travel and Colonial Writing*,
66 and n. 125).

the Sultan was "merely absolute and in the highest degree Tyrannicall, using all his Subjects as borne-slaves,"[169] and the Turks were, of course, "addicted to sexual pleasures, particularly sodomy" (Hadfield, *Amazons*, 160).

Rycaut also includes some standard references to classical historians, although his use of them is quite sparing as well as revealing; they include Tacitus and Quintus Curtius Rufus. The most frequently cited classical authority by far is Tacitus; what Rycaut no doubt found attractive was the Roman historian's reputation for paying close attention to documentary source material and his sometimes rather cynical, or at least pessimistic take on the vicious political infighting that characterised the opening century of Roman imperial rule and the emergence of absolutism. Tacitus, who died in 117, would have been very much aware of the implications of the tyrannical rule of emperors like Domitian as compared with the more enlightened rulers who followed him, Nerva and Trajan, whose reign ended in the same year as the historian's death. There is also a rather interesting, if somewhat tenuous parallel between Tacitus and Rycaut; Michael Grant noted in his perceptive introduction to *The Annals of Imperial Rome* that whilst Tacitus's "observation of facts. . .is often invidious," what he actually records is "generally accurate," and these facts, according to Grant, "involuntarily contradict his sinister innuendos."[170] Rycaut, for his part, often makes assertions that suggest that he is perpetuating stereotypes, making errors, or simply engaging in purple prose, but the reader knows that he is not mistaken or reporting from ignorance or lack of knowledge. As Linda Darling puts it, "authorities have used Rycaut's maxims as a description of Ottoman government realities while dismissing his account of real Ottoman politics as an aberration, or, worse, a corruption of reality" ("Ottoman Politics" 93), thus missing the point that what he is actually doing is reversing the stereotypes to show how changes in the Ottoman government had been gradually happening. Tacitus, as Grant says "was writing under enlightened emperors" (*Annals*, 21), just as Rycaut was writing under Charles II, and he, like Rycaut, is well aware of this whilst at the same time knowing that the situation could change in the blink of any eye. Tacitus, like Rycaut, "is not really able to believe that an autocrat *can* be good," Grant explains (*Annals*, 21). Rycaut tellingly cites the emperor Tiberius's remark about being surrounded by slavish people, but, as Tacitus put it, "Tiberius was transformed and deranged by absolute power" (*Annals* 6, 48). This could have been easily said by and about Sultan Ibrahim, and if Charles II were to move too closely to the Ottoman model, it would be said about him as well. Of course, there is also the obvious parallel between the power and extent of the Roman and Ottoman Empires, together with

---

[169] Fynes Moryson, *Itinerary*, cited in *Amazons, Savages and Machiavels: Travel and Colonial Writing in English 1550–1630*, ed. Andrew Hadfield (Oxford: Oxford University Press, 2007), 167.

[170] Introduction to Tacitus, *The Annals of Imperial Rome*, trans. Michael Grant, rev. ed. (Harmondsworth: Penguin Books, 1989), 20.

the perceived tyranny of such rulers as Tiberius and Ibrahim when power went to their heads. Perhaps Rycaut, living as he did under the rule of the restored Stuarts, saw himself in the same position as Tacitus; both had endured civil war and tyranny, and both ended their careers serving regimes promising more hope of enlightenment than they actually delivered.

Of modern authorities Rycaut cites Guez de Balzac and Hugo Grotius. The former is known for his collection of letters and for *Le Prince,* a self-serving eulogy of Louis XIII written in 1631, and the latter for his great treatise on international law, *De jure belli ac pacis* (1625) as well as other works on political philosophy. Balzac's *Aristippe, ou De la cour* (1658), is the work cited by Rycaut; it was dedicated to ex-Queen Christina of Sweden, who had abdicated, converted to Catholicism and settled in Rome, where, until her death in 1689, she set about leading a very interesting, if tumultuous life. Balzac's book is part panegyric of Cardinal Richelieu, who had died in 1642, and part a manual of statesmanship and good manners. As we have noted, Balzac had already paid tribute to Richelieu's master in *Le Prince,* and the dedication to the intellectual Christina, who had employed Descartes (at least until the cold Swedish winter killed him), would not have been lost on Rycaut, who seems, like Balzac and Tacitus, to have been on a quest for enlightened rulers. *Aristippe* has some quasi-Machiavellian overtones to it; in "Discours VI," for example, Balzac states that when circumstances demand it, "Poison sometimes cures" (*Le venin guerit en quelques rencontres*).[171] Its title figure is the philosopher Aristippus, historically a pupil of Socrates and precursor of Epicurus; he taught that what we seek in life is pleasure, which we should not deny to ourselves under any circumstances. Rycaut may have been suggesting that the self-indulgence supposedly recommended by the historical Aristippus and by extension the contemporary Balzac was exemplified by the present moral state of the Ottoman Empire, or, by not too large a stretch of the imagination, the immorality of the court of Charles II if its course continued, and certainly that of Louis XIV, whom many Englishmen believed Charles wanted to emulate. The subtext in Balzac, too, is ironic, as the quotation above might suggest; his book appeared just five years after the end of the Fronde, a period of civil war and political unrest which had darkened the minority of Louis XIV. As well, it may not be going too far to note that John Evelyn, a fellow-member of the Royal Society and Rycaut's "ghost" on the Sabbatai Zevi book, remarked on this topic over and over again in his diaries. Evelyn and Rycaut, though royalists, shared a puritanical streak which from time to time surfaces in their writings, but which stems not so much from bigotry or even genuine religious convictions but from a desire to see a return to normalcy after the devastation of the Civil War years.

There are two references to Hugo Grotius in Rycaut's book, both of which cite *De jure belli ac pacis.* In one Rycaut lifts a quotation from Aristotle concerning

---

[171] Jean-Louis Guez de Balzac, *Aristippe, ou De la cour* (Coulogne: Etienne de la Place, 1704), 181.

the treatment of slaves, and the other is about the treatment of ambassadors. Rycaut's reading of Grotius went considerably further than pilfering quotes from Aristotle. In this work Grotius tells us that "there is a common law among nations which is valid alike for war and in war," and further that he found "a lack of restraint in relation to war, such as even barbarous races should be ashamed of."[172] As Linda Darling states, "the Ottoman system was considered abhorrent by definition, while any admirable qualities in it were customarily held up as a reproach to Europeans lacking those virtues" ("Ottoman Politics," 92), and, without naming it, Grotius surely meant by "barbarous races" the Ottomans and others like them. However Europeans, for Grotius, were as bad as Turks, and sometimes even worse; in 1625 Europe was seven years into the Thirty Years War. Rycaut deals in some detail with the still formidable Ottoman war machine in Book 3; he believed that "this government, being wholly founded upon martial discipline and the law of arms," would "never be nourished by softness and the arts and blandishments of peace." By the time the edition presented here was published, the Ottomans had laid siege to Vienna, the climax to a series of conflicts with the Hapsburgs which had begun in 1663 when Ahmet Köprülü advanced on Belgrade with what Lord Kinross described as "the largest and most imposing [army] assembled since Süleyman's time" (_Ottoman Centuries_, 334). This campaign ended in the defeat at St. Gothard, but three years later there was war in Crete, followed by two wars against the Poles (1672, 1676) and so on until the culmination with the defeat before the walls of Vienna. However, it was not to be the end by a long way; Venice declared war on the Ottoman Empire in 1684 and the Austrians moved to attack the Ottoman territories in Croatia. In Hungary at Mohács the Turks sustained a massive defeat at the hands of Charles V of Lorraine (1687), but by 1691 they were back in the field again, this time advancing rapidly up the Danube, and so it went on.

At this point history passes beyond the chronology of Rycaut's book, but events certainly bore out his point about the bellicose nature of the Ottoman Empire. "I observe," Grotius had written, "that men rush to war for slight causes, or no cause at all" ("Prolegomena," sec. 28); as Kinross put it, Ottoman policy under Mehmet IV and his Köprülü viziers was one of "deflecting [the army] from troublesome dissensions at home to campaigns abroad in renewal of the Ottoman conquering spirit" (_Ottoman Centuries_, 333). What Grotius is saying here may well have been applied by Rycaut to the Dutch wars being sporadically waged by his own country, or indeed any wars for which the causes were somewhat obscure and which he believed may have been a pretext to divert attention from problems at home. This edition of Rycaut's book, for example, appeared on the heels of the Duke of Monmouth's rebellion against James II (1685), and by

---

[172] Hugo Grotius, "Prolegomena, section 28," in _The Law of War and Peace in Three Books_ (1625) [_De jure belli ac pacis_], trans. Francis W. Kelsey, et al (1925), http://lonang. com/library/reference/grotius-law-war-and-peace/gro-100/.

that time England had fought three naval wars with the Dutch for which the cause was simply a combination of maritime competitiveness and trading rivalries. Wars, however, keep armies occupied, and since the Janissaries seemed often to be in a state of dissatisfaction and turmoil, a foreign war provided the government with a breather from their troublesome dissentions and potentially dangerous political interventions. For Grotius, and for Rycaut himself, however, these reasons would not have been considered justifications for engaging in wars that cost lives and money.

One of the most interesting and less prejudiced sources upon which Rycaut drew was not a book at all, but his personal interaction with the Polish exile Woyciech Bobowski or Albertus Bobovius (1610–1675), whom we have briefly met in connection with Grelot. He was taken prisoner by Crimean Tatars (1638), then sold to the Turkish court. Known to the Turks by the name of Ali Ufki, Bobowski, whom Rycaut in his address to the reader calls "an understanding Polonian, who had spent nineteen years in the Ottoman court," converted to Islam and served Sultans Ibrahim and Mehmet IV initially as a musician, becoming familiar with Turkish music. He played the *santur* and made an extensive collection of Turkish music as well as composing a great deal of his own. In addition to his musical skills, Bobowski was a talented linguist; he learned the Turkish language and, it is said, fourteen others as well,[173] amongst which would certainly have been English. He was released from formal service by Mehmet IV in 1657. Bobowski wrote, amongst other things, a Turkish grammar[174] and an exposition of Islam in Latin, which was designed, unlike the majority of books on that subject, to foster a better understanding between Muslims and Christians. He also translated the psalter and the Bible into Turkish, as well as works by Grotius and Jan Amos Comenius, the eminent Bohemian educator. Just how much information Bobowski gave Rycaut and how accurate it was cannot be determined, but we know that he was, of course, fluent in Turkish and that he had a good knowledge of Islam.

As a westerner, Bobowski had likely arrived in Turkey with all the misconceptions and prejudices of any European newcomer, which he had learned to modify by studying the language and immersing himself in Ottoman culture, not to mention eventually changing his faith.[175] He was the ideal source of

---

[173] Anderson states that Bobowski spoke seventeen languages (*English Consul,* 41).

[174] For further details, see Hannah Neudecker, "Wojciech Bobowski and his *Turkish Grammar* (1666)," *Dutch Studies in Near Eastern Languages and Literatures* 2 (1996): 169–92. Sonia Anderson noted that "one of the best accounts of Bobowski's career" may be found in the first volume of the *Travels* of Cornelio Magni (1679), which also included Bobowski's description of the Sultan's seraglio (*English Consul,* 41, n. 64).

[175] The question of validity in Christian conversions to Islam has been recently addressed by Tijana Krstić, *Contested Conversions to Islam: Narratives of Religious Change in the Early Modern Ottoman Empire* (Stanford, CA: Stanford University Press, 2011).

information for Rycaut; Bobowski was sufficiently latitudinarian in his outlook to give the Englishman a very good idea of what was going on and how things worked in the Ottoman court. There is no proof of this assertion, but it was probably Bobowski who at least helped Rycaut with his Turkish if he did not actually teach him. Bobowski also had some English credentials in his own right. Through the good offices of the cleric Isaac Basire,[176] who was chaplain both to the English community in Constantinople and personally to Sir Thomas Bendysh, he had entered the service of the English ambassador, and it may have been Basire who introduced Bobowski to Rycaut. At this stage of his career Bobowski had begun the work of translating the Bible, and in this project he was assisted financially by the Dutch ambassador Levinus Warner, with whom Bobowski became good friends and who seems to have been highly respected by all the Europeans. Bobowski eventually returned to Egypt, the site of his original capture, and he may have also gone on a pilgrimage to Mecca, which would have made his exploit predate that of Sir Richard Burton by over two centuries.

As well as Bobowski, Rycaut also tells the reader that he had help from "the mouth and argument of considerable ministers" as well as "some of the most learned doctors and preachers of their law, with whom for money or presents I gained a familiarity and appearance of friendship" and "several sober persons, trained up in the best education of the Turkish language." Even if Rycaut could have read Turkish by the time he came to write *The Present State of the Ottoman Empire* in 1665, he had only been in Constantinople for five years, and would certainly have needed help with Ottoman official documents. Linda Darling suggests that even if Rycaut had been allowed to examine written records, some of them "were handwritten. . .in a loopy scribble" or "in a script combining the characteristics of a shorthand and a secret code," and he probably relied on Şeytan Ibrahim Pasha, who was one of the treasurers (*defterdars*), for assistance in reading these government documents ("Ottoman Politics," 75–76), as it is unlikely that Bobowski would have had access to them. Rycaut also knew the ex-prince of Moldavia and Wallachia, Gheorghe I Gica, who was then resident in Constantinople and could have supplied him with information about the lands he had once ruled. Prince (*voivode*) Gheorghe, who died in 1664, had, according to Rycaut, "for many years been employed for *voivode* both in Moldavia and

However, if Bobowski was willing to risk the ordeal of a pilgrimage to Mecca, his sincerity probably should not be doubted.

[176] Isaac Basire (1607–1676) was a French Protestant minister who moved to England and served both Charles I and Charles II. He had travelled extensively in Europe and from 1650 to 1661 he was in the Ottoman Empire, where he settled in as a chaplain in Istanbul. He eventually returned to England and became Archdeacon of Northumberland. For further details see Hannah Neudecker, "From Istanbul to London? Albertus Bobovius's Appeal to Isaac Basire," in *The Republic of Letters and the Levant*, eds. A. Hamilton, et al (Leiden: Brill, 2005), 175–196.

Wallachia by the Turks;" Gheorge had actually only ruled Moldavia in 1658–
1659 and Wallachia 1659–1660, but he had nonetheless gained the close friendship and trust of the Köprülüs, and remained in Constantinople until his death
in 1664. His son and successor Grigore would also end his career in the Turkish capital, arriving there in 1673 after the Turkish defeat at the battle of Hatin.

Still another important source for Rycaut was a close friend and erstwhile
next-door neighbour Giovanni Mascellini or Marsellini (1612–1675), whom Rycaut calls "a worthy learned man" and "a good Christian" (*Turkish History*, 312).
Mascellini, who had started his overseas career in 1644 as physician to the Venetian ambassador, had subsequently been court physician to Mateiu Bassarab,
prince of Wallachia (1652–1654), but the prince, recognising his great merits,
had appointed him his private secretary as well. When the country became unstable under the Ghica rule, Mascellini moved to the Pera district in Constantinople, where he met Rycaut. He practiced medicine there, and his clients included Sultan Mehmet IV and the Grand Vizier as well as a wide variety of Turks
and resident Europeans. The Italian doctor, it was said by Antoine Galland, the
French orientalist who spent many years travelling in the Levant and the Ottoman Empire, "enjoyed an unprofessional gossip about his eminent patients,"
but "without forfeiting their confidence."[177] Rycaut also befriended another expatriate Italian, Marc' Antonio della Torre, known as Mamucha, who served
Mehmet IV as Imperial Grand Dragoman and whose task was to interpret and
translate foreign languages for the Turks, who were, reputedly, unwilling to learn
them. It was certainly true, as Bernard Lewis tells us, that even "the first Ottoman resident diplomats in Europe were. . .ignorant of Western languages" (*Muslim Discovery of Europe*, 132). Their European counterparts, on the other hand,
often did not lack language skills, as the case of Bobowski and indeed of Rycaut
himself, demonstrates. When della Torre was forced to accompany Mehmet IV's
army on its Hapsburg campaign in 1683 "he solved this conflict of loyalties by
making secret copies of all the more important dispatches given him to translate," and after the siege he decided to remain in Vienna, from where he kept up
his contact with Rycaut (Anderson, *English Consul*, 258).

There were also, of course, embassy staff, colleagues in Smyrna, other travellers and interpreters, all of whom could have contributed to Rycaut's work and
some of whom may have known Turkish, but he mentions few by name. In the
"Epistle Dedicatory," however, he also credits his former employer, the earl of
Winchilsea, "who often rectified my mistakes, supplied me with matter, and
remembered me of many material points which I might otherwise have most
unadvisedly omitted." The "matter" supplied by Winchilsea no doubt consisted

---

[177] *Journal d'Antoine Galland pendant son séjour à Constantinople (1672–1673)* [Paris:
Schafer, 1881], cited in Anderson, *English Consul*, 236 and n. 6. For further details on
Mascellini, see Maria Denisia Liușnea, "V. A. Urechia—a Pioneer of the Conservation
of the Historical Patrimony in Galati," *Axis Libri* (June, 2010): 6–7.

of letters, state papers, notes, and evidently included verbal confirmation or corrections of what Rycaut had written. If Rycaut is telling the truth, and there is no reason to believe he is not, then his book would have been considered very authoritative, containing as it does information from both Turkish and foreign sources, references to previous travellers and historians, and the author's own on-the-spot experience. Rycaut's book is indeed designed to be "history" in the seventeenth-century sense, that is, the plain truth as plain as he could make it, unembellished by fiction and uninformed by any particular agenda on the part of the author. What else the book might have been was left to perceptive readers who could turn their scrutiny on what they believed might have been written between the lines.

### England and the Ottoman Empire II: "Fact" and Fiction

It was always conceded by European writers that the Turks and other Muslims could, on occasion, behave nobly (that is, according to western notions of what behaving nobly meant) and that they could sometimes show up the shortcomings of Christianity and western civilisation. Shakespeare's *Othello* (c. 1603), for example, has for a hero a "Moor," a man from North Africa, perhaps Morocco or Tunisia, who fights for the Venetians in their wars against the Ottoman Empire, the enemy whom the Christian convert Othello describes as the "malignant and. . .turbaned Turk" (V, 2, 362).[178] Othello's own virtuous conduct, at least up until his fall from grace, shows up the shallowness and hypocrisy of Venetian society, which in no way, on reading this play, can be considered the epitome of decorum, Christian virtue, or even courage. Shakespeare's view of Venice in *Othello* is very much, like his view of Moors, a construct of his own anti-Catholic prejudices and environment. "English Protestant texts," Daniel Vitkus notes, "conflated the political/external enemies, associating both the Pope and the Ottoman Sultan with Satan or the Antichrist."[179]

---

[178] An interesting point is made by Virginia Vaughan that Othello's actions against the Turks represent "on a mythic level" a "Manichean" conflict between good and evil, as represented by Venice and the Ottoman Empire respectively. This view had modified somewhat by Rycaut's time, but is still significantly present in the writings of people like Smith. See Virginia Vaughan, *Othello: A Contextual History* (Cambridge: Cambridge University Press, 1994), 22, cited in Andrew Hadfield, *Literature, Travel, and Colonial Writing in the English Renaissance 1545–1625* (Oxford: Oxford University Press, 1998), 227.

[179] Daniel Vitkus, "Turning Turk in *Othello*: The Conversion and Damnation of the Moor," *Shakespeare Quarterly*, 48, no. 2 (1997), 145.

These prejudices were not present in all forms of east-west discourse. For example, as Nabil Matar points out, "Government documents, prisoners' depositions, and commercial exchanges show little racial, sexual or moral stereotyping. . .It was plays, masques, pageants, and other similar sources that developed in British culture the discourse about Muslim Otherness" (*Turks*, 13). As Francis Bacon noted with some annoyance, "let the suits of the masques be graceful. . .Not after examples as Turks, soldiers, mariners and the like."[180] Andrew Hadfield makes the point that in the particular case of drama, its "ephemeral nature. . .at a time before plays had obtained the literary status of other types of writing," made it "more politically topical" and even "subversive," as it attracted a much wider audience than other less public art-forms or courtly entertainments (*Literature, Travel, and Colonial Writing*, 202). Many of the Venetians in *Othello* display what we would term today "racial, sexual, or moral stereotyping,"[181] which is also reflected to a degree in some histories and travel accounts of the Ottoman Empire, where there are usually references to Turkish lust, unnatural sexual practices, corruption, and the absolutism of oriental rulers. Shakespeare, in this regard, was in tune with his contemporaries and saw no reason to differ from them.

Islam, of course, is often denigrated and attacked as a "false" religion, and in many cases writers display a fear and loathing of Ottoman exoticism which is also mixed with vicarious envy and a certain amount of voyeurism. As Matar puts it, "as long as Tasso, Camoes [*sic*], Ariosto, Cervantes, Marlowe and Shakespeare, along with *El Cid*. . .were viewed, rightly, as the supreme icons of European imagination. . .the polarization with Islam and Muslims could only continue" (*Turks*, 13). Even books specifically intended for travellers were not exempt; we find, for example, the learned physician and traveller Andrew Borde informing his readers in doggerel verse through a character in his book that "I am a Turke, and Machomytes law to kepe, / I do proll for my pray whan others be aslepe,"[182] which amusingly, albeit unintentionally, links the Turk's piety with his alleged propensity for sneakily doing evil things at night. In Matar's view, the literature of the times unduly influenced the way people viewed Muslims, and this influence was often reflected in the works of historians who tackled the subject of the

---

[180] Francis Bacon,"Of Masques and Triumphs," in *The Major Works*, ed. Brian Vickers (Oxford: Oxford University Press, 2002), 43.

[181] In *Othello*, this can easily be seen in the opening scenes of the play, where Iago goads Brabantio into rage by using racial and sexual stereotyping.

[182] Andrew Borde, *The First Book of the Introduction of Knowledge*, ed. J. Furnivall (1547; repr. London: Early English Text Society, 1870), 214. Borde or Boorde (c. 1490–1549) was a lapsed Catholic who had even been Suffragan Bishop of Chichester, although he apparently did not take up the post and was freed from his religious vows in 1529. He wrote on such diverse subjects as personal hygiene and foreign travel, which is in fact the subject of the work from which this quotation is taken.

Ottoman Empire. In travel-writings, authors certainly had preconceived ideas before they set out to "discover" the Ottoman Empire for themselves, and, as we shall see, Rycaut's book went to some lengths to change those ideas.

By the time that Rycaut was writing *The Present State of the Ottoman Empire*, "Turk" literature, particularly drama, had proliferated into a literary sub-genre of its own and indeed, some of its later practitioners would draw on Rycaut's own work for its background. As well as *Othello*, Rycaut, had he been a theatre-goer (and many educated people were), could have seen or known of such productions, which dated from Thomas Kyd's *Soliman and Perseda* (1592) and Robert Greene's *Selimus, Emperor of the Turks* (1594), to Robert Daborne's *A Christian Turned Turk* (1612), and Philip Massinger's *The Renegado* (1623),[183] as well as a host of others such as Thomas Goffe's *The Raging Turk* or *Bajazet II* (1613–1618) through to Mary Pix's *Ibrahim, the Thirteenth Emperor of the Turks* (1696), one of the works which drew directly from Rycaut's book, although, as the author admitted, her memory had failed her, as Ibrahim was, in fact, the twelfth ruler.[184] "I read some years ago. . .," Pix wrote apologetically in her preface, "Sir Paul Ricaut's *Continuation* of [Knolles's] *Turkish History*, and ventured to write upon it, but trusted too far to my memory."[185] We will discuss Rycaut's influence on literary works later on in this introduction; suffice it to say here that there was plenty of material around to influence the attitude of the general public in England towards the Ottoman Empire.

In addition to plays, English readers had at their disposal works such as Camoens's *Lusiads* (1572), translated by Sir Richard Fanshawe (1655), and John Foxe's *Acts and Monuments* (1563), popularly known as *The Book of Martyrs*, where Turks are described as being usually savage and bloodthirsty when it came to dealing with Christians. On the subject of Islam itself, there was William Percy's

---

[183] These plays have been edited by Daniel Vitkus in *Three Turk Plays from Early Modern England* (New York: Columbia University Press, 2000).

[184] Some titles of other "Turk" plays include Thomas Dekker's *Lust's Dominion* (1618); George Peele's *Battle of Alcazar* (1589) and *The Turkish Mahomet and Hiren the Fair Greek* (?1594); Fulke Greville, Lord Brooke's *Mustapha* (1608), a closet drama; John Mason's *The Turk* (1609); Ludowick Carlell's *Osmond the Great Turk* (1638); Elkanah Settle's *Ibrahim, the Illustrious Bassa* (1676), based on a four-part romance by Madeleine de Scudéry which had itself been translated into English by Henry Cogan (1652); and Henry Payne's *Siege of Constantinople* (1675). The range of dates would indicate that "Turk" plays were more than a passing fad.

[185] Cited in Ros Ballaster, *Fabulous Orients: Fictions of the East in England 1662–1785* (Oxford: Oxford University Press, 2007), 84. Mary Pix (c. 1666–1720) was a successful novelist and dramatist who returned to the Oriental theme with her play *The Conquest of Spain* (1705), based on a translation of Miguel de Luna's *The Life of the Most Illustrious Monarch Almanzor* (1693). For further information, see Bernadette Andrea, ed., *English Women Staging Islam, 1696–1707: Delarivier Manley and Mary Pix* (Toronto: University of Toronto Press, 2011).

play *Mahomet and his Heaven* (1601), remarkable not for its literary merit, but for being the only play to actually put Muhammad on stage as a character, thus making the work a predecessor to some of the literary controversies of our own times, although Percy did not have to live with a *fatwa* and a possible assassination attempt. Percy does not simply make the Prophet a caricature, but seems to suggest that he actually had some supernatural power, at one point depicting him in heaven with the angels, just as the Prophet's journey is described in the Qu'ran. It may be that Percy had intended to show Muhammad as a kind of evil mirror-image of Christ, as some critics have noted. [186]

The "Turk," then, was seen as cruel, lustful, ambitious, devious, self-serving and, of course, someone who belonged to the wrong religion, although sometimes, as in Thomas Goffe's *The Courageous Turke, or Amurath the First* (1618, published 1632) a Turkish ruler, here Murad I, is elevated to quasi-heroic status, in spite of the fact that he has performed some murderous deeds. This positive portrayal was, however, unusual; in Scene 12 of Robert Greene's *Selimus*, for example, the beylerbey Mahomet asks his uncle Acomat what will happen if he doesn't surrender the city of Iconium to him. The reply is unequivocal:

> MAHOMET: What craves our uncle Acomat of us?
> ACOMAT: That thou and all the city yield themselves;
> Or by the holy rites of Mahomet,
> His wondrous tomb and sacred Alcoran,
> You all shall die: and not a common death,
> But even as monstrous as I can devise.
> (Vitkus, *Three Turk Plays*, 97)

Here is the famous cruelty of the Turk, linked, as always, with the Muslim religion. In *The Renegado*, Philip Massinger solves the "Turk" problem by having Donusa, the Turkish princess, attempt to convert her lover Vitelli to Islam, but ending up being herself converted to Christianity. "I'll undertake / To turn this Christian Turk and marry him," Donusa confidently tells Mustafa and Arambeg, Vitelli's gaolers (IV, 2, 156–59), but after a fairly lengthy conversation with Vitelli, she says "I perceive a yielding in myself/ To be your prisoner," and shortly afterwards converts to Christianity, declaring "Then thus I spit at Mahomet" (IV, 3, 158). In the end, with the help of the repentant "renegado" Grimaldi, all the Christian characters, together with the newly-converted Donusa, escape from captivity. Lust and Islam are sometimes combined. For example, in Scene 7 of Daborne's *A Christian Turned Turk*, Voada offers herself to the pirate captain

---

[186] Percy's play has been recently edited by Matthew Dimmock (Aldershot, UK: Ashgate, 2006). Percy (1574–1648) was a son of the earl of Northumberland, and wrote a number of plays for child actors at St. Paul's School including this one, which was originally entitled *Arabia sitiens, or A Dream of a Dry Year: A Tragicomedy*. Sitiens means thirsty.

Ward in explicit terms; "If you'll enjoy me," she says, "Turn Turk—I am yours" (Vitkus, *Three Turk Plays*, 193), and after Ward converts she does indeed marry him, although, of course, things do not end happily ever after because Ward has succumbed to lust and Islam all at once. In Gilbert Swinhoe's *The Unhappy Fair Irene* (1640, published 1658), the author kills off all the Christian characters, and emphasises the cruelty of the Turks through their love for war, as Sultan Mahomet lops off (albeit reluctantly, as he protests) Irene's head to show the Janissaries that he is more interested in expanding the Ottoman Empire than he is in making love and sinking into luxurious inactivity with a beautiful consort, although, of course, he gets nowhere with the virtuous Irene. Mahomet exhibits lust to the end; "O had thou but look'd," he says regretfully, "I never could have struck this fatal blow," but his followers, happy to see him chose war, exultantly chorus "To arms; our / Emperor is himself, with his falchion severs head and body." [187] Turks, particularly Sultans, are supposed to make war, not love. Ironically, Swinhoe begins the play with an ordinary Ottoman soldier offering Irene favours if she will permit him to have sex with her, and the sub-text of this play, like that of so many others, serves up a liberal dose of cruel and lustful Turks alongside more likeable figures, such as the chivalrous Turkish officer who rescues Irene from the clutches of the boorish private and decides to present her to the Sultan, thus unwittingly starting the whole tragedy.

Not all "Turk" fiction was dramatic in nature. Between 1687 and 1694, for example, there appeared eight volumes of a very popular work (Jacob Crane calls it a novel) entitled *Letters Writ by a Turkish Spy, who lived five and forty years undiscovered at Paris: giving an impartial account to the Divan at Constantinople, of the most remarkable transactions of Europe: and discovering several intrigues and secrets of the Christian courts (especially that of France)*, purporting to be written by one "Mahmut the Arabian" and covering the years 1637 to 1682. In all likelihood it was the work of Giovanni Paolo Marana (1642–1693), a Genoese nobleman who was living in political exile at the court of Louis XIV. [188] Marana had apparently

[187] Gilbert Swinhoe, *The Tragedy of the Unhappy Fair Irene* (London: Early English Books Online Editions, 2012), 28. For a rare discussion of Swinhoe's play, see Bridget Orr, *Empire on the English Stage* (Cambridge: Cambridge University Press, 2001), 80–81. Swinhoe found his plot in Knolles, and the story surfaces again in Samuel Johnson's one and only attempt at drama, *Irene* (1749), which seemed to have been a commercial success at the time, but otherwise believed to be one of the least performed plays, lying moribund until 1999. However, I have not been able to trace any signs that Gilbert Swinhoe's version is faring much better than Johnson's. George Peele's *The Turkish Mahomet and Hiren (Irene) the Fair Greek* was also based on Knolles.

[188] Marana's authorship, at least for the first volume, seems to have been undisputed. An article on the work in Isaac D'Israeli's *Curiosities of Literature* (1792), confirms it, and subsequent scholarship seems to bear him out. For a full text of D'Israeli's essay, see http://www.spamula.net/col/archives. See also Jacob Crane, "The Long Transatlantic Career of the Turkish Spy," *Atlantic Studies* 10 (2013): 228–46.

been caught fabricating plans by Victor Amadeus II of Savoy for an invasion of Venetian territory, which he had presented as authentic to the Doge of Venice. It is not known whether Marana was responsible for all the volumes; an English translation of the first volume by William Bradshaw appeared in 1687, followed in 1696–1697 by a French version which claimed to be translated from English. This gave rise to speculation that Bradshaw himself, whom we know was still active in 1700, might have written the continuation, hoping to capitalise on the resounding success of the first volume. The "letters" included political observations, court gossip, satire, and a great deal of anecdotal information about various rulers and others in power. "Mahmut," as the title tells us, was collecting the information and passing it on by letter to contacts in Turkey. As the work was fictional, it supplies an interesting intermediate "bridge" between the imaginative world of the drama and factual accounts of the Ottoman Empire such as Rycaut's, and the latter would have been a mine of information for Marana, who, as far as is known, never himself visited the Ottoman Empire. Some writers have noted that the *Letters* are very favourable towards moderate and enlightened government, which was, as we have seen, an important part of Rycaut's analysis of the implications of anything resembling "Ottoman-style" government. The book was widely-read and went into several editions, so successful that Daniel Defoe even wrote a continuation of it (1718). Montesquieu's well-known *Lettres Persanes* (1721), might also have owed something to Marana; indeed C. J. Betts believed it to have been "the model for Montesquieu's *Lettres Persanes*."[189]

All in all, fictional "Turk" literature, with some exceptions, tended to reinforce and exaggerate the distorted views about the Ottoman Empire and Islam that many people already had. As Daniel Vitkus notes, "the early modern demonization of Islam tends to focus upon the overwhelming, absolute power of Islamic culture," which, he tells us, "is often embodied in an Islamic ruler, Sultan or king whose authority over his subjects is compared to a cruel master's over his slaves" (*Turk Plays*, 11), a stereotype more often than not found in histories (including Rycaut's) and travel-accounts as well, although there is no doubt that writers and observers also admired certain aspects of the Ottoman Empire, its power, wealth and energy. As the seventeenth century progressed, however, it would be accurate to state that a more tolerant attitude towards Islam was slowly being developed, although the established stereotypes still made for successful plays and the image of the "lustful Turk" with his harems, polygamy and insatiable sexual appetites remained embedded in the literary consciousness of Europe until well into the nineteenth century.

---

[189] C. J. Betts, *Early Deism in France* (The Hague: Martinus Nijhoff, 1984), 97–8.

## *The Present State of the Ottoman Empire*: An Overview

Rycaut begins in part 1 with a discussion of the way the Turkish government, "being different from most others in the world," is set up, and he intends to explain the "peculiar maxims and rules" under which it operates. He states from the outset that doing this will be difficult; even in the best-ordered commonwealth, he says, one "supported with reason and religion," it would be a formidable task, as he would have to "unriddle and resolve a mystery." He implies here that the Ottoman state is not "supported with reason and religion," and goes on to elaborate, declaring that it is ruled by "an emperor without reason, whose speeches may be irrational, and yet must be laws, whose actions irregular and yet examples, whose sentence and judgment. . .are most commonly corrupt." Everything, he tells the reader, is subject to chance, and everyone in government is, to a degree, a slave to the whim of the Sultan. "Do not revile the Sultan, for he is God's shadow on God's earth," Muhammad is reported to have said (cited in Lewis, *Middle East Mosaic*, 120). These views are not Rycaut's alone. George Sandys, for example, had noted that the Empire was governed by the Sultan's slaves; "among these slaves is no nobility of blood, no known parentage, kindred nor hereditary positions, but, as it were, of the Sultan's creation" (*Travels*, 37). Furthermore, "virtue and moral honesty," Rycaut states bluntly, "are rare in a Turk." Merit and noble blood account for nothing.

The Ottoman Empire, so the reader might have thought at this point in the discourse, was little but a hotbed of corruption, slavery, fear, and near-anarchy, barely holding itself together and completely dependent on the whims of a ruler whose mental capacities could on occasion be questionable. However, Rycaut explicitly states that in spite of appearances, "one might admire the long continuance of this great and vast empire," one which has "stability. . .without change in itself." Indeed, he goes on, the Ottomans have over a period of years increased their domains and are continuing to do so at the present time. Could the cause of this apparently contradictory, indeed almost irrational, state of affairs be supernatural, he asks rather disingenuously, "as if the divine will of the all-knowing Creator had chosen for the good of his church and chastisement of the sins and vices of Christians to raise and support this mighty people?" A hundred years earlier Busbecq, too, had voiced a similar concern; the Turks, he wrote, were "a scourge sent against us by the anger of heaven" (*Turkish Letters*, 161). This was a common rationalisation of the fact that the Turks won the battles as often as the Europeans did, and that in spite of setbacks they seemed always able to expand their empire. As God could not possibly be aiding the Muslim Turks, he must be punishing the Christian Europeans for their sins.

Rycaut's answer to the riddle of Turkish unity is simple enough. "That which cements all breaches and cures all those wounds in this body politic," he declares, "is the quickness and severity of their justice." The latter, Rycaut states with a little hyperbole, "makes almost every crime equal, and punishes it with the last and extremest chastisement, which is death." He believes that "without this remedy. . .this mighty body would burst with the poison of its own ill humours, and soon divide itself." Some modern historians share his view. Najwa al-Qattan, for instance, points out that, for at least those courts presided over by a *kadi*, which were the courts an ordinary person would be most likely to deal with, there was "levelling of the legal playing field" (Aksan and Goffman, *Early Modern Ottomans*, 210) on which all Ottoman subjects would have equal and swift justice. Nevertheless, as Rycaut saw it, the Ottoman Empire operated through fear and intimidation, keeping its people in a perpetual state of "servitude and slavery." Sandys, too, remarked that "the punishments for offenders will be either pecuniary or corporal" (*Travels*, 49). Rycaut believed that "not only is tyranny requisite for this people," but it is "as natural to them as to a body to be nourished with that diet which it had from its infancy or birth been acquainted with." At the very beginning of his book, Thomas Smith wrote of the Turks' "natural fierceness" which he believed could only be restrained by "the cruelty and severity of their punishments" (*Remarks*, 1). It would appear, then, that so far Rycaut has made little attempt to depart from the commonplaces and generalisations of his predecessors and contemporaries. As Nabil Matar expresses it, "English. . .representation of the Muslims was particularly adept at subduing facts to categories of polarization and antipathy." These categories, Matar suggests, were "syncretic and interchangeable;" they also "totally disregarded geographical, ethnographical and military differences" (*Turks*, 106–7). So far, we have been informed by Rycaut that the Turks are "most happy, prosperous and contented under tyranny," that "severity, violence and cruelty are natural to [the Ottoman government], and that "most of their customs should run in a certain channel and course most answerable to the height and unlimited power of the governor," whose absolute supremacy is reinforced by "the lesson of obedience to the emperor," which is "a principle of religion rather than of state." These remarks certainly reinforce John Marshall's contention that Rycaut "not only identified the greatness of the empire with its tyrannical nature. . .but also used the concept to analyse the Turkish maxims of government" (*John Locke*, 204). Rycaut suggests that the Ottoman system, even if it was essentially despotic and "tyrannical," was not necessarily evil, and could provide a measure of fair government and swift justice. To make this claim, however, does not make Rycaut an advocate of absolutism; he could, however, be accused of being "Machiavellian," as he seems to approve of the means justifying the ends. As Asli Çirakman states, "within the historical-empirical perspective of Rycaut this sort of regime could very well produce a well-ordered, legitimate government and virtuous governors," and he likely realised that if the tyranny were also corrupt and oppressive it would contribute to the inevitable decline of the regime (*Terror*, 204–5). As an empiricist, Rycaut looks at the results, which show a still-powerful empire, a justice system which worked efficiently, and subjects who were not constantly in revolt. The Köprölü vizierate, with which Rycaut was very familiar, appeared to provide good government according to the rule of law and backed by the traditional obedience to the will of the Sultan. In broader terms, Rycaut's analysis might be seen as an attempt by an outsider at a systematic understanding of human nature from the point of view of Ottoman culture and institutions, and a willingness to admit that there may be good things in a non-Western state's way of running itself. One person's "tyranny" might, in some cases, be seen as another's "order and good government," depending on the cultural background of the person making the judgment.

We have alluded above to several of Rycaut's comments about Islam, which he deals with at some length in Book 2, so this will be by way of summary and recapitulation. "There is no consideration more abstruse and full of distraction," Rycaut tells us, "than the contemplation of the strange varieties of religions in the world." He finds it strange, too, that "nations who have been admirably wise, judicious and profound in the maxims of their government should yet, in matters of religion, give themselves over to believe the tales of an old woman, a Pythoness, or the dreams and imaginations of a melancholy hermit." He emphasises that in the Ottoman Empire, religion and "civil laws" are "so confounded into one body that we can scarce treat of one without the other." Rycaut explains that the Turks believe that their law actually came from God via Muhammad, with a little help from "Sergius the monk," a Christian apostate who is conventionally associated with Muhammad by writers who wish to discredit the credibility of Islam's prophet. However, Rycaut, whilst admitting that divine inspiration was often used by those who wished to ensure that their man-made laws were obeyed, nonetheless states that "all laws which respect right and justice and are tending to a foundation of good and honest government, are of God." The question is, of course, whether the Ottoman government was, in fact, "good and honest," the answer to which depended at least partly on its foundation under the principles of Islam, which Rycaut, for all his seeming tolerance elsewhere in the book, routinely calls "superstition" and which he believes was invented by a man whose life was "infamous," as opposed, of course, to the unsullied life of Christ. However, there is no out-and-out condemnation of Turkish law simply because it is based on non-Christian foundations. Indeed, Rycaut notes in several places that the Turks, and Muslims in general, were often quite tolerant of Christians and even of Jews, at least compared to other powers at the time. Rycaut states, for example, that "in all places where [Ottoman] arms were prevalent and prosperous," the Turks "proclaimed a free toleration to all religions." A little further on in the same chapter he explains how the "Muhammadan religion tolerates Christian churches and houses of devotion," and allows repairs even though it does not permit new ones to be built. It was this broad-minded quality in religious questions which would recommend Rycaut to writers on the subject of toleration such as John Locke and Pierre Bayle.

Rycaut expends a great deal of space in book 2 on Islamic sects of various kinds, following a precedent set in earlier treatises. Similar information can be found in Knolles, Sandys, or Ottavio Bon, and Rycaut does not have anything

very new to add, in spite of his claims that he had access to first-hand information. The discussion of Islamic sects may be there simply to indicate that the religion of the Ottoman Empire was not monolithic, and that westerners could
not speak of it as if all its practitioners were the same. Rycaut may also have
been implying that Islam, like Christianity, could at some point be weakened
by schisms, although he makes no mention of the possibility of such conflicts as
we see today with Sunnis and Shi'as, or the persecution in Iran and other states
of Ahmadiyya Muslims. Readers would have likely been quite interested in the
differences between the sects regarding their views of God or their interpretations of the Qur'an, not to mention Rycaut's descriptions of some of the rituals
they practised, which would have seemed quite strange to westerners. The sects
would have been, for Rycaut as for other writers, just a proliferation of "false doctrines" derived from the ultimate "false doctrine" laid down by Muhammad in
the Qur'an. In short, his discussion of Ottoman religion supports Nabil Matar's
charge of "polarization and antipathy." It also counterbalanced, to a degree, what
the Turks already knew about Christians, namely that "Christendom, even more
than Islam, was divided into petty, warring sovereignties, whose internecine
conflicts might be used to some advantage" (Lewis, *Islam and the West*, 32).

In book 3 Rycaut presents a discussion of the "Turkish Militia," which, he
states in the final sentences of book 2, is "that by which their empire is more supported than either by their policy in civil government or profession in religion."
This section is important because Rycaut conceives of the Ottoman state as "begot by arms" and that because of this it "will never be nourished by softness and
the arts and blandishments of peace." However, he stresses that at the present
time it is difficult for a westerner to form an accurate opinion; Ottoman strength
is often seen as not having changed since the time of Süleyman the Magnificent,
but "that ancient sublimity and comely majesty," Rycaut tells us, "is much abated." It is here that Rycaut discusses the notion that the Ottoman Empire has "become degenerate" because the "court" no longer takes an interest in the military
power which made it great in the first place. "In brief," Rycaut laments, "there
are no relics of ancient justice or generosity of discreet government or obedience
to it." There is no "courtesy or concord," "valour or counsel," "confidence, friendship or generous fidelity" left. In 1686, after the defeat by the Austrians and the
virtual transformation of Mehmet IV from a *ghazi* to a Sultan who no longer had
much to offer, this certainly looked like the case. Rycaut blames the situation
on "the tyranny and rapine of the *beylerbeys* and pashas, who. . .expose the poor
inhabitants [of the various Ottoman territories] to violence and injury," and also
"the insolence of the horse and foot," who march around extorting "money and
clothes" as well as "taking. . .children to sell as slaves."

Rycaut believes that "there is no question but a standing army of veteran and
well-disciplined soldiers must be always useful and advantageous to the interest
of a prince," but that if the government loses control of it, "licentiousness and
restiness" prevails, and the state's welfare is endangered. It is possible that Rycaut

might have been alluding to the last years of the Protectorate, when Richard Cromwell, not a soldier himself, was unable to assert civilian authority over the army, but fear of powerful standing armies was, in any case, endemic in Rycaut's England because of the Civil War. In the Ottoman Empire, the danger was posed by the Janissaries and Sipahis, which Rycaut traced back, rather self-contradictorily, to the time of Süleyman the Magnificent, who, he said (citing Busbecq as his authority), "trembled at nothing more than the apprehension of some secret ulcer of perfidiousness which might lie concealed within the retirement of the Janissaries," who were, in large part, recruited from the Christian areas of the empire. The Ottomans became powerful, Rycaut thinks, because the Christian powers were not well-led or properly organised. He cites "the sloth of the Germans and other nations in their counsels against the Turks," and he condemns "the liberty given to Christian soldiery," which he attributed, rather naïvely, to an excessive "intemperance in wine"! Again citing Busbecq, Rycaut seriously argued that the reason the Christians were losing battles was because their men were constantly drunk, a vice which Rycaut states has now taken over the Ottoman army and which accounts for the decline in Ottoman power. "Drunkenness is now become so common a vice amongst them," he tells us, "that scarce one in ten but is addicted to a brutish intemperance."

The book concludes with a reminder to readers that England itself has "never felt any smart of the rod of this great oppressor of Christianity," and that "amicable correspondence and friendship" have prevailed because England does business with the Ottomans through "the excellent conduct and direction of that right worshipful Company of the Levant Merchants." This has brought "employment and livelihood to many thousands of people in England," increased the Crown's revenues, and prevented wars. It also increased the prestige of England, which has been "preserved by the prudence and admirable discretion of a series of worthy ambassadors." This paean to the Levant Company ends Rycaut's treatise, and supports Filiz Turhan's contention that Rycaut's book not only "echoes the tone of its predecessors," but also "anticipates the attitudes of the future" (*The Other Empire*, 12). Whatever the Turks might be morally, their empire offered huge possibilities for English commerce and trade; the economic advantages, as Rycaut sees them, far outweighed any ethical considerations. As we move into the eighteenth-century, that great age of banking, speculation, and, ultimately, empire, and come down to our own age of capitalism, where trade with dictators and totalitarian states has never stopped, we can perhaps imagine Sir Paul Rycaut's approving shade hovering over it.

## Why did Rycaut write this book?

In his address to the reader, Rycaut himself gives some reasons for having written this particular book and establishes his qualifications for doing so in no uncertain terms. He denies, first, that he is writing a mere travel account, but rather presenting "a true system or model of the Turkish government and religion, not in the same manner as certain ingenious travellers have done." Travellers, Rycaut believes, are not very systematic; their accounts are conversational or anecdotal rather than analytical, therefore "consequently subject to many errors and mistakes." This is exactly the claim made by John Greaves in his edition of Robert Withers's book; he writes scornfully in his preface of the "vain garbes, & modes, and disguised fashions, the onely objects, and idols, of phantastic Travellers" (*Description*, A4). It is rather a pity that Rycaut (and Greaves, for that matter) are so hard on travellers, whose accounts at least give readers the pleasure of the exotic, and interesting anecdotes as well as descriptions of local people and customs. Rycaut, had he been a little more the traveller and a little less a collector of facts and figures, might have produced a more accessible book for modern readers, but of course this was not his purpose, and he obviously believed that his readership wanted facts, not stories.

Scholars have also long speculated on what Rycaut's "hidden agenda" might have been in his book, and their conclusions are surprisingly uniform. He does not simply attack the Ottoman system of government for being despotic whilst praising that of Charles II for not being despotic. Linda Darling, for example, points out that if "Rycaut's picture of the Ottoman Sultan is uncompromisingly negative," this view is not the result of simple "ignorance or prejudice." Sir Dudley North, former treasurer at Constantinople and Smyrna, who sniffed at Rycaut's book for being "very superficial" (MacLean and Matar, *Britain*, 201), was simply wrong, as was Lady Mary Wortley Montagu in the next century, who criticised Rycaut for being often inaccurate in his views. There is much more to it than that, because "contradictions in Rycaut's view of the Ottomans are matched by equivocation and hesitancy in his praise of English kingship" ("Ottoman Politics," 73). What makes Rycaut's opinions about the Ottoman Empire important is that they were gathered whilst he was actually there, unlike, for example, those of Richard Knolles and most other English historians of the Ottoman Empire. Certainly Rycaut must have known about the travellers' accounts, histories, and even the plays mentioned in the previous paragraphs, but he has taken some pains to align himself against blind prejudice, hearsay, and ignorance, and it would not be correct to designate Rycaut's book as a mere "travel account." It is part the autobiography of an Englishman abroad in foreign service, part a handbook for merchants, politicians, diplomats, and others who wished to know something about the Ottoman Empire, and, if the reader exercises some imagination, part travel-book, too. Filiz Turhan praises Rycaut for his objectivity, noting his "balanced tone and fair reporting" (*The Other Empire*, 12). As Darling states further, if Rycaut nonetheless expresses some of the traits of other writers about the same subject, "he was using an old stereotype for new purposes" ("Ottoman Politics," 74). Putting it simply, what Rycaut is saying is that the Ottoman government is a despotic model we know and fear, whether the accounts are exaggerated or not; if we look at our own government carefully, we should get worried as to how far it might go in the same direction unless it modifies its present course. "Look at Turkey," Rycaut seems to be saying; "do you want us to proceed down the same path?" As Andrew Wheatcroft puts it, Rycaut's book was "not just a plain history but an extraordinarily powerful and complex polemic, which has resonated throughout Europe down the centuries;" if the English "failed to protect their ancient freedoms," Rycaut suggests, they might as well subscribe to Ottoman tyranny.[190]

Rycaut was writing in the second half of the seventeenth century, and he was, when push came to shove, a royalist through and through, in spite of the privations he and his family had suffered for their loyalty to the royal cause. England had come through a long period of civil wars and failed attempts to establish a non-monarchical system of government, yet in a few years after the Restoration of 1660 it was obvious to many Englishmen that things would not simply go back to the way they had been under King Charles I "of blessed memory," but would be following, to an extent, the trends set by the rest of Europe. Charles II was in many ways an extremely astute ruler; it was that astuteness that would let him keep both his throne and his head. He had spent eleven years in France watching and waiting, and he had had plenty of time to observe the way Louis XIV governed. Given that, he would certainly have known what aspects of French absolutism not to imitate in England. If Charles was a man who harboured absolutist tendencies, he certainly did a reasonably good job of keeping them mostly to himself when he needed to, and when anything went awry, it was his ministers who usually bore the brunt of the blame. In this sense, he was more of a Louis XIII than a Louis XIV. At the same time, many political actions were motivated by what seemed to many a real danger that a civil war might at some point break out again; there is no doubt that Charles II himself was aware of that fear and indeed shared it to a degree, given his own personal experiences. He also knew how to raise the spectre of civil war when it might contribute to his own cause. Others, like Rycaut, believed that despotic rule was what caused civil unrest, and that a tendency towards it, however slight, must be watched carefully and, ultimately, scotched before the country exploded again into civil war. As Rycaut lived through the reign of James II and the so-called Glorious Revolution of 1688, the deposition of James and his own precarious position in that year, his words might have come back to him as strangely prophetic.

---

[190] Andrew Wheatcroft. *The Enemy at the Gate: Hapsburgs, Ottomans and the Battle for Europe* (New York: Basic Books, 2008), 76.

For Rycaut, the kind of government that prevailed in England immediately after the Restoration was probably the best, but, as we shall see, it had short-comings, and these could be subtly pointed out by, for example, praising some aspects of the Ottoman system of government which look comparable, but without directly criticising the English government. This was, of course, an old trick; Sir John Mandeville, for example, had presented a dialogue between his narrator and an Arab ruler in which the faults of Christianity are clearly laid bare for all to see. It does not matter whether "Mandeville" was a fictitious character or not—what his character says is the important point. And Rycaut can do the same thing in *The Present State of the Ottoman Empire* by, for example, praising the way things in Turkey used to be, but which, under Mehmet IV, appear to have declined, although the notion of the Ottoman Empire in decline seems to be rather relative, as historians have more recently pointed out. Rycaut could thus patriotically praise the English system of government as it then was whilst at the same time covertly criticise it for not doing some things as well as they were done in the Ottoman Empire. He could also suggest that as things were supposedly "better" in the days of Süleyman the Magnificent, so they were for England in, say, the reign of Elizabeth I, and that we would do well to look back on those days and perhaps try to emulate or re-create them after the devastation of the Civil War and the alleged "misrule" of the Commonwealth and Protectorate. What he did not wish to see was any English version of the legendary absolutism of the Ottoman Sultan, where the only constraint upon the ruler's power, as he pointed out, was in religious matters.

This is not to suggest, however, that Rycaut's text is either deliberately or provocatively "subversive;" it is, in the end, a subtly suggestive and surprisingly objective yet critical discourse that invites both positive and negative comparisons, but does not usually directly draw them. Indeed, Wheatcroft notes that Rycaut "always presented himself as a humble but reliable chronicler of Ottoman affairs" (*Enemy at the Gate*, 76). An example of suggestiveness would be Rycaut's unspoken invitation for readers to think about the deposition and murder of Osman II by Janissaries and the Grand Vizier of in 1622, the Ottoman Empire's first regicide, or, even closer to home, that of Ibrahim in 1648, which occurred almost at the same time that Charles I suffered a similar fate at the hands of Parliament and its military supporters, although the judicial murders were different in kind. As Ros Ballaster points out, "oriental courts function alternately as both analogue and opposite" (*Fabulous Orients*, 47). Indeed, Rycaut alluded more directly to this in his continuation of Knolles's *Turkish History* (1678), where he stated that Ibrahim's fate "puts me in mind of the saying of a wiser and a better King than he, *that there is little distance between the prisons and the graves of princes*" after which he goes on to record how the Grand Vizier expressed shock at the execution of Charles I just a few months before the murder of Ibrahim, whom, he claimed disingenuously, was "revered and observed" (ii, 79; cited by Ballaster, 46). For Rycaut, the execution of both king and Sultan would have been a fla-

grant act of regicide; Charles had been condemned by a self-constituted court of
his enemies with no constitutional or legal authority and Ibrahim more or less
sentenced to death by the mufti, the Grand Vizier, and his own mother. The circumstances may have been different in kind, but the comparison would not have
gone unnoticed, and it was no accident that Rycaut wrote in detail of the murder
of Ibrahim and the resulting factionalism involving female power brokers and
military factions. When Rycaut is a little more specific, it is usually to display
his royalist leanings and his abhorrence of anarchy or non-royal forms of government, which in his view are usually the product of civil wars and dissentions of
various kinds, but could also be the result of overreaching absolutism. As for the
women, one need look no further than Charles's predilection for womanising;
even if he did not allow his mistresses to run the government in actual fact, it
might not have looked that way to outside observers, and the ambitions of a Barbara Castlemaine or a Louise de Kérouaille, at least for the advancement of their
friends and relations, were very well known. Rycaut's detailed description of the
roles of Kösem Sultan and Turhan Hadice would have invited obvious comparisons. How do we know what they did or did not say or do behind the scenes or,
more accurately, behind the curtains of the four-poster bed? Could English history repeat itself with the same dire consequences?

Rycaut, as the continuer of Knolles, had probably also read the latter's translation of Bodin's *Six livres de la république* (1576), which he must have viewed
with some misgivings or ambivalence. After all, Bodin had argued that the only
legitimate form of rule was that invested in a single person (or, on rare occasions, an oligarchy), because sovereignty itself should not be divisible. Bodin,
like James I in *The True Law of Free Monarchies* (1598), assumed that fear of divine retribution would make the ruler restrain himself morally or politically, but
that there could be no legal recourse to act against him if his tyranny were le-
gitimately constituted, which, to Rycaut's mind, neither the Commonwealth nor
Protectorate were. About England itself, Bodin had written, not quite accurately
as it turned out, that "the entire sovereignty belongs undivided to the kings of
England and that the Estates (i.e. Parliament) are only witnesses."[191] Later on, in
*Patriarcha*, which was published in 1680, seventeen years after its author's death,
Sir Robert Filmer, following Bodin, advocated near-absolutism, and, again like
James I, argued that rulers, no matter how they got their power, were like fathers
who had the right of life and death over their family or subjects. "It skills not
which way kings come by their power," Filmer declared; "for it is still the man-
ner of the government by supreme power that makes them properly kings,"[192]

---

[191] Jean Bodin, *On Sovereignty: Four Chapters from The Six Books of the Commonwealth*, ed. and trans. Julian H. Franklin, (Cambridge: Cambridge University Press,
1996), 23.

[192] Sir Robert Filmer, *Patriarcha and Other Writings*, ed. Johann P. Somerville
(Cambridge: Cambridge University Press, 1996), 44.

recalling Bodin's earlier phrase "genuine monarchs," amongst whom he lists, perhaps ominously for Rycaut when he read it, the Ottoman Sultan and the king of England (*On Sovereignty*, 115). The year in which Filmer's book was published might also have raised a red flag for Rycaut; it was the same year that Charles II had dissolved Parliament (for the second time in a year) after it had tried to pass the Exclusion Bill, which aimed at making sure that Charles's brother, the Catholic James, duke of York, would never succeed, and whose opponents had argued that its passing could occasion another civil war.

The posthumous first publication of Filmer's book in that year might be seen as part of the propaganda machine of the Stuart monarchy, raising fears of civil war in order to justify the arbitrary dissolution of Parliament and the reassertion of the king's power. As Darling puts it, "the later Stuarts and their supporters used order-centered language to justify royal action independent of Parliament" ("Ottoman Politics," 79), and Filmer's book exactly fitted that bill. "Government of a people," Filmer clearly declared, "be a thing not to be endured" (*Patriarcha*, 31), a maxim with which Rycaut would have heartily concurred, but that did not mean he was a supporter of complete royal independence from Parliament. He does call the Sultan a "tyrant," and he uses phrases like "the absoluteness of an emperor without reason" (Ibrahim, in this case), or "servitude and slavery." Rycaut was showing his readers what tyranny would be like, whether it was personal tyranny of rulers like Ibrahim or too-powerful ministers exercising quasi-monarchical power under Mehmet IV. Rycaut wanted a compromise. He liked neither oriental despots nor French-style absolutists, but he did not want power to reside entirely in either a parliament, an all-powerful favourite, or an oligarchy of some kind, and he was certainly no democrat. It had never, in any case, been decided in England just *how* supreme the king (or any other single person, such as a Lord Protector) was, despite the plethora of books arguing both sides of the question.[193] After the debacle that was the reign of Charles I it had become abundantly clear that his father's theory of divine right did not hold up to close scrutiny, but just to what extent, on the other hand, was Parliament, as it embodied the laws of the land, the supreme authority, and did it even have the right to establish itself as such? Certainly writers like Filmer thought it did not. These questions, moreover, had not been resolved by the failed experiments of either Commonwealth or Protectorate and were raising their heads again during the reign of Charles II. Rycaut, a royalist whose very livelihood depended upon those

---

[193] Two well-known examples of the most notable books arguing against divine right were John Milton's *Tenure of Kings and Magistrates* (1649) and Algernon Sidney's *Discourses concerning Government* (1680), which was a direct reply to Filmer. Milton's book merely contributed to the poet's political and personal difficulties after the Restoration, but Sidney found himself charged with high treason and was executed in 1680, implicated in the Rye House Plot, allegedly hatched to assassinate Charles II and his brother James.

immediately above him on the rungs of the ladder of power, must have been very nervous, and he himself resorted to some off-the-job juggling to make sure that he ended up in the right place. To this end Clarendon and Halifax, as we have seen, needed reconciling; as one's power was waning and the other's waxing, Rycaut was caught in the middle, and his solution was to bring the two together.

There were other reasons, too, why Rycaut wished to hold up the Ottoman government as an example of what should *not* happen in England. Linda Darling persuasively argues that in Rycaut's case, as in that of others like him, there was grave concern about "tyrannical power" being exercised by the monarchy over property. In chapter 2 Rycaut spends considerable time discussing questions of land ownership in the Ottoman Empire, where he tells us that it lay within the power of the Sultan to dispose of any land that was not religious property. The Sultan actually allowed people a temporary right to possess land, which he could revoke at any time; this reduced Ottoman landowners to the status of "servants" in the English understanding of the word, as they could not own any property that was not under someone else's control. As Darling states, "The term *liberty* was used in the seventeenth century to refer not to freedom in the abstract, but to the concrete ability to do whatever you wanted with yourself and your property" ("Ottoman Politics," 84). Furthermore, "the Ottoman Sultan owned all the land and claimed all its taxes," Jason Goodwin states, "but he lent some of its revenues directly to his men in return for service" (*Lords of the Horizons*, 68), the operative word being "lent." George Sandys spoke of "a world of people" dependent entirely on Ahmet I's bounty (*Travels*, 60), and Rycaut himself described the "doctrine of submission to the will of [the] great master," the absolute command over life and death exercised by the Sultan. He tellingly quotes from Tacitus a scathing remark uttered by the emperor Tiberius about his senators, "*O homines ad servitutem paratos!*" and then goes on to suggest that while, like the Roman emperor, Ottoman Sultans must have become impatient with "this slavish compliance," at the same time they maintained their absolute power and "desired not the public liberty."

For English people, the individual's life, land, and goods were basic rights, and if the English king were to become absolute, these fundamentals could be under threat and people would be reduced to "slavish compliance." It was not for nothing that the Levellers, Diggers, and others who had advocated the end to private property in the 1640s were blocked by property-owning Parliamentarians from gaining any real power when the monarchy was gone. And it was supremely ironic when Charles I, accused of "tyranny" by his detractors, had declared on the scaffold that whilst he desired the "liberty and freedom" of the people, "I must tell you that their liberty and freedom consists in having of government those laws by which their life and goods may be most their own,"[194]

---

[194] *King Charles His Speech Made upon the Scaffold at Whitehall-Gate* (London: Peter Cole, 1649), n.p.n.

a statement with which Rycaut would have heartily agreed. At the same time, however, Charles I had governed in many instances as if he were above the law, which did indeed constitute a form of tyranny in many English eyes. Rycaut also cites Justinian's *Digest of Roman Law*, in which that emperor stated clearly "*Etsi legibus solute sumus, attamen legibus vivimus*," namely that we may be free from the law, but nevertheless must live within it. A ruler, Rycaut says, needs to apply his power "like physic, when the ordinary force of nature cannot remove the malignancy of some peccant humours." Along with this went liberty of religion, which in England had come under threat from time to time, and the question of who paid for the upkeep of the armed forces. Charles I, for instance, had illegally levied Ship Money in 1637 to pay for naval expansion, and later on people began to understand that paying taxes to support an army was tantamount to paying the cost of their own subjection. Later, the institution of regional rule by major-generals under Oliver Cromwell certainly looked like that; in fact, people referred to them as "satraps and bashaws," titles in the Safavid and Ottoman Empires. [195] Questions were also asked as to whether the king had the right to declare war at all. Rycaut diplomatically raised these issues by descanting on how wonderful it was to live under a ruler who voluntarily limited his own power within the law and "who doth not punish the innocent with the guilty," as the Ottoman Sultans frequently did.

From the above we may see that Rycaut's book serves a number of purposes; as a travel-book it would have helped readers acquire knowledge of Ottoman customs, religion, and social structure, but there was also a political purpose. This, in turn, would invite readers to make comparisons with their own, more familiar territory, and to reflect on their own situation. Rycaut stresses this last aspect by his repeated references to England's form of government and the freedom he believes it represents. In this, Rycaut was not alone and, indeed, he was not the first writer to do this. According to Andrew Hadfield, early modern travel writing, which is (in part) what Rycaut's book is, "reflected on contemporary problems within the English—sometimes, the British—body politic," thus making the book not only "anthropological speculation," but also "the study of comparative government" (*Literature, Travel and Colonial Writing*, 1–2). Thus *The Present State of the Ottoman Empire* stands as a book which was, as Hadfield suggests in his discussion of earlier modern texts, written "in order to participate in current pressing debates about the nature of society" and to preserve "religious toleration" as well as "individual liberty" (*Literature, Travel and Colonial Writing*, 12). The present work demonstrates that the thematic material of earlier writings was continued by Rycaut, and that the underlying sub-text was also a continuation of former practices found in the works of earlier travellers and historians.

---

[195] David Sharp, *Oliver Cromwell* (London: Heinemann, 2003), 51.

Another question that Rycaut addresses is that of Ottoman "decline," a subject which has always fascinated outsiders and has been variously analysed by historians. Lord Kinross dated "the seeds of decline" from the accession of Süleyman the Magnificent's son Selim II "the Drunkard" (1566), whom he calls "a nonentity, absorbed in himself and his pleasures" (*Ottoman Centuries*, 260). Ogier de Busbecq, writing during Süleyman's reign (1555–62), had actually believed that only the emerging power of the Safavids in Persia posed any kind of threat to Ottoman expansion, and when the Sultan's son Bayezid, a capable military commander, revolted against his father, Busbecq noted that it was to Persia he turned for help, although he found none and was imprisoned, the Persians seeing him as more of a threat than a potential ally. Busbecq thought that the Persians had seized Bayezid in order that Süleyman's son Selim, "naturally gluttonous and slothful" would ascend the throne, which is what in fact happened. Busbecq predicted a "promise of peace and lasting security" (*Turkish Letters*, 111) if Selim succeeded. As long as the Persians had Bayezid, Busbecq hoped "the Turks will not readily turn their arms against us" (*Turkish Letters*, 112). He was wrong; regardless of Bayezid, who was eventually turned over to his father and executed, or the potential power of the Safavids, the Turks did come against Europe, and Lepanto (1572) only temporarily stopped them. Busbecq recommended that the Hapsburg emperor employ delaying tactics against the Turks, rather than "hurl[ing] oneself precipitately against such a foe with a small and hastily-levied army" (*Turkish Letters*, 161). Bernard Lewis, however, believed that Busbecq was "profoundly wrong in his global perspective," and that the power displayed by the Ottomans under Selim I and Süleyman I had "passed its peak,"[196] thus concurring with Kinross that the decline began with Selim II's accession.

As we have seen, Sir Thomas Roe had been convinced some years later that Ottoman decline had begun when the unfortunate Sultan Osman II was murdered by members of his own court. Rycaut, too, connects absolutism not with prosperity and power, but with rebellion and consequent loss of political power. This is not simply a royalist's reaction to the aftermath of the English Civil War and the judicial murder of a monarch, but a general observation on the nature of power, and the paradox of absolutism when handled badly by the wrong rulers. A Sultan who was "brave and wise," Rycaut thought, would use his absolute powers to expand his empire and create a good life for his subjects, whilst one that was "effeminate" would simply become self-indulgent, immoral, and rule by or through various favourites, whose power depended on how much they abetted and encouraged their lord's misdeeds. Soldiers, viziers, ministers of state, and the royal family, especially eunuchs or powerful women such as a Sultan's mother, wives or concubines could all end up jockeying for power and contributing to instability, unrest, and ultimately rebellion. There were even factions within fac-

---

[196] Bernard Lewis, *Islam and the West* (New York: Oxford: Oxford University Press, 1993), 16.

tions, as the quarrels within the Ottoman military indicated; Sipahis and Janissaries were often at odds with one another, as the turmoil surrounding the young Mehmet IV at the beginning of his reign demonstrated. The recent past under the reigns of mentally unstable Sultans such as Mustafa I and Ibrahim, young rulers with unrealistic ambitions like Osman II coming to grief when his actions upset the Janissaries, and the rule of women over Mehmet IV in those early years, notably Kösem Sultan and Turhan Hadice, and that same ruler's propensity for leaving affairs of state to others were all significant negative examples of autocracy in decline or going wrong. His major example, given in chapter 4 of the first part of his book, was an account of the murder of Kösem Sultan, her rivalry with Turhan Hadice and the wavering loyalty of the Janissaries. These events speak to what Rycaut termed "the decay of discipline" which was eroding the strength of the Ottoman Empire and which could, in a parallel way, undermine the strength of England.

Rycaut's political position rides uncomfortably upon the fence between royal absolutism and Parliamentary government, neither of which he sees as entirely desirable. It might be uncomfortable being a trimmer, but sometimes it was the right thing to do. The Ottoman Empire represented what absolutism at its worst might produce, and thus served as a warning to any English ruler who might seriously consider it. Yet, without the monarchy as a kind of legitimate lynchpin, government might fall into tyranny or anarchy when taken over by all-powerful politicians, favourites, or military leaders. The nobility and landed classes also played their part in Rycaut's scheme of things, enjoying their liberty and property without fear of losing it to the monarch, to whom, in the Ottoman Empire, it ultimately belonged anyway. Even in the Ottoman Empire, Rycaut could point to the rise to power of the Köprülü viziers, who would begin the transformation of the absolute power of the Sultan into their own form of leadership over which the Sultan benignly presided and the Vizier took his own decisions. The Grand Vizier became more like a prime minister; Mehmet IV "presented the vizier with a building, which served him both as an official residence and an office" (Lewis, *Istanbul*, 95). Mehmet Köprülü and his successor Fazil Ahmet were such men; the former "set about to restore the state" by "the simple notion that there must be an end to corruption and graft,"[197] and his son, within fifteen years, made the Grand Vizierate "more absolute and powerful than it ever had been" (Shaw, *Ottoman Empire* 1, 211), even more powerful than the able Mehmet Sokollu Pasha, who had been Grand Vizier under Selim II. Ottoman bureaucracy in general flourished, too, and the whole structure actually worked more efficiently under a modified system where the Sultan's whims could not affect its day-to-day operations. At the same time, however, as Darling notes, "Ottomans continued to talk and write as if sultanic absolutism were still in place" ("Ottoman Politics,"

---

[197] Norman Itzkovitz, *Ottoman Empire and Islamic Tradition* (University of Chicago Press, 1972), 78.

95), and there were, no doubt, some who wished it was. Furthermore, as Caroline Finkel puts it, "after the deposition of Mehmet IV in 1687, Sultans engaged themselves more closely in the day-to-day running of the empire and enjoyed at least the illusion of ruling as well as reigning" (*Osman's Dream*, 325). A final Köprülü vizier, Numan Pasha, the son of Fazil Ahmet, would hang on to a semblance of power for a short time in 1710 under Ahmet III, but the Köprülü glory days had been effectively over for some time before that. Caroline Finkel dates the decline of the vizierate to 1699, when the Ottomans signed the Treaty of Karlowicz, effectively ending hostilities with the Hapsburgs at the expense of a large amount of Turkish territory (*Osman's Dream*, 328).

At the same time, as we have already seen, Rycaut did not make the mistake which Tsar Nicholas I would in 1853 when he remarked to Lord John Russell that "we have a sick man on our hands," of ruling the Ottoman Empire out as a significant power, and he was likely not surprised sixteen years later in 1681 when he learned that Kara Mustafa's army was encamped outside the walls of Vienna. The Ottoman Empire of the later seventeenth century, even if it looked to overly-hopeful outsiders like it was in decline, was still more powerful than most European countries. It had recovered quite handily from defeats such as Lepanto and St. Gothard, and would recover again even after the Poles finally lifted the siege of Vienna. "Decline," Rycaut knew, was a relative term, and it was not for nothing that he included a section in his book on the strength of the Ottoman army. He promised, indeed, to give readers "an exact computation of their forces both by sea and land," a promise he delivers in book 3. In spite of the fact that the Turks' armed forces are not the way they were in the time of Süleyman the Magnificent, Rycaut warned his readers that "if they have lost ground in one place, like the sea, they have recovered it in another," and he gives plenty of examples, thus failing to relieve any anxiety his readers migh have had about Ottoman power. "European observers," Norman Itzkowitz writes, "were convinced that [the Köprülüs] had not only restored the empire to health, but that they had placed new power and glory within its grasp" (*Ottoman Empire*, 81), which, if the observation is correct, certainly suggests that they did not see much of a decline in Ottoman power. Rycaut emphasised, however, that the real decay was in the Ottoman naval forces, which in itself was good for the Christian powers, but his description of the land forces available to an able Sultan would likely have served as a caution.

In the end, Rycaut reveals himself as the loyal Levant Company man, deciding firmly in favour of cultivating the Ottoman Empire as a trading partner rather than worrying about whether it is a potential enemy. He points out that the English "have never felt any smart of the rod of this great oppressor of Christianity," but have rather "tasted of the good and benefit which hath proceeded from a free and open trade and amicable correpondence with this people, which have been maintained for the space of above eighty years." Rycaut is certainly not interested, as some previous writers such as Grelot were, in looking for a weak spot to exploit in a war against the Turks in order to destroy the Ottoman Empire, because that would be very bad for trade. "As some study several ways and prescribe rules by which a war may be advantageously managed against the Turk," Rycaut says, "I, on the contrary, am more inclined to give my judgment in what manner our peace and trade may best be secured and maintained." If the Turks have subjected Christians in the remoter part of Europe, Rycaut is willing to overlook it, because, for him, there are infinitely more advantages to cultivating trade-relations and diplomatic ties than there are to waging war, as the continuing and constant struggle in Europe between the Ottomans on one side and the Hapsburgs and their allies on the other surely demonstrated. Then, as now, it was a trade-off; we in the West negotiate with communists in China, seventeenth-century England sent diplomats to the Muslim Sultan's court in Constantinople. There was also, as Bernard Lewis observes, another reason, namely that after their defeat at the walls of Vienna the Ottomans "were faced with the need to negotiate a peace treaty, and to do so from a position of weakness," but, because England, France, and the Netherlands stood to gain by keeping the Austrians from "the full fruits of their victory," the Turks were, thanks to diplomatic manoeuvres from these countries, "able to get rather better terms than they might have been able to achieve through their own unaided efforts" (*Islam and the West*, 33).

Rycaut dedicated the book to Lord Arlington, who had, after all, once spoken of his "good parts,"[198] although he had failed to do anything further to help Rycaut's career. Not much attention has been paid to this dedication, but it may, if readers do not dismiss it as egregious flattery or apple-polishing, give some information as to where Rycaut's political sympathies lay at the time and thus shed some more light on the purposes of the book. Henry Bennett, earl of Arlington (1618–1685) had been a staunch supporter of the royal cause since the early days of the Civil War, in which he was wounded in 1644. He seems to have enjoyed advertising this fact, because for a long time he sported a black plaster on his nose which appears in several portraits. After the execution of Charles I, Bennett went to France with the court of the exiled Charles II, where he became secretary to Charles's brother James, Duke of York. After the Restoration he seems to have become a kind of royal procurer, finding suitable (or not-so suitable) mistresses for the king whilst at the same time holding the office of Keeper of the Privy Purse. People liked Arlington; by all accounts he had a charming and polished manner, and by 1663 he was a peer, taking the title of Baron Arlington, which Charles II later elevated into an earldom. His easy-going personality, rather like Winchilsea's, concealed great political ambitions but also, unlike Winchilsea, a marked propensity for putting his personal interests first, no matter what the cost to former friends and allies.

---

[198] Lord Arlington to Lord Winchilsea, 13 October 1666. *Finch Report*, 442, cited in Abbott, *Under the Turk,* 52.

Arlington's politics, too, were often contradictory. For example, in 1665 he came across as a religious liberal advocating liberty of conscience, but this may have simply been a ruse to persuade more people to donate money for the second instalment of the Anglo-Dutch War, which broke out the same year. Later on he became ardently anti-Catholic, in spite of his friendship with the Duke of York. He is best-known for being a member of the so-called "Cabal" government, which consisted alphabetically of Lord *C*lifford of Chudleigh, *A*rlington, the duke of *B*uckingham, Lord *A*shley (later Shaftesbury) and the earl of *L*auderdale. Those in this group who were Catholics were in favour of the secret Treaty of Dover which Charles II signed with Louis XIV in 1670. This treaty provided for English assistance to the French in their war with the Dutch, and secured Louis XIV's promise that he would assist in the restoration of the Catholic faith in England. Arlington also became involved in a number of political movements and machinations which included a plan for making Charles II absolute, ignoring the debts incurred by the state, and first opposing any deals with the Dutch whilst later becoming their advocate. His relentless pursuit of his own advantage finally led to a falling-out with his colleagues, and although he was able to play a part in his associate Clifford's dismissal, he himself was impeached in 1674. However, his career was not yet over. The next year found Arlington on the anti-Catholic side, against a French alliance, and travelling to the Netherlands to make peace and secure an alliance with William III. His total failure as an ambassador put paid to any further credit he might have had, and he gradually lost all his former prestige and influence at court. The consensus of opinion is that Arlington turned himself into an advocate of absolutism because, as a favourite of the king, he saw it would be an easier way for him to get whatever offices or privileges he wanted. Under the system he found himself, and constantly playing both sides against the middle, Arlington never realised his ambition to become Lord Treasurer, and in the end became known as a bitter and jealous intriguer, which in fact he had always been, but had managed to conceal it under a charming and urbane veneer.

Having read this, one might be forgiven for wondering why Rycaut, who was firmly against absolutism and all it entailed, would dedicate his book to someone like Arlington. Was he simply naïve, or perhaps himself an opportunist? Like any intelligent observer of the political milieu of the time (and there were several), Rycaut likely saw through the façade of this consummate political manoeuverer; Arlington, Rycaut says in silken tones, "penetrates into the designs and knows the cabinet-councils of neighbouring principalities," he possesses "profound wisdom" together with "experience and judgment." The book, furthermore, "seems naturally to appertain to the patronage of Your Lordship, whose faculties of wisdom and virtue have given you the blessing of your Prince's favour and the reputation as well abroad as at home of an eminent and dexterous minister of state." Even here, however, we can, without too much imaginative reading, see a subtext; the word "dexterous" is both complimentary and suggestive of political sleight of hand. Arlington may well be sharp or clever, but these characteristics are double-edged, even as Rycaut protests his own "great presumption" in writing them. Rycaut wrote these words in 1665, the same year in which Arlington was working with the Duke of York, the Lord Admiral, to capitalise on English victories in the First Dutch War by starting another one and extending English power even further; even after this there would be two further wars, the last one in the next century. This one was precipitated in December 1664 by Sir Thomas Allin, who was based in Tangier, with an attack on the Dutch Smyrna fleet near that city in which several Dutch ships were sunk and others captured. The Dutch consulate in Smyrna was an important one; of course Rycaut was working in Smyrna at the time of this event, and it was in 1665 that the Dutch consul there, Levinus Warner, with whom Rycaut was well-acquainted, was said, by Rycaut's source Bobowski, to have been mysteriously murdered in Constantinople.

If Rycaut wrote *The Present State of the Ottoman Empire* as a warning and a negative example, Arlington, the man who would support absolutism to feed his own ambitions was the ideal dedicatee, and had his first priority been political ambition, his continued friendship with Winchilsea already gave him an entrance to the highest court circles, and his membership in the Royal Society may also have enabled him to glean information about politics in high places, as many of its members had court connections. Arlington, as one of Charles II's intimates, would have been in a good position to apprise the king of the book's contents, but at the same time Rycaut may have been delivering a very subtle hint to Arlington himself. One may only speculate how deeply Rycaut really understood Arlington's political views and his leanings towards supporting absolutism to gain his own ends; the warnings in the book are clear enough. He certainly would have known more about Arlington's intentions than the hindsight of modern historians could gather. Favourites, through whom absolutists often ruled, were, at least in the Ottoman sense, slaves; even viziers, grand or otherwise, could be highly-favoured one day and headless the next. What is more, Rycaut gives such details of court-intrigue involving women that the connections with Arlington's unofficial duties as royal procurer and the potential danger of royal mistresses attempting to convert sexual power into political power can, as we have seen, hardly be overlooked. Lastly, Rycaut may have also seen Arlington as a man who would soon become very powerful indeed, and thus in a position to influence the English government in whatever way he chose. There is, of course, no concrete evidence for what has just been suggested, but there seems no other likely explanation for Rycaut's dedication of the book to a man whose political principles were, in the end, so opposed to his own. The dedication, moreover, remained in the sixth edition of Rycaut's book (1686), published some months after Arlington's death the previous year.

Rycaut's ambitions were, in fact, reasonable. He does not seem to have made many enemies, and men from both sides of the political spectrum were his friends. It was true that he seemed to be allied temperamentally, at least at first, with the Tories, who supported the accession of James II, but Rycaut could never reconcile himself with the king's closeness with Louis XIV. Lord Arlington, as we have seen, was ever the "dexterous" politican, and Rycaut's other friends in high places or society included the ex-Cromwellian Lord Fauconberg as well as Halifax "the Trimmer," the great proponent of the *via media*, the Finches and a number of senior Anglican clergymen, one of whom, William Sancroft, then Archbishop of Canterbury, had been tried and imprisoned in 1688 for opposing James II's Declaration of Indulgence. In the end Rycaut supported the accession of William of Orange, and dedicated the 1699 volume of his *Turkish History* to the king. Even Abbott's accusation that Rycaut lacked a sense of humour is mistaken, too; when he was forced into inferior lodgings on his arrival in Hamburg, due to the fact that Sir Peter Wyche was not ready to leave, Rycaut commented wryly "that it was impossible to have been so cold anywhere, unless under the Northern Pole" (Cited in Anderson, *English Consul,* 271).

## Influence of *The Present State of the Ottoman Empire* and an Overview of Later Works

Rycaut's book was widely read and served as a source book and reference for writers of both literary works, as we have seen above, and histories. For over a hundred years it was the standard reference work for anyone who wanted to know or write about the Ottoman Empire, and it played a major part in modifying the way in which European readers regarded Islam and the Turks. It was translated into Polish (1678), German (1694), Dutch, Italian, and Russian, with paraphrased versions appearing in Hungarian (1794) and Romanian (Anderson, *English Consul,* 294–97). We have mentioned the names of Kelemen Mikes, Prince Demetrie Cantemir, and Martin Vogel as having used Rycaut as a source. "Attempts were made in seventeenth- and eighteenth-century Europe to correct errors about Muhammad and Islam," Ros Ballaster writes, "but largely in order to protect the Christian case against it from countercharges of imposture, extravagant fictionalizing, and invention" (*Fabulous Orients,* 50). However, Rycaut does not do this; in his chapters on Islam he sought to explain, as objectively as he could, how the various sects differed in their beliefs and activities, and how Islam was subject to sectarianism in a similar way to Christianity. It was always a given, for Rycaut as well as Knolles and earlier writers, that Turkish power and success could be explained as a punishment inflicted on divided Christianity (Catholic or Protestant) by God, and it therefore made sense to show that Islam was not united either, and was, in fact, even more divided than Christianity because there were so many sects. At the same time, schisms and splits in Christianity could still pose dangers and would allow Islam to take advantage of the consequent weakness of both Eastern and Western Christianity. Rycaut, writing as a Protestant at a time when religion in England seemed to be undergoing change, particularly through the perceived Catholic sympathies of Charles II and the reality of those of James II, may well have, like others, seen Islam as "a mask through which they denounced their arch-enemy, the Church of Rome," as Ahmad Gunny points out (cited in Ballaster, *Fabulous Orients*, 51), and his dedication of a work to James II, as we have seen, was not accidental.

Interest in the Ottoman Empire and in the Orient in general appears to have tapered somewhat in England,[199] and it was the French who came to focus on it; Ros Ballaster notes that this was true particularly with "Middle Eastern languages, literatures and theology" (*Fabulous Orients*, 77), but it was also the case with travel-accounts and other forms of literature. French writers had been interested in Turkish matters for some time, of course; Rycaut is directly mentioned in the preface to Jean Racine's *Bajazet* (1672) as a source, and John Sayer further points out that it was the "inaccurate rendering of Rycaut" by Racine's French translator Pierre Briot (1670)[200] which gave rise to some of the most spectacular scenes in that play, including "a vivid account of the conspiracy of the Grand Vizir."[201] Molière has a mock-Turkish scene in *Le malade imaginaire* (1673), complete with someone impersonating a mufti, to which Charpentier provided some "Turkish" music which features a chorus of Turks repeating the word *yok*, meaning something which does not exist or is not so. Later on Voltaire would take up Middle Eastern, if not quite Turkish, themes in plays such as *Zaïre* (1732), whose heroine is a Christian slave of the "Sultan of Jerusalem," and *Mahomet* (1741). The French historian Antoine Galland (1646–1715), best-known for his famous translation of *The Thousand and One Nights*, and who would become one of the most distinguished of all orientalists, was in Constantinople as part of the French embassy (1670–1675), where he learned Arabic and Persian as well as Turkish. He was also in Smyrna (1678) and left an unpublished account of his experiences there which finally saw the light of print in the twenty-first century.[202] Rycaut had left Smyrna in 1677; whether or not he met Galland we do not know, although it is quite possible that they could have known each other in

---

[199] Apparently not for English dramatists, however; after Pix's *Ibrahim* (1695), we find, amongst others, the following, all of which have Turkish themes or characters: Eliza Heywood, *The Fair Captives* (1721); Joseph Trapp, *Abra-Mule* (1735); Isaac Bickerstaff, *The Sultan* (1775); and Hannah Cowley, *A Day in Turkey* (1791). For details of these and other later plays, see Mohammed Ahmed Rawashdeh, "A Confined Amorous Being: The Eastern Woman between Travel Literature and English Drama," *Damascus University Journal* 28 (2012): 91–114.

[200] Briot's translation was revised and corrected by the Sieur Bespier in 1677. The earlier translation appeared three times, in 1670, 1671, and 1678.

[201] John Sayer, *Jean Racine: Life and Legend* (Bern: Peter Lang, 2006), 186–87.

[202] Antoine Galland, *Voyage à Smyrne*. Introduction by Frédéric Bauden (Paris: Editions Chandeigne, 2000).

Constantinople. In 1700, the year of Rycaut's death, the French botanist, medical writer, and diplomat Joseph Pitton de Tournefort (1656–1708) visited Greece and Constantinople, where he stayed for two years; after his unfortunate death in a carriage accident his *Rélation d'un voyage du Levant* appeared posthumously in 1717. The historical background given by de Tournefort owed something to Rycaut, and his book is also notable for its maps and illustrations, which included a city map of Ankara.

There were, of course, a number of other English writers on the Ottoman Empire who followed in Rycaut's footsteps, such as Aaron Hill (1685–1750), whose *Full and Just Account of the Present State of the Ottoman Empire in all its Branches: With the Government, and Policy, Religion, Customs, and Ways of Living of the Turks in General, in general faithfully related from serious observations taken in many years travels thro' those countries* appeared in 1709. Hill, who would become a well-known theatre manager, essayist, dramatist, and opera impresario (he worked with Handel), was being a little disingenuous with his lengthy title. He did indeed go to Constantinople, but it was in 1700 when he was only fifteen years old, and he stayed only until 1703, making short supervised trips to Palestine and Egypt whilst in the care of his relative Lord Paget, the ambassador in Constantinople, and on his way back also travelled in Europe. Hill, described as "a man of amiable manners and of great moral worth,"[203] paraphrased a great deal from Rycaut's book, and apparently regretted later that he had rushed into print at such an early age as well as, probably inadvertently, misrepresenting himself as a seasoned traveller. Hill, like other writers, constantly emphasised the idea of Turks being slavishly obedient; indeed, as Asli Çirakman noted, he believed that "slavishness" was "the sole defining feature of Turkish character," but which, for Rycaut, is simply one part of something much more complex (*Terror*, 198).

The most notable and probably the best-known English writer on Turkey was, of course, the highly-observant, redoubtable, and gossipy Lady Mary Wortley Montagu (1689–1762), whose colourful and informative *Turkish Embassy Letters* were written between 1716 and 1718, when she lived in Constantinople as the wife of the British ambassador there. Montagu's letters refer more than once to Rycaut, but usually to admonish or correct, because she believed that as a woman she could gain a more intimate perspective than a man on such subjects as the seraglio, the baths, and other domestic matters. There is no doubt that Montagu "had first-hand knowledge of Ottoman court life and the harem that previous European male travellers lacked,"[204] and consequently she takes Rycaut to task for some of his information, such as the Sultan dropping a handkerchief in the seraglio to select his partner for the night or that Turkish women have

---

[203] Nathan Drake, *Essays, Biographical, Critical and Historical Illustrative of The Rambler, Adventurer, and Idler* (London, 1809–10), vol. 1, 53.

[204] Humberto Garcia, *Islam and the English Enlightenment* (Baltimore: Johns Hopkins University Press, 2012), 70. For further details on Montagu, see 60–93.

no souls. On a more serious note, she reverses Hill's pronouncements about the slavishness of the Turks and the submissiveness of Turkish women, claiming that from what she can gather it is the Sultan, at that time Ahmet III (1703–1730) who is the slave, of both the Janissaries and his ministers (Ballaster, *Fabulous Orients*, 182), and in fact Ahmet III was eventually deposed.[205] Lady Montagu's book, like Busbecq's, being epistolary in nature, is much more personal than Rycaut's, and of course the writing is far more consciously literary and autobiographical. For a real "feeling" of Turkish life in the early part of the eighteenth century Lady Montagu may well be the best authority, at least from the point of view of a female British expatriate moving in high society, and we learn at least as much about the writer of the letters as we do about the Turks. Rycaut's prose, compared with hers, is often plain, almost self-effacing for the purpose of objectivity and bordering sometimes on dull, but he was not an ambassador's wife and the Ottoman Empire was not, for him, an exotic place of amusement. Rycaut's book, in places, reads rather like a government report or even a handbook, although there are personal passages, too.

One further eponymous work which owed an obvious debt to Rycaut was *The Present State of the Ottoman Empire* (1784), by one Elias Habesci, in which the author claimed to offer "a more accurate and interesting account of the religion, government, military establishment, manners, customs and amusements of the Turks than any yet extant." Habesci went on to tell readers that his book would make them think they were actually in Constantinople at the Sultan's court, and that he would regale them with "many singular and entertaining anecdotes."[206] Whether this can be read as an indirect criticism of Rycaut's rather pedestrian style we have no way of knowing, but Habesci does take Lady Mary Wortley Montagu to task for "deception and misinterpretation" (A3), and is at pains to make sure readers will think that his book is the best one. Habesci (c. 1743–1811) was an interesting character in his own right; according to Liviu Bordas, "Habesci" was a name concocted from an anagram of Sahib el-Sicia, an Arabic title, and he also claimed to be a Moldavian prince. Habesci, unlike Hill, was widely-travelled; by his own account he had been to India, China, and south

---

[205] As an interesting aside, Voltaire featured the ex-Sultan in *Candide* (1759), along with some other jobless kings, meeting Candide on a boat.

[206] Elias Habesci, *The Present State of the Ottoman Empire* (London, 1784), A2. Habesci claimed to be Prince Alexander Ghica, the son of Prince Grigore Ghica III, who ruled in Moldavia 1764–1767, 1774–1777 and Wallachia 1768–1769. Habesci began his career in Constantinople as secretary to the Grand Vizier. After his defection to Russia he embarked on his travels, an account of which appeared in *Objects Interesting to the English Nation*. From 1789 to his death he lived in India.

east Asia, as well as Europe and even the Americas.[207] When war broke out between Russia and Turkey (1768), he defected to the Russians, after which he travelled further, visiting England and America. In 1789 he finally left the west altogether and settled in India, where he spent the rest of his life, modestly using the title "count." In his book, which he originally wrote in French, Habesci claimed to have used Arabic sources, and his book, which uses Rycaut's title, follows the same outline as Rycaut's. Habesci discusses Islam at length (negatively), describes all the "sects" and has a special section on the seraglio which repeats much of the information found in Rycaut's book, although he updates it to the reign of Abdul Hamid I (1774–1789). Habesci also spends a fair amount of time on the Ottoman military's strength and organisation, a practice often found in earlier books on the Ottoman Empire, including Rycaut's.

The eighteenth century also produced an English translation by Abraham Hawkins (1787) of Vincent Mignot's *History of the Turkish or Ottoman Empire from its Foundation in 1300 to the Peace of Belgrade in 1740*, a work based largely on translated sources and French foreign affairs documents.[208] This book went through four French editions between 1771 and 1773 as well as two of Hawkins's translation. By the time these works appeared, there was, finally, an English translation of the Qur'an available, by George Sale (1734). A few years later the baron de Tott[209] went to Constantinople with his uncle the comte de Vergennes, the newly-appointed French ambassador, charged with learning Turkish and investigating the state of affairs in the Crimea. De Tott did both, and in fact produced two books; his combined volumes, *Mémoires du Baron de Tott sur les Turcs et les Tartares* (1785) appeared in English the following year.

"Rycaut's. . .Turks were to reappear in a great many English works of sociological or anthropological complexion," María Antonia Garcés tells us (Di Biase, ed., *Travel and Translation*, 219); his readers also included a number of philosophers and intellectuals from both England and France who found his

---

[207] Liviu Bordas, "An early ideologist of British supremacy in south and south-east Asia: Elias Habesci (1793)." Paper presented at the Fifth International Convention of Asian Scholars, Kuala Lumpur (2–5 Aug. 2007).

[208] Abbé Vincent Mignot (c. 1730–1791) was Voltaire's nephew. He had no knowledge of Turkish and had never travelled to the Ottoman Empire. However, he was an important orientalist and collected Chinese manuscripts. For further details see Urs App, *The Birth of Orientalism* (Philadelphia: University of Pennsylvania Press, 2010), 494, n. 24. Mignot is perhaps best-remembered for having arranged Voltaire's burial in sacred ground over the objections of the clerical establishment. Abraham Hawkins, a justice of the peace, is also known for having produced a mediocre translation (1817) of the complete poetry of Claudian.

[209] François, baron de Tott (1733–1793) made himself useful to Sultan Abdulhamid I by helping him reform the Janissaries and modernise weapons in the army. De Tott also designed and built fortifications for the Turks and travelled extensively in the Ottoman Empire and ended his days in Hungary. He also wrote a book on the Crimean khanate.

broad-minded interpretation of Islam and his willingness to commend the Turks for their toleration of Christians to their liking. John Locke in his *Letter Concerning Toleration* (1689) "celebrated 'Mahometan' toleration" and Pierre Bayle, who "cited Rycaut on Muslim issues in his *Dictionary* more extensively than any other author," also "used Rycaut's arguments in his case for toleration" (Marshall, *John Locke*, 395). Rycaut was thus in good company, insofar as "Locke and Bayle tower over their contemporaries in late seventeenth-century defenders of religious toleration" (Marshall, *John Locke*, 468). Sir William Temple, on the other hand, returned to the subject of tyranny. In an essay entitled "Of heroic virtue" (1690) where he wrote of the "divine designation of the Ottoman line," and in a discussion of the Sultan's power, where "they held obedience to be given in all things to the will of the Ottoman prince," the section on the *timariot* system and the organisation of the Janissaries all indicate that he had a copy of Rycaut's book at his side when he wrote.[210]

In the eighteenth century, when Montesquieu came to write his seminal treatise *Défense de l'ésprit des lois* (1748), he, too, "depended on Rycaut's work and his theory of despotism," and had a copy of *The Present State* in his library (Çirakman, *Terror*, 204). A later English work by Sir William Eton, *A Survey of the Turkish Empire* (1799), purporting to be deduced, like Rycaut's, "from facts recorded in their own history," followed Rycaut's pattern by including information on the structure of the Ottoman government, now under the ill-fated reforming Sultan Selim III (1789–1807), and came to the same conclusion about why the Turks were still powerful. "The power of the Turks was once formidable to their neighbours," Eton wrote, "not by their numbers only, but by their military and civil institutions, far surpassing those of their opponents,"[211] eventually deciding that the Turks were not as well-organised as they used to be, and were, again, therefore, in decline. As Eton put it in his introduction to the *Survey*, his "abstract of history is mostly from Ricaut [*sic*]," whose "antiquated though faithful relation" he considers amongst the best accounts, along with those of Busbecq, Leunclavius, and some others (*Survey*, vi). At the same time, however, Eton sniffed at Lady Montagu's account as being "the production of a warm imagination" (*Survey*, v). Some years later Eton's rather negative outlook on the Ottomans prompted a blistering reply from Thomas Thornton[212] in *The Present State of Turkey* (1807), in which he argued that the Ottomans were still a power

---

[210] Sir William Temple, "Of heroic virtue," in *The Works of Sir William Temple, Bart.*, vol. 3 (London, 1814), 87–90.

[211] Sir William Eton, *A Survey of the Turkish Empire* (1799; repr. Boston: Adamant Media, 2004), ii, 3, 62. Eton was for some years a commercial agent of the Levant Company in Constantinople, and, by his own account, also served in Russia, where he enjoyed "the confidence of the late Prince Potemkin" (*Survey*, ii).

[212] Thomas Thornton (1762–1814) spent more than a decade in Constantinople as an agent, then consul of the Levant Company. After a short time back in England (1813),

to be reckoned with and that prejudiced views such as Eton's were both misleading and dangerous. Thornton's book, which elicited in its turn an indignant reply from Eton, also followed Rycaut's pattern, containing chapters on religion, customs, government and the state of the Turkish military.

From the above we can see that Rycaut's outline of analysing the Ottomans was followed at least into the early nineteenth century, and that his book, given his experience and qualifications, was considered the best account of the conditions in Turkey. Anyone wishing to write on the subject of the Ottoman Empire was obliged to consult Rycaut, the man who had been there and lived there; his work came to replace that of Knolles, and as the eighteenth century progressed, his more tolerant and balanced assessment came to replace those which displayed prejudices and preconceived notions. Those who read his continuation of Knolles would be able to discern the shift in the attitude taken by later writers towards the Ottomans as due in part to Rycaut, whose calm and reasonable tone now replaced the shrillness and vituperation of many earlier writers on the subject. Rycaut, who was after all a man of his own era, did not create an unrealistically favourable view of the Turks, but he did succeed in demonstrating that they were a people with whom the British could do business and who might even, if the times allowed it, become allies and trading partners rather than the frightening Islamic bogeymen of former ages. If Sir Paul Rycaut did nothing else, he depicted the Turks about objectively as anyone in his time could have done, and did a great deal towards moderating the prejudices and ignorance which had coloured the western view of the east for so long.

At the same time, Rycaut's subtler purposes did not go undetected, as the use of his book by Locke, Bayle and Montesquieu demonstrated; these writers were well-acquainted with Rycaut's polemical sub-text, and the age of Louis XIV in particular saw France moving nearer and nearer to an almost quasi-oriental despotism, where such ancient freedoms as existed seemed to be receding into oblivion as royal power grew and the thirst for conquest went unchecked. Rycaut showed his readers that it was no longer the Ottomans themselves who were dangerous, but what they symbolised, namely raw power, imperial designs, and lack of individual liberty for subjects. When this was coupled with a ruler who had absolute power of life and death over his subjects, there would be no more ancient freedoms, no more guarantees that peoples' property and lives were at their own disposal. Rycaut's gift to readers was that he pointed this out clearly and logically, and that his subtle warnings, ostensibly presented as history, were not lost either on contemporary readers or on his illustrious successors.

---

Thornton prepared to return to the Levant, but died suddenly before his departure. For details, see Elizabeth Baigent, "Thomas Thornton, 1767?-d. 1814," *ODNB*, 27363.

## A Note on the Illustrations

There is little doubt that engraved illustrations, especially of portraits and costumes, were an important part of books such as Rycaut's and that they helped increase circulation, especially when they dealt with unfamiliar or "exotic" topics. Prints showed what people in foreign lands looked like, how they dressed, and how they differed from the readers; they also showed what the traveller had actually perceived. They might create stereotypes or even idealise, but they might also counteract those stereotypes, and any idealisation would serve to create a more positive image of the people and places depicted. In an illustration, the "other" was there in person, available for all to see and to judge, more or less accurately represented by the engraver. Some seventeenth-century travellers, such as George Sandys, John Greaves, and Sir Thomas Herbert, actually did their own illustrations, which were then engraved, often anonymously, and these add a more personal and intimate sense of immediacy to the text. The quality of the illustrations, dependent as it was on the engraver, could vary from the mediocre to the highly accomplished; we know, for example, that John Milton complained bitterly about the skill, or lack thereof, of his engraver William Marshall, but the high artistic quality of engravings by, for example, Wenceslas Hollar or William Faithorne cannot be denied, and the representation of the pyramids of Egypt by John Greaves is also exceptional. The illustrations for Rycaut's book, described on the title page as "divers pieces of sculpture representing the variety of habits amongst the Turks" in *The Present State of the Ottoman Empire* are not signed either by an artist or an engraver. In style they look very much like those in Claes Rålamb's book, which were executed by a Turkish artist in Constantinople, or the album of Turkish costumes compiled by Peter Mundy in his *Brief Relation of the Turks* (1618). There is also a similar group of illustrations in Sir Hans Sloane's collection, which is dated by scholars to about 1620.[213] In Savage's abridgment of Rycaut's continuation of Knolles's *History of the Turks* (1701) the engravings were by William Elder (fl. 1680–after 1700), best-known for his portraits, many of which were reworked from older engravings, but these are signed. We do know that the Rycaut material from *The Present State of the Ottoman Empire* was engraved (or re-engraved) for Briot's French translation by Sébastien Leclerc (1637–1714), a distinguished artist who held the post of *Graveur du roi* under Louis XIV.

As Elder was not responsible for the engravings in *The Present State of the Ottoman Empire* there is another candidate, and that is Frederick van Hove (c. 1628–1698), a Dutch artist and engraver from either Haarlem or The Hague (scholars dispute his birthplace) who had trained in Antwerp and had relocated

---

[213] There are one hundred and twenty-four paintings in this collection at the British Museum, London. It is entitled *The Habits of the Grand Signor's Court*. Its accession number is 1928,0323,0.46.

to London. Like Elder, he too was known for his portraits, which included royalty, politicians, and celebrities of the day. Van Hove evidently became naturalised, and by the 1690's he had a daughter living in Blackfriars and married to an Englishman. David Alexander believes that van Hove had "moved to London in the 1660s" and that he "also carried out unsigned work,"[214] which suggests further that he could have been Rycaut's illustrator. Furthermore, the rare December 1666 folio edition of *The Present State of the Ottoman Empire* has a signed title page illustration by van Hove; although that does not necessarily prove that he did all the unsigned engravings, it strongly suggests that it might be the case. Van Hove issued a series of biblical engravings bearing his name in book form, *The History of the Old and New Testament in Cuts* (1671), which proved so popular that people often inserted them in their bibles. He also illustrated William Bradshaw's translation of Marana's *Letters Writ by a Turkish Spy*, which may be an indication that he had some interest in oriental material. The illustrations in Rycaut's book are all of people, not places or buildings, in keeping with the description on the title-page, which tells us that they will be "representing the variety of habits amongst the Turks." They depict important court officials, military personnel and religious figures, and they are all full-page size. They are probably not meant to portray anyone in particular; it is not known, for example, whether the illustration entitled "The Prime Vizier" is an attempt to represent one of the Köprülüs. Portraits of individual Sultans, including Mehmet IV, appear in Rycaut's continuation of Knolles's *Turkish History*.

## Editorial Practices

This is a modern spelling version of "the sixth edition corrected" of the work (1686), which contains all of Rycaut's revisions and corrections, and is the last edition to be issued during the author's lifetime. Some of Rycaut's sentences are exceptionally long, punctuated with many semi-colons denoting subordinate clauses, and these have been broken up, wherever possible, into full sentences, although in some cases the placement of the main verb did not permit this. Punctuation has been modified to conform to current practice. There has been absolutely no alteration of the actual words. Turkish names have been emended for modern readers; "Mahomet" becomes "Muhammad" when denoting the prophet, but "Mehmet" as a Turkish name, this spelling being the usual modern

---

[214] Michael Hunter, ed., *Printed Images in Early Modern Britain: Essays in Interpretation* (Farnham, UK: Ashgate, 2010), 299. Professor John Astington of the Department of English, University of Toronto, stated in a letter to the editor (17 June, 2012) that van Hove "was in London for the Restoration, and quite possibly earlier." I am indebted to Professor Astington for his help with the vexed question of Rycaut's engraver's identity; he first suggested that it could have been van Hove.

rendering. Ottoman Turkish words have either been changed to modern Turkish (if they are similar) or footnoted; all effort has been made to check these for accuracy with Turkish-speaking experts in the field. Footnotes have been used to identify persons, places, and terms which may be unfamiliar to readers. They also provide background information, correct errors which may be found in Rycaut's text, and suggest further reading. English words which have become obsolete or which have changed their meanings have also been glossed at the foot of the page where they occur. Translations from Latin are either the editor's own, or have, whenever possible, been taken from reputable modern versions, particularly with Busbecq and Tacitus, who are Rycaut's most-quoted authorities. Glosses of unfamiliar words have also been supplied. It is the hope of the editor that readers of Rycaut may be encouraged to look further into the literature of English-Ottoman relations, and that perhaps some of the prejudices about English views of Turkey and any misapplication of "orientalist" theory to earlier writers like Rycaut by scholars following Edward Said may be vitiated by their reading of this important work.

# TO THE RIGHT HONOURABLE HENRY, LORD ARLINGTON,

## His *Majesty's* Principal Secretary of State

*My Lord,*

After five years residence at Constantinople in service of the embassy of the Earl of Winchilsea[1] (my ever-honoured Lord), and this my second journey from thence by land into my own country, I judged it a point of my duty and of my religion, too, to dedicate this following treatise, as the fruits of my travels, negotiations and leisure in those remote parts, to the noble person of Your Lordship, as that *votiva tabula*[2] which many, both in ancient and in the modern times, after some signal deliverance or happy arrival at their desired port, used to offer to their gods, their saints or their patrons. And truly, my Lord, this discourse, treating chiefly of the Turkish polity,[3] government and maxims of state, seems naturally to appertain to the patronage of Your Lordship, whose faculties of wisdom and virtue have given you the blessing of your Prince's favour and the reputation, as well abroad as at home, of an eminent and dexterous minister of state.

It were a great presumption in me to offer any observations of my own in the courts of Christian princes to the test of Your Lordship's experience and judgment, who not only is acquainted with the customs and manners, but penetrates into the designs and knows the cabinet-councils of neighbouring principalities with whom our divided world may possibly be concerned. But perhaps, without disparagement to Your Lordship's profound wisdom or over-value of my own abilities, I may confidently draw a rude[4] scheme before Your Lordship of the Turkish government, policies, and customs, a subject which travellers have rather represented to their countrymen to supply them with discourse and admiration than as a matter worthy the consideration or concernment of our kings or governors.

---

[1] Sir Heneage Finch, third earl of Winchilsea (1628–1689). See Introduction.
[2] Votive tablet, a stone inscribed with words of thanksgiving to a deity.
[3] The state or government.
[4] Rough, sketchy.

It hath been the happy fortune of the Turks to be accounted barbarous and ignorant, for upon this persuasion Christian princes have laid themselves open and unguarded to their greatest danger, contending together for one palm of land, whilst this puissant enemy hath made himself master of whole provinces and largely shared in the rich and pleasant possessions of Europe. This contempt of the Turk on one side caused the Emperor to be so backward in opposing that torrent of the Ottoman force which in the first year of the late war broke in upon him, and the suspicion of designs from France on the other, altered the resolutions and councils of the Emperor for prosecution of the war, which then running favourably on the Christians' part, was no less than with the astonishment of the whole world and of the Turks themselves, on a sudden understood to be clapped up[5] with articles of a disadvantageous peace, admiring to see the Emperor give a stop to the current of his victories and relinquish the game with a lucky hand. But this will seem no riddle to those who penetrate affairs with the same judgment that Your Lordship doth, and consider the unfirm condition the House of Austria was in, by a daily expectation of the death or fall of so main a basis of it as the King of Spain,[6] and the division amongst the Princes of the Empire, the League of the Rhine,[7] the French practices to make the Duke of Enghien[8] king of Poland, and the extravagant demands of the French and Rhenish League for winter quarters and places of strength, not only in Hungary but also in Styria[9] and the adjacent places, and at the same time look on the factions in Hungary and a considerable army of the French in the bowels of Germany, who

---

[5] Put together carelessly or hastily.

[6] The impending death of Carlos II of Spain, who had succeeded Philip IV in 1665, was a continuous topic of speculation. That unfortunate monarch, by all accounts a decent person, was afflicted by a whole host of mental and physical diseases, but managed to hang on, contrary to all expectations, until 1700, when he expired in his thirty-ninth year and the thirty-fifth of his reign. He was succeeded by Philip V, the grandson of Louis XIV.

[7] The League of the Rhine was a confederation formed by Louis XIV and Cardinal Mazarin in 1658, which allied France with more than fifty German princes, ostensibly to counteract the power of the Holy Roman Empire, but, as Rycaut notes, to promote the interests of a French candidate for emperor. However, in 1664 the League, which was dominated by France, contributed troops to fight the Ottomans at St. Gotthard, and was disbanded in 1667–1668.

[8] Louis II de Bourbon, fourth prince de Condé (1621–1686), usually known as "the Great Condé," was one of France's greatest military commanders, particularly in the Thirty Years War, when he obtained victories over the Spaniards at Rocroi (1643) and over the Bavarians at Nördlingen (1645), after which he went on to win many other important battles. Condé was responsible for reducing the power and influence of Spain in Europe after 1648. He was interested for a number of years in becoming king of Poland, and obtained the support of Louis XIV in this ambition, but he never succeeded.

[9] The former Duchy of Styria is in the southeastern part of modern Austria.

were supposed in those parts to have rather come with design to overawe the next Diet[10] and force the German Princes to elect the French king for King of the Romans[11] than with sincere and simple intentions of opposing themselves to the enemy of the faith, for then it will appear that the best use the Emperor could make of his good success was moderation in victory and reconciliation with his powerful enemy. And hereupon, Earl Leslie[12] being dispatched for extraordinary ambassador from His Imperial Majesty to the Grand Signior, though the Turk was elevated with the thoughts of the necessity the Christians had of a peace, yet did so happily manage his charge and employment as created in the Turks an extraordinary reverence towards his person, and obtained such honours and treatments from them as the Turkish court never bestowed before on the Emperor's or any other Christian ambassador, exhorting this compliment from the Grand Vizier, that he was more satisfied that the Emperor had sent so brave and illustrious a person than if he had sought to reconcile his affections with a hundred thousand dollars more of present. And, to do justice to this worthy person, he hath brought a reputation to the British nation above any in our age, whose virtues and industry have acquired the highest trusts and preferments in foreign parts, and done the same honour to his King, under whom he was born a subject, as to the present Emperor and his ancestors, under whom he is and hath always been a faithful minister, having deserved so eminently for saving the whole German Empire from the treason of Wallenstein[13] by his own single act of bravery,

---

[10] The assembly of the princes of the Holy Roman Empire.

[11] Holy Roman Emperor.

[12] Count Walter Leslie (1606–1667), a Scottish soldier and diplomat, began working for the Hapsburgs in 1630, when he participated in the Mantuan War. He also served in the Thirty Years War and was captured by the Swedes, who evinced great admiration for his bravery and soon released him. In 1634 he took part in the assassination of Wallenstein (see below), and soon afterwards was appointed Imperial Chamberlain by Ferdinand II. Leslie pursued a military career, but was dismissed for absenteeism, which did not, however, stop him either from acquiring large tracts of land and several castles (including one of Wallenstein's in Prague) or from gaining influential diplomatic friends and being made a *Reichsgraf* (Count) in 1637. He knew, amongst others, Sir Thomas Roe and Rycaut's employer, the Earl of Winchilsea. The Turkish mission Rycaut refers to took place in 1665, when Rycaut went to meet Leslie in Vienna.

[13] Albrecht von Wallenstein (1583–1634), a Bohemian soldier and politician, was one of the greatest military commanders of the Thirty Years War. As supreme commander of the Imperial forces, he gained numerous victories for the Catholic cause in 1625–1629, and became Duke of Friedland. In 1634 he was suspected of secretly negotiating with the Protestant powers and was charged with treason by Emperor Ferdinand II, whose cause he may have been preparing to desert. This led to his assassination, which may or may not have been ordered by the Emperor. Rycaut evidently believed that Wallenstein was a traitor and praises Leslie for his involvement in the murder.

a story notoriously known to all the world, as can never be forgot by that nation, nor want its due record and place in the history of that country.

The speculation of what is contained in this following discourse may seem unworthy of Your Lordship's precious hours, in regard of that notion of barbarity with which this Empire is styled, yet the knowledge hereof will be like a turquoise or some other jewels set within the rose of those many gems of Your Lordship's wisdom and virtues.

This present, which I thus humbly consecrate to Your Lordship, may be termed barbarous, as all things are which are differenced from us by diversity of manners and custom, and are not dressed in the mode and fashion of our times and countries, for we contract prejudice from ignorance and want of familiarity. But Your Lordship, who exactly ponderates[14] the weight of human actions, acknowledges reason in all its habits and draws not the measures of economy or policy from external appearances or effects, but from fundamental and original constitutions, so that Your Lordship will conclude that a people as the Turks are, men of the same composition with us, cannot be so savage and rude as they are generally described, for ignorance and grossness is the effect of poverty, not incident to happy men, whose spirits are so elevated with spoils and trophies of so many nations.

Knowing, my Lord, that this work which I have undertaken is liable to common censure, I have chosen to shroud my name under the patronage of Your Lordship to protect me from the ill-understanding and misconceptions of our countrymen both at home and abroad, which I doubt not but to be sufficiently armed in all parts where I travel, when the countenance Your Lordship affords me is joined to the authority of His Excellency the Earl of Winchilsea, His Majesty's Ambassador Extraordinary,[15] now actually resident at Constantinople, my ever-honoured lord, to whom I read, a long time before being published to the world, the greatest part of this following treatise. And as I received his favourable approbation and assent to the verity of most matters herein contained, so I must ingenuously confess to have been beholden to that quick and refined genius of his, who often rectified my mistakes, supplied me with matter, and remembered me of many material points which I might otherwise have most unadvisedly omitted. And His Excellency, knowing that in his absence this book might want a favourable patron, left me to myself to seek out one who might concur with him in the same innocent defence. And as, My Lord, you are a public person and under our gracious sovereign are one of those generous spirits which have espoused the common interest of the nation, so I presume on this present occasion not to want[16] your protection also in a single capacity, for which excess

---

[14] Considers.
[15] The personal representative of the king, he is also known as the plenipotentiary.
[16] Lack.

of favours I shall ever pray for the exaltation of the greater glory of Your Lordship and ever acknowledge myself,

*My Lord, Your Lordship's most humble, most faithful and devoted servant,*
**PAUL RYCAUT**

## TO THE
# READER

*Courteous Reader,*

I present thee here with a true system or model of the Turkish government and religion, not in the same manner as certain ingenious travellers have done, who have set down their observations as they have obviously occurred in their journeys, which being collected for the most part from relations and discourses of such who casually intervene in company of passengers, are consequently subject to many errors and mistakes. But, having been an inhabitant myself at the imperial city for the space of five years, and assisted by the advantage of considerable journeys I have made through divers parts of Turkey, and qualified by the office I hold of Secretary to the Earl of Winchilsea, Lord Ambassador, I had opportunity, by the constant access and practice with the chief ministers of state and variety of negotiations which passed through my hands in the Turkish court, to penetrate farther into the mysteries of this polity, which appear so strange and barbarous to us, than hasty travellers could do, who are forced to content themselves with a superficial knowledge.

The computations I have made of the value of their offices, [and] of the strength and number of their soldiery, according as every city and country is rated, are deduced from their own registers and records. The observations I have made of their polity are either maxims received from the mouth and argument of considerable ministers or conclusions arising from my own experience and considerations. The articles of their faith and constitutions of religion I have set down from the mouth of some of the most learned doctors and preachers of their law, with whom, for money or presents, I gained a familiarity and appearance of friendship. The relation of the Seraglio and education of their youth, with divers other matters of custom and rule, were transmitted to me by several sober persons trained up in the best education of the Turkish learning, and particularly by an understanding Polonian who had spent nineteen years in the Ottoman court.[17]

If, Reader, the superstition, vanity and ill-foundation of the Muhammadan[18] religion seem fabulous as a dream or the fancies of a distracted and wild brain, thank God that thou wert born a Christian and within the pale of an holy and orthodox church. If the tyranny, oppression and cruelty of that state, wherein reason stands in no competition with the pride and lust of an unreasonable minister, seem strange to thy liberty and happiness, thank God that thou art born

---

[17] Woyciech Bobowski, see Introduction.

[18] Rycaut uses the standard seventeenth-century "Mahometan" throughout. This has been emended to conform to modern orthographical practices.

in a country the most free and just in the whole world, and a subject to the most indulgent, the most gracious of all the Princes of the universe; that thy wife, thy children and the fruits of thy labour can be called thine own, and protected by the valiant arm of thy fortunate king, and thus learn to prize thy own freedom, by comparison with foreign servitude, that thou mayst ever bless God and thy king, and make thy happiness breed thy content without degenerating into wantonness or desire of revolution. Farewell.

# THE MAXIMS OF THE TURKISH POLITY

## Book I.

**Chapter I.** *The constitution of the Turkish government, being different from most others in the world, hath need of peculiar maxims and rules whereon to establish and confirm itself.*

I have begun a work which seems very full of difficulty and labour, for to trace the footsteps of government in the best-formed and moulded commonwealths (such as are supported with reason and with religion) is no less than to unriddle and resolve a mystery. For as a commonwealth by many authors hath not been unaptly compared to a ship in diverse respects and proper allegories, so principally the small impression or sign of track the floating habitation leaves behind it on the sea in all the traverses it makes according to the different winds to attain its port, is a lively emblem of the various motions of good government, by which reason of circumstances, times and multiplicity of chances and events, leaves little or no path in all the ocean of human affairs.

But there must be yet certain rules in every government which are the foundations and pillars of it, not subject to the alteration of time or any other accident, and so essential to it that they admit of no change until the whole model of polity suffer a convulsion, which is either effected by the new laws of a conqueror or by intestine and civil revolutions. Of such maxims as these, obvious to all who have had any practice in the Ottoman court, I have made a collection, subjoining to every head some reflections and considerations of my own, which at my leisure hours I have weighed and examined, bringing them, according to the proportion of my weak judgment and ability, to the measure and test of reason and virtue, as also to a similitude and congruity with the maxims of other empires to which God hath given the largest extent of domination.

But indeed, when I have considered seriously the contexture of the Turkish government, the absoluteness of an Emperor without reason,[19] without virtue, whose speeches may be irrational and yet must be laws; whose actions irregular and yet examples; whose sentence and judgment, if in matters of imperial concernment, are most commonly corrupt, and yet decrees irresistible;[20] when I

---

[19] Rycaut refers here to Sultan Ibrahim, whose reign (1640–1648) was held up as an example of government by a capiricious and unpredictable madman.

[20] Lord Kinross cites a story about Sultan Ibrahim which Rycaut must have known, and which may well have prompted this opinion. It concerns the Grand Vizier Sultan-zade Mehmed Pasha, who held office 1644–1645, "a flatterer so obsequious as to prompt

consider what little rewards there are for virtue and no punishment for profitable and thriving vice; how men are raised at once by adulation, chance and the sole favour of the prince, without any title or noble blood or the motives of previous deserts or former testimonies and experience of parts and abilities, to the weightiest, the richest and most honourable charges of the empire; when I consider how short their continuance is in them, how with one frown of the prince they are cut off; with what greediness above all people in the world they thirst and haste to be rich, and yet know their treasure is but their snare; what they labour for is but as slaves for their great patron and master, and what will inevitably effect their ruin and destruction though they have all the arguments of faithfulness, virtue, and moral honesty (which are rare in a Turk) to be their advocates and plead for them. When I consider many other things of like nature, which may more at large hereafter be discoursed of, one might admire the long continuance of this great and vast empire and attribute the stability thereof without change in itself and the increase of dominions and constant progress of its arms rather to some supernatural cause than to the ordinary maxims of state or wisdom of the governors, as if the Divine Will of the All-knowing Creator had chosen for the good of his church and chastisement of the sins and vices of Christians to raise and support this mighty people. "*Mihi quanto plura recentium seu veterum revolve, tanto magis ludibria rerum mortalium cunctis in negotiis observantur.*"²¹

But that which cements all breaches and cures all those wounds in this body politic is the quickness and severity of their justice, which not considering much the strict division of distributive and commutative,²² makes almost every crime equal and punishes it with the last and extremest chastisement, which is death — I mean those which have relation to the government and are of common and public interest. Without this remedy, which I lay down as a principal prevention of the greatest disorders, this mighty body would have burst with the poison of

----

his master's question: "How is it that you always approve my actions, good or evil?" To this he received and accepted the reassuring reply: "Thou art Caliph. Thou art God's shadow upon earth. Every idea which your spirit entertains is a revelation from heaven. Your orders, even when they appear unreasonable, have an innate reasonableness which your slave always reveres although he may not always understand it" (Lord Kinross, *The Ottoman Centuries: The Rise and Fall of the Turkish Empire* [New York: Harper Perennial, 2002], 314).

²¹ "For my part, the more I think about the events of late or of the past, the more I am persuaded that human affairs are the sport of superior powers" (Tacitus, *Annals*. Translated by Michael Grant [Harmondsworth, UK: Penguin Books, 2003], 3.10).

²² Rycaut is probably referring to the distinction made between the two forms of justice by Aquinas, who adapted it from Aristotle. Distributive justice "distributes common goods proportionately," whilst commutative justice "is the order of one part to another, which corresponds to the order of one private individual to another" (Thomas Aquinas, *Summa theologiae, Questions on God*, ed. Brian Davies and Brian Leftow [Cambridge: Cambridge University Press, 2006], 58.7–8).

its own ill humours and soon divide[d] itself into several signories, as the ambition and power of the governors most remote from the imperial seat administered them hopes and security of becoming absolute.

In this government, severity, violence, and cruelty are natural to it, and it were as great an error to begin to loose the reins and ease the people of that oppression to which they are their forefathers have since their first original been accustomed as it would be in a nation free-born and used to live under the protection of good laws and the clemency of a virtuous Christian Prince to exercise a tyrannical power over their estates and lives and change their liberty into servitude and slavery.

The Turks had the original of their civil government founded in the time of war, for when they first came out of Scythia[23] and submitted unto one general it is to be supposed that they had no laws but what were arbitrary and martial, and most agreeable to the enterprise they had then in hand. When Toghrul Beg[24] overthrew the Persian Sultan, possessed himself of his dominions and power, and called and opened the way for his companions out of Armenia; when Kutlumish[25] revolted from him and made a distinct kingdom in Arabia; when other Princes of the Seleucian family[26] in the infancy of the Turkish power had by wars among themselves or by testament made division of their possessions; when (1300) Osman, by strange fortunes and from small beginnings swallowed up all

---

[23] Modern scholarship seems to be of the opinion that the Turkic peoples in general originated in an area stretching from Central Asia to Siberia. Ancient Chinese chronicles from the seventh century mention them as living in China. For details, see, for example, Peter B. Golden, "Some Thoughts on the Origins of the Turks and the Shaping of the Turkic Peoples," in *Contact and Exchange in the Ancient World,* ed. V. H. Mair (Honolulu: University of Hawaii Press, 2006).

[24] Toghrul Beg was Sultan of the Seljuk Turks 1037–1093. He captured Baghdad and overran most of Persia after defeating the Ghaznavid Sultan Abdul Rashid near Marv (1053). The rendering of his name as "Tagrolipix" may have originated with Thomas Newton's *Notable History of the Saracens* (1575), a work partly translated from the work of Celio Curione (1538–1567) but containing material from "sundry other good authors." The odd spelling seems to have been common, however, in other histories of the time. Also see George Sandys, *Sandys' Travels: Containing an History of the Original and Present State of the Turkish Empire* (London [1615], 1673), 34.

[25] Kutlumish (d.? 1079) was a nephew of Toghrul Beg and a successful general until he was defeated in Arabia. Fearing the wrath of his uncle, he fled to the Persian part of Armenia and raised a rebellion, carving out for himself an independent kingdom in the area. Some accounts have him being defeated and killed by Toghrul Beg, others insist that he ruled his territory for fourteen years until his death. Also see Sandys, *Travels* 34,

[26] Rycaut means the Great Seljuk Empire, which lasted from the eleventh to the fourteenth century. It was named for Seljuk (d. c. 1038), whose tribe had split from the Oghuz Turks and formed their own country.

the other governments into the Oghuzian tribe and united them under one head until it arrived to that greatness and power it now enjoys.[27]

The whole condition of this people was but a continued state of war, wherefore it is not strange if their laws are severe and in most things arbitrary, that the Emperor should be absolute and above law and that most of their customs should run in a certain channel and course most answerable to the height and unlimited power of the governor, and consequently to the oppression and subjection of the people. And that they should thrive most by servitude, be most happy, prosperous, and contented under tyranny, is as natural to them as to a body to be nourished with that diet which it had from its infancy or birth been acquainted with. But not only is tyranny requisite for this people and a stiff rein to curb them, lest by an unknown liberty they grow mutinous and unruly, but likewise the large territories and remote parts of the Empire require speedy preventions without processes of law or formal indictment, jealousy and suspicion of misgovernment being license and authority enough for the Emperor to inflict his severest punishments, all which depends upon the absoluteness of the Prince, which because it is that whereby the Turks are principally supported in their greatness and is the prime maxim and foundation of their state, we shall make it the discourse and subject of the following chapter.

---

[27] Osman I or 'Uthman (1280–1324) initially ruled over the Kayi people of the Ogusian tribe. In 1299 he announced his independence from the Seljuk Turks and united the various peoples in the area to found what eventually became the Ottoman Empire. He defeated the Byzantines several times and is considered the founder of the Ottoman Empire.

**4**      *The Maxims of the* Turkiſh *Politie.*

C H A P. **II.**
*The abſoluteneſs of the* Emperour *is a great ſupport of the* Turkiſh
Empire.

Sultan Mahomet Han the present Emperour of the Turks
aged 23 years Anno 1666

### Chapter II. *The Absoluteness of the Emperor is a great support of the Turkish Empire.*

The Turks, having, as is before declared, laid the first foundation of their government with the principles most agreeable to military discipline, their generals or Princes, whose will and lusts they served, became absolute masters of their lives and estates, so that what they gained and acquired by the sword with labours, perils, and sufferings was appropriated to the use and benefit of their great master. All the delightful fields of Asia, the pleasant plains of Tempe and Thrace, all the plenty of Egypt and fruitfulness of the Nile, the luxury of Corinth, the substance of Peloponessus, Athens, Lemnos, Skios, and Mitylene with other isles of the Aegean Sea, the spices of Arabia and the riches of a great part of Persia, all Armenia, the provinces of Pontus, Galatia, Bithynia, Phrygia, Lycia, Pamphylia, Palestine, Coelo-Syria, and Phoenicia, Colchis and a great part of

Georgia, the tributary principalities of Moldavia and Wallachia, Romania, Bulgaria and Serbia, and the best part of Hungary concur all together to satisfy the appetite of one single person.[28] All the extent of this vast territory, the lands and houses as well as the castles and arms, are the proper goods of the Grand Signior.[29] In his sole disposal and gift they remain, whose possession and right they are; only to lands dedicated to religious uses the Grand Signior disclaims all right or claim, and this he so piously observes (to the shame of our sectaries[30] in England who violate the *penetralia* of the sanctuary), that when a pasha,[31] though afterwards convicted of treason, bestows any lands or rents on any certain mosque or temple, that grant or gift is good, and exempted from any disposal or power to the Grand Signior. The lands being thus originally in the Grand Signior, after the conquests were made and the country secured and in condition to be distributed, divisions were made of the houses, manors, and farms among the soldiery, whom they call *timariots*,[32] as the reward and recompense of their valour and labour, in consideration of which everyone proportionably to

---

[28] The Vale of Tempe is in northern Thessaly. Lemnos and Skios are two of the larger Greek islands; Mitylene is the capital city of the island of Lesbos; Pontus was a kingdom on the south coast of the Black Sea, now in Turkey; Galatia, now the province of Angora, is in the central Anatolian highlands of Turkey; Bithynia is in central northern Turkey, adjoining Pontus; Phrygia was a kingdom in west central Anatolia; Lycia is on the south coast of Turkey; Pamphylia was situated between the Mediterranean Sea and Mt. Taurus in south Asia Minor; Coelo-Syria covered that part of modern Syria and Lebanon where Mt. Libanus (or the Western Mountain Range) is situated, and Colchis is in the western part of modern Georgia. The other locations are likely familiar enough to the reader.

[29] This Italianate title, which is also sometimes rendered in its French form (*Grand Seigneur*) means, of course, "great lord," and was used throughout the sixteenth and seventeenth centuries to denote the Ottoman Sultan. The Sultan's actual title was *padishah*, derived from two Persian words, *pad* (protector) and *shah* (king), and the title *khan* (sometimes spelled *han*, as in Rycaut) was added in the fifteenth century. Rycaut quite often refers to the Ottoman Sultan as the Emperor, thus avoiding the issue altogether.

[30] A sectary (now usually rendered "sectarian") is a dissenter from the Church of England. Rycaut criticizes sectarians for their attitude towards the inner sanctuaries (*penetralia*) of churches. He is likely referring to the damage done to statues, altars, pulpits, and other objects by various radical or puritan elements during the Civil War.

[31] A pasha ranked above a bey or aga in the Ottoman peerage system. The title was usually bestowed on high officials, governors and army officers, and later on was even given to foreigners in the Ottoman service (General Gordon was one, for example). The English rendition *bashaw*, used by Rycaut, seems to have entered the language about 1650. The Turkish word is *paşa*.

[32] The land granted by a Sultan to soldiers was known as a *timar*. It came with tax revenues which could be collected as compensation for military service. Those who held one were known as *timariots*. Rycaut actually calls the soldiers themselves *timars*, which is, strictly speaking, incorrect.

his revenue and possession is obliged to maintain horse and men to be always
ready when the Grand Signior shall call him forth to serve him in the wars. By
which means the whole country, being in the hands of the soldiery, all places are
the better strengthened and the conquered people more easily kept from mutiny
and rebellion, not much unlike our tenure of knights' service in England and
lands held of the Crown, but with this difference, that we enjoy them by the
title of a fixed and settled law never to be forfeited but upon treason and rebellion. They enjoy them also by inheritance derived from the father to the son, but
yet as usufructuary[33] during the pleasure of the Emperor, in whom the propriety is always reserved and who doth often, as his humour and fancy leads him to
please and gratify a stranger, dispossess an ancient possessor whose family hath
for many generations enjoyed that inheritance. Sometimes I have heard, with the
sighs of some and the curse of others, how the Grand Signior, heated in his hunting[34] and pleased with the refreshment of a little cool and crystal water presented
him by a poor peasant, hath in recompense thereof freed the tenant from the rent
of his landlord and by his sole word confirmed to him the cottage he lived in, the
woods, gardens, and fields he manured, with as sound a title as our long deeds
and conveyances[35] secure our purchases and inheritances in England. And this
the former master does not dare name injustice, because this tenant is now made
proprietor by the will of the Grand Signior, which was the same title and claim
with his, prescription,[36] tenant right and custom[37] availing nothing in this case.
For, if the inheritance hath been anciently derived from father to the son, the
more is the goodness and bounty of the Emperor to be acknowledged, that hath
permitted so long a succession of his favours to run in one family, in whose power
it was to transfer it to others.

The absolute and unlimited power of this Prince is more evident by the titles they give, as "God on Earth," "the Shadow of God," "Brother to the Sun
and Moon," "the Giver of all Earthly Crowns," etc.[38] And though they do not

---

[33] A usufructuary is someone who has a legal right to use something which does not
actually belong to him, such as (in this case) land.

[34] Mehmed IV, the ruler with whom Rycaut was most familiar, was a Sultan known
to be particularly fond of hunting, which often prevented him from taking care of state
affairs. He was nicknamed *Avci*, "the hunter." For further discussion, see introduction.

[35] A deed of conveyance allows property to be transferred from one person to another and indicates the legal right to possess that property.

[36] Prescription, in the legal sense, means the right to acquire land which one does
not actually own through long-term continuous usage of that land.

[37] This refers to the right of compensation which tenants have against landowners
for improvements made when the tenancy is terminated.

[38] Rycaut has omitted a few, such as Commander of the Faithful, Custodian of the
Holy Sanctuaries of Mecca and Medina, Sultan of Sultans, Khan of Khans, Righteous
Lord of Arabs, Helper of the State and People, and Sovereign of the House of Osman,
not to mention the vast list of territories over which the Sultan was lord.

build and erect altars to him, as was done to the Roman emperors when that people degenerated into a fashion of deformed adulation wherein Italy is at present corrupted,[39] yet the conception they have of his power, the ray they consider him to be of divine illumination, is a kind of imagery and idolatrous fancy they frame of his divinity. It is an ordinary saying among the Turkish *kadis*[40] and lawyers that the Grand Signior is above the law, that is, whatsoever law is written is controllable and may be contradicted by him. His mouth is the law itself, and the power of an infallible interpretation is in him, and though the *Mufti*[41] is many times for custom, formality, and satisfaction of the people consulted with, yet when his sentences have not been agreeable to the designs intended, I have known him in an instant thrown from his office to make room for another oracle better-prepared for the purpose of his Master.[42] Some maintain that the very oaths and promises of the Grand Signior are always revocable when the performance of his vow is a restriction to the absolute power of the Empire. And I remember, when my Lord Ambassador hath sometimes complained of the breach of our capitulations[43] and pleaded that the Grand Signior had no power by single commands to infringe articles of peace to which he had obliged himself by solemn oaths and vows, the interpreters have gently touched that point and been as nice[44] to question how far the power of the Grand Signior extended, as we ought to be in the subtle points of divine omnipotence, but rather in contemplation of the Grand Signior's justice, wisdom, faith, and clemency, insinuated arguments of honour, convenience, and justice in maintaining the league inviolate with the King of England.

It was Justinian's rule concerning the prerogative of Princes, "*Etsi legibus soluti sumus, attamen legibus vivimus,*"[45] that is, although the majesty of Princes and the necessity of having a Supreme Head in all governments did free and privilege them from the censure and correction of the law, that no earthly power could call them to account for their errors or disorders in this world, yet it is necessary

[39] Presumably Rycaut is referring to the Catholic Church and the pope's "infallibility."

[40] A *kadi* or *cadi* is an Islamic magistrate.

[41] The *Mufti*, usually a distinguished scholar, is the interpreter and expounder of Islamic law for Sunni Muslims.

[42] For example, in 1683 Mehmed IV "removed from office the Grand Mufti who had given Kara Mustafa Pasha the *fetva* or authorization to attack the Christian emperor 'contrary to the disposition of their laws, inasmuch as he [had] asked for peace'" (Giambattista Vico, *Statecraft: The Deeds of Antonio Carafa*, ed. and trans. Giorgio A. Pinton [New York: Peter Lang, 2005], 466).

[43] Summary of points, here of an agreement between the English and Turkish governments. Nowadays, we might use the word "recapitulations."

[44] The meaning of "nice" here is "precise," as in "a nice distinction."

[45] "Although we are free from the law, yet we live within the law" (Justinian, *Digest of Roman Law* 10). Editor's translation.

to the being of an absolute monarch to be a severe executioner of the laws of his country, and it is more his interest and security than to act without rule and always to make use of the power of absolute dominion, which is to be applied like physic when the ordinary force of nature cannot remove the malignancy of some peccant[46] humours.

The Grand Signior himself is also restrained by laws, but without impeachment[47] to his absolute jurisdiction. For when there is a new Emperor, it is the custom to conduct him with great pomp and triumph to a place in the suburbs of Constantinople called Job,[48] where is an ancient monument of some certain prophet or holy man, whom the Turks, for want of knowledge in antiquity and history, style that Job who was recorded for the mirror of constancy and patience, for they confound all history and chronology, saying that Job was Solomon's judge of the court and Alexander the Great captain of his army. At this place, solemn prayers are made that God would prosper and infuse wisdom into him who is to manage so great a charge. Then the Mufti, embracing him, bestows his benediction, and the Grand Signior swears and promises solemnly to maintain the Muslim faith and laws of the Prophet Muhammad, and then the viziers of the bench and other pashas, with profound reverence and humility kissing the ground first and then the hem of his vest, acknowledge him their lawful and undoubted Emperor. And after this form of inauguration, he returns with the like solemnity and magnificence to the Seraglio,[49] which is always the seat of the Ottoman emperors. And thus the Grand Signior retains and obliges himself to govern within the compass of laws, but they give him so large a latitude that he can no more be said to be bound or limited than a man who hath the world to rove in can be termed a prisoner because he cannot exceed the enclosure of the universe. For though he be obliged to the execution of Muhammadan law, yet

---

[46] Sinning.

[47] Here, used in the sense of "challenging the validity" of the Sultan's absoluteness.

[48] Now known as Eyüp, this location is, as Rycaut states, associated with "some certain Prophet or holy man." He was Abu Ayub (c. 576–674), a famous military commander and one of the chosen companions of Mohammed. He died at a very advanced age of an illness whilst participating in the siege of Constantinople under caliph Yazid I, and was buried outside the walls. There is little evidence, however, that the Turks actually mixed him up with the Biblical Job or associated him with Solomon; Rycaut may be referring to the fact that in the Quran both Solomon and Alexander were hailed as prototypes of Muhammad. The spot is still holy ground for Muslims.

[49] This is the Italian rendition of the Persian word *saray*, which denotes a palace or, as European writers usually saw it, an enclosed court for the ruler's *harem*. Here, it is used in its general sense as a palace, not only for the place where the imperial concubines lived. "In Ottoman usage," Bernard Lewis states, "it denotes the whole complex structure of the imperial palace, court, and household," and further that "Turkish usage. . .applies the term *Saray* to the whole and not just part of the palace" (*Istanbul and the Civilization of the Ottoman Empire* [Norman: University of Oklahoma Press, 1963], 66).

that law calls the Emperor the mouth and interpreter of it, and endues[50] him with power to alter and annul the most settled and fixed rules, at least to waive and dispense with them when they are an obstacle to his government and contradict, as we said before, any great design of the Empire.

But the learned doctors among the Turks more clearly restrain the imperial power only to the observation of that which is religious in the Muhammadan law, saying that in matters which are civil his law is arbitrary and needs no other judge or legislator than his own will. Hence it is that they say the Grand Signior can never be deposed or made accountable to any of his subjects under the number of 100 a day, and in like manner hence it is that though the Muhammadan law determines the testimony of two witnesses of that faith to be valid for the determination of all cases of difference, yet by our capitulation it is provided that no Turkish witnesses of what number of quality soever can avail any of the English nation, by reason that the case, being civil, is dispensable by the imperial power. But I doubt, were any matter in question criminal, as we have never, God be praised, had occasion to put to trial, the capitulations would be forced to yield to the Muhammadan law as being both religious and divine, with which the Sultan hath no power to dispense. Of what consequence and benefit this absolute power hath been to the Turks is evident by the extent of their Empire and success of their arms, for if the Sultan pleases the soldiery, no matter how the people in this constitution is contented, and this was the conclusion of Machiavel[li] upon this government in the 19th chapter of his book *del Principe*.[51] And it must needs be a great advantage to a commander, when the *utile* and *iustum*[52] are reconciled and made the same, that he meets no contradiction or opposition at home which may retard or cross the great designs abroad. The Emperor of Germany had doubtless sooner encountered the Turk and given a stop to his free entrance the first year of the late war into Hungary had he been absolute of the whole Empire and not necessitated to expect the consent of his several Princes and the result of a Diet when the Turks were even ready to enter Germany. For when many heads or hands are required, all business moves slowly and more time is spent in

---

[50] Archaic form of "endows."

[51] The relevant passage reads: "I have excepted the Turk, who always keeps around him twelve infantry and fifteen thousand cavalry, on which depend the security and strength of his kingdom, and it is necessary that, putting aside every consideration for the people, he should keep them his friends" (Machiavelli, *The Prince*, trans. W. K. Marriott, http://www.worldcat.org/title/prince-translated-by-wk-marriott). French and Latin translations of Machiavelli were available to Rycaut, and by 1640 there were several manuscript translations, notably one by William Fowler, but there is no evidence that Rycaut knew them. See Alessandra Petrina, *Machiavelli in the British Isles: Two Early Modern Translations of* The Prince (London: Ashgate Press, 2009).

[52] Rycaut is paraphrasing a Latin tag *"Quod iustum, non quod utile,"* which may be translated as "[Do] what is fair, not what is expedient."

agreement of the manner of action, in arguments and debates, which are most commonly carried on by faction, than in the most difficult point of execution. It would seem a great clog to the Grand Signior to be obliged to depend on the bounty of his subjects when he would make a war or on the judgment of a lawyer that should contradict and censure the actions of his Prince as irregular and exceeding the privileges of his prerogative.

It is very difficult to understand how it is possible with these fetters for any country or city ever to arrive at that height as to be termed the mistress of a great empire, or a Prince be said to have a long arm or embrace the compass of the globe who is pinioned with the bands of his own laws. But I confess, it is a blessing and wonderful happiness of a people to be subjects of a gracious Prince, who hath prescribed his power within the compass of wholesome laws, acknowledged a right of possession and propriety of estate as well in his subjects as himself, who doth not punish the innocent with the guilty nor oppress without distinction, nor act the part of that king whom God gives in his wrath.[53] But then they must content themselves with their own borders or some neighbouring conquest, and this is better and a greater glory and content than the honour of being slaves to the lust of a monarch whose titles comprehend the greatest part of the world.

### Chapter III. *The Lesson of Obedience to the Emperor is taught by the Turks as a Principle of Religion rather than of State.*

The absolute power in the Prince implies an exact obedience in the subjects, and to instil and confirm that principle no art or industry is wanting in the education of those who are placed in the Seraglio, with design of preferment to offices and great charges, so that even the oath of obedience which friars and other religious men vow to their superiors at their first initiation into ecclesiastical orders is not more exactly or devoutly observed or professed by them than this doctrine of submission to the will of their great master is carefully taught to his young scholars who stand probationers[54] and candidates for all the government of the Empire. To die by the hand or command of the Grand Signior, when the blow is submitted to with entire resignation, is taught to be the highest point of martyrdom, and whose good fortune it is to suffer is immediately transported to Paradise. Kara Mustafa Pasha,[55] a Great Vizier, after he had been so successful

---

[53] An oppressive monarch was seen as a punishment sent by God for the people's sins, and, of course, had to be endured because he was there by divine right.

[54] Someone who is new on the job and is being tested.

[55] Kara Mustafa Pasha (c. 1634–1683) was a distinguished military commander and Grand Vizier to Mehmed IV (1676–1683). He successfully fought the Poles (1672) and was employed to suppress a Cossack rebellion (1678–1681), but had difficulties doing so and was obliged to make peace. In 1683 he was in command of the Turkish army which reached Vienna and laid siege to the city, where he was decisively defeated by the Polish

in all matters of his charge and proved so excellent an instrument of victories and services to his master that he was applauded by all to be a most happy and fortunate minister, was so sensible of his own condition and the favour of his Prince that he confessed he was now arrived to the greatest glory and perfection he could in this life aspire to, and only wanted the holy martyrdom, to die by the order and sentence of the Grand Signior as the reward of his faithfulness and the consummation of all his honours.

Such as receive any wages or pay coming from the Exchequer or any office depending on the Crown have the title of *Kul*, which is the Grand Signior's slave.[56] Such is the Great Vizier and all the pashas of the Empire, and it is more honourable than the condition and name of subject, for they have a privilege over these and can revile, beat, and abuse them with authority, but the subject cannot offer the least injury to the slave without danger of severe punishment. Slavery amongst the Turks denotes a condition of entire resignation to the will and command of the Emperor, to perform whatever he signifies or, if possible, what he conceives, though he command whole armies of them to precipitate themselves from a rock or build a bridge with piles of their bodies for him to pass rivers, or to kill one another to afford him pastime or pleasure. They that have been where they have seen and known the manner of this blind obedience may well cry out *"O homines ad servitutem paratos!"*[57] And doubtless, the flattery used in the Seraglio towards the Prince by those that are near his person is proportionable to this condition of slavery they profess, and cannot but fancy a strange kind of projected baseness in all the deportment within the walls of the Seraglio, when there appears so much condescension abroad to all the lusts and evil inclinations of their master, so that a generous Prince (as some have been found among the Ottoman emperors), though he desired not the public liberty, would yet be weary of this slavish compliance and seek other counsel and means to inform himself of the true state of his own and other kings' dominions than such as proceed from men inexperienced in any other court of country than that they live in." *Qui libertatem publicam nollet, tam proiecta servientium patientiae taedebat.*[58]

This flattery and immoderate subjection hath doubtless been the cause of the decay of the Turkish discipline in the time of Sultan Ibrahim, when women governed, and now in this present age of Sultan Mehmed [IV], whose counsels

---

king Jan Sobieski. He retreated in disgrace to Hungary, and soon afterwards was executed in Belgrade by strangulation; his head was presented in a velvet bag to Mehmed IV.

[56] The word *kul* can indeed mean "slave boy" or "male slave," but it also denotes "a servant or vassal," which perhaps makes a little more sense in the context.

[57] "O men fit only for slavery!" (Tacitus, *Annals* 3.65). Tacitus records this as a comment made by the Emperor Tiberius about senators who never thought for themselves or took initiative.

[58] "Even he [Tiberius], who denied any public freedom, got tired of such abject servility" (Tacitus, *Annals* 3.65).

are given chiefly by his mother,[59] negroes, eunuchs, and some handsome young *mosayp*[60] or favourite. Seldom any from without being permitted or have their spirits emboldened to declare a truth or are called to give their counsel in matters of greatest importance, so that this obedience, which brave and wise Emperors have made use of in the advancement of noble exploits and enlargement of their Empire, is with effeminate Princes, delighted with flattery, the snare of their own greatness and occasion of weak counsels and means in the management of great designs.

If a man seriously consider the whole composition of the Turkish court, he will find it to be a prison and barnyard of slaves, differing from that where the galley-slaves are immured only by the ornaments and glittering outside and appearances. Here their chains are made of iron, there of gold, and the difference is only in a painted shining servitude from that which is a squalid, sordid, and noisome slavery. For the youths educated in the Seraglio, which we shall have occasion to discourse of in the next chapter, are kept as it were within a prison, under a strange severity of discipline, some for twenty, thirty, others forty years, others the whole time of the age of man, and grow grey under the correction of their *hodjas*[61] or tutors. The two brothers of this present Grand Signior are also imprisoned here, restrained with a faithful and careful guard, and perhaps are sometimes permitted out of grace and favour into the presence of their brother to kiss his vest and to perform the offices of duty and humility before their Prince.[62] The ladies also of the Seraglio have the liberty of enjoying the air which passes through grates and lattices, unless sometime they obtain license to sport and recreate themselves in the garden, separated from the sight of men by walls higher than those of any nunnery.

Nay, if a man considers the contexture of the whole Turkish government, he will find it such a fabric of slavery that it is a wonder that any amongst them

---

[59] For the reign of the "crazy" Sultan Ibrahim (1640–1648) and the regency of Mehmed IV's mother, the Valide Sultana Turhan Hatice (c. 1628–1683), see Introduction and Caroline Finkel, *Osman's Dream*, 223–28. Ibrahim was the subject of a near-contemporary play by the German dramatist Daniel Casper von Lohenstein (1635–1683) entitled *Sultan Ibrahim* (1671); Lohenstein treated the reign as a tragedy with a happy ending. In England, Mary Pix wrote a play entitled *Ibrahim, the Thirteenth Emperor of the Turks* (1696), for which see introduction.

[60] For further details, see Rycaut's "Story of Asan Aga, the *Mosayp* or Favourite," in his continuation of Knolles's *Turkish History* (II, 141 ff.).

[61] An honorific title of respect for an *imam*. It can also be spelt *khoja* or *khwaja*.

[62] Rycaut is referring to the *kafes* (cage) in the Topkapi Palace compound, in which Sultans kept relatives, especially brothers, under a kind of luxurious house-arrest in order to avoid possible trouble. Mehmed IV's two brothers, Süleyman (1642–1691) and Ahmet (1643–1695), whom Rycaut mentions here, both succeeded him, as Süleyman II (1687–1691) and Ahmet II (1691–1695).

should be born of a free ingenuous[63] spirit. The Grand Signior is born of a slave, the mother of the present being Circassian, taken perhaps by the Tatars in their incursions into that country. The Viziers themselves are not always free-born by father or mother, for the Turks get more children by their slaves than by their wives, and the continual supply of slaves sent in by the Tatars, taken from different nations by way of the Black Sea, as hereafter we shall have occasion to speak more fully, fills Constantinople with such a strange race, mixture and medley of different sorts of blood that it is hard to find many that can derive a clear line from ingenuous parents. So that it is no wonder that amongst the Turks a disposition be found fitted and disposed for servitude, and that is better-governed with a severe and tyrannous hand than with sweetness and lenity unknown to them and their forefathers, as Grotius takes this maxim out of Aristotle: "*Quosdam homines natura esse servos;* i. e. *ad servitutem aptos, et ita populi quidem, eo sunt ingenio, ut regi quam regere norint rectius*"[64] But since it appears that submission and subjection are so incident to the nature of the Turks, and obedience taught and so carefully-instilled into them with their first rudiments, it may be a pertinent question how it comes to pass that there are so many mutinies and rebellions as are seen and known amongst the Turks, and those commonly the most insolent, violent and desperate that we read of in story. To let pass the mutinies of former times in the Ottoman camp and the usual, though short rebellions of ancient days, I shall instance in the causes and beginnings of two notorious disturbances, or rather madnesses of the soldiery not mentioned in any history, which, being passages of our age, deserve to be recorded.

This obedience, then, that is so diligently taught and instilled into the Turkish militia as to the Sipahis[65] in their seraglios or seminaries,[66] the Janissaries[67] in their chambers sometimes is forgot, when the passions and animosities of the court, by which inferior affections are most commonly regulated, corrupt that discipline which its reason and sobriety instituted. For the affections of Princes are endued with a general influence when two powerful parties, aspiring both to greatness and authority, allure the soldiers to their respective factions and engage them in a civil war amongst themselves, and hence proceed seditions, destruction

---

[63] Here, "native" or perhaps "free-born." This usage is now obsolete.

[64] "Some people are slaves by nature, born to be governed, not to govern" (Aristotle, *Politics*, trans. T. A. Sinclair, rev. Trevor Saunders [Harmondsworth, UK: Penguin Books, 1981], 3.7). Grotius discusses in this chapter the question of prisoners-of-war being used as slaves and how they should be treated.

[65] Sipahis: the Turkish horse (Rycaut's note). The word often appears in English as *spahi*, actually the French term for cavalrymen recruited from Algeria.

[66] Here, the word "seminary" means a training school.

[67] I have retained the English "Janissary" throughout the text as it is well-known; the Turkish word is *Yeniçeri*, which translates literally as "new soldier."

of empires, the overthrow of commonwealths and the violent death of great ministers of state.

And so it happened, when ill government and unprosperous successes of war caused disobedience in the soldiery, which some, emulous of the greatness of those that were in power, nourished and raised to make place for themselves or their party. For in the time of Sultan Mehmed [IV], the present Grand Signior, when the whole government of the Empire rested in the hands of one Mulki Kadin,[68] a young audacious woman, by the extraordinary favour and love of the Queen Mother, who, as it was divulged, exercised an unnatural kind of carnality with the said Queen, so that was nothing was left to the counsel and order of the Vizier and grave seniors but was first to receive approbation and authority from her. The black eunuchs and negroes gave laws to all, and the cabinet councils were held in the secret apartments of the women, and there were prescriptions made, officers discharged or ordained as were most proper to advance the interest of this feminine government. But at length the soldiery, not used to the tyranny of women, no longer supporting this kind of servitude, in a moment resolved on a remedy, and in great tumults came to the Seraglio, where, commanding the Grand Signior himself to the *kiosk*[69] or banqueting-house, they demanded without farther prologue the heads of the favourite eunuchs. There was no argument of rhetoric to be proposed to this unreasonable multitude, nor time given for delays, but every one of the accused, as he was entered into the soldiers' roll or catalogue and required, being first strangled, was then afterwards thrown headlong from the wall of the garden and committed to the farther satisfaction of their enemies' revenge, by whom they were dragged to the hippodrome, and before the new mosque cut into small pieces and their flesh roasted and eaten by them.

The day following they apprehended Mulki Kadin and her husband Shaban Kalfa, both whom they put to death, nor ended this tumult here until by means of dissention between the Sipahis and Janissaries, the principal ministers found means and opportunity to interpose their power, and having executed several of the Sipahis and performed other exemplary parts of justice, reduced matters to some kind of quietness and composure, and thus order results from confusion and tumults in commonwealths have operated good effects to the redress of several evils. But besides this insurrection or mutiny of the Janissaries have succeeded divers other, but because there hath been no disorder amongst them so

---

[68] Mulki Kadin was, indeed, a favourite of Mehmed IV, and Rycaut's account of her rise and fall is accurate enough, although the accusation of "unnatural" sexual practices is typical of European writers (for details, see introduction). An account of her career appears in Louis Moreri's *Le grand dictionnaire historique ou mélange curieux de l'histoire* (1731) which is taken word-for-word from the French translation of Rycaut.

[69] The word actually means "pavilion" or "summer house."

notorious and memorable as that which occasioned the death of Kösem,[70] grandmother to the present Sultan, we have thought fit to record the certain particulars of it to all posterity.

---

[70] Kösem Sultan [*Kiosem*], also known as Mahpeyker Sultan (1585–1651) was a consort of Ahmed I (1603–1617) and mother of the crazy Sultan Ibrahim (1640–1648). She was a Bosnian Greek by birth, whose original name was Anastasia. Ahmet appointed her Valide Sultana, and she served as Regent for the first nine years of the reign of Murad IV (1623–1632), the first woman in Turkish history to hold formal power over the Empire, and was known for her charity work. She was again Regent during the first three years of Mehmed IV (1648–1651). Her downfall was brought about by her rival Turhan Hatice, who eventually had her strangled. Rycaut's account of her rise and fall is fairly accurate. An epic film about her has been made recently in Turkey.

Chapter IV. *A True Relation of the Designs managed by the old Queen, wife of Sultan Ahmed and Mother of Sultan Murat and Sultan Ibrahim, against her grandchild Sultan Mehmed, who now reigns, and of the death of the said Queen and her Complices.*

After the murder of Sultan Ibrahim by conspiracy of the Janissaries, Sultan Mehmed [IV], eldest son of the late deceased Emperor, a child of nine years old, succeeded in the throne of his father, and the tuition of him and administration of the government during his minority was committed to the old Queen, the grandmother called Kösem, a lady who through her long experience and practice in affairs was able and proper for so considerable an office. And so the young Sultan was conducted to the mosque of Ayub,[71] where with the accustomed ceremonies his word was girt to his side and he proclaimed Emperor through all the kingdoms and provinces of his dominions.

For some time this old Queen governed all things according to her pleasure, until the mother of the young Sultan, as yet trembling with the thoughts of the horrid death of her lord, and fearing lest the subtle and old politician[72] and grandmother, who had compassed the death of her husband, should likewise contrive the murder of her son, grew hourly more jealous of his life and safety, which suspicion of hers was augmented by the knowledge she had of the ambitious and haughty spirit of the grandmother and the private treatise and secret correspondence she held with the Janissaries, which compelled her to a resolution of making a faction likewise with the Sipahis and pashas and beys who had received their education in the Seraglio, being a party always opposed to the Janissaries. These she courted by letters and messages, complaining of the death and murder of the Sultan her husband, the pride and insolence of the Janissaries and small esteem [which] was had of her son their undoubted Prince, adding that if they provided not for their own safety the old Queen would abolish both the name and order of Sipahis. The Asiatic Sipahis, awakened hereat, with a considerable army marched to Scutari[73] under the conduct of Gürcü Nebi[74] and

---

[71] Now known as the Mosque of Eyüp Sultan, it was erected over the site of Ayub's tomb by Mehmed II in 1458, the first mosque to be built after the capture of Constantinople. The girding of Sultan Osman I's sword on to the newly invested Sultan's side symbolized dynastic continuity and also the victory in a holy war of Islam over the Christians.

[72] Here, the sense is of someone who is seeking personal power and is often unscrupulous about getting it. See, for example, "this vile politician Bolingbroke" (Shakespeare, I *Henry IV*, 1.3, 252).

[73] Scutari, now known as Üsküdar, is on the Anatolian shore of the Bosphorus.

[74] Gürcü Abdül Nebi (d. 1650), whose first name means "the Georgian," was a brother of Gürcü Mehmed Pasha, who served as Grand Vizier 1651–1652. A former cavalryman, he apparently went to Istanbul to see the Sultan and protest against a massacre of Christians that had occurred in the Hippodrome, and their bodies had been thrown

demanded the heads of those who had been the traitors and conspirators against the sacred life of their late sovereign, all which were then under the protection of the Janissaries and supported by the powerful authority of the Queen Regent. Upon this alarm, the Grand Vizier Murat Pasha,[75] who had had his education among the Janissaries, being adored by them as an oracle and engaged with them in the late treason against the Sultan, speedily passed over from Constantinople to Scutari with an army of Janissaries and others of his favourites and followers, transporting likewise artillery and all necessaries for entrenchment. Some skirmishes passed between the vanguard of the Sipahis and the Deli,[76] which are the Vizier's guard, and thereby had engaged both the armies, but that the two Chief Justices of Anatolia and Greece, interposing with their grave and religious countenances, preached to them of the danger and impiety there was in the effusion of Muslims' or believers' blood, and that had they any just pretenses their plea should be heard and all differences decided by the law. These and like such persuasions made impression on Nebi and other Sipahis, and the posture they found their adversaries in to give them battle made them inclinable to proposals for accommodation. But especially their courages were abated by what the Justices had declared, that in case they repaired not to their own homes the Vizier was resolved to burn all the Rolls and proclaim a general *nesiraum* through the whole Empire, which is an edict of the King and Mufti commanding all the Turks of his kingdom from seven years old and upward to follow him to the war.

The Sipahis hereupon dispersed themselves and from their retreat increased the pride of the Janissaries' faction and of their chief commanders, *viz.* Bektaş Aga,[77] highly-favoued by the Queen Regent, [the] Kul Kiahia, Lieutenant of the Janissaries, and Kara Cavuş,[78] a follower of Bektaş, who now esteemed

into the sea, although the contemporary chronicler Evliya Celebi thought that he "harboured a personal grievance against the government, having been deprived of a lucrative state job" (Caroline Finkel, *Osman's Dream: The History of the Ottoman Empire* [New York: Basic Books, 2005], 236).

[75] Kara Dev Murad Pasha (1611–1655), an ethnic Albanian, served as Grand Vizier 1649–1651. It was actually his predecessor, the Sofu Mehmed Pasha. who had ordered Sultan Ibrahim strangled. Kara Dev was succeeded for a short time by Mehmed Pasha.

[76] The word *deli* means "mad" or "wild," and was used to denote irregular troops as well as the Captain of the *akinji* (irregular cavalry). One of Sultan Ibrahim's nicknames was *Deli*. Rycaut discusses them in Part 3, Chapter 10.

[77] Bectaş or Bektaş Aga (d. 1651) was in fact a former commander-in-chief of the Janissaries. He was instrumental in depositing the Grand Vizier Melek Ahmed Pasha and replacing him with Abaza Siyavus Pasha (1651), whom he assumed would be more pliable. Bektaş was later made sub-governor of Bursa. Rycaut's account of his activities here is accurate.

[78] Kara Cavuş Mustafa Pasha (d. 1651) was the commander-in-chief of the Janissaries. As Rycaut notes later on, he was appointed governor of Temeşvar, although he did not live long to enjoy the position.

themselves absolute masters of the Empire.[79] These three now verned all matters, contriving in their secret councils the destruction of the Sipahis, especially those famed for riches and valour, and as one of the first rank gave order to the Pasha of Anatolia to take away the life of Gürcü Nebi, whom accordingly he one day assaulted in his quarters, and, [he] being abandoned by his soldiers, shot him with a pistol and sent his head to Constantinople. The Sipahis, exasperated hereat, entered into private councils and conspiracies in Anatolia against the Janissaries, drawing to their party several beys and pashas or Asia, and particularly one İpşiri,[80] a Circassian born but educated in the Seraglio, a person of a courageous spirit and powerful in men and treasure, assaulted many quarters of the Janissaries in Asia and, cutting off their arms and noses, miserably slaughtered as many as fell into their hands.

On the other party, Bektaş Aga, secure in his condition, amassed wealth with both hands by new impositions, rapine, and other arts, causing to be coined at Belgrade 300 thousand aspers, one-third silver and two of tin. These aspers he dispersed amongst the tradesmen and artisans, forcing others to exchange his false metal for gold, at the value of 160 aspers for the Hungarian ducat.[81] The people, sensible of the cheat, began a mutiny in the quarter of the soldiers at Constantinople, which increased so fast that the whole city was immediately in a general uproar. This tumult was violently carried to the place of the Mufti, whom they forced, with the Sheikh who is the Grand Signior's preacher and the *Nakib ül-Eşraf*,[82] a primate of the Mohammedan race, to accompany them to the Seraglio, where at the inward gate of the royal lodgings with clamours and outcries they made their complaint. In this danger the Grand Signior was advised by the Capi Agassi[83] and Süleyman Aga, the *Kizlar Aga* or Chief Eunuch[84] of all

---

[79] *Kul-kiahia* is actually a title, and means "lieutenant-general." Sometimes Rycaut's knowledge of Turkish is not perfect.

[80] İpşiri Mustafa Pasha (d. 1658) later served for a short time as Grand Vizier, May-August, 1655.

[81] An asper (Turkish *akçe*) was a small silver coin, the main currency of the Ottoman Empire until 1688, when the *kurus* (piastre) was introduced. A Hungarian ducat was a gold coin which would be worth approximately 25p today. One can easily understand why people objected to this radical debasement.

[82] The Nakib ül-Eşraf was the marshal or recorder of the descendants of the Prophet.

[83] Governor of the royal pages.

[84] Lala Süleyman Aga (d. 1656) was raised to his office by Turhan Hatice, but was dismissed nine months later. He was the person who carried out her orders to strangle Kösem Sultan, and was later put to death by Mehmed IV. He would be the power behind the vizierate of Siyavuş Pasha. He believed, together with Turhan Hatice, "that strong leadership was needed if the empire that supported them was to be saved" (Sandford Shaw, *History of the Ottoman Empire and Modern Turkey* [Cambridge: Cambridge University Press, 1988], 1, 205) and to this end they replaced Gürcü Mehmed Pasha as Grand Vizier with Tarhonçu Ahmed Pasha.

the women, that this happy conjuncture was to be embraced for the destruction of Bektas and his complices, but fear and too much caution hindered that design for the present. Only it was judged fit, for satisfaction of the multitude, that Melek Ahmed Pasha,[85] then Prime Vizier and yet a slave to the lusts of the Janissaries, should be deprived of his office, which was immediately effected, and the seal taken from him was delivered to [Abaza] Siyavus Pasha,[86] a stout and valiant person. This Vizier, being jealous of his own honour and jealous for the safety of the Empire, cast about all ways to suppress the arrogance of Bektaş and his adherents, lest the like shame and misfortune should befall him as did to [Kara Dev] Murat Pasha, one of his late predecessors in the office of Vizier, who, for dissenting from Bektaş in opinion, had lost his life had he not escaped his fury by flying into Greece.

The times were also troublesome and full of danger; the Janissaries kept guard in the streets, not suffering so much as two citizens to walk together for prevention of secret consultations. Many artisans or handicraftsmen were imprisoned, as principally in the later tumult against the order of the new Vizier. The court also was divided; the Sultan's party contrived to surprise and kill the rebellious commanders of the Janissaries, and that day following the Lieutenant of the *Baltaçis* or Hatchet-men should encounter [the] Kul-kiahia as he came according to the custom to the Divan and slay him, but the old Queen, being of a contrary faction, with threats and menaces frightened that officer from his design. The two queens were exasperated highly against each other, one to maintain the authority of her son and the other her own. In the city the confusion grew greater; the Janissaries were not pleased with the election of Siyavuş Pasha, knowing him to be averse to their faction, but yet considering the state of the times, they endeavoured with fair promises to allure him to their party.

The old Queen by letters advised Bektaş of all matters that were discoursed in the Seraglio, intimating that the young Queen was author of all these disturbances, and that therefore, as a remedy of all these evils, it was necessary that Sultan Mehmed should be deposed and his younger brother Süleyman placed in his stead, who, having a mother, would be absolutely subject to her tuition. She added likewise that Süleyman was a lusty youth, corpulent and majestical, whereas Mehmed was lean, weakly, and unable for the crown. Bektaş, having

---

[85] Melek Ahmed Pasha served as Grand Vizier 5–22 August, 1651.

[86] Siyavuş Pasha (d. 1657) served as Grand Vizier in 1651 and 1656. After his dismissal from the second term he was made Governor of Damascus, but ran into trouble when he refused to resign this post on the orders of Mehmed Köprülü, who had recently been appointed Grand Vizier, retaliating by raising a revolt against the vizier. The vizier asked Mehmet IV to order Siyavuş's execution, but he escaped this fate temporarily through the intercession of friends at court. Köprülü then resigned, saying that he could not do his job, and as he was on the point of leading an army against the Venetians, the Sultan changed his mind and Siyavuş was executed.

received this message from the Queen Regent, assembled a council at Orta-tza-mi, that is, the Janissaries' mosque, where was a great and solemn appearance both of the soldiery and lawyers (which latter are of the spiritual function among them), some out of friendship to their party and others for fear of their power. Only the Vizier was wanting, whom they sent to invite out of an opinion that he might be drawn to their side, and in case they found him opposite, then not to suffer him to escape alive from their councils. It was then two hours in the night when this message came to the Vizier, and though it was against the state and gravity of a Vizier to go to any but his master, yet he thought it now time to dissemble and overcome the greatness of his mind, and so with a private retinue went to the mosque, where the first he encountered was a guard of ten thousand Janissaries armed with their muskets and matches lighted, which at first so dismayed him that he had some thoughts of returning, but afterwards recovered himself, and, taking courage, resolved to proceed. And coming to the mosque, Bektaş vouchsafed not to meet him, but sent another to perform that ceremony, at which neglect, though the greatness of his spirit could scarce contain itself, yet suppressing his choler he addressed himself to the feet of Bektaş, who, scarce arising, gave him a faint welcome, and setting him on his left hand, which is the upper hand with the Turkish soldiers, began to propound to him new designs. And first, that it was necessary that the present King should be deposed and Sü-leyman crowned in his place, that the canons of the Imperial Seraglio should be reformed and that whereas the children of diverse nations were yearly collected for the service of the Grand Signior, none should for the future have admission there but the sons of Janissaries. The Vizier consented to all that was proposed, professing a sincere affection and reality to them and their party, swearing upon the Qur'an with the most horrid imprecations on himself and his family if he were not faithful to him and his designs, which gave Bektaş that satisfaction that he began to persuade himself that the Vizier was really a confiding person and one affectionate to their interest. And so, partly from this consideration and partly out of a confidence of his own strength and inability of the Vizier to hurt him, fairly took leave of him and so dismissed his *kalaba Divan*,[87] or his confused council. But the [Kul-] Kiahia Bey or Lieutenant-General of the Janissaries and Kara Khiaus reproved very much Bektaş for permitting the Vizier to escape with his life, saying he had done ill in suffering the bird to escape out of the cage, that he had released one and permitted him to carry his head on his shoulders who would shortly take off theirs, with many words of the like effect. But Bektaş slighted their reproof as proceeding from want of courage and the ignorance of their own power, and that the time until morning was so short that should the

---

[87] "The next day we were summoned to the Divan, which is their Council of State" (Ogier de Busbecq, *Turkish Letters*, trans. E. S. Forster [London: Eland, 2001], 61). *Ka-labalik* means "confused mass."

Vizier intend to counter-mine them, he was wholly unable, being unprovided both of power and counsel.

The Vizier, being got free, went apace to the Seraglio with two men only, thanked God as he walked that he was freed from the hands of those tyrants and villains, and, coming to the iron gate, intending to pass through the garden, he found it open, contrary to the custom, and enquiring of the *bostancis* or gardeners the reason, he could learn nothing farther from them than that it was the order of the old Queen, who, as it appeared afterwards, expected her confidants, who might withdraw her that night into some retirement where she might remain secure from the dangers of the ensuing day. The Vizier, being entered, went softly to the Sultan's apartments, and in his way by good chance met with the Kizlar Agassi Süleyman Aga, the Chief Eunuch of the Women, who in the dark was making his rounds about the old Queen's lodgings. By the Vizier's voice Süleyman knew who he was, but was amazed at his unseasonable visit, yet understanding the business thanked him for his vigilance, adding that he had also observed that the old Queen, contrary to her custom, was not yet gone to bed, who did at other times at two hours in the night dispose herself to rest; only this evening she had entertained herself in the company of her eunuchs and favourites with music, singing, and other unusual delights. Wherefore, after some short deliberation, the Vizier, Süleyman Aga, and others of the King's eunuchs went to the quarters of the old Queen, and, offering to enter forcibly, were repulsed by the Queen's eunuchs. But Süleyman Aga, being a stout[88] man, drew his dagger and struck the chief Chamberlain, Kapa Oğlar Pasha, on the face, upon which the other eunuchs who accompanied Süleyman entered furiously with their daggers, at which, the eunuchs of the Queen flying, she remained alone in the chamber, where she was committed to the custody of the King's eunuchs.

The fugitive eunuchs would have immediately escaped out of the Seraglio, but the gates were first shut by order of Süleyman Aga, so that they, with all other favourites of the said Queen were taken and secured in safe hands. This victory was so secretly obtained that they received no alarm in the royal lodgings, though near adjoining, so that the Vizier and Süleyman Aga went to the chamber where the King slept, and lifting up the anteport[89] made a sign of silence to the ladies of the guard, commanding by dumb motions that the young Queen should be awakened. For it is the custom in the Grand Signior's court to speak by signs to prevent noise, and as if there were some point in it of majesty and decency they have practiced this mute language so fully that they are able to recount stories in it. The ladies hereupon, gently rubbing the Queen's feet, raised her out of her sleep and gave her to understand that Süleyman Aga would speak with her, whereat the Queen, surprised, leapt from her bed to speak with him and was scarce informed of the business before she became so affrighted that she

---

[88] Strong, brave.
[89] Outer door.

could not contain herself within the bounds of moderation or silence, but with a great cry ran to take her son as one distracted, and catching him up in her arms cried out "O son, thou and I are dead!" The Grand Signior likewise, as a child bewailed himself, and falling at the feet of Süleyman Aga says "*Lala, lala, kurtar-beni*," which is "Tutor, tutor, save me!" He, not without tears, took his lord into his arms, and with the Vizier encouraged the child and his mother, protesting that they would rather die than live to behold so horrid a ruin, and so accompanied him (some ladies carrying before torches lighted in their hands) to the *hoz oda*, which is the presence-chamber or place where the principal officers of the court attend.

Upon the approach of the torches the guard which watched in this chamber was amazed, and, walking towards the light to discover what there was, perceived that the Grand Signior was coming thither, and thereupon returned again with all haste to awaken their companions, and calling them immediately to repair to their due service. The Grand Signior being seated on a throne which is always remaining in the presence-chamber, the officers hereof, which are in number forty, presented themselves before him, desiring to know if His Majesty had anything wherein to employ their fidelity and service. Hereat, Süleyman Aga said, "He that eats the King's bread should apply himself to the King's service. We suffered the traitors to destroy Sultan Ibrahim, and now they would also take this [Sultan] out of our hands. To you it belongs, who are His Majesty's principal servitors, to afford him your utmost assistance." Mustafa Pasha, sword-bearer and Chief of the Presence-Chamber, a man of a lion's heart and undaunted resolution, understanding something formerly of the bad intentions of the old Queen towards the King, readily replied, "Great master, be not troubled; tomorrow you shall see (God willing) the heads of your enemies at your feet."

The Vizier and others in the meantime, after a short consult fell to act, the exigency of their affairs admitting no delays, and in the first place, pen and ink being brought, an order was presented to the Grand Signior to be subscribed for the arresting of the *Bostançi* Pasha as a traitor, for having against the rule of the night kept open the gate of the King's garden. This was done in an instant, he removed from his office and another constituted in his place, and at the same time the Oath of Allegiance was administered to him, who, calling together the gardeners, in number about 500, caused them also all to swear faithful obedience to the Grand Signior and to remain all that night keeping good guard at the gates and walls of the gardens. In the next place the *içoğlans*[90] were called up, who are the Grand Signior's pages, and to proceed with the more privacy and least confusion, they went first to the chamber of the Kapi Agassi, who by his office is over all the youth of the Seraglio, and, knocking gently at the window,

---

[90] They were boys recruited as pages (sometimes by coercion) from non-Muslim families living in the Balkan areas of the empire. Rycaut gives more details in chapter 5. The Turkish word is *içoğlani*.

the guards came at the noise and demanded what the matter was. They answered, "Awake the Kapi Agassi and let him speak to us at the window." But the Kapi Agassi would first know who they were that would speak with him, and when it was told him that it was the Vizier and the Kizlar Agassi, he answered, "I am indisposed and cannot rise. But utter what you have to say at the window." So they said, "By His Majesty's order go and raise all the *içoğlans* in the Seraglio; our King is ready to be taken out of our hands upon an important occasion!" And yet the Kapi Agassi would not stir, so that some believed him confederate in the conspiracy, but the truth was he was an ancient man of ninety years and unhealthful in his body. Wherefore Süleyman Aga cried out with a loud voice, "Aga, raise the *içoğlans*! Our King is ready to be taken out of our hands!" But the Kapi Aga persisted that he would not raise the *içoğlans* or pages unless he brought a command in writing from the King.

In this interim the servants of the Kapi Aga awakened, and, hearing this discourse, could not contain themselves, but without farther order ran to both the greater and lesser chamber of the pages. The butler came to that which is called the greater chamber; it was then five hours in the night when he entered in, and running to the middle of the chamber, which was 80 paces in length, he made a stop and clapped his hands together. To make such a noise in the Seraglio at night was a high misdemeanor, at which some, being awakened, raised up their heads, and, startled at such an unusual alarm, enquired the reason of it, at which he, again clapping his hands and crying out, "Arise! The Grand Signior is likely to be taken out of our hands!," the whole chamber was raised, so that you might have seen the *içoğlans*, in number about 600, to rise and run in a confused manner, some without clothes, some without arms to fight, some supposing the Janissaries were already entered the Seraglio. In this amaze came a guard of black and white eunuchs [91] to the door, advising them to arm themselves with what weapons were near at hand, and there to remain until they received farther orders.

All the other chambers of the pages and officers were in the same confusion, and were commanded in the like manner to arm themselves. The Grand Signior, fearing all the while he should be put to death as his father was, could not be pacified until Mustafa Pasha his sword-bearer, taking him by the hand, showed him his attendants all armed and ready at his command, and, passing by one of the windows of the lodgings, was descried by a young man, who cried out with a loud voice "God grant our King ten thousand years of life!," at which all the chamber shouted "Allah! Allah!" [92] This acclamation rang through all the

---

[91] Black eunuchs were recruited from prisoners of war taken in Egypt, Sudan, or Ethiopia; the white eunuchs were from Armenia, Georgia, Hungary, and other European parts of the Ottoman Empire.

[92] A shout used by the Turks when they fight (Rycaut's marginal note).

Seraglio, so that it reached the more remote quarters of the druggists,[93] cooks, poleaxe-men,[94] falconers, and others, who, being ready and armed as the others, answered with the like shout.

These preparations were not only in the Seraglio but likewise without, for the Vizier had given order to all the pashas and beylerbeys[95] and other his friends, that without delay they should repair to the Seraglio with all the force they could make, bringing with them three days' provision, obliging them under pain of death to this duty. In a short space so great was this concourse that all the gardens of the Seraglio, the outward courts and all the adjoining streets were filled with armed men. From Galata and Tophana[96] came boats and barges loaded with provender and ammunition and other necessaries, so that in the morning by break of day appeared such an army of horse and foot in the streets and ships and galleys on the sea as administered no small terror to the Janissaries, of which, being advised and seeing the concourse of the people run to the assistance of the King, they thought it high time to bestir themselves and therefore armed a great company of Albanians, Greeks, and other Christians, to whom they offered money and the title and privileges of Janissaries, promising to free them from *harach*,[97] or impositions paid by the Christians, which arguments were so prevalent that most taking arms, you might see the court and city divided and ready to enter into a most dreadful confusion of a civil war.

In the Seraglio all things were in good order. The morning devotions being finished, the *baltacis*,[98] who are a guard that carry poleaxes, called to the pages to join with them and accompany them to the Presence-Chamber. These *baltacis* were in number about 200 strong, of large stature and of admirable agility, at whose beck the pages ran with all alacrity to the door of the Chamber, where they at first received a repulse from the Master of the Chamber, who was an eunuch and one faithful to the old Queen's interest, who, to yield all possible

---

[93] "Druggist" does not mean pharmacists, but "dragomen" or "druggermen," the court interpreters and translators.

[94] A poleaxe is a long handled war hammer.

[95] *Beylerbey* is the highest grade of pasha. It is also spelled *beglerbeg*.

[96] Galata and Tophana are suburbs in the Beyoğlu district of Istanbul, on the European side. Galata, which is also known as Pera (see below) is described by Mansel as "the Shanghai of the Levant," which "resembled a small Italian city, with Catholic churches, straight streets, well-built stone houses and a piazzetta" (Philip Mansel, *Constantinople, City of the World's Desire 1453–1924* [Harmondsworth, UK: Penguin Books, 1997], 12).

[97] A yearly tax on agricultural commodities levied on Christians.

[98] The Turkish word *baltaci* means "someone skilled with an axe." They were "responsible for various duties at the court, for example cutting wood, hence their name" (Karin Ådahl, ed., *The Sultan's Procession: The Swedish Embassy to Sultan Mehmed IV in 1657–1657* [Istanbul: Swedish Research Institute, 2006], 212). They also formed the Sultan's guard in the Topkapi Palace, where they were "chiefly concerned with the protection of the harem" (Lewis, *Istanbul*, 72).

furtherance to the protection of her person, reproved the insolence of the rout in coming so boisterously to the royal lodgings, to which they unanimously answered that they would speak to His Majesty, that it was their desire to have the old Queen, enemy to the King and the Mohammedan faith, put to death. At which words he, being enraged and relying on this authority, reproved them with terms of "rebels" and "traitors" to their master. "What have you to do with the Queen?," said he; "Are you worthy to open your mouths against her serene name?" He, reiterating these and like words, one of this rabble said, "Kill that cuckold, for he also is an enemy of the faith!" And, whilst one lifted up his hand to strike him, he fled by way of the terrace, whither, being pursued by five or six of them, he was overtaken, and catching him by the collar would have cut his throat, but that at his earnest entreaty they gave him so much liberty as first to cast himself at the feet of the Sultan, whither being dragged he delivered to the King a seal and a key of secret treasure, and, being about to say something in his own behalf and defence of his life, a bold youth of these *baltacis* called Jalch-Leferli struck him on the head with his axe and cleft it in two pieces. The others, seeing this first blow given him, fell on him with their scimitars and cut him to pieces; his blood and brains were dashed on the rich carpets, which moved fear in many who were secretly of the conspiracy with the old Queen.

The young King himself, ignorant of the good intentions of his servants, at the sight of bloodshed being yet tender-hearted, cried and closely embraced the *Silahdar*[99] who then held him in his arms, but upon the removal of the corpse out of his sight and some smooth words, as that it was a sacrifice of love to him and the like, his childish tears were soon wiped away. In this interim the new-created Mufti and Kenan Pasha, one of the Viziers of the Bench[100] and Karaçelibizade Effendi,[101] who was formerly Lord Chief Justice and well-affected to the Sipahis' party, entering the *haz oda* or Presence-Chamber, perceiving a tumult in His Majesty's presence with different voices and languages, for some

---

[99] Also spelled *selictar*. He was the Sultan's sword-bearer.

[100] The six Viziers of the Bench make up the Sultan's *divan*; they were drawn from both civilian and military ranks. Kenan Pasha (d. 1659), a favourite of Sultan Ibrahim and apparently a Russian or Circassian convert to Islam, was Governor of Egypt (1632–1635). As *Kapitan-i Derya* (Captain of the Seas). he would suffer a resounding defeat by Christian forces at the battle of the Dardanelles (1656). Rycaut discusses them in some detail in Chapter 11.

[101] Kara Çelebizade Abdülaziz Effendi (1591–1653) was the Şeyhülislam or Sheykh ul-Islam, the chief religious authority in the Empire. He was the person responsible for instructing the Sultan in Quranic law. He was a former chief justice of Anatolia and Rumeli. A reluctant and fearful supporter of the Janissaries, he disobeyed the Sultan's summons and was dismissed from his position in 1650, then exiled to the island of Chios. He wrote an account of the events that Rycaut describes here. For details, see Caroline Finkel, *Osman's Dream*, 240–43.

cried in Georgian, others Albanian, Bosnian, Mingrelian,[102] Turkish, and Italian, remained in great confusion on how to proceed with order and reason in this important affair, for the Mufti and others were of opinion that the sentence against the old Queen was not rashly to be pronounced, and so the matter might calmly be debated, and, if possible, an expedient might be found for saving her life and securing the Sultan. But the rabble, impatient of delay, cried out, "Defer not the sentence, for otherwise we shall esteem thee as one of her adherents!"

By this time news was come to the young Queen that there had been a fight in the streets, who, as yet doubting of the success and fearing if the Janissaries should gain the advantage, Bektaş would revenge the blood of the old Queen by her death, came covered with a veil into the Presence-Chamber, saying as she passed, "Is this the reverence you owe to the King your lord? Do you know the place where you are? What would you have of a woman? Why do you busy yourselves in the King's affairs?" Some presently apprehended that this was only a plot of the young Queen to make the world believe she would rather assist the grandmother than contrive against her, which made the pages more importunately to persist with the Mufti for the *fetva* or sentence against her. But one of the pages, suspecting that this woman so veiled might be the old Queen herself, cried out, "This is she you seek for; she is in your hands! Take your revenge upon her!" At which, some bestirring themselves to seize her, she ran to the feet of her son, and laying hold on him cried out, "No, no, I am not the grandmother! I am the mother of this His Majesty!," and, wiping the tears from the eyes of her son with her handkerchief, made signs to keep back, which restrained the forwardness of some who pressed to lay violent hands upon her.

The Mufti, who observed the carriage of the rout and their earnest desires which could not be resisted, feared if he gave not his concurrence he himself should be killed, and the rather because he had heard old Kenan Pasha discourse with the Vizier to the like effect, so that after some pause and consultation with the other chief ministers it was resolved to supplicate His Majesty for his consent, which was done in these words: "Sir, the will of God is that you consign your grandmother into the hands of justice if you would have these mutinies appeased. A little mischief is better than a great one; there is no remedy. God willing, the end shall be prosperous." Pen and ink being brought, the Mufti wrote the sentence and the Grand Signior subscribed it, which was that the old Queen should be strangled but neither cut with sword nor bruised with blows. The writing was delivered into the hands of one of the chamberlains, to whom by word of mouth it was ordered that they should carry the Queen out by Kushana, or the Gate of the Birds, so as she might not die in sight or hearing of the Grand Signior.

---

[102] Mingrelia was a former independent principality in the western part of Georgia, with its own language and culture.

The *içoğlans*, advancing the royal command on high with their hands, went out of the presence with a great shout, crying "Allah! Allah!" to the door of the Women's Lodgings, where they met some black eunuchs keeping guard, who, upon the sight of the imperial *firman* and the command of Süleyman Aga, gave them admittance upon condition that twenty persons only should enter the chamber. Those who were best-armed went in, and passing through the chambers of the virgins, were met by the Queen's *buffone*[103] with a pistol in her hand, who demanded what they would have. They answered, "The King's grandmother;" she replied, "I am she," and with that offered to discharge her pistol, but it took fire only in the pan. With that, the *içoğlans* laid hold on her, supposing her to be the Queen, but, being better-advised by Süleyman the Kizlar Aga, and directed to the chamber where the Queen was. The door being opened, they perceived the room to be dark, for the women's quarters in the Seraglio, for the most part, are made obscure and close, and lights are burnt in them day and night, and the old Queen had, at the approach of these officers, extinguished her candles and got into a great press[104] and there covered herself with quilts and carpets. But, torches being brought in, they looked all about and descried nothing, at which they were enraged against Süleyman and would have killed him, saying that he was the cause the Queen had escaped. But Süleyman advising them to search more narrowly, one called Deli *Dogangi*[105] got upon the press, and removing the clothes discovered the Queen, who had thrust herself into a corner, at which she shortly thus entreats him, "O brave man, be not cruel unto me," and promised she would give to every *içoğlan* five purses a man, each purse consisting of 500 dollars,[106] if they would save her life. "It is not the time of ransom," said he, and taking her by the feet drew her forth. The Queen, rising up, put her hand into her pocket and threw out handfuls of sequins,[107] hoping that whilst they were scrambling for the gold she might have an opportunity to escape. Some of the young men gathered up the money, but the *dogangi*, like a dog of the game, left her not, and at length, though she were heavy, cast her down. The others offered at her life, and particularly an Albanian called Ali *Bostanji*,[108] who, seeing two great jewels at her ears, immediately catched at them and tore them thence. They were two diamonds of the bigness of chestnuts, cut angularly, and beneath each diamond was a ruby to set it off. Those earrings were given her by Sultan Ahmet in the time of her most flourishing age and his greatest affection. 'Tis said that such jewels cannot be found in all the Great Turk's treasure, and were

---

[103] Jester or fool (Italian).
[104] A large wardrobe used for storing clothes.
[105] A *dogangi* is a falconer. This name means "the crazy falconer."
[106] The Dutch "lion" silver dollar or *daalder* circulated throughout the Middle East as a coin for trading. It had a lion on the reverse side, facing right.
[107] The gold sequin [*zaichin*] was introduced in 1535.
[108] A *bostanji* is an Imperial guard.

esteemed by the most skillful jewellers worth a year's revenue of Grand Cairo. This Ali showed the jewels to his comrade, demanding the value of them and his counsel whether to reveal or conceal them, but the comrade prized them at that rate that the stout young man could not sleep day nor night, being always in fear lest the jewels should not be kept hid, and apprehending that they became none but the Grand Signior to wear, went and delivered them to Süleyman Aga, who in recompense thereof presented him with 16 sequins, which he accepted, desiring also to be admitted into the chamber of the Treasury, which was granted him. Others also plucked her, some by the hands, others by the feet; some rifled her clothes, for she was furnished throughout with things of great value sewed in her garments, and especially in her sable furs, which contained also certain magic spells by which she conceived she had tied the tongues of all the Emperors living in her time. The person who gave me this relation informed me that he had seen a lock admirably made and engraved with the names of Murad[109] and Sultan Ibrahim; it was made by a famous *gindgi*, a very ignorant fellow but a superstitious crafty liar, by which arts finding access. In short time he became a chief favourite of Sultan Ibrahim, and from a poor student, called by the Turks a *softa*,[110] he grew so rich in two years that none in Constantinople was comparable to him.

But to return to the Queen, now assaulted by furious young men, greedy of riches: she was in a moment despoiled of her garments, her furs were torn off into small pieces, and, being stripped of her rings, bracelets, garters and other things, she was left without a rag to cover her and dragged by her feet to the Kushana. And, being at the place of execution, the young officers found themselves unprovided of a cord to strangle her, so that crying out for a cord, one ran to the royal chapel and thence took the cord that upheld the great antiport of the mosque, which, being twined about the Queen's neck, the aforesaid dogangi, getting on her back, pitched her neck with his hands whilst the others drew the cord. The Queen, though she were by this time beside her senses and worn out with age, being above 80 years old[111] and without teeth, yet she with her gums only did bite the thumb of his left hand, which by chance came into her mouth, so hard that he could not deliver himself, until with the haft of his poniard he struck her on the forehead near her right eye. There were four that strangled her, but being young executioners labored long to dispatch her, till at length the Queen, leaving to struggle, lay stretched out and was supposed to be dead. And so, crying "*Uldi, uldi!* (She is dead, she is dead),"[112] [they] ran to carry the news thereof to His Majesty, but, being scarce out of sight, the Queen raised herself up and turned

---

[109] Probably Murad IV, who reigned from 1623 to 1640.

[110] A *softa* was usually a student either of religion or Islamic law.

[111] Rycaut is wrong; Kösem Sultan was sixty-six. She was murdered 2 September 1651. Finkel has "nearly seventy," which is also wrong (*Osman's Dream*, 242). Shaw says she was born in 1585 (*Ottoman Empire* 1, 339).

[112] Modern Turkish is [*kadin*] *ölü*.

her head about, at which the executioners, being called back again, the cord was a second time applied and wrung so hard with the haft of a hatchet that at length she was dispatched and the news carried to the royal chamber. The black eunuchs immediately took up the corpse, and in a reverent manner laid it stretched forth in the royal mosque, which about 400 of the Queen's slaves, encompassing round about with howling and lamentations, tearing the hair from their heads after their barbarous fashion, moved compassion in all the court.

This work being over, the Vizier having given thanks to the *içoğlans* or pages for their pains, gave order to produce the banner of Muhammad, which is carefully and reverently kept in the treasury, which, being produced, obliges all of that faith from seven years and upward to arm and come under it. The banner being brought forth with a rich covering, was advanced with great shouts of "Allah, Allah!," and carried by the *içoğlans* out of the chief gate of the Seraglio, where it was shown to the people, who with wonderful admiration and devotion beheld their glorious standard. Order was also given to proclaim through the whole city the procession of the holy banner, for they say that the angel Gabriel brought it to Muhammad in the time of a great war made against the Christians as an infallible sign and evidence of victory. The opinion of this superstitious flag so prevailed as it brought not only the young and healthful to fight under it, but sick and old and women judged themselves obliged to run to the defence of this holy ensign.[113]

The news hereof and the death of the old Queen coming to the Old Chamber of the Janissaries, several of them and those also of the principal heads began to murmur that it was now necessary to lay aside their private interests and have a respect to their faith and to their souls. For, should they oppose the heavenly banner, they should run themselves into the state of *giaours*[114] and infidels and become liable to the same censure or punishment which is inflicted upon unbelievers. But in the New Chambers Bektaş endeavoured to remove this apprehension from the minds of his soldiers by large presents both of gold and silver, persuading them to uphold their fortune and reputation, for that the Grand Signior and his mother were enemies to their name and designs, and resolved to abase or destroy the order of that militia, and with assurance of victory and encouragement against a people unarmed and undisciplined, animated them to fight, and

---

[113] The banner of Muhammad [*Sançak-ı Şerif*] was a battle flag which was supposed also to have been used as a tent flap for Muhammad's wife Aïsha. It was taken from Mecca by Selim I (1512–1520), who kept it in the Grand Mosque in Damascus, after which Murad III sent it to Hungary. It was finally housed in the Topkapi Palace, together with the standard of caliph, by Mehmed III (1595), who had it placed in an ornamented box and entrusted the key to the Kizlar Aga.

[114] This is a pejorative term used to denote Greek or Balkan Christians. Readers of Byron may recollect that it is the title of one of his best-known poems. The modern Turkish word is *gâvur*.

to make the business more easy, advised them to fire the city in several parts, so that the people might be diverted and divided for the safety of their own goods and dwellings. But this proposition took not with the officers and soldiers, who had many of them houses and possessions of their own in Constantinople, but put them into great distractions and divisions in their counsels. In this pause came an officer from the Grand Signior, who, to venture his life, had the promise of a great reward, with a command in writing which he threw in amongst them, and galloped away as fast as he could, crying out as he rode, "He that comes not under the banner of the Prophet is a pagan, and his wife divorced!" The writing was taken up and carried to the presence of the principal officers, which, being opened and read, was to this purpose: "Bektaş Aga I have made Pasha of Bosnia,[115] Kara Cavuş I have made Pasha of Temeşvàr,[116] and Kara Hassan Oğlu I have made *Yeniçeri Agasi*,[117] and I require, at sight of these presents, that every one of you, upon pain of death and ruin of his family, repair to his duty and station." In this instant came news that the Old Chamber of Janissaries had left their station and were run under the banner without arms, and had refused Bektaş's money and deserted his cause, and that the Sipahis in great troops and the *Gebegis* (who command the ordnance), approached with artillery to beat upon their chambers. The Sipahis came thundering in upon the Janissaries in remembrance of their past injuries, and had certainly cut them off, had not the Vizier with his sword in his hand by good and bad words restrained them and appeased their animosity. The Janissaries of the New Chamber proclaimed their new commander and visited him with their usual form of congratulation, running afterwards confusedly under the banner. Kara Hassan, the new-elected aga of the Janissaries, went to the Seraglio to thank the Grand Signior for the honour done him, and with ten of his principal friends was admitted to the Grand Signior's presence, who, humbly kissing the ground, received the accustomed vests, and with some admonitions was fairly dismissed and ordered to reduce his Janissaries to better obedience.

By this time Bektaş, [the] Kul-kiahia and Kara Cavuş, with some of their favourites, remained wholly abandoned, looking one upon the other full of complaints and railings, each at other for the miscarriage of the action, but since it was not now time to condole but to save their lives, everyone made to his house. First Bektaş fled to his home, where, having ordered his affairs, he clothed himself in the Albanian fashion and escaped to the house of a poor man formerly his friend and confidant, but the next day, being discovered by a youth, was taken, and, being set on a mule, was with the scorn and derision of the people conducted

---

[115] This is incorrect. It was Kara Cavuş's second-in-command, Mustafa Aga, who was elevated to this rank (Finkel, *Osman's Dream*, 244). Rycaut has confused Bosnia with Bursa (see note above).

[116] Timisoara, now in Romania.

[117] Commander-in-chief of the Janissaries.

to the Grand Signior's Seraglio and there strangled. This person was held in so much detestation by the common people that after his death the cooks and inferior sort of servants run spits and pitchforks through his body, and, plucking the hairs out of his beard, sent them for presents to their acquaintance through all Constantinople, saying "These are the hairs of that traitor who gloried that before he would lose his head there should be raised a mountain of heads as high as St. Sophia."

But the Kul-kiahia, being come to his house, filled his portmanteaux with gold and jewels, and accompanied with 60 horse resolved to fly to the mountains of Albania, places so inaccessible that they have never yielded to Turkish yoke. But finding himself hotly-pursued in his journey, and that it was impossible to escape with so great a number, freely distributed a great part of his gold upon his retinue, and, thanking them for their affection and good intentions, dismissed them all excepting one servant, with whom he journeyed with four laden horses with gold, jewels, and other riches. And perceiving that this also was too great an encumbrance, they buried a treasure to the value of 600 thousand dollars in the country as they travelled, which was afterwards found out by certain shepherds, who disagreeing about the division thereof, the matter came to be known to the judge of that country, who seized upon it all and sent it to the Grand Signior's treasury. But the Kul-kiahia, travelling still farther with his single page, came to a town, where, wanting bread and forced for the payment of it to exchange gold, fell into a suspicion of being one of those rebels lately escaped from Constantinople, which news being brought to a captain of horse that commanded the place, he came immediately with some men to take him, but the Kul-kiahia, resolving not to fall into their hands alive, resisted them until he was killed by a musket-shot, and so his head, being severed, was sent to the Grand Signior.

Kara Cavuş in this interim, being with 200 men retired into his garden, was assaulted by an aga of the Sipahis called Parmaksiz[118] with 500 men, but that this enterprise might be acquired with a little blood, a person was sent secretly to advise that party that if they opposed the royal command they should everyone be put to death, at which the people fled and dispersed themselves. At that instant came in this aga and took him, yet comforted him with the clemency and mercy of the Grand Signior, promising also himself to intercede for him. And so, bringing him to the Seraglio by the garden gate, His Majesty had notice of it, and, looking out of the window and seeing him upon his knees begging pardon, the Grand Signior gave a sign to the executioner to strangle him, which was accordingly performed.

The new Janissar Agassi, who knew all the officers formerly affected to the rebellious party, for several nights caused some or other of them to be strangled, to the number of 38 persons, which struck such a terror into the Janissaries that

---

[118] This was Parmaksiz Huseyn Aga, whose name means "fingerless Huseyn."

for a long time they kept themselves within the bounds of humility and obedience. And thus concluded this tragedy, remarkable as well for the dispatch as for the action itself, being but the work of fourteen hours. And in this manner it is apparent how the lessons of obedience which are so carefully taught and instilled into the minds of those who serve and depend upon the Grand Signior are corrupted, and by the pride, discord, and faction of the governors seduced from their natural principles.

By the premises we may consider more generally that it hath always been the misfortune of unlimited powers to be subject to dangers and violence arising from the discontents and unconstancy of the soldiery. For they, coming to be sensible of their own strength and knowing that the power of the Emperor is but fortified with their hands and heart, like unruly beasts throw their riders and show that the principles of obedience taught them are easily corrupted and defaced by evil persuasions or sedition in a commander or common soldier. Thus we see in the time of the latter Roman emperors, who usurped power unknown in the days of the pure and happy constitution of that commonwealth, and governed by the sword or their own lusts. Few of them ended their days fortunately or died in their beds and peace, without becoming a sacrifice to the same power that proclaimed them emperors.[119] And though the mutinies and rebellions in the Turkish militia can hardly operate any durable alteration in the state, as we shall more at large hereafter discourse, yet doubtless the tyranny in the Ottoman emperors had provoked the people long since to have proved the benefit of another race, but that there is a strange kind of devotion in their minds as to the Ottoman blood, which, having been the original of their empire and greatness, will ever be maintained in high reverence and honour. Nor is it likely that the fair speeches and allurements of a rebellious slave will ever prevail to persuade this people from their religion to this Prince, or that their arms can ever be prosperous under the ensign and conduct of an usurper. And may all Christians learn this lesson from the Turks and add this principle to the fundamentals of their religion as well as to their laws. None can more experimentally preach this doctrine to the world than England, who no sooner threw off her obedience and religion to her Prince but, as if that virtue had been the only bar to all other enormities and sins, she was deprived of all other ecclesiastical and civil rights, and in all her capacities and relations deflowered and profaned by impious and unhallowed hands.[120]

---

[119] Rycaut refers here to the period immediately following the Antonine era and the "five good emperors," from Nerva to Marcus Aurelius (96–180), traditionally thought to have been the best time to have been alive in the ancient world. The third century was a time of predominantly short-lived military emperors who ruled, lived and died in violence. Many of them were murdered by the very soldiers who had brought them to power.

[120] This is the first of Rycaut's attacks on the recent past in English history. His point here is, of course, that had the wrong side not won the Civil War and put Charles

And thus, having given a relation of the Turks' religion and first principles in order to show their obedience to their Prince, let us proceed a little into the *penetralia* of their Seraglio and there see what farther care is taken of the youth in all points of their education to fit and prepare them for the management and performance of the highest and weightiest offices of state, which I judge to be one of the chiefest of the Turkish polities, and is certainly an extraordinary support and security of the empire.

---

I to death, England would not have suffered deprivations. The "impious and unhallowed hands" are those of the two Lords Protectors (Oliver and Richard Cromwell) and the Commonwealth, which took power after the abolition of the monarchy, Church of England and House of Lords. Note how Rycaut personifies England as a virgin undergoing a process of defloration by these political rapists.

**Chapter V.** *The Education of young men in the Seraglio, out of which those who are to discharge the great offices of the Empire are elected, it being a maxim of the Turkish polity to have the Prince served by such whom he can raise without envy and destroy without danger.*

It is a special point of wisdom in princes to provide and prefer men of deserving parts and abilities to the discharge of great and important offices of state, not such whom chance and fortune casually throws on them, because they will not take the pains of a narrow and severe scrutiny to seek men able and fit for trust, nor such whom flattery, riches, gifts, or nobility promote, but those whom the Prince, by his own experience of their wisdom, virtues and diligence, or the testimony of his councilors and other confidants, judges capable to improve their advancement to the honour of the King and the blessing of their country, and not like vast mountains which hide their heads in the clouds and yet remain without fruit or herbage, whose barrenness makes their height accursed. Some wise princes and great ministers of our modern times have kept rolls and registers of the most eminent men famed for their virtue and knowledge in any parts, with an account of their family, lineage, and condition, out of which, in their own jurisdiction, they culled and elected such proper for their occasions and vacant offices.[121]

The youths, then, that are designed for the great offices of the empire, called by the Turks *içoğlans*, must be such as are of Christian parents taken in war or presented from remote parts, as I have observed that the Algerians, always amongst other gifts, present some youths whom they have taken by piracy. The policy herein is very obvious, because the sons of Christians will hate their parents, being educated with other principles and customs, or, coming from distant places, have contracted no acquaintance, so that starting from their schools into government they will find no relations or dependences on their interest than that of their great master, to whom they are taught, and necessity compels them to be faithful. In the next place, these youths must be of admirable features and pleasing looks, well-shaped in their bodies and without any defects of nature, for it is conceived that a corrupt and sordid soul can scarce inhabit in a serene and ingenious aspect. And I have observed, not only in the Seraglio, but also in the courts

---

[121] Rycaut's marginal note: *"Balzac de la Cour, leur sterilite fait maudire leur elevation. Cardinal Richelieu."* Jean-Louis Guez de Balzac (1597–1654), was a French writer famous for his epistolary essays, the *Lettres* (1636) and the work cited here, *Aristippe, ou de la Cour* (1658), which was translated into English as *Aristippus* by R. W. in 1659. The phrase, which Balzac attributes to Richelieu, translates "Their fruitlessness makes their elevation [to office] accursed." Balzac refers to the Greek philosopher Aristippus (c. 435–356 BCE), a pupil of Socrates, who maintained that as pleasure is the goal of life, people should adapt themselves to those circumstances which produce the most of it. For a further discussion, see introduction.

of great men, their personal attendants have been of comely, lusty youths, well-habited, deporting themselves with singular modesty and respect in the presence of their master, so that when a pasha, aga, Sipahi travels, he is always attended with a comely equipage, followed by flourishing youths well-clothed and mounted in great numbers, that one may guess the greatness of this Empire by the retinue, pomp and number of servants which accompany persons of quality in their journeys, whereas in parts of Christendom where I have travelled I have not observed, no, not in attendance of princes, such ostentation in servants as is amongst the Turks, which is the life and ornament of a court. And this was always the custom in the eastern countries; as Q. Curtius Rufus reports, *Lib.* 6, *"Quippe, omnibus barbaris in corporum maiestate veneratio est, magnorumque operum non alios capaces putant, quam quos eximia specie donare natura dignata est."*[122]

But these youths, before they are admitted, are presented before the Grand Signior, whom, according to his pleasure, he disposes in his seraglio at Pera[123] or Adrianople[124] or his great Seraglio at Constantinople, which is accounted the imperial seat of the Ottoman Empire, for these are the three schools or colleges of education. Those that are preferred to the last-named are commonly marked out by special designation and are a nearer step to degrees of preferment are delivered to the charge of the Capi Agassi, or chief of the White Eunuchs. The eunuchs have the care of these scholars committed unto them, whom they treat with an extraordinary severity, for these, being the *censores morum*,[125]

---

[122] Quintus Curtius Rufus (d. c. 53 CE or later) was a Roman politician and historian, whose only extant work, the *Historiae Alexandri Magni*, originally written in ten books, survives now in eight incomplete books. Tacitus says that some people claimed that Curtius was the son of a gladiator (*Annals* 11.21). There is a standard Loeb edition, with translation by John C. Rolfe (Cambridge, MA: Harvard University Press, 1946), and a good recent translation by John Yardley (Harmondsworth, UK: Penguin Books, 1984). Translation: "For all barbarians have respect for physical presence, believing that only those on whom nature has thought fit to confer extraordinary appearance are capable of great achievements" (*The History of Alexander* 6.29; Yardley translation, 128).

[123] Pera was part of the district in Istanbul now known as Beyoğlu; the name Pera persisted until the early part of the twentieth century. "Pera," Lynn Levine tells us, to this day "recalls a bygone era of wealth, entitlement and gaiety" (*Frommer's Istanbul* [Indianapolis: Wiley Publishing, 2008], 46). Orhan Pamuk remembered the poet Yahya Kemal, who lived there, describing Pera as "the district where one never hears a call to prayer" (*Istanbul*, 257).

[124] Adrianople, now called Edirne, is located in Eastern Thrace near the Bulgarian border. An ancient city, it was later adorned with buildings by Hadrian, who changed its name to Hadrianopolis, and it was the Ottoman capital from 1365 to 1453. "The extent of this city, as enclosed by the ancient walls, is not very great," Busbecq wrote in 1555; "but it has spacious suburbs, the buildings of which, added by the Turks, greatly increase its size" (*Turkish Letters*, 16).

[125] The censors of morals.

punish every slight omission or fault with extreme rigour. For eunuchs are naturally cruel, whether it be out of envy to the masculine sex which is perfect and entire or that they decline to the disposition of women, which is many times more cruel and revengeful than that of men. They will not let slip the smallest peccadillo without its due chastisement, either by blows on the soles of the feet or long fastings, watchings or other penance, so that he who hath run through the several schools, orders and degrees of the Seraglio must needs be an extraordinary mortified[126] man, patient of all labours, services, and injunctions, which are imposed on him with a strictness beyond the discipline that religious novices are acquainted with in monasteries, or the severity of Capuchins[127] or holy votaries. But yet, methinks these men that have been used all their lives to servitude and subjection should have their spirits abased, and when licensed from the Seraglio to places of trust and government, should be so acquainted how to obey as to be ignorant how to rule, and to be dazzled with the light and liberty and overjoyed with the sense of their present condition and past suffering, passing from one extreme to another, that they should lose their reasons and forget themselves and others. But in answer hereunto the Turks affirm that none know so well how to govern as those who have learned to obey; though at first the sense of their freedom may distract them, yet afterwards the discipline, lectures, and morality in their younger years will begin to operate and collect their scattered senses into their due and natural places.

But to return from whence we have a little digressed. These young men, before they are disposed into their schools, which are called *oda*,[128] their names, country and parents are registered in a book, with their allowance of four aspers a day. The copy of this book is sent to the *defterdar*,[129] or Lord Treasurer, that so quarterly they may receive their pension. Being thus admitted, they are entered into one of two schools, that is to say into the *bojuk oda*, which is the Great Chamber, or the less. The former commonly contains 400 and the other one 200 or 250. These two schools may be said to be of the same form or rank, and what is taught in one is likewise in the other; neither of them hath the precedency, all of them equally near to preferment. Their first lessons are silence, reverence, humble and modest behavior, holding their heads downwards and their hands across before them; their masters the khojas instruct them in all the rites, discipline and superstition of the Muhammadan religion and to say their prayers and understand them in the Arabic language, and to speak, read and write Turkish perfectly. Afterwards, having made proficiency in the former, they proceed in the

---

[126] Here, "disciplined by self-denial" or even asceticism.

[127] The Capuchin order of friars, founded in 1520, was known for its extreme austerity and severe rules of conduct.

[128] *Oda* signifies a chamber (Rycaut's note).

[129] Literally, "book-holder." The term may be applied to any financial official in the Ottoman bureaucracy.

study of the Persian and Arabic tongues, which may be of benefit to them if their lot chance to call them to the government of the eastern parts, and is a help to the improvement of their knowledge in the Turkish, which, being itself barren, is beholding to those tongues for its copiousness and enrichment.

Their clothing is good English cloth and linen, neither fine nor coarse; their diet is chiefly rice and other wholesome meats which become the table of scholars, where there is nothing of superfluity as there is nothing of want. Their manners and behavior are strictly watched by the eunuchs their careful guardians, so as they cannot be familiar with one another at any time without modesty and respect to the presence they are in. If they go to perform the necessary offices of nature or to the bath, they are never out of the eye of an eunuch, who will admit none of their nearest relations to speak with them or see them unless special license be obtained from the Capi Agassi, or chief of the eunuchs. Their bedchambers are long chambers where all night lamps are kept burning; their beds are laid in ranks one by another upon *safras* or boards raised from the ground, and between every five or six lies an eunuch, so as conveniently to see or overhear if there be any wanton or lewd behavior or discourse amongst them.

When they are arrived to some proficiency and almost to man's estate and strength of body, fit for manly exercises, they are trained up in handling the lance, throwing the iron bar, drawing the bow and throwing the *gerit* or dart. In all these exercises they spend many hours being constant in all or some of them, and are severely corrected by their eunuch if they seem to be remiss or negligent therein. Many of them spend much time principally in drawing the bow, in which they proceed from a weaker to one more strong, and by continual exercise and use come at last to draw bows of an incredible strength, more by art and custom than of pure force, and thus by constant bodily exercise they become men of great strength, health, and agility, fit for wars and all active employments.

Amongst their other exercises, horsemanship is a principal lesson, both to sit in a handsome posture and to manage their horse with dexterity, to draw the bow on horseback forwards, backwards, and on either side, which they learn with that agility and pliantness of their joints in the full career or speed of the horse as is admirable. They learn also to throw the *gerit* or dart out of their hands on horseback, which, because it is a sport of recreation the present Grand Signior delights in above all others, everyone in hopes of preferment and in emulation one of the other, endeavours to be a master in it, and most are so dexterous that they will dart a stick of above three-quarters of a yard long with that force that where it hits it will endanger breaking a bone. The Grand Signior every day passes his time with seeing his pages exercised in this sport, in which ordinarily one knocks another from his horse, and seldom a day passes in which some receive not bruises or desperate wounds. The Sultan doth many times appoint days of combat between the Black Eunuchs and some of his White Pages on horseback in this manner with the *gerit*, and then happens such a skirmish with such emulation, each side contending for the honour of his colour, race, and dignity with that heat and courage as if they contended for the empire, this pastime seldom concluding without some blood. But it is to be noted that none of these exercises are performed by any of those that belong to the two Chambers, unless within the walls of the Seraglio. The other pages, who accompany the Grand Signior abroad, are such as are preferred to farther and higher Chambers, as hereafter we shall discourse.

To the former lessons of school-learning and exercise abroad are added some other accomplishments of trade, handicraft, or mystery in which a man may be useful to the service of the Grand Signior, as to sew and embroider in leather (in which the Turks exceed all other nations), to make arrows and embroider quivers and saddles and make all sorts of furniture. Some learn to fold up a turban, others to fold up, clean, and brush vests, to wash and clean in the bath, to keep dogs and hawks, others to excel in the Turkish manner of music, and all other services which may keep them from idleness and wherein they may be of future use to their great master. And according hereunto, pashas and great men have been denominated and surnamed after their departure from the Seraglio to their places of office and trust.

Such as before have made good proficiency in their studies and attained to a dexterity in their bodily exercises are transplanted to the first step of preferment, which is the washing the Grand Signior's linen, and here they first change their cloth for satin vests and cloth of gold, and their pay and salary is augmented from four or five aspers a day to eight or more. Thence they pass, as places fall, to the *hazine oda*, or Chamber of the Treasury, or to the *kiler* or dispensatory, where the drugs, cordials and rich drinks for the Grand Signior's service are kept. Out of those two chambers they are elected in order to the highest and supreme place in the Seraglio, which is called the *haz oda*, which consists of 40 pages; these attend immediately on the person of the Grand Signior, and amongst them twelve hold the chief offices of the court, *viz.*

1. The *Silahdar-Aga*, the King's Sword-bearer.
2. The *Çokadar-Aga*, he who carries his cloak or vest for rainy weather. [130]
3. The *Rikabdar-Aga*, he that holds his stirrup.
4. The *Mataraci-Aga*, he that carries his water to drink or wash.
5. The *Telbendar-Aga*, he that makes up his turban.
6. The *Çamaşir-Aga*, he who keeps the wardrobe and oversees the washing the linen.
7. The *Caşnigir-Aga*, the chief sewer. [131]

---

[130] Head valet: çokadar means "waterproof" (Ottavio Bon, *The Sultan's Seraglio*, trans. George Withers, intro. and ann. Geoffrey Goodwin [London: Saqi Books, 1996], 157). For Rycaut's indebtedness to this work, see the Introduction.

[131] Actually he was the chief taster, not the steward or sewer (Ådahl, *Sultan's Procession*, 227).

Cbrists Aga or he that brings the bason to the Grand Signior

Selictar Aga or Sword bearer

Tulbentar Aga or he who makes the Grand Signior Turbant

A page of the Hazoda     .29. P

8. *Zagarcişi Başi,*[132] the chief over the dogs.
9. *Turnaci Başi,* he who pares his nails.
10. *Berber Başi,* chief barber.
11. *Muhasebeci Başi,* the chief accountant.
12. *Tezkereci Başi,* his secretary.[133]

There are also two other officers in the court of great respect, the Doğanci başi or chief falconer, and the Hamamci başi, or chief over the baths, but these have their offices and lodgings apart, and, not entering into the royal chamber, are not capable of higher preferment.

There are nine also, called *Ars agalar,* who have the privilege of presenting petitions like masters of the requests; of these, four are of the *haz oda,* as the *Silahdar-Aga, Çokadar-Aga, Rikabdar-Aga, Telbendar-oğlani,* and the others are of different offices, as the *Hazna Kiahiasi,* who is the second officer of the Treasury, [the] *Kiler Kiahaisi,* who is overseer of the provisions of sherbets, sugars, sweetmeats etc., [the] *Doğanci başi,* or chief falconer, the *Haz oda başi,* or principal commander of the royal chamber, and [the] *Kapi Agassi,* or chief commander of the pages, all which are first and nearest to preferment and to be employed abroad in the office of pasha, as places are void.

Those that are thus through the grace and favour of the Sultan arrived to the dignity of being of the royal chamber, where they enjoy the honour and privilege of being constantly in his eye and presence, are often presented by him with swords, vests, bows, and the like, and are permitted to take rewards for the intercessions and applications they make in behalf of others. Sometimes he sends them on message to pashas, sometimes for the confirmation of the princes either in Transylvania, Moldavia, or Wallachia, sometimes to carry presents to the Vizier and great men, in all which employments they are greatly entertained with money, jewels, and rich furniture for horses, so that very few of these forty but in a short time gain estates of their own fir to equip and furnish them to enter into any offices of the empire. As offices fall in order, supplies are made out of these, others arising from lower chambers successively in their places, whether it be to the four most considerable governments, which are Cairo, Aleppo, Damascus, and Buda, or, if none of these places be void, to be *beglerbegs* of Greece or Anatolia. To be aga of the Janissaries, *Sipar Salar* or general of the horse, or to some small *pashaliks* or governments scattered in several places of the empire. But

[132] *Başi* means "head."
[133] Rycaut seems to have got this list almost verbatim from Ottavio Bon, although Withers translated some of the titles slightly differently. Bon has the same number of officials listed in exactly the same order up until 12, when he adds two more (Bon, *The Sultan's Seraglio,* 73–74). However, he might also have consulted Baudier, *History of the Serraill and of the Court of the Grand Seigneur,* trans. Edward Grimeston (London, 1635; repr. La Vergne, TN: Nabu Reprints, 2012), 128–29. Here, as with Bon, the list is almost identical.

we shall not need here to discourse of the particular offices and dignities within the power and gift of the Grand Signior, intending to make a distinct chapter of the several offices, governments, dignities, and places from whence the Grand Signior's profits arise, that so we may the better describe the wealth of this empire and the importance of those offices for discharge of which young men are educated with the care aforementioned.

But before the conclusion of this chapter it will be necessary to add that none, unless by special grace, are advanced from the Seraglio until the age of about 40 years, by which time they are ripe and mature for government and the wantonness and heat of youth allayed. Before their departure to their places of trust they are courted and honoured by all with presents; the Queen Mother, the Sultanas, the rich eunuchs, the Great Vizier, and officers abroad concur all to adorn them with gifts and riches at their advancements, as undoubted consequents of the Grand Signior's favour. And at the farewell, with much submission they visit the Kapi Agassi or chief of the eunuchs and other principal officers of the Seraglio, recommending themselves in the time of their absence to their good grace and favour, desiring to live in their good opinion and friendship. And this is done with much ceremony and compliment, as is exercised in the most civil parts of Christendom, for though the Turks, out of pride and scorn, comport themselves to Christians with a strange kind of barbarous haughtiness and neglect, they are yet among themselves as courtly and precise in their own rules of compliment and civility as they are at Rome or any other parts of the civilized world.

## Chapter VI. *Of the Method of the Turkish Studies and Learning in the Seraglio.*

We have rather showed in the foregoing chapter the education of young scholars in reference to exercise of body and dexterity in arms than the method of their studies and speculations according to the manner of our seminaries and colleges, which more respect the cultivation of the mind with the principles of virtue and morality and the notions of sublime reason than the improvements of the body by assiduity of exercise, which makes them become more active and begets an agility in the management of arms. And though the latter is a business most attended to by sprightly and ingenious spirits, who know preferments in the Ottoman court have always depended, and still do, on the virtue of the sword, yet speculation and knowledge in sciences are not wholly estranged from their schools, which we shall in brief touch upon to satisfy the curiosity of our academies, who I know would gladly be resolved what sort of physical or moral philosophy, what sort of tongues and sciences fall within the contemplation of that barbarous ignorance of the Turks. To elucidate which, the most clearly that I can, according to the best information of the learned Turks, it is reported by the kalfas[134] or pedagogues of the Seraglio that their chief design is to instruct their scholars in reading and writing, so as they may have some inspection into the books of their law and religion, especially the Alcoran, whereby may be produced in their minds a greater reverence to them. For being once passed from the first form of their ABC and joining syllables, they are then instructed in the Arabian tongue, wherein all the secrets and treasure of their religion and laws are contained and is a necessary accomplishment of a pasha or any great minister in relation to the better discharge of his office, being thereby enabled to have an inspection into the writings and sentences of the kadis[135] or other officers of the law within his jurisdiction, as well as furnished with knowledge and matter of discourse concerning religion.

And to adorn these young candidates of the Grand Signior's favour with more polity and ingenious endowments, the next lesson is the Persian tongue, which fits them with quaint[136] words and eloquence becoming the court of their prince and corrects the grossness and enriches the barrenness of the Turkish tongue, which in itself is void both of expression and sweetness of accent. It teaches them also a handsome and gentle deportment, instructs them in romances,[137]

---

[134] Assistant schoolmasters.

[135] Magistrates or lawgivers.

[136] Here, perhaps, "charming," but may also suggest "old-fashioned" or even "formal." Persian words are often found in poetry, as Turkish words frequently do not fit the Persian poetic meters employed by Ottoman writers.

[137] Here Rycaut means fiction about chivalry, or "high" romances. A famous Turkish example might be the *Gul ü Navruz,* en epic romance about Timur (Tamerlane)

raises their thoughts to aspire to the generous and virtuous actions they read of in the Persian novellaries,[138] and endues them with a kind of Platonic love each to other, which is accompanied with a true friendship amongst some few and with as much gallantry as is exercised in any part of the world. But for their amours to women, the restraint and strictness of discipline makes them altogether strangers to that sex; for want of conversation with them they burn in lust one toward the other, and the amorous disposition of youth, wanting more natural objects of affection, is transported to a most passionate admiration of beauty wheresoever it finds it, which, because it is much talked of by the Turks, we will make it a distinct discourse by itself.[139] The books they read commonly in the Persian language are: *Danisten, Schaidi, Pend-attar, Giulistan, Bostan, Hafiz,* and the Turkish books called *Mulamma,* or a mixture of the Arabian and Persian words both in prose and verse, fectious and full of quick and lively expressions. Of these sorts of books, those most commonly read are called *Kirkwizir, Humaiun-name* or *Delile wa Kemine, El fulceale, Seid-batal,* and various other romances.[140] These are usually the study of the most airy and ingenious spirits amongst them.

---

composed in about 1411 by the poet Lutfi (c. 1367–1463) and based on a Persian original. Rycaut discusses some more of these below.

[138] Collections of stories.

[139] This passage (and the next chapter) has occasioned some controversy. For example, James Neill remarks that "The fact that some of the boys were sent to be trained for service in the Sultan's harem illustrates the extent to which the boys were regarded as sexual objects" (*The Origins and Role of Same-Sex Relations in Human Societies* [Jefferson, NC: McFarland, 2008], 313). That the word *seraglio* can refer to a palace or court in general, not just the women's quarters, has evidently escaped this writer, who also thinks that Rycaut is a French author.

[140] These books (left here in Rycaut's spelling) are as follows. *Danisten* may refer to the the *Danişmend-nameh,* a work which celebrates the exploits of the Danishmend emirs of Anatolia; *Schaidhi* probably refers to the *Thousand and One Nights* and its heroine Scheherezade; the *Pend-nameh* or *Book of Counsels* is by the Persian poet Farid ud-din 'Attar (c. 1145–1221); the *Gulistan* or *Rose-Garden* of Muslih ed-Din Sa'adi (c. 1184–1283) is a very well known Persian work containing a great deal of wisdom, and had already been translated into English by Rycaut's time; the *Bostan* or *Fruit-Orchard* is also a work of anecdotes and wisdom by Sa'adi; Hafiz (c. 1325–1390), of course, is the great Persian poet, not his book, which is called the *Divan; Mulemma* is simply a word used to denote narrative romances in general; *Kalila wa Dimna* is a collection of didactic fables originating in India and known also, after multiple redactions, as *Fables of Bidpai* and available in an English as *The Moral Philosophy of Doni* by Sir Thomas North (1570). This has been edited by D. Beecher, J. Butler, and C. Di Biase (Ottawa: Dovehouse Editions, 2006). The connection with the *Humayun-nama* by Princess Gulbadan Begum (1523–1603), the life of the Mughal Emperor Humayun (d. 1556), seems to be a mistake; they are separate books. The *Qirk Wazir,* or *History of Forty Viziers,* is a collection of folk tales. There is now an English version by E. W. Gibb (1886), but Rycaut could only have known Charles Perrault's translation of the "Twenty-ninth Vizier's Tale;" *El fulceale* is probably *Al-Kanz*

Those others who are of a complexion more melancholic and inclinable to contemplation proceed with more patience of method and are more exact in their studies, intending to become masters of their pen and by that means to arrive to honour and office either of *Reis Effendi* or Secretary of State, Lord Treasurer or Secretary of the Treasury or Dispensatory etc., or else to be *imams* or parish priests of some principal mosques or royal foundation, in which they pass an easy, quiet and secure life with a considerable competency of livelihood. Others aim in their studies to become *hafizi*,[141] which signifies a conserver of the Alcoran, who get the whole Alcoran by heart and for that reason are held in great esteem and their persons as sacred as the place which is the repository of the law.

Those who are observed to be more addicted to their books than others are named by them *talibulilmi*[142] or lovers of philosophy, though very few amongst them arrive to any learning really so-called, yet they attain to the degree of Readers of the Alcoran for benefit and relief of the souls of those departed, who for that end have bequeathed their legacies. At certain hours they read books that treat of the matters of their faith and render them out of Arabic into Turkish, and these books are: *Shurut, Salat, Mukad, Multeka, Hidaie* etc.,[143] which they descant upon[144] in an expository manner, instructing the more ignorant and of lower form by way of catechism. They have also some books of poetry written both in Persian and Arabic, which run in rhyme and meter like the "Golden Verses" in Pythagoras,[145] containing excellent sentences of morality, being

---

*al-madfn wa al-Fulk al-mashn*, by Yunus al-Malik (d. 1349); the *Battal Ghazi* refers to epic poems about an Arab hero of that name (c. 690–740) who fought against paganism and whose exploits were considered a great example. Several Turkish films based on it have been made. For more information, see, for example, Carter V. Finley, *The Turks in World History* (Oxford: Oxford University Press, 2005), 72–74.

[141] Rycaut is correct; the term *hafiz* means "one who has memorised the Quran." He spells it *hazifizi*.

[142] Young men preparing to become imams. The word may be familiar in its more sinister Farsi or Pushtun form, *taliban*, which translates as "students."

[143] Some of these terms, which are left in Rycaut's spelling, are not books. The *shurut*, which means "pre-conditions," are instructions for Muslims as they get ready for prayer, which is the *salat*. The term *mukad* likely refers to a book, the *Muqaddimah* or *Universal History* of Ibn Khaldun (1332–1406), which may be found in a modern translation by Franz Rosenthal and N. J. Dawood (Princeton, NJ: Princeton University Press, 1967). *Multeka* may be Rycaut's version of *multaqa*, which means "meeting-place." *Hidaie* has not been identified, but may mean *hadith*.

[144] Discuss at great length.

[145] The so-called "Golden Verses" comprises seventy-one lines of moral precepts in dactylic hexameters attributed, probably falsely, to Pythagoras (c. 570–495 BCE) and available to Rycaut in various editions. There is an English translation by Nayan Louis Redfield (Whitefish, MT: Kessinger Reprints, 1992); the eminent playwright Nicholas Rowe issued a version in 1726, a little too late for Rycaut.

directions for a godly life and contemplation of the miseries and fallacies of this world, which many of them do commit to memory and repeat occasionally as they fall into discourse. For other sciences, as logic, physic, metaphysic, mathematics, and other our university learning, they are wholly ignorant, unless in the latter, as far as music is a part of the mathematics, whereof there is a school apart in the Seraglio. Only some that live in Constantinople have learned some certain rules of astrology, which they exercise upon all occasions and busy themselves in prophecies of future contingencies of the affairs of the empire and the unconstant estate of great ministers, in which their predictions seldom divine grateful or pleasing stories.

Neither have the wisest and most active ministers or soldiers amongst them the least inspection into geography, whereby to be acquainted with the situation of countries or disposition of the globe, although they themselves enjoy the possession of so large a proportion of the universe.[146] Their seamen, who seldom venture beyond sight of land unless they be those of Barbary, who are renegades and practiced in the Christian arts of navigation, have certain sea-charts ill-framed, and the capes and headlands so ill laid-down that in their voyages from Constantinople to Alexandria, the richest place of their trade, they trust more to their eye and experience than the direction of their maps, nor could I ever see any chart of the Black Sea made either by Turk or Greek which could give the least light to any knowing seaman so as to encourage him, according to the rules of art, to lay any confidence thereon in his navigation.

The art of printing, a matter disputable whether it hath brought more of benefit or mischief to the world, is absolutely prohibited amongst them[147] because

---

[146] Rycaut is completely wrong here. Bernard Lewis tells us that "the first serious reports in Arabic about western Europe that have survived appeared during the ninth century" and were based on Arabic translations of Ptolemy. He notes that "the first Muslim geographer whose work has come down to us was a certain Ibn Khurradadbheh" (*The Muslim Discovery of Europe* [New York: Norton, 2001], 137–38). In fact, the whole of Chapter 5 in Lewis's book, (135–70) gives the lie to any notions of ignorance, if not of accuracy. Furthermore, Rycaut does not seem to have known, for example, the Ottoman admiral Piri Ra'is's map (1513), which showed parts of Africa, South America, and even Antarctica, which, assuming it is genuine, indicates that some Ottomans were very much aware of the world around them. See Svat Soucek, *Piri Reis and Turkish Mapmaking after Columbus* (London: Nour Foundation, 1996).

[147] Rycaut is correct; the first Turkish printing press appeared in 1729, only to be closed down by the government in 1742, and re-opened finally in 1784. For details, see Bernard Lewis, *Muslim Discovery*, 168–70. However, Rycaut did not seem to know that the Jews had had their own press since 1494, the Armenians since 1567 and the Greeks since 1627. None of these groups, however, was allowed to print anything in Turkish or Arabic. Much opposition to the introduction of printing came from religious authorities, and the result was, in part, the ignorance which Rycaut discusses above, coupled with illiteracy.

it may give a beginning to that subtlety of learning which is inconsistent with as well as dangerous to the grossness of their government, and a means to drive many of their livelihood who gain their bread only by their pen, and occasion the loss of that singular art of fair writing, whereof they excel or equal most nations, the effect of which is evident amongst the Western people, where printing hath taken footing. And though there be few historians among them who have any knowledge of past times or the beginning of other empires before the Ottoman, mixing all stories in confusion together, as we have said before, without distinction of persons or respect of chronology, yet as to the success and progress of affairs in their own dominions, they keep most strict registers and records, which serve them as precedents and rules for the present government of their affairs.

And thus the reader may sound the depth of the Turks' philosophy, who though they reach not those contemplations of our profound sophies, have yet so much knowledge as neither to be overreached in their treaties with the wits of the world, nor for want of good conduct of affairs lose one inch of their empire.

**Chapter VII.** *Of the Affection and Friendship the Pages in the Seraglio bear each other.*

Since in the foregoing chapter we have made mention of the amorous disposition that is to be found among these youths to each other, it will not be from our purpose to acquaint the reader that the doctrine of Platonic love hath found disciples in the schools of the Turks, that they call it a passion very laudable and virtuous, and a step to that perfect love of God whereof mankind is only capable, proceeding by way of love and admiration of his image and beauty enstamped on the creature. This is the colour of virtue they paint over the deformity of their depraved inclinations, but in reality this love of theirs is nothing but libidinous flames to each other, which they burn so violently that banishment and death have not been examples sufficient to deter them from making demonstrations of suchlike addresses, so that in their chambers, though watched by eunuchs, they learn a certain language with the motion of their eyes, their gestures, and their fingers to express their amours. And this passion hath boiled sometimes to that heat that jealousies and rivalries have broken forth in their chambers without respect to the severity of their guardians, and good orders have been brought into confusion, until some of them have been expelled the Seraglio with the tippets[148] of their vests cut off, banished into the islands and beaten almost to death.

Nor is this passion only amongst young men each to other, but persons of eminent degree in the Seraglio become inveigled in this sort of love, watching occasions to have a sight of the young pages that they fancy, either at the windows of their chambers or as they go to the mosque or to their washings or baths, offer them service and presents, and so engage them as to induce them to desire to be made of the retinue of him that uses this courtship towards them, which they many times obtain, and being entertained in the service of a master who so highly fancies and admires them, they become often sharers with him in his riches and fortune.

The Grand Signiors themselves have also been slaves to this inordinate passion. For Sultan Murad [IV] became so enamoured of an Armenian boy called Musa as betrayed him, though otherwise a discreet prince, to a thousand follies, and at another time preferred a youth for his beauty only from the novitiate of Galata to be one of the pages of his *haz oda* or Chamber of his Royal Presence, and in a short time made him *Selihtar Aga* or sword-bearer, one of the greatest offices in the Seraglio. And this present Sultan became so enamoured of a Constantinopolitan youth called Güloglü, or son of a slave, that he made him his chief favourite, never could content himself without his company, clothed him like himself, made him ride by his side, commanded all to present and honour him in the same manner as if he had made him companion of the Empire.

---

[148] A tippet, in this case, is probably a long sleeve, although it can refer to a scarf or any other dangling appendage on a coat or jacket.

This passion likewise reigns in the society of women. They die with amorous affection one to the other; especially the old women court the young, present them with rich garments, jewels, money, even to their own impoverishment and ruin, and these darts of Cupid are shot through all the Empire, especially Constantinople, the Seraglio of the Grand Signior, and the apartments of the Sultans.[149]

---

[149] Love between women seems to have fascinated and appalled European writers in the seventeenth century. Michel Baudier, for example, has a chapter headed "Of the Loves of the great Ladies of the Turk's Court, and of their violent affections among themselves," and describes in some detail how the women "embrace one another and do other actions which love seeks and modesty forbids to write" (*The History of the Imperial Estate of the Grand Seigneurs*, trans. Edward Grimeston [London, 1635], 166). George Sandys is even more explicit, and writes nervously that "Much unnatural and filthy lust is said to be committed daily in the closets of these darksom *Bannias*, yea women with women, a thing incredible, if former times had not given thereunto both detection and punishment" (*Travels*, 54).

# GHAP. VIII.

## *Of the Mutes and Dwarfs.*

*A mute*     *A dwarf*

## Chapter VIII. *Of the Mutes and Dwarves.*

Besides the pages, there is a sort of attendants to make up the Ottoman court called [dilsiz][150] or mutes, men naturally born deaf, and so consequently for want of receiving the sound of words are dumb. These are in number about 40, who by night are lodged amongst the pages in the two chambers, but in the daytime have their stations before the mosque belonging to the pages, where they learn and perfect themselves in the language of the mutes, which is made up of several signs in which by custom they can discourse and fully express themselves, not only to signify their sense in familiar questions, but to recount stories,

---

[150] Rycaut uses the Persian word *bizebani*, but the Turkish word for a mute is *dilsiz* (Ádahl, *Procession*, 221). For details, see M. Miles, "Signing in the Seraglio: Mutes, Dwarfs [*sic*] and Jestures [*sic*] at the Ottoman Court 1500–1700," Santa Barbara, CA: Independent Living Institute, 2000.

understand the fables of their own religion, the laws and precepts of the Alcoran, the name of Muhammad and what else may be capable of being expressed by the tongue.

The most ancient amongst them, to the number of about eight or nine, are called the favourite mutes, and are admitted to attendance in the *haz oda*, who only serve in the place of buffoons for the Grand Signior to sport with, whom he sometimes kicks, sometimes throws in the cisterns of water, sometimes makes fight together like the combat of Clineas and Damoetas.[151] But this language of the mutes is so much the fashion in the Ottoman court that none almost but can deliver his sense in it, and is of much use to those who attend the presence of the Grand Signior, before whom it is not reverent or seemly so much as to whisper.

The dwarves are called *cüce*.[152] These also have their quarters amongst the pages of the two chambers until they have learned with due reverence and humility to stand in the presence of the Grand Signior, and if one of these have that benefit as by Nature's fortunate error to be both a dwarf and dumb, and afterwards by the help of art to be castrated and made a eunuch, he is much more esteemed than if Nature and art had concurred together to make him the perfectest creature in the world. One of this sort was presented by a certain pasha to the Grand Signior, who was so acceptable to him and the Queen Mother that he attired him immediately in cloth of gold and gave him liberty through all the gates of the Seraglio.

---

[151] This is probably a reference not to some ancient Greek myth but to Samuel Butler's satirical poem *Hudibras* (1680, begun 1660), which bears the subtitle "The incomparable Poem of *Gundibert* vindicated from the Wit Combat of 4 Esquires, Clinias, Damoetas, Sancho and Jack-Pudding" (1665).

[152] Rycaut renders this as *giuge*. For details of the dwarves, see Miles, "Signing in the Seraglio."

# Chapter IX. *Of the Eunuchs.*

1. The libidinous flame of depraved nature is so common a disease among the Turks and so ancient a vice that both for state and prevention of this unnatural crime it hath not been esteemed safe or orderly in the courts of eastern princes to constitute others for the principal officers of their household than eunuchs. The like is observed in the Seraglio of the Grand Signior, where two eunuchs especially have the principal command and are persons of the highest and eminentest esteem, *viz.* the Kizlar Ağassi, who is superintendent over the women and is a black eunuch. The other is [the] Kapi Ağassi or Master of the Gate, who is white and commands all the pages and white eunuchs residing in the court. Under him are all the officers that are eunuchs, as first the *haz oda başi* or Lord Chamberlain, who commands the Gentlemen of the Bedchamber.

2. The *Serai Kiahiasi*, Lord Steward of the Household, who oversees the chambers of the pages and the *seferli odasi* or the chambers of those pages who are designed to follow the Grand Signior upon any journey, and of these he hath care to see them provided of clothes and all other necessaries for the service they undertake.

3. The *Haznadar Başi*, or Lord Treasurer of the Seraglio, who commands those pages that attend the treasury. I mean not that which is of present use, as to pay the soldiery or serve the public and present occasions of the empire, for that is in the hands of the *Defterdar*, but that riches that is laid apart for the expenses of the court and that which is amassed and piled up in several rooms of the Seraglio, of which there have been collections and additions in the time of almost every emperor, distinguished and divided by the names of the Sultans through whose industry and frugality they had been acquired. But this wealth is conserved as sacred, not to be used or exposed unless on occasions of extreme emergency.[153]

4. The *Kilargi Başi*, that is, Chief Commander over the Pages, to whose care the charge of the dispensatory is committed, or expenses for the daily provisions. Other officers there are of eunuchs, as he that is first Master of Scholars for their books, called *Ikinji Kapu-oğlani*,[154] and his usher, the chief *Mesjidji* or Priest of the Grand Signior's Mosque, under whom are two other assistants for cleaning and well-ordering of the mosques.

These are the only officers of the White Eunuchs; the others are of commonality, which are in number about fifty, and have ordinarily twelve aspers per day

---

[153] According to Baer, these "riches" were "the precious cloaks such as sable furs of honor kept under the watchful eye of the palace treasurer," which were used "on significant occasions, including conversion ceremonies" (David Baer, *Honored by the Glory of Islam: Conversion and Conquest in the Ottoman Empire* [Oxford: Oxford University Press, 2007], 200). He believes that Rycaut's surmise about "extreme emergency" is not quite correct.

[154] The White Eunuch, who is in charge of the second gate of the Sultan's palace.

**36**                *The Maxims of the* Turkiſh *Politie.*

*Kuzlir-Aga or Black Eunuch of the women*

pay, which also are augmented according to the *wakfi* or legacies of the deceased. Those that are curates of the royal mosques and have pluralities of benefices of that nature have sometimes a revenue of 100 sequins a day. Among these also due order is observed, the younger or juniors in the Seraglio always giving respect and reverence to seniority.

### Of the Black Eunuchs

1. The Black Eunuchs are ordained for the service of the women in the Seraglio, as the White are to the attendance of the Grand Signior, it not seeming a sufficient remedy by wholly dismembering them to take the women off from their inclinations to them as retaining some relation still to the masculine sex, but to create an abhorrency in them. They are not only castrated but black, chosen with the worst features that are to be found among the most hard-favoured of that African race. The prime officer, as we have said before, is the Kizlar Ağassi, or Master of the Maids or Virgins.

2. *Valide Ağassi*, the eunuch of the Queen Mother.

3. *Shahzadeler Ağassi*, or the eunuch to whose charge is committed the royal progeny, and in whose custody at present are three sons of Sultan Ibrahim, brothers to the present emperor, *viz.* Süleyman, on whom the Turks at present found their principal hopes and expectation, Bayezid and Orhan, the mother of which two is still living and confined to the Old Seraglio[155] in Constantinople, which is the monastery of the decayed wives and mistresses of former Grand Signiors, from whence there is no redemption until either their sons die or by good fortune one becomes emperor.[156]

4. *Fazna Ağassi*, or the eunuch that is Treasurer to the Queen Mother, and commands those damsels that are servants in the said chamber.

5. *Kiler Ağassi*, or he that keeps the sugar, sherbets, and drugs of the Queen Mother.

6. *Bujuk Oda Ağassi*, Commander of the Greater Chamber.

7. *Kulchuk Oda Ağassi*, Commander of the Lesser Chamber.

8. *Başi Kapa Oğlani*, the Chief Porter of the Women's Apartment.

9 and 10. Two *Mesjidji Başi*, or the two imams or priests of the royal mosque belonging to the Queen Mother, ordained for the women's prayers.

### The Apartments of the Women

And since I have brought my reader into the quarters of these eunuchs which are the black guard of the sequestered ladies of the Seraglio, he may chance to take it unkindly if I leave him at the door and not introduce him into those apartments where the Grand Signior's mistresses are lodged. And though I ingenuously confess my acquaintance there, as all other my conversation with women in Turkey, is but strange and unfamiliar, yet not to be guilty of this discourtesy I shall to the best of my information write a short account of these captivated ladies, how they are treated, immured, educated, and prepared for the great achievements of the Sultan's affection, and as in other stories the knight consumes himself with combats, watching, and penance to acquire the love of one fair damsel, here an army of virgins make it the only study and business of their life to obtain the single nod of invitation to the bed of their great master.

The reader then must know that this assembly of fair women, for it is probable that there is no other in the Seraglio, are commonly prizes of the sword, taken at sea and at land, as far-fetched as the Turk commands, composed almost of

---

[155] The Old Seraglio was built by Mehmed II (1451–1481). In 1549 Süleyman I made over half the grounds to a religious foundation and built a great mosque there.

[156] Rycaut is a little confused here. The mother of Süleyman [II], Saliha Dilâşub Sultan (1627–1689) was very much alive. A Serbian native originally known as Katarina, she was made Valide Sultan when her son ascended the throne in 1687. Orhan and Bayezid were sons of concubines.

38     *The Maxims of the Turkish Politie.*

*The Apartments of the Women.*

*The habit of a Lady in the Seraglio*

as many nations as there are countries of the world, none of which are esteemed worthy of this preferment unless beautiful and undoubted virgins.

As the pages before-mentioned are divided into two Chambers, so likewise are these maids divided into two *odas*, where they are to work, sew and embroider, and are there lodged on *safawes*, everyone with her bed apart, between every five of which is a *kadin* or grave matron laid to oversee and hear what actions or discourse passes, either immodest or undecent.[157] Besides this school, they have their chambers for music and dancing, for acquiring a handsome air in their carriage and comportment, to which they are most diligent and intent, as that which

---

[157] "By every ten virgins there lies an old woman; and all the night long there are many lamps burning, so that one may see plainly throughout the whole room; which doth keep the young wenches from wantonness" (Bon, *Seraglio* 47).

opens the door of the Sultan's affections and introduces them into preferment and esteem.

Out of these the Queen Mother chooses her court, and orderly draws from the schools such as she marks out for the most beauteous, facetious,[158] or most corresponding with the harmony of her own disposition, and prefers them to a near attendance on her person or to other officers of her court. They are always richly-attired and adorned with all sorts of precious stones, fit to receive the addresses and amours of the Sultan. Over them is placed the *Kadin Kahya* or Mother of the Maids, who is careful to correct any immodest or light behavior amongst them in all the rules and orders of the court.

When the Grand Signior is pleased to dally with a certain number of these ladies in the garden, "*helvet*"[159] is cried, which rings through all the Seraglio, at which word people withdraw themselves at a distance and eunuchs are placed at every avenue, it being at that time death to approach near those walls. Here the women strive with their dances, songs, and discourses to make themselves mistresses of the Grand Signior's affection, and then let themselves loose to all kind of lasciviousness and wanton carriage, acquitting themselves as much of all respect to majesty as they do to modesty.

When the Grand Signior resolves to choose himself a bedfellow he retires into the lodgings of his women, where, according to the story in every place reported, when the Turkish Seraglio falls into discourse, the damsels being arranged in order by the Mother of the Maids, he throws his handkerchief to her where his eye and fancy best directs, it being a token of her election to his bed. The surprised virgin snatches at this prize and good fortune with that eagerness that she is ravished with joy before she is deflowered by the Sultan, and, kneeling down, first kisses the handkerchief and then puts it in her bosom, when immediately she is congratulated by all the ladies of the court for the great honour and favour she hath received. And after she hath been first washed, bathed, and perfumed, she is adorned with jewels and what other attire can make her appear glorious and beautiful. She is conducted at night with music and songs of her companions chanting before her to the bedchamber of the Sultan, at the door of which attends some favourite eunuch, who upon her approaching gives advice to the Grand Signior, and, permission being given her to enter in, she comes running and kneels before him, and sometimes enters in at the foot of the bed, according to the ancient ceremony, or otherwise as he chances to like her, is taken in a nearer way with the embraces of the Grand Signior.

This private entertainment being ended, she is delivered to the care of the *Kadin Kahia* or Mother of the Maids, by whom she is again conducted back with the same music as before, and, having washed and bathed, hath afterwards the lodging and attendants that belong to *Hunkiar Asa-kisi*, that is, the Royal

---

[158] Here used in the sense of "playful" or "witty;" it is not a pejorative term.

[159] This word literally means "solitude."

Concubine. If it be her good fortune to conceive and bring forth a son she is called *Haseki Sultana*[160] and is honoured with a solemn coronation and crowned with a small coronet of gold beset with precious stones. Other ladies who produce like fruits from the Grand Signior's bed have not the like honour, but only the name of *Baş Haseki, Inkingi Haseki*, the First and Second Concubine and so forward.

The daughters that are born from the Grand Signior are oftentimes at four or five years of age wedded to some great pasha or *beylerbey* with all the pomp and solemnities of marriage, who from that time hath care of her education, to provide a palace for her court and to maintain her with that state and honour which becomes the dignity of a daughter to the Sultan. At this tenderness of age Sultan Ibrahim married three of his daughters, one of which, called Gevher Han Sultan, hath already five husbands and yet, as is reported by the world, remains a virgin. The last husband was Ismail Pasha, who was slain in the passage of the river Raab,[161] and is now again married to Gürcü Mehmed Pasha of Buda,[162] a man of 90 years of age, but rich and able to maintain the greatness of her court, though not to comply with the youthfulness of her bed, to which he is a stranger, like the rest of her preceding husbands.

After the death of the Grand Signior the mothers of daughters have liberty to come forth from the Seraglio and marry with any person of quality, but those who have brought forth sons are transplanted to the old seraglio, where they pass a retired life without redemption, unless a son of any of those mothers, by death of the first heir succeeding, release his mother from that restraint and make her sharer with him in all his happiness and glory.

---

[160] Princess-Favourite. The title was usually given only to the first six women who bore sons.

[161] This is the battle of St. Gothard (1664), in which the Austrians and French defeated the Ottoman army under the Grand Vizier Fazil Ahmet Köprölü. The battle took place near the Raba or Raab river on the Austrian-Hungarian frontier. Lord Kinross states that this battle was "the first great defeat in a pitched battle of the infidel Turks by the Christian forces of Europe. It broke that spell of Turkish victories which had started at Mohacs in 1526" (*Ottoman Centuries*, 334). Ismail Pasha, who had married the Sultan's sister and is discussed later by Rycaut, was the second-in-command of the Ottoman army. He "had won notoriety on account of his pitiless inspection tour of Anatolia a few years earlier" (Finkel, *Osman's Dream*, 268).

[162] Gürcü Mehmed Pasha had been Grand Vizier for a short time (1651–1652). He was later made governor of Aleppo, and participated in the battle of St. Gothard.

## Chapter X. *Of the Aciemoğlani.*

We have hitherto spoken of the *içoğlans* or pages, mutes, dwarves, eunuchs and the feminine court; it will now be necessary to speak of the under-officers and servants called *aciemoğlans*, who are designed to the meaner uses of the Seraglio.[163] These are also captives taken in war or bought of the Tatar, but most commonly the sons of Christians taken from their parents at the age of ten or twelve years, in whom appearing more strength of body than of mind, they are set apart for labour and menial services. These are:

1. Porters.[164]
2. *Bostançis* or gardeners.
3. *Baltaçis* or hatchet-men, who cut and carry wood.
4. *Aşçis* or cooks, with all the officers of the kitchen.
5. *Peyks* and *solaks*.[165]
6. Butchers.
7. *Halvajis* or confectioners.
8. The attendants of the hospital of sick pages. And all other set apart for servile offices.

These are seldom the sons of natural-born Turks, but yearly collected, as I said, from the increase of poor Christians in the Morea[166] and Albania, by which means those countries are greatly dispeopled. The yearly number of those collected amount most commonly, as I am given to understand, to about 2000, which, being brought to Constantinople, are first presented before the Vizier, who, according as his humour directs him, are placed in divers stations, either in the seraglios of Galata, Okmeydani[167] or Adrianople. Others are put forth to learn divers trades in the city, others to be seamen and learn navigation; others especially are placed in the great Seraglio, where they are made to serve in the stables, in the kitchen, to dig in the gardens, to cleave wood, to row in the Grand Signior's barge, and to do what other services they are commanded by the superiors set

---

[163] Much of this chapter, including the lists, is derived from Michel Baudier, who has two chapters on these people (*History of the Imperial Estate*, sections 2.1–2.2, 115–24).

[164] The Turkish word is *hammal.*

[165] A *peyk* is a running messenger or a halbardier; a *solak* is a Janissary archer. The word *solak* means "left-handed."

[166] The Morea is a name for the Peloponessus in southern Greece, which was under Ottoman rule.

[167] Okmeydani, which means "place of the arrow," (Jane Taylor, *Imperial Istanbul: A Traveller's Guide* [London: I. B. Tauris, 1998], 192) was originally a lodge built by Mehmed II (1451–1481) where archery contests were held. It is now a neighbourhood in Istanbul, bordered by Kağithane and Şişli districts on the European side of the city; the building is just a few ruins.

The Bustange: Bashaw or Head of the Gardiners

A Helvagi or Confectioner of the Seraglio

A Hasaki or an Officer employed by the
Grand Signor on Pages etc.

The habit of an Agiamoglan

over them, called *oda baçis*, who are men of ancienter standing than the rest, having about fifteen aspers a day salary, two vests of cloth a year, and two pieces of linen cloth for shirts and handkerchiefs etc., and these are subject to the *Bostançi Paşa*, who is the head and absolute commander of all those who have the name of *bostançis* or gardeners, of which there may be 10,000 in and about the seraglios and garden of the Grand Signior.

Of these *bostançis*, some are raised to a higher degree and called *haseki*, which signifies "royal," and attend only to messages sent by the Grand Signior himself, and are men of special authority. Their habit of clothing nothing differs from the *bostançis* unless in the fineness of their cloth, their collar and girdle, according to this picture.

The power of the *Bostançi Paşa* is very great, for though he himself arose but from the *aciemoğlans* and wore a felt cap, yet he hath the command of all the Grand Signior's gardens and houses of pleasure, oversees all his waterworks and hath power and jurisdiction along the Bosphorus unto the mouth of the Black Sea, commands also the country at a large distance from Constantinople, having power to punish all debaucheries and extravagancies in and about the country villages, and is capable by the Grand Signior's favour to become pasha of Grand Cairo, Babylon, Buda etc., and of the first degree, which is Vizier *Azem*.[168]

The *aciemoğlans* who are designed to the Grand Signior's seraglio are of the choicest amongst the whole number, the strongest bodies and most promising aspects, and are distributed into several companies as they want to make up their complement. This discipline is very severe and strict, so that they are taught obedience and readiness to serve with watchings, fastings, and other penances.

Their clothing is of coarse cloth made at Salonica, anciently called Thessalonica, their caps of felt after the form of a sugar-loaf,[169] of a hair colour according as the picture here describes. Some of them are taught to read and write, who are esteemed the most acute and fit to receive ingenious learning, but the most part are exercised in activity of body, in running, leaping, wrestling, throwing the iron bar, and other agility wherein the strength and activity of body is best practiced. Their lodgings are under several pent-houses[170] or sheds built under the walls of the Seraglio. Their diet is flesh and rice, sufficient though not luxurious. Out of these belonging to the Seraglio, none are drawn out for the Janissaries but are sometimes preferred to service of pashas for their fidelity or good deserts, and by those masters arise to considerable riches and commodious manner of livelihood. Others of these, in great numbers, are made use of for attendance on the Grand Signior's tent when he goes to the wars, and in other journeys are

---

[168] Grand Vizier.

[169] A sugar-loaf is tall and conical with a rounded top. It was the traditional shape in which sugar was sold.

[170] Here, an outhouse attached to the wall of a building, probably with a sloping roof.

useful for the management of the Grand Signior's carriages and travelling necessaries. Such *aciemoğlans* (as we have said before) that are distributed into other quarters besides the royal Seraglio are principally designed, as they grow ripe and of strength of body, to be made Janissaries in the place of the deceased, so that their principal education is in order thereunto, of whom we shall speak more largely when we treat of the militia. The names of the *aciemoğlans* are written in a book with the places where they are distributed, their several pays of two, three, or five aspers a day, which book is underwritten by the Grand Signior and consigned to the *Defterdar* or Lord Treasurer, who pays their salaries every three months, being obliged at that time to inquire who is dead or removed, and so accordingly to make a true report to the Grand Signior.

And thus I have given you a brief account of the Grand Signior's Seraglio and the regiment of it, which, if well-considered and weighed, is one of the most politic constitutions in the world and none of the meanest supports of the Ottoman Empire, which relation I had from the mouth of one who had spent nineteen years in the schools of the Seraglio. I must confess I have not treated so amply thereof as the subject might require, because the rules and economy observed among the women, mutes, eunuchs, and other of the retired apartments I conceive to be a kind of digression from my purpose, my intention being principally to describe the government, maxims, and polities of the Turk. And therefore I proceed to treat of the diversities of offices and places of great riches and trust which remain in the power of the Sultan to confer on those favourites, minions and creatures whom thus at his own charge he hath nourished like a father from their infancy to invest in their riper years with great honours, for security of his own person and flourishing estate of his dominions.

*The* ~*Maxims of the* Turkiſh *Politie.*    43

## CHAP. XI.

*Of the* Viſier Azem *or* Prime Viſier, *his Office, the other ſix Vi-ſiers of the Bench, and of the* Divan *or place of* Judicature.

*The Prime Vizier*

## Chapter XI. *Of the Vizier Azem or Prime Vizier, his Office, the other six Viziers of the Bench, and of the Divan, or place of Judicature.*

The Prime Vizier, called in Turkish Vizier *Azem*, is as much as chief counsellor. He is sometimes termed the Grand Signior's deputy or representative. or *Vicarius Imperii*,[171] because to him all the power of the Sultan is immediately devolved. There is no other solemnity, as I know of, in the creating a vizier other

---

[171] Deputy of the Empire. This title was used in Rycaut's time by the Elector of Saxony, and may have been familiar to some of his readers.

than the delivery of the Grand Signior's seal, which he always carries about him in his bosom, on which is engraved the emperor's name, by which he becomes invested in all the power of the empire and can, without the formality and process of law, remove all obstacles and impediments which hinder the free sway of his government. It hath always been the policy of the great princes of the East to erect one as superintendent over all the rest of their ministers; so Daniel was constituted by Darius[172] over the presidents and princes because of the admirable spirit and wisdom that was in him, and Joseph was made chief governor and absolute commander over all Egypt, and by this means those princes who gave themselves over to softness and luxury could with more ease demand account of miscarriages in the rule of their empire, it being their policy to constitute one on whom all the blame of miscarriages in government might be thrown.

The first constitution that we meet with in history of the first Vizier was in the time of Amurath the Third, king of the Turks, who, passing into Europe with his tutor called Lala Shabin,[173] he made him his chief councillor and committed to him the charge of his army, with which he won Adrianople, formerly called Orestias,[174] and ever since the Grand Signior hath continued to maintain the office of vizier, using that common appellation of *Lala*, which signifies "tutor," whenever in familiar discourse he speaks to him.

There are, besides the first, commonly six other viziers who are called Viziers of the Bench, that have no power or authority in the government, but only are grave men that have perhaps had charges and offices and are knowing in the laws and sit, together with the first vizier, in the *divan* or court where causes are tried, but are mute and cannot give their sentence or opinion in any matter unless the First Vizier please to demand their counsel or judgment in point of law, which he seldom does, not to disparage his own reason and experience. Their pay proceeds from the Grand Signior's treasury and is not above 2000 dollars a year; any of these six can write the Grand Signior's *firman* or *tughra*[175] upon all commands or decrees that are sent abroad, and because their riches are but moderate and the office they are in treats not much with the dangerous parts of state,

---

[172] Dan[iel] c. e. (Rycaut's note).

[173] The first Grand Vizier was Çandarli Kara Halil Sayeddin Pasha, who served 1364–1387 under Murad (Amurath) I, not III, and whom Rycaut must mean by *Shabin*. The Ottomans captured Adrianople under Murad I in 1365. The first Grand Vizier to have the prefix "Lala," which means "tutor to the Sultan's son," was Kara Mustafa Pasha (c. 1500–1580), who *was* Grand Vizier 28 April–7 August, 1580 under Murad III (1574–1595). Rycaut appears to have mixed them up, although several members of the Çandarli family served as viziers from the time of Murad I onwards..

[174] This was a name given to the city by Byzantine writers.

[175] The *firman* is an imperial decree; the *tughra* is an elaborately designed calligraphic monogram denoting the name of each Sultan, which serves as a seal or signature on documents and decrees.

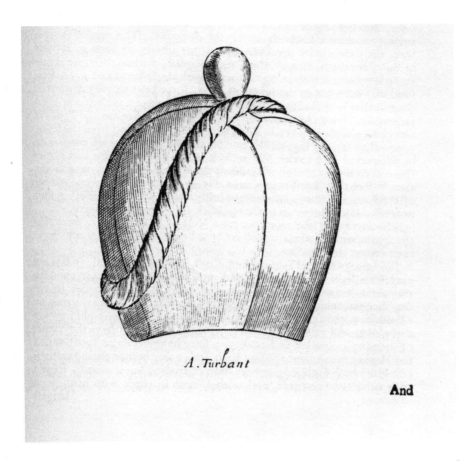

*A. Turbant*

**And**

they live long without envy or emulation or being subject to that unconstancy of fortune and alteration to which greater degrees are exposed. And yet, when any great matter is in consult and of considerable importance, these six, with the first vizier, the Mufti and *Kaziaskers* or Lord Chief Justices, are admitted into the Cabinet Council and are often permitted freedom to deliver their opinions on matters of question.

The state and greatness the Prime Vizier lives in is agreeable to the honour of him whom he represents, having commonly in his court about 2000 officers and servants. When he appears in any solemnity or public show, he carries on his turban before[176] two feathers as the Grand Signior wears three set on with a handle of diamonds and other rich stones, and before him are carried three horsetails, called the *tugh*, upon a long staff, upon the top of which is a gilded knob. The like

---

[176] In front.

distinction of honour is permitted only to the three other principal pashas within
their jurisdiction, *viz.* the Pasha of Babylon, of Cairo, and of Buda. The other
inferior pashas have only one horsetail carried before them, without any other
distinction or badge of authority, and these three forementioned pashas have a
right to be Viziers of the Bench and can take their places in the *divan* when the
time of their offices is expired and any of them found at the court in entire grace
and favour.

The Prime Vizier, as he is the chief representative of the Grand Signior, so
he is the head and mouth of the law. To him appeals may be made, and anyone
may decline the ordinary course of justice to have his case decided by his determination, unless the Vizier, through the multiplicity of his affairs and the small
consideration of the case, thinks fit to refer it to the law. And that he may evidence his care of the public good, he is always present at the *divan* four times a
week, that is Saturday, Sunday, Monday, Tuesday, and the other days, excepting
Friday, keeps *divan* in his own house, so diligent and watchful are these men to
discharge the acts of justice and their own office.

He is attended to the *divan*, which is the chamber of the Seraglio, by a
great number of çavuşes[177] and their commanders-in-chief, who are a sort of
pursuivant,[178] and other officers who only serve to attend him to the *divan*, called
*müteferrika*,[179] and may be termed serjeants or tipstaffs,[180] and as he descends
from his horse and enters the *divan*, he is with a loud voice of his attendants
prayed for and wished all happiness and long life, not unlike the salutations the
Roman soldiers used to their emperors: "*Cum sub auspiciis Caesaris omnia prospera
et felicia precabantur.*"[181] When he is set upon the bench, all causes are brought
before the *Kaziasker*,[182] who is Lord Chief Justice, and by him all judgments pass,
unless the Prime Vizier shall think the cause proper for his cognizance or shall
disapprove at any time the sentence of the judge, and then by virtue of his unlimited power he can reverse the verdict and determine how he pleases. All officers
in the *divan* wear a strange sort of dress upon their heads called in Turkish *mu-
gevezi*, which for the more lively description is delineated in the preceding page.

---

[177] A çavuş [*khiaus*] is an usher or messenger, although it can also denote an ambassador or emissary.

[178] A follower or attendant.

[179] These are actually cavalry officers.

[180] A serjeant keeps order in the courts. Tipstaffs are court officers; however, the
term may also refer to law clerks.

[181] When they prayed for everything to be prosperous and happy under Caesar's
supervision.

[182] See also below. A *kaziasker*, or "army judge," is the second-highest rank in the
Ottoman judiciary system.

The Lord Chief Justices which sit with the Grand Vizier are two, of Rumelia[183] and Asia, called *kaziasker* or Judges of the Army. And this shall, in short, serve for what is necessary to speak of the *divan* in this place, in regard we only touch upon it for the better explanation of the Vizier's office.

The Prime Vizier hath his power as ample as his master who gives it him, except only that he cannot, although he is the elder brother of all the pashas, take off any of their heads without the imperial signature or immediate handwriting of the Grand Signior, nor can he punish a Sipahi or Janissary or any other soldier but by means of their commanders, the militia having reserved themselves that privilege, which secures them from several oppressions. In other matters he is wholly absolute, and hath so great a power with the Grand Signior that whomsoever he shall think fit of all the officers in the empire to proscribe he can speedily obtain the imperial hand to put it in execution.

Whatsoever petitions and addresses are made in what business soever ought first to pass through the hands of the Vizier, but yet, when a party hath suffered some notorious injury in which the Vizier is combined or hath rendered him justice, he hath liberty then to appeal to the Grand Signior himself, which is permitted by an ancient custom: the aggrieved person, putting fire on his head, enters the Seraglio, runs in haste, and can be stopped by nobody until he comes into the presence of the Grand Signior, to whom he hath license to declare his wrong. The like was done by Sir Thomas Bendysh[184] when ambassador at Constantinople, putting pots of fire at the yard-arms of some English ships then in port and coming to an anchor near the Seraglio. The reason thereof was the violent seizure of the merchants' goods as soon as arrived in port for the service of the Grand Signior without bargain or account of them, which, being taken up by those officers and great persons who were out of the reach of law, forced the worthy ambassador at that time resident to represent his grievances with much resolution, signifying them to the Grand Signior by fire on the yards of eleven English ships then in port, which were drawn off from the scale where they usually lay to the side of the Seraglio, which coming to be discovered first to the Vizier before the Grand Signior had notice thereof, he immediately extinguished those fires by a fair accommodation before they burst into a more dangerous flame by the knowledge of the Grand Signior, who might justly destroy him for suffering injustice to run to that public and known extremity. The Persians in like cases put on a vest of white paper, signifying the aggravation of their injury is not to be described in as much paper as can cover their bodies.[185]

---

[183] The term Rumelia, derived from *Rum* (Rome or Byzantium) denotes Ottoman territories in the southern part of the Balkans.

[184] For Sir Thomas Bendysh, second baronet (c. 1607–1674), see introduction.

[185] Much of this material may also be found in chapter 2 of Bon's *Sultan's Seraglio* (33–41).

This great office of charge and trust, as it is the highest, so it is the nearest to Jove's thunderbolt, and most exposed to envy and emulation.[186] Strange stories are read and confirmed by eyewitnesses in our days concerning the unexpected rise and ascent of unworthy men on a sudden without degrees, steps or approaches to this mighty power and glory, and as soon have been thrown down and been the subject of the people's cruelty and revenge. Some have been the sons of but a few days' growth, and the sun hath scarce set before their greatness and glory hath declined. Others have continued but a month, some a year, others two or three, and withal even in those who have lived longest and happiest, fortune sports with that wantonness and inconstancy that it may serve to be the mirror and emblem of the world's vanity and uncertain riches. It is the fate of great favourites with barbarous princes to be but short-lived, for either the prince delights to exercise his power in debasing some and advancing others, or hath bestowed so largely that his bounty is at a stop, and begins to be wearied with heaping of favours as the other is glutted and satiated with receiving them, *"Fato potentiae raro sempiternae, an satias capit aut illos cum omnia tribuerunt, aut hos cum iam nihil reliquam est quod cupiant."*[187] Emulation and flattery are likewise great and the factions are commonly many in the Ottoman court, whereby the state of the first minister is endangered, *"Insita mortalibus natura recentem aliorum felicitatem acribus oculis introspicere, modumque fortunae a nullis magis exigere, quam quos in aequo videns."*[188] Sometimes the Queen Mother rules, sometimes the Kizlar Aga commands; perhaps a beautiful woman is mistress of the power as well as of the affections of the Sultan. Every one of these have some favourites, some or other who watch preferments and are intent to observe all miscarriages of state which may reflect on or question the judgment or honesty of the first author, by which means the unhappy Vizier, either by the Sultan's immediate command or tumults of the soldiery raised by the powerful factions aforementioned, yields up his life and government together, whose power and greatness being only borrowed from his master and depending on another's pleasure verifies that true

---

[186] Here, "emulation" means ambition to surpass someone.

[187] ". . .so rarely is it the destiny of power to last, or whether a sense of weariness steals over princes when they have bestowed everything, or over favourites when there is nothing left for them to desire" (Tacitus, *Annals* 3.30). Rycaut's printer missed out *cum iam* and has *quod* instead; he also writes *capiant* instead of *cupiant.*

[188] "They were acting on the instincts of human nature, which prompt men to keep sharp eyes on the recent elevation of their fellows and to demand a moderate use of prosperity from none more vigorously than from those they are seeing as on a level with themselves" (Tacitus, *Annals* 2.20). Rycaut cites it as *"lib. 3,"* which is mistaken, and has *aegris* instead of *acribus.*

saying of Tacitus: *"Nihil rerum mortalium tam instabile ac fluxum est, quam famae potentiae non sua vi nixae."*[189]

But it doth not always happen that the Prime Vizier, because he is deprived of his office, should therefore lose his life, for many times, especially if he be a man whose disposition is not greatly suspected of malice or revenge to the contrivers of his fall, or be not of a generous spirit and great ability and popularity, whereby he may be capable of raising rebellion or mutiny, he is permitted calmly to retire and quietly to descend from his high throne of honour, to enter into a lower region and air of a small and petty government of a pasha, as not many years past the predecessor of Köprölü, father to this present Vizier,[190] being degraded, had the *pashalik* of Kanisza,[191] which is accounted one of the meanest of all the governments which are subject to a pasha conferred on him. And here I cannot tell whether such a Vizier hath not more reason to bless and congratulate his fortune than accuse it, for in this condition he is more free from cares and dangers and much more happy if his ambition and greatness of spirit render not his repose and ease less pleasing because it is not in the highest lodgings of honour and command. But it is seldom so among the Turks, for with them it is esteemed no disgrace to be transplanted from the mountains to the valleys; they know their original and composition partakes not much of heavenly fire, and that the clay they are framed of is but of common earth, which is in the hand of the Grand Signior as the pot to frame and mould, as is most agreeable to his present will. And as it is no disparagement to decline and go backward in honour amongst the Turks, so it is no new thing or absurdity in their politics to see men rise like mushrooms in a night without degrees or convenient approaches, and from the meanest and most abject offices leap into the seat and quality of the Prime Vizier.

I shall instance one example worthy of record which was of late days, and as yet that I know of, hath had no place in history. It happened that in Constantinople there was either great scarcity of flesh or the negligence of the butchers had made it so, so that they who were not so early abroad as to watch their usual time of making their day's provision, or came anything late, were necessitated to pass

---

[189] "Of all human matters the most precarious and transitory is a reputation for power which does not have any strong support of its own" (Tacitus, *Annals* 13.19). Rycaut cites this as "*lib.* 12."

[190] Köprölü Mehmed Pasha was Grand Vizier 1656–1661; his predecessor was Boynuyarali Mehmed Pasha, an eighty-year-old who was Grand Vizier only from 26 April to 16 September 1656. During Rycaut's time the Grand Vizier was Köprölü Fazil Ahmed Pasha, son of Mehmed, who held the position from 1661 to 1676. For details, see introduction.

[191] Kanisza [*Kanisia*], also known as Nagykanisa, was a walled fortress-town on the southern Hungarian border. It would have been considered a remote outpost. It was a site of fighting with the Hapsburgs in the 1670s.

that day with a Lenten diet. Among those who had missed one morning their common proportion of flesh was one Dervish,[192] a cook of a chamber of Janissaries. This man knew the blows and punishment he was to suffer from the chief of the chamber, that through his sloth and want of care the whole company should that day pass without their dinner, which caused him in great passion with loud exclamations as he passed the streets to accuse the ill-government and little care was had to rectify those common abuses. It fortuned that at that time that Dervish was lamenting his care to all the world and cursing the principal officers, the Grand Signior in disguise passed by, and, seeing a man in such disorder of mind, came in a courteous manner to demand the reason of his passion, to whom Dervish replied it was vain for him to be inquisitive, "Or for me," said he, "to inform you what you are able to afford no remedy unto, for none but the Grand Signior himself is of sufficient power to redress that for which I have so much cause to be troubled." At last, with much importunity, he told what great abuse there was in the butchery, that the shambles[193] were ill-served, that he had missed the usual proportion of flesh that morning for his Janissaries' chamber, and what punishment he was likely to suffer for having come short only one moment of his due time. He added farther that the Vizier and other officers were negligent in rectifying these mean and low disorders, being wholly taken up in enriching themselves and intent to their own interest. "But if I were First Vizier, I would not only cause great plenty of flesh in this city, but at all times of the day it should be found by those who wanted it. And now, what benefit have either you," said he, "by hearing this story, or what release am I likely to have of punishment by repeating it to you?"

The Grand Signior, afterwards returning home and considering of the discourse the Janissaries' cook had made him, whether to prove the abilities of the man or because he conceived Providence had offered this encounter or that princes delight to exercise their power in creating great men from nothing, he sent immediately for Dervish, who being come into his presence and sensible of the familiar discourse he had made him, trembling cast himself down at his feet, supposing that the free language he used of the Vizier and the government was the cause he was now to lose his life. But it happened quite contrary, for the Grand Signior, encouraging him to lay aside his fear, told him he was resolved to make him First Vizier, to try an experiment whether he was able to amend those abuses he complained of, and that herein he might not transgress the degrees whereby he was gradually to pass, he first made him chief of his chamber, the next day captain, the day following aga or general of the Janissaries, and

---

[192] There were two Grand Viziers of this name. Derviş Mehmet Pasha, a former Bosnian, was Grand Vizier in 1606. Koca Derviş Mehmet Pasha, a military man and Kapudan Pasha from 1652, served Mehmet IV as Grand Vizier 1653–1654. If this story is true, it likely applies to the earlier man, because Mehmet IV was still a minor in 1653.

[193] Slaughterhouses.

thence with one step to the Great Vizier, who not only remedied the abuse in the shambles according to his promise, but proved a famous and excellent minister of state. And though examples of the like nature are frequent among the Turks, yet this may serve at present to show in part the fortune and fate by which men are raised, and the unconstancy of greatness and glory amongst the Turks above any other part of the world besides.

It was a hard problem in the Turkish policy which, as a wise Prime Vizier proposed to certain pashas amongst other questions, what courses were possible to be found out for a First Vizier to maintain and continue his office and acquit this so dangerous charge from the hazard and uncertainty to which it is liable. "For you see, brothers," said he, "how few enjoy or grow old herein. Their virtue, their care, and their innocence are no protection; some remain a day, a week, a month, others protract the thread to a year or two, but at length they are (to use our own proverb) like the ants to whom God gives wings for their speedier destruction." The pashas were for a while all silent, not knowing what reply to make, until Köprülü, who was then the most ancient and perhaps the wisest pasha, as the actions of his following life have sufficiently testified, replied that in his opinion the only and most probable means for a tottering Vizier to secure himself is to divert the mind of the Grand Signior and other working brains upon some foreign war, for peace is that which corrupts the dispositions of men and sets them on work to raise themselves with intestine and civil evils. When war busies their spirits and employs them to gain renown by martial actions, by which means plots and treachery are driven from our homes, "*consiliis et astu res externas moliri, arma procul habere.*"[194] And it is possible that [Fazil] Ahmed the son of Köprülü, who began the last war with Germany, might go upon this maxim of his father's, for in all matters of his government he is observed to walk by the same rules and directions which were bequeathed to him as well as his inheritance.

And yet, for all this doubtful estate of the Prime Vizier, some have been known to manage this office 18 or 19 years, and afterwards, wearied with care and pains, to acquit it by a natural death, from whence this question may arise, whether the favour or displeasure of the prince depends on the destiny or fortune we are born to, or whether human counsel can assign a way between contumaciousness[195] and flattery, wherein to steer free from danger and ambition? "*Unde dubitare cogor, fato et sorte nascendi, ut caetera, ita principum inclinatio in hos, offensio in illos, an sit aliquid in nostris consiliis, liceatque inter abruptam contumaciam et deforme obsequium pergere iter, ambitione ac periculis vacuum.*"[196] But we find but few

---

[194] "He clung to his purpose of regulating foreign affairs by a crafty policy and keeping war at a distance" (Tacitus, *Annals* 6.32).

[195] Disobedience, rebellion.

[196] "From which I am forced to doubt whether the liking of rulers for some people and their antipathy towards others depends, like other contingencies, on the fate and destiny we are born to, or, to a degree, on our own plans, so it is possible to steer a course

examples of this kind, for if Viziers have been evil, their own cruelty and covetousness have hastened their fate; if good, their merits have been their ruin. Lest the great benefits their merits have procured to their prince should seem to want reward or be dangerous or difficult to requite, "*beneficia eo usque laeta, dum videntur exsolvi posse; ubi multum antevenere pro gratia odium redditur.*"[197]

The revenues of the First Vizier, which issued immediately from the Crown and are certain appendages to the offices, are not great, being not above 20,000 dollars yearly, which arise from certain villages in Rumelia. The rest of the immense riches which accrues to this charge so full of cares and danger flows from all quarters of the Empire, for no pasha or minister of trust enters his place without his present and offering to the First Vizier to obtain his consent and purchase a continuance of his favour. Those that have governments abroad have always their agents at court, who with gifts continually mollify the Vizier's mind, entreating him to represent their service to the Grand Signior in an acceptable and grateful manner. And though at the equinoctial in the spring all pashas and any that have governments of note are obliged to make their presents to the Grand Signior of considerable value, at which time the First Vizier neither will not want his own acknowledgments, he is yet farther treated by all persons with sums of money as the nature of their business is, which is not secretly but boldly and confidently demanded, and the bargain beaten as in matters of merchandise and trade, and justice and favours made as vendible and set as public to sale as wares and commodities are in the shops and places of common mart, so that if the First Vizier proves covetous, as commonly they do who are raised from nothing and used always to thrift and resolve to lose nothing of what he may get, his income is incredible, and may equal that which is in the rent of the Grand Signior, and in a few years amass immense riches and wealth. But of this the prince and the Turkish polity is not ignorant, and accordingly provides remedies to drain the inundations of the Vizier's coffers, at first by extorting great sums of money from him at his entrance to the charge, then under colour of friendship and favour the Grand Signior makes him visits, in requital whereof rich presents are made him as gratitude for so much honour. Next, he many times sends to him for a gift of 100,000 dollars, for jewels, horses and other things of great value, and in this manner several contrivances are used to turn these rivulets to pay their tribute to the great ocean. Amongst which this present Grand Signior, Mehmed IV, hath found out one way amongst the rest, putting the Vizier often to charges of his dinner, sending to his kitchen for 20 dishes of meat, which is the usual proportion of the Grand Signior's ordinary table, and by inviting himself to a banquet

---

between defiant independence or undignified servility" (Tacitus, *Annals* 4.20). Rycaut's translation is certainly more than adequate.

[197] "Benefits are acceptable insofar as the recipient thinks he can make an adequate return, but if that is exceeded, hatred instead of gratitude is given back" (Tacitus, *Annals* 4.10).

many times at the Vizier's expense, and, this being done so frequently, gives the world occasion to believe that he demands it our of no other design than narrowness of soul to save the charges of his own dinner. And the rather, it is so believed because this Emperor is reputed of a covetous disposition and of no affinity with Süleyman the Magnificent. But the ways and means by which the Grand Signior comes in the end to be possessed of the gains and profits collected by his Vizier and other officers requires a particular discourse apart, which shall in its due time and place be treated of, and this shall for the present suffice to have spoken concerning the Prime Vizier and his office.

## Chapter XII. *The Offices, Dignities and several Governments of the Empire.*

He that will describe the polities of a country must endeavor especially, in the most exact and punctual manner possible, to declare the several offices, dignities and riches of it, that a computation may be calculated of its strength, numbers of men, fortifications, forces by sea, where best defended, and where most easily vulnerable and exposed.

The next to the Vizier *Azem* or First Vizier are the several *beylerbeys*. Which may not unaptly be compared to archdukes[198] in some parts of Christendom, having under their jurisdiction many *sanjaks* or provinces, beys, agas, and others. To every one of these the Grand Signior in honour bestows three ensigns, called in Turkish *tugh*, which are staves trimmed with the tail of a horse with a golden bull on top, and this is to distinguish them from pashas, who have two ensigns, and the *sanjak bey*,[199] who also hath the name of pasha and hath but one. When a pasha is made, the solemnity used at the conferring of his office is a flag or banner carried before him and accompanied with music and songs by the *Mir Alem*,[200] who is an officer for this purpose only, the investiture of pashas in their office.

The government of *beylerbeys*, who have several provinces called *sanjaks* under their command, is two sorts. The first is called *hazile beylerbeylik*, which hath a certain rent assigned out of the cities, countries and seigneuries[201] allotted to the principality; the second is called *saliane beylerbeylik*, for maintenance of which is annexed a certain salary or rent collected by the Grand Signior's officers with the treasure of the whole government, out of which are paid the *sanjak beys*, that is the lords of the several counties, towns or cities and the militia of the country.

It is impossible to describe the wealth and ways of gains exercised by these potent governors to enrich themselves, for a Turk is ingenious to get wealth and hasty to grow rich. Howsoever, we will succinctly set down the certain sums of revenue which are granted them by the commission from the Grand Signior, assigned them out of every particular place of their government, besides which they have profits of all wefts[202] and strays, goods of felons, sale of vacant church-offices,

---

[198] Actually, the comparison is not quite apt. The title "archduke" (*Erzherzog*) was only used for Hapsburg-Lorraine royalty. It ranks below the king or emperor but above dukes, and exists only in the Austrian peerage. Its Russian equivalent is "grand duke." *Beglerbegs* were not necessarily people of royal blood.

[199] *Sanjak beys* were rarely pashas; they were military or civilian administrators in control of a district and directly under the *Vali* or governor. Sometimes, however, they functioned as governors in their own right and answered to the Sultan directly.

[200] The Sultan's standard-bearer.

[201] A *seigneury* (French *seigneurie*; Rycaut uses Italianate *signiorie*) is a freehold estate.

[202] Anything floating around or cast away.

mules, horses, and cattle, which by mortality or other accidents have no certain master, to which may be added the benefit of their *avanias*[203] or false accusations, whereby they invade the right and estates of their subjects by their own slaves and servants, whom they send abroad with that design. And, having committed the robberies themselves, under pretense of discovery of the crime and doing justice, they seize the innocent people, torture and imprison them, and perhaps put some to death for expiation of their own offences. To come nearer then to this purpose: the *beglerbegs* of the first sort are in number 22, who have their revenue allotted them in the places that they govern, collected by their own officers according to commission, of which the first is Anatolia, anciently called Asia Minor, afterwards Anatolia, ἀπό ἡ'Ανατολῆς from its more eastern situation in respect of Greece, the yearly revenue which is in the Grand Signior's books called the old canon, is a million of aspers,[204] and hath under its jurisdiction 14 *sanjak kiotahi* where the *beylerbey* resides in Phrygia Major, Saruhan, Aydin, Kastamonu, Hüdavendigar, Bolu, Menteşe, Angora (otherwise Ancyra), Karabysar, Teke, Kiangri, Hamid, Sultan Ughi, Karesi, with the command of 22 castles.[205]

2. Karamania, anciently called Cilicia, and was the last province which held out belonging to the Caramanian princes when all places gave way to the flourishing progress of the Ottoman arms. The revenue hereof is 660,074 aspers, and hath under its jurisdiction 7 *sanjaks*, *viz.* Iconium, which is the court of the *beglerbeg* in Cappadocia, Niğde, Kaisani (otherwise called Cesanca), Yeneşehir, Kirşehir, Hasibektaş, Aksaray, and in this principality are three castles, at Iconium one, at Laranda and Mendui under the pasha's immediate command, and 17 others in several *sanjaks*.[206]

---

[203] An *avania* or *awâni* was an extortionate tax levied on Christians and some Turkish merchants; the word came to denote any kind of tax that was unjustly levied.

[204] "An asper is about the value of a halfpenny" (Rycaut's marginal note). In Turkish it is *akçe*.

[205] Phrygia is in west central Anatolia; Saruhan was a former emirate in western Anatolia; Aydin is a city in the Aegean region; Kastamonu, known to the Romans as Timonium, is in the Black Sea region; Hüdavendigar is in the modern Eskisehir region, northwestern Turkey; Bolu is in the Black Sea region; Menteşe is a former emirate, now in Muğla Province, southwestern Anatolia; Angora or Ancyra is present-day Ankara; Teke is a former emirate whose capital was Antalya; Hamid emirate is in southwest Turkey, corresponding to present-day Isparta province; Karesi, later Bergama, is on the northern Aegean coast.

[206] Karamania is an interior province of Turkey, east of Anatolia; Iconium, now Konya, is in central Anatolia; Cesanca is in Cappadocia; Niğde is an ancient city in central Anatolia, once a Hittite town; Kayseri was known as Caesarea Mazaca and was the royal capital of ancient Cappadocia; Kirşehir was known as Justinianopolis until 1071, when it was captured by Ottoman forces; Yenişehir or "New City" is a town fifty-five kilometres east of Bursa in southwest Anatolia, the Ottoman capital until 1402; Haçibektaş in central Anatolia was named for the Sufi saint of the same name (c. 1209–1271); Ak-

3. Diyarbakir, otherwise Mesopotamia, hath a revenue of a million two hundred thousand and sixty aspers, and hath under its jurisdiction 19 *sanjaks* with five other governments, called *hukumet* in Turkish, eleven of which *sanjaks* are properly belonging to the Ottoman royalties, and eight are Kurdian countries of the people called Kurds, for when Kurdia was conquered the country was divided and distinguished into the nature of *sanjaks*, but with this difference, of right inheritance and succession to the goods and possessions of their parents and succeed as lords of manors or to other petty governments by blood and kindred. And as other lords of *sanjaks*, *timariots* or barons pay the Grand Signior's duties and hold their lands in knights' service or other tenure, whereby they are obliged to attend and follow their commanders to the wars whensoever they are called thereto by the Grand Signior. These that are registered for *hukumet*[207] have no *timariots* or lords to command them, but are free from all duties and impositions and are absolute masters of their own lands and estates. Those *sanjaks* which are properly belonging to the Ottoman royalties are Harput, Ergani, Çernik, Nusaybin, Çetmkaya, Çemişgezek, Si'irt, Mayafaraqin, Akçakale, Kala, Habur, Sangiar, otherwise Diyabakir, which is the place of residence of the *beylerbey*. Those *sanjaks* which are entitled upon families are Sağman, Kulab, Mehranieh, Tarjil, Ataq, Pirtek, Chiachqur, Çirmek.[208]

4. Of Sham, otherwise Damascus, the certain revenue of which is a million of aspers and hath under it *sanjaks* 7 with *khaṣṣ*,[209] where the contributions by the *beylerbey*'s officers are collected upon the country and are al-Quds aš-Šharif, alias Jerusalem, Gaza, Safed, Nablus alias Naples in Syria, Ajloun, Bahrulbyaz and Damascus, the city where the *beylerbey* resides. He hath farther three with Saliane, for account of which he is paid by the king's officers, and those are Kadmus, Saida, Beirut, Kirkük, and Çubuk, where there are no *timariots* but the

---

saray in central Anatolia was once a major way station on the Silk Road and is known for Seljuk period buildings. Laranda was the old name for Karaman, which became the capital of Carmania in 1250.

[207] This word translates as "government."

[208] Harput, in eastern Anatolia, is five kilometres from modern Elâziğ, which was built as an extension because the old town, on top of a hill. was difficult to get to in winter. Ergani, also known as Arghana, is now a district of Dyabakir province; Nusaybin is ancient Nisibis, a major city of the old Armenian kingdom, now in Mardin province; Çetmkaya is a rural area in Sivas province; Çemişgezek is listed in 1520 as a *sanjak* of Diyarbakir; Si'irt is also a *sanjak* in Diyarbakir province at the same date; Mayafaraqin is the Syriac name for Martyropolis, now known as Silvan, and one of the possible locations peculated for Tigranocerta, the old capital of Armenia; Akçakale is probably the urban district of that name (there are three districts with the same name in Urfa and Diyabakir, but only one is a *sanjak*) which is now a rural district; Kala is a city in Ceyazir province; Habur is in southeastern Turkey on the Turkey-Iraq border; the others are small towns and villages in the Kurdish region of Anatolia. I have given the modern names.

[209] *Khaṣṣ* is a customs levy which could be collected by the governor.

inhabitants are true and absolute masters of their own estate in the same manner as the Kurds are which we have before-mentioned.[210] The castles here are for the most part demolished and scarcely worth our notice.

5. Is of Sivas, a city in Armenia Major, hath a revenue of nine hundred thousand aspers, and hath under his dominions six *sanjaks, viz.* Amasya, Çurum, Borçka, Demirki, Yanik, Kuyucak, Arapgir, the castles of which are 19.[211]

6. Is the government of the Pasha of Erzurum on the confines of Georgia, hath a revenue of a million two hundred thousand six hundred and sixty aspers, and hath under his government 11 *sanjaks, viz.* Kuruçay, Çerkeş, Kiği, Pasinler, İspir, Hinis, Tercan, Tortum, Meginkerd, Namervan, Kuzucan-Pülümür, Malazgirt, and hath 13 castles.[212]

---

[210] Al-Quds aš-Šharif, an Arab name for Jerusalem, means "the holy sanctuary;" Safed is in the northern district of modern Israel; Nablus is a Palestinian city on the West Bank; Ajloun or 'Aglun is located in modern Jordan; the other names are no doubt familiar to readers. Bahrulebyaz is in the province of Egypt, now named Tevfikiye; Kadmus was listed in 1517 as an urban centre in the province of Tripoli, Syria; Saida (ancient Sidon), which came under Ottoman rule in the seventeenth century, was an urban centre in Damascus province; Beirut is in the province of Damascus, which in 1598 became a *sanjak* of Sayda; Kirkük, now in Iraq, was the capital city of Şehrizor province from the seventeenth century. Çubuk was listed in 1530 as a township in the province of Anatolia, but may also refer to Saubak (see Andreas Birken, *Die Provinzen des Osmanischen Reiches* [Wiesbaden: Reichert, 1976], 246). I am grateful to Professor Virginia Aksan of McMaster University for providing me with a copy of this invaluable and hard-to-find book.

[211] Sivas, now an industrial town, was the capital of Armenia Minor (not Major) under Diocletian (285–305) and was captured by Bayezid I in 1398; Amasya or Amasia, the birthplace of the geographer Strabo, is in northern Turkey above the Black Sea coast; Çorum is an Anatolian city in the central Black Sea area, near the ancient Hittite capital Hattusa, which has been Ottoman since the fourteenth century. Borçka is a township in Trabzon (Trebizond) province, which in 1530 is described as a *kaza*, an area ruled over by a judge; Demirci is in modern-day Manisa province in the Aegean region, and is famous for its carpets; Yanik or Yanik Köy is a town in Aiolis, which may have been the old Greek settlement of Neonteichos (see Birken, *Provinzen*, 143); Kuyukak was, by the sixteenth century, a district in Anatolia; Arapgir, a town in Malatya province at the confluence of the east and west Eurphrates river, was founded by the Vaspurakan Kingdom of Armenia, passed to the Byzantines, and was captured by the Seljuks in 1070.

[212] Kuruçay is now known as Kuruçay Koyu; Çerkeş is in central Anatolia, modern-day Çankin province; Kiği is in eastern Anatolia, modern-day Bingöl province; Pasinler, also known as Hasankale, is forty kilometres east of Erzurum. It is known for Hasankale Castle; İspir, in Erzurum province, is known also as Sper in Armenian (it had a large Armenian population) was captured by the Ottomans from the Persians in 1555; Hinis is in Erzurum province, and boasts ruins of the mosque of Ala-ad-din Bey, constructed in 1735; Tercan was the old capital of the Saltukids of Erzurum, and formerly bore the name of its female ruler Mama Hatun (1191–1200). Tortum is famous for being the site of the Khakuli Monastery, built in the twelfth century by the Georgians, and is situated

7. Is the government of the Pasha of Wan or Van, a city in media, hath a revenue of one million one hundred and thirty-two thousand two hundred and nine
aspers, and commands 14 *sanjaks, viz.* Adilcevaz, Erçis, Muş, Bargiri, Kirikân,
Keşan, Espiye, Ağakis, Ekrad-i Çorum, Benkudre, Kale-i Bayezid, Bardu and
Ogek.[213]
     8. Is the government of the Pasha of Çildir on the confines of Georgia,
hath a revenue of nine hundred twenty-five thousand aspers and commands
nine *sanjaks, viz.* Oltu, Hirtis, Ardanuç, Ardahan, Hacrek, Poshov, Maçlay,
Acarya-yi Ulya, Panak, Perterek.[214]
     9. Is the government of Şehrizor in Assyria, the pasha of which hath a rev-
enue of a million in aspers and commands 20 *sanjaks, viz.* Sörütçuk, Arbil,
Keşap, Shehribazar, Saidile, Köstere, Hezarmard, Dulkadir, Markâve, Hanikin,
Al-Awja, Nurettin, Sepeuzengire, Evren, Tond, Badeberend, Belkis, Biçnik,
Garikula, Renghene.[215]

---

in the Black Sea region of Erzurum province. Namervan is now called Narman. It is in
Erzurum province and was the site of an Armenian massacre; Kuzucan-Pülümür, now
known as Pülümür, is a small town in Tunceli province, eastern Anatolia; Malazkerd,
now Meydan, is mid-way between Erzurum and Van. Known to the West as Manzikert,
it was the site of a huge battle (1071) in which the Seljuk ruler Alp Arslan defeated and
captured the Byzantine emperor Romanus IV Diogenes.
     [213] Adilcevaz is now a township in Bitlis province; by 1550 it was a *sanjak*. Erçis
was a *sanjak* in the province of Van, as was Muş, now a province and provincial capital in
eastern Turkey; Bargiri, also known as Muradiye, was a township in Van, which by 1548
was a *sanjak*; Kirikân was an urban centre in Erzerum province; Keşan was a township in
Sivas province; Espiye was a rural district in the province of Rum near Trebizond; Ağakis
is now a town in Van, which in 1550 was listed as a *sanjak*; Ekrad-i Çorum is in Sivas
province, and is inhabited by Kurds; Benküdre is another Kurdish settlement near the
city of Hanikin in Şehrizor province; Kale-i Bayezid was in 1578 a *sanjak* of Van; Berdi'a
is a town in the Caucasus and Ogek is a township in Anatolia.
     [214] Rycaut has listed ten, not nine *sanjaks*, and there were in fact more (see Birken,
*Provinzen*, 210–12). Oltu is now in north-eastern Erzerum province. It was captured
from Georgia in the sixteenth century; Hirtis is modern-day Camili in Artvin province;
Ardanuç is in the Black Sea region of Artvin province; Hacrek is a *sanjak* of Çildir province; Poshov is in Samtskhe province in the southwest Caucasus region; Maçlay is an
urban centre in Bosnia; Acarya-yi Ulgi is in the southeast; Perterek, where settlements
date back to the Bronze Age, is modern day Yusufeli on the Black Sea region of Artvin
province. The others could not be found in Birken.
     [215] Şerizhor is the old name for Kirkuk, a city and area in Iraq north of Baghdad;
Sörütçuk is a district in Edirne; Arbil is eighty kilometres east of Mosul, and is the largest Kurdish settlement in modern day Iraq, and one of the oldest continually inhabited
sites in the world; Keşap is a district in Trabzon province near Geresun; Shehribazar is in
the Kurdistan district of Iraq; Saidili (tentative identification) was an urban centre near
Konya; Köstere or Tomarza was a district in Kars province; Hezarmard was a *sanjak* of
Şehrizor; Dulkadir is an old emirate situated between the Ottoman border and Egypt;

10. Is the government of Halep or Aleppo, hath eight hundred and seventeenth thousand seven hundred and seventy-two aspers revenue and commands 7 *sanjaks* with *khaṣṣ* and 2 with *salyane*[216] Of the first sort are Adana, [Beled]-Ekrat, Kilis, Birecik, Ma'arra, Gaziantep. Of the other are Matik and Turman, which is Turcomania;[217] of these at this day the revenue is farmed and are not called *sanjaks* but *agalik*,[218] for in them are no *timariots* but every man is lord and master of his own lands. This government hath five castles.

11. Is the government of Maraş near the river Euphrates, situated between Mesopotamia and Aleppo, otherwise called by the Turks Zûlkâdiryye, hath a revenue of 628,450 aspers, and commands four *sanjaks* only, *viz.* Malatya, Asab, Kars, and Samsad, and hath four castles.[219]

12. Is the government of Kibris, otherwise called Cyprus, hath a revenue of five hundred thousand six hundred and fifty aspers and commands five *sanjaks*, *viz.* four with *khaṣṣ*, and are Içili, Tarsus, Alanya, Sîs. The other three, with

---

Markâve was a *sanjak* of Şehrizor; Hanikin (tentative identification) was a district in the provinces of Baghdad and Şehrizor; al-Awja is on the Euphrates, thiorteen kilometres from Tikrit in Iraq; Nurettin (tentative identification) was a district in Bitlis province, near Muş; Evren is near modern-day Ankara; Tond was a district in Karaman province; Belkis or Balkiz is on the Euphrates and is thought by some scholars to be the site of Seleucia, a city built by Seleucus I in 300 B.C.E.; Biçnik was a district in Trabzon province; Garikula is in modern-day Georgia, and Renghene is unidentified.

[216] A *salyane*, which means "annual" in Persian, is territory that can be held on a year-to-year basis.

[217] Aleppo in Syria is the oldest continually inhabited place in the world and was the end point of the Silk Road; Adana is thirty kilometres inland from the Mediterranean Sea in south-east Anatolia; Kilis is on the (modern) Turkey-Syria border, and now is the name of a Turkish province. It has been inhabited since Assyrian times; Birecik, known as Bir and Macedonopolis, is on the Euphrates in Şanliurfa province; Ma'arra, known now as Ma'arat al-Numan, is between Aleppo and Hama in western Syria. It was the site of a massacre during the Second Crusade (1085–1095); Beled-Ekrat is a name for the Kurdish areas; Gaziantep, sixty kilometres north of Kilis, has been settled since Hittite times, and is the site of Antiochia ad Taurum. It is Turkey's sixth-largest city and now has its own province; Turcomania is a general term for the land now occupied by Turks of Syrian descent, known as Yöruks.

[218] An area ruled by an aga.

[219] Mar'aş, also known as Zulkadiriye, is in southeastern Turkey, now in Kahrranmaraş province. It fell to the Ottomans in 1515; Kars is in north-eastern Turkey, and was captured by the Ottomans in 1534 and is now capital of an eponymous province; Malatya is in eastern Turkey. It was in ancient times the Assyrian city of Meliddu, and was captured by the Ottomans in 1515; it is also now capital of an eponymous province. Samsad is on a major trade route to Syria and was also an important station on the pilgrim route. It became a *sanjak* in 1522. Asab could not be identified. For details on this area, see C. E. Bosworth et al, eds. *The Encyclopedia of Islam*, vol. 6 (Leiden: Brill, 1988), 506–10,

*salyane,* are Kyrenia, Bas Musa, Lefkoşia or Larnaka. The place of the pasha's residence is Nicosia.[220]

13. Is the government of Tarablus Sham, otherwise Tripoli of Syria, hath a revenue of eight hundred thousand aspers. At this place the pasha resides and hath under him 4 *sanjaks, viz.* Homs, Hamā, Hermel and Salamiyeh, and hath only one castle in the *sanjak* of Hams called Fazlul Ekrak.[221]

14. Is the government of Terbozan, otherwise Trebizond, encompassed with a ridge of mountains. According to a poet born in that place, *"Vertice montano Trapezus inclusa recessit,"* formerly the imperial seat of the Comneni reigning over Cappadocia, Galatia and other parts of Pontus, founded by Alexius Comnenus, who upon the taking of Constantinople by western Christians fled to this place, which flourished until taken by Mehmed the Great.[222] It is situate on the Euxine or Black Sea and still a place of considerable traffic, especially made rich for fishing, out of which and the customs, the pasha, though he hath no *sanjaks* under his government, hath yet a revenue allotted of 734,850 aspers, with 14 castles to defend the city and the dominions belonging thereunto.

15. The government of the Pasha of Kars, a city near Erzurum, hath a revenue of eight hundred twenty thousand six hundred and fifty aspers, and

---

[220] Larnaka is a city on the south coast of Cyprus, but it is not called Lefkoşia (see Nicosia); Tarsus is in south-central Turkey, twenty kilometres from the Mediterranean and the birthplace of St. Paul. Selim I captured it in 1516. Alanya, on the southern Turkish coast, became a *sanjak* in 1571. It has been continuously inhabited since Palaeolithic times; Sîs became a *sanjak* in 1571; also called Kozan, it is now known as Larnakas tis Laipthous. Içili or Içil Sansagi is in Karamania on the southeastern coast of Asia Minor; Nicosia or Lefkoşia is now the capital of Cyprus, and has been inhabited since Assyrian times.

[221] Tarablus is the Arab name for Tripoli, now in modern Lebanon, its second largest port. Rycaut adds "Sham," which is a name for Damascus; Hama is is central Syria on the Orontes river north of Damsacus. It was once a very important trading-centre; Homs in western Syria is 162 kilometres north of Damascus. By "Fazlul Akrad," Rycaut may mean the famous Krak des Chevaliers, built for the emir of Aleppo in 1031, and subsequently one of the most significant crusader strongholds in the east. There is also a citadel in Homs, built by Saladin. Hermel is a town in northern Lebanon; Salamiyeh, settled since Assyrian times, is in western Syria, close to Homs.

[222] The Empire of Trebizond, which consisted of territory on the south coast of the Black Sea, was founded in 1204 by Alexius I Comnenus (r. 1204–1222), a scion of the Byzantine imperial family. He did not flee to Trebizond after the capture of Constantinople by the Fourth Crusade, but had, with Georgian help, declared Trebizond a separate empire some weeks before that event. The empire lasted until 1461, when its last emperor, David Comnenus (r. 1459–1461), surrendered the city to Mehmed II "the Conqueror."

commands six *sanjaks, viz.* Ardahan-Kitutchuk, Giugevan, Sarikamiş, Gedegara, Kağizman, Pasinler.[223]

16. The government of the Pasha of Mosul, otherwise called Nineveh in Assyria, hath a revenue of six hundred eighty-one thousand fifty-six aspers, and commands 5 *sanjaks, viz.* Baguwanlu, Tikrit, Irbid, Eski Mosul or Old Nineveh, and Houran.[224]

17. The government of the Pasha of Rakka hath a revenue of 680,000 aspers and commands seven *sanjaks, viz.* Gümüs, Khabour, Cezire, Banirebia, Serugh, Birecik, Ani.[225]

These are all the governments which are in Asia with *khaṣṣ.* Let us now pass into Europe.

18. Is the government of the Pasha of Rumelia, otherwise Romania, which is the most honourable Turkish charge in Europe, hath a revenue of a million and one hundred thousand aspers. The seat of the pasha is Sofia, and commands 24 *sanjaks, viz.* Güstendil, otherwise Justiniana [Prima], Mora otherwise Morea, Iskenderiye, Tirhala, Silistra, Nicopolis, Okhri, Valona, Ioannina, Il-bessan, Chermen, Selanik otherwise Salonica, Vize, Delonia, Uskub, Kirkkilissa, Ducagia, Vidin, Alagehizar, Perserin, Vulçitrin, Akkerman, Özü, Azaq. But it is to be observed that though Morea, according to the ancient canon, was under the jurisdiction of the Pasha of Romania, yet now it is divided and made part of the

---

[223] This pashalik was merged with that of Samtshke in 1604; Rycaut's information is not completely accurate. Ardahan, annexed by the Ottomans in 1555, is also listed by Rycaut under the pashalik of Çildir (see above). Sarikamiş in eastern Anatolia was captured by the Ottomans in 1534; Gedegara or Vezirköprü is a township in the province of Rum; Kağizman is another city in eastern Anatolia; Pasinler is forty kilometres from Erzurum and the home of Hasankale Castle.

[224] Baguwanlu became a *sanjak* in the sixteenth century; it is west of Kirkuk on the Zab river. Mosul in Iraq is the site of Nineveh, the capital of Assyria, established by Asshur-nasir-pal II in about 850 B. C. E. It was captured by the army of Süleyman I in 1535; Tikrit, 140 kilometres northwest of Baghdad, has been settled since Assyrian times and was the birthplace of Saladin; Irbid, seventy kilometres north of Amman, Jordan, is ancient Arbela, site of a battle between Darius III and Alexander the Great; Houran is an area now stretching from southwest Syria to northwestern Jordan, and includes the Golan Heights.

[225] Rakka, now ar-Raqqah in north central Syria, was the Hellenistic settlement of Kallinokos, and is 160 km east of Aleppo; Gümüs is a town in the province of Amasya; Khabour, now Nahr Khabour, is in north-eastern Syria; Cezire is a district in Baghdad province; Banirebia, also known as Diyar-i Beni Rabia, was a *sanjak* in 1520; Serugh or Suruç, birthplace of the fifth-century Syrian mystic Jacob of Serugh, is in the eastern part of the old kingdom of Commagene and forty-six kilometres from modern Şanliurfa in eastern Anatolia; for Birecik, see above under Aleppo; Ani, now Ani'am, is an Israeli settlement in Syria.

revenue of the Valide or Queen Mother, where a farmer[226] of her rents and incomes now resides.[227]

19. Is the charge of the Kapudan, otherwise Captain Pasha, or, as the Turks call him, General of the White Seas, hath a revenue of 885,000 aspers. He is admiral of the Grand Signior's fleet and commands as far as the Turkish power by sea extends, and commands 13 *sanjaks, viz.* Gallipoli, which is the proper place of the pasha's residence, Eğriboz, otherwise Negroponte, Karleli, Ainabachit, Rhodes, Midillü or Mitylene, Khoja-ili, Sifta, Mistra, Sakis or the island of Skios, Beneschke or Malvatia. Some others add Nicomedia, Lemnos, and Naxos.[228]

---

[226] "Farmer" here means a revenue-collector; in France, for example, the farmer-general had the right to levy taxes.

[227] Sofia is now, of course, the capital of modern Bulgaria; Güstendil or Justiniana Prima was a Byzantine city in southern Serbia, now known as Caričingrad; Morea or Mora is the Peloponesse in southern Greece; Iskenderiye or Shkodër (also known, confusedly, as Scutari) is a city in northwestern Albania; Tirhala or Trikkala in north-western Thessaly was a city with a large Jewish population; in 1453 many of them were forcibly relocated to Constantinople, where they founded a significant community. Silistra is a port in northeastern Bulgaria near the Romanian border; Nicopolis, founded by Philip II of Macedon, was the site of a great defeat of the French by Bayezid I (1396). It is in eastern Bulgaria on the Danube; Valona is now Vlorë in Albania, and was the capital of an eponymous independent principality until 1417; Ioannina is in Epirus, north-western Greece. It was probably founded by Justinian I, and fell to the Ottomans in 1430; Ilbessan, also known as Sandzak or Albanopolis, is an area and town along the present border between Serbia and Montenegro; Vize is in what used to be Thrace, the Marnara region of Turkey, now Kirklareli province; Kirkkilissa or Lozengrad, also known as Kirklareli, is a town in eastern Thrace; it was captured by the Ottomans in 1363; Vidin, a town in northwestern Bulgaria, fell to the Ottomans in 1392; Vulçitrin was a *sanjak* in the provinces of Rumelia and Buda listed from 1545; Bender is in modern-day Moldavia, but in 1538 was listed as a *sanjak* of Rumelia; Akkerman was a district in Silistre province which was captured by the Russians in 1812 and renamed Belgorod-Dinestrousky; Özü or Ocakov was made the capital city of Özü Eflâk province, Romania, in 1593; Azaq was a town in Kefe province at the mouth of the river Don; it was captured from the Ottomans by the Russians in 1736.

[228] Gallipoli, made famous by the battle in 1915–1916, is in the Dardanelles Peninsula, Turkish Thrace; Negroponte is the ancient Greek city of Euboea in the Euripus Strait off Boeotia; Karleli was once the ancient Greek city of Agrinion in Aetolia, western Greece; Ainabachit is the Turkish name for Lepanto or modern Naupaktos on the Gulf of Corinth, the site of Don John of Austria's famous naval victory over the Turks in 1571; Rhodes, an island in the Aegean Sea, is eighteen kilometres south-west of Turkey and known for the Colossus of Rhodes, one of the Seven Wonders of the World; Mitylene is the capital of Lesbos, a Greek island in the Aegean Sea and the birthplace of the poet Sappho; Khoja-ili, an area in Ottoman hands since 1337, had as its capital Nicomedia, now Izmit, 100 kilometres from Istanbul, which is sometimes counted as a separate

20. Is the government of the Pasha of Budin, otherwise Buda in Hungary, hath a revenue[229] — [sic] commands 20 *sanjaks, viz.* Eger, Kanije, Semendire, Petchui, Ustunubilgrad or Stuhlweissenburg, Esztergom or Strigonium, Sekdin, Caqan, Simontornya, Szérem, Koppány, Fülek, Szigetver, Siklos, Novigrad, Sekçay, Belgrade or Alba Regalis. And now lately, in the year 1663 that Székesfehévár was taken, a new *sanjak* is since added.[230]

21. The Pasha of Temesvar in Hungary hath a revenue — and hath under his command six *sanjaks, viz.* Lipva, Çanad, Göle, Morava, Varad, to which also Yanova is added, conquered in the year 1663.[231]

22. Is the government of the Pasha of Bosnia, which is part of Illyria, divided formerly into Liburnia and Dalmatia, now called Slavonia.[232] His rev-

---

*sanjak*; Sifta is modern Sivota, a town in Lefkada (Leucas) in the Ionian Sea, western Greece; Mistra is a historical city located near Sparta; Skios is the island of Mykonos in the Celebes; Malvatia is also known as Monemvassia, a town in Laconia on the eastern Peleponnesus; Lemnos and Naxos are two well-known Greek islands.

[229] There is a blank space here and in the next two descriptions, where no revenue information is given.

[230] Eger, known to tourists for its thermal baths, is a city in northern Hungary; Kanije, now Nagykanisza, is in south-western Hungary near Lake Balaton; Semendire is now Smederevo, a city in Serbia on the right bank of the Danube, forty kilometres from Belgrade. It was captured by the Turks in 1459; Stuhlweissenburg is the German name for Székesfehérvér in central Hungary, sixty-five kilometres south-west of Budapest (see again below). It was occupied by the Ottomans from 1453 to 1688; Esztergom, the birthplace of Hungary's founder-king Stephen I, who was crowned there in 1000, is a city sixty kilometres northwest of Budapest; Simonotrnya is in central Hungary on the west bank of the Danube; Szérem or Srijem is an area now in eastern Croatia and northwestern Serbia; Koppány, now Kis-Koppány, is part of the city of Pest, across the river from Buda; Fülek is a town now on the Slovakian-Hungarian border; Novigrad is now in Croatia, on the western coast of Istria; Belgrade is now the capital of Serbia, but Rycaut has mixed it up with Stuhlweissenburg, which was actually known as Alba Regalis. The German name means literally "a white castle with a chair," which may be translated into Serbo-Croatian as Beograd, hence Belgrade, also the name for the city in central Hungary.

[231] Temesvár (Romanian Timişoara) is in the Banat region of Romania in western Transylvania. The Hungarians ruled it from 1030, the Turks occupied it from 1552–1716; Lipva or Lipova is now in western Transylvania, Romania. Ottoman occupation occurred twice: 1552–1595 and 1613–1716; Göle (Hungarian Gyula) is in south-eastern Hungary on the Romanian border; Morava is a district of northern Bulgaria; Varad or Arad is in western Romania, and was under Ottoman rule 1551–1699; Yanova (Romanian Ineu) is in West Transylvania, 100 kilometres from Arad.

[232] Slavonia or Slovenia came under Ottoman rule between 1529 and 1552. However, the old medieval kingdom, which extended to the Sutla river on the modern Slovenian-Croatian border, remained independent.

enue is—[*sic*] and commands 8 *sanjaks, viz.* Hersek, Kilis, Izvornik, Požega, Vrhovine, Çernik, Kirka-Lika, Bihać.[233]

There are other pashas, of Caffa, Theodosia in Taurica Chersonesus,[234] which, having no *sanjaks*, no *timàriots* nor *ziamets*[235] under them, but only a few beggarly villages which we shall purposely omit as not worthy the notice. And so much shall be said for the pashas or *beylerbeys* with *khaşş* or with the revenue imposed upon countries under their command, collected by their own officers.

1. The Pasha of Grand Cairo, called by the Turks *Mýsýr*,[236] hath a revenue of six hundred thousand sequins a year which he may justly and honestly pretend to. As much is the tribute yearly paid the Grand Signior from that place, which is most commonly brought since the war with Venice[237] upon camels' backs by land with a guard of 500 men, not to expose it to the danger of being intercepted at sea. Another sum of six hundred thousand sequins yearly goes to the payment of the Turks' forces in Egypt, besides the vast sums of money this pasha extorts with insupportable avarice and tyranny from the natives of the country during the space of his three years' government, by which means he grows excessive rich and able to refund a good stream into the Grand Signior's coffers at his return, as hereafter shall be the subject of our more large discourse. He commands 16 *sanjaks*, as is reported, but not being registered in the king's book, I let them pass without naming them.

2. Is the government of Baghdad, otherwise Babylon, and hath a revenue of a million and seven hundred thousand aspers and commands 22 *sanjaks, viz.* Dertenk, Gozé, Gawariz, Renk, Amadiye, Gilan, Samawah, Ramallah, Bayán,

---

[233] Illyria was the Roman name for the western region of the Balkan peninsula; Liburnia was the Roman name for the northeastern Adriatic coastal region, now in Croatia; Dalmatia, the Roman territory on the eastern Adriatic, is also in modern Croatia; Hersek is Herzegovina, the southern region of modern Bosnia; Kilis or Klis is in central Dalmatia, Croatia, and was the *sanjak* centre of Bosnia; Izvornik is on the Drina river in northeastern Bosnia; Požega is a city in eastern Croatia, captured by the Turks in 1537; Vrhovine is a village on the Adriatic coastline of Croatia; Çernik is in the southern Slavonian region of Croatia; Kirka-Lika is in central Croatia; Bihać is in north-western Bosnia, captured by the Turks in 1592.

[234] Theodosia is a port on the Black Sea in the Crimea, now in Ukraine; it was captured by the Ottomans in 1475 and renamed Kefe or Caffa. Taurica Chersonesus is the Crimean area.

[235] Lands or revenues granted by the Sultan to individuals who had performed military services for the state.

[236] This is (technically) incorrect. Rycaut gives the Turkish name for "Egypt;" Cairo is known as *Kahire* in Turkish. However, the name of the capital city did sometimes stand for the whole country.

[237] The Turko-Venetian war lasted from 1648 to 1669. There were, however, intermittent outbreaks between the two powers until 1699.

Darne, Dehbala, Wasit, Gankule, Gu'aidiyah, Kerend, Qara Tag, Ghilan, Karaj, Aná, Al-Ahsa, Deirberhiie, Qazaniya.[238]

3. Is the government of the Pasha of Yemen, which is in Arabia Felix, whose place of residence is at Aden on the Red Sea, which place and country being recovered for the most part again from the Turk by the Arabians, it is neither needful to mention the revenue nor the *sanjaks* it formerly commanded.[239]

4. The Pasha of the Abyssinias hath his residence at Suakin, a small isle in the Red Sea, and commands the ports of Massawa and Hergigo. But this pasha, being very poor and far distant from the succours of the Turks, we cannot assign any *sanjaks* or render anything certain of his estate.[240]

5. In the government also of Basra on the confines of Persia were reckoned 26 *sanjaks*, but not now held by the Turk, who hath no other power there nor benefit thence excepting only that prayers are made constantly for the Sultan.[241]

---

[238] Gawariz (modern al-Gazira) is a river plains area of Iraq near Mosul; Amadiya, a Kurdish mountain town, has been a settlement since the time of the Assyrian Empire. It had a large Jewish population at one time. Amadiye or 'Imadiye was a Kurdish area; Gilan was a *sanjak* without a fief but with its own *beylerbey*, as were Bayán or Bayát, both now in Iran, Debhala, and Qazaniya; Samawah, built on both sides of the Euphrates, is the capital of modern al-Muthanna governorate, in Iraq. Ramallah, now well-known as a Palestinian enclave, was founded in the sixteenth century by the Haddadins, who lost it to the Ottomans in 1595; the British took over in 1917. Darne, now Derne in Libya, was settled in 1493 by Muslim refugees from Spain. Wasit, in eastern Iraq on the Tigris, is described as a place "without feudal cavalry" by Birken (*Provinzen*, 220), presumably because it was originally established as a military base in 702 by the Baghdad caliphate, and by the seventeenth century its shipbuilding industry had been destroyed when the river's course changed. Gankule or Čankūlak is in present-day Iran; Kerend, now known as Kerend-é Gharb, is now in western Iran on the border with Iraq. Al-Ahsa is now in Saudi Arabia; in 1521 it was captured by the Muntafiqs from southern Iraq, who ruled it for the Ottoman Empire until 1670, when the Turks were expelled. It was reoccupied in 1818.

[239] Yemen was Ottoman territory from 1517 to 1630, when it was recovered by the Zaidi imam al-Mu'ayyad Muhammad (r. 1620–1644). The Turks remained in control of a few coastal areas.

[240] Abyssinian territory under the Ottomans was known as Habeš; a list of its *sanjaks* may be found in Birken (*Provinzen*, 254–55). Suakin, now on the west coast of Sudan, was in important Red Sea port. It is now deserted, due to a devastating earthquake in 1918, but the ruins were still impressive when the editor was there in 1964. Hergigo, also known as Arkiko, is a Red Sea port in modern Eritrea situated on the mainland across from Massawa, which was actually the capital of Habesh. Now in Eritrea, it was captured by the Ottomans in 1557.

[241] Basra is, of course, Iraq's second-largest city and is near the Iranian border. It was finally captured by the Ottomans in 1668; the *vilayet* of Basra was quite extensive, covering the area of what is now southern Iraq, Kuwait, and Qatar, as well as parts of eastern Saudi Arabia. For a list of the *sanjaks*, see Birken, *Provinzen*, 226–30.

6. In the government of Lahsa on the confines of Hormuz in Persia are counted 6 *sanjaks*, *viz.* Aiwen, Sakul, Negeniyah, Netif, Bandarazir, Giriz, but these countries are poor and have scarce any place in the Grand Signior's registers.[242]

To these we should add the governments of Algiers, Tunis, and Tripoli in Barbary,[243] but that being much fallen-off from the Turk's obedience and become almost independent of themselves, we shall pass by the discourse of them, especially because of late years the mutual treaties with Barbary and interchanges of war and peace with these countries hath made the state and condition of that people well-known and familiar in England.

The use of the particular catalogue foregoing is to demonstrate the greatness and power of the Ottoman Empire, which hath so many considerable governments and principalities in its possession wherewith to encourage and excite the endeavours of heroic spirits to an ambition of great and noble enterprises whereby to merit the rewards which remain in the power of the Sultan to gratify them with. And also, to help in the just computation of the number of men the Turk can bring into the field, every pasha being obliged for every 5000 aspers rent to bring a soldier to the war, though notwithstanding they often appear for ostentation and gain of the Grand Signior's favour with more men than their own complement, as in the last war with Germany, the *beylerbey* of Romania brought 10,000 effective men into the field. Of these *beylerbeys* five have the title of viziers, which signifies as much as "counsellor," *viz.* the pashas of Anatolia, Babylon, Cairo, Romania, and Buda, which are charges of the greatest riches, power and fame. The others have their pre-eminence, rank or order according to the priority of conquest and antiquity in the possession of the Turks.

These are all the great governments of the empire, in whose respective jurisdictions are always three principal officers, *viz.* the *Mufti*, the *Ra'is Effendi*, otherwise called *Ra'is Kitab*, which is Lord Chancellor or Secretary of State, or rather those two offices united into one. The third is [the] *Defterdar Pasha*, or Lord Treasurer. These three officers are near counsellors and attendants on their

---

[242] Lahsa or al-Hasa is the Turkish name for the areas now known as Kuwait and Qatar, but the main city in the area was al-Ahsa, now known as al-Hofuf. It was under Ottoman rule from 1551 to 1663, when the Turks were expelled by the Bani Khalid tribal confederation under Barraq ibn Ghurayr, whose clans went on to establish the present-day ruling dynasties in Qatar, Kuwait, and Bahrain. It was actually an *eyalet*, not a *sanjak*.

[243] Barbary was a catch-all term used to denote the middle and west-coastal area of north Africa, namely Algeria, Tunisia, Morocco, and Libya in modern times. Algiers came under Ottoman control in 1517, but in 1671 the Dey of Algiers became semi-independent from the Ottoman pasha, although still nominally under the Sultan's rule. Tunis was conquered in 1574 and ruled from Algiers, as was Tripoli (in modern Libya). In 1705 the Bey of Tunis became an independent ruler. Rycaut is correct in describing these places as "almost independent."

pashas, and so also they are on the Prime Vizier, whose *mufti, ra'is effendi,* and *defterdar* have a superiority and dignity above others and are to them as the original to the copy.

Of the *Mufti* we shall speak in due place. The *Reis Effendi,* which signifies "chief of the writers or book-men," for the Turks call always men of the law and professors of the pen and parochial priests by the title of *effendi,* is always present and attending on the Vizier, for passing orders, decrees, patents, and commissions into all parts of the empire, which are duly dispatched in those numbers into all places, as is incredible, for the Turks governing more by their arbitrary power and according to the exigencies of affairs than by a set rule or form, every business requires its distinct order, and the very courts of justice are moderated according to the commands and directions they receive from above. By which means the *Reis Effendi's* hands are filled with a multitude of business, as employs great numbers of writers and consequently brings in riches flowing to his coffers, some in which office who by their parts industry and courage have gained authority and respect, have amassed wealth which might compare with the riches and treasure of princes. We shall here instance in one of late years, famous in Turkey for his knowledge and riches, called Samizade, one who had piled those heaps of all things that were rich and curious as were too tedious and long to insert in a catalogue in this place. It may suffice, that being executed in the time of the last wars against the emperor of Germany for some conspiracy against the Great Vizier, such a treasure was found appertaining to him (all which was confiscated to the Grand Signior) as was sufficient to have enriched and raised his prince, had he been impoverished and in a declining condition.

The other great officer is the *Defterdar* or Lord Treasurer, who receives the revenue of the Grand Signior and pays the soldiery and makes other public disbursements. This office is different from the Treasurer of the Seraglio, of whom we have already spoken, who attends to nothing else but the expenses of the court and to gather in the accidental profits and presents paid to the Grand Signior, which is so considerable that every Sultan, for the most part, amasses a particular treasure of his own, which after his death is lodged in a particular chamber, shut with an iron gate, the keyhole stopped with lead, and over the port is written in golden letters "The treasure of such a Sultan." And this shall suffice to have spoken of the offices and dignities of the empire.

Chapter XIII. *Of the Tatars and Tatar Khan, and in what manner they depend upon the Turks.*

The Tatars[244] may very well be accounted amongst the other princes subject to the Ottoman power. I mean not the Asiatic Tatars or the Tatars of Uzbek, though so much Muhammadans as to wear green turbans and to deduce their race from the line of Muhammad himself, for having conquered China and possessing a greater empire than the Ottomans, they are far from acknowledging any subjection or degree of inferiority to the Turk. Nor are all the European Tatars subjects to the Sultan, for the Kalmyk and Citrahan Tatars,[245] men of strange barbarity and countenance different from all the other race of mankind, though possessors of the Muhammadan religion, are yet faithfully and piously obedient to the [Grand] Duke of Muscovy,[246] their lawful prince.

The Praecopensian[247] Tatar, which inhabits Taurica Chersonesus, now called Crim[ea], the principal city of which is Theodosia, now Caffa, and the Nagaentian Tatar, which inhabits the Palus Maeotis[248] between the rivers of Volga and Tanais,[249] are the people which may be accounted the subjects, or at least confederates of this empire, though only the city of Caffa of all those dominions is immediately in possession and government of the Turk, which in my opinion appears to be a cautionary town and pledge for their obedience. And though the khan or prince of the country is elective, yet he is chosen out of that true line and confirmed by the Grand Signiors, who have always taken upon them a power to depose the father and in his place constitute the son or next of the lineage when found remiss in ordering their auxiliary helps to the war, or guilty of any disrespect or want of duty to the Ottoman Porte.[250]

---

[244] Tatars or Tartars (Rycaut uses the second spelling, but it has been here modernised to conform to current usage) are Turkic tribes and peoples who inhabit a widespread area, including parts of Russia, Turkmenistan, Uzbekistan, Turkey, Kazakhstan, Kyrgyzstan, Tajikistan, and Azerbaijan. In Rycaut's time it was something of a catch-all term.

[245] The Kalmyks or Oirats are a western Mongolic people who inhabit parts of Russia, China, and Mongolia. Citrahan is an old name for Astrakhan, which is in southern European Russia on the left bank of the Volga.

[246] By Rycaut's time he would have been the Tsar of Russia.

[247] These are Tatars from the Crimea, "known to the common people as Tartaria Praecopensis" [*quae vulgo Tartaris Praecopensis vocatur*] (Joseph de Jouvency, *Epitome historiae Societatis Jesu*, vol. 2 [Ghent: J. Poelman-De Pape, 1853], 326.

[248] The Azov Sea.

[249] The river Don.

[250] This is the first time Rycaut uses this rather odd term. "Sublime Porte" was a western diplomatic term for the *Bab i-Ali*, meaning "High Gate of the Divan," which was the vizier's court in the Topkapi palace, the place where the Sultan would receive foreign ambassadors. There was also the "High Porte," which was the private court of the Sultan.

This present khan which now governs, called Muhammad Giray[251] (for that is the surname of his family) remained during the life of his father, according to the custom of the eldest son of this prince, a hostage to the Turk in Yanbolu, a town in Thrace,[252] four days' journey from Adrianople, situate on the Euxine or Black Sea, but from thence, upon jealousy of too near a vicinity to his own country, was removed to Rhodes, where he passed an obscure and melancholy life until the death of his father, and then, being recalled to Constantinople, had there his sword girt on, swore fealty to the Grand Signior with all other formalities performed according to their custom of regal inauguration. But, being settled in his kingdom and mindful of his sufferings at Rhodes, he had ever stomached the pride of the Ottoman emperor, by which, and the dissuasion of the Polonians and the other neighbouring Tatars, as a thing dishonourable to so ancient and powerful a people, to resign the heir of their kingdom a hostage to their neighbours. This present prince hath refused this part of subjection, which the Vizier Köprülü often complained of, but not being in a condition to afford a remedy unto it, thought it prudent to dissemble.

But yet these people are esteemed as brothers or near allies with the Turk, to whom for want of heirs male in the Ottoman line the empire is by ancient compact to descend, the expectation of which, though afar off and but almost imaginary, doth yet conserve the Tatar in as much observance to the Turk as the hopes of an estate doth a young gallant who is allured to a complacency and obsequiousness with the petulant humour of a father who adopts him, who is resolved never to want heirs of his own family. And thus the Tatar is as obedient as other subjects, and though the Turk exercises not his power there by commands as in other places of his dominions, but treats all his business by way of letters, yet these letters serve in the place of warrants for the signification of the Grand Signior's pleasure, and are as available as the *tughra*[253] and other formalities of the imperial edict are in other places in subjection to the Turk. When the Sultan writes to the Khan of Tatary, he uses this style:

---

[251] Khan Muhammad Giray IV (1610–1674), a talented poet (under the name of Karim) and philosopher who was surnamed *Sofu* (the Sufi) reigned twice, from 1641 to 1644 and again from 1654 to 1666. Between his two reigns he was deposed and succeeded by Islam III (1644–1654); he was deposed again and replaced by Adil Giray (1666–1671). His father was Bahadir I, who reigned 1637–1641. Rycaut's account is not wholly accurate. "The frequent succession struggles among the family of the Tatar khans of the Crimea—in which one member would seek allies among their neighbours against another," Caroline Finkel writes, "often provoked the Ottomans to intervene to ensure that their preferred candidate was on the throne" (*Osman's Dream*, 221).

[252] Now Yambol in southeastern Bulgaria, it was conquered by the Seljuks in 1364 and by Rycaut's time was situated in the *sanjak* of Silistre.

[253] The great character of the emperor's name affixed at the top of every command (Rycaut's marginal note). Rycaut calls it the *autogra*.

To that Government wherein flourishes the Mass and Original of Regency, on which fortune depends and by which felicity is obtained, possessor of excellent power and established glory, elected by the favour of that King from whom succours are to be demanded, the King of Crimea, Jani Beg Giray Khan,[254] whose height be forever maintained.

After respect had to those blessings, which are freighted[255] with amber, and salutations perfumed with narcissus,[256] proceeding from the Imperial Grace, "Be it known unto you, etc."

By ancient compact between the empire and the kingdom of Tatary it is agreed that whenever the Grand Signior goes in person to the wars the Tatar khan is to accompany him in person with an army of one hundred thousand men, but if the Vizier or some other general be in the field, then is he only obliged to send forty or fifty thousand under the command of his son or some principal officer of his kingdom, who are paid and maintained out of the booty and pillage they acquire. In the year 1663 the Tatar, called on occasion of the war in Hungary to the assistance of the Turk, they made such incursions into that country, Moravia and Silesia, sacking and burning all cities and towns, that they carried away one hundred and sixty thousand captive souls in one year, which precise number I am informed from those who had received good information of the *tandik*[257] or certificates that were given upon every head, for the Tatar, being an absolute freebooter,[258] makes prize of all that comes within his power, and lest he should prey on the subjects of the Turk they are bound to take out attestations from certain registers of the names, countries and age of their captives, lest they should deceive the Turk with the sale of those who are already their own subjects and slaves.

The Tatar is to the Turk as the jackal is to the lion, who hunts and finds prey for the lion to overcome and feed on. And so the Tatars make incursions into the neighbouring countries round about, and pass in great bodies sometimes ten or twelve days without doing the least damage or spoil in their journey outwards, but as soon as they turn their faces home they rob, spoil, burn, and carry all the inhabitants of what age or sect soever like a torrent before them, and every one of them leading three or four horses apiece on which they mount their captives and load their prey, make a running march day and night with a few hours intermission for natural repose, too fast for any orderly army to overtake, and any other that is not so is not able to give them battle. Such of their slaves as in their

---

[254] Khan Jani Giray ruled from 1610 to 1623. Why Rycaut has used this name instead of a more recent one is uncertain.
[255] Weighed down or laden.
[256] Daffodil. The Turks called it *fulya* or *nergis*, and sometimes "the golden bowl."
[257] This is the modern Turkish word for "certificate." Rycaut uses *pengik*.
[258] Here not a pirate, but a general term for someone who plunders or pillages.

journey are wounded and infirm and not able to accompany the camp they kill; those which they bring safe into their own country they sell to the Turks, who come hither to trade for this merchandise, which is the most profitable commodity that Tatary affords. Young boys and girls are rated at the highest price, the latter of which, being beautiful, are like jewels held at an unknown value, but few of them escape the lust of the Tatars, who deflower them even in the years of their very infancy.

This sort of people were by the ancients called Sarmati, and were always famous for their exploits on horseback, but heavy and ignorant of foot-service, which character Tacitus gives of them: "*Omnis Sarmatum virtus quasi extra ipsos, nihil ad pedestrem pugnam, tam ignavum ubi per turmas advenere, vix ulla acies obstiterit, iners videtur sudore acquirere, quod possis sanguine parare, mira diversitate natura cum iidem homines sic ament inertiam, et oderint quietam.*"[259] They live very hardly and feed especially on horseflesh, which, dying in their march, they never examine his diseases, whether surfeited or over-heated, but, distributing his flesh amongst their companions, place it under their saddles, and thus baked between the heat of the man and the horse, chafed with the day's labour is at night judged sufficiently prepared as a dish fit for the table of their prince. And as the men are nourished with a diet of raw flesh, herbs, and roots, or such as the earth naturally produces without concoction of the fire to prepare it for their stomachs, so also their horses are of a hardy temperament, patient of hunger and cold, and in the sharp winter of those countries when the ground is covered with snow, nourish themselves with the barks of trees and such herbage as they can find at the bottom of the deep snow.

Their towns and villages consist of huts rather than houses, or hurdles made with sticks and covered with a coarse hair cloth, of which villages there are accounted two hundred thousand, so that taking one man out of every village, as is their custom when they go to war, they speedily form an army of two hundred thousand fighting men. But now, having carried great riches out of Poland and gained considerable wealth by the market of their slaves, some of them throw off their homely plaids to wear sables, and some, more frugal, employ their money for building houses. The riotous and dissolute are addicted to strong waters and a drink called *boza*[260] made of a certain feed (which drank in a great quantity doth

---

[259] Rycaut seems to be conflating passages here, but in *Germania* 15 Tacitus states (in Mattingly and Handford's translation): "When not engaged in warfare, they [the Germans, not the Sarmatians, ed.] spend a certain amount of time in hunting, but much more in idleness, thinking of nothing else but sleeping and eating. For the boldest and most warlike men have no regular employment. . .in thus dawdling away their time they show a strange inconsistency—at one and the same time loving indolence and hating peace (114).

[260] A thick drink made from fermented wheat, which actually has quite a low alcohol content. The Turks call it *bosa*, and its name gave rise to our term "booze."

intoxicate and is now much in use amongst the Turks) and give themselves up to a gluttony as brutish as that which is natural unto swine, having no art of sauces to provoke their appetite, but rest delighted with the mere contentment of idleness and a full stomach.

But this shall be sufficient to have spoken of the relation the Tatars have to the government of the Turk and their subjection to this empire, their customs and manners being more amply and fully described in other books.

**Chapter XIV.** *Of the tributary princes to the Grand Signior, viz. Moldavians, Wallachians, Transylvanians, Ragusians,*[261] *etc.*

The power and puissance of an empire is not more judged of by the many governors, the rich offices it can dispose of, the multitude of provinces it contains in obedience, and the necessity it can impose on other princes to seek its confederacy, which we have already treated of, than it is by the many tributaries which, to redeem the remainder of their worldly goods, willingly sacrifice the best part to appease his fury in whose power it is to master all. And so these distressed nations, long wearied-out with tedious wars, oppressed between the emperor of Germany, the Polander, and the Turk, and more damaged by their own civil dissentions and domestic perfidiousness than vanquished by the force of arms, were forced at last to surrender up their fruitful provinces to the devotion of the Turk, which are now harassed and oppressed beyond all expression and are the merest slaves to the Turk of all other his subjects, and may well be compared to the industrious bee and profitable sheep, whom he cares for and maintains alive for the sake of their honey and the interest of their wool. And, as if this were all too little, when it shall be thought fit he opens the gate to the incursions of the Tatar, who, having gained a considerable booty of goods and captives, sells to the Turks for slaves those which were before his subjects. These three poor provinces, formerly called the Daci,[262] which withstood so long the Roman arms, were always esteemed a valiant and warlike people, according to that of Virgil, *lib. 8 Aeneid*: "*Indomitique Dacae et pontem indignitatis Araxes,*"[263] and Juvenal, *Satires* 6, "*Dacicus et scripto radiat Germanicus auro,*"[264] which countries have been the graves and cemeteries of the Turks, and in these modern times been the stage on which so many tragedies of war have been acted, being defended with as much valour and variety of successes as could humanly be expected in so unequal a match as was between these provinces singly and the Ottoman Empire. But now at last they are forced to yield and become not only tributaries but slaves and subjects to the Turk, who, having deprived them of the true line of their natural princes succeeding in lawful inheritance, place over them some Christians of the Greek Church, without consideration of their conditions or riches or qualifications,

---

[261] The Republic of Ragusa, with its capital at Dubrovnik, Dalmatia (now in modern Croatia), lasted from 1358 to 1808. It enjoyed the protection of the Ottoman Empire. For further details, see below.

[262] The Dacians inhabited the region of northern Thrace. They fought several wars with the Romans, until they were finally conquered by Trajan in 106 CE, when Dacia became a Roman province after its king, Decebalus, committed suicide following fierce resistance to the Roman invaders.

[263] Translation: "the untameable Dahae and the Araxes, chafing at a bridge."

[264] "I write of the Dacian and the German, glittering with gold." (Juvenal, *Satires* 6.105). Rycaut has "*Dacius & scripto radiat Germanicus antro.*"

nay, rather choose to give the standard (which is the sign of the Grand Signior's confirmation of the prince) to some inferior person, as taverners, fishmongers or other meaner professions, purposely to disparage the people with the baseness of their governors and expose them to the oppressions of men of no worth or dexterity in their office.

It hath been several times under the consideration of the Turks at length to reduce these three provinces to the command of so many pashas, contrary to the original capitulations agreed on at the time that these people first submitted to the Ottoman yoke, but as yet it hath been carried to the contrary, as more profitable and better serving the ends of the empire. For hereby Christians become the instruments of torment to their own brethren; outrages and spoils may be the more boldly-acted, more Turkish officers employed on every slight occasion on gainful messages, and the people, by long oppressions living under the jurisdiction of a prince who can rather spoil than protect, may be reconciled more willingly to the Turkish government and learn to value the gentleness and power of a pasha compared with the remembrance of their former aggrievances. But of this government they will rather let them imagine the ease and sweetness than enjoy it, for were a pasha the governor, the power of a Turk would be concerned for their protection, he would esteem himself their patron and his honour engaged in their defence, by which means these countries would be relieved in a great measure of extortions and violences, which is not so beneficial to the Turk as the present miserable estate in which they remain.

Moldavia, called by the Turks *Bugdan*, was first made tributary to the Turks by Mehmed [II] the Great, but under the small tribute of 2000 crowns *per annum*. Afterwards Bogdan, *voivode*[265] thereof *Anno* 1485, fearing to become absolute vassal to the Turk, taking his association the kingdom of Poland, took up arms against Selim the Second, by whom, being drawn out of the country, John, a Moldavian born but one who had embraced the Muhammadan superstition, was preferred by Selim to the principality, but no sooner was he settled therein but he returned to his former religion, for which cause the Turk, taking into his assistance the province of Wallachia, made war upon Moldavia. But John the *voivode* by treachery losing his life, this province fell totally into the power of the Turk and was united to his empire in the year 1574.[266]

---

[265] The word *voivode* signifies as much as *praefectus militia* or the general of an army (Rycaut's marginal note). Modern historians usually render it as "prince," although Rycaut's Latinisation is strictly correct. It can also mean "governor."

[266] Rycaut's chronology is confused here. In 1485 the ruler of Moldavia was Stephen III (r. 1457–1504), who won several notable victories over the Turks, notably at Vaslui (1475) and Lake Catlabuga (1485). He eventually agreed to pay tribute to Bayezid II in order to preserve Moldavian self-rule. He was succeeded by Bogdan III, who reigned from 1504 to 1517. Bogdan IV (r. 1568–1572) was replaced by Ioan III the Brave (r. 1572–1574), the son of Bogdan III, who had been living in Constantinople for many

The tribute in those days of this province is recorded in the Turkish history to have been 40,000 sequins or 80,000 dollars, but now, whatsoever may be reported the tribute of those countries is or was, the reader may take this following account for what is certainly paid, being related to me from one who had many years been employed for *voivode* both in Moldavia and Wallachia by the Turk.[267] The yearly tribute of Moldavia is:

1. To the Grand Signior 120 purses of money, each purse containing 500 dollars, makes 60,000 dollars.
2. Ten thousand *okes* of wax, each *oke* being two pounds and a half English weight.[268]
3. Ten thousand *okes* of honey.
4. Six hundred quintals[269] of tallow for the arsenal.
5. Five hundred ox-hides.
6. Five hundred pieces of canvas for clothing and shirts for the slaves, and other services for the galleys.
7. One thousand three hundred and thirty *okes* of wax for the service of the arsenal.
8. To the Chief Vizier ten purses of money or 5000 dollars, and a sable's fur for a vest.
9. To the Vizier's *kiahia* or Chief Steward, one purse or 500 dollars.
10. To the *Defterdar* or Lord Treasurer the same as to the *kiahia*.

This is the ordinary and annual tribute this country acknowledges to the supremacy of the Sultan, and it were well and happy for this people were it all, but there are so many accidental expenses, pretensions, and artifices of the Turks, framed and contrived messages merely to extract money and presents from this oppressed and harassed people, as do more than equal and sometimes double the charge of their yearly tribute. To which you may add the price paid for the prin-

---

years and may have actually been a merchant there. He defeated Ottoman incursions several times but was captured and killed through treachery, as Rycaut states. Selim II the Drunkard was Sultan from 1566 to 1574, and through a treaty with Austria in 1568 had been allowed more authority over Moldavia.

[267] Rycaut is referring here to Prince George Ducas (d. 1685), who ruled Moldavia 1665–1666, 1668–1672, and 1678–1684 and was also *voivode* of Wallachia 1673–1678. Ducas was a Greek from a fairly humble background (although he was not a taverner or fishmonger) and had ably served Prince Vasile Lupu (r. 1634–1653). He allied himself with the Ottomans, and even after his depositions remained loyal to them, fighting in the Turkish army at the siege of Vienna (1683). He was captured and sent to exile in Poland, where he died.

[268] The Turkish *oke* is the one Rycaut means here; the Wallachian and Hungarian *oke* was a liquid measure of about two pints.

[269] A quintal is equivalent to a hundredweight, or 50.8 kilograms.

cipality, which is every three years set to sale, and is to the Grand Signior 150 purses or 75,000 dollars, to the Valide or Queen Mother 50 purses or 25,000 dollars, to the Grand Signior's favourite, who is commonly some handsome young youth, 10 purses or 5000 dollars, and to the Kizlar Aga or chief Black Eunuch who is superintendent over the ladies in the Seraglio, 10 purses of money, and lastly to the Prime Vizier amd other officers for as much as they can beat the bargain. All which money is taken up at interest at 40 or 50 *per cent*, and sometimes on condition it be doubled, and this is done by men who, having no estates of their own, the debt comes to be charged on their country, which is pillaged and polled for it to the very bones, first to satisfy the price of the principality with the with the interest-money for what it is valued, then to pay the annual tribute, then to satisfy the multitude of covetous Turks, who like so many vultures pursue after the skeleton of this consumed carcass. And lastly, the prince himself must take his accounts and take his measures to be capable for the future after he hath laid aside the ornament of his office to live in some proportion agreeable to his past condition. And this is neither done moderately or modestly, but with a covetous and greedy appetite commonly incident to the nature of men born of mean parentage and educated with the parsimony of a scanty house, who also thereunto add many grains of allowance to the limits of their gains, in consideration of the yearly gratuities they must make to reconcile the friendship of the Turkish ministers, whereby they may enjoy protection for their persons and estates.

The state and condition of the province of Wallachia is not better, but rather worse and more afflicted than that of Moldavia, for this country is now equally with the former in the sole and entire disposal and possession of the Turk, to whom it became first tributary under their own princes in the time of Sultan Bayezid. Afterward, in the year 1462, Mehmed the Great undertook the entire conquest of it, then governed by its *voivode* Vlad [III], whose younger brother, supported by the Turk and factious party in the country, possessed himself of the principality, contenting himself to be vassal to the Turkish Empire. Afterwards, in the year 1595, Michael the *voivode* thereof joining himself with Sigismund of Transylvania and with the *voivode* of Moldavia, waged a long and terrible war against the Turks, until revolutions, unquietness, and factions have so spent them as that they are at length become another addition to the empire of the Turks, who now impose on them a heavy yoke and strait curb, not to be imputed to anything more than divine justice, which takes occasion to exercise a hand of severity against the unseasonable negligence, sedition, and variance of Christians amongst themselves at a time when the common enemy to their possession attended only the opportunity of their own dissentions to enter and devour them.[270]

---

[270] The chronology is a little confusing here. Prince Vlad IV (or III) Țepeș of Wallachia (r. 1448, 1456–1462, 1476), otherwise known as Vlad the Impaler of *Dracula* fame, fought determinedly against the Turks all his life. He was deposed by his brother

The tribute of Wallachia to the Grand Signior was formerly 120 purses of money or 60,000 dollars yearly, according to that of Moldavia, and so still continued had not lately Matthew[271] the *voivode* about the year 1655 grown rich, and therefore forgetful of his condition, having by friends and large presents at the Porte procured a continuation of his office for the space of nineteen or twenty years, rebelled against the Turk, taking false measures of his wealth and power as able to encounter with the puissance of the Ottoman Empire, but being soon put to the worst and forced to yield, his life was spared and the safety of his country redeemed upon the augmentation of their tribute, so that now, that which yearly paid being 120 purses of money,

1. Is become to the Grand Signior 260 purses or 130,000 dollars.
2. There is paid 15,000 *okes* of honey.
3. Nine thousand *okes* of wax.
4. To the Prime Vizier ten purses of money or 5000 dollars, and a vest of sables.
5. To the Defterdar or Lord Treasurer one purse of money or 50 dollars, and a vest of sables.
6. To the Kizlar Aga, or Chief Eunuch of the Women, 12,000 aspers.
7. To the Vizier's *kiahia* or steward, 500 dollars and a vest of sables.

The other charges and value set on this province, when triennially sold, is less than that of Moldavia. The method used for extorting money from thence are the same, the oppression in every point equal, unless the remembrance of the extravagant disorder of Matthew the *voivode* still kept in mind emboldens the Turk with more confident pretences to work more desolation and impoverishment in this province.

Now lately a prince was settled there by order of the Grand Signior in the year 1664 called Stridia Bey by the Greeks,[272] which signifies a lord that

---

Radu III the Handsome (r. 1462–1473), who was a Turkish supporter and convert to Islam. Michael the Brave (r. 1593–1601) was also ruler of Transylvania (1599–1600) and Moldavia (1600), having replaced the reigning *voivode* of Moldavia, Ieremia Movilă (r. 1595–1600). Sigismund Báthory was *voivode* of Transylvania 1581, 1586–1598, 1600, a vassal of the king of Hungary.

[271] Matei Basarab ruled Wallachia from 1632 to 1654. He seems to have had some idea about breaking free from Ottoman domination, forming a strong tie with George II Rácoczi of Transylvania (r. 1648–1660), although it would appear that the Moldavians gave him more trouble than the Turks. It was actually his successor Constantin Şerban (r. 1654–1658) who fought the Turks until his deposition by Mihnea III in 1658. Constantine then became ruler of Moldavia (1659 and 1661).

[272] This is Prince Radu Leon "the Oyster-Seller," who reigned from 1664 to 1669. He did not speak Romanian very well, but he was the son of Prince Leon Tomşa (r. 1629–1632) and he had powerful support from the Greek merchant community in Constanti-

had gained some fortune from selling oysters and fish. This person succeeded Gregorasco[273] the late prince, who, fearing the anger of the Prime Vizier for returning home with his army without licence, defeated by General Souches near Leva,[274] fled for safety of his life into the dominions of the Emperor. The Turks, who always avenge the crimes of the governors on the people or of the subjects on the governors, raised the price of the principality to a higher value, causing Stridia Bey, who, as I am confidently informed, was contented to accept it at any rate, to pay for it 800 purses of money or 400,000 dollars, to which being added the interest before-mentioned, the sum may easily be computed that this new *voivode* engulfed himself in, and I leave the reader to imagine with what glad hearts and blessings the people of that country went forth to receive their bankrupt prince.

Nor is Transylvania wholly exempted from the oppression of the Turk, for after several revolutions from the time of Hunyadi,[275] made *voivode* by Ladislaus,[276] king of Hungary, *anno* 1450, a great defender of his country against the infidels, until the time of Stephen the Seventh, surnamed Rácóczi, patronized by the Turks, *anno* 1450.[277] This principality remained sometimes at the devotion

nople, known as the Phanariots. Radu's reign came to an end after anti-Greek riots forced his abdication. The nickname comes from the Greek στρειδια, which means "oyster."

[273] Grigore I Ghica was *voivode* of Wallachia 1660–1664 and 1672–1674. Rycaut's account is correct, and see below.

[274] Leva is the Hungarian name for Levice, where the Ottoman army under Ali Pasha was defeated by the Hapsburg general Jean-Louis Raduit de Souches on 19 July, 1664. The Ottoman commander was killed in the battle.

[275] John or János Hunyadi (c. 1407–1456) was regent of Hungary from 1446 to 1450 and *voivode* of Transylvania from 1440 to1456. He was one of the greatest and most successful opponents of Ottoman power, and developed new strategies and training for his armies which had wide-reaching effects in Europe.

[276] Ladislaus V "the Posthumous" was king of Hungary 1440–1457. Rycaut has "Ladislaus the Fourth," which is incorrect, as Ladislaus IV reigned 1272–1290. However, given the date, Rycaut may have meant Vladislaus III, king of Poland, who also ruled Hungary (1440–1444) in opposition to Ladislaus V, a child, after being elected by the Hungarians. The names are somewhat similar, and Hunyadi's term as *voivode* overlaps both kings' reigns.

[277] This account is inaccurate, as is the chronology. Stephen VII Báthory (not Rácóczi) was Palatine of Hungary 1519–1523 and 1525–1530. During his time the Hungarian forces were decisively defeated by the Turks at Mohacs (1526) and Lajos II of Hungary was killed. Rycaut seems to have conflated him with Stephen Báthory of Ecsed, who ruled as *voivode* of Transylvania 1479–1493, and who fought successfully against the Turks on several occasions, having procured the alliance of Vlad III of Wallachia and other local leaders. He helped re-establish Vlad's rule in Wallachia (1476) after the latter was deposed by the Turks, and gained a great victory over the Ottomans in 1479 at Sebeş on the Mureş river. He was eventually deposed by Vladislaus II of Hungary and died a few months later. However, there were two princes of Transylvania called George (György) Rácóczy; George I reigned 1630–1648, and his son George II 1648–1660. The

and disposal of the king of Hungary, of Poland, of the Emperor, and sometimes of the Turk, until by the growing greatness of the Ottomans the Turks became masters of the best part of this country. But yet Transylvania is more honourably treated than the two other provinces, their tribute being much less and their princes chosen for the most part more regularly from the ancient line or at least from the honourable houses of the *boyars* or nobility, who have an affinity or alliance with the true blood of the former *voivodes*. Their ancient tribute was only 6000 sequins yearly, but afterwards were added 9000 more annually for acknowledgment of certain castles which [Stephen] had taken from Poland, which the Turk demanded to have resigned into his possession, were for that sum redeemed and still detained in the hands of the Transylvanians, over and above which they only pay 300 dollars and two silver bowls to the Viziers of the Bench. And this is all the acknowledgment they make to the Turk, who demonstrates more respect always to this prince and his messages than those of the neighbouring provinces, by reason that that country is not totally in his power (certain strong fortresses being in the hand of the emperor of Germany), for whose sake this people is more gently dealt with, lest too much severity should occasion them to revolt. And this consideration induced the Turks to treat modestly with Michael Apafi,[278] the prince of the country in the late wars in Hungary, by trusting much to his conduct and using him like an honourable confederate by permitting him freely to possess Székelyhid[279] after its voluntary surrender in a mutiny, without the controlment or superintendency of a Turk as his superior, and for his farther encouragement gave out that when the Sultan had totally subdued Hungary, those parts which were not subject to pashas should be annexed to his dominions and be honoured with the title of King of Hungary.

These princes of the three foregoing provinces are farther obliged to serve the Grand Signior in his wars whensoever summoned thereunto, but with what

---

latter allied himself with Moldavia, Wallachia, and the Cossacks against Poland, which he invaded in 1657, capturing Cracow and then, with Swedish help, Warsaw as well. However, he was decisively defeated by the Poles at Czarny Ostrów the same year, and was deposed by the Sultan for waging an unapproved war. Soon restored, George II was again deposed by the Turks (1658) and two years later died of wounds received at the battle of Gyalu (now in Romania), fighting against the Turks. Rycaut must be referring to George II in his discussion of the "two castles." For further details, see Finkel, *Osman's Dream*, 256–258.

[278] Michael III Apafi was Prince of Transylvania 1661–1690. He was supported by the Turks against his rival János Kemény, who was backed by the Holy Roman Emperor but was killed in battle. After the Ottomans were defeated at Vienna (1683), Michael drew closer to the Austrians, finally concluding an alliance with Leopold I in 1687. The latter then officially recognized Apafi's position.

[279] Now Sacueni in western Romania, this town had a castle which was destroyed in 1656.

number and in what manner we reserve for its due place in the treatise of the
Turks' militia and auxiliaries.

The city and small dominion of Ragusa is also another tributary to the Turk,
which is a petty commonwealth not vouchsafed the title of a republic neither by
the Venetians nor the Pope, and only styled *la communità di Ragusi*, which is a
town in Dalmatia commanding over a narrow and barren territory of a few villages which extends itself along the sea coast, and some little islands of no great
consideration. It was anciently called Epidaurus, of which name there were two
other cities in Peleponessus, but that being razed by the Greeks, the inhabitants after their departure rebuilt again this city of Ragusa, giving it a new name
as well as a new foundation. The government of it, in the nature of a commonwealth, is more ancient than that of Venice, having preserved itself more by art
and submission to some powerful protector than to its own force, which caused
them to court the friendship of the Turk before he was master of many parts
of Europe. And, as their records report, it was upon the advice of a holy nun,
esteemed a great saint amongst them, who prophesying of the future greatness
of the Turkish Empire, assured them that the only means to preserve for many
ages their commonwealth free and happy was to submit themselves to one of the
most prosperous of princes, to whose dominion the best part of the world should
be subdued. Whereupon two ambassadors were dispatched to the city of Prusa,
then the regal seat before the utter ruin of the Grecian Empire, with presents
to the Sultan Orhan,[280] desiring to become his tributaries, and in consideration
thereof to strengthen their weak commonwealth with assistance under the shadow of his prevalent protection. There is no doubt but the Sultan then received
them the more courteously and promised the maintenance of a former league.
By how much the distance they were at as yet gave them the less cause to fear his
arms, wherefore, the tribute being agreed on of twelve thousand and five hundred sequins yearly, they were returned home with all demonstrations of courtesy and assurances of defence. Orhan entered into articles with them, bestowed
on them a grant of all the immunities and privileges they desired, the which he
signed with the form of his own hand wetted in ink and clapped on the paper,
which was all the firm and seal in those days,[281] and is now reverenced amongst

---

[280] Orhan reigned from 1324 to 1362; he was the second Ottoman Sultan. During
his time the Ottoman Empire started expanding into Byzantine territory, and by the end
of Orhan's reign most of northwestern Anatolia was in Turkish hands, including the cities of Nicaea and Nicomedia, captured in 1331 and 1337 respectively. Prusa, now Bursa,
was captured from the Byzantines in 1326 and became the capital of the Ottoman Empire. It is in northwestern Turkey in its eponymous province.

[281] It may be worth noting here that the first known imperial *tughra* is that of Sultan Orhan.

the Turks with the same esteem as the Jews do the Tables of Moses[282] or we the most sacred and holy relics. Ever since that time this tribute hath yearly continued and been brought always in the month of July by two ambassadors, who reside at the Turkish court for the space of a year. The former returning home, these are relieved at the same season of the following year by the accession of two others with the like tribute, which with the presents they also bring to the Prime Vizier, Chief Eunuch of the Women, the Queen Mother and other Sultans, with the charges and expenses of the embassy, is computed to amount yearly to the sum of twenty thousand sequins.

They were, in time past, before the war between the Republic of Venice and the Turk, very poor and put to hard shifts and arts to raise the Turkish tribute, but this war hath opened their seal and made it the port for transmitting the manufactures of Venice and all Italy into Turkey, which yields them such considerable customs as thereby their tribute is supplied with advance and other necessities provided for, so that now the old ornaments of the ambassadors, as their black velvet bonnets and gowns of crimson satin lined with marten's fur but now with sables, are not laid up in the common wardrobe for the ambassadors of the succeeding year, but a new equipage and accoutrements are yearly supplied at the common charge. And thus they pass honestly and in good esteem at the Ottoman court, being called the *dowbrai Venedik* by the Turks, or "the good Venetian."

This petty republic hath always supported itself by submission and addresses for favour and defence to divers powerful princes, courting the favour of everyone, never offering injuries, and, when they receive them, patiently support them, which is the cause the Italians call them *le sette bandiere*, or "the seven banners," signifying that for their being and maintenance of the name of a free republic they are contented to become slaves to all parts of the world. And it is observable on what a strange form of jealous policy their government is founded, for their chief officer, who is an imitation of their Doge at Venice, is changed every month, others weekly, and the governor of the principal castle of the city is but of 24 hours continuance. Every night one is nominated by the Senate for governor, who is without any preparation or ceremony taken up as he walks the streets, is led away blindfold to the castle so that no man can discover who it is that commands that night, and by that means all possibility of conspiracy of betraying the town prevented. These people in former times were great traders into the western part of the world, and it is said that those vast carracks called argosies, [283] which are so much famed for the vastness of their burden and bulk, were corruptly so

---

[282] The Jews call these the Tables of the Law (Torah); they are the two tablets said to have been handed to Moses by God, which contained the law and the Ten Commandments. See Exodus 24:12.

[283] A carrack is a three or four-masted merchant ship; an argosy is a very large one of the same.

denominated from "Ragosies," and from the name of this city, whose port is rather forced by art and industry than framed by nature.

Some of the provinces also of Georgia, formerly Iberia but now supposed to be called from St. George the Cappadocian martyr[284] and the poor country of Mingrelia are also tributaries to the Turk, who every three years send messengers with their sacrifice to the Grand Signior of seven young boys and as many virgins apiece, besides other slaves for presents to great men. This people choose rather this sort of tribute than any other, because custom hath introduced a forwardness in the parents without remorse to sell their children and to account slavery a preferment and the miseries of servitude a better condition than poverty with freedom. Of the whole retinue which these beggarly ambassadors bring with them (for so the Turks called them) being about seventy or eighty persons, a crew of miserable people are all set to sale to the very secretary and steward to defray the charge of the embassy and bring back some revenue to the public stock, so that the ambassadors return without their pomp, reserving only the interpreter as a necessary attendant to their voyage home.

The Emperor of Germany may also not improperly be termed one of the tributaries to the Ottoman Empire, whom for honour's sake we mention in the last place in so ungrateful an office, being obliged, according to the articles made with Süleyman the Magnificent, to pay a yearly tribute of 3000 *hungars*,[285] but it was only paid the first two years after the conclusion of the peace. Afterwards, it was excused by the Germans and dissembled by the Turks, until, taking a resolution to make a war on Hungary, made that one ground and occasion of the breach, for upon the truce made for eight years between Sultan Süleyman and the Emperor Ferdinand, as Ogier de Busbecq reports in those capitulations that the tribute is made the foundation of the accord: "*Cuius concordiae hae conditiones sunto primo, ut tua dilectio quotannis ad aulam nostrum pro arca induciarum 3000 Hungaricos ducatos mittere teneatur, una cum residuo, quod nobis proxime praeterlapsum biennium reservetur.*"[286]

---

[284] St. George of Cappadocia (c. 270–303) was said to have been a Christian Roman soldier who suffered martyrdom under the emperor Diocletian. There are numerous legends about him, and he is, of course, the patron saint of England as well as of Georgia and a number of other places. All information about his life, including the dates given for his birth and death, is either legendary or conjectural.

[285] The Austrian gold one ducat coin, so called because the emperor's title as king of Hungary is abbreviated as HUNGAR[iae]. In Venice they were known as *ongri*.

[286] For Ogier Ghislen de Busbecq (1549–1591), the Hapsburg ambassador to the court of Süleyman the Magnificent, see Introduction. Translation: "Of this agreement, the conditions are: first, that it is our pleasure that 3000 Hungarian ducats should be sent to our court for the treasury every year, and the rest every two years."

**Chapter XV.** *The desolation and ruin which the Turks make of their own countries in Asia, and the parts most remote from the Imperial Seat, esteemed one cause of the conservation of their empire.*

This position will appear a paradox at first sight to most men who have read and considered the Roman conquest, whose jurisdiction and dominions were far larger than this present empire, and yet we do not find that they so studiously endeavoured to dispeople and lay waste the nations they subdued, but rather encouraged industry in plantations, gave privileges to cities meanly-stored, invited people to inhabit them, endeavoured to improve countries rude and uncultivated with good husbandry, and maritime towns with traffic and commerce, made citizens of their confederates and conferred on their conquered subjects oftentimes greater benefits than they could expect or hope for under their true and natural princes. And certainly, the Romans thrived and were richer and more powerful by their policy, and therefore why the Turk might not proceed in the same manner and yet with the same advantage is worth our consideration, for the solution of which difficulty it will be necessary to consider that these two empires, being compared, there will be found a vast difference in the original, foundation, progress, and maxims each of other.

The Romans built their city in peace, made laws by which the arbitrary will of the prince was corrected, and afterward, as their arms succeeded and their dominions were extended, they accommodated themselves often to present necessities and humours and constitutions of the people they had conquered, and accordingly made provision and used proper arts to keep them in obedience. And next, by their generosity and wisdom won those nations to admire and imitate their virtues and to be contented in their subjection. But the Turks have but one sole means to maintain their countries, which is the same by which they were gained, and that is the cruelty of the sword in the most rigorous way of execution, by killing, consuming, and laying desolate the countries and transplanting unto parts where they are nearest under the command and age of a governor, being wholly destitute and ignorant of other refined arts which more civilised nations have in part made serve in the place of violence. And yet the Turks made this course alone answer to all the intents and ends of their government.

For the subjects of this empire, being governed better by tyranny than gentleness, it is necessary that courses should be taken whereby these people may remain more within compass and reach of authority, which they would hardly be were every part of this empire so well-inhabited to afford entertainment within the fortifications of its vast mountains and woods to the many unquiet and discontented spirits that live in it. And this may be one cause that so rarely rebellions arise amongst the Turks though in the remotest parts of Asia, and when they do are easily suppressed. This also is one cause why great men so easily resign themselves up to the will of the Grand Signior to punishment and death whether the sentence be according to law or only arbitrary. This is the reason that fugitives and homicides cannot escape, for, having no place for flight, neither the inhabited cities which are immediately under

the eye of a vigilant commander will afford them refuge, nor can the desolate countries entertain them, and Christendom is so abhorred by them that they will never
take it for their sanctuary. And thus, deprived of all means of safety, they wholly attend to please and serve their great master, in whose favour and hands alone is the
reward and punishment.

Another advantage, and that not inconsiderable, that this manner of dis-
peopling the country brings to this empire, is the difficulty an enemy would find in
their march should they with a land army attempt to penetrate far into the country,
for without great quantities of provision they could not possibly be sustained. From
the country none can be expected; what little it affords the inhabitants will conceal
or carry away, and leave all places as naked and barren of food for man as the sea
itself. And though it is known often that in Asia the troops of some discontented
bey or *agha* to the number of three or four hundred men, in the summertime having their retirements in the woods and mountains, assault caravans and rob all passengers from whom there is any hope of booty, yet in the winter they are dispersed,
because they have no quarters against the weather nor provisions for sustenance,
everyone shifting for himself in some place where his condition is the least known
or suspected.

And it may not be here from our purpose to admonish the reader that as the
Turks account it one good part of their policy to lay a considerable part of their
empire desolate, so on the contrary they observe in their new conquests to fortify,
strengthen and confirm what they have gained by numbers of people and new colonies of their own. And when they have reduced any considerable country to their
subjection, they commonly are inclined to make peace with that prince from whom
they have won it, so as to have time to settle and secure their bow conquests, for
countries overrun in haste are almost as speedily again recovered, and are like tem-
pests and sudden storms, which are the sooner dispersed for being violent. Augustus
Caesar, who was a wise and judicious prince, considering the extent of the Roman
Empire, wrote a book, saith Tacitus, which was published after his death, wherein
he described the public revenue, the number of citizens and confederates listed for
war, the fleets, kingdoms, provinces, tributes, customs etc. "*Addidteratque insuper
consilium coercendi intra terminus imperii, incertum,*" saith that author, "*metu, an per
invidiam,*"[287] which doubtless this wise emperor meant of a moderate and not a precipitate progress of their arms, as well as of prescribing fixed limits to the ultimate
confines of the empire, beyond which a statute should be made of *non plus ultra,*[288]
notwithstanding the most promising designs and incitements that could offer.

---

[287] "He had added a clause advising that the empire should not be extended beyond
its present frontiers, fearing danger or jealousy" (Tacitus, *Annals* 1, 11). Tacitus states that
it was a "document," not a book, and that it contained "a list of the national resources."
Works by Augustus are largely lost.

[288] Nothing further or to the utmost point.

**Chapter XVI.** *All hereditary succession in government, as also the preservation of an ancient nobility, against the maxims of the Turkish polity.*

Having formerly entered into discourse of the several great officers of state, it will be necessary to declare what care the Turks take to preserve their empire free of faction and rebellion, for, there being many provinces in the Sultan's gift which are remote, rich, and powerful and so administer temptation to the governors to throw off the yoke of their dependence and make themselves and their posterity absolute. Great care is taken to prevent this mischief by several arts, none of which hath been more effectual amongst the Turks nor more sedulously practiced than the destruction of an ancient nobility and admitting no succession to offices of riches. As my Lord Verulam says, "A monarchy where there is no nobility at all, is ever a pure and absolute tyranny, as that of the Turks. For nobility attempers[289] sovereignty, and draws the people somewhat aside from the line royal."[290] By which means it comes to pass that [a] pasha's education in the Seraglio, in the manner we have said before, without knowledge of their blood or family and without the support of powerful relations or dependencies, being sent abroad to foreign governments, where they continue but for a short season, have no opportunity or possibility of advancing any interest of their own above the Sultan. And though some have, out of an aspiring and ambitious spirit, assumed a blind confidence of renting away part of the empire, as [Abaza] Hassan Pasha of Aleppo[291] of late years with a strong and powerful army marched as far as Scutari, threatening the imperial city, and the *Turkish History*[292] tells us of the revolt of several pashas. Yet all these rebellions have been but of short durance, the Grand Signior never designing by open force by dint of sword to try his title to the empire with his own slaves, but only by some secret plot and stratagem getting the head of the rebel, he is assured of the victory without other hazard or dispute of war, for immediately thereupon the whole army disperses and everyone shifts by flight to save himself from the Sultan's anger. Nor is it imaginable it

---

[289] Modifies.

[290] Francis Bacon, baron Verulam, "Of Nobility." *The Major Works*, ed. Brian Vickers (Oxford: Oxford University Press, 2002), 365.

[291] Abaza Hassan Pasha (d. 1659) was a supporter of the disgraced Grand Vizier Ipşir Mustafa Pasha and an opponent of the increasing power and influence of Grand Vizier Mehmed Köprülü. Gathering an army of some 30,000 men in Konya, he refused to lead them either to Transylvania or to Baghdad, as Mehmed IV had ordered. The revolt resulted in a number of small battles, but Abaza Hasan was betrayed and murdered after accepting mediation by Murteza Pasha, who commanded the Sultan's army. For details see Finkel, *Osman's Dream*, 257–261.

[292] Richard Knolles, *The Turkish History, Comprehending the Origin of that Nation, and the Growth of the Ottoman Empire, with the Lives and Conquests of their several Kings and Emperors* (London, 1603). This book was, of course, expanded and brought up to date by Sir Paul Rycaut.

can be otherwise, for these men are but strangers and foreigners in the countries they ruled, have no relations there or kindred to second or revenge their quarrel, have no ancient blood or possessions which might entitle their heirs to the succession or out of affection or pity move their subjects to interest themselves in their behalf, but, being cut off themselves, all falls with them, which affords the strangest spectacle and example of fortune's inconstancy in the world. For a Turk is never reverenced but for his office—that is made the sole measure of his greatness and honour, without other considerations of virtue or nobility. And this is the reason the Turks value not their great men when taken by the enemy, for not otherwise looking on them than on ordinary soldiers, they exchange them not with commanders and persons of quality on the Christians, for the favour of the Sultan makes the pasha and not the noble blood or virtues, so that the pasha imprisoned, losing the influence of his sovereign's protection and greatness, loses that also which rendered him noble and considerable above other persons.

There are, notwithstanding, some pashas of petty governments who have obtained to themselves, through some ancient grace and privilege from the Sultan, an hereditary succession in their government, and as I can learn, those are only the pashas of Gaza, Kurdistan and three *sanjaks* formerly mentioned under the pasha of Damascus, and Turkmenistan under the pasha of Aleppo. And since I have mentioned the pasha of Gaza, it will be but requisite to call to mind one lately of that place with much honour and reverence, being one whose actions and devotion to the Christian worship might conclude him not far from the Kingdom of God, for besides his favourable inclination in general to all who professed the Christian faith, he was much devoted to the religious of Jerusalem, to whom he often made presents, as provisions of rice and other supplies for their monasteries. And when once the Father Guardian of the Holy Sepulchre[293] came to make him a visit, he met him at a good distance from his house, giving him a reception much different from what the Turks usually bestow on any who profess other than the Muhammadan faith, and might deserve the character that Tacitus gives of L. Volusius, that he was *"Egregia fama, cui septaginta quinque anni spatium vivendi, praecipuaeque opes bonus artibus, inoffensa tot imperatorum malitiae fuit."*[294]

---

[293] There were six or seven of these at one time, all Franciscans. As well, there were six or seven lay guardians.

[294] Lucius Volusius Saturninus (37 B.C.E.–56 C.E.) was a distinguished Roman statesman who served every emperor from Augustus to Nero. Rycaut has changed the quotation, which reads: *"egregia fama concessit, cuit tres et nonaginta anni spatium vivend praecipuaeque opes bonus artibus inoffensa tot imperatorum amicitia fuit."* Translation: [Volusius] died with a glorious name; there was his long life of ninety-three years, his conspicuous wealth honourably acquired, and his friendship with so many emperors" (Tacitus, *Annals* 13.30). Rycaut substitutes *malitia* (bad faith) for *amicitia*. Rycaut is most likely referring to Husayn Pasha, who was governor of Damascus in the 1660s and respected for his tolerance of both Christians and Jews.

And yet this good man, having for seventy-five years lived innocently in that government and received the inheritance from his father, was by promise of fair treatment allured to the Porte, where without farther process or any accusation, his hoary head was severed from his body for no other reason than lest the permission and indulgence to this long continuance and succession in office should prove too ample deviation from the rules of the Turkish polity.

And that means of attaining ancient riches, which is the next degree to nobility, may be cut off, the Turk observes this maxim of Machiavel[li], *"A reprimere la insolenza di uno [che surge in una reppublica potente] non vi è piu sicuro, e meno scandaloso modo, che preoccupargli quelle vie, per le quali e'viene a quella potenza."*[295] And so the Grand Signior suffers no possibility of arriving to ancient wealth, for as eldest brother to great men he makes seizure of the estates of all pashas that die, who, having children, such part is bestowed upon them for their maintenance as the Grand Signior shall think fit and requisite. If a pasha dies that is married to a Sultana, which is the Grand Signior's sister, daughter, or other relation, her *kabin* or dowry is first deducted from the estate (which is commonly 100,000 dollars), and the remainder accrues to the Sultan as heir to the rest, and by this means all ancient nobility is suppressed, and you shall find the daughters of ancient Greek houses espoused to shepherds and carters, and the ancient relics of the noble families of Cantacuzenus and Palaeologus[296] living more contemptuously at Constantinople than ever Dionysius[297] did at Corinth.

But not only in pashas and great men is care taken to clip their wings, which may hinder them from soaring too high, but also in the Ottoman family itself greater severity and strictness is exercised than in others to keep them from growing great in offices or wealth whereby to have possibility of aspiring to the supreme power, and therefore by the original and fundamental law of the Turks the children of a Sultana married to a pasha are not capable of any office in the empire, and at most cannot rise higher than to be in the quality of a *kapucibaşi*, which is one of the porters of the Grand Signior's gate. They that are of this race never dare vaunt of their pedigree; it is a contumaciousness and almost treason to name it, nor have I learned that there is any family amongst the Turks of this line of any account or esteem, but one alone, who is called Ibrahim Han Ogleri, or the offspring of Sultan Ibrahim, their father being the son of the Grand Signior's

---

[295] "To reprimand the insolence of someone powerful [who springs up in a republic], there is no more secure or less troublesome way than to forestall him in those ways by which he came to power" (Machiavelli, *Discourses*, 1, 52 [chapter heading]). Rycaut omitted the words in brackets.

[296] Both these families had supplied a number of Byzantine emperors.

[297] Dionysius II (d. 344 BCE) was tyrant of Syracuse. After his deposition he lived in Corinth in much-reduced circumstances, ending his life as a teacher of philosophy and rhetoric. Plutarch, in his "Life of Dion," holds Dionysius (who had been Dion's rival) up as an example of the reversal of fortunes.

sister and married to a Sultana, and are said to be of the race of the Tatars, so that proceeding by the women's side only their rent or revenue is yearly about 70,000 dollars *"quibus magnae opes innocenter partae et modeste habitae,"*[298] which they manage with prudence and discretion, live honourably without ostentation, seek no office or intermeddle in affairs of state, by which means they have preserved themselves from envy and suspicion in the revolutions of the Turkish government.

The Grand Signior many times, when he fears the greatness of any pasha, under colour and pretense of honour prefers him to the marriage of his sister or some other of his feminine kindred, by which means, instead of increasing power and glory, he becomes the miserablest slave in the world to the tyranny of a proud and insulting woman. For first, he cannot refuse the honour, lest he should seem to neglect and condemn the Sultan's favour, then, before the espousals, he must resolve to continue constant to her alone and not suffer his affection tos to wander on other wives, salves or distractions of his love. If he hath a wife whom he loves, whose long conversation and children she hath brought him have endeared his affections too far to be forgotten, he must banish her and all other relations from his home to entertain the embraces of his unknown Sultana. Before the espousals, what money, jewels, or rich furs she sends for he must with compliment and cheerfulness present, which is called *ağirlik*.[299] Besides this, he makes her a dowry called *kabin*, of as much as friends that make the match can agree. When the *kabin* is concluded and passed before the Justice in form or nature of a recognisance, the bridegroom is conducted to the chamber of his bride by a Black Eunuch, at whose entrance the custom is for the Sultana to draw her dagger and imperiously to demand the reason of his bold access, which he with much submission replies to and shows the *emir e-padishah*[300] or the imperial *firman* for his marriage. The Sultana then arises, and with more kindness admits him to nearer familiarity. The eunuch takes up his slippers and lays them over the door, which is a sign of his good reception, then he bows with all reverence before her to the ground and retires a few paces back, making some brief oration to her full of compliment and admiration of her worth and honour, and remaining afterwards a while silent in a humble posture, bowing forward with his hands before him until the Sultana commands him to bring her water, which he readily obeys, taking a pot of water provided for that purpose, and, kneeling before her, delivers it to her hand. Then she takes off her red veil from before her face, embroidered with gold and silver flowers, and so drinks. In the meantime her serving-maids bring in a low table on which are set a pair of pigeons roasted and

---

[298] "[he] attained great wealth which was blamelessly acquired and modestly enjoyed" (Tacitus, *Annals* 4.44). The reference is to Gnaeus Lentulus (d. 25 C. E.), Roman general and statesman.

[299] Literally, "weight."

[300] Literally, "command of the Sultan."

a plate of sugar-candy. The bridegroom then invites his coy spouse to the collation, which she refuses until other presents are brought her which lie prepared in the outward room, with which, her modesty being overcome and her stomach brought down, she is persuaded to the table, and sitting down receives a leg of a pigeon from the hand of her bridegroom, tastes a little and then puts a piece of sugar-candy into his mouth, and so, rising up, returns to her place. All the attendants then retire and leave the bridegroom alone with his Sultana for the space of an hour to court her singly.

That time being past, the music sounding, he is invited forth by his friends to an outward room where, having passed most of the night with songs and sports, at the approach of morning the Sultana, weary of her pastime, retires to her bed, which is richly-adorned and perfumed, fit to entertain nuptial joys. The bridegroom, advised hereof by nod of the eunuch, creeps silently into the bedchamber, where, stripping himself of his upper garments, he kneels awhile at the feet of the bed, and then by little and little turning up the clothes, gently rubs her feet with his hand, and, kissing of them, ascends higher to the embraces of his spouse, which she willingly admits him to and wishes herself and him a happy bedding. In the morning betimes the bridegroom is called by his friends to the bath, at whose call arising he is presented by the bride with all sorts of linen to be used in bathing. After these ceremonies are past they are better acquainted, yet in public she keeps him at a distance, wears her *hançer* or dagger by her side in token of her superiority, and so frequently commands gifts and riches from him until she hath exhausted him to the bottom of all his wealth. Nor is this esteemed sufficient, to mortify these poor slaves by women's tyranny, but they are always put forward upon deliberate attempts, as lately Ismail Pasha who was killed passing the river Raab in the overthrow given the Turks by the Emperor's forces under Montecuccoli,[301] and others I could name in like manner, lest the honour of their marriage in the royal family without the crosses and mortifications which attend it should puff them up with the ambition and proud thought which is not lawful for them to imagine.

But it may well be objected how it came to pass that the present Prime Vizier called Ahmed should succeed his father Köprülü in the government of the empire. 'Tis true it was a strange deviation from the general rule of their policy and perhaps such a precedent as may never hereafter be brought into example, but accidents occur oftentimes to the fortune of some men without order or reason. And yet Köprülü the father had so well-deserved of the Sultan and his whole dominions, for having by his own wisdom and resolution saved the empire from

---

[301] Prince Raimondo Montecuccoli (1608/09–1680) was an Italian general in the service of the Holy Roman Empire. Rycaut describes his victory over the Turks at St. Gothard earlier on (see above). He fought against the French (1674) and gained notable victories over Marshal Turenne. Montecuccoli also wrote books on military history and strategy.

being rent in pieces by the faction and ambition of some aspiring persons and by the blood of thousands of mutinous heads, had cemented and made firm the throne of his master that no honour could be thought sufficient to be paid to his ghost unless it were the succession of his son in his place, which, the more unusual and irregular it was esteemed, the greater glory it was to that family. And herein also this subtle fox played his masterpiece, by representing the state of affairs to remain in that posture as was necessary to be carried on with the same method as begun, which he had entrusted to the knowledge of his son, and this was the reason what this young vizier, then scarce arrived to thirty years and but an ordinary *cadi* or justice of the law, was both as to his age and relation thus irregularly preferred to the office of [Grand] Vizier.

Nor hath hereditary succession nor long continuance in authority been only avoided amongst the Turks, but we find the Romans often changed their governors and never suffered them to continue long in one province, and so the king of Spain doth at present in the government of Flanders, the Indies, the Kingdom of Naples, and other parts, the space of three years being commonly allotted them for their residence. But amongst the Turks there is no fixed term of time appointed to their pashas, but only they remain as tenants at will of the Grand Signior, who according to his pleasure and as he sees reason cuts them off, recalls them, or transplants them to another province. Only the pasha of Grand Cairo in Egypt hath a certain space of three years appointed, to which his government is confined, and there may be very good reason for it, for it being a place of great trust, riches, and power in which pashas grow in a short time vastly wealthy, the revenue of which we have had occasion to discourse of. And therefore the Grand Signior doth often not only abbreviate their time, but also at their return shares in the best part of the prizes they have made. The Romans had that opinion of the wealth and power of Egypt that Augustus made a decree and held it "*inter alia dominationis arcana*"[302] that it should not be lawful for any without particular license to enter Egypt, and expressly forbids senators and gentlemen of Rome without order from the prince or for the affairs of state to visit those parts. And Tacitus gives this reason for it, "*ne fama urgeret Italiam quisquis eam provinciam claustraque terrae ac maris, quamvis levi praesidio adversum ingentes exercitus insedisset.*"[303]

Another danger to the empire, which the Turks sedulously avoid, besides hereditary succession of office, is rivalry among princes of the blood during the time of their father's life, for afterwards the successor takes care to secure his brethren beyond possibility of competition. The story of Selim and Bayezid, the

---

[302] "Amongst other secrets of imperial policy" (Tacitus, *Annals* 2.59).

[303] "Lest anyone who held a province containing a key of the land and sea might, with ever so small a force, occupy Italy by famine against the most powerful army" (Tacitus, *Annals* 2.59).

sons of Süleyman the Magnificent,[304] is a perfect experiment of the feud and dissension which is bred in the desires of barbarous princes, so that when they arrive to any maturity of age they are always transported to different seraglios abroad, where they keep their courts distinct and cannot enter within the walls of Constantinople during the life of their father, lest by interview with each other their minds should be moved with emulation, or, inhabiting the imperial city, should be provided with means before their time to attempt the throne of their father. And for this reason the Grand Signior hath scarce performed the ceremonies of his inauguration before he hath seasoned his entrance to his throne with the blood of his brothers, which began in the time of Sultan Bayezid.[305] But if the brothers are but few and the Grand Signior of a disposition more naturally inclined to clemency than cruelty, he secures them in the seraglio under the tuition of masters and care of a faithful guard, differing nothing from imprisonment but in the name, prohibiting them the society and conversation of all. And thus the two brothers of this present Sultan Mehmed live in as much obscurity and forgetfulness as if they had never been born, or, having passed a private life, were departed to the place where all things were forgotten.

It is no great digression from our purpose here to take notice of two sorts of governments purely popular. The one hath already had its period and the other is of late beginning and at present flourishes, and those are the commonwealths of Egypt under the Mamluks[306] and the other, in our day, in the dominion of Algiers. The first not only deposed the whole family of their prince from having power in the government and from all succession but also made it an immutable law that the sons of the Mamluks might succeed their father in the inheritance of their estates as lands and goods, but could not assume the title or government of a Mamluk. Nor not only so, but that all that were born in the Muhammadan or Jewish faith were incapable *ipso facto* of the Order of a Mamluk, and only such preferred thereto who had been sons of Christians and become slaves instructed and educated in the Muhammadan superstition or else men of mature age, who,

---

[304] Süleyman gave his sons Selim and Bayezid military commands, but they soon began a rivalry. In 1559 Selim (later Selim II "the Drunkard") defeated Bayezid near Konya, and the latter, afraid to face his father, fled to Persia with his family, where the Shah permitted him to be executed two years later by an agent sent from Istanbul. It was Selim who eventually succeeded his father in 1566. Both Bayezid and his brother Mustafa, who was also executed, "were endowed with such inherited qualities as to make either of them worthy to carry on the line of the first ten Ottoman Sultans" (Kinross, *Ottoman Centuries*, 259).
[305] Bayezid I, who came to the throne in 1389, had his younger brother Ibrahim strangled in 1390.
[306] Al-Ashraf Tuman Bey II (r. 1516–1517), the last Burji Sultan of Egypt, was defeated by Selim I at the battle of Ridnieh outside Cairo, then betrayed to the Turks and executed.

having abjured God and their country, were come thither to seek preferment in that kingdom of darkness. And this slavish and strange constitution of government flourished for the space of 267 years[307] until overthrown in the year of Our Lord 1517 by the arms of Selim [I], that victorious emperor of the Turks. The present government of Algiers is but of a few years, the first original of which was by one Barbarossa, a famous pirate,[308] and afterwards by the accession of great quantities of Turks out of the Levant. The protection of the Grand Signior was craved and a pasha received from the Porte, but now the pasha remains without any power, the whole government being transferred to the scum of the people, who, fearing lest the power should at last become subject to the natives, have made it a law that no son of a Turk born in that country, whom they call *coulouglies*,[309] can be capable of an office in their commonwealth, but only such who, having been born Christians, are perverted to the Turkish sect or else such who come from parts of the Turkish dominions to be members of their republic. And this much shall serve to have declared how much the Turks are jealous of all successions in office and authority which may prejudice the absolute monarchy of their great Sultan.

---

[307] Rycaut is correct. The first Mamluk dynasty was founded by Shajar al-Durr in 1250.

[308] Oruç Reis (c. 1474–1518), a famous Turkish pirate and privateer born in Lesbos, was the eldest of three brothers, two of whom were known as Barbarossa, or "Redbeard." He took over Algiers in 1516, and ceded it as a *sanjak* to the Ottoman Empire the next year, in return for which he was appointed its governor, and subsequently became the governor of the West Mediterranean region. He was killed fighting the Spaniards at the battle of Tlemcen in Algiers. He was succeeded by his brother Hayreddin Barbarossa.

[309] The *coulouglies* were "half-Turks. . .sons of such soldiers who had been permitted to marry at Algiers. . .excluded from the honour of being Dey, Agha of the Janissaries and other considerable offices" (Sir Robert Lambert Playfair, *The Scourge of Christendom: Annals of British Relations with Algiers prior to the French Conquest* [London: Smith, Elder and Co., 1884], 17).

**Chapter XVII.** *The frequent exchange of officers,* viz. *the setting up of one and degrading another, a rule always practiced as wholesome and conducing to the welfare of the Turk.*

He that is an eyewitness and strict observer of the various changes in greatness, honours, and riches of the Turks hath a lively emblem of contemplation before him of the unconstancy and mutability of human affairs. Fortune so strangely sports with his people that a comedy or tragedy on the stage with all its scenes is scarce sooner opened and ended than the fate of divers great men, who in the daytime being exalted to high sublimity by the powerful rays of the Sultan's favour in the nightfall vanish like a meteor. The reason hereof, if duly considered, may be of great use as things stand here, that is, to the power of the Grand Signior, for in this constitution the health and benefit of the Emperor is consulted before the welfare of the people. And the power of the Emperor is in no action more exercised and evidenced than by withdrawing and conferring his favours, for by these means having many whom he hath educated and prepared for offices and stand candidates to receive them, his power would seem to be at a *non plus*[310] and appear like an inconsiderable father who had spent more money in the breeding of his sons than the patrimony amounted to he had to bestow upon them. And therefore the Grand Signior, to imitate the sun, benights some parts of the world to enlighten others, that so by a general influence and communication of his beams he may be acknowledged the common parent of them all.

And this course doth not evidence the power of the Grand Signior but likewise increases it, for none are advanced in these times to office but pay the Grand Signior vast sums of money for it according to the riches and expectations of profit from the charge. Some pay, as the pashas of Grand Cairo and Babylon, 3 or 400,000 dollars upon passing the commission; others one, others 200,000, some 50,000 as their places are more or less considerable, and this money is most commonly taken up at interest at 40 or 50 per cent for the year and sometimes double, when they are constrained to become debtors to the covetous eunuchs of the seraglio, so that everyone looks on himself, as indeed he is, greatly indebted and obliged by justice or injustice, right or wrong, speedily to disburden himself of the debts and improve his own principal in the world. And this design must not be long in performance, lest the hasty edict overtake him before his work is done and call him to account for the improvement of his talent. Think, then, taking all circumstances together of the covetous disposition of a Turk, the cruelty and narrowness of soul in those men commonly that are born and educated in want, what oppression, what rapine and violence must be exercised to satisfy the appetite of these men, who come famished with immense desires and strange considerations to satisfy! *"Diu sordidus repente dives mutationem fortunae*

---

[310] Here, the phrase means something like "at a standstill."

*male tegebat, accensis egestate longa cupidinibus immoderatus,"*[311] so that justice in its common course is set to sale and it is very rare that when any lawsuit is in hand but bargains are made for the sentence, and he hath most right who hath most money to make him *rectus in curia*[312] and advance his cause. And it is the common course for both parties at difference, before they appear together in presence of the judge, to apply themselves singly to him and try whose donative and present hath the most in it of temptation, and it is no wonder if corrupt men exercise this kind of trade in trafficking with justice, for having bought the office, of consequence they must tell the truth, *"vendere iure potest, emerat ille prius."*[313] Add hereunto a strange kind of facility in the Turks for a trifle or small hire to give false witness in any case, especially, and that with a word, when the controversy happens between a Christian and a Turk, and then the pretense is, for the *Müslümanlik,*[314] as they call it, for the cause is religious, hallows all falsehood and forgery in the testimony, so that I believe in no part of the world can justice run more out of the current stream than in Turkey, where such maxims and consideration corrupt both the judge and witnesses. *"Turcae magnae pietatis loco ducunt dicere falsum testimonium adversus hominem Christianum; non expectant ut rogentur; iniussi adsunt seque ultro ingenerunt."*[315]

This consideration and practice made an English ambassador, upon renewing the capitulations, to insert an article of caution against the testimony of the Turks, as never to be admitted in evidence in the case, but only a *hoget* or recognizance[316] made before a judge, or a bill of writing under the hand of him on whom the demand is made. Which article, as it was very advisable and with great prudence and wisdom obtained, so it hath proved of admirable consequence and security to the traffic of merchants' estates, which before being liable to the

---

[311] "For a long time being poor and suddenly becoming wealthy, he could hardly conceal the change in fortune and indulged immoderately the appetites which a lengthy poverty had inflamed" (Tacitus, *Histories* 1.66). Rycaut's version has *regit* where it should read *tegebat*.

[312] Literally, "upright in court," that is, having clean hands.

[313] "He may lawfully sell that which he previously bought." The origin of this Latin tag is most likely a pasquinade against Pope Alexander VI Borgia (1492–1503) cited in various places: *"Vendit Alexander claves, alteris, Christum / vendere iure potest, emerat ille prius,"* which translates as "Alexander sells the keys, the altars, and Christ / He may lawfully sell what he previously bought." This in turn may be derived from Martial, *"Carmina Paulus emit, recitat sua carmina / nam quod emas possis iure vocare tuum,"* which says "Paulus buys poems and recites them as his own / so you see, whatever you buy, you can lawfully call your own" (Martial, *Epigrams* 2.22).

[314] The Islamic religion.

[315] "For the Turks regard it as an act of great piety to bear false witness against a Christian; they do not wait to be questioned but come of their own accord" (Busbecq, *Turkish Letters*, 149).

[316] Conditional obligation.

forgeries and false pretenses of every dissolute Turk, have now this point as a defence and fortification by which false pretenses and suits for considerable sums of money and matters of great value have been blown away and decided with great facility and little expense.

In the time of Bayezid [I], the fourth king of the Turks, the courts of justice were in like manner corrupted, as at present, for reformation of which the prince resolved to execute a great number of his lawyers, until it was pleasantly represented by his jester, to whom between jest and earnest he had given liberty to speak the truth, which soberer men durst not, that all the cause of bribery and corruption in the judges proceeded from want of stipends and necessary maintenance. Whereupon Bayezid, growing cooler and sensible of the cause of that evil, by granting their pardon, allowing them salaries and stipends with additional fees of twenty aspers in all causes exceeding a thousand and twelve aspers for every writing and instrument out of court. And in the time of the best emperors, when virtue and deserts were considered and the empire flourished and increased, men had offices conferred for their merits and good services were rewarded freely and with bounty, without sums of money and payments to be a foil to the lustre of their better parts. But now it is quite contrary, and all matters run out of course, a manifest token, in my opinion, of the declension and decay of the Ottoman Empire. As Livy saith: "*Omnia prospera evenisse sequentibus deos, adversa autem spernentibus.*"[317] Howsoever in part this serves the great end of the empire, for pashas and great men, having a kind of necessity upon them to oppress their subjects, the people thereby lose their courages, and by continual taxes and seizures on what they gain, poverty subdues their spirits and makes them more patiently suffer all kinds of injustice and violence that can be offered them, without thoughts or motion to rebellion. And so the Lord Verulam says in his *Essays* that "it is impossible for a people overladen with taxes ever to become martial or valiant, for no nation can be the lion's whelp and the ass between burthens,"[318] by which means the Turk preserves.so many different sort of people as he hath conquered in due obedience, using no other help than a severe hand joined to all kind of oppression. But such as are Turks and bear any name of office or degree in the service of the empire feel but part of this oppression and live with all freedom. Having their spirits raised by a license, they attain to insult over others that dare not resist them.

---

[317] "You will find that everything works out well for those who follow the gods, whilst adversity dogs those who spurn them" (Livy, *History of Rome* 5.51.5).

[318] The whole passage from Bacon reads: "The blessing of Judah and Issachar will never meet; that 'the same people or nation should be both the lion's whelp and the ass between burthens,' neither will it be, that a people overlaid with taxes should ever become valiant and martial" (Bacon, *Essays* [1625 edition], *The Major Works*, 398–399). The quotation is inverted by Rycaut.

But the issue and conclusion of the spoils these great men make on sub-jects is very remarkable, for as if God were pleased to evidence his just punish-ment more evidently and plainly here than in other sins, scarce any of all those pashas who have made haste to be rich have escaped the Grand Signior's hands but he either divests them of all or will share the best part of the prey with them. Amongst which, I have observed none passes so hardly as the pashas of Grand Cairo, because it is the richest and most powerful of all the governments of this empire, and so either in his journey home or after his return he loses his life by public command or at least is rifled of his goods as ill-got, which are condemned to the Grand Signior's treasury. And it is strange to see yet with what heat these men labour to amass riches which they know by often experiences have proved but collections for their master, and only the odium and curses which the op-pressed wretches have vented against their rapine remain to themselves: *"rebus secundis avidi, adversis autem incauti."*[319] And this is like the policy that Cesare Borgia[320] used, otherwise called *Il Duca Valentino*, who, the better to reduce Romagna, lately subdued to obedience, made one Messer Ramiro de Lorca[321] his deputy, a man of a cruel and tyrannical disposition, who by rigour and force reduced affairs to the will and order of his prince. And the work now done, and the people remaining extraordinarily discontented, the duke thought it time to purge the minds of his people of the ill apprehension they had of his government by demonstrating that the former hard usage proceeded from the bad inclination of his minister, and commanded the same Ramiro de Lorca at Cesena to be cut in pieces and exposed to the public view of the people with a piece of wood and a bloody knife by his side. This saith Machiavelli: *"fece aquelli popoli in un tempo remanere stupidi e sodisfatti,"*[322] and the Turk understands well how profitable in

---

[319] "As unprepared for adversity as they had been elated by success" (Tacitus, *An-nals* 1,68).

[320] Cesare Borgia (1476–1507), well-known from Machiavelli's *The Prince*, was a statesman, general, and churchman, the first cardinal ever to resign his title. He was created duc de Valentinois by Louis XII, and carved out territory for himself in the Romagna district of southeastern Italy. He was a byword for ruthless efficiency as a ruler, and has been cited for many crimes by various historians. After a successful military ca-reer, he was imprisoned when on his way to Romagna to put down a rebellion, his lands were seized by the Papal States, and he himself exiled to Spain in 1504. He died fighting for the king of Navarre.

[321] Ramiro de Lorca (c. 1452–1502), a Spaniard, was Cesare Borgia's majordomo and governor of Romagna in his master's absence. At the sieges of Forli and Cesena he displayed conspicuous cruelty by hanging hundreds of their citizens, and eventually found himself in trouble after continued complaints from the people he oppressed, as Ry-caut tells us. He was murdered, probably on Cesare Borgia's orders. Rycaut's account of his death is lifted from Machiavelli (see below).

[322] "Causing the people to be at once satisfied and dismayed" (Machiavelli, *The Prince*, 7).

the same manner it is for the constitution of his estate to use evil instruments who may oppress and poll his people, intending afterwards for himself the whole harvest of their labours, they remaining with the hatred, whilst the prince, under colour of performing justice, procures both riches and fame together.

If it be supposed that any great man intends to make combustion or mutiny in his government or that his wealth or natural abilities render him formidable, without further inquisition or scrutiny all discontent of the Grand Signior is dissembled and perhaps a horse, a sword, or sables is reported to be presented and all fair treatment is counterfeited until the executioner gets the bowstring around his neck, and then they care not how rudely they deal with him, just like the birds in Plutarch who beat the cuckoo for fear that in time he should become a hawk.[323] And to make more room for the multitude of officers who crowd for preferments and to act the cruel edicts of the empire with the least noise, [there are] times when a great personage is removed from his place of trust and sent with a new commission to the charge, perhaps, of a greater government. And though he depart from the regal seat with all demonstrations of favour, before he hath advanced three days in his journey, triumphing in the multitude of his servants and his late hopes, the fatal command overtakes him, and without any accusation or cause other than the will of the Sultan he is barbarously put to death and his body thrown into the dirt of a foreign and unknown country without the solemnity of funeral or monument, that he is no sooner in the grave than his memory is forgotten. And this, methinks, is somewhat agreeable to the crafty policy of Tiberius, who sometimes would commissionate men for government of provinces to whom beforehand he had designed not to permit licence to depart the city.

Hence are apparent the causes of the decay of arts amongst the Turks, of the neglect, want of care in manuring and cultivating their lands, why their houses and private buildings are made slight, not durable for more than ten or twenty years, why you find no delightful orchards and pleasant gardens and planations, and why in those countries where Nature hath contributed so much on her part there are no additional labours of Art to complete all and turn it to a paradise. For men knowing no uncertain heir nor who shall succeed them in their labours contrive only for a few years' enjoyment, and, moreover, men are fearful of showing too much ostentation or magnificence in their palaces or ingenuity in the pleasures of their gardens lest they should bring on them the same fate that Nabal's vineyard occasioned to his master.[324] And therefore men neglect all applications to the study of arts and sciences, but only such as are necessary and conducing to the mere course of living, for the very fear and crime of being

---

[323] The original fable may be found in Aesop. Plutarch retells it in his "Life of Aratus," *Lives of Noble Greeks and Romans*, 11.

[324] For the story of Nabal, his vineyard and his daughter Abigail, victims of King David's greed, see 1 Samuel 25.

known to be rich makes them appear outwardly poor and become naturally stoics and philosophers in all the points of a reserved and cautious life. And here I am at a stand and cannot conclude this chapter without contemplating awhile and pleasing myself with the thoughts of the blessedness, the happiness, the liberty of my own country, where men under the protection and safe influence of a gracious and the best of princes in the world enjoy and eat of the fruit of their own labour and purchase to themselves with security fields and manors, and dare acknowledge and glory in their wealth and pomp, and yet leave inheritance to their prosperity.

**Chapter XVIII.** *The several arts the Turks use to increase their people is a principal policy, without which the greatest of their empire cannot continue to be increased.*

There was never any people that laid foundations and designs of a great empire but first thought how to make it populous and by which means they might best supply them with people, not only sufficient for the sacrifice and slaughter of war, but for the plantation of colonies, possession and security of what the sword hath conquered. We never understood how one people alone that was martial and by successes in war had framed a large empire, was able from the mere original of its own stock to abound with issue of natural subjects, to bear proportion with the stronger nations, nor how a handful of people with the greatest policy and courage in the world was able to embrace a large extent of dominion and empire. It is true that Alexander did, with an army for the most part composed of Macedonians, as it were in a rant[325] make a conquest of the best part of the eastern world, but this empire, like a ship that had much sail and no ballast, or a fair tree overcharged with boughs too heavy for its stem, become a windfall on a sudden.

The Turks therefore, during the continuance of their empire, have not been ignorant of this truth, for no people in the world have ever been more open to receive all sorts of nations to them than they, nor have used more arts to increase the number of those that are called Turks. And it is strange to consider that from all parts of the world some of the most dissolute and desperate in wickedness should flock to these dominions to become members and possessors of the Muhammadan superstition, in that manner that at present the blood of the Turks is so mixed with that of all sorts of languages and nations that none of them can derive his lineage from the ancient blood of the Saracens.

The Romans, who well knew the benefit of receiving strangers into their bosom, called this freedom they gave *ius civitatis*,[326] whereby foreigners became as lawful possessors of estates and inheritances and had as much right to the common privileges as any that were born in the walls of Rome, and this *ius civitatis* was given to whole families, so that as Sir Francis Bacon says well, that the Romans did not overspread the world but the world itself. The English call it naturalization, the French *enfranchisement* and the Turks call it "becoming a believer," for they, joining with it a point of religion, not only the proffers of the goods of this world but also of delights in the world to come, make the allurements and arguments the more prevalent. And, it being an opinion amongst them, as over all the world, that it is a meritorious work to create proselytes, scarce any who hath money to purchase a slave but will procure one young and fit for any

---

[325] In an extravagant but empty manner.

[326] In Roman law, this term refers to those laws which must be observed by everyone in a nation.

impression, whom he may name his convert and gain reputation amongst his neighbours of having added to the number of the faithful.

Of all this number, which yearly are added to the professors of Muhammad, none can retreat on lower terms than death and martyrdom for Christ, which causes many whose consciences, though touched with the sense of the denial of their savior, yet having not grace or courage to assert their faith on so hard a lesson, grow desperate and careless and die in their sin. This sort of people become really Turks, and some through custom and their own lusts are really persuaded of the truth of this profession and have proved more inveterate and fatal enemies to Christianity than the natural Turks, which will appear, if we consider that all the successes they have had and exploits they have done at sea have been performed by such who have denied the Christian faith, as, namely, Cigalazade, Uluç, and others.[327]

It was the custom formerly amongst the Turks every five years to take away the Christians' children and educate them in the Muhammadan superstition, by which means they increased their own people and diminished and enfeebled the force of the Christians. But now that custom in a great part is grown out of use, though the abundance of Greeks, Armenians, Jews and all nations where the iron rod of the Turks' tyranny extends, who flock in to enjoy the imaginary honour and privilege of a Turk. And indeed it is no wonder to human reason, that considers the oppression and contempt that poor Christians are exposed to and the ignorance of their churches occasioned through poverty in their clergy, that many should be found who retreat from the faith, but it is rather a miracle and a true vindication of those words of Christ, that the gates of Hell shall not be able to prevail against his Church,[328] that there is conserved still amidst so much opposition and in despite of all tyranny and arts contrived against it, an open and public profession of the Christian faith, which next to God's providence, considering the stupid ignorance of the Greek and Armenian churches, their conservation of their faith is not to be attributed to any instance more than

---

[327] Cigalazade Yusuf Sinan Pasha (c. 1545–1605) was born Scipione Cicala in Messina, Sicily, and was one of the most successful Ottoman admirals of his time. He had been captured at the battle of Djerba (1560) and eventually converted to Islam, married two great-grand-daughters of Süleyman the Magnificent and rose to the rank of *silahtar*, after which he became *aga* of the Janissaries (1575), *beylerbey* of Damascus and Van, and finally, for a short time, Grand Vizier (1596), as well as being *Kapudan Pasha* or admiral of the fleet. Uluç Ali or Kiliç Ali (1519–1587), born Giovanni Galeni, became pasha and *beylerbey* of Algiers (1568) and *Kapitan-I Derya* (1571) after successfully extricating part of the Ottoman fleet from the disaster at Lepanto. He then initiated the rebuilding of the fleet, and led an expedition to the Crimea (1584), afterwards putting down revolts in Syria and Lebanon (1585).

[328] This is a paraphrase of "thou art Peter, and upon this rock I will build my church. And the gates of hell shall not prevail against it" (Matthew 16:18).

to the strict observation of the feasts and fasts of their churches. For having rarely the helps of catechisms or sermons, they learn yet from these outward ceremonies some confused notions and precepts of religion, and exercise with severity and rigour this sort of devotion, when through custom, confusion, and scarcity of knowing guides, all other service is become obsolete and forgotten amongst them.

The Turks have another extraordinary supply of people from the Black Sea, sent them by the Tatars, who with their light bodies of horse make incursions into the territories of the neighbouring Christians and carry with them a booty of whole cities and countries of people, most of which they send to Constantinople to be sold, and is the chief trade and commodity of their country, as we have already discoursed. It is sad to see what numbers of *sayaks*[329] or Turkish vessels come sailing through the Bosphorus freighted with poor Christian captives of both sexes and all ages, carrying on the maintop a flag either as a note of triumph or else as a mark of the ware and merchandise they carry. The number of slaves brought yearly to Constantinople is uncertain, for sometimes it is more and sometimes less, according to the wars and successes of the Tatars, but as it is apparent in the registers of the customs at Constantinople only, one year with another, at the least 20,000 are yearly imported, amongst which the greatest part, being women and children, with easy persuasions and fair promises become Turks. The men, being ignorant and generally of the Russian or Muscovite nation, who are reported not to be over-devout or of famed constancy and perseverance in religion, partly by menaces and fear, partly by good words and allurements of rewards, despairing of liberty and return to their own country, renounce all interest in the Christian faith.

Of this sort of mettle most of the Turks are composed, and by the fecundity of this generation the dominions of this empire flow, for the Turks of themselves, though they have the liberty of polygamy and freer use of divers women allowed them by their law than the severity of Christian religion doth permit, are yet observed to be less fruitful in children than those who confine themselves to the chaste embraces of one wife. It is true we have heard how in former times there have been particular men amongst the Turks that have severally been fathers to a hundred sons, but now, through that abominable vice of sodomy, which the Turks pretend to have learned from the Italians and is now the common and professed shame of that people, few fecundious[330] families are found amongst them, especially amongst the persons of the greater quality, who have means and time to act and contrive their filthiness with the most deformity. And in this manner, the natural use of the women being neglected amongst them, as St. Paul saith, "Men burning in lust one towards another,"[331] so little is mankind propagated

---

[329] A *sayak* is a type of ketch, or two-masted sailing boat.
[330] Fertile.
[331] Romans 1:27.

that many think that were it not for the abundant supplies of slaves which daily come from the Black Sea, as before we have declared, considering the summer-slaughters of the plague and destructions of war, the Turk would have little cause to boast of the vast numbers of his people, and that a principal means to begin the ruin of this empire were to prevent the taking of so many captives or intercept those numbers of slaves which are daily transported to nourish and feed the body of this great Babylon. By which means, in time they would not only find a want of servants but a decay and scarcity of masters, since as it is before-mentioned, these slaves, becoming Turks, are capable of all privileges, and being commonly manumitted by their patrons, through the help of fortune arrive equally to pre-ferments with those who are of the ancient Muhammadan race. This is the true reason the Turk can spend so many people in his wars, and values not the lives of ten thousand men to win him but a span of ground, and yet almost without any sensible diminution of his people. And, on the contrary, the invention of an In-quisition and the distinction between *cristianos viejos* and *nuevos*[332] in Spain and Portugal have caused that decay and scarcity of people in those countries as hath laid the best part of those fruitful soils desolate and forced them to a necessity of entertaining a mercenary soldiery.

It is no small inducement to the vulgar people, who is most commonly one with outward allurements, to become Turks, that when they are so by a white turban or such a particular note of honour they shall be distinguished from other like sects, all people amongst the Turks being known by their heads of what re-ligion and quality they are, and so may the better be directed where they may have a privilege to domineer and injure with the most impunity. If we consider how delightful the mode is in England and France, especially to those who are of a vain and gay humour, and that nothing seems handsome or comely but what is dressed in the fashion and air of the times, we shall not wonder if the ignorant and vain amongst Christians born and educated in those countries should be catched and entrapped with the fancy and enticement of the Turkish mode and be contented to despoil themselves of the garment of Christian virtues to assume a dress more courtly and pleasing to the eyes of the world. For so the Britons and other nations after conquered by the Romans began to delight themselves in their language and habit, their banquets and buildings, which they accounted to be humanity and refinement of their manners, but Tacitus says: *"pars servitutis esset,"*[333] a signal symptom of their subjection.

And it is worth a wise man's observation how gladly the Greeks and Arme-nian Christians imitate the Turkish habit and come as near to it as they dare,

---

[332] These terms denote respectively "pure" (old) Christians, that is, not converts, and "new" Christians, those Iberian Jews and Muslims who converted to Christianity after the Spanish conquest of Granada and all their baptised descendents.

[333] "It would be part of their servitude" (Tacitus, *Agricola* 1.21). Rycaut has *erat* in-stead of *esset*.

and how proud they are when they are privileged upon some extraordinary occasion to appear without their Christian distinction. And thus the Turk makes his very habit a bait to draw some to his superstition: riches to allure the covetous, rewards and hopes to rule the ambitious, fears and terrors of death the cowardly and timorous, and by all means works on the dispositions and humours of men to make additions to his kingdom. Such as adhere to the Christian faith the Turk makes no account of, and values no otherwise in the place of subjects than a man doth of his ox and ass, merely to carry the burdens and to be useful and servile in slavish offices. They are oppressed and are subject to all advantages and pretences, and their goods and estates gained with labour and the sweat of their brows, liable to the rapine of every great man. They are disarmed and never exercised in war, by which means they become effeminate and less dangerous in rebellion. Only the people of Transylvania, Moldavia and Wallachia, under the conduct of their respective princes that the Grand Signior sets over them, serve him in their persons in the war and are the first thrust forward in all desperate enterprises, so that the oppression of poor Christians under the Turk is worthy our compassion. How poor they are become, how their former wealth is exhausted, how the fatness of their rich soil is drained and made barren by poisonous suckers, so that it is evident that the Turk's design is no other than by impoverishment and enfeebling the interest of Christianity to draw proselytes and strength to his own kingdom.

Wherefore some sort of poor Christians, either actually subjects to the Turkish tyranny or borderers on them, who often feel the misery of their incursions, being fearful of their own constancy in the faith, have contrived ways to preserve themselves from any other profession, wherefore in Mingrelia the Christians at the baptism of their children make a cross on their hands. And in Serbia their custom is to make it on their foreheads with the juice of a certain herb, the stain of which never wears out, so that some of these nations who become renegades to the Christian faith bear always a badge and note of designation about them to a holy profession, which may serve to upbraid their perfidious desertion of the faith, the cross on their forehead appearing for a shame and discountenance to the white turban on their heads. By which pious art many of these distressed Christians have, notwithstanding fear and despair of liberty and promises of reward, through the apprehension of this incongruity between the cross and the banner of Muhammad, preserved themselves firm to their first colours.

**Chapter XIX.** *The manner of reception of foreign ambassadors amongst the Turks, and the esteem they have of them.*

There was no nation in the world ever so barbarous that did not acknowledge the office of an ambassador sacred and necessary, "*Sanctum populis per saecula nomen*,"[334] and Cicero saith "*Sic enim sentio ius legatorum eum hominum praesidio munitum, tum etiam divino iure esse vallatum.*"[335] And it is a Turkish canon, "*elehi zaval yoketer*," do not hurt an ambassador, so that the Turks confess themselves obliged by their own law to rules of civilities, courteous treatment, and protection of ambassadors. The greatest honour they show to any foreign minister is to him who comes from the Emperor, because his confines are contiguous with theirs and have had occasion more frequently than with any other Christian princes to try the power of the imperial sword. An ambassador coming from the Emperor, as soon as he enters the Ottoman dominions, hath his charges defrayed by the Sultan according to the importance of the business and negotiation he is designed to until the time of his return, and a Resident continuing in ordinary hath in like manner his constant allowance. As it hath always been a custom amongst the eastern princes to send presents to one another as tokens of friendship and amity, so the Emperor is by an ancient custom and agreement obliged to accompany his ambassador to this court with presents and gifts as offerings of peace. And, on the contrary, that the Emperor may not remain with the disadvantage, the Grand Signior is bound to recompense the embassy with another from himself and adorn it with presents of equal value with those that were sent him. But ambassadors and representatives from other princes who have their dominions more remote and whose principal design is esteemed for the promotion of trade and commerce, as the English, French, and Dutch, are always admitted with their presents, which the Turk by custom calls his right, and judges not himself obliged to return the like, esteeming his capitulations and articles he makes with those princes privileges and immunities granted their subjects.

The ceremonies they use at the audience of every ambassador are acted, as in all parts of the world, most to set off the glory of the empire and represented with such advantages as may best afford a theme for an ambassador's pen to describe the riches, magnificence and terror of the Ottoman power. The audience with the Grand Signior, having first passed a compliment with the Prime Vizier, is commonly contrived on days appointed for payment of the Janissaries, which is every three months, and with that occasion the order and discipline of the militia, the money and stipends that are issued forth are there exposed to the observation of the public minister. The money is brought into the divan and there piled

---

[334] "A name reverenced by people through the ages" (Statius, *Thebaid* 2.486).

[335] "I think that the right of ambassadors is not only safeguarded by human protection but also strengthened by divine law" (Cicero, *On the Responses of the Soothsayers* 16.34).

in heaps, where the ambassador is first introduced and seated on a stool covered with crimson velvet, placed near the first Vizier and other Viziers of the Bench. As soon as the money is paid out to the chief of every *oda* or chamber, who afterwards distribute it amongst their soldiers, a plentiful dinner is prepared for the ambassador, who, together with the First Vizier and other Viziers of the Bench and *defterdar* or Lord Treasurer are seated at the same table, which is not raised as high as the tables we use but something lower, covered over with a capacious voider[336] of silver in which the dishes are set without ceremony of tablecloths or knives. In the same room are two tables for the principal attendants of the ambassador and other personages amongst the Turks of chief note and quality. The dishes are served in by one at a time, which as soon as touched or tasted are taken off to make room for another, and thus there is a succession of threescore or fourscore services, all the dishes being of china worth about 150 dollars apiece, which are reported to have a virtue contrary to poison and to break with the least infusion thereof, and for that reason esteemed more useful for the service of the Grand Signior, "*Nam ulla aconita bibuntur / fictilibus.*"[337]

The banquet being ended, the Çavuş başi or Chief of the Pursuivants[338] conducts the ambassador with some of his retinue to a place apart, where several gay vests or long garments made of silk with divers figures are presented them as a sign of the Grand Signior's favour, which the ambassador first putting on, and then the others to the number of 18 or 19, attended with two *capuşi başis* or Chief of the Porters, persons of good esteem in that court with silver staves in their hands, he is conducted nearer towards the Grand Signior's presence. Then follow the presents brought by the ambassador, which are carried to the best advantage for appearance and are delivered to officers appointed to receive them. The courts without are filled with Janissaries, amongst whom is observed such a profound silence that there is not the least noise or whisper understood, and the salutations they give their principal officers as they pass, bowing all together at the same time, is warlike and yet courtly, and savours of good discipline and obedience.

The ambassador is then brought to a great gate near the audience, the porch of which is filled with White Eunuchs clothed in silks and cloth of gold. Farther than this none is suffered to proceed besides the secretary, interpreter, and some other persons of best quality. At the door of the chamber of audience is a deep silence, and the murmuring of a fountain nearby adds to the melancholy, and no other guard is there but a White Eunuch. And here they tread softly in token of fear and reverence, so as not to disturb with the least noise the majesty of the Sultan, for access to the eastern princes was always difficult and not permitted

---

[336] Usually a voider is a container for food scraps and leftovers; here it is the actual container for the dishes.

[337] "They will drink no aconite out of earthenware cups" (Juvenal, *Satires* 10.25). Aconite or aconitine is a poison derived from the monkshood plant.

[338] A pursuivant is an attendant; in England he is a heraldry officer.

with the same familiarity as hath been practiced amongst the Romans and at present with us, where the sight of the King is his own glory and the satisfaction of his subjects. For it is with the Turks as it was with the Parthians when the received Vonones their king, educated in the Roman court, who, conforming to those manners, saith Tacitus, "*irridebantur Graeci comites,[ac vilissima utensilium annulo clausa] prompti aditus, obvia comita, ignotae Parthis virtutes,*" the affability and easiness of address to their prince was a scandal to the nation.[339]

At the entrance of the Chamber of Audience hangs a ball of gold studded with precious stones, and about it great chains of rich pearl. The floor is covered with carpets of crimson velvet embroidered with gold wire, in many places beset with seed-pearl. The throne where the Grand Signior sits is raised a small height from the ground, supported with four pillars plated with gold; the roof is richly-gilded, from which hang balls that seem to be of gold. The cushions he leaned upon, as also those which lay by, were richly-embroidered with gold and jewels. In this chamber with this occasion remains no other attendant besides the First Vizier, who stands at the right hand of the Grand Signior with modesty and reverence. When the ambassador comes to appear before the Grand Signior he is led in and supported under the arms by the two *capuçi başis* before-mentioned, who, bringing him to a convenient distance, laying their hands upon his neck, make him bow until his forehead almost touches the ground, and then, raising him again, retire backwards to the farther part of the room. The like ceremony is used with all the others who attend the ambassador, only that they make them bow somewhat lower than him. The reason of this custom, as Busbecq saith, was because that a Croat, being admitted near to Murat to communicate something to him, made use of that opportunity to kill him in revenge of the death of his master Marcus,[340] but the Turkish history saith that this was done by one Miloš Orbilić, who after the defeat given to Lazar[341] the despot of Serbia, rising from amongst the dead, had near access to the presence of Murat.[342] The ambassador

---

[339] "They laughed at his Greek entourage and because he locked up the most ordinary household objects; the Parthians, unfamiliar with his virtues of accessibility and affability, took them for unusual vices" (Tacitus, *Annals* 2.2). Rycaut omits the words in brackets. Vonones I, who was indeed Roman-educated, reigned 8–12 CE. He was driven out by Artabanus and later assassinated.

[340] "On our arrival we were introduced to [the Sultan's] presence by his chamberlains, who held our arms—a practice which has always been observed since a Croatian sought an interview and murdered the Sultan Amurath in revenge for the slaughter of his master, Marcus the Despot of Serbia" (Busbecq, *Turkish Letters*, 39).

[341] Prince Lazar Hrebeljanović (1329–1389) was the ruler of the Moravian Serba from 1371–1389, although he was virtually king in Serbia because of the weakness of the monarchy at the time. He was killed along with Sultan Murat I at the battle of Kosovo. Lazar was elevated into both an epic hero and a saint of the Serbian Orthodox Church.

[342] Rycaut is retelling an old story which is recorded in many sources. Murad I was killed after the battle of Kosovo (1389) by someone, but scholars are not sure who. Miloš

at this audience hath no chair set him, but standing informs the Grand Signior by his interpreter the several demands of his master and the business he comes upon, which is all penned first in writing, which, when read, is with the letter of credence consigned into the hands of the Great Vizier, from whom the answer and farther treaty is to be received.

This was the manner of the audience given to the earl of Winchilsea when ambassador there for His Majesty, and is, as is there said, the form used to others who come from a prince equally honoured and respected. But though the Turks make these outward demonstrations of all due reverence and religious care to preserve the persons of ambassadors of ambassadors sacred and free from violence, yet it is apparent by their treatment and usage towards them in all emergencies and differences between the prince they come from and themselves that they have no esteem of the law of nations or place any religion in the maintenance of their faith. For when a war is proclaimed the ambassador immediately is either committed to close imprisonment or at least to the hands of a careful guard confined to the limits of his own house. In this manner the representative of Venice, called there the *bailo*, by name Soranzo,[343] in a strait[344] chamber of a castle situated on the Bosphorus endured a severe imprisonment, having his interpreter strangled for no other cause than performing his office in the true interpretation of his master's sense. Afterwards this *bailo* (for so they call there the ambassadors from Venice) was removed to another prison at Adrianople, where he continued some years, and in fine, by force of presents mollifying the Turks with money, with which their nature is easily made gentle and pliable, he obtained liberty to remain in the house appropriated to the representatives of Venice, but under a guard, whose office was to secure him from escape and observe his actions. And yet, with liberality and presents, which overcome the Turks more than any consideration in the world, he enjoyed as he pleased license for his health to take fresh air and use what freedom was reasonable.

Nor less injurious to the law of nations have been the examples of violence and rage acted on the persons of the French ambassadors, first on the sieur Sancy,[345]

---

Obilić was a probably a Serbian hero in the service of Prince Lazar Hrebeljanović who was alleged to have pretended to surrender to Murad and then killed him. There are several versions of the story, both Serb and Croat, and there is uncertainty as to the identification or even nationality of Obiliç.

[343] The title *bailo*, which probably derives from the Latin *baiulus*, "porter," was given to all the Venetian ambassadors who were sent to Constantinople. It was sometimes anglicised to "baillie" or even "baily." For details of Soranzo's dealings with the Turks and his imprisonment, see Kenneth M. Setton, *Venice, Austria and the Turks in the Seventeenth Century* (New York: American Philosophical Society, 1991), 112–20.

[344] Narrow, cramped.

[345] Achille de Harlay, sieur de Sancy (1581–1646), a friend of Cardinal Richelieu's, was ambassador to the Ottoman Empire from 1610 to 1620. Accused of fraudulent

accused upon suspicion of having contrived the escape of Koniećpolski,[346] general of the Polish army, taken captive in a fight and sent prisoner to the above-said castle on the Bosphorus. The means was by a silken cord sent in a pie with limes, and files to cut the iron bars, and, having first secured his guard with the strength of wine, in the dead of night let him down by the cord from the highest tower, where, finding horses ready, he got safe into Poland. The contrivance of this stratagem and the instruments of the escape was laid to the charge of the French ambassador, who was committed for that reason to the Prison of the Seven Towers,[347] where he remained for the space of four months until his money and the French king his master mediated for him, promising to send another speedily to succeed him. He was delivered from his imprisonment and returned home by the way of Poland. The successor of this ambassador was the count Cézy,[348] a man too generous and splendid to live long amongst covetous and craving Turks, exhausted most of his wealth in gifts and presents, to which, adding a vanity and ambition to court the Grand Signior's mistresses in the Seraglio (as is said), he paid such vast sums of money to the eunuchs for his admittance that in a few years he became so indebted and importuned with the clamours of his creditors as wholly discredited, and lost the honour and authority of his embassy, so that the French king, thinking it dishonourable to continue his minister in that charge who was failed and undone in the reputation of the world, sent his

behavior, he was ordered to be given the bastinado by Sultan Mustafa I, and was recalled in 1620. He accompanied Henriette Marie to England to marry Charles I, but was sent back by the king in 1627. Louis XIII appointed him bishop of St-Malo in 1630.

[346] Stanisław Koniećpolski (c. 1590–1646) was an eminent Polish nobleman, statesman and military commander. He was captured by the Turks at the battle of Cecora (1620) and held captive until 1623. He went on to become one of the greatest Polish generals of his time, defeating the Tatars in 1624 and 1626, and finally destroying an Ottoman army at the battle of Ochmatów (1644). He also served as governor of Sandomierz from 1625, and was appointed Crown Grand Hetman of the Polish-Lithuanian Commonwealth by king Władysław IV of Poland, who wanted to start a crusade against the Ottoman Empire.

[347] The Fortress of the Seven Towers, now known as the Yedikule, was originally a triumphal arch and tower built by the Byzantine emperor Theodosius I. In 412 Theodosius II added two more towers, and the number seven was reached in 1470 by Mehmed II, who used it as a treasury and a prison. It was often used to confine foreign ambassadors who had offended the Turks, and was also the scene of the murder of Sultan Osman II in 1622. Nowadays one can still see "sad graffiti elegantly scrawled" on the walls of the East Tower or Tower of the Ambassadors by those imprisoned foreign ambassadors (Taylor, *Imperial Istanbul*, 29).

[348] Philippe de Harlay, comte de Cézy (1582–1652), a cousin of de Sancy, was French ambassador at the Ottoman court from 1620 to 1631. He shows up as a source for Racine's tragedy *Bajazet* (1672), and is credited by the author in his preface for providing him with information about the death of Bayezid.

letter of revocation to recall him home. But the Turks gave a stop to his return, pretending that their law, which was indulgent to the persons of ambassadors, did not acquit them from payment of their debts or privilege them with impunity to rob the believers and other subjects of the Grand Signior, contrary to that rule of Grotius, who not only exempts the persons but the servants and moveables of ambassadors from attachments, and no law can compel him to the satisfaction of debts by force, but by friendly persuasion only, till being returned to his own country and put off the quality of a public person he becomes liable to common process: "*Si quid ergo debiti contraxit et ut sit res soli eo loco nullas possideat, ipse compellandus erit amice, et si detrectes, is qui misit, ita ut ad pstremum usurpentur ea, quae adversus debitores extra territorium positos usurpari solent.*"[349]

Nor less remarkable was the barbarous usage of the sieur la Haye,[350] ambassador for the French king to the Porte under the government of the Great Vizier Koprülü. The court being then at Adrianople and the treaty in hand between the Grand Signior and the Republic of Venice through the mediation of the French ambassador by consent and command of his master, certain letters of his were intercepted by the Turks, by what means and upon what information the matter was too evident then to be apprehended other than an Italian contrivance. The cipher, as containing matter prejudicial to the state, was carried to Adrianople, and, being known by examination and confession of the messenger to have been delivered to him by the Secretary of the French Affairs, immediately in all haste the ambassador, then at Constantinople, was cited to appear at court, but being ancient and indisposed in his health with the gout and the stone, dispatched his son as his procurator with instructions and orders how to answer what might be objected, hoping by that means to excuse the inconvenience of a winter's journey.

The son, being arrived there, immediately was called to audience, accompanied with the chancellor or secretary for the merchants, for the other secretary of the private affairs of the embassy, apprehending the fury and injustice of the Turks, had timely secured himself by flight. Discourse was first had concerning

---

[349] "If [an ambassador] has contracted a debt and, as is usual, has no possession in the country where he resides, then friendly application must be made to him, and, in case he refuses, to his sovereign. But if both these methods of redress fail, recourse must be had to those means of recovery which are used against debtors residing out of the jurisdiction of the country" (Grotius, *De jure belli ac pacis* 2, 18.9).

[350] Jean de la Haye, seigneur de Vantelet (d. 1667) was French ambassador to the Ottoman court from 1639 to 1665. Rycaut's account of his misadventures is largely accurate. He was actually succeeded as ambassador by his son Denis. In addition to what transpires in this story, la Haye had apparently failed to send gifts or offer congratulations to Mehmed Koprülü Pasha when he was appointed Grand Vizier in 1656, which may have been just as important as his perceived sympathy with the Venetians a few years later. The story was repeated to Antoine Galland a few years later (*Journal d'Antoine Galland pendant son séjour à Constantinople 1672–1673*, ed. Charles Schafer [Paris: Leroux, 1881], I, vii–viii).

the contents of the characters; the Turks, insolent in their speeches, provoked this sieur la Haye the younger to utter something tending towards a contempt of that power the Turks had over him, encouraging himself with the thought of the protection of the king his master, who was soon sensible and moved with the least injuries offered his ministers. The Turks, who can endure nothing less than menaces, and Koprülü, through natural cruelty and choler of old age and particularly malice against the French nation, moved with this reply, commanded the Çavuş baçi, who is chief of the pursuivants, to strike him on the mouth, which he did with that force, being a rude robustious fellow, that with a few blows of his fist he struck out two of his teeth before, and in a most undecent and barbarous manner dragged him with the secretary of the merchants to a dungeon so loathsome and moist that the ill vapours oftimes extinguished the candle.

The old ambassador, the father, was with the like Turkish fury sent for, the Turks executing all they do with strange haste and violence: "*barbaris cunctatio servilis, statim exequi regium videtur*,"[351] and being arrived at Constantinople was also committed to custody, although not with that rigour and severity of imprisonment as the son, until the space of two months passing, with presents and solicitations the both obtained their liberty and returned again to Constantinople. Scarce were they arrived before news coming of a French ship which had laden goods of the Turks and run away with the cargo, the ambassador was again committed to another prison in Constantinople called the Seven Towers, where he remained until gifts and money the anger of the Turks was abated. And still the malice of Koprülü persecuted this sieur la Haye, until after his 25 years continuance, unfortunate only at the conclusion, he was dispatched home obscurely and in disgrace without letters of revocation from his master or other intimation to the Grand Signior which might signify the desire of this ambassador's return.

The reason of this irreverent carriage in the Turks towards the persons of ambassadors, contrary to the custom of the ancient Romans and other gallant and civilised people, is an apprehension and maxim they have received that an ambassador is endued with two qualifications, one of representing to the Grand Signior the desires of his Prince, the breach of articles or league, the aggrievances and abuses of merchants trading in his dominions that so satisfaction may be made, and the other, that he remains in the nature of a hostage, called by themselves *mahapous* or pledge, by which he becomes responsible for what is acted by his prince contrary to the capitulations of peace, and remains for a pawn for the faithful and sincere carriage of his nation and as security to insure what goods belonging to Turks are loaden on their vessels. The resident from Holland was in the year 1663[352] imprisoned at Adrianople for miscarriage of a ship belonging to

---

[351] "Delay is seen as servile, prompt action as kingly" (Tacitus, *Annals* 6.32).

[352] This was Levinus Warner (1619–1665), a scholar and antiquarian who was Dutch ambassador to the Ottoman court (1654–1665) as well as being a great collector of Islamic and Judaic manuscripts. A German by birth, Warner studied oriental languages at the

his nation taken by the Maltese men-of-war, whereon at Alexandria were goods loaden belonging to the Grand Signior and other considerable persons of state, and was not released until he engaged to eighty-five thousand dollars in the space of one hundred and twenty days, which was the full import of the Turkish interest.

Nor hath this Law of Nations to the sacred esteem of ambassadors found better observation towards the representatives of the German Emperor, who have upon all conjunctures of discord and breaches of peace between those two powerful Princes been subject to confinements and custody of a guard, nothing differing from formal imprisonment, or else, as happened to the German Resident in the last war, transported from place to place according to the motions of the armies as a barbarous trophy in the time of their prosperous successes and as a means at hand to reconcile and mediate when evil fortune compels them to composition.

What ill fate soever hath attended the ministers of other Princes in this court, the ambassadors from His Majesty of Great Britain, our sacred King, have never incurred this dishonor and violation of their office. The negotiations and differences since the English trade hath been opened in Turkey have been various and considerable, and matters as to the security of the ambassadors and merchants have been often reduced to a doubtful condition as far as words and rude speeches full of menaces and choler might make a sober man suspicious of a greater ruin, and yet, through the constancy, prudence, and good fortune of ambassadors, the Turkish rashness hath not drawn upon themselves the guilt of violating their persons, but have either prevented troubles in the beginning or wisely compounded them before they made too far a breach.

It is worth observation that the Turks make no difference in the name between an ambassador, resident, agent, or any petty messenger sent or residing upon a public affair. The name *elçi* serves them to express all, although they have the name of *kapikahya*, which signifies an agent at court and is commonly attributed to those who reside at the Porte for the Princes of Transylvania, Moldavia and Wallachia and also for the agents of pashas, every one of which hath his minister at the court to send him advices and to answer for him if

---

University of Leiden and wrote several scholarly works on the Middle East. He died in Istanbul, possibly poisoned, as a letter from Woyciech Bobowski to Isaac Basire suggests (Hannah Neudecker, "From Istanbul to London: Albertus Bobovius's Appeal to Isaac Basire," in *The Republic of Letters and the Levant*, ed. A. Hamilton, M. van den Boogert, and Bart Westerveel [Leiden: Brill, 2005]), 181. His memoirs were posthumously edited by G. N. Du Rieu as *De rebus Turcicis: epistolae ineditae* (Leiden: Brill, 1883). Rycaut gives more details of Warner in Chapter 21. Also see Mehmed Bulut, "Business, Correspondence, Organisation and Composition between Atlantic and Levant during the Age of Merchant Capitalism" (paper, International Economic History Conference, Helsinki, 2006), 4–5.

anything should be amiss represented. And though the Turks on occasion of rup-
tures and other discontents lose their respect towards the person of ambassadors,
yet still it is commendable in them that they commonly abstain from the spoil
and plunder of the merchants' estates with whose princes they are at enmity. For
they look upon merchants as men whose protection is best advanced by peace,
and as their own comparison is, like to the laborious bee which brings honey to
the hive and is innocent, industrious, and profitable, and therefore an object of
their compassion and defence.

**Chapter XX.** *How ambassadors and public ministers govern themselves in their negotiations and residence amongst the Turks.*

Ambassadors in this country have need both of courage and circumspection, wisdom to dissemble with honour and discreet patience seemingly to take no notice of affronts and contempts, from which this uncivilised people cannot temperate their tongues even when they would seem to put on the most courteous deportment and respect toward Christians. The French ambassador Monsieur la Haye sent once to advise the Great Vizier Koprülü that his master had taken the strong city of Arras from the Spaniard[353] and had obtained other victories in Flanders, supposing that the Turk would outwardly have evidenced some signs of joy and returned an answer of congratulation. But the reply the Vizier gave was no other than this: "What matters it to me whether the dog worries the hog or the hog the dog, so my master's head be safe?" intimating that he had no other esteem of Christians than as savages or beasts, and with no other answer than this, due to an officious courtship towards a Turk, the messenger returned. There is no doubt but of all those means wherewith kingdoms and states are supported, there are two more principal and chief of all others: the one is the substantial and real strength and force of the prince, which consists in his armies and interest, and the other is the honour and reputation he gains abroad, which hath sometimes proved of that authority and consequence as to make the state of the weaker prince to appear more considerable, or at least equal to the greater forces of the other. This reputation is principally maintained by a prudent manner of negotiation and depends on the discretion of the representative, in which for many years the Republic of Venice had great advantage in the Turkish court through the caution and policy of their ministers, who nourished in the Turks an opinion of their strength of arms and source of wisdom beyond the reality thereof, that before the war broke forth no nation in amity with the Turk had their affairs treated with more honour and respect than this commonwealth.

An ambassador in this court ought to be circumspect and careful to avoid the occasion of having his honour blemished or of incurring the least violation of his person, for afterward, as one baffled in his reputation, he becomes scorned, loses his power and interest and all esteem of his worth and wisdom. For, having endured one affront, their insolence soon presumes farther to trespass on his patience, for certainly Turks, of all nations in the world, are most apt to crush and trample on those that lie under their feet, as on the contrary those who have a reputation with them may make the best and most advantageous treaties of any part of the world. According to that of Busbecq, *Epistle 1, "sunt Turci in utramque*

---

[353] Arras was captured in 1640 by the combined French forces of Marshals de Châtillon and de La Meilleraye. The siege was an important victory against the Spanish occupation of the Netherlands, and made even more significant by the fact that both Louis XIII and Cardinal Richelieu were present.

*partem nimii sive indulgentia, cum pro amicis se probare volunt, sive acerbitate cum irati sunt.*[354] To reply according to the pride and ignorance of a Turk is to blow up fire into a flame; to support with submission and a pusillanimous spirit his affronts and indignities by negotiations by negotiating faintly or coldly is to add fuel and wood to the burning piles, but solid reason and discourse accompanied with cheerful expressions, vivacity, and courage in arguments, is the only way of dealing and treating with the Turks. That which is called good nature or flexible disposition is of little use to a public minister in his treaty with Turks; a punctual adherence to former customs and examples, even to obstinacy, is the best and safest rule, for the concession of one point serves to embolden them to demand another, and so their hopes increase with the success, having no modesty or wisdom to terminate their desires. One act or two of favour is enough afterwards to introduce a custom, which is the chiefest part of their law, and to make that which is merely voluntary and of grace to become of obligation. But a principal matter which a public minister ought to look to is to provide himself of spirited, eloquent and intelligent interpreters, I say, because many times the presence is great they appear before, and the looks big and sour of a barbarous tyrant, and it hath been known that the ambassador hath been forced to interpose his own person between the fury of the Vizier and his interpreter, whose offence was only the delivery of the words of his master, some of whom have, notwithstanding, been imprisoned or executed for this cause.

As we have partly intimated in the foregoing chapter, the reason of which tyranny and presumption in these prime officers over the interpreters is because they are most commonly born subjects of the Grand Signior, and therefore ill-support the least word misplaced or savouring of contempt for them, not distinguishing between the sense of the ambassador and the explication of the interpreter. And therefore it were very useful to breed up a seminary of young Englishmen of sprightly and ingenious parts to be qualified for that office, who may, with less danger to themselves, honour to their master and advantage to the public, express boldly without the usual mincing and submission of other interpreters whatsoever is commanded and declared by their master. The French nation hath taken a very good course in breeding up youths to make their druggermen[355] or interpreters. Some few years past, twelve were sent to Smyrna, where, being awhile instructed in the convent of Capuchins and there taught the Turk-

---

[354] "The Turks are very extreme on both sides, whether with tenderness when they wish to show themselves as friends, or with harshness when they are angry."

[355] This is an alternative English spelling of the more familiar word "dragoman." The word is derived from the Turkish *turcüman*, which means "interpreter," "translator," or "guide" (modern Turkish *çevirmen*). There is some speculation amongst scholars that the Turks were reluctant to learn European or non-Muslim languages, which is why interpreters were often ethnic Greeks, and thus subjects of the Ottoman Empire, hence vulnerable to abuse.

ish and vulgar Greek, they are afterwards dispersed to the several factories, such as were of most pregnant[356] parts being placed with the ambassador at Constantinople. Such a provision of young druggermen, at least twelve, ought to be allowed, for some of them die, some grow weary of the country and are desirous to return home; others, not having a sufficiency of parts nor health, answer not expectation, so that if two or three of such a number happen to succeed well, they are a great help to the ambassador and the consul where they serve. The English ambassador once had three youths sent abroad on this design, but they are now all three dead, and one alone came into employment.

It is certainly a good maxim for an ambassador in this country not to be over-studious in procuring a familiar friendship with Turks. A fair comportment towards all in a moderate way is cheap and secure, for a Turk is not capable of real friendship towards a Christian, and to have him called only and thought a friend who is in power is an expense without profit, for in great emergencies and times of necessity, when their assistance is most useful, he must be bought again and his friendship renewed with presents and farther expectations. Howsoever, this way of negotiating by presents and gratuities is so much in custom amongst the Turks that, to speak truly, scarce anything can be obtained without it. But it is the wisdom of the minister to dispose and place them with honour, decency, and advantage, for there are, and have been always, two or three powerful persons in this court which in all times carry the principal sway and command of all. These must necessarily be treated with respect and often sweetened with gratuities; he that hath money may doubtless make friends when he needs them, and with that secure, his capitulation and privilege purchase justice, and if his stock will hold out, act anything that can reasonably be imagined, yet it is the most profitable and prudent way to refer something to friendship and good correspondence, and not at all to mere force and strength of money.

---

[356] Most-developed skills.

**Chapter XXI.** *How foreign princes in particular stand in the esteem and opinion of the Turks.*

The Turks, as we have occasionally instanced before, are naturally a proud and insolent people, confident and conceited of their own virtue, valour and forces, which proceeds from their ignorance of the strength and constitution of other countries, so that when the danger which may arise from the conjunction and union of Christian princes to Muhammadan interest is discoursed of, they compare the Grand Signior to the lion and other kings to little dogs which may serve, as they say, to rouse and discompose the lion, but can never bite him but with their utmost peril. They say farther, as by an ingenuous confession, that they are unable to encounter the Christians at sea, to whom God hath given that unstable element for dominion and possession, but that the earth is the lot and inheritance of the Turks, which is demonstrable by that great circuit of empire obedient to the Muhammadan arms. These are the thoughts and apprehensions of the commonalty concerning Christendom in general, which I have heard often discoursed amongst them, but the opinion and esteem which knowing men and ministers frame of foreign kingdoms and states distinctly is, for the most part, according to these following particulars.

Of all the princes so far remote as England, none amongst this people stands in better account than His Majesty of Great Britain, not only for the convenience of the trade, which provides the empire with many necessary commodities, but for the fame of his shipping and power at sea, which makes him, though divided from all parts of the world, yet a borderer on every country where the ocean extends. And this esteem and honour the Sultan bears towards His Majesty hath been evidenced in several particulars, and by none more than by the security and freedom his merchants live in in these dominions, and a readiness always, in every reasonable request, to gratify His Majesty's ambassadors.

As for the Emperor, the Turk knows that his own proper and peculiar force is, in itself, inconsiderable, but that with the conjunction and assistance of the German princes they are assured, and have proved it to their experience in the year 1664, that his strength is equivalent to the Ottoman power. But yet they are not ignorant that the diversity of religions and sects in Germany abate much of that vigour and co-operation amongst themselves which is requisite to the vigorous opposition of so potent an enemy. And it is evident that the Emperor's unseasonable severity against the Protestants in Hungary, disobliging his whole dominion there by depriving them of their churches and exercising other courses for suppression of the reformed religion, ripened the Turks' design of war, first laid in the year 1663, conceiving in that conjuncture holding forth the specious pretence of liberty in religion and conscience, the Hungarians would either wholly defeat the Emperor or very coldly and faintly apply themselves to his succour, the effect of which was in the succeeding wars plainly verified and known that the Hungarians were not only sparing in their contribution and supplies of men in service of the Emperor, but held secret juntos and councils whether it were not better to accept the Turks' sovereignty on the conditions proposed, with liberty of their religion, rather than to continue in allegiance to the Emperor, who neither afforded them freedom of conscience, which is the destruction of their spiritual estate, nor was able to withstand the Turk, which argued insufficiency to yield them protection in their temporal. The Emperor sends his ambassador to the Turk under notion of the King of Hungary,[357] because at his installment as Emperor, he swears to make a perpetual war with the Turk, and indeed their peace is little better than a war, considering their frequent incursions into each other's territories, and that to skirmish or fight in bodies under the number of 5000, not taking forts or bringing cannons in the field, is no breach of the capitulations.

The French king, though the first Christian prince that having no confines bordering on these dominions entered into capitulations with the Turk for a free and open commerce and traffic and obtained the title of *Padishah*, which signifies as much as "emperor" and is denied to all other Christian kings and even to the German Emperor himself, being adjudged an honour amongst the Turks proper and peculiar only to the Grand Signior. Yet their esteem of the French is not so great as some would persuade the world it is, having, as we have at large declared in the foregoing chapter, given ample testimonies in the persons of the ambassador of their scorn and neglect of the prince he represented. I have heard the wise Lord Chancellor Samizade say that the French gained that title of *Padishah* to their king by craft and subtlety, and was never fully examined nor considered, and in that business there is a strange romance told of a fair French lady preferred to the Seraglio whom the Turks were willing to receive for a princess, and thence challenging affinity with the King of France was the more profuse in the honour of his titles. It is true there was a time when the French ambassador was called to secret councils and admitted within the walls of the Seraglio to private meetings and debates of the Turk, but it was when the French plotted and openly assisted in transportation of the Turks for the invasion of Italy, but since that time, and especially in the year 1664, through the force given the Emperor and the bravado upon Barbary, the French hath always, and that not without some reason, gone declining in the good opinion and esteem in the Ottoman court.

The Pope is more esteemed as a prince able to blow the coals and excite other princes to the damage of the Muhammadan state rather than by his own power or force to effect anything himself, and having no confines bordering on the Turks, his riches, power or greatness seldom falls as a subject for their consideration.

---

[357] The Holy Roman Emperor was also King of Hungary, so the latter part of him could treat with the Turks, whilst the former part could not, having sworn a coronation oath to war with them.

As little account would they make of the King of Spain, but that the Granadine Turks, of which there remains in Constantinople a considerable number since their expulsion,[358] through an extreme affection naturally inherent in them to Spain discourse of it with a passion not altogether free of a little rodomontade and vainglory, vices incident to their country, whereby they create in the Turks a conceit of the greatness, riches and force of Spain, according as it flourished in the time that the Moors possessed their seat and habitation there. But yet the Turks, though a people injurious and negligent of the accurate state of other places besides their own, are not altogether ignorant of the decay of Spain, the wars in Portugal and the menaces from France, which makes them aim at one of the Venetian ports in Dalmatia to have the better prospect and easier passage unto Sicily or the Kingdom of Naples.

The esteem the Venetians are in at this time amongst them is greater than when the war first began, for then they entertained an opinion of their force much inferior to the real estimation thereof as they do now the contrary beyond their true strength, making always calculations from the effect and success of things. Yet the Turk knows that the Venetian power is not comparable to his by land, and that nothing but Friuli[359] stands between him and the mastery of Venice, which makes him ashamed and angry that after so many years' wars no greater additions should be acquired to the empire than his footing in Candia,[360] the whole possession of which was imagined at the beginning of the war would upon a bare demand have been quietly presented as the price and purchase of peace.

The King of Poland is none of the least amongst the Christian princes esteemed at the Ottoman court by reason of his great power, consisting chiefly in horse, which in the opinion of the Turks is the most warlike, and looks upon the people as martial and with much difficulty brought under their subjection. But by reason of the great combustions and intestine troubles of that country, the Polanders apply themselves with much dexterity and caution in their treaties with the Turks, and especially, being borderers with them and subject to their incursions and robberies of men and cattle, they endeavour all means of fair and reasonable compliance. And on the other side, the Turk is well-inclined to the Polander and desires his prosperity beyond others of his neighbor-princes, because he looks on

---

[358] The final expulsion of Moors from Spain took place from 1610 to 1614.

[359] Friuli is in the north-east of Italy, with its former capital at Udine. By 1516 the eastern part was controlled by the Emperor, whilst the central and northern areas were Venetian.

[360] Candia was a city in Crete (the name was also used to denote the whole island) which sustained what was probably the longest siege in history (1648–1669) until it was finally taken by the Ottomans. Crete had been controlled by Venice since 1204, and even after Candia the last Venetian outpost did not fall until 1718.

him as the only curb upon all occasions of the Muscovites, and whom they make use of to give some stop and arrest unto the progress of his arms.

The Muscovite hath yet a greater fame and renown with the Turks, being reported to make one hundred and fifty thousand horse, so that he treats with the Turk on equal terms and fills his letters with high threats and hyperbolical expressions of his power and with as swelling titles as the Turk. The Greeks also have an inclination to the Muscovite beyond any other Christian prince, terming him their emperor and protector, from whom, according to the ancient prophecies and modern predictions, they expect delivery and freedom of their church. But the greatest dread the Turk hath of the Muscovite is from the union with the Sophy[361] or Persian, which two, uniting together, would be too unequal a match for the Ottoman Empire.

But above all the great potentates of the world the King of Persia was most feared and esteemed by the Turk, not only by reason of his great force and that the borders of his dominions run a long space on the confines of the Turks, but because it is almost impossible, by reason of vast deserts and uninhabited places, to carry the war into his country without the cumbersome carriages of all necessary provisions, which with how much difficulty and incommodity were performed in the last wars between these two great princes the history sufficiently relates. But, since the conquest of Babylon[362] and decay of their riches, they are now the subjects of the Turkish scorn and contempt. The nearness of their faith, though derived from the same founder but afterwards receiving some difference by the interpretation of Ali, is in nowise a reconcilement of their affections but rather a ground and matter of their fear and jealousy, lest at any time waging a war against the Persians that heresy should be set on foot amongst the people, which, like a spark that causes the conflagration of a whole city, may breed those intenstine civil distractions, which may prove of more danger and ruin than the former war.

"It will not be necessary to speak much of the Hollanders, in regard that though they have a resident there, they are scarce taken notice of as a nation different, but depending on the English." These foregoing words of Holland have been liable to censure amongst the Dutch, but for my apology therein, I have this much to say, that though the assertion may seem strange in these our times, yet when it was first wrote, which is now above 17 years past, it might have passed for common truth. *Distingue tempora et bene doces.*[363]

When I came first into Turkey, which was in the year 1660, there were very few of the Dutch nation then in Turkey, and their trade very inconsiderable. At

---

[361] This is the usual name used by English writers to denote the Shah of Persia. It was derived from the name of the ruling dynasty, the Safavids, who reigned in Persia from 1499 to 1722.

[362] Babylon was captured by the Turks in 1637.

[363] Separate the times and you are well-informed.

Aleppo they had no consul till some years after my arrival Levinus Warner, resident at Constantinople, sent his brother first to that place, but before that time they always lived under the English protection. At Smyrna they had no other for their consul than one Evan Ogle, a Greek, of whom either the Dutch or Turks took little notice, having recourse very often to the English consul for his advice and assistance. At Constantinople for many years the Dutch lived under the English ambassador, which was the occasion of those differences debated in the divan between ours and the French ambassador. Likewise Levinus Warner, a German born, lived for some years in the house of the English ambassador until afterwards that by the Lords the States he was promoted to be their Resident at the Porte, all of which, happening in so short time after my arrival in Turkey, it will not appear strange to considering men that the Dutch nation should not at that time by the generality of the people (though the Ministers of State might know otherwise) be distinguished from ours or their puissance and greatness so well-understood as it is at present, the Heer Colyer[364], formerly resident but now dignified with the title ambassador at the Porte, and the several consuls in their respective factories being much-respected and esteemed. And these are all the nations considerable with whom the Turk hath occasion to treat or that fall under his cognizance or business.

When the Grand Signior hath occasion to write unto any of the Christian princes, he commonly uses these expressions at the beginning of the letter:

> To the Glory of the great Princes of JESUS, elected by the Reverend Senators of the Religion of the Messiah, Composer of the Public Affairs of the Christian Nation, Patron (or Master) of a courteous and modest Train, Lord of those Ways which Lead to honour and glory whose end, may it be happy, &c.

---

[364] Justinus Colyer (1624–1682), a distinguished lawyer and diplomat, was first Dutch resident and then ambassador at Constantinople from 1667 to 1682. He died in Istanbul and was succeeded as ambassador by his son Jacobus. He arranged the third capitulation between the Netherlands and the Ottoman Empire in 1674. In 1668 Colyer presented a copy of Blaeu's great atlas to Mehmed IV, who ordered it translated into Turkish and printed. Colyer's journals covering his time in Constantinople were translated into French (1672) by Vincent Minutoli. Further details on Colyer and his son may be found in Mehmet Bulut, "Business" 4–5.

**Chapter XXII.** *The regard the Turks have to their leagues with foreign princes.*

As the Christian religion teaches humility, charity, courtesy, and faith towards all that are within the pale of human nature to be φιλόθεος κάι φιλάνθροπος,[365] so the Turkish superstition furnishes its followers with principles not only to abhor the doctrines but also the persons of such whom they term not believers. The sordidness of their blood and ungentleness of their education makes them insolent and swelled in prosperity, and their victories and spoils upon Christians render the arms and force of other parts contemptible in respect of theirs. Upon these considerations of the vileness of Christianity and scorn of their power they assume this into a maxim that they ought not to regard the leagues they have with any prince or the reasons and ground of a quarrel, whilst the breach tends to the enlargement of their empire, which consequently infers the propagation of their faith.

Many and various are the examples and stories in all ages since the beginning and increase of the Turkish power, of the perfidiousness and treachery of this people, that it may be a question whether their valour and force hath prevailed more in the time of war or the little care of their faith and maintenance in their leagues hath availed them in the time of peace. Thus Didymoticum,[366] in the time of peace under Murat, third king of the Turks, whilst the walls and fortifications were building, was by the Asian labourers which were entertained in the work, and the help of other Turks which lay near in ambush, surprised and taken. So also Rodestum[367] in the time of peace by command of Murat was by Eurynoses assaulted and taken by stratagem, so Adrianople[368] in the reign of the same emperor, after peace made again and assurances given of better faith, was by the art and disguise of Chassis-Ilbeg, pretending to be a discontented captain and a fugitive from the Turks, by fair speeches and some actions and speeches abroad gained such confidence among the credulous Greeks as enabled

---

[365] A lover of God and man.

[366] This city, now known as Didymoteicho, is in the eastern part of Thrace and southeast of modern Edirne in Turkey. In 1352 it was the site of the first victory of Ottoman arms in Europe, although Murad I did not capture Didymotichum until 1361. It even became the Ottoman capital for a short time, and remained in Turkish possession until 1912, when it was captured by the Bulgarians.

[367] "Now called Rhodesto" (Rycaut's marginal note). It is a city in eastern Thrace on the Sea of Marmara and now called Tekirdağ, described by Roger of Wendover as being "four days journey from Constantinople" (*Chronice, sive Flores historiarum*, ed. Henry O. Coxe, vol. 2 [London, 1814–24], 78). It was twice (813, 1206) captured by the Bulgarians; from 1204 to 1235 it was under Venetian rule, from which it passed to the Ottomans. "Eurynoses" has not been identified.

[368] Murad I captured Adrianople in 1362, renaming it Edirne and making it his capital in place of Bursa.

him afterwards to set the gates open to Murat's army, which after some conflict was taken and never recovered again by the power of the Greeks.

It is an old and practiced subtlety of the Turks, immediately after some notable misfortune to entreat of peace, by which means they may gain time to recollect their forces and provisions to prosecute the war. It is notable and worthy of record the treachery used the year 1604, begun in the time of Mehmed the third and broken off by Ahmed his successor. The overtures for a treaty were first propounded by the Turks and commissioners from the Emperor appointed and met the Turks at Buda. Twelve days' truce were concluded for consideration of the articles and presents sent by the Turks to the Emperor to persuade of the reality of their intentions. Mehmed dying, Sultan Ahmed renews his commission to the Pasha of Buda to continue the treaty, whereupon the Christians and Turks commissioners have another meeting at Pest, where, whilst the Christians were courteously treating the infidels in tents near the town and they, to create in the Christians an assurance of their faithful dealings, were producing letters from their Sultan and Prime Vizier filled with oaths and protestations as by the God of Heaven and Earth, by the Book of Moses, by the souls of their ancestors and the like, and that their intentions for peace were real and meant nothing but what was honourable and just. At that very time the Turks of Buda, conceiving that in the time of this great jollity and confidence the walls of Pest were neglected and lightly-manned, issued out in great numbers to surprise it, the alarm of which ended the banquet, and the Turks, finding matters contrary to their expectation, returned only with the shame of their treachery.

It is no wonder the disciples should in a point of so great liberty and advantage follow the example and doctrine of their master, for the like Muhammad did when overthrown and repulsed at the siege of Mecca, [and] made a firm league with the inhabitants of strict peace and amity, but the next summer, having again recruited his forces, easily surprised and took the city, whilst the people, relying on the late agreement, suspected nothing less than the Prophet's treachery.[369] And that such perfidiousness as this might not be chronicled in future ages in disparagement of his sanctity, he made it lawful for his believers, in cases of like nature, when the matter concerned those who are infidels and of a different persuasion, neither to regard promises, leagues, or other engagements. And this is read in the book of institutions of the Muhammadan law, called *Kitab al-'Ataya*.[370] It is the usual form and custom, when a noble advantage is espied on any country with which they have not sufficient ground of quarrel, to demand the opinion of the Mufti for the lawfulness of war, who, without consulting other

---

[369] Muhammad actually "conquered" Mecca without a battle.

[370] The *Kitab al-'Ataya* or *Book of Benefactions* forms Part 13 of the *Da'a'im al-Islam* (*The Pillars of Islam*), by al-Qadi al-Nu'man (c. 903–974), a North African-born jurist and the official historian of the Fatimid caliphs. This section deals with human relations. There is a modern translation by Asaf Fyzee (Oxford: Oxford University Press, 2007).

consideration and judgment of the reasonable occasions than the utility of the empire, in conformity to the foregoing precedent of his Prophet, passes his *fetva* or sentence, by which the war becomes warrantable and the cause justified and allowed.[371]

It is not to be denied but even amongst Christian princes and other the most gallant people of the world advantages have been taken contrary to leagues and faith, and wars commenced upon frivolous and slight pretences, and the states have never wanted reasons for the breach of leagues, though confirmed by oaths and all the rites of religious vows. We know it is controverted in the schools, whether faith is to be maintained with infidels, with heretics and wicked men, which in my opinion were more honourable to be out of question. But we never read that perfidiousness by act and proclamation was allowable until the doctors of Muhammadan law, by the example of their Prophet, recorded and commanded this lesson as a beneficial and useful axiom to their disciples.

And here I cannot but wonder at what I have heard and read in some books of the honesty and justice of the Turks, extolling and applauding them as men accomplished with all the virtues of a moral life, thence seeming to infer that Christianity itself imposes none of those engagements of goodness on men's natures as the professors of it do imagine. But such men, I believe, have neither read the histories nor consulted the rules of their religion, nor practiced their conversation, and in all points being ignorant of the truth of the Turks' dealing. It is not strange if, through a charitable opinion of what they know not, they err in the apprehension and character they pass upon them.

---

[371] Rycaut must surely have been familiar with the opening scene of Shakespeare's *Henry V*, when the king asks the Archbishop of Canterbury and the Bishop of Ely to find just cause for his projected war against France.

# OF THE TURKISH RELIGION

## Book II.

### Chapter I. *Of the religion of the Turks in general.*

The civil laws appertaining to religion amongst the Turks are so confounded into one body that we can scarce treat of one without the other, for they conceive that the civil law came as much from God, being delivered by their Prophet, as that which immediately respects their religion, and came with the same obligations and injunctions to obedience. And though this polity was a fiction of some who first founded certain governments, as Numa Pompilius, Solon,[372] and the like, to put the greater engagements and ties on men as well as of conscience, as though fear of punishment. Yet in the general that proposition is true that all laws which respect right and justice and are tending to a foundation of good and honest government are of God, "for there is no power but of God, and the powers that be are ordained of God."[373] And then, if God owns the creation and constitution of all princes and rulers, as well the pagans as Christians, the tyrants as the indulgent fathers of their people and country, no less doth he disallow the rules and laws fitted to the constitution and government of a people, giving no difference to their obedience because their prince is a tyrant or their laws not founded according to true reason but to the humour of their corrupted judgments or interest.

It is vulgarly known to all that their law was compiled by Muhammad with the help of Sergius[374] the monk, and hence this superstition is named

---

[372] Numa Pompilius was the second semi-legendary king of Rome, reigning 715–673 BCE. He is credited with codifying Roman religion and the law codes. Solon (c. 638–558 BCE) was a distinguished Athenian statesman and poet who reformed the laws and fought against the moral decline of the state. Both men are held up as paragons of wisdom and ethical rectitude.

[373] Romans 13:1 (Rycaut's marginal note).

[374] That Muhammad had assistance from a heretical Christian monk is an old tradition. For example, Celio Curione's *Notable History of the Saracens*, translated by Thomas Newton (1576) states that "Mahomet patched together his Alcoran (a book containing his pestilent doctrine and gross opinions) through instinction and procurement of two heretical monks, John of Antioch and Sergius of Italy" (120). Muslim tradition holds that Muhammad met one Bahira, a Nestorian monk, who foretold that he would become a great prophet and leader, and in subsequent Christian polemics Bahira becomes a heretic monk, thus depriving the Quran of any possible legitimacy in the eyes of Christians. The name Sergius seems to have been first used by the eminent Muslim philosopher al-Kindi

Muhammadanism, whose infamous life is recorded so particularly in many other books that it were too obvious to be repeated here. And therefore we shall insist and take a view of the rites, doctrines, and laws of the Turkish religion, which is founded in three books, which may not improperly be called the codes and pandects[375] of the Muhammadan constitutions.

The first is the Qur'an, the second the content or testimony of wise men, called the *Al-Sunnah,* or *The Traditions of the Prophets,*[376] and the third the inferences or deductions of one thing from another. Muhammad wrote the Qur'an and prescribed some laws for the civil government; the other additions or superstructures were composed by their doctors that succeeded, which were Abu Bakr, Omar, Osman, and Ali.[377] The caliphs of Babylon and Egypt were other doctors and expositors whose sentences and positions were of divine authority amongst them, but their esteem of being oraculous failing with their temporal power, that dignity and authority of infallible determinations was by force of the sword transferred to the Turkish Mufti. And though there is great diversity amongst the doctors as touching the explication of their law, yet he is esteemed as a true believer who observes these five articles or fundamentals of the law, to which every Turk is obliged. The first is cleanness in the outward parts of their body and garments; secondly, to make prayers five times a day; thirdly, to observe the *Ramazan*[378] or monthly fast; fourthly, to perform faithfully the *zakat,*[379] or giving of alms according to the proportion prescribed in a certain book written by four doctors of theirs; fifthly, to make their pilgrimage to Mecca if they have means and possibility to perform it.[380] But the article of faith required to be believed is but one, *viz.* that there is but one God and Muhammad his prophet. Other rites such as circumcision, observation of a Friday for a day of devotion, abstinence from swine's flesh and from blood, as they say, amongst the five principal points, because they are enjoined as trials and proofs of man's obedience to the more necessary law.

---

(801–873), after whose time the names became conflated. There is a grain of truth in all this, as it is quite possible that Muhammad could have encountered Christian mendicants during his wanderings and even listened to some of them preaching..

[375] A complete body of laws.

[376] The *sunnah* means "usual practices." It consists of what Muhammad believed, taught, or implied, and is written down in the *Hadith.* It is referred to after first consulting the Quran, when that book does not have an answer.

[377] These are the first four caliphs. Their dates are as follows: Abu Bakr (632–634), Omar I (634–644), Osman I (644–656), and Ali (656–661).

[378] The usual (Arabic) form is *Ramadan*; I have used the Turkish form throughout.

[379] The *zakat* dictates that 2.5 percent of a Muslim's possessions or income should be given to the poor and needy.

[380] These rules are known as the Five Pillars of Islam.

**Chapter II.** *The toleration that Muhammadanism in its fancy promised to other religions, and in what manner that agreement was afterwards observed.*

When Muhammadanism was first weak and therefore put on a modest countenance and plausible aspect to deceive mankind, it found a great part of the world illuminated with Christianity, endued with active graces, zeal, and devotion, and established within itself with purity of doctrine, union, and firm possession of the faith, though greatly shaken by the heresies of Arius and Nestorius.[381] Yet it began to be guarded, not only with its patience, long-suffering, and hope, but also with the fortifications, arms, and protection of emperors and kings, so that Muhammadanism, coming them on the disadvantage and having a hard game to play either by the lustre of graces or good examples of a strict life to outshine Christianity, or by a looseness and indulgence to corrupt manners, to pervert men dedicated to God's service, or by cruelty and menaces to gain those who accounted martyrdom their greatest glory and were now also defended by the power of their own princes, judges it best policy to make proffers of truce and peace between the Christian and its own profession. And therefore, in all places where its arms were prevalent and prosperous, proclaimed a free toleration to all religions, but especially, in outward appearance, courted and favoured the Christian, drawing its tenets and doctrines in some conformity to that rule, confessing Christ to be a prophet and greater than Moses, that he was born of a virgin, that Mary conceived by the smell of a rose, that the Blessed Virgin was free from original sin and the temptations of the Devil, that Christ was the word of God and is so styled in the Qur'an, and cured diseases, raised the dead, and worked many miracles, and by his power his disciples did the like. And I have heard some speak of him with much reverence and with heat to deny Christ's passion, saying it were an impiety to believe that God, who loved and had conferred so much power and so many graces on Christ, should so far dishonor him as to deliver him into the hands of the Jews, who were the worst and most scorned of men, or to the death of the cross, which was the most infamous and vile of all punishments.

In this manner they seemed to make a league with Christianity to be charitable, modest, and well-wishers to its possessors, and Muhammad himself says in his Qur'an thus: "O infidels, I do not adore what you adore, and you adore not what I worship. Observe your law and I will observe mine."[382] And for a farther

---

[381] Arius of Alexandria (c. 250–336) denied that Jesus was of the same substance as God, but affirmed that he was only the highest form of human being. Nestorius (c. 386–451) was bishop of Constantinople. His "heresy" rested on his belief that no union between the human and divine was possible.

[382] Rycaut would have known something of the history of Quranic translations, which is as follows. Abraham Hinkelmann printed an Arabic text, *Al-Coranus, seu lex*

assurance of his toleration of Christianity and evidence to the world that his intention was neither to persecute nor extirpate their religion, he made this following compact,[383] the original of which was found in the monastery of friars on Mount Carmel,[384] and, it is said, was transported to the king's library in France, which, because it is ancient and of curiosity, it will not be impertinent to be inserted here:

> Muhammad, sent from God to teach mankind and declare the Divine Commission in truth, wrote these things that the cause of Christian religion determined by God might remain in all parts of the East and of the

---

*Islamitica* in Hamburg (1649), but not a Latin translation. The first Latin version, *Lex Mahomet[ae] pseudoprophetae*, was commissioned by Peter the Venerable and translated by Robert of Ketton and Hermann of Dalmatia (1143); it appeared in print quite early (1543). The same mediaeval Latin translation was published by Theodore Bibliander and was also translated into Dutch, Italian (1547), and German. Scholars as early as Juan de Segovia in the 1440s had questioned the accuracy of the translation. Rycaut likely knew André du Ryer's French version (1647) and there was also another German translation by Salomon Schweiger (Nurnberg, 1616). The first English translation, which Rycaut probably used, was hardly a translation at all; Alexander Ross (1592–1654), Charles I's chaplain, issued *Mahomet's Alcoran, Translated out of Arabique into French, by the Sieur du Ryer. . .and newly Englished, for the satisfaction of all that desire to look into the Turkish vanities* (London, 1649). It should always be remembered that early translations of the Quran were undertaken often with the specific intention of proving that it was false doctrine and that Muhammad was not a prophet of God. See further T. E. Burman, *Reading the Qu'ran in Latin Christendom 1140–1560* (Philadelphia: University of Pennsylvania Press, 2007).

[383] This may refer to the *Achitname of Muhammad*, which is a document claiming to be an agreement made between the monks of St. Catherine's monastery on Mt. Sinai and Muhammad in 628, but is only one page long and quite terse. It has a handprint purporting to be the Prophet's on it. Rycaut prints a much-expanded version, which may well be, as scholars have claimed, a forgery, probably from the tenth century. The story goes that Muhammad granted the monastery his protection after he had conquered Egypt, and that he further ratified all the rights and privileges of the monks as well as of pilgrims and church officials. The original document is lost, but there are copies in the monastery library, and the agreement was reaffirmed by Egyptian rulers as being genuine. Muhammad's letter, together with other documents, was translated and printed by Gabriel Sionita (1577–1648), a Lebanese Maronite scholar and theologian, as *Testamentum et pactiones inter Mohammedanem et Christianae fidei cultores* (1630). This book may have been Rycaut's source.

[384] Now the site of the Stella Maris Monastery, built in 1886 over the ruins of the older church. The Carmelites, who picked the site because of its association with the prophet Elijah, were officially recognized by Pope Honorius III in 1226, but there is speculation that monks had settled in the area earlier than this date. The monks had mostly left by 1290, when some were massacred by Muslims, but in 1631 they returned and re-established the monastery.

West, as well as amongst the inhabitants, as strangers near and remote, known and unknown. To all those people I leave this present writing as an inviolable league, as a decision of all farther controversies and a law whereby justice is declared and strict observance enjoined. Therefore, whoever of the Muslim faith shall neglect to perform these things and violate this league and after the manner of the infidels break it and transgress what I command therein, he breaks the compact of God, resists his agreement and condemns his testament, whether he be a king or any other of the faithful. By this agreement, whereby I have obliged myself and which the Christians have required of me, and in my name and in the name of all my disciples, to enter into a covenant of God with them and league and testament of the prophets, apostles, elect and faithful saints and blessed of times past and to come. By this covenant, I say, and testament of mine, which I will have maintained with as much religion as a prophet missionary or as an angel next to the Divine Majesty is strict in his observance to his law and covenant, I promise to defend their judges in my provinces with my horse and foot, auxiliaries and other my faithful followers, and to preserve them from their enemies whether remote or near, and secure them both in peace and war and to protect their churches, temples, oratories, monasteries and places of pilgrimage, whether mountain or valley, cavern or house, a plain or upon the sand or in what sort of edifice soever. Also, to preserve their religion and their goods in what part soever they are, whether at land or sea, east or west, even as I keep myself and my scepter and the faithful believers of my own people. Likewise, to receive them into my protection from all harm, vexation, offence and hurt. Moreover, to repel those enemies which are offensive to them and me, and stoutly to oppose them both in my own person, by my servants and all others of my people and nation. For since I am set over them, I ought to preserve and defend them from all adversity, and that no evil touch them before it first afflict mine who labour in the same work. I promise farther to free them from those burdens which confederates suffer either by loans of money or impositions, so that they shall be obliged to pay nothing but what they please, and no molestation or injury shall be offered to them herein. A bishop shall not be removed from his diocese or a Christian compelled to renounce his faith, a monk his profession or a pilgrim disturbed in his pilgrimage or a religious man in his cell. Nor shall their churches be destroyed or converted into mosques, for whoever doth so break this Covenant of God opposes the Messenger of God and frustrates the Divine Testament. No impositions shall be laid upon friars or bishops, nor any of them who are not liable to taxes unless it be with their consent. And the tax which shall be required from rich merchants and from fishermen of the pearl, from miners of their precious stones, gold and silver, shall not exceed above 12 shillings yearly. And it shall also be from them who are constant inhabitants of the place and not from travellers and men of an uncertain abode, for they shall not be subject to impositions or contributions unless they are possessors of inheritance of land or estate, for he which is lawfully subject to pay money to the Emperor shall pay as much as another and not more, nor more required from him above his faculty and strength.

In like manner, he that is taxed for his land. Houses or revenue shall not be burdened immoderately nor oppressed with greater taxes than any others that pay contribution. Nor shall the confederates be obliged to go to the war with the Muslims against their enemies either to fight or discover their armies, because it is not of duty to a confederate to be employed in military affairs, but rather this compact is made with them that they may be the less oppressed, but rather the Muslims shall watch and ward and defend them. And therefore, that they be not compelled to go forth to fight or encounter with the enemy or find horse or arms unless they voluntarily furnish them, and he who shall thus willingly contribute shall be recompensed and rewarded. No Muslim shall infest[385] the Christians nor contend with them in anything but in kindness, but treat them with all courtesy and abstain from all oppression or violence towards them. If any Christian commits a crime or fault, it shall be the part of the Muslim to assist him, intercede and give caution for him and compound for his miscarriage. Liberty shall also be given to redeem his life, nor shall he be forsaken nor be destitute of help because of the Divine Covenant which is with them that they should enjoy what the Muslims enjoy and suffer what they suffer, and on the other side that the Muslims enjoy what they enjoy and suffer what they suffer. And according to this Covenant, which is by the Christians' just request and according to that endeavor which is so required for confirmation of its authority, you are obliged to protect them from all calamity and perform all offices of good will towards them so that the Muslims may be sharers with them in prosperity and adversity. Moreover, all care ought to be had that no violence be offered to them as to matters relating to marriage, *viz.*, that they compel not their parents to match their daughters with Muslims, nor shall they be molested for refusal either to give a bridegroom or a bride, for this is an act wholly voluntary, depending on their free will and pleasure. But if it happen that a Christian woman shall join with a Muslim, he is obliged to give her liberty of conscience in her religion that she may obey her ghostly[386] Father and be instructed in the doctrines of her faith without impediment. Therefore he shall not disquiet her either by threatening divorce or solicitations to forsake her faith, but if he shall be contrary thereto and molest her herein, he despises the Covenant of God, rebels against the Compact of the Messenger of God, and is entered into the number of liars. Moreover, when Christians would repair their churches or convents or anything else appertaining to their worship and have need of the liberality and assistance of the Muslims hereunto, they ought to contribute and freely to bestow according to their ability, not with intention to receive it again, but *gratis* and as a good will towards their faith, and to fulfill the Covenant of

---

[385] Either "overrun with numbers" or "live on like a parasite."
[386] Spiritual father, i. e. God.

the Messenger of God, considering the obligation they have to perform the
Covenant of God and the Compact of the Messenger of God. Nor shall
they oppress any of them living amongst the Muslims, nor hate them nor
compel them to carry letters, or show the way or any other manner force
them, for he which exercises any manner of this tyranny against them is an
oppressor and an adversary to the Messenger of God and refractory to his
precepts. These are the covenants agreed between Muhammad the Messenger of God and the Christians.

   But the conditions upon which I bind these covenants on their consciences are these. That no Christian give any entertainment to a soldier,
enemy to the Muslims, or receive him in his house publicly or privately; that
they receive none of the enemies of Muslims as sojourners into their houses,
churches or religious convents, nor underhand furnish the camp of their
enemies with arms, horse, men, or maintain any intercourse or correspondence with them by contracts or writing, but betaking themselves to some
certain place of abode shall attend to the preservation of themselves and to
the defence of their religion. To any Muslim and his beasts they shall give
three days entertainment with variety of meat, and, moreover, shall endeav-
or to defend them from all misfortune and trouble, so that if any Muslim
shall be desirous or be compelled to conceal himself in any of their houses
or habitations, they shall friendly hide him and deliver him from the danger
he is in and not betray him to his enemy. And in this manner the Christians
performing faith on their side, whoever violates any of these conditions and
doth contrarily, shall be deprived of the benefits contained in the Covenant
of God and his Messenger, nor shall he deserve to enjoy these privileges indulged to bishops and Christian monks and to the believers of the contents
of the Qur'an. Wherefore I conjure my people by God and his Prophet to
maintain these things faithfully and fulfill them in what part soever of the
world they are. And the Messenger of God shall recompense them for the
same, the perpetual observation of which he seriously recommends to them
until the Day of Judgment and dissolution of the world. Of these conditions
which Muhammad the Messenger of God hath agreed with the Christians
and hath enjoyed, the witnesses were Abu Bakr as-Siddiq, 'Umar ibn al-
Khattab, 'Uthman ibn Affan, Ali ibn Ali Talib, with a number of others.
The secretary was Mu'awiya ibn 'Abi Sufyan, a soldier of the Messenger of
God,[387] the last day of the moon of the fourth month, the Fourth year of
Hegira in Medina. May God remunerate those who are witnesses to this
writing. Praise be to God, the Lord of all Creatures.

This covenant or articles with Christians, howsoever denied by the Turks to have
been the act and agreement of Muhammad, is yet by very good authors taken for

[387] Abu Bakr, 'Umar, 'Uthman, and Ali are the four early caliphs, for whom see
above. Caliph Mu'awiya I reigned from 661 to 680, and founded the 'Umayyad dynasty
of caliphs.

real, and to have been at that time confirmed when his kingdom was weak and in its infancy, and when he warred with the Arabians, and fearing likewise the enmity of the Christians (not to be assaulted by two enemies at once) secured himself by this religious league made in the monastery of friars in Mount Carmel, from whence that strict order have their denomination.

But mark how well Muhammad in the sequel observed this law. As soon as his government increased and that by arms and bad arts he had secured his kingdom, he writes this "Chapter of the Sword,"[388] called so because the first words spoken are often engraved on the Turks' scimitars made at Damascus and other their bucklers[389] and other sort of arms. And another chapter in the Qur'an, called "The Chapter of Battle,"[390] which is always read by the Turks before they go to fight, and therein his modest words, "If you adore not what I adore, let your religion be to you and mine to me," and other promises of toleration and indulgence to the Christian religion were changed to a harsher note and his edicts were then for blood and ruin and enslavement of Christians. "When you meet with infidels," saith he, "cut off their heads, kill them, take them prisoners, bind them until either you think to give them liberty or pay their ransom, and forbear not to persecute them until they have laid down their arms and submitted."[391] And that is the sort of toleration the Turks give to the Christian religion; they know they cannot force men's wills nor captivate their consciences as well as their bodies, but what means may be used to render them contemptible, make them poor, their lives uncomfortable and the interest of their religion weak and despicable are practiced with divers arts and tyranny, that their toleration of Christianity is rather to afflict and persecute it than any grant of favour or dispensation.

The Muhammadan religion tolerates Christian churches and houses of devotion in places where they have been anciently founded, but admits not of holy buildings on new foundations. They may repair the old coverings and roofs, but cannot lay a stone in a new place consecrated to divine service, nor, if fire or any accident destroy the superstructure, may a new strength be added to the foundation wherewith to underprop for another building. And, as it happened in the great and notable fires of Galata first, and then of Constantinople in the year 1660,[392] that many of the Christian churches and chapels were brought to ashes

---

[388] Sura 9:1–8. It is more accurate to call 9:5 the "verse" of the sword: "When the sacred months have passed, slay the idolaters wherever ye find them. . . .."

[389] A buckler is a small, usually round shield. It was often used in hand-to-hand combat and continued in use until the Renaissance.

[390] Sura 61, known as *al-Saff,* or "Array of Battle."

[391] Sura 9:5. This is not, as can be seen, the "Battle" chapter, but a quote from the sura mentioned previously.

[392] For details, see Marc David Baer, "The Great Fire of 1660 and the Islamization of Christian and Jewish Spaces in Istanbul," *International Journal of Middle Eastern Studies* 36 (2004): 159–81.

and afterwards by the piety and zeal of Christians scarce re-edified before by public order they were thrown down again in heaps, being judged contrary to the Turkish law to permit churches again to be restored of which no more remained than the mere foundation.

**Chapter III.** *The arts wherewith the Turkish religion is propagated.*

The Turks, though they offer the specious outside of the foregoing toleration, yet by their law are authorized to enforce men's consciences to the possession of their faith, and that is done by various arts and niceties of religion, for if a man turn Turk, his children under the age of 14 years, though educated with other principles, must be forced to the same persuasion. Men that speak against the Muhammadan law, that have rashly promised at a time of distraction or drunkenness to become Turks, or have had a carnal knowledge of a Turkish woman must either become martyrs or apostates, besides many other subtleties they have to entrap the souls of Christians within the entanglements of their law.

It is another policy wherewith the Muhammadan sect hath been increased, the accounting it a principle of religion not to deliver a city or fortress by consent or voluntary surrender where mosques have once been built and Muhammadanism professed. And therefore the Turk no sooner enters a town by conquest but immediately lays foundation for his temples, thereby imposing an obligation of an obstinate and constant resolution on the conscience of the defendants, which many times hath been found to have been more forcible and prevalent on the spirits of men than all the terrors and miseries of famine, sword or other calamities.

It is well known upon what different interests Christianity and Muhammadanism were introduced into the world; the first had no other enforcements than the persuasions and sermons of a few poor fishermen, verified with miracles, signs and inspiration of the Holy Ghost, carrying before it the promises of another life and considerations of a glorified spirituality in a state of separation. But the way to it was obstructed with the opposition of emperors and kings, with scorn and contempt, with persecution and death. And this was all the encouragement proposed to mankind to embrace this faith, but Muhammadanism made its way with the sword. What knots of argument he could not untie he cut, and made his spiritual power as large as his temporal, made his precepts easy and pleasant and acceptable to the fancy and appetite as well as to the capacity of the vulgar, representing heaven to them not in a spiritual manner or with delights inexpressible and ravishments known only in part to illuminated souls, but with gross conceptions of the beauty of women with great eyes, of the duration of one act of carnal copulation for the space of sixty years and of the beastly satisfaction of a gluttonous palate, things absurd and ridiculous to wise and knowing men but yet capable to draw multitudes of its professors and carnal defenders of its verity.[393]

---

[393] This passage is typical for European writers of the time. The descriptions of Paradise in the Quran (see, for example, Sura 56:10–38; Sura 76:12–21) occasioned the assumption of Christians that Islam was a "sensual" religion which attracted its followers by promising things in the afterlife that everyone wants in this life. "And Mahomet promiseth," wrote George Sandys, for example, "magnificent palaces spread all over with silk carpets, fields and crystalline rivers, trees of gold still flourishing, pleasing the eye

And this doctrine, being irrational to the better sort of judgments, causes the lawyers, who are men of the subtlest capacities amongst the Turks, to mistrust much of the truth of the doctrine of Muhammad, especially the assertions relating to the conditions of the other life. For the representation of the delights of the next world in a corporeal and sensual manner being inconsistent with their reason leads them to doubt the truth of that point, and so wavering with one scruple proceed to a mistrust of the whole system of the Muhammmadan faith. One would think that in such men a way were prepared for the entertainment of a religion erected on more solid principles and foundations and that the Jews might gain such proselytes to their law, from which a great part of the Muhammadan superstition was borrowed, or that the Christians might take advantage in so well-disposed subjects to produce something of the mystery of godliness. But the first are a people so obnoxious to scorn and contempt, esteemed by the Turks to be the scum of the world and the worst of men, that it is not probable their doctrine can gain a reputation with those to whom their very persons and blood are vile and detestable. Nor is it likely that the Christians will ever be received by them with greater authority and more favourable inclination until they acquit themselves of the scandal of idolatry which the images and pictures in their churches seem to accuse them of in the eyes and judgment of the Turks, who are not versed in the subtle distinctions of schoolmen, in the limitations and restrictions of that worship and the evasions of their doctors, matters not only sufficient to puzzle and distract the gross heads of Turks but to strain the wits of learned Christians to clear them from that imputation.

But to return to our purpose. The propagation of the Muhammadan faith having been promoted wholly by the sword, that persuasion and principle in their catechism that the souls of those who die in the wars against the Christians[394] without the help of previous acts of performance of their law or other works are immediately transported to Paradise must necessarily whet the swords and raise the spirits of the soldiers, which is the reason that such multitudes of them, as we read in history, run evidently to their own slaughter, esteeming their lives and bodies at no greater price than the value of stones and rubbish to fill rivulets and ditches that they may erect a bridge or passage for their fellows to assault their enemies.

The success of the Muhammadan arms produced another argument for the confirmation of their faith, and made it a principle that whatever prospers hath God for the author. And by how much more successful have been their wars, by

---

with other goodly forms and taste with their fruits,. . .Under whose fragrant shades they shall spend the course of their happy time with amorous virgins who shall alone regard their particular lovers, not such as have lived in this world but created of purpose with great black eyes and beautiful as the hyacinth" (*Travels*, 46). For further information, see introduction.

[394] See, for example, Sura 3:195.

so much the more hath God been an owner of their cause and religion. And the same argument, if I am not mistaken, in the times of the late rebellion in England was made use of by many to entitle God to their cause[395] and make him the author of their thriving sin because their wickedness prospered and could trample on all holy and human rights with impunity. And I have known that the Romanists have judged the afflictions and almost subversion of the Church of England to be a token of God's desertion and disclaim of her profession, forgetting the persecutions and martyrdoms of the primitive saints and that the church of God is built in sorrow and established with patience and passive graces. But these men, rather than want an argument, their malice will use the weapons of infidels to oppugn[396] the truth. And on this ground the Turks horribly detest and abhor the Jews, calling them "the forsaken of God" because they are vagabonds all over the world and have no temporal authority to protect them. And though according to the best inquiry I could make that report is not true that they permit not a Jew to become a Turk but by turning a Christian first as a nearer step and previous disposition to the Muslim's faith.[397] Yet it is certain they will not receive the corpse of a regenerate Jew into their cemeteries or place of burial, and the Jews on the other side disowning any share or part in him, his loathed carcass is thrown into some grave distant from all other sepulchres as unworthy the society of all mankind.

---

[395] Rycaut refers here, of course, to the Civil War and the "Good Old Cause," the phrase used by former Parliamentary soldiers and supporters to characterize what they fought for.

[396] Call into question; we would now use "impugn."

[397] Another example of a common misconception. ". . .no Jew can turn Turk until he first turn Christian, they forcing him to eat hog's flesh and calling him Abdullah, which signifieth the son of a Christian, who after two or three days, abjuring Christ, is made a Mahometan" (George Sandys, *Travels*, 42).

**Chapter IV.** *The power and office of the Muftis and of their government in religious matters.*

The Mufti is the principal head of the Muhammadan religion or oracle of all doubtful questions in the law, and is a person of great esteem and reverence amongst the Turks. His election is solely in the Grand Signior, who chooses a man to that office always famous for his learning in the law and eminent for his virtues and strictness of life. His authority is so great amongst them that when he passes judgment or determination in any point, the Grand Signior himself will in no wise contradict or oppose it. The title which the Grand Signior gives unto the Mufti when he writes to him is:

> To the Es'ad,[398] who art the Wisest of the Wise, instructed in all knowledge, the most Excellent of the Excellent, abstaining from things unlawful, the Spring of Virtue and True Science, Heir of the Prophetic and Apostolical doctrines, Resolver of the Problems of Faith, Revealer of the Orthodox Articles, Key of the Treasures of Truth, the Light to Doubtful Allegories, strengthened with the grace of the Supreme Assister and Legislator of Mankind. May the most High God perpetuate thy virtues.

His power is not compulsory, but only resolving and persuasive in matters both civil and criminal and of state. His manner of resolves is by writing, the question being first heard in paper briefly and succinctly. He underneath subscribes his sentence by yes or no or in some short determination called a *fetva*, with the addition of these words, "God knows better," by which it is apparent that the determinations of the Mufti are not esteemed infallible. This being brought to the *qadi* or judge, his judgment is certainly regulated according thereunto, and lawsuits of the greatest moment concluded in an hour without arrests of judgment, appeals or other dilatory arts of the law.

In matters of state the Sultan demands his opinion, whether it be in condemnation of any great man to death or in making war or peace or other important affairs of the empire, either to appear more just or religious or to incline the people more willingly to obedience. And this practice is used in business of greatest moment; scarce a vizier is proscribed or a pasha for pretence of crime displaced or any matter of great alteration or change designed but the Grand Signior arms himself with the Mufti's sentence, for the nature of man reposes more se-

---

[398] Es'ad Effendi (1570–1625) was a former Grand Mufti of Constantinople (1613–22, 1623–25), whose daughter Agile married Sultan Osman II (1617–22) in 1622, shortly before the Sultan's murder. Esad had been instrumental in bringing Osman II to the throne. Rycaut seems to think that "Esad" is a title, and may have copied this from an older source, although both Es'ad's son and grandson occupied the position. For details, see Baki Tezcan, *The Second Ottoman Empire: Political and Social Transformation in the Early Modern World* (Cambridge: Cambridge University Press, 2010), 63–65.

curity in innocence and actions of justice than in the absolute and uncontrollable power of the sword. And the Grand Signior, though he himself is above the law and is oracle and fountain of justice, yet it is seldom that he proceeds so irregularly to contemn that authority wherein their religion hath placed an ultimate power of decision in all their controversies.

But sometimes, perhaps, queries are sent from the Grand Signior to the Mufti which he cannot resolve with satisfaction of his own conscience and the ends of the Sultan, by which means affairs important to the wellbeing of the state meet delays and impediment. In this case the Mufti is fairly dismissed from his infallible office and another oracle introduced who may resolve the difficult demands with a more favourable sentence. If not, he is degraded like the former, and so the next, until one is found to prophesy according to what may best agree with his master. This office was in past times esteemed more sacred by the Ottoman princes than at present, for no war was undertaken or great enterprise set on foot but first, like the oracle or augur, his determination with great reverence was required as that without which no blessing or success could be expected. But in these days they are more remiss in this manner of consultation; sometimes it is done for formality, but most commonly the Prime Vizier, conceited of his own judgment and authority, assumes the power to himself and perhaps first does the thing and afterwards demands the approbation of it by the sense of the law. And herein the Mufti hath a spacious field for his interpretation, for it is agreed that their law is temporary and admits of expositions according to times and state of things. And though they preach to the people the perfection of their Qur'an, yet the wiser men hold that the Mufti hath an expository power of the law to improve and better it according to the state of things, times and conveniencies of the empire, for that their law was never designed to be a clog or confinement to the propagation of faith, but an advancement thereof, and therefore to be interpreted in the largest and farthest-fetched sense when the strict words will not reach the design intended.

So it was once propounded to the Mufti what rule should be observed in the devotion of a Turk carried slave into the northern parts of the world, where in winter is but one hour of day, how he might possibly comply with his obligation of making prayers five times within the twenty-four hours, viz. morning, noon, afternoon, sunset, and at an hour and half in the night, when the whole day, being of but one hour, admitted not of these distinctions. For resolution of which, the Mufti answered that God commanded not things difficult as it is in the Qur'an, and that matters ought to be ordered in conformity to time and place, and making short prayers once before day, then twice in the hour of light and twice after it is dark, the duty is complied with. Another question of the same nature was proposed to the Mufti concerning the qiblah or holy place of Mecca, to which they are obliged to turn their faces in their prayers, how at sea, where they had no mark, especially such bad geographers as the Turks commonly are, it is possible to comply with that necessary formality required in their devotion. The Mufti resolved this doubt almost like the former, prescribing a kind of circular motion in prayers, by which means they cannot miss of having at some time their faces towards the holy city, which in a case of so much difficulty is a sufficient compliance with the duty.

Many cases of this nature are proposed to the Mufti and many particular rules of conscience required, one of which is remarkable that Busbecq relates that occurred in his time during the wars between the Emperor of Germany and Sultan Süleyman [I], whether a few Christians taken captives by the Grand Signior might be exchanged with many Turks in the hand of the Emperor.[399] It seems the Mufti was greatly perplexed and puzzled in the resolution, for sometimes it seemed a disesteem to the value of a Turk to be rated under the price of a Christian. On the other side it appeared want of charity and care of the interest of the Muslims to neglect real terms of advantage on such airy and subtle points of formality. In fine, he consulted his books, and declared that he found two different authors of greater authority of contradictory opinions in this controversy, and therefore his judgment was to incline to that which had most of favour and mercy in it.

The Mufti, whilst qualified with that title, is rarely put to death, but first degraded and then becomes liable to the stroke of the executioner, but in cases of notorious crimes or conviction of treason he is put into a mortar,[400] for that intent remaining in the prison called the Seven Towers at Constantinople, and therein beaten to death and brayed[401] to the contusion of all his bones and flesh.

The next office to the Mufti is the *Kaziasker* or Judge of the Militia, otherwise Judge Advocate,[402] who hath yet power of determination in any other lawsuits whatsoever, for this privilege the soldiery of this country enjoys, to have power extensive over all other conditions of people, but to be only subject themselves to the government of their own officers. This office a Mufti must necessarily pass through and discharge with approbation before he ascends to the top and height of his preference.

The next inferior degree is a mullah,[403] and these are of two sorts, one of three hundred aspers and the other of five hundred aspers, so-called for distinction sake. The first sort are principal judges in petty provinces, containing under them the command of *qadis* of poor and inconsiderable places; the others have their jurisdiction over the whole dominion of a *beylerbey*, and have the *qadis* of several rich and renowned places under their government. These rise often to the

---

[399] Busbecq himself had proposed the exchange, stipulating that "no fewer than forty Turkish captives—ordinary soldiers, it is true, and men of no position—should be given in exchange" (Busbecq, *Turkish Letters*, 148 ).

[400] A vessel used for crushing material.

[401] Crushed or pounded.

[402] A legal adviser seconded to the armed forces.

[403] Literally, vicar or guardian.

Mufti's office, but proceed by several degrees and steps, and must first gradually command where the imperial seats have been, as first to be mullah in Prusa, then in Adrianople and lastly in Constantinople, at which time he is next to the office of *kaziasker* and thence to that of the Mufti.

The Sultan, when he writes to any of his mullahs or qadis of the first degree, he uses this following style:

> To the most perfect Judge of the Faithful, the best President of believers in God, the Mine of Virtue and True Knowledge, the Distributor of all just sentence to all human creatures, Heir of the Prophetic and Apostolical Doctrines, elected by the singular Grace of God for our Governor and Judge, of whose virtues may they ever flourish.

These and qadis, which are the lower and ordinary sort of judges, are as much to be reckoned in the number of religious men as the Mufti himself, for as I have said before, the civil law of the Turks is conceived by them to be derived from their Prophet and the other expositors of their law with as much engagement and obligation as these which immediately concern the divine worship, and therefore are to be treated and handled together.

The imams or parochial priests must be able to read in the Qur'an and be counted men of good fame and moral lives amongst their neighbours before they can be promoted to this function, and must be one of those who have learned at the appointed times of prayer to call the people together on the top of the steeple, by repeating these words: *"Allahu akbar, ash-had al-la illaha illalah, ash-hadu anna Muhammadan rasulullah, haya 'alah-salah, haya 'ala 'l-felah, Allahu akbar, Allahu akbar, la illaha illalah,"* that is, "God is great, God is great, I profess that there is no deity but God and confess that Muhammad is the Prophet of God." In this manner the people of a parish, recommending anyone to the Prime Vizier, declaring that the former imam is dead and the office vacant and that this person is qualified in all points to the function or better and more knowing than the present incumbent. He receives immediate induction and establishment in the place, but for better proof or trial of the truth of the testimony that accompanies him he is enjoined to read in presence of the Vizier some part of the Qur'an, which, being done, he is dismissed and approved, and takes the Vizier's *tesrif* or *mandamus*[404] for the place.

This is all the ceremony required in making an imam, for there is no new character or state of priesthood, as they hold, conferred upon them, nor are they a different sort distinguished from the people by holy orders or rites, but merely by the present office they manage, when, being displaced, they are again numbered with the laity. Their habit is nothing different from others, but only that

---

[404] The Turkish word *tesrif* means "legislation." A *mandamus* is a judicial writ which orders someone to perform a public function.

they wear a larger turban like the lawyers, with some little variety in folding it up, and put on a grave and serious countenance. Their office is to call the people to prayers and at due hours to be their leader in the mosque and to read and repeat upon Fridays certain sentences or verses out of the Qur'an. Few of them adventure to preach unless he be well-conceited[405] or really well-gifted, but leave the office to the *sheikh*, or him that makes preaching his profession, who is one commonly that passes his time in the convents that we shall hereafter treat of.

The Mufti hath no jurisdiction over the imams as to the good order or government of the parishes, nor is there any superiority or hierarchy as to rule amongst them, everyone being independent and without control in his own parish, excepting his subjection in civil and criminal causes to the chief magistrates. And considering the manner of their designation to the religious office, the little difference between the clergy and the laity and the manner of their single government in parochial congregations may not unaptly seem to square with the independency[406] in England, from which original pattern and example our sectaries and fanatic reformers appear to have drawn their copy.

The churchmen and lawyers are generally in esteem amongst them, as is apparent by the title they use towards them in their writings and commands, directed to them in this manner: "You that are the glory of the judges and sage men, the profound mines of eloquence and excellence, may your wisdom and ability be augmented."

---

[405] Witty, intelligent.

[406] An "independent" minister in the seventeenth century is difficult to define. A Protestant nonconformist, he would likely reject both the established Church of England and the stricter, Calvinistic Presbyterianism of puritan elements. Rycaut lumps all of these characteristic together, and is of course referring to the kind of preacher in the Civil War and Protectorate period (1642–1660) who might not have any formal theological training. For people like Rycaut, John Bunyan and Milton would have been classed as "fanatics." Whatever the case, Rycaut's linking independents with Muslim imams is clearly prejudicial.

## Chapter V. *Of the Mufti's revenue and from whence it doth arise.*

After the Mufti is elected there is no ceremony used in his investiture than this: he presents himself before the Grand Signior, who clothes him with a vest of rich sables of one thousand dollars price, and one thousand more he presents him with gold made up in a handkerchief which he delivers with his own hand, putting it in the fold of his undergarment doubled over his breast, and bestows on him a salary of two thousand aspers a day, which is about five pound sterling money, besides which he hath no certain revenue unless it be the power of preference to some prebendaries or benefices[407] of certain royal mosques, which he sells and disposes of as is best to his advantage without the scruple of corruption or simony.[408] By the sentences he gives, called *fetvas*, he receives not one asper benefit. Though every *fetva* costs eight aspers, yet the fee thereof goes to his officers, that is, to his *musewedegi* or he who states the question, is paid five aspers; to his *mumeiz* or he who copies or transcribes the question fair, two aspers; to him that keeps the seal, one asper. Other benefits the Mufti hath little, excepting only that at his first entrance to his office he is saluted by all the ambassadors and residents for foreign princes, as also the agents of several pashas residing at the Porte, none of which come empty-handed but offer their accustomed presents, by which he collects at least fifty thousand dollars.

When any Mufti is deprived of his office without any motive than the pleasure of the Grand Signior, he is gratified with an *arpalik*, which is the disposal of some judicial preferment in certain provinces and the superintendency of them, from which he gathers a competent revenue for his maintenance. And because he is a person whose advice and counsel is of great authority with the Grand Signior and Vizier, and that his word and candid report of matters is considerable, he is therefore courted by all the grandees of the empire, who know no other way of reconciling and purchasing the affection of a Turk than by force of presents, which have more power in them than all other obligations or merits in the world.

---

[407] A prebendary is money drawn from the revenue of a cathedral; a benefice is a parish which comes with some property rights for its incumbent, such as a vicarage or parsonage. In Rycaut's time it might also include other lucrative rights.

[408] Simony is committed when one pays for or sells a benefice or any other holy office.

## Chap. VI.
### *Of the* Emirs.

*Emir Bashee or Head of Mahomets kindred.*

## Chapter VI. *Of the Emirs.*

We may here bring in the emirs, otherwise called *ulad rasul*,[409] into the number of the religious men, because they are of the race of Muhammad, who for distinction's sake wear about their heads turbans of a deep sea-green,[410] which is the colours of their Prophet. Out of reverence to his esteemed holy blood, many privileges are indulged by the secular authority that they cannot be vilified,

---

[409] Descendents of the Prophet.
[410] For an illustration, see Ådahl, *The Sultan's Procession*, 223, Fig. 40.

affronted or struck by a Turk upon forefeiture of his right hand. But lest they should be licentious by his impunity, they have a chief head or superior amongst them called *Nakib ül-Eşraf*, who hath his serjeants[411] or officers under him and is endued with so absolute a power over them that as he pleases it extends both to life and death, but he never will give the scandal to this holy seed to execute or punish them publicly. And though few of them can derive his genealogy clearly from Muhammad, yet those who can but only pretend to it are often helped out in their pedigree. As often as the *Nakib* desires to favour any person or can have any colour to acquire a new subject, then to clear all scruple from the world he gives him a tree of his lineage and descent. The Turks, being well-acquainted with this abuse, carry the less respect to the whole generation, so that as often as they find any of them drunk or disordered they make no scruple to take off their green turbans first, kissing them and laying them aside with all reverence, and afterwards beat them without respect or mercy.

Their second officer is called *alemdar*, who carries the green flag of Muhammad when the Grand Signior appears with any solemnity in public. They are capable of any offices; few of them exercise any trade unless that which is *esirgi*,[412] or one who deals in slaves, to which sort of traffic this sainted offspring is greatly addicted, as being a holy profession to captivate and enslave Christians. These are the most abominable sodomites and abusers of masculine youth in the world, in which sin against nature they exceed the foulness and detestable lust of a Tatar.

---

[411] Officers who keep people in order.
[412] Modern Turkish *esir tuccan*, "dealer in slaves."

112                 *The* Turkiſh *Government*

### Chap. VII.

*Of the endowments of Royal Moſches, and in what manner*
*Tithes are given for Maintenance of their Prieſts and Re-*
*ligion.*

*An Emaum or Parish Prieſt of one of the*
*Royall Moſchs.*

**Chapter VII.** *Of the endowments of royal mosques and in what manner tithes are given for maintenance of their priests and religion.*

The Turks are very magnificent in their mosques and edifices erected to the honour and service of God, and not only in the buildings but in the endowments of them with a revenue which records the memory of the donor to all posterity and relieves many poor who daily repeat prayers for the souls of such who died with a persuasion that they have need of them after their decease. For those, I say, who die of that belief, for the condition of the soul until the Day of Judgment is controverted amongst the Turks and the question not decided as a matter of faith or as revealed or determined by the Qur'an. For so large benevolence is given to places destined to God's service that, as some compute, one-third of the lands of the whole empire are allotted and set out to a holy use, much to the shame of those who pretend to the name of Christians and yet judge the smallest proportion to be too large a competence for those who serve at the altar.

The principal mosques and those of richest endowment, as in all reason ought, are those of royal foundations, called in Turkish *selatin camileri*,[413] over which the prime superintendent is the Kizlar Aga or Chief Black Eunuch of the Sultan's women, and in his power it is to distribute all considerable offices of ecclesiastical preferment relating to the royal mosques, which office makes a considerable addition to his power and revenue, for there are many of those mosques in divers places of the empire, but especially where the Sultans do or have resided, as Prusa, Adrianople, or Constantinople. The royal mosques of Constantinople are Santa Sophia, Sultan Mehmed, Sultan Selim, Sultan Süleyman, Şehzade or the son of Sultan Süleyman, Sultan Ahmed and three other mosques built by the Queen Mothers, one of which was lately erected and richly endowed by the mother of the present Sultan.[414]

I shall scarce adventure to acquaint my reader with the particular revenue belonging to all these royal edifices, but certain it is they have rents as noble and splendid as their founders, for example of which I shall instance only in that of Santa Sophia, built by Justinian the Emperor and rebuilt by Theodosius, and was the metropolis of old Byzantium and the mother-church belonging to the Patriarchal See of Greece, [and] is still conserved sacred and separate for use of divine service. Of the revenue of which, Muhammadan barbarism and superstition hath made no sacrilegious robbery, but maintained and improved, and

---

[413] A mosque or *camii* built by a *selatin*, who is a Sultan, his wife, or one of his children.

[414] The mosque built by Mehmed II in 1463–1470 was completely destroyed by fire in 1766, after two previous fires. The oldest original mosque in Istanbul is now that of Sultan Bayezid II, which was built in 1501–1506 (see Taylor, *Imperial Istanbul*, 115–16); Selim I's mosque (1522) was not completed until after his death (see Taylo,r 122–24); the impressive Sülimaniye mosque , a building of "majestic assurance" (Taylor, 161) was completed in 1557 (Taylor 161–66); the Şehzade or Prince's mosque was built by a grieving Süleyman the Magnificent for his son Mehmed (1521–1543) and was completed in 1548 (see Taylor 156–58); the Sultan Ahmed mosque, known popularly as the Blue Mosque, is still Istanbul's most popular mosque. It was built in 1617 (Taylor, 173–77). Mosques built by the Queen Mothers include the Yeni Valide Camii near the Galata Bridge, which was started in 1597 by Săfiye Sultan, wife of Murad III, and completed in 1663 by Turhan Hatice, wife of Sultan Ibrahim and the mother of Mehmed IV. Rycaut might also be referring to the Atik Valide Camii, built in 1583 under the auspices of Sultana Nur Banu (1525–1583), wife of Selim II.

added to it in that manner that the income may equal any religious foundation of Christendom.[415] For, when I had the curiosity of procuring from the registers of that church distinctly all the particular gifts, benefices, lands, monies at interest and other endowments belonging thereunto, and offered according to my ability something considerable to have a true copy of the riches and annual rent of the place, the keepers of those lists would persuade me, whether out of ostentation or scruple of sin to make one of my faith acquainted with the particulars of their religious offerings, that the wealth, rent, and account of all those royal endowments are so many, that as they are distinctly set down fill a volume, and the knowledge of them is the study alone of those who are designed to this service. But, in general, I am given to understand by those who magnify not matters beyond their due computation that the revenue amounts to about one hundred thousand sequins a year, which proceeds not from any lands or duties raised without the walls of the city, but all from within, the Sultan himself being a tenant to that place, paying or acknowledging a rent of one thousand and one aspers a day for the ground which the Seraglio stands on, being in times of the Christian emperors some parts of the sanctuary or gardens dedicated to the use of that stately temple which the Turks esteemed sacrilegious to separate entirely from the holy service to which it was assigned. Though the admirable situation thereof rendered it unfit for other habitation, they did therefore think fit to oblige the land to a rent, adding the odd asper as a signification that the thousand aspers were not a sufficient consideration for the use of the church lands, and might therefore be augmented as the piety and devotion of succeeding emperors should move them.

It is reported by the Turks that Constantinople was taken upon Wednesday[416] and that on the Friday following, which is their Sunday or Sabbath (as we call it) the victorious Sultan, then first entitled emperor, went with all magnificent pomp and solemnity to pay his thanksgiving and devotions at the church of Santa Sophia, the magnificence of which so pleased him that he immediately added a yearly rent of 10,000 sequins to the former endowments for the maintenance of imams or priests, doctors of their law, talismans[417] and others who con-

---

[415] Rycaut has a few problems with his chronology concerning the Hagia Sophia church. Theodosius II (408–450) rebuilt a church originally founded by Constantius II in 360 that burned down in 404; the new church was consecrated in 415, and lasted until 532, when rioters burned it down. Justinian I (527–565) rebuilt it in 537, and in 1453 it became the Mosque of Aya Sofia after Mehmed II captured Constantinople. The Turks, as Rycaut states, did no damage to the edifice and in fact repaired and improved its interior. For further details, see Taylor, *Imperial Istanbul*, 49–61.

[416] The city actually fell on Tuesday, 29 May 1453, according to the Julian calendar. That would mean that Mehmed II would have probably entered it on the following day, which would of course be Wednesday.

[417] People who perform religious rites.

tinually attend there for the education of youth, teaching them to read and write, instructing them also in the principles of their law and religion.

Other emperors have since that time erected near unto it their *türbes* or chapels of burial, in one of which lies Sultan Selim, surnamed *Sarkhosh* or the Drunken, with his one hundred children,[418] and therewith have conferred a maintenance of oil for lamps and candles which burn day and night, and a provision for those who attend there in prayer for their souls departed, to which opinion the Turks, as I have said already, are generally inclinable, though not preached or enforced on any man's belief as an article of faith. Over and above this expense there is daily provision made for relief of a multitude of poor, who at certain hours appear at the gates of this temple and receive their daily sustenance. Whatsoever advances as yearly great sums are laid up in the treasury is numbered with the riches of the mosque, and remains for the service of that place as for the reparation or building thereof in case of fire or other accidents. Besides the sumptuous edifices of the body of the royal mosques, there are annexed unto them certain colleges for students in the law, called *temele*,[419] outhouses for kitchens where the poor's meat is dressed, hospitals called *timarhaneler*,[420] *hanes* or houses of lodgings for strangers or travellers, public fountains, shops for artisans and whole streets of low cottages for habitation of the poor, whose stock reaches not to a higher rent.

All these appendages bring some revenue to the mosque, which is constantly paid to the Rector or President thereof, called *Muteveli*,[421] but because this is not a sufficient maintenance there are divers lands, villages, mountains, woods and whole countries assigned to this use, called *vakfiye*,[422] which are hired out at certain rents for the behoof[423] and benefit of the mosques, some rents being paid in corn, others in oil and all sorts of provisions. And out of every new-conquered country some part thereof is assigned to the use of mosques of modern fabric, as now from the country gained lately about Neuhausel,[424] (which, as I am informed from those who gave in the account to the Grand Signior, there are 2000

---

[418] Selim II reigned 1566–1574. His tomb was finished in 1577. There are actually only forty-two of his children and grandchildren buried here, some of whom were "reluctantly" ordered strangled by Murad III on his accession. His wife Nur Banu (see above) is also buried here (Taylor, *Imperial Istanbul*, 60).

[419] Literally, "a foundation."

[420] Literally, "houses [belonging to] a timariot."

[421] Administrator.

[422] Religious foundations.

[423] Advantage.

[424] Neuhausel, also known as Nové Zamky (or Uyvar in Turkish), is a city on the Nitra River some 100 kilometres from Bratislava in modern-day Slovakia. The Turks attacked it several times in the sixteenth and seventeenth centuries, finally succeeding in capturing it in 1663 with a force under Ahmed Köprülü. It was recaptured in 1685 by Charles of Lorraine. For details, see Finkel, *Osman's Dream*, 266–67.

villages which pay contribution to the Turk), are assigned certain lands for in-crease of the rent of the mosques built in Constantinople by this present Queen Mother, which rents are sometimes raised by the way of tenths or tithes. Not that the Turk makes tithes a duty or rule for the maintenance of persons, places and things consecrated to divine service, but as they find it convenient and equal expedient in some countries for alleviation of their rents. Such countries and vil-lages as these which are called *vakfiye* are greatly blessed and happy above others, in regard that the inhabitants enjoy not only particular privileges and immunities from thence, but freedom likewise from the oppression of pashas and the Turkish soldiery in their march or of great persons in their journey or passage from one country to another, who out of reverence to that lot to which they are separated, abstain from all kind of disturbance and abuse towards that people.

Other mosques of inferior quality founded by private persons and the consents of dervishes[425] and other orders which cannot have their revenues in land like the mosques of royal foundation, have their estates in money be-queathed by testament or by gift of the living, which, being lent out at eighteen in the hundred *per annum*, produces a constant rent. And though interest for the most part is forbidden by the Muhammadan law, yet for the uses of mosques and support of orphans it is allowed; in all other cases [it] is *haram*[426] and abomina-ble. And because the taking-up of money upon loan is in some manner necessary and conducing to the better subsistence and being of trade and that men will not lend without a consideration of benefit, the usual manner is to borrow money for a certain time, and in the writing or obligation to acknowledge the receipt of as much as the principal and interest may amount unto, and oftentimes double of the capital sum, which, being delivered before witness in a bag or in gross, the creditor declaring the sum to be so much contained and the debtor acknowledg-ing it, the testimony is valid when the debt comes to be demanded. And thus much shall serve in brief to have declared concerning the endowments and man-ner of enriching the Turkish mosques, from whence the constitution of others of the like nature may easily be collected.

---

[425] Dervishes, who are usually Sufis, were often mendicants who observed a particular ascetic form of Islam.

[426] This is an Arabic word meaning "forbidden." Rycaut is quite correct about the taboo on interest in Islam.

## Chapter VIII. *The nature of predestination according to the Turkish doctors.*

The doctrine of the Turks in this point seems to run exactly according to the assertion of the severest Calvinists, and in proof hereof their learned men produce places of scripture which seem to incline to their opinion, as, "Shall the vessel say to the potter, why hast thou made me thus?;" "I will harden the heart of Pharaoh;" "Jacob have I loved and Esau have I hated," and the like.[427] For the Turks attribute no small reverence and authority to the Old Testament as wrote by divine inspiration, but that the Qur'an, being of later date and containing the will of God more expressly and perfectly, the former is now abrogated and gives place unto this. Some are so positive in this assertion that they are not afraid to say that God is the author of evil, without distinction or evasions to acquit the divine purity of the foulness of sin according to the doctrine of the Manichees.[428] And all in general concur in this conclusion, that whatsoever prospers hath God for the author, which was the reason they destroyed not Bayezid's children during the time of his war against his brother Selim, expecting to receive an undoubted argument of the will of God therein from the good or bad fortune of the father.[429] And from the same rule they conclude much of the divine approbation and truth of their religion from their conquests and present prosperity.

They are of opinion that every man's destiny is writ in his forehead, which they call *nasip*[430] or *takdir*,[431] which is the book writ in heaven of every man's fortune, and is by no contrary endeavours, counsels or wisdom to be avoided, which tenent[432] is so firmly radicated[433] in the minds of the vulgar[434] that is causes the

---

[427] Rycaut seems to be quoting from memory, at least in the first passage, which reads (in the King James translation): "Shall the thing formed say to him that fashioneth it, What makes thou?" (Isaiah 45: 9). The other quotes, in sequence, are Exodus 7:3 and Romans 9:13. Given the next sentence, it is odd that he thought the quote about Jacob and Esau was from the Old Testament.

[428] The Manichees were the followers of Mani (c. 216–276), a Persian mystic. They believed in a syncretic dualism incorporating elements from various religious systems, that after a primal struggle in which Satan (matter, darkness) separated from God (spirituality, light) there was a continuing battle between the two, and man, composed of matter and spirit, was caught in the middle. The spirit could be released from the material through asceticism. They regarded evil as something physical, not moral.

[429] In the later years of the reign of Bayezid II (1481–1512), his sons Selim and Ahmed fought against each other, and Bayezid took the field against Selim, defeating him in 1511. However, Selim defeated and killed Ahmed (there were rumours of poisoning), which brought about Bayezid's abdication in 1512.

[430] Lot, predestination.

[431] Understanding.

[432] Obselete form of "tenet."

[433] Entrenched, rooted.

[434] Ordinary people (no pejorative context).

soldiers brutishly to throw away their lives in the desperate attempts and to esteem
no more of their bodies than as dirt or rubbish to fill up the trenches of the enemy.
And to speak the truth, this received assertion hath turned as much account to
the Turks as any other their best and subtlest maxims. According to this doctrine,
none ought to avoid or fear the infection of the plague, Muhammad's precepts being not to abandon the city-house[435] where the infection rages because God hath
numbered their days and predetermined their fate, and upon this belief they as
familiarly attend the beds and frequent the company of pestilential persons as we
do those that are affected with the gout, stone or ague. And though they evidently
see that Christians, who fly into better airs and from infected habitations survive
the fury of the year's pestilence when whole cities of them perish and are depopu-
lated with the disease, yet so far is this opinion rooted amongst them that they
scruple not to strip the contagious shirt from the dead body and to put it on their
own. Nor can they remove their abode from the chambers of the sick, it being the
custom in the families of great men to lodge many servants on different palettes in
the same room, where the diseased and the healthful lie promiscuously[436] together, from whence it hath happened often that three parts of a pasha's family, which
perhaps consisted of two hundred men most youthful and lusty, have perished in
the heat of July and August. And in the same manner many whole families every
summer hath perished and not one survivor left to claim the inheritance of the
house, for want of which the Grand Signior hath become the proprietor.

Though the Muhammadan law obliges them not to abandon the city or their
houses nor avoid the conversation of men inflicted with the pestilence where their
business or calling employs them, yet they are counselled not to frequent a contagious habitation where they have no lawful affair to invite them. But I have observed, in the time of an extraordinary plague, that the Turks have not considered
so much the precept of their prophet as to have courage enough to withstand the
dread and terror of that slaughter the sickness hath made, but have under excuses
fled to retired and private villages, especially the qadis and men of the law, who,
being commonly of more refined wits and judgments than the generality, both by
reason and experience have found that a wholesome air is a preserver of life and
that they have lived to return again to their own house in health and strength,
when perhaps their next neighbours have through their brutish ignorance been
laid in their graves. And this is the opinion most general and current with the
Turks who are called *jabare*;[437] there is another sort amongst them called *kadere*.[438]

---

[435] Shelter or hospital for plague victims.

[436] Randomly.

[437] From the Arabic *al-jabariyah*, a sect "who deny free agency in man" (Thomas
Hughes, *A Dictionary of Islam* [1886; reprint Chicago: Kazi Publications, 1994], 223).

[438] From the Arabic *al-qadariyah*, a sect "who deny absolute predestination and believe in the power (*qadr*) of man's free will" (Hughes, *Dictionary*, 478).

**Chapter IX.** *The difference of sects and disagreement in religion amongst the Turks in general.*

There is no consideration more absolute and full of distraction than the contemplation of the strange variety of religions in the world, how it is possible that from the rational soul of man, which in all mankind is of little difference in itself and from one principle, which is the adoration of a deity, should proceed such diversities of faiths, such figments and ideas of God that all ages and countries have abounded with superstitions of different natures. And it is strange to consider that nations who have been admirably wise, judicious, and profound in the maxims of their government should yet in matters of religion give themselves over to believe in the tales of an old woman, a pythoness[439] or the dreams and imaginations of a melancholy hermit. And it is strange that men who embrace the same principles in religion and have the same infallible and true foundation should yet raise such different and disproportionate fabrics that most should make their superstructure of straw and stubble, but few of a substantial and durable building without uniformity, harmony or agreement each to other. For resolution of which difficulties nothing can be said more than that "the God of this world hath blinded the hearts of them which believe not, lest the light of the glorious gospel of Christ who is the image of God should shine unto them."[440]

The Muhammadan religion is also one of the prodigious products of reason's superstitions, which hath brought forth nothing good nor rational in this production more than the confession of one God. And yet even herein also are diversities of sects, opinions and orders which are maintained in opposition each to another with emulation and zeal by the professors, with heats, disputes and separations terming the contrary parties profane and unholy, the particulars of which sects and diversity in their tenents I shall, as far as I have seen or could learn, set down and describe, having with the more curiosity and diligence made the stricter inquiry, because I have not read any author which hath given a satisfactory account of such sects as are sprung up amongst them in these latter and modern times.

It is a common opinion that there are seventy-two sects[441] amongst the Turks, but it is probable that there are many more, if the matter were exactly known and scanned. The Turkish doctors fancy that the seventy-two nations, which they call

---

[439] A prophetic priestess from Apollo's oracle in Delphi.

[440] 2 Corinthians 4:4 (Rycaut's note).

[441] In the *Mishkatu'l-masabih*, compiled by Husain al-Baghawi, who died around 1122, it is stated that Muhammad prophesied that Islam would be divided. "The Children of Israel were divided into seventy-two sects," he is said to have declared, "and my people will be divided into seventy-three. Every one of these sects will go to Hell except one sect" (Hughes, *Dictionary*, 567). However, the number is, as Rycaut thinks, much larger than that.

*yetmiş iki millet*,[442] into which the world was divided upon the confusion of the languages of Babel, was a type and a figure of the divisions which in after ages should succeed in the three most general religions of the world. In this manner they account seventy different sects among the Jews, seventy-one amongst the Christians, and unto the Muhammadans they assign one more, as being the last and ultimate religion, in which, as all fullness of true doctrine is completed, so the mystery of iniquity and the deviation of man's judgment by many paths from the right rule is here terminated and confined. The Turks have amongst themselves, as well as in other religions, sects and heresies of dangerous consequence which daily increase, mixing together with them many of the Christian doctrines, which shall in their due place be described, and in former times also a sort of fanatic Muhammadans, which at first met only in congregations under pretence of sermons and religion, appeared afterwards in troops armed against the government of the empire.

So one Sheykh Bedreddin,[443] chief justice of Musa, brother of Mehmed, the fifth king of the Turks,[444] was banished to Nicaea[445] in Asia, where, consulting with his servant Börklüce Mustafa[446] by what means they might raise sedition

---

[442]  Seventy-two countries.

[443]  Sheikh Bedreddin bin Abdulaziz (1359–1420) was a Sufi who led a revolt in Anatolia against high taxation and unfair land distribution. His forces defeated an Ottoman army but he was eventually captured and hanged in Serez, Macedonia. Centuries later (1961), the Turkish government had his body reburied in the mausoleum of Sultan Mahmud II. He was not a Sultan's brother, but his father, a qadi, was the great-grandson of Sultan Kaykaus II of Rum (r. 1246–1460). His memory is very much alive today; the great modern Turkish poet Nazim Hikmet has written *The Epic of Sheykh Bedreddin* (1935), in which he extolled the proto-socialistic ideas of Bedreddin. Because it was read by a number of Turkish soldiers Hikmet was imprisoned for fourteen years. Bedreddin's writings are contained in his book, the *Varidat*; there does not seem to be an English translation.

[444]  Prince Musa Çelebi (d. 1413) was the brother of Sultan Mehmed I (r. 1413–1421). After the death of Bayezid I (1403) Musa, Mehmed and other sons of the late Sultan battled for the throne. Musa made himself Sultan of Edirne, and for a time ruled as co-Sultan with Mehmed I (1411–1413) in the European part of the Ottoman Empire. He was finally defeated by Mehmed at the battle of Çamurlu Derbent in Bulgaria and was killed while fleeing after the battle. The interregnum ended with Musa's defeat. It was also Mehmed I who suppressed the revolt of Sheikh Bedreddin. Musa had appointed Bedreddin as his chief military judge.

[445]  Now known as Iznik; it is in modern Bursa province near the Sea of Marmara.

[446]  Börklüce Mustafa (d. 1420) went into exile to Nicaea with Bedreddin, and is said to have had a fair amount of influence on the latter's communalistic doctrines. He served as Bedreddin's chief commander, and managed to defeat several Ottoman armies before withdrawing to the Karabarun Peninsula in Albania, where he was finally defeated in a battle at a place called the Valley of the Torment. He was crucified after the battle. Rycaut could have found accounts of this man in various places, including Johann Löwenklau

and a second war, they agreed the readiest course was by broaching a new sect and religion, and by persuading the people to something contrary to the ancient Muhammadan superstition, whereupon Börklüce, masking his villainy under a grave and serious countenance, took his journey into Aydin, otherwise Caria,[447] where he vented doctrines properly agreeing to the humour of the people, preaching to them freedom and liberty of conscience and the mystery of revelations. And you may believe he used all arts in his persuasions, with which subjects used to be allured to a rebellion against their Prince, so that in a short time he contracted a great number of disciples beyond his expectation. Bedreddin, perceiving his servant thrive so well with his preaching, fled from his place of exile at Nicaea into Wallachia, where, withdrawing himself into a forest like a devout religious man, gathered a number of proselytes composed of thieves, robbers and outlawed people. These he, having instructed in the principles of his religion, sent abroad like apostles to preach and teach the people that Bedreddin was appointed by God to be King of Justice and Commander of the Whole World, and that his doctrine was already embraced in Asia. The people, taken with these novelties, repaired in great numbers to Bedreddin, who, conceiving himself strong enough to take the field, issued from his desert with colours displayed and an army well-appointed, and, fighting with his deluded multitude a bloody battle against those forces which Mehmed sent to suppress him under his son Murat.[448] The deluded rebels were overthrown, Bedreddin taken prisoner and his pretences of sanctity and revelation were not available to save him from the gallows.

And thus we see that the name of God's cause, revelations, liberty and the like have been old and common pretences and delusions of the world, and not only Christians but infidels and Muhammadans have wrote the name of God on their banners and brought the pretence of religion in the field to justify their cause.

---

(Leunclavius), *Historia musulmanae Turcorum* (1591), where he could read of *"praefectum rei domesticate quemdam, cui nomen erat Burgluzes Mustapha"* (477). For further details, see H. I. Cotsonis, "Aus der Endzeit von Byzanz: Bürklödische Mustafa, ein Märtyrer für die Koexistenz zwischen Islam und Christentum," *Byzantinische Zeitschrift* 50 (1957): 397–404.

[447] Caria was a region in western Anatolia; it reached south from Ionia to Lycia and Phrygia. Aydin (formerly Tralles) was a city in the region, renamed Güzelhisar when it was taken over by the independent beys of Menteş in the early part of the thirteenth century. They submitted to the Ottoman Empire under Bayezid I in 1390.

[448] Afterwards reigned as Murad II (1421–1444).

Chapter X. *Of the two prevailing sects,* viz. *Of Muhammad and Ali, that is, the Turk and the Persian. The errors of the Persian recounted and confuted by the Mufti of Constantinople.*

The two great sects among the followers of Muhammad which are most violent each against other, the mutual hatred of which diversity of education and interest of the princes have augmented are the Turks and the Persians. The first hold Muhammad to have been the chief and ultimate prophet; the latter prefer Ali before him, and though he was his disciple and succeeded him, yet his inspirations they esteem greater and more frequent and his interpretations of the law most perfect and divine. [449]

The Turk also accuses the Persian of corrupting the Qur'an, that they have altered words, misplaced the commas and stops, that many places admit of a doubtful and ambiguous sense, so that those Qur'ans which were upon the conquest of Babylon brought thence to Constantinople are separated and compiled in the great Seraglio in a place apart, and forbidden with a curse on any that shall read them. The Turks call the Persians "forsaken of God, abominable and blasphemous of the Holy Prophet," so that when Selim I made war in Persia he named his cause "the Cause of God" and proclaimed the occasion and ground of his war to be the vindication of the cause of the Prophet and revenge on the blasphemies the Persians had vented against him. And so far is this hatred radicated[450] that the youth of what nation soever is capable of admittance into the schools of the Seraglio, excepting only the Persian, who are looked upon by the Turk as a people so far apostasised from the true belief and fallen into so desperate an estate by the total corruption of the true religion that they judge them altogether beyond hopes or possibility of recovery and therefore neither give them quarter in the wars nor account them worthy of life or slavery.

Nor are the Persians on the other side endued with better nature of good will to the Turks, estranging themselves in the farthest manner from their customs and doctrines, rejecting the three great doctors of the Muhammadan law, *viz.* Abu Bakr, 'Uthman and Omar, as apocryphal and of no authority, and have a custom at their marriages to erect the images of those three doctors of paste or sugar at the entrance of the bridal chamber, on which, the guests first casting their looks, leave the impression of any secret magic which may issue from their eyes to the prejudice or misfortune of the married couple, for in the eastern parts of the world they hold that there is a strange fascination innate to the eyes of some people, which, looking attentively on any, as commonly they do on the

---

[449] This is not quite accurate. Shi'a Muslims believe that Ali was the first real khalifa (caliph) or successor to Muhammad, and they do not recognize the three other khalifas (Omar I, Abu Bakr, and 'Uthman I), which the Sunnis do. The Shi'as also consider that Ali, who was the Prophet's cousin, was directly appointed by Muhammad to be his successor.

[450] Planted deeply.

bridegroom and bride in marriages, produce maceration[451] and imbecility in the body and have an especial quality contrary to procreation. And therefore, when the guests are entered, having the maliginity of their eyes arrested on these statues, they afterwards cut them down and dissolve them.

And that it may the more plainly appear what points of religion are the most controverted amongst them and what anathemas and curses are by both sides vented each against the other, this following sentence, pronounced by the Mufti Esad Effendi[452] upon Saru Khalifeh, tutor to Shah Abbas [II], the king of Persia[453] and all the Persians will be a sufficient testimony and evidence of the enmity and hatred that is between these two nations, an extract of which is here drawn from the book itself, licensed and approved at Constantinople.

> If you had no other heresy than the rejection of those elevated familiars of Muhammad, *viz*. 'Umar, 'Uthman and Abu Bakr, your crime would notwithstanding be so great as were not expiable by a thousand years of prayer or pilgrimage in the sight of God, but you would be condemned to the bottomless abyss of hell, and be deprived forever of celestial bliss. And this sentence of mine is confirmed by the same opinion of the Four Imams, *viz*. Imam Azam, Imam Shafi, Imam Malik and Imam Hanbal,[454] and therefore I friendly admonish you to correct this error in yourselves and likewise in your scholar, king Abbas.
>
> Nor are you contented to pass with this single error whereby you have gained the name of *qizilbashi*,[455] that is, Persian heretics, but you are become

---

[451] Softening.

[452] See Chapter 4, n. 1.

[453] Rycaut appears to be referring to Shah Abbas II (r. 1642–1666), who was ten years old when he succeeded his father Shah Safi. The "tutor" to whom Rycaut refers could be either Saru Taqi, Abbas II's Grand Vizier and regent to 1645, or his successor Khalifeh Sultan. The names seem to have been mixed up. For details, see David Blow, *Shah Abbas: The Ruthless King Who Became an Iranian Legend* (London: I. B. Tauris, 2009), 232.

[454] The Four Imams were each the founder of an Islamic school of jurisprudence, known as a *madhhab*. Their full names are Azam Abu Hanifa (699–767); Muhammad al-Shafi (767–820); Malik ibn Anas (711–795), and Abu Abdullah ibn Hanbal (780–855). Imams are scholars, not "clergymen" or "priests" as Rycaut sometimes describes them, because Islam does not have clergy who are the equivalent of Christian priests. Sunni Muslims belong to one of the four schools and recognize the first four caliphs as the rightful successors of Muhammad.

[455] Literally, "red-heads," so-called from the twelve-gored (a gore is a triangular piece of cloth) red or crimson headdresses they wore wrapped around their turbans or protruding from the top of them, symbolizing their adherence to the Twelve (Shi'a) Imams rather than the Four of the Sunnis, and also their connection with the Safavids, who ruled Persia and were, of course, mortal enemies of the Turks.

as abominable as the Druzes, a people that live about Mount Libanus,[456] of
bad esteem and reputation, corrupted in all points of doctrine and manners,
so that I cannot but pass this black sentence upon you, that it is lawful in a
godly zeal to kill and destroy you for the service of God, your tenets being
refuted by Ja'afar Effendi, who hath branded the Persians for pagans, and
in seventy several places of the Qur'an and the very words of Muhammad
demonstrated the clearness of their error.

If the Christian, only for saying there is a Trinity in God, is condemned for life and estate, why should the Persian expect better quarter,
who is stigmatized for heresy in seventy places of the Qur'an? And one
of your detestable opinions of the first rank is that you esteem yourselves
obliged to assemble at the mosques if not to prayers, for what signifies your
meeting if not to prayers? Muhammad himself says that he who repairs to
the congregation without a desire of prayer is a hypocrite and a dissembler,
is accursed of God, nor shall be blessed in his house or estate. The good angels shall abandon him, the devils shall attend him, nor shall he ever prosper in this world or in the world to come.

In answer hereunto you say that the ancient order of priests is extinct,
that you have none whose pious lives enable to preach and instruct you or
to be your leader to holy prayer in the public assembly. Do there want pious
and holy persons of the race of Muhammad? If there do not, why do you
not imitate and follow them? But you are enemies, and in open hostility to
the Muhammadan family, and excuse yourselves from the use of priests or
imams, because their innocence cannot equal that of infants. In this point it
is true you have something of reason, for your imams are not only infidels in
doctrine but defiled in their conversation, and your king is your high priest,
frequents stews and the sties of deformed lust, ravishing fair and chaste
wives from the embraces of their husbands, and that publicly, in the face of
the world, maintaining concubinage with them. And where the example of
a Prince makes such things lawful, his subjects, whether soldiers or lawyers,
will make no scruple to imitate his actions.

You deny the verse called "The Covering of the Qur'an" to be authentic.[457] You reject the eighteen verses which are revealed to us for the sake of

---

[456] Hughes defines the Druzes as "a heretical mystic sect" (*Dictionary*, 100) of Is-
lam whose founder was one Hamza ibn Ali (985–after 1040), a Persian mystic. They live
today in Syria, Lebanon, Jordan, and Israel, and may be considered an offshoot of the
Ismaili Muslim sect, a Shi'a group which accepts Ismail ibn Ja'afar as the successor to
Ja'afar as-Sadiq (702–765), a jurist who was a direct descendent of Muhammad. Mount
Libanus is actually the whole Western Mountain Range of Lebanon.

[457] Sura 24:30–31. This deals with the way women are supposed to cover their heads
and bodies.

the holy Aisha.[458] At the *abdest* or washing you hold it not lawful to wash the bare feet but only lightly stroke them over.[459]

Your moustachios or hair on the upper lip you never cut, but the beard on the chin, which is the honest ornament of a man's countenance, you cut and clip into what form you please.[460]

That holy colour of green, appropriated to the banner of Muhammad,[461] which ought only to adorn the nobler parts, you despite of the honour of the Prophet with an irreverent negligence, place it on your shoes and breeches.

Wine, which is an abomination to the true observers of the law, you drink freely of without scruple of conscience, as also in meats you make no distinction between clean and unclean, but use all with a like indifferency. In short, should I mention all those seventy points wherein you err and are without comparison corrupt and erroneous, I should swell my writing to a volume and not attain my end, which is brevity.

Another sinful custom you permit amongst you is for many men to be joined to one woman, for to whom of them can be appropriated the offspring that is born?[462] What book have you, or law, or example of any nation to produce in approbation of this vile and unnatural custom? How vile must those children be who are the issue of such parents, that it is no wonder there be none found amongst you worthy the holy character of a priest or judge.

But you cannot be so irrational as to deny that the assembling in mosques to prayer is necessary to divine service; Muhammad himself prayed together with the people and sometimes preferred Abu Bakr to celebrate the divine service, following him as others of the people did.

Why do not you ask your pilgrims who come from Mecca what mean these four altars in the mosque which are the places of prayer designed to

---

[458] Aisha bint Abu Bakr (612–678) is believed by Sunnis to have been Muhammad's favourite wife, and is held in great esteem by them. She is often referred to as "Mother of the Believers." There are several references to her in the Quran, notably Sura 33:6, which discusses Muhammad's wives.

[459] Rycaut uses the Turkish term *abdest*; the Arabic word for the washing of the feet is *wudhu*. Sunnis and Shi'as perform different actions as they carry out this ritual. Shi'as do not take more water to wash their feet after they have washed their head and hands first.

[460] Shah Abbas II had a moustache but no beard, which must have upset the Mufti considerably.

[461] Muhammad's own banner was actually black, but his armies used various solid colours, including green, for their flags.

[462] No Islamic sects ever permitted polyandry. However, in pre-Islamic Arabia there was *nikah ijitmah*, a form of marriage contracted by a woman with no more than ten men; if she became pregnant she would simply summon the men and name whichever one she liked as the father of the child.

the four several orthodox sects? Why take you not example from these? But you are still perverse and obstinate haters of God and his Prophet: what will you answer at the day of judgment before Muhammad and his four friends, who, long since dead, you revive their ashes with ignomy, erecting their statues at your marriages in vulgar, and afterwards in contempt hew them down to yield pastime and occasion of laughter to the spouses and their guests?

Was not the first converted to the faith Abu Bakr? Was not 'Umar the bravest champion of the Muhammadan religion against the Christians? Was not he who disposed and distinguished the chapters of the Qur'an the chaste 'Umar? Was not the bravest and most learned bearer of the *zulfikar* or the sword with two points, was it not Ali? And were not Imam Hassan and Imam Husain martyrs of the faith in the deserts of Karbala?[463]

Did not Muhammad say with his own mouth, "O Ali, for thy sake there are two sorts of people predestinated to hell, one that loves thee and one that loves thee not"? Are not you then that wear red turbans much to be condemned, being of evil life and conversation and not well-inclined to the House of the Prophet nor the family of the faithful as it is written in the book called *Hadith*?[464] The Christians conserve the hoofs of that ass on which Christ rode and set them in cases of gold and silver and esteem it an extreme honour to have their faces, hands or heads touched with so holy a relic. But you, who profess yourselves disciples of the Prophet of God and derived from the blood and family of his friends, despise so glorious a title, commanding after the repetition of your prayers, that is, after the *azan*,[465] that curses and blasphemies be proclaimed against these holy friends and associates of the Prophet.

Besides this, your books maintain and avouch it is lawful to pillage, burn and destroy the countries of the Muslims, to carry their wives and families into slavery and from a principle of malice and reproach to carry them

---

[463] Abu Bakr was the first person outside Muhammad's immediate family to become a Muslim. Caliph 'Uthman (Osman) I formed a committee which standardized the text of the Quran in order, at least he hoped, to avoid schism amongst Muslims. The *zulfikar* was presented to Ali by Muhammad himself. Hassan ibn Ali (625–669) was the son of Caliph Ali, and reigned briefly as caliph in 661; he is also regarded as the second Sh'ia imam (661–669). He died in Medina of poison said to have been administered by his wife Ja'ada on the instigation of Caliph Mu'awiya I. His brother Hussein (626–680), regarded by Shi'as as the third Imam, refused to acknowledge the authority of caliph Yazid I (680–683) and was defeated at the battle of Karbala (680), after which he was beheaded. Both men are regarded as martyrs of the Sh'ia sect.

[464] The *hadith* are sayings or acts ascribed to Muhammad and collected in various books. They are regarded as authentic and have authority.

[465] The *azan* or "announcement" is the summons to public prayers.

naked through your markets and expose them to sale to any chapman.[466] Pagans themselves esteem not this honest nor decent, by which it is apparent that you are the most mortal and irreconcilable enemies to us of all the nations in the world. You are certainly more cruel to us than the Zeidiyehs, the Kafirs, the Zindiqs,[467] than the Druzes, and in brief you are the kennel of all uncleanliness and sin. A Christian or a Jew may hope to become true believers, but you can never.

Wherefore, by virtue of that authority I have received from Muhammad himself, in consideration of your misdeeds and incredulity, I pronounce it lawful for anyone of what nation soever that is of the believers to kill, destroy and extirpate you, so that as he who slays a rebellious Christian performs a meritorious action in the sight of God, much rather he who kills a Persian shall obtain a reward seventy-fold from the fountain of justice. And I hope that the Majesty of God in the day of judgment will condemn you to be the asses of the Jews, to be rode and hackneyed[468] in hell by that despised people, and that in a short time you will be exterminated both by us, the Tatars, the Indians and Arabians, our brothers and associates in the same faith.

---

[466] A wandering salesman.

[467] Zeidiyehs are a sect who believe that prayers can only be led by one of Ali's descendents (Hughes, *Dictionary*, 568). The term *kafir* or *kaffir* denotes an unbeliever; *zindiqs* are atheists or freethinkers. Druzes we have met already.

[468] Hired out.

**Chapter XI.** *Of the ancient sects and heresies amongst the Turks.*

There are four sects into which the Muhammadans of the esteemed orthodox belief are divided, and those are these:

The first is called Hanafiyah, which is professed in Turkey, Tatary, Uzbekistan and on the other side of Jihon, Bactorus and Oxus.[469] The second is
Shafi'iyah, whose customs and rules the Arabians follow.[470] The third is Malaki-
yah, to which Tripoli, Tunis, Algier, and other parts of Africa devote themselves.
The fourth is Hanbaliyah, of which are but few and is known only in some parts
of Arabia.[471]

These four are all accounted orthodox and are followers of certain doctors (as
we may say amongst Christians, scholars of Augustine, Thomas Aquinas, Domi-
nic or the like), and have only differences as to ceremonies, postures in their
prayers, washings, diversities in some points of their civil laws, and each maintains a charitable opinion of the other as true believers and capable of entering
into Paradise if their life and conversation be regulated according to their profession and tenents. All Muhammadans, according to the countries wherein they
live, come under the notion of one of these four preceding professions, but yet
are nominated with other names and differences of sects according as they follow the opinions which some superstitions and schismatical preachers amongst
them have vented. Those commonly-known and marked with the names of ancient heresies by the respective opponents, which may properly be called so because they are conversant in their doctrines concerning the attributes and unity
of God, his decrees and judgments, his promises and threatenings, and concerning prophecies and gifts of faith, are especially these which stand in opposition
each to other, *viz.* Mu'tazilah to Sifatiyah, Qadariyah to Jabariyah, Murjiyah to
Waridiyah, Shi'a to Kharijiyah. From each of these sects, as from so many roots,
arise several branches of different doctrines, as according to the tenents of the
Turkish doctors, complete the number of seventy-two.

Mu'tazilah signifies as much as "separatists." The reason of which denomination was from al-Hasan, the scholar of Wasil ibn 'Ata, the author and master
of this sect, to whom the question being proposed whether those who had committed a gross sin were to be adjudged condemned and fallen from the faith,

---

[469] The Oxus river, now known as the Amu Darya, is in Central Asia, running
north-west to the Aral Sea; its Hebrew name is Jihon. Bactorus is another name for the
Vaksh river, one of the Oxus's main tributaries, which is located in north central Tajikistan. Rycaut's information about the locations of these sects is largely accurate; their
founders have been mentioned and noted in the preceding chapter..

[470] According to Hughes, they are found in southern India and Egypt (*Dictionary*,
567). However, they may also be found in Yemen.

[471] Rycaut is correct about this being the smallest sect; Hughes does note that there
are also some in Africa (567).

the scholar al-Hasan, instead of expecting the resolution of his master, with-drew himself and began to interpret his sense thereof to his other fellow-disciples, from which withdrawing of himself they were afterwards denominated Mu'tazilah, which is "separatists." But the name they give themselves is "the Defenders of the Equity and unity of God," in declaration of the manner of which they so differ among themselves that they are divided into two and twenty sects, which are maintained with that passion on all sides that every party accuses his opposites of infidelity. But the principle in which their wrangling sophisters accord in common is this, that God is eternal and that eternity is an attribute most properly agreeable to his essence. Yet they reject the attribute itself, saying that God is eternal, wise, powerful and the like by his own entire and single essence, but yet they say he is not eternal by his eternity nor wise by his wisdom nor powerful by his power, for fear of admitting any multiplicity in the Deity or incurring the like error as they say of the Christians, who divide and dishonor the unity of God by the conceptions they frame of the three persons in the Trinity. And if Christians are to be blamed for introducing three eternals, how much more are those who frame as many eternals as there are attributes to the Deity? [472]

Another sort derived from this sect, called Ha'itiyah, [473] hold that Christ assumed a true and natural body and was eternal and incarnate, as the Christians profess, and in their creed or belief have inserted this article, "That Christ shall come to judge the world at the last day," and for proof hereof allege an authority out of the Qur'an in these words, "Thou, Muhammad, shalt see thy Lord return in the clouds," which, though they fear expressly in plain terms to interpret of Christ, yet they confidently affirm it to be prophesied of the Messiah, and in discourse confess that Messiah can be no other than Christ, who shall return with the same human flesh again into the world, reign for forty years upon earth, confound Antichrist and afterward shall be the end of the world.

---

[472] Rycaut's writing is a little confusing on this point. Wasil ibn 'Ata (700–748) was actually the founder of the Mu'tazilah, separating from the school of Hasan al-Basri (642–728), a prominent Sunni scholar and theologian. Hughes, citing the *Sharhu 'l-Muwaqif* of al-Jurjani (d. 1413), lists only twenty sects (*Dictionary*, 425). However, Rycaut's description of the Mu'tazilahs' beliefs is accurate; Hughes notes, for instance, that "they entirely reject all eternal attributes of God, to avoid the distinction of persons made by the Christians, saying that eternity is the proper or formal attribute of his essence, that God knows by his essence, and not by his knowledge" (425).

[473] This sect was founded, Hughes tells us, by Ahmed ibn Ha'it, who believed that there were two Gods, Allah and al-Masih, Christ the Messiah, who would come to judge the world. Allah is eternal, al-Masih was created (*Dictionary*, 154). See also Ahmad Shafaat, "Islam's View of the Coming/ Return of Jesus," *Islamic Perspectives* (May 2003), http://www.islamicperspectives.com. The story of Jesus defeating the Antichrist (*Dajjal*, which means "false") may be found in various *hadiths* and is believed by Sunnis.

Another sort of the professors of the sect of Mu'tazliyah are Ash'ariyah, whose first author was al-Ashari.[474] These maintain that the Qur'an was created, contrary to the word of Muhammad, who anathematises all who are of this persuasion, saying "Let him be reputed an infidel who believes the Qur'an created," for solution of which difficulty and to concur with the words of their Prophet, they say that the Qur'an delivered by Muhammad was but a copy transcribed out of that wrote by God and laid in the library of heaven, and that when their Prophet denies the creation of the Qur'an, he hath no reference to the original but to his own handwriting which he had copied and extracted from the first and infallible exemplar. These also further proceed to deny against the common tenent of the Muhammadans, the incomparable and matchless eloquence of the Qur'an, asserting that were it not prohibited, other Arabians might be found who could far transcend every line of it in wisdom and rhetoric, which in my opinion is a strange kind of impudence in the very face of their Prophet, who seems to be so proud of the exact disposition and full signification of every word that he judges it not less charming for the sweet sound of its eloquence than it is convincing for the purity and truth of its doctrine.

The great anatagonists to the Mu'taziliyah are the Sifatiyah,[475] who assign in God eternal attributes of knowledge, power, life etc., and some of them proceed so far and grossly herein that they frame conceptions of corporeal organs of sense, as of hearing, seeing and speech to God, affirming that those expressions of God's sitting in his throne, creation of the world by the work of his hands, his anger against sin, repentance for man's conversion, which we call ἀνθρωποπάθεια,[476] are to be taken in the literal and plain sense, and have no need of farther-fetched interpretations to clear the true notions of them. But yet, herein their doctors seem not to agree, some defining a body to be the same as *per se subsistens*,[477] denying it to be an essential propriety of a body to be circumscribed

---

[474] The Ash'ariyahs are not a sect of the Mu'tazilyahs, but followers of Abu al-Hasan al-Ashari (872–936), who held that "the attributes of God are distinct from his essence, yet in such a way as to forbid any comparison being made between God and his creatures" (Hughes, *Dictionary*, 25), and they agreed with the Mu'tazilyahs on other points as well. They did hold that the Quran was created, but that the actual speech of Allah was uncreated, another point on which both groups agreed.

[475] The name is derived from the Arabic *sifat*, which means "attributes." Hughes calls the Sifatiyah "a school of thought rather than a sect," and notes that all Sunnis think of themselves as "attributists," whilst Mu'taziliyahs deny that God's attributes are eternal. An attributist "maintains that the attributes of God are eternally inherent in His essence without separation or change" (*Dictionary*, 582).

[476] The attribution of human emotions to a non-human being.

[477] Subsisting *per se*. The full sentence from Aquinas states that "*individua substantia,*" the individual substance, "*substantia, complete, per se subsistens, separata ab alia.*" [is] "a substance complete, subsisting *per se*, existing apart from others" (*Summa theologiae* III, Q. xvi, a. 12 ad 2 um).

and finite. Others conclude that it is enough to say that God is great, without argument of his circumscription or determination to any particular place, with many other strange conceits whereby are made apparent the roving fancies of ignorant men without the rules or grounds of philosophy or metaphysics. But the soberer sort amongst them, who would appear more moderate and wiser than the rest, forbid their scholars to make comparison of the senses in God with whose of the creature, who, being more subtly urged by their severe opponents to the Mu'taziliyahs, they were forced to declare themselves more clearly in this manner, that the God which they worshipped was a figure visible and an object of the sight, consisting of parts spiritual and corporeal to whom local motion might be agreeable, but that his flesh and blood, his eyes and ears, his tongue and hands were not of any similitude with created substances, but were of another crasis[478] and mixture, which subjected them to no distemper or corruption. In proof whereof they allege the words of Muhammad, "That God created man after his own likeness," and all other of those examples drawn from the Holy Scriptures with which the Qur'an is filled, and where in familiar expressions the Divinity is pleased to condescend to the infirmity of human capacity.

The next sect is that of the Qadariyah,[479] who deny wholly the divine decree or predestination, affirming that every man is a free agent from whose will, as from the first principle, all good and bad actions flow and are drived, so that as with just reason God crowns man's good works with the rewards of bliss and felicity, so on the other justly punishes his evil actions in this world and in the next to come. And this they style the Doctrine of Equity, and define it to be a measure of man's actions, according to the rectitude and disposition of that right line which the prime intellect hath drawn out by wisdom's proportions. This opinion is absolutely rejected as heterodox in the Muhammadan religion, and yet it is not fully determined how Muhammad moderated in the dispute between Adam and Moses, whom an Arabian doctor[480] comically introduced, pleading

---

[478] Combination.

[479] The name comes from *qadr*, meaning "rights." This sect is one of the more extreme advocates of free will in man, arguing that God gave it to us because how else could we take responsibility for our actions? They also believe that God cannot know our actions in advance, and they deny the concept of "punishment in the grave," a belief that God punishes sinners in the period immediately following death, before judgment.

[480] "Ebnol Athir, Mr. Pocock *De moribus Arabum*" (Rycaut's marginal note). Ali ibn al-Athir al-Jazari (1160–1233) was a Kurdish scholar of Islamic traditions and historian based in Mosul and chiefly-known for his monumental *Al-Kamil fi t-tarikh*, a universal history. This book has been translated and edited by Carl Tornberg in fourteen volumes (Leiden, 1851–1876). Edward Pococke (1604–1691) was a historian, orientalist, linguist and Professor of Hebrew at Oxford. He had a long and distinguished career which included two stints in Turkey, one as chaplain to the English traders in Aleppo (1630–1636) and another in Constantinople (1637–1640) as chaplain to Sir Sackville Crowe, the ambassador to the Ottoman court. His *Specimen historiae Arabum, sive Gregorii Abulfarajii*

and justifying themselves before God. Moses, beginning first, reproached Adam
that he was one immediately created by the proper hand of God, in whom the
Divine Nature breathed the breath of life, whom angels were made to adore,
placed and seated in Paradise and fortified with actual graces against the enormities and crooked irregularities of inferior affections, from which happy state
that he should fall and precipitate mankind together with himself, his crime was
aggravated with all the degrees of his former perfection. Adam, to excuse himself, replied in this manner. "Thou, Moses, whom God hath called to a familiar
parley, revealed his will and pleasure unto in those engraven tables where all morality and virtue is contained, resolve me this one query and difficult problem.
How many years before I was created dost thou find that the law was wrote?"
Moses answered, "Forty." "And did you find," replied Adam, "that Adam rebelled against his law and sinned?" To which Moses answering in the affirma-
tive, "Do you blame me, then," said he, "for executing that which God forty years
before hath predestinated and assigned me unto? And not only forty years, but
many myriads of ages before either the heavens or earth were framed?" Muhammad, confounded, as the Qadariyah report, with this argument, left the question
undetermined, though his followers, as men are most prone to error generally,
entertain the contrary tenent.

The great enemies dismetrically opposed to thes are the Jabariyah,[481] who
maintain that a man hath no power over his will or actions but is wholly moved
by a superior agent, and that God hath a power over his creatures to design them
to happiness or to misery as seems best to his divine pleasure. But in the explication of this opinion they proceed in the most rigorous manner and say that man
is wholly necessitated and compelled in all his actions, that neither his will, nor
power nor election is in himself, and that God creates in him his actions as he
doth in inanimate and vegetable creatures the first principle of their life and essence. And, as the tree may be said to produce fruit, the water to run, the stone to
move downwards, so are the actions in man, for which there is a reward and punishment properly and necessarily allotted. This point is very subtly controverted
by the Arabian doctors, to which how the Turks are addicted we shall farther
discourse in the Chapter of Predestination.

The sect of Murjiyah[482] are the great favourers and patrons of the Muhammadan religion, maintaining that a Muslim or believer, though guilty of the

---

*de origine et moribus Arabum succincta narratio* (1648), is a series of essays based on an extract from al-Faraj's historical writings.

[481] Their name is derived from *jabr*, which means "necessity." They deny free will
and believe that God's decrees control human actions. Hughes adds that there are more
moderate versions of Jabariyah belief in which humans have some power, but no influence
over actions. Humans can commend or blame an action. Rycaut seems to be familiar only
with the "pure" Jabariyahs (Hughes, *Dictionary*, 223).

[482] The name means "procrastinators" (Hughes, *Dictionary*, 421).

grossest sins, is not punished for them in this world nor receives his absolution or condemnation after death until the day of resurrection and judgment, and farther, that as impiety with the true belief shall never be punished, so piety and good works proceeding from a false and erroneous faith is of no validity or power conducing to the fruition of the joys of Paradise. And to these may not improperly be compared some sectaries in England who have vented in their pulpits that God sees no sin in children, and that the infidelity of Sarah,[483] being of the house of the faithful, is more acceptable to God than the alms, prayers and repentance of an erroneous believer without the pale[484] and covenant of grace.[485]

The opposite sect to these are the Waridiyah,[486] who esteem that a man fallen into any great or mortal sin is put into the condition of a deserter of his faith, and, though he be a professor of the true belief, shall yet without recovery forever be punished in Hell, but yet that his torments shall be in a more remiss degree than that of infidels. But that opinion which in this point is esteemed orthodox amongst the Turks is this, that a sinner in a high nature, going out of this world without repentance, is wholly to be committed to the pleasure of God, either to pardon him for his mercy or for the intercession of the Prophet Muhammad[487] according to what he saith in the Qur'an, "My intercession shall be for those of my people who have greatly sinned," that, being first punished according to the measure of their iniquity, they may afterwards in compassion be received into Paradise. For it is impossible they should for ever remain in the eternal flames with the infidels, because it is revealed to us that whoever hath but the weight of an atom remaining in his heart of faith shall be in due time released from fiery torments, for which cause some sects amongst the Turks use prayers for the dead and place their cemetaries always by the side of highways that passengers may be remembered of their own mortality and pray for the souls of those departed, of which we shall have occasion to discourse hereafter.

---

[483] The sources for the story of Sarah (Abraham's wife) and her relationship with Pharaoh are not biblical, but are found in the *Genesis Rabbah* and the *Sefer ha-Yashar* or *Book of Jasher*, commentaries and exegeses (*midrash*) of Genesis. If Rycaut had known Hebrew, he could have found his material in the printed version of the latter, which appeared in 1625.

[484] An enclosed or fenced area, as in the phrase "beyond the pale."

[485] The underlying doctrine of Christianity, which teaches that people may be saved through the grace of God.

[486] The name denotes "spiritual inspiration" (*Dictionary of Spiritual Terms*, http://www.dictionaryofspiritualterms.com).

[487] See, for example, in a *hadith* narrated by Ma'abad ibn Hilal al-Anzi and other extra-Quranic texts. It is not in the Quran. "None shall meet [on the Day of Judgment]," says the Quran, "save he who hath entered into covenant with the God of mercy" (Sura 19:90). Hughes notes that "According to the Sunnis, the intercession of Muhammad is especially for those who have committed great sins" (*Dictionary*, 215), which makes Rycaut correct on this point.

The fictions the Muhammadans frame of Hell are as ridiculous as those they fancy of Paradise, for they imagine when they shall be called by Muhammad from this Purgatory⁴⁸⁸ at the day of judgment the way to him is over iron bars red-hot with fire, over which they must pass with naked feet. Only the paper which they in their lifetime have taken from the ground and conserved from being trampled on by the foot of men or beasts shall at that day be strowed on the bars of this hot passage that they may pass that fire ordeal with less torment, which is the reason the Turks see no small piece of paper on the ground but they immediately stoop for it and place it in some secret corner of a wall to redeem that, as they say, from the dishonour of men's feet, on which the name of God is or may be wrote, and with expectation to enjoy the benefit promised when the soles of their feet shall try the intense heat of this burning iron. The same respect they show to rose leaves, in consideration, as they believe, that a rose was produced from the sweat of Muhammad.⁴⁸⁹

The Shi'ites are the sect spoken of before, opposed by the subjects of the whole Ottoman Empire as the most heretical of any of the rest in regard they prefer Ali before Muhammad in the prophetical office, and restrain the prophetic gift to the natural line derived from Ali and that none is worthy of the title of prophet who is guilty of sin, though of the lower nature. Some of which professors call Nusairi⁴⁹⁰ affirm that God appeared in the form of Ali and with his tongue proclaimed the most hidden mysteries of religion, and some have proceeded yet further to attribute to their prophets divine honours, asserting them to be elevated above degree and state of the creatures. These expect the return of their prophet Ali in the clouds, and have placed that belief as an article of their faith, from whence may seem to be grounded that mistake amongst our vulgar that the Turks believe Muhammad shall again return into the world.

To the foregoing are apposed the Khawarijiyah,⁴⁹¹ who deny that there is or hath been any such function as that of a prophet allowed by God in any particular person nor any ever sent into the world endued with that power of infallibility

---

⁴⁸⁸ According to Muslims, Hell is divided into seven parts. Rycaut here refers to *Jahannam*, the area of Hell where the dead person is purged before moving on. It is the first region, through which all Muslims must pass.

⁴⁸⁹ As Muhammad ascended into Heaven, each drop of his sweat was said to have produced a rose. The connection between Muhammad's sweat and roses persisted, according to some Islamic scholars, only as far as the twelfth century.

⁴⁹⁰ The Nusairi are followers of the eighth Shi'a imam, Hasan al-'Askari (d. 873) and his disciple Abu Shayb ibn Nusayr (d. 868). Known today as Alawiysh or Alawites, they may be found mostly in Syria, and are, as Rycaut says, Shi'a Muslims, although other Muslims, including some Shi'a sects, say they are not Muslims at all because they have some Trinitarian views. They deify Ali and Muhammad, as Rycaut points out.

⁴⁹¹ Their name means "the revolters," and they believe that anyone can be a khalifa or successor to the Prophet as long as he is chosen by Muslims. We are told that twelve thousand of Ali's men revolted when Ali allowed his claim to be a khalifa to "the

to resolve doubts and teach and impose a law on mankind. But, if at any time such an office should be necessary, it can never be restrained to one lineage,[492] for the person, being faithful and just, no matter whether he a servant or free, a Nabataean or a Quraishite.[493]

These are ancient sects amongst the professors of the Muhammadan religion, out of which arose so many others as by the confession of the Turkish doctors complete the number of seventy-three. But, because the accurate search into so many is of little delight or profit to the reader, I shall content myself with having given him a taste of these foregoing premises, and shall now give an account how busy these modern times have been at Constantinople in hammering out strange forms and chimaeras of religion, the better to acquit England from the accusation of being the most subject to religious innovations, the world attributing much thereof to the air and constitution of its climate.

arbitration of man" rather than of God. Some also said that there need not be any khalifas at all (For details, see Hughes. *Dictionary*, 270).

[492] Many Muslims believed that only a member of the Quraish tribe, which was Muhammad's tribe, could be a prophet or successor to Muhammad if there were no qualified family members.

[493] Rycaut defines these respectively, in a marginal note, as "One of the vulgar or rude sort amongst the Arabians" and "One of a noble family amongst the Arabians." The Nabataeans are inhabitants of modern-day Jordan. For Quraish, the tribe of Muhammad, see above.

**Chapter XII.** *Concerning the new and modern sects amongst the Turks.*

All ages and times have produced their sects and heresies in every religion, and therefore we shall proceed in declaring some few that are of a fresher date than those in the foregoing chapter, and so shall continue to descend to others which this present age hath begot.

The Zaidiyah[494] maintain that God will send a prophet of the Persians with a law which shall be annulled the law of Muhammad.[495] A second to this is derived from the Mutaziliyah, who deny any man can be styled a saint in this world excepting the prophets, who were without sin. And that the true believers shall in the next world see God as clearly as we see the moon at full, against the doctrine of Muhammad, who says God is invisible either to us in this world or the next. There are also those called Malumiyah, who maintain God is perfectly to be known in this world, and that by the doctrine of *cognosce te ipsum*[496] the creature proceeds to the perfect knowledge of the Creator. The opponents to these are *Mezzachuliya*,[497] who hold that they which know God only in this world by some glimmerings and rays of his glory and essence is sufficient to lead them into Paradise and rank them in the number of the faithful. Another sort there are called Jaba'iyah,[498] which denies God's omniscience, affirming that God governs the world by chance and accidents, not comprehending from eternity or at the creation of the world, a perfect certainty of the particular affairs that were to be transacted in it, and that God improves in knowledge by time as men do by constant practice and experience.

But these modern times have produced other sects amongst the Turks, some of which seem in part dangerous and apt to make a considerable rupture in their long-continued union, when time changes and revolutions of state shall animate some turbulent spirits to gather soldiers and followers under these doctrines and other specious pretences, one of which is called Kadizadeli,[499] a sect sprung up in

---

[494] They are the followers of Zayd ibn Ali al-Husain (695–740), whom they believed to be the rightful successor to Zayd as imam over his half brother Muhammad Baqir. Zayd revolted against the 'Umayyad caliph Hisham ibn Abd al-Malik and was killed in battle.

[495] Rycaut's sentence is unclear. He adds a marginal note: "That called Zeidi is one of the latter edition."

[496] The full phrase is *"cognosce te ipsum et disce pati,"* which means "Know yourself and learn to suffer." It was originally inscribed (in Greek) on the temple of Apollo at Delphi.

[497] Unidentified.

[498] Followers of Abu Ali Muhammad ibn 'Abd al-Wahab al-Jabai.

[499] The Kadizadeli believed in a kind of mixture of Christianity and Islam, and were seen by some as stoics; they were staunch opponents of the Sufis. Their founder was actually Kadizade Mehmed (1582–1658), who was inspired by the teachings of Mehmed of Birgili (d. 1573). He gained the attention and eventually the favour of Murad IV, and from 1630 to 1680 the new faith flourished, after which it seems to have died down. There were adherents in Syria and Bosnia as well as in Russia.

the time of Sultan Murat [IV] whose chief propagator was one Birgili Effendi, who invented many ceremonies in praying for the souls departed at the burial of the dead. Those that are of this sect cause their imam to cry loud in the ears of the inanimate body to remember that God is one and his Prophet one. Those who are principally devoted to this sect are the Russians and other sort of renegade Christians, who amongst their confused and almost-forgotten notions of the Christian religion retain a certain memory of the particulars of Purgatory and prayers for the dead.

But the opinion esteemed orthodox and most generally allowed amongst the Turks is that no Muhammadan goes eternally to Hell, but after a certain space of years is delivered thence and passes into Paradise. After death they assign two sorts of punishments. The first is called 'Adhab al-Qabr or the punishment of the grave, which, being the bed of wicked men, binds with its earth so fast as it crushes their bones and thus shuts the pores and crevices through which they should see into Heaven, but the bodies of good men enjoy the comfort of having a window from their dark enclosures to behold the vision of God's glory. The other is the pain of Hell, where the souls remain until their torments are accomplished and divine justice satisfied.

There is an opinion of late years principally maintained amongst the gallants of the Seraglio and common in Constantinople, the professors of which are called Chupmessahi or "the good followers of the Messiah." These maintain that Christ is God and the Redeemer of the World. The young scholars in the Grand Signior's court are generally devoted to this tenet, especially those which are the most courteous, affable, and best-disposed. That it is grown into a proverb amongst them, when they would commend and praise gentleness and courtesy of each other's nature, they do it with the expression of *hûp mesîhisin*, as if they would say "You are gentle, accomplished and excessive in your favours," as one who professes the Messiah. Of this sort of people there are great numbers in Constantinople, some of which have so boldly asserted this doctrine that they have suffered martyrdom under this denomination, which is still maintained and secretly professed by such multitudes as wear white turbans, that upon some notable opportunity were this cause and religion made the ground of some toleration and insurrection amongst its disciples and professors, it might take an unexpected footing and prepare a way for the plantation of the Gospel. But of this we shall speak more hereafter in its due place.

And because it is our intent here to declare the several religions amongst the Turks, it will not be from our purpose to mention how far atheism hath spread itself in these countries, and, as logicians elucidate one contrary with another and painters set off the whiteness of their colours with a foil of jet or other blackness, so the privation[500] of all religion is not unaptly placed in the same chapter with the various and different professors of it.

These, then, give themselves the title of Muserin, which signifies "the true secret is with us,"[501] which secret is no other than the absolute denial of a Deity, that nature or the intrinsical principle in every individual thing directs the orderly course which we see and admire, and that the heavens, sun, moon, and stars have thence their original and motion, and that man himself rises and fades like the grass or flower.[502] It is strange to consider what quantities there are of men that maintain this principle in Constantinople, most of which are *qadis* and learned men in the Arabian legends, and others are renegados from the Christian faith who, conscious of the sin of their apostasy and therefore desirous that all things may conclude with this world, are the more apt to entertain those opinions which come nearest to their wishes. One of this sect, called Mehmed Effendi, a rich man educated in the knowledge of the Eastern learning, I remember was in my time executed for impudently proclaiming his blasphemies against the being of a Deity, making it in his ordinary discourse an argument against the being of a God, for that either there was none at all, or else not so wise as the doctors preached he was in suffering him to live who was the greatest enemy and scorner of a Divine Essence that ever came into the world. And it is observable that this man might, notwithstanding his accusation, have saved his life would he but have confessed his error and promised for the future an assent to the principles of a better, but he persisted still in his blasphemies, saying that though there were no reward, yet the love of truth obliged him to die a martyr. I must confess until now I never could believe that there was a formal atheism in the world, concluding that the principle of the being of a God was demonstrable by the Light of

---

[500]  Here, a condition resulting from the lack of something.

[501]  The term for atheist is actually *dahri*, defined by Hughes as "one who believes in the eternity of matter and asserts that the duration of this world is from eternity" (*Dictionary*, 64). Some years after Rycaut (1717) we find Lady Mary Wortley Montague correcting him; "The most prevailing opinion if you search into the secrets of the effendis," she writes in a letter to the Abbé Conti, "is plain deism, and goes on to note that "Sir Paul Rycaut is mistaken, as he commonly is, in calling the sect *muserin* (i. e. the secret within us) atheists, they being deists, whose impiety consists of making a jest of their prophet" (*Turkish Embassy Letters*, ed. Malcolm Jack. [London: Pickering, 1993], 62). Like Rycaut, however, Lady Mary found it hard to believe that there actually were atheists at all. Thomas Smith, on the other hand, discussed atheism in Islam at some length (*Remarks upon the Manners, Religion and Government of the Turks* [London, 1678], 114–20), and remarked that many of the *qadis* were atheists.

[502]  Rycaut is echoing Job 14:2: "He cometh forth like a flower, and is cut down: he fleeth like a shadow and continueth not."

Nature,[503] but it is evident now how far some men have extinguished this light and lamp in their souls.[504]

This pernicious doctrine is so infectious that it is crept into the chambers of the Seraglio, into the apartments of the ladies and eunuchs and found entertainment with the pashas and their whole court. This sort of people are great favourers and lovers of their own sect, courteous and hospitable to each other, and if any by chance receives a guest within his gates of their own judgment, besides his diet and fare, with much freedom he is accommodated with a handsome bedfellow of which sex he most delights. They are very frank and liberal and excessive in their readiness to do each other service. It is said that Sultan Murat [IV] was a great favourer of this opinion in his court and militia, desirous withal to propagate that of Kadizadeli amongst the vulgar, that they, being a severe, morose, and covetous people, might grow rich and spare for the benefit of his exchequer, for the sect of Kadizadeli before-mentioned is of a melancholy and stoical temper, admitting of no music,[505] cheerful or light discourses, but confine themselves to a set gravity. In public as well as private they make a continual mention of God by a never-wearied repetition of these words "*Illahu illah Allah*," that is, "I profess there is one God." There are some of these that will sit whole nights bending their bodies towards the earth, reciting those words with a most doleful and lamentable note. They are exact and most punctual in the observation of the rules of religion and generally addict themselves to the study of their civil law, in which they use constant exercises in arguing, opposing and answering, whereby to leave no point undiscovered or not discussed. In short, they are highly pharasaical[506] in all their comportment, great admirers of themselves and scorners of others that conform not to their tenents, scarce according them a salutation or common communication. They refuse to marry their sons with those of a different rite, but amongst themselves they observe a certain policy: they admonish and correct the disorderly, and such who are not bettered by their persuasions they reject and excommunicate from their society. These are for the most part tradesmen, whose sedentary life affords opportunity and nutriment to a melancholy and distempered fancy.

But those of this sect who strangely mix Christianity and Muhammadanism together are many of the soldiers that live on the confines of Hungary and

---

[503] Reason.

[504] This whole passage, and others following, appears cited verbatim and without credit to Rycaut in James Creagh, *Armenians, Koords, and Turks*, vol. 1 (London: Samuel Tinsley, 1880), 148–50.

[505] This is a curious observation, as Murad IV was himself a composer and poet; otherwise, Rycaut's information is broadly correct. It is known, for example, that Mehmed IV's spiritual mentor was Vani Seyyid Mehmed Effendi, a Kadizadeli, whom the Sultan eventually expelled from his court in 1683 (see below, Chapter 13, n. 12).

[506] Censorious and self-righteous.

Bosnia, reading the Gospel in the Slavonian tongue, with which they are supplied out of Moravia and the neighbouring city of Ragusa, besides which they are curious to learn the mysteries of the Qur'an and the law of the Arabic tongue, and, not to be accounted rude and illiterate, they affect the courtly Persian. They drink wine in the month of fast called Ramazan, but to take off the scandal they refuse cinnamon or other spices in it and then call it *hardali* and passes current for lawful liquor. They have a charity and affection for Christians and are ready to protect them from injuries and violences of the Turks. They believe yet that Muhammad was the Holy Ghost promised by Christ and that the descending of the Holy Spirit on the day of Pentecost was a figure and type of Muhammad, interpreting in all places the word παράκλητος[507] to signify their Prophet, in whose ear the white dove revealed the infallible directions to happiness.[508] The Potures[509] of Bosnia are all of this sect, but pay taxes as Christians do; they abhor images and the sign of the cross. They circumcise, bringing the authority of Christ's example for it, which also the Coptics, a sect of the Greek church imitated, but have now, as I am informed, lately disused that custom.[510]

Another subtle point about the divine attributes hath begot a sect amongst the Janissaries called Bektaşi, from one Bektaş,[511] which seems an improper

---

[507] Paraclete: this word usually denotes the Holy Ghost as counselor or advocate.

[508] A white dove, which represented peace and contentment, was believed to have acted as Muhammad's oracle by whispering in his ear.

[509] The derivation of this word has been variously discussed. A *poture* is form of Turkish breeches or shoes, but it is more likely that the word came from the Serbo-Croatian *poturčite se*, which means "to turn into a Turk," hence people who have adopted Turkish customs and religion. Of course, it might also refer people who wore Turkish shoes or breeches.

[510] In our own day, I am informed that Copts still (voluntarily) circumcise for reasons of hygiene, not religion.

[511] Hajji Bektaş Veli may have been a mystic and philosopher from Nishapur in Persia who lived and taught in Anatolia during the reigns of Sultans Orhan (1324–1362) and Murat I (1362–1389), although there is a "lack of historical evidence for Hajji Bektaş's existence" (John Pair Brown, *The Darvishes, or Oriental Spiritualism* [London: Frank Cass (1868), rep. 1968], 216). The Bektaşis are Sufis, believing in the Unity of Being and in a mystical interpretation of the Quran. They also incorporate beliefs from other religions into their own. Bektaş's biography, the *Walayatnama*, was written in the sixteenth century by Uzun Ferdowsi. Rycaut is correct about the Bektashis and the Janissaries; "It was only in the late sixteenth century that the *Bektaşis* were officially attached to the [Janissary] corps through its ninety-ninth battalion, with its Grand Master appointed as its *çorbaci*" (Stanford J. Shaw, *History of the Ottoman Empire and Modern Turkey*, vol. 1 [Cambridge: Cambridge University Press, 1988], 123). Also see Huseyin Abiva, trans. *The Saintly Exploits of Bektas Veli* (Djakarta: Babagan Books, 2006). In 1826 Sultan Mahmud II banned the Bektaşis altogether from the Janissary corps. The present headquarters of the Bektaşis is in Tirana, Albania.

subject so deep in the metaphysical speculation to trouble such gross heads as theirs. They began, it is said, in the time of Süleyman the Magnificent, and are called by some *Zerati*, that is, "those that have copulation with their own kindred," and by the vulgar *Mumsöndüren*, or "extinguishers of the candle."[512] This sect observe the law of Muhammad in divine worship with a strictness and superstition above any of the precisians of that religion, but hold it unlawful to adjoin any attributes to God by saying that God is great or God is merciful, by reason that the nature of God, being infinite and incomprehensible, cannot fall under the weak and imperfect conceptions of man's understanding, which can imagine nothing applicable to his nature. Of this sect there was a famous poet amongst the Turks called Nesimi[513] that was flayed alive for saying, when the imam called the people to prayers at the ordinary hours from the steeple with the usual words *"Allahu akbar,"* God is one, that he lied, upon the supposition that no epithets can be predicated of the Divine Essence. Amongst the Janissaries are at present many commanders of this sect, but formerly were more in the time of Bektaş Agha, the Kul Kiahia, Mehmed Agha and others, who for their rebellion in Constantinople, as we related before, were put to death under the historical pillar in the time of this present Emperor's minority.

These people, against the instinct of nature, use carnal copulation promiscuously with their own kindred, the fathers mixing with their sons and daughters without respect to proximity of blood or nearness in the degrees of relation, suffering themselves to be transported contrary to the abhorency of nature by a weak and illogical comparison of the lawfulness and reason that he who engrafted the tree and planted the vine should rather taste of the fruit than resign the benefit of his labours to the enjoyment of others, and in this argument act against the

---

512 This refers to the Turkish phrase *mum söndü,* "the candle went out." In the *Cem* ceremony, which celebrates Muhammad's ascent into heaven at night, the Bektaşis put out twelve candles, which represent the twelve Shi'a imams. There follows singing and dancing. Opponents of the sect maliciously claimed that after the candles were out people then engaged in incestuous and adulterous orgies. Rycaut evidently believed this, too, as the following paragraphs indicate, and other Western writers followed him. For example, "They hold it lawful," James Creagh wrote, "to forget the instincts of nature. . .in defiance of every law of consanguinity or even of natural modesty" (*Armenians, Koords, and Turks*, 149).

513 Ali Imad ed-Din Nasimi (c. 1369–1417) was a mystical poet who used the name Nesimi. His birthplace is shrouded in mystery; he may have been born in Aleppo or Baghdad, but his parents seem to have been from Azerbaijan, and there is a statue of him in modern-day Baku, the capital. He was a member of the Hurufi movement, which taught that human beings can become one with God, and this got him into trouble with the religious authorities in Aleppo, who ordered him flayed, as Rycaut relates, but not before reciting a satirical poem about his persecutors. A legend grew up that after his ordeal he picked up his skin, put it over his arm, and walked calmly off.

inclination of innate modesty according to that of Seneca, *"Ferae quoque ipsae Veneris evitant nefas, / Generisque leges inscius servat pudor."*[514]

These people are easily induced to give false witness or testimony in the favour of their sect without consideration of equity or reasonableness of their cause, by which means, invading the light of others, they became rich and powerful until they were debased by the deprivation of Bektaş's authority, and though afterwards upheld by Sudgi Bekr, a standard-bearer of the Janissaries, a rich and learned man, they received a second blow by his death, he executed by [the] Vizier Mehmed Köprülü for his diversity in religion and wealth together. But further animosity against this sect was dissembled at that time by reason of the multitude of those professors in Constantinople and because reason of state saw it at that time necessary to draw blood in many parts of the empire for other causes than for errors in religion.

The sect called Sabins,[515] though Muhammadans in profession, seem yet to run contrary to the stream and general content of all its professors who give themselves commonly the title of "Enemies and Confounders of Idolatry." And yet these, notwithstanding, seem from the influence of the sun and moon have on sublunary[516] bodies, of all living sensitive creatures to conclude a certain divinity in those common lights of the world. In Constantinople there are some few astrologers or physicians of this sect, but in Parthia and Media they are numerous, the men commonly worshipping the sun, and the women the moon and others the Arctic pole. They are not strict in a severity of life or in the conformity to the prescriptions of their law, but govern themselves with morality and prudence. They are not apt to believe in the immortality of the soul nor the reward of virtue or punishment of vice in the next world, nor prone to vindicate themselves from injuries, reproachful language or other evil actions of men, but, regarding them as the natural effects of the celestial influences, are no more provoked by them than we are with a shower of rain for wetting us or the intense heat of the sun in the summer solstice.

---

[514] "Even animals shun incestuous love / and instinctive chastity guards nature's laws" (Seneca, *Phaedra* 913–14 [Scene vi]). Rycaut is wrong about incest, which is strictly forbidden by Islam. However, a Muslim may marry a first cousin, which is forbidden in some forms of Christianity, or an ex-wife of an adopted son. Muhammad himself married the ex-wife of his adopted son Zeyd.

[515] They are the followers of Abu Muhammad al-Haqq ibn Sabin (1217–1259). He was the last Sufi philosopher from Andalusia, although he died in Mecca. He is renowned for his great knowledge of world religions, and apparently studied Hinduism and Zoroastrianism in addition to Judaism and Christianity. Ibn Sabin's philosophy was blended with Gnostic elements and astral religion, as Rycaut points out. He is also famous for his theological correspondence with the Holy Roman Emperor Frederick II (r. 1220–1250), although scholars have disputed its authenticity.

[516] In the old Ptolemaic cosmology, "sublunary" referred to the spheres below the moon, hence earthly or physical bodies subject to change and decay.

Munasihi[517] is a sect purely Pythagorical which believes the metempsychosis or transmigration of souls, of which there are some in Constantinople. One [Wojtiech] Albert Bobowski,[518] a Polonian by nation but educated in the Seraglio and instructed in all the learning of the Turkish literature, from whom I freely confess to have received many of my observations, related to me a pleasant discourse that passed between him and a druggist at Constantinople touching this subject. This druggist, being learned, was the occasion that Albert frequented his shop, and once, being after some familiar acquaintance at a collation together, it chanced that a black dog giving them interruption at their banquet, that Albert kicked him to drive him to a further distance, at which the druggist, growing pale and disordered, Albert guessed by his countenance that he was displeased at this unkindness towards the dog, and therefore desired his pardon if thereby he had given him any subject of offence. The druggist, being thus pacified with the courtesy of his guest, advised him to ask pardon of God, for that it was no small crime and sin that he thereby committed. This, happening at the same time that the funerals of a mufti called Behai Effendi were then solemnising, afforded an occasion of discourse concerning the soul of the mufti and dog together, the druggist demanding the opinion of his guest whether he conceived the soul of that mufti was predestinated to remain within the confines of the grave until the day of resurrection? In the knowledge of which question Albert seeming wholly ignorant and desirous to understand the solution from him, the druggist began freely to declare that the souls of men deceased enter into the bodies of beasts which are in temperament most agreeable to the dispositions of those whom before they animated. As the soul of the glutton enters into the swine, the soul of the lascivious into the goat, of the generous into the horse, of the vigilant into a dog, and so the like, in proof of which he produced a book treating of all the distinctions of nature and the proper assignments for their habitation after death, adding moreover that of his opinion it was pity there were so few in Constantinople. Some there were, and those all of his own trade and profession, but that at Grand Cairo were great numbers, strict adherers to this doctrine; that for his part he prayed to God with the rest of his brothers of the same trade that their

[517] The Munasihi are mentioned also by Giovanni Paolo Marana, an Italian living in France, in his *Letters Written by a Turkish Spy* (1684), where he states that they "seem to me the only orthodox and illuminated of GOD, who. . .walk in the high road of pristine justice and piety" (80). Arthur J. Weizman has edited Marana's book (New York: Temple University Press, 1970). Most later authorities simply follow Rycaut; Thomas Salmon, for example, in his *Modern History of the Present State of all Nations* (1744), calls them "Pythagoreans believing in the transmigration of souls" (I, 529), Salmon, like Creagh, simply lifts large chunks from Rycaut and lists the sects in the same order. Elements of Greek thought, including of course Pythagoreanism, were introduced to Muslim thinkers in medieval times and often translated into Arabic.

[518] For Bobowski, see Rycaut's "To the Reader," n. 1, and Introduction.

souls may hereafter be so honoured as to inform the body of the camel, because they are beasts that are laborious, abstemious, patient and meek, and bring their drugs from the remotest part of the East, and that he did not doubt but after the circle of 3365 years through the world and wandering from the body of one camel to animate another, it should, with the vicissitude of time, return again to a human body more purified and refined than in its first principles. And this was the credo of the druggist, to which opinion it is said all China is greatly devoted.

Ishraqi,[519] which signifies "illuminated," is a sect purely Platonical, contemplative of the divine idea and the number in God. For though they hold the unity, yet they deny not the trinity as a number preceding from the unity, which conception of theirs they illustrate by three folds in a handkerchief, which may have the denomination of three, but being extended is but one entire piece of linen. These men are no great admirers of the composition of the Qur'an; what they meet therein agreeable to their principles they embrace and produce as occasion serves in confirmation of their doctrine, other parts which with difficulty are reconciled they reject and style abrogated.[520] And because they apprehend that the true beatitude and bliss of Paradise consists in the contemplation of the Divine Majesty, they condemn all the fancies and gross conceptions of Heaven which Muhammad hath framed to allure and draw the minds of rude and gross men. Of this sect are all the sheykhs or able preachers that belong to the royal mosques or churches, who are men constant in their devotions, abstemious in their diet, of a cheerful countenance and taking behavior, great lovers of harmony and music, of an indifferent strain in poetry, whereby they compose certain songs in metre for entertainment of their auditory. They are likewise generous and compassionate of human frailty and are not covetous, stoical, or conceited of themselves, by which means their behavior is rendered extremely taking through all Constantinople. They are greatly delighted with an ingenious aspect in youth, and from thence gather matter of contemplation on the comeliness of increated[521] beauty. They are addicted to entertain a charitable affection for their neighbor because, as they say, he is a creature of God, from whom our love is converted to the Creator. Their disciples they procure as much as possible to be men of comely and pleasing countenance and majestic presence, who they instruct in all the rules of

---

[519] This sect follows the teachings of Shahab al-Din Yahya as-Suhrawardi (1155–1191), a Kurdish Sufi and philosopher who founded a school known as *Hikmat al-Ishraq*, or "illuminism," hence Ishraqi. He believed, amongst other things, that all created being originates from a Supreme Light, and also taught that each soul existed previously as an angel before it became a body as we know it. When it becomes a body, the angelic part stays in heaven until it once again detaches itself from the world and becomes one again. His teachings have some elements in common with Neoplatonism. Suhrawardi was executed in Aleppo for heresy.

[520] Done away with.

[521] Self-existent or inherent; not created by anyone or anything.

abstinence, gravity and other virtues most appropriated to their sect. And these of all sorts of Turk seem worthy of the best character, whom I compassionate for not being born within the pale of a Christian church, to which they seem by their morality and virtues already to have prepared many previous dispositions.

A sect most different to that immediately foregoing is the Hayreti,[522] signifying "amazed," and doubtful in determination of all controversies, who can endure anything rather than to controvert opinions and dispute one question in chase of truth. They will neither undertake to persuade or dissuade, but like the academics affirm that falsity may by the wit and contrivance of man be dressed in a habit as not to be distinguished from truth itself, and, on the contrary, truth may be so disguised with sophistry and delusions as to be rendered as deformed and ugly as falsehood. And therefore they conclude all questions to be merely probable and no way admitting of certain demonstration, so that in points of dubious controversies their common sayings are *Allah biliyor*, "God knows," *bize karanuk*, "it is unknown to us," and suchlike expressions savouring of negligence and a brutish want of curiosity to search into the studies of art and science. Of this sect some, notwithstanding, are preachers, and from that degree are promoted to the office of mufti, in which they behave themselves according to their affected carelessness with a readiness and facility to subscribe all sentences to the satisfaction and in favour of the demandant, adding for the most part these words, *Wellahu alem bissenah*, "God knows that which is best." As to the manner of their life and practice, they are punctual observers of the rites of the Muhammadan religion and constitutions of their civil law, but much-inclined to yield to the course of their own nature and the force of passion. They drink wine not to appear cynical or unsociable, but more generally addict themselves to electuaries[523] composed of opium, which tends to augment their natural stupefaction, and when they are overcome with the obscurity of this vapour whatsoever you affirm, though never so contradictory, they readily assent to, not so much, as they confess, from a persuasion to one proposition more than another, but of a pleasing compliance to their companions, which humour the nature of their sect allows of. And though they style the Ishraqi dogmatical and obstinate opinionators, yet by experience it is observed that the muftis educated in the Ishraqi schools have been much more fortunate than those of the Hayreti sect, because the former, having a certain foundation of principles, have been cautious in signing *fetvas* or delivering their sentence in the resolution of weighty matters of state, choosing rather to renounce their office than their reason. But the others, being negligent and incurious in their determinations, as if fortune did direct them more to the true part than solidity of judgment, have always been free and open in their sentences, by which means events of state falling out unhappily and the miscarriage attributed

---

[522] From the Turkish *hayret etmiş*, "amazed," as Rycaut states.
[523] Medicinal pastes.

to the counsel of the muftis, they have been oftener subjected to the punishment of banishment or death than their opponents.

We shall not proceed to swell this work with a longer catalogue of these sects lest we should seem over-tedious to the reader and instead of pleasing his palate should overcharge his stomach, otherwise we might proceed to recite as many sects as there are towns or schools in the empire, in every one of which some pragmatical preacher or other have always started a new opinion which can never want disciples. And certainly the diversity of opinions in Turkey is almost infinite and more numerous than in England or other parts of Christendom, though commonly not proceeding from the same malice nor laid with the same design to the prejudice of the state. The reason of this variety amongst the Turks I attribute to the many religions which voluntarily and for interest or by force have entered into the Muhammadan superstition, many of which being Grecians and instructed in the arts and sciences with which that empire once flourished which was the mine and treasury of philosophy and learning, did afterwards mix with their new religions, not being wholly satisfied with the Qur'an, certain traditions and opinions of the ancient philosophers. And several other nations, as Russians, Muscovites, Circassians and the like, retaining some few remembrances of their first notions and principles, make a farther addition to this ill-compounded medley, which also receiving some difference and variety as they increased and were propagated, have multiplied into a number both uprofitable and tedious to search farther into.

## Chapter XIII. *Of the dervishes.*

It is commonly-known and received that the Turkish religion is an absurd composition of the Christian and Jewish rites, in imitation of the former of which doubtless their monasteries and orders of religious men were introduced, most of which incline to a pretended mortification and strictness of life, to poverty and renunciation of the world's enjoyments according to the devotion of Christians a thousand years past, whose piety and exemplary lives drew infidels to extract a rough copy of their elevated virtues.

I have been the more curious in making an exact inquiry into the customs, institutions and doctrines of the Muhammadan convents because I find relations hereof sparingly-featured in other books, and that obscurely without punctuality[524] or certainty. But I shall promise my reader to deliver nothing herein but what I have good authority for and taken from the mouth of the most learned of their sheykhs or preachers, which are the heads or superiors of these societies. The doctors of the Muhammadan law inform me that their religious houses and institutions are as ancient as Muhammad, from whom general orders and instructions were derived from their economy, first to his disciple Ali. But our *Turkish History* and other records make no mention of these monasteries till within these three hundred and fifty years, in the time of Orhan, second king of the Turks, who is famed to have been the first founder of houses of these orders.

Those of the Muhammadan faith who first framed rules and instiotutions for these religions were two, *viz.* Khalwatiyah and Naqshbandi, which, after Muhammad, are esteemed the two fountains from whence other orders are produced, which are these following. From Khalwatiyah are derived Nimatullahiyah, from Nimatullah; Qadiriyyah, from al-Qadir; Qalandariyah, from Qalandar; Adhemiyah from Adhem; Hizrevi from al-Herewi; Bektashi from Bektaş.[525]

---

[524] Precision.

[525] The Khalwatiyah are named for their founder 'Umar al-Khalwati (d. 1397), a Persian; the name means "withdrawal from the world." Over the years this sect distanced itself from common people and by Rycaut's time had been embraced by the wealthy and the upper classes of Turkish society, particularly in Istanbul. However, Rycaut is incorrect in deriving the other sects from the Khalwatiyah .It does have many branches, however. Naqshbandi is named for Baha al-Din Naqshband (1318–1389), and is the only Sufi order connected by lineage to both Muhammad and Ali. This order is widespread today all over Islam. The Nimatulliyah were founded by Nur al-Din Nimatullah or Nimatullah Shah (1330–1431) as a Sunni order, but became Shi'a in the sixteenth century. He died in Iran, and his shrine may be seen today. His followers are known for their strict observance of Sharia law. The Qadiriyyah order was founded by Abd al-Qadir Gilani (1077–1166), another Persian, and quickly spread all over the Islamic world. It, too, professes as strong adherence to the fundamentals of Islam. A notable foreign adherent of this very popular Sufi sect was the explorer Sir Richard Burton. Hughes calls them "an ascetic order of Faqirs" (*Dictionary*, 478). Qalandariyah are wandering Sufis, although there is a small x

From Naqshbandi proceed only two, *viz.* Abubakriyah from Abu Bakr, Mevlevi from Mevleva,[526] their original founders.

The Mevlevi,[527] otherwise and most commonly named dervish, which word signifies "poor" and "renouncers of the world,"[528] have their chief and superior foundation in Iconium, which consists of at the least four hundred dervishes and governs all the other convents of that order within the Turkish Empire by virtue of a charter given them by Osman, first of the Muhammadan kings, who out of devotion to their religion once placed their prior or superior in his royal throne because, having been his tutor and he who girded on his sowrd, which is the principal ceremony of coronation, he granted him and his successors ample authority and rule over all others of the same profession.

They pretend[529] to great patience, humility, modesty, charity, and slence in presence of their superior or others; their eyes are always fixed downwards, their heads hanging towards their breast and their bodies bending forwards. Their shirts are of the coarsest linen can be made, with a white plaid or mantle about their shoulders, but most wear a loose kind of garment made of wool at Iconium

---

of this name. Currently the main branch of this group is in Pakistan. The Adhemiyah are named after Ibrahim ibn Adhem (seventh century), a Sufi who may have been from Balkh (now in Afghanistan) and whose life and exploits are commended by Rumi in the *Masnavi* and by Farid ud-Din Attar in the *Tadhkiratul Awliya*, a collection of biographies of Sufi saints. Not much is known about this semi-legendary figure, who was said to have left behind a life of great wealth and privilege, possibly as king of Balkh, after an encounter with a Christian ascetic. The Hizrevi were founded by Ismail Abu al-Herewi (1005–1089), a chemist and orthodox Hanbali Muslim who lived and died in Herat. They practiced abstinence and were prominent in Istanbul. The Bektaşi we have already encountered. Rycaut discusses these sects in turn below.

[526] These are the followers of Abu Bakr Shibli (861–946). He was a wealthy and high-ranking official in Baghdad who gave everything up to become a religious mystic and teacher. After undergoing imprisonment and privation he met the great Persian Sufi al-Junayd (830–910) and became his disciple. Like his mentor, Abu Bakr emphasized the annihilation of the self in order to become one with the divine. The Mevlevi, for whom see below, are probably best-known for their connection with the poet Rumi.

[527] The Mevlevi order was founded in Konya (Iconium) by Hüsamettin Celebi in 1273, immediately after the death of its inspiration, the great poet Jalal ed-Din Rumi (1207–1273) or Mowlana, author of the *Masnavi*. After Celebi, the movement was taken over by Rumi's son Baha al-Din Muhammad (1226–1312), also known as Sultan Veled. They are probably the best-known order, familiar today as "whirling" dervishes, who symbolize spiritual ascent to perfection through dance and music. Sultan Osman's sword was girded on by Sheykh Edebali (1206–1326 [*sic*]), a Mevlevi who was Sharif of Konya, and the Sultan later married his daughter. A further, more direct royal connection with Rumi himself came when Devlet Hatun (d. 1411), a descendant of Sultan Veled's daughter, married Bayezid I.

[528] The Turkish word *derviş* means "beggar."

[529] Undertake, practice. The word does not carry a pejorative sense here.

thern girdle with fome fhining ftone upon the Buckle before, either of
Marble or Alablafter, Porphyry, Ivory, or fome thing that makes a
great fhew or lufter.

The Prior over a Comv of Dervifes

The Habit of Dervifes

or in Anatolia, of a dark colour. Their caps or what they where on their heads is
like the crown of a hat of the largest size, made of a coarse felt of a whitish colour;
their legs are always bare and their breasts open, which some of them burn or
sear in token of greater devotion. They wear also a leather girdle with some shining stone upon the buckle before either of marble or alabaster, porphyry, ivory,
or something that makes a great show or lustre. They always carry with them a
string of beads which they call *tesbih*, and oftener run them over than our friars do their rosary, at every bead repeating the name of God. When the Prior of
their order dies, they commonly set a hearse for him in a chapel and upon it lay
a long string of beads as big as walnuts. It is also common amongst other Turks
to carry beads in their hands to play with, and they say that when they have no
other employment that kind of divertissement drives away idle and evil thoughts.
Besides their fast of Ramazan, they keep a weekly fast on every Thursday, on
which day none, unless for some indisposition of health or other lawful cause,
hath license to eat until after sun-setting.

Every Tuesday and Friday the Superior of the convent makes a sermon or exposition of some verses in the Qur'an or out of the books wrote by the founder or some other prime doctor of the Muhammadan law, after which is done the dervishes, with marvellous modesty and reverence bowing to their Superior, begin to turn round, some of them with that swift motion that their faces can scarce be seen, a certain pipe made of a cane[530] sounding all the time of this motion. And, of a sudden, when the music ceases, they all stop with that exactness and firmness, showing no symptoms of a disordered or swimming brain, to which, having accustomed themselves from their infancy or youth, in some years that motion becomes as natural, with as little disturbance to their head or stomach as to walk forward or to use any other exercise which nature is delighted with. This custom, as they say, they observe with great devotion in imitation of the first founder Mevlana,[531] who for fourteen days together and without taking any nourishment used this vertiginous[532] motion by a miraculous assistance, his friend Hamza[533] or companion all that time sounding by him with his flute or pipe until at last, falling into ecstasy, he received strange revelations and divine commands for the institution of this his order.

The pipe they play on they esteem for an ancient sanctified sort of music and to be that on which Jacob and other holy shepherds in the Old Testament praised God. It hath a doleful melancholy sound, but their constant exercise and application thereunto makes it as musical as can be imagined in such an instrument. The best of these canes are esteemed to come from Iconium, and are of twenty-five dollars price. But this sort of devotion with instrumental music is by Turks themselves disputed against, denying that their founder, who was so spiritual a man, did ever institute or himself use music is his turning around, because the Qur'an expressly forbids all devotion and service of God with music, but only with the natural and living voice,[534] and that is the reason why in calling people to prayers they use no bells but only the voice of a man. And for this cause I remember that in my time prohibitions have been made by public authorities against this practice of the dervishes. But they, on the contrary, alleging David's example and his dancing before the ark as arguments for their music and gyration, have, by the

---

[530] This would be the *ney*, an end-blown flute, the usual accompaniment for the "whirling" dervishes.

[531] Mevlana or Mowlana is the usual name given to Rumi (see above). In Persian and Arabic it means "Our lord."

[532] Whirling or revolving.

[533] This may refer to Rumi's mentor and friend Shams i-Tabrizi (d. 1248).

[534] The Quran does not forbid music. Several *hadiths* do, however, claiming that it distracts people from thinking about God. Some scholars argue that this applies more to public entertainments and female musicians than to music directly connected with religion. Clearly the Afghanistan Taliban place great authority in these *hadiths*, as under their regime all music was strictly forbidden.

help of several persons in power, many of them being greatly affected with their devotion, maintained from time to time this custom and institution of the first founder of this order, notwithstanding that one Vani Effendi,[535] a great sheykh or preacher esteemed as a knowing person by the Grand Signior and all the court, hath by his authority endeavoured to reform this corruption, as he calls it, amongst them. They profess poverty, chastity and obedience like Capuchin friars or other orders of St. Francis, but if any have not the gift of continence he may obtain license to leave his convent and marry. But of these they observe that none ever thrived or lived happily with contentment that renounced this dedication to God's service.

The novices serve in the most servile offices, and in time others supply their places. They lie as companions two together in a cell, some of which employ their time in learning to read and write in Turkish, Arabic, and Persian, but most yield to the slothful temperament to which they are naturally addicted. But because the nature of man is restless and must employ itself either in good or bad actions, most of these associates exercise some kind of legerdemain[536] or tricks to amuse the minds of the common people, and some really apply themselves to sorceries and conjurations by help of familiar spirits. Busbecq tells strange stories of one with which he was acquainted, that he would strike a stone of great weight and bigness against his bare breast with that force and violence as were sufficient to knock down an ox or break the bones of the stoutest giant, and that the same man he hath seen take an iron bar red-hot from the fire and hold it in his mouth, and, though the spittle and moisture of his mouth hissed with the heat, yet he seemed to take it thence again without the least hurt or burning imaginable.[537]

This sort of people, of all other Turks, addict themselves to drink wine, strong waters, and other intoxicating liquors, and eat opium in that quantity, by

---

[535] For a detailed discussion of Vani Effendi and Mehmed IV, see Marc Baer, *Honored*, 105–21; also Paolo Marana, *Letters written by a Turkish Spy*, 165. Marana addresses a letter to "Sephat Abercromil Vani Effendi" and commends him on his piety and devotion; also see Thomas Smith, *Remarks*, where he is described as a man "famous for his eloquence, [and] who had gained a mighty opinion in the Court for his pretensions to extraordinary piety" (172). He is discussed in detail by Caroline Finkel, from whom the following information comes. Mehmed Vani Effendi, otherwise known as Mehmed ibn Bistan, was a preacher from Van who operated in Erzerum. He became preacher in Turhan Sultan's mosque (1665) and the spiritual guide to Fazil Ahmed Pasha, the Grand Vizier and subsequently close to Mehmed IV. Vani Effendi moved against mystical orders and did manage to prohibit the some of the Mevlevis from singing and dancing. "The descendants of his followers," Finkel writes, known as Dönme. . .remain an identifiable group in Turkey today" (*Osman's Dream*, 276–80). Vani Effendi was expelled from court by Mehmed IV in 1683. Interestingly, he tried to convert Sir John Finch to Islam (See G. F. Abbott, *Under the Turk*, 156–57).

[536] Sleight-of-hand.

[537] Busbecq, *Turkish Letters*, 141.

degrees using their bodies thereunto that no mountebank[538] or Mithridates[539] himself, who was nourished with poison, are capable to digest half that proportion that these men will do, the effect of which is, at first like men drunk or mad, to raise their spirits to a sort of distracted mirth and afterwards, when the subtle vapours are consumed and spent and a dull stupefaction overcomes them, they name it an ecstasy, which they account very holy and divine in imitation of their first founder, who was often observed to put himself in this condition. And therefore, what helps may be found to excite mirth or distraction is lawful and allowable in this order.

There is a famous monastery of these in Egypt, invocating for their saint one Khidr, which by the stories they tell of him should be St. George,[540] in conformity with whom all other dervishes maintain a reverent esteem of this saint, affirming that in his lifetime he was a valiant horseman, killed dragons and all sorts of venomous beasts, and now being departed this life, God, for preservation of good men, hath given him power to deliver such as, being in distress, invoke his assistance, especially those who are at sea and at the point of shipwreck, and that he, with extraordinary swiftness of motion, flies from one part of the world to another in the twinkling of an eye and seasonably comes in to their succour. These, by virtue of that blessing Khidr confirms on them, pretend to charm serpents and adders, and handle them as familiarly as we do the most innocent and domestic creatures, which art, as I have heard from good authority, is not peculiar in Egypt only to dervishes, but to other men who are said to be naturally endued with a virtue against the poisonous bites of vipers and other venomous beasts, who, putting great numbers of them into a bag together, do cull and sort them out with their hands as one would do worms or mussels. And others with a word charm serpents from moving as they crawl along the banks of the Nile, which gifts these men pretend to inherit from their parents and others to possess in reward of their virtue and sanctity. This sort of Egyptian dervishes have

---

[538] A charlatan or con-man, usually one who tricks people out of their money and who often sold patent medicines.

[539] Mithridates VI "the Great" was king of Pontus 120–63 BCE. As a young man, he is said to have tried out small doses of many poisons in order to build up immunity. After his defeat by the Romans he tried to commit suicide but failed, presumably because his experiments had worked. He is alleged to have developed a universal remedy, the *antidotum mithridaticum*, recipes for which appear in the writings of Pliny the Elder and Celsus.

[540] For St. George of Cappadocia, see Book 1, Chapter 14, n. 13. Khwaja al-Khidr, who is described in the Quran (Sura 18:65–82) and in the *hadiths*, is a Sufi prophet often identified with St. George or Elijah or believed to have been a contemporary of Moses. He is venerated as someone who received enlightenment without human mediation, and is looked upon as an initiator of people who wish to become Sufis. The Mevlevis were established in Egypt after the Ottoman conquest (1517) and the order built many *tekkes* or monasteries. The centre was the Madrassa of Sunqur Sadi in Cairo.

## 140  *The Turkish Monasteries and Votaries.*

sainted the horse of St. George[541] and have seated him in Paradise with the other three beasts in high respect and esteem amongst the Turks, *viz.* the ass on which Christ rode, the camel of Muhammad[542] and the dog of the Seven Sleepers.[543]

These dervishes have monasteries in the most famous places in the Turkish Empire, which serve the travelling pilgrims of this order for inns and places of

---

[541] Khidr, like St. George, is sometimes associated with a mysterious green horse, on which he comes down to offer assistance to people in distress..

[542] Muhammad was said to have been very attached to his camel, which he named Qaswah.

[543] The Seven Sleepers were Christian youths from Ephesus who hid in a cave to escape the the persecution ordered by Emperor Decius in 250. They woke some one hundred and fifty or two hundred years later in a Roman Empire which was Christian. In the Quran (Sura 18:9–26) their story is retold with the addition of a dog, which kept watch over the entrance to the cave. Their dog's name (in the Arabic version) was al-Rakim.

entertainment. For they above all other religious Turks journey and travel from one place to another where the Muhammadan religion is professed under pretence of preaching and propagating their faith. And thus they travel upon charity of their monasteries and alms of others into Persia, China and all the dominions of the Mongol, by which means they become the best spies and intelligencers of any that are found in the Eastern parts of the world.

I remember at Adrianople to have seen the ruin of one of their monasteries, situated on a pleasant hill and in good air, that oversees the whole city and plains round about, which upon inquiry I understand was demolished by the famous vizier Köprülü because it was discovered to be a rendezvous of the lewd women of the town and a stew where the young gallants debauched the wives of the richest Turks, to whom their husbands had given liberty in honour to the sanctity of the place to be often present at the devotion of the dervishes. But their way of practice being too public and scandalous, the foundation of their house by order of the Vizier was raised to the ground.

**Chapter XIV.** *Of the order of religious Turks called Abubakriyah.*

The order of Abubakriyah was first instituted by their founder and institutor Abu Bakr, from whom they have their denomination, who herein followed the precepts and rules of his master Naqshbandi, from who in like manner the order of Mevlevi or dervishes are derived.[544] For the better understanding this sort of people, the reader may take this following as an authentic discourse relating to their manners and original, which I shall deliver *verbatim* as given me in writing by one esteemed learned amongst the Turks and was a *hajji* or pilgrim and made it his business to inform me of this sect.

"Sultan Bayezid," said he, "in the year of Muhammad nine hundred and eleven,[545] erected a mosque and convent in Constantinople dedicated to this holy emir Abu Bakr, that is, the race of Muhammad, upon whom rest the mercy of the Creator. This man, both extrinsically as to appearance in the world and intrinsically as to his devout soul, was famous and renowned for the miracles he worked, on which fabric Sultan Selim afterwards bestowed a fountain of water. This Abu Bakr, scholar of Naqshbandi, taking into his company the assistance of Abdullah and Illahi and Vefa, preachers and heads of other convents, came out of Asia to propagate their doctrine in Europe. Their actions were governed with meekness, gravity, and silence, and, laying aside all superstitious worship, they exercise themselves in pious actions. Their discourses amongst themselves were nothing in relation to the things of the world but of matters relating to a future life. These poor religious fast for the most part on Mondays and Thursdays, and both they and those devoted to their order abstain from all meats that carry with them any feculent[546] or ungrateful[547] smells, and in this manner these devout people exercised in abstinence and a moral life and swallowed up or transported with the illumination of God and, attending to their daily prayers, commemoration of God's mercy and other offices of devotion, acquire a holy disposition and preparation for celestial glory. As to the holy emir Abu Bakr, whose mysterious life may God sanctify to us, he was nourished with bread made of barley, oil of olives, honey, and grapes, and abstained from all things of a strong scent or flavor. He ate but three times a year, giving himself continually to fasting and prayer. He was a man of great sanctity, full of divine revelation; his attractive virtue was grateful to all. To his feet from divers countries were many diseased persons brought, which afterwards returned sound and healthful to their own

---

[544] For Baha al-Din Naqshband, see chapter 13, n. 2.
[545] 1505 CE. The mosque is the Bayezid II Mosque and is located in Bayezid Square. It is the second-largest imperial mosque complex in the city as well as being the oldest. For details, see Taylor, *Imperial Istanbul*, 115–17.
[546] Foul-smelling or connected with faeces.
[547] Unpleasant.

homes, all which is the relation of my doctor and great admirer of the Muhammadan religion."

In commendation of the religious of this order are these verses in the Persian tongue: "*Gher hakiki iahi der geban bulendi / Nakshbendi kiun Nakshbendi,*" that is, "If thou wouldst find in the world one accomplished as a true hero, / Make thyself a Naqshbandi, who is the true pattern of a servant of God." And, notwithstanding this great pretended purity and sanctity of these men, they are yet by the generality esteemed heretics in the Muhammadan superstition, because they judge themselves not obliged to the pilgrimage of Mecca by reason of their pretended purity of soul and seraphic raptures, which elevate them above the world and enable them in their very cells to be present or have a clear prospect into their holy Mecca.

## Chapter XV. *Of the Nimatullahiyah.*

One of those who are accounted in the number of Khalwatiyah is the Nimatullahiyah. They had their beginning in the Hegira or Year of Muhammad 777[548] and their denomination from one of that name, famous for his doctrine and severity of life in the time of Sultan Mehmed,[549] son of Bayezid called by the Turks *Yildirim* or the "Son of Thunder." He was an excellent physician and renowned for his virtues amongst the vulgar; for better knowledge of his life and doctrine, the reader may take notice of what one of this order related to me in admiration of his master.

"He was one," said he, "who preached and published the truth, mortified his body, followed not the affections of carnal appetite, knew the intrinsic nature and quiddity[550] of all creatures, rendered continual prayers and praises to his Creator, and so long resigned himself entirely to speculation until he arrived to the ravishment of ecstasies and raptures, in which he oftentimes obtained the happiness to discourse with God. He ate of all those things that God made lawful for human nourishment without observation of fasts or strictness in diet, but day and night continued his prayers and devotions. While he slept he extended not his feet like beasts of sense who eat corn and hay in the stables; sometimes the fear of God made him tremble and his countenance become melancholy and affrighted with the apprehension of his majesty. And to this perfection none ever arrived, nor to that intimate knowledge of the divine secrets."

The professors of this order assemble every Monday night to praise the unity of the Divine Nature and celebrate the name of God with hymns and songs. Those that would initiate themselves into this order are obliged to make a quarantine first, or remain sequestered in a chamber for the space of forty days with twenty-four drams[551] of meat a day, during which time they see the face of God, the sublime Paradise and praise the Creator and Framer of the Universe. At the expiration of their term they are taken forth by the rest of the fraternity who, taking hands, dance in a morris,[552] in which vagary,[553] if any vision appear to the novices from God, they throw their clothes behind them and fall flat with their faces on the ground like men astonished or struck with an apoplexy,[554] until such time as their Prior of chief of their order coming and making prayers for them, they return to their sense again, and, taking them up with their eyes red

---

[548] 1375 CE. For Nimatullah, see Chapter 13, n. 2.

[549] Sultan Mehmed I, son of Beyezid I, reigned from 1413 to 1421. *Yildirim* means "lightning," not "thunder."

[550] The essence of an object, literally its "what-ness."

[551] About 1.7 grams.

[552] A kind of rhythmic stepping.

[553] Erratic motion.

[554] A fit.

and distorted, they remain a while like men drunk, distracted or stupid. But afterwards, their scattered spirits being better-collected, the Prior demands in secret their visions and revelations, which they communicate to him or some other serious and grave person well-instructed in the mysteries of their profession.

## Chapter XVI. *Of the Qadiriyah.*

This is another of those six religions which are derived from Khalwatiyah, which had one Abdul Qadr Gilani[555] for its first founder, a man greatly admired for wisdom and abstinence, whose sepulcher is found without Babylon,[556] to which place many of those who enter into the regular orders of these convents make their pilgrimages.

Those who enter into this religion must perform their novitiate with degrees of abstinence and fasting, wherefore when first they take the profession upon them there is bestowed upon them a small cudgel made of the wood of a willow, weighing, when fresh and green, about four hundred drams, which they are always to carry about with them hung at their girdle. By the weight of this they take their daily allowance of bread, until such time as the wood, becoming exceeding dry, is also much the lighter, and so, according as the weight thereof lightens, their proportion of bread diminishes.

Besides their prayers of five times a day, to which all Muhammadans are bound, they are obliged to spend the whole or best part of the night with turning round at the sound of a little pipe and to utter this word. *"Hai, hai,"*[557] which signifies "Alive, alive," being one of the attributes of God, and this they do in imitation of the custom used by their founder, who is said to have pronounced this word *hai* so often and with that vehemency that the vein of his breast bursting, the blood gushed out upon the wall and made the word *hai*. Wherefore, all his disciples, to follow the example of their master, taking hands together in a ring repeat this word *hai hai* with so much violence and so often, until they fall on the ground without breath or life. Those who last longest carry off the dead from the chamber and lay them to recover their spirits after their strained exercise, and this they do every Friday night. Every one of these are obliged once in the year to a retirement of forty days in a little cell, free from all company or conversation, during which time they are wholly to give themselves to their Superior, who studies the interpretation of them and from them divines of future things. They have many times license from their Superior to be drunk or intoxicate themselves with *aqua vitae*,[558] opium or any stupefying drugs, to be better able to perform with more spirit and vehemency their mad dance.

These fellows are of a refined wit, notable sophisters and hypocrites; their secrets they reveal to none but those of their own profession, by which means they are subtle to cheat those of other religions. They are not debarred from the liberty of marriage, but if they do marry they are excluded from the covenant and may wear any sort of habit, yet for distinction's sake they wear black buttons. Those

---

[555] See Chapter 13, n. 2.

[556] Abdul Qadr's burial place is a madrassa in Baghdad.

[557] Modern Turkish *hayatta*.

[558] A general term for any distilled alcohol (such as ethanol), literally "water of life."

that live in the convent carry a certain white plaid of a coarse cloth, their heads with hair unshaven, without caps or other covering and their feet bare. These are called Qadiriyah, and have a convent at Tophana in Constantinople.

The founder of this order, called, as we have said before, Abdul Qadr Gilani, was born in the Hegira or year of Muhammad five hundred and sixty-one and died in the year six hundred and fifty-seven.[559] He was esteemed both a lawyer and a philosopher; his master of instructor was Ghazali, who composed two books, one called *Maghrib* or *The Arabian Grammar* and another called *Andalus*.[560] At that time Hulagu son of Genghis Khan[561] came to Babylon; he caused him to kill one al-Alqami,[562] then Vice-King of that city, for being of the Persian sect called by the Turks Rafizi[563] or heretics because they reject Abu Bakr, 'Umar, and 'Uthman as apocryphal writers and attribute not to them that honour of holy men which is given by the Turks.

The Priors of chiefs of the convent of this order teach the disciples a certain prayer, which they whisper in their ears that it may not be overheard or known by others. This they are obliged to repeat every moment with little intermission, unless the times set apart for the offices of nature, and boast that it hath so much of efficacy in it that by virtue thereof they obtain the enjoyment of divine visions and revelations. Their posture is like other religious Muhammadans, to sit with their heads hanging down and their noses in their breasts, which they call *murakabe*,[564] the better to keep them from distraction or wandering thoughts during their contemplations of Heaven and the vanity of satisfying the carnal appetite.

Amongst the many miracles that the followers of this order report of their master, one is this, that coming once to Babylon to inhabit amongst the other

---

[559] Rycaut has the dates wrong. Abdul Qadr Gilani was born AH 471 (1078) and died in 561 (1166).

[560] He was not, as far as can be determined, a pupil of the great Arab philosopher Abu Hamad al-Ghazzali (1058–1111). *Maghrib* means either North Africa in general or Moroccco in particular; it does not mean *Arabian Grammar*. *Andalus* refers, of course, to the Arab part of Spain.

[561] Hulagu Khan was Ilkhan from 1256 to 1265; his father was Tolui Khan, son of Genghis Khan. In 1258 Hulagu captured Baghdad (not Babylon) and had caliph al-Mu'tasim put to death (see below). Babylon is about 110 kilometres south of Baghdad. The information given in this paragraph is wrong, as is Rycaut's chronology.

[562] Ibn al-Alqami (1195–1258) was a minister of the caliph al-Muta'sim, whom he betrayed by inviting Hulagu to come and besiege Baghdad. After the capture of the city, al-Alqami volunteered to kill his old master by rolling him in a carpet and beating him to death, as the blood of the sacred caliph could not be spilled. He hoped to become Hulagu's viceroy over the conquered territory but instead was executed. Rycaut's details are incorrect.

[563] Literally, "rejecters."

[564] Literally "supervision."

superstitious persons and santones[565] of that city, they, hearing of his approach, went forth to meet him, one of them carrying in his hand a dish filled with water, from whence they would infer that as that dish was full to the brim so as to be capable of containing no more, so their city was so replenished with learned and religious persons that there was no place to receive him. Whereupon, this subtle sophister, studying to confute this hieroglyphic whereby they would excuse the courtesy of due hospitality, stretching his arms first towards Heaven and then bowed down and gathered a rose-leaf which he laid on the water, which before had filled the dish, by which piece of ingenuity he not only confuted the parable of the churlish Babylonians but also so took with them that they registered it as a miracle of wisdom, and, bringing him into their city with triumph, made him the Superior of all their orders.

---

[565] Holy men (Italian).

## Chap. XVII.
### Of the Order of Kalenderi.

a Santone or Holy man

**Chapter XVII.** *Of the order of the Qalandariyyah.*

This order may rather be termed the sect of Epicureans than men retired to mortify their appetites and deny the world, as all other of the religious and regulated Turks pretend. But yet this sort of fanatics pretend to religion by a different way of libertinism and looseness in their conversation, which they act so publicly that they are not ashamed to profess their institution and customs to be after this manner.

In the time of Muhammad Mansur, son of Malik al-Aziz the son of Saladin, being ready to resign up his last breath, bequeathed to his son Malik al-Kamil the government of Cairo and all the other parts of the Kingdom of Egypt, Damascus and Jerusalem to his son Malik al-Muazzam and Diyarbakir to his third son al-Ashraf Musa,[566] there lived a certain santone who always mentioned the name of God with the sound of his pipe, and with that music recreated himself day and night, not after a cheerful and merry humour, but with sad and melancholy tunes accompanied his pipe with tears and sighs. He was an excellent musician and a deep philosopher endued with those supernatural virtues as enabled him to work miracles clear and notorious[567] to all the world. He was a hermit, called in Arabic Abdul, went with his head bare and his body full of wounds, without a shirt or other clothing beside a skin of some wild beast thrown upon his shoulders. At his girdle he wore some fine-polished stone; on his wrists he wore counterfeit jewels which carried a lustre and fair appearance with them. This man was called Santone Qalandari, who was constantly fingering Arabic sonnets and according to them musical airs, making also harmonious compositions so artificially[568] that he seemed another David.

But how strict and sober this santoon was, his disciples or proselytes are of another temper. Being wholly given up to jollity and delights, they banish all kind of melancholy and sadness and live free of cares, passions or torments of the mind, and have this saying amongst them, "This day is ours; tomorrow is his who shall live to enjoy it," and therefore studiously attend to lose no moment or least part of their pleasure, but continue their time in eating and drinking. And to maintain this gluttony they will sell the stones of their girdles, their earrings and bracelets. When they come to the house of any rich man or person of quality they accommodate themselves to their humour, giving all the family pleasant words and cheerful expressions to persuade them to a liberal and free entertainment. The tavern by them is accounted holy as the mosque, and [they] believe they serve God as much with debauchery or liberal use of his creatures, as they call it, as others with severity and mortification. And the Turks say that in the

---

[566] Rycaut's information is somewhat confused here. Saladin (Salah al-Din), the most famous opponent of the crusaders, was Sultan of Egypt 1171–1193. He was succeeded by his brother al-Aziz (1193–1198), followed by al-Mansur (1198–1200). Malik al-Kamil was the son of al-Adil I (1200–1218), and reigned 1218–1238. Saladin had divided up his territory between several of his sons; al-Muazzam ruled over Damascus and Syria (1193–1219), and al-Awhad over Diyarbakir (in southeastern Turkey) from 1193 to 1214. Upon his death Awhad was succeeded by another son of al-Adil, al-Ashraf Musa (d. 1237). There was a fair amount of infighting between Saladin's sons and other members of the Ayyubid dynasty.

[567] Here, "well-known," without the pejorative meaning.

[568] Skilfully.

Hegira 615[569] the Christians became masters of Jerusalem by reason that the institutor of this order of the Qalandariyyah, who had a chief hand in the government of the city, was found drunk when it was assaulted.

---

[569] The Christian army under Raymond of Toulouse and Godfrey of Bouillon captured Jerusalem in 1099. It was recaptured by Saladin in 1187.

CHAP. XVIII.

*Of the* Edhemi.

A Religious man of the Order of Edhemi

## Chapter XVIII. *Of the Adhemiyah.*

The original founder of this order was one Ibrahim ibn Adhem,[570] concerning whom the disciples themselves or followers recount things very obscurely and tell us stories that his father was a slave and Abyssinian by nation, and went one

---

[570] See Book 2, Chapter 13, n. 2.

day under the fort Haranan to discourse with ibn Malik,[571] King of Cairo, that
he was a man very comely, facetious[572] and sober in his carriage, always desiring
to please God, continued in the mosques reading the Qur'an and in prayer day
and night with his face prostrate on the ground and often repeating these words:
"O God, thou hast given me so much wisdom as that I know clearly that I am in
thy direction. And therefore, scorning all power and dominion, I resign myself
to the speculation of philosophy and a holy life."

His servants, seeing this his devout way of living, applied themselves to the
imitation of his austerity, and abandoning all greatness and vanities of the world,
applied themselves to solitude and mortification. Their superfluous garments
they bestowed on the poor, giving to those whose necessities required them.
Their food is bread made of barley, [they] pray frequently with fasting, and their
priors apply themselves much to a faculty in preaching. Their principal convents
are in cities of Persia, especially Khorasan.[573]

Their clothing is of a coarse, thick cloth; upon their heads they wear a cap
of wool with a turban round it, and about their necks a white linen cloth striped
with red. In the deserts they converse with lions and tigers, salute them and make
them tame, and by the miraculous power of divine assistance entertain discourse
with Enoch[574] in the wilderness. This and many other wild discourses they make
of this Adhem, but because there are but few of this order in Constantinople, being most appropriated to Persia, I could not receive so particular account of their
rule and institutions as I have done of others.

[571] Probably the Umayyad ruler of Egypt Abd al-Malik (714–717; 727). Fort
Haranan is unidentified.

[572] Pleasantly witty.

[573] Khorasan was a region which covered parts of modern Iran, Afghanistan,
Uzbekistan, and Tajikistan.

[574] Enoch was Adam's great-grandson, said to have escaped death and been taken to
Heaven by God. Some Muslims identify him with the prophet Idris, who is mentioned
twice in the Quran (see Suras 19 and 21).

## Chapter XIX. *The Order of Bektaş.*

The original founder of this religion is of no ancient memory or standing, nor had his birth or education amongst the santones of Arabia, from whence most of these superstitious pretenders have had their beginning, but one of those that was an army preacher that could fight as well as pray, of whom my learned *khoja* gives this account:

"In the time," says he, "that the warlike and victorious Sultan Murat [I] passed with his army into Serbia and overcame Lazar,[575] the despot of that country, Bektaş was then a preacher to Murat,[576] who amongst his admonitions warned him of trusting the Serbians. But Murat, out of his courageous spirit relying on his own wisdom and force, admitted a certain nobleman called Orbilič, upon presence of doing him homage, to approach near him and kiss his hand, who, having his dagger ready and concealed, stabbed Murat to the heart and with that blow made him a martyr. Bektaş, knowing that this treacherous death of his Prince must needs also be the cause of his for being so near his person and prophesying this fatal stroke, sought not to prevent it but made preparations for his own death, and in order thereunto provided himself with a white robe with long sleeves which he proffered to all those which were his admirers and proselytes to be kissed as a mark of their obedience to him and his institutions. From this action the custom hath been introduced of kissing the sleeve of the Grand Signior.[577]

The religious of this order wear on their heads white caps of several pieces with turbans of wool twisted in the fashion of a rope. They observe constantly the hours of prayer, which they perform in their own assemblies; they go clothed in white and praise the unity of God, crying *hu!*, which is, "may he live," and by these means obtain the grace of God. This santone hath many millions of disciples and followers; now all the Janissaries of the Ottoman Porte are professors of the same religion. This Bektaş at his death cut off one of his sleeves and put it upon the head of one of his religious men, part of which hung down on his shoulders, saying "After this you shall be Janissaries, which signifies a new militia," and from that time begun their original institution, so this is the reason why the Janissaries wear caps falling behind in the manner of sleeves, called *ketche.*[578]

---

[575] For Prince Lazar Hrebeljanovič, Milos Orbilič and the aftermath of the battle of Kosovo, see Book 1, Chapter 19, n. 9.

[576] For further information, see Book 2, Chapter 12, n. 17, and Brown, *Darvishes*, 215–18, where Rycaut's account is discussed in full.

[577] There is also a report saying that Bektaş died in the presence of Sultan Orhan.

[578] The origins of the Janissary corps are obscure. "Most traditional accounts credit Orhan with creating the Corps," David Nicolle writes, "and almost all give the *Bektaşi* dervish sect a major role, if only in the design of the Janissaries' distinctive *börk* or white felt cap" (*The Janissaries* [Oxford: Osprey Publishing, 1995], 7).

This Hajji Bektaş was a person exceedingly attractive in his conversation, holy to admiration, a man of great worth and majestic in his comportment. He was buried in the city Kir,[579] where they have many convents and religious followers who always praise God." And thus far my *khoja* informs me.

But, whatsoever he says, this order is the most abhorred in the world by the Kadizadeli, because that Bektaş left it to the free will of his disciples either to observe the constant hours of prayer or not, by which great liberty and licentiousness is entered amongst the Janissaries, who are, soldier-like, not over-zealous or devout in their prayers, little attendant to the offices of devotion. In some songs which this Bektaş is said to have composed it is often repeated "That none hath known God, because none hath seen him," and for this reason the most zealous Muhammadans call the Jamissaries *kafirs*, which signifies "without faith," and a certain mufti called Ebujnud delivered his sentence or *fetva* to the question demanded him if a Muslim or believer should say to a Janissary, "Thou art a pagan," what punishment he should merit by the law? He replied that a man is an infidel who holds a Janissary for a true believer.

Some friars of this order of Bektaş do in all public shows and solemnities march near the person of the Janissar Aga, crying "*Hu, hu,*" with their daggers drawn. They are a most licentious sort of people, much given to sodomy, for which the ignorant and loose sort of Janissaries are willingly their disciples, and are now grown into that vast multitude as is almost impossible to extirpate them or their vices, though corrosives are laid to eat away this gangrene in the militia, which goes creeping on with an unsensible pace, as we shall discourse more largely in our next book of the Turkish militia.

---

[579] There is a city of Kir in Syria, which had an ancient Assyrian fortress. The actual place of the saint's death is unknown.

## Chapter XX. *Of the order of Herewi or Hizrevi.*

In the time of Orhan, the second king of the Turks, who governed thirty-five years and reigned eighty-three[580] and died in the Hegira of Muhammad seven hundred and sixteen, there lived in Prusa, then the regal seat, a famous santone called Herewi,[581] who used to walk up and down and as an act of charity to buy the livers and lights[582] of beasts to feed cats and dogs. He professed poverty and severe mortification with tears and sighs, which he acted with that fervency that the angels, leaving heaven, came to be witness of his holy penance, the fame of which moved Sultan Orhan to discourse with him and to know the story of his past life, which he, smiling, began to recount, and told him that he formerly was a king derived from the line of Muhammad, had compassed with his arms the rivers of Nile, Euphrates, and Tigris, had governed provinces with his sword and sceptre and had been triumphantly adorned with precious stones and glittering arms, and had made the world tremble at the very mention of his name. But at last, considering the vanity of this world, he resolved on a solitary life and to renounce all the follies and small satisfaction of riches and empty honours. At which saying Sultan Orhan was amazed, and said, "We ought not to despise those who under the guise and appearance of mad and distracted persons wander through the world, for their virtues are rare, and in this man particularly I discover so much of sanctity that I judge myself unworthy of the name of one of his servants." And this is the reason why fools and frantic people have ever since been had in honour and reverence amongst the Turks as those whom revelations and enthusiasms[583] transported out of the ordinary temperament of humanity.

This Herewi was very learned and experienced in chemistry, and to those who professed his order and entered into the regular life of his religion, instead of aspers he bestowed gold. He wore a green vest and lived very abstemiously; he mended his own clothes and dressed the diet for his convent. He endowed many

---

[580] Rycaut has this wrong. Sultan Orhan ruled for thirty-eight years (1324–1362) and lived for eighty; he was born in 1282.

[581] The story of Herewi and Sultan Orhan cannot be true, as al-Herewi lived from 1005 to 1089. For further details, see Book 2, Chapter 13, n. 2. Interestingly enough, however, this story from Rycaut is quoted in full by one "Nestor," writing in *The Scots Magazine*, Volume 3 (February 1741): 65–68, who also appends a "manuscript" expanding on exactly what Herewi was supposed to have said to the Sultan. How authentic this is, we have no way of knowing. "Nestor" claims that he is near death and wants to impart this eastern wisdom to the readers of the magazine, and he is puzzled that Rycaut did not know about the manuscript.

[582] Usually, lights are the lungs of sheep or pigs. They were still used in the twentieth century as pet food.

[583] In the seventeenth century, an "enthusiast" was a religious fanatic; the term was often used to denote various forms of puritanism or nonconformity. The term could also apply to religious ecstasy.

mosques and several hospitals of charity at Grand Cairo and Babylon. His sepulchre is at Prusa, which is greatly visited by pilgrims and adorned by the bounty
and munificence of those who reverence the memory of this holy santone.

This is the best relation I could procure from one of the sheykhs or preachers,
and one that was prior of this order, whose example as the original copy others
of this order imitate. They have a monastery in Constantinople, as all the others before-mentioned, besides which in this capital city nor in any parts of the
Turkish dominions in Europe have I observed any *teke* or monastery where Turks
profess to lead a religious life but is one of the orders before-mentioned. Some
others there may be about Babylon and Egypt and remotest parts of Asia whose
names and constitutions I have not repeated here, who have, as I am informed,
somewhat more of ridiculous and superstitious work amongst them than I have
declared in the account I have given of those I have been acquainted with in the
parts I have travelled, yet it is observable they all of them pretend to poverty as
the nearest way to arrive to the happiness of Paradise. But with their poverty, as
I have seen in some of their *tekkes*[584] where I have been, especially those removed
from cities, they mix so much negligence in their living, not caring for neatness
in their houses, but leave things in a disorderly and confused manner as testifies
their laziness as well as poverty, and are not like the cells of Capuchins, who,
having nothing to attend to besides their prayers and gardens, improve all things
with that advantage as graces poverty and convinces the world that in a moderate enjoyment of it there is more satisfaction than in those vexations which attend the disposal and government of heaps of riches and the satiety of opulency
and plenty. It is worth noting also that on the monuments of the santones and in
the gardens or before the gates of these religious there is always some ridiculous
adornment such as agrees with the fancy of bedlams,[585] as crowning the hearse
of the dead with beads and horns and ribbons and pieces of tinsel etc., and their
doors with the like, accounting it a chief disposition to divine service to have a
mind endued with an humour inclining to the fancy of hypochondriacal or distracted heads, so that I shall not enlarge further in this discourse nor glut my
reader with so insipid[586] and fulsome a subject.

---

[584] A dervish convent. As Ottavio Bon pointed out in 1607, "Among the Turks there
are no religious houses, or monasteries, unless the *teckhes* of the *Mevleves*, which are an
order of *Derveeshes*, that turn round with musick in their divine service" (*The Sultan's Seraglio*, 143). Rycaut, however, frequently uses the word "monastery" (see, for example,
above).

[585] Bedlams are mad people; the name is derived from the medieval Priory of Beth-
lehem or Bethlem in London, which became a home for mentally-disturbed people in the
sixteenth century, although some scholars believe that there had been patients there since
the mid-fourteenth century.

[586] Lacking any interest.

## Chap. XXI.

*Of Marriages and Divorces, and how far Concubinage is in-dulged amongst the Turks.*

*The Habit of the Women in Constantinople*

The

**Chapter XXI.** *Of marriages and divorces, and how far concubinage is indulged amongst the Turks.*

The state of marriage is accounted both honourable and holy amongst the Turks, by which the race of mankind is both increased and maintained, yet the priest, as I may call him, or their churchman, hath the least hand in the solemnity. The matter, as an action wholly civil, is performed before the *kadi* or judge, not unlike the manner practiced in England for some few years according to that absurd Act of Marriages by a Justice of the Peace,[587] and it is in the nature of a recognizance whereby the husband doth personally oblige himself before the judge to take such a wife, and in case of his death or divorce, to endow her with a certain estate to remain to her own disposal. The woman is not there present, but appears by her father or some of her nearest relations, and if afterwards by a great attendance of women brought covered, sitting astride on horseback under a canopy, to the habitation of her bridegroom, who remains at the gate with open arms to receive her. There is great rejoicing and feasting hereat. The night before she is brought to the company of her husband, but when the precedent ceremonies to the marriage are performed and completed, the house is all silent and she is brought into the bride-chamber by an eunuch, if she be of quality; if not, by some women of near relation, and delivered to her husband, who is himself to untie her drawers and undress her for his bed, not unlike the custom amongst the Romans of *zonam solvere.*[588]

Polygamy is freely indulged to them by their religion as far as the number of four wives, contrary to the common report that a Turk may have as many wives as he can maintain, though Muhammad had nine wives and Ali had fourteen,[589] as being men more spiritual and of a more elevated degree had greater privileges and indulgences for carnal enjoyments. This restraint of the number of wives is certainly no precept of their religion, but a rule superintroduced upon some politic considerations as too great a charge and weakening to men's estates, everyone that takes a wife being obliged to make her a *kabin* or dowry, as we have said before, or else, for better regulation of the economies and to prevent and abate somewhat of the jealousies, strifes, and embroilments in a family which must necessarily arise between so many rivals in the affection of one husband, who

---

[587] Under the Commonwealth and Protectorate (1649–1660) marriages could be carried out by Justices of the Peace, a practice which originated in the Puritan belief that marriage was not a sacrament. After the Restoration the practice was reversed.

[588] Literally, "to undo the marriage-girdle." George Sandys writes, "But the bridegroom himself must untie her buskins (as among the Romans they did with their girdles)," adding, amusingly, "to which he is fain to apply his teeth" (*Travels*, 34). Rycaut's account of marriage is quite close to that of Sandys.

[589] The number of Muhammad's wives actually varies from eleven to thirteen. Scholars disagree on the exact count, some arguing that one or two at least of these marriages was political in nature. Likewise, the number of Ali's wives is also disputed. "Marry what seems good to you of women," the Quran states rather confusedly; "by twos, or threes, or fours, or what your right hand possesses" (Sura 4:88). In practice, according to Hughes, Muhammad restricted his followers to four wives but Muslims could have as many concubines as they could afford (*Dictionary*, 671). Present-day Sharia laws allow four wives, but many modern Muslims have just one wife. Christian writers always used this to condemn Muhammad for his carnal appetites and lustful demeanour.

is obliged by law and covenants to deal and bestow his benevolence and conjugal kindness in an exact proportion of equality. And lest this confinement to a certain number of wives should seem a restriction and impeachment of that liberty and free use of women which they say God hath frankly bestowed on man, everyone may freely serve himself of his women slaves with as much variety as he is able to buy or maintain, and this kind of concubinage is no ways envied or condemned by the wives so long as they can enjoy their due maintenance and have some reasonable share in the husband's bed, which once a week is their due by law. For if any of them hath been neglected the whole week before, she challenges Thursday night as her due and hath remedy in that case against her husband by the law. And if she be so modest as not to sue him for one week's default, she is yet so ingenious as to contrive a supply of her wants. And whereas these women are educated with much retiredness from the conversation of men and consequently with greater inclinations towards them and with no principles of virtue, of moral honesty or religion as to a future estate relating to the rewards or punishments of their good or bad actions, they are accounted the most lascivious and immodest of all women, and excel in the most refined and ingenious subtleties to steal their pleasures. And, as in Christendom, the husband bears the disgrace and scandal of his wives' incontinency; here, the horns[590] are by the vulgar adjudged to the father, brother, and wives' kindred, the blood of her family is tainted and dishonoured, and the husband, obtaining a divorce, quits himself of his wife and dishonour altogether.

No question but the first institutor of this easy religion, next to the satisfaction of his own carnal and effeminate inclination and this taking freedom amongst his disciples, his first consideration was the increase of his people by polygamy, knowing that the greatness of empires and princes consists more in the numbers and multitudes of their people than the large extent of their dominions. This freedom, if it may be called so, was granted at the beginning of the world for the propagation and increase of mankind, and the Jews had that permission and indulgence to their loose and wandering affections. And we read that the eastern parts of the world have abounded with children of divers mothers and but one father, and that ordinarily a great personage in Egypt hath been attended with an hundred lusty sons in the field proceeding from his own loins, well-armed and daring in all attempts of war. But yet, this course thrives not so well amongst the Turks as formerly, whether it be thought their accursed vice of sodomy, or that God blesses not so much this state of life as when the paucity of mankind induced a sort of necessity and a plea for it.

But, chiefly through the irreconcilable emulation and rivalry which is amongst many wives, those witchcrafts and sorceries, which in this country are very frequent, are prepared against the envied fruitfulness each of other,

---

[590] The horns are, of course, those of a cuckold.

that either they make an abortive birth or otherwise their children pine and macerate[591] away with secret and hidden charms, by which means they are now observed not to be so fruitful and numerous as is the marriage-bed of a single wife. Nor is the family so well-regulated and orderly as under the conduct and good housewifery of one woman, but contrarily filled with noise, brawls, and dissentions, as passes the wisdom of the husband to become and equal umpire and arbitrator of their differences, which consideration restrains many, though otherwise inclinable enough to gratify their appetites, from encumbering themselves with so great an inconvenience. And I have known some, though childless, [who] have adhered to a single wife and preferred quiet and repose before the contentment of their offspring.

The children they have by their slaves are equally esteemed with those they have by their wives: "*Neque vero Turcae minus honoris defereunt natis ex concubinis aut pellicibus quam ex uxoribus, neque illi minus in bona paterna iuris habent,*"[592] but yet, with this difference in esteem of the law, that unless the father manumits them by his testament and confers a livelihood upon them by legacy, they remain to the charity of their elder brother that is born from the wife and are his slaves and he their lord and master. And it is with them as in the civil law, "*Partus ventrem sequitur,*"[593] so that from the loins of the same father may proceed sons of a servile and ignominious condition. There is also another sort of half-marriage amongst them which is called *kabin,* when a man takes a wife for a month or for a certain limited time, and an agreement is made for the price before the *kadi* or judge, and this strangers oftentimes use, who have not the gift of continency and are desirous to find a wife in all places where they travel, and is the same which they term in Spain to be *emancipado* or *casado de media carta,*[594] only the act there is not made allowable by the laws as in Turkey. There is another sort of marriages commonly used amongst the Turks (if we may give it that honourable title) which is the conjunction of an eunuch with a woman; such as are wholly disarmed of all parts of virility do notwithstanding take many wives and execute lusts of an unknown and prodigious nature.

There is also one point or restriction of matrimony in the Turkish religion which is observable, that is, a Muhammadan may marry himself with what woman soever, though esteemed an infidel, as a Christian, Jew, or any other different profession, so it be of those who are of a learned religion of which books are wrote to defend it. But such women who are of a religion which hath nothing of learning or written law, as the sect of *Meiuzi,*[595] who adore the fire, conserving

---

[591] Become emaciated.

[592] Busbecq, *Turkish Letters.* Rycaut has already translated the quotation.

[593] Literally, "that which is brought forth follows the womb." It is usually interpreted, in legal terms, as "the children follow the condition of the mother."

[594] Literally "married in a half-way respect."

[595] Zoroastrians or Parsis.

it always burning in their temples, and are to be found in parts of Persia but principally in some countries of the Mughal, and also the gypsy women are prohibited, of which great numbers are amongst the Turks, a vagabond people without religion but what is fabulous and ridiculous, and, having no literature or knowledge amongst them, are reputed as abominable amongst the Turks.[596]

And here the Turks, upon occasional discourses of the severity and strictness of the Christian discipline in matters of concupiscence, telling them that no copulation is allowable but in the marriage-bed, and that restrained and confined to one wife without the additions of slaves to satisfy with variety the corrupted fancy, that the very thoughts of lust or concupiscence pollute the purity of the soul, "And that whosoever looketh upon a woman to lust after her, commits adultery in his heart."[597] They presently deride these our precepts and our laws, which Christians not only by their actions and corrupted lives contemn as invalid, but authority itself not by a simple connivance only but by indulgence and privileges foments and encourages persons walking contrary to that which is confessed to be an indispensable law, for proof whereof they mention the stews of Italy, whoredom made an allowable trade and profession in Venice, Naples, and the city of Rome, and the *cantoneras*[598] in Spain, and framed into a politic body , as is related and apprehended by the Turks, from whence taxes and impositions are raised. The Turks comprehend not the politic grounds hereof with which in Italy this maxim is defended, nor is it fitting to produce the reasons or argue it with them, since the benefit which accrues to the Roman Church and the profits that arise thence, being employed in maintenance of galleys and forces against infidels, is the best than can be said to hallow this permission. But 'tis an improper argument with a Turk to excuse this license and authority to sin upon considerations of being better able to war against the professors of his religion! And therefore the Turk will hardly be convinced but that this manner of concubinage hath much more of sanctity, order, and policy in it, as being free from disease and foulness, than the wandering lusts of stews or impudence of courtesans made bold and hard-foreheaded by concession of authority.

Amongst all the privileges that the Sultan enjoys above his subjects, this one hath less than they, that he cannot marry, but yet he hath as many women as serves his use, though never so libidinous, or are requisite for the ostentation and great magnificence of his court, according to the custom of the eastern princes, who placed a great part of their pomp in the multitude of their women. This disuse of marriage in the Sultan hath been a maxim of state, and reckoned amongst

---

[596] For an historical overview of Turkish attitudes towards gypsies see Sirat Kolukinik, "The Gypsy Image and Bias in the Turkish Society," *Sociology Research Journal* vol. 8, No. 2 (2005).

[597] Matthew 5:28.

[598] Literally, "women who stand on street corners."

the Turks *inter arcana imperii*[599] from the time of Bayezid [I] until this very age. The reasons thereof are diversely related; Busbecq saith[600] that Bayezid, after the great victory obtained against him by Timur, to his other great misfortunes and disgraces had this one added, of having his wife Despina, whom he dearly loved, to fall into the hands of the conqueror, whose ignominious and indecent treatment before the eyes of her husband was a matter of more dishonour and sorrow than all the rest of his afflictions, so that ever since that time the Sultans, to free themselves from being capable of that disgrace on occasion of like fortune, take no feminine companion of their empire in whom they may be more concerned than as in slaves or the loss of goods, riches, or estate.[601] But, in my opinion, this policy is of a deeper reach and design than the considerations of matters so merely possible, for, as I have heard, the only sign and ceremony of the Sultan's making a wife is the endowing of her with riches agreeable to her condition and quality, not called *kabin*, which is dowry, but *paşmaluk*, or money for her shoes, which, besides presents, jewels, and rich garments for herself and great attendance, her revenue ought to be equal to that of a *valide* or Mother of the Grand Signior, which is four or five hundred thousand dollars yearly rent. So that were the custom in use, and meeting with the dispositions of some princes that are amorous and prodigal, the chief revenue of the empire would be expended in chambers of women and diverted from the true channels in which the channel ought to run for the nourishment of the politic body of the commonwealth. Besides, were it the custom for Sultans to take wives, it would contradict that main principle of policy amongst them of avoiding alliances and relations of the Grand Signior abroad. And this

---

[599] "Amongst the secrets of the empire" (Tacitus, *Annals* 2.30).

[600] Rycaut paraphrases the whole passage about Despina (see below) from Busbecq, who writes: "Bajazet, having been defeated and having fallen, together with his wife, into the hands of Tamerlane, underwent many intolerable sufferings, but there was nothing which he regarded as more humiliating than the insults and affronts to which his wife was subjected before his very eyes. Mindful of this, the Sultans who followed Bajazet on the throne abstained from marrying wives, so that, whatever fate befell them, they might not suffer a similar misfortune" (*Turkish Letters*, 19).

[601] Bayezid I was defeated and captured by Timur at the battle of Ankara (1402). In 1390 he had married Princess Marja Olivera Despina (c. 1377–1444), daughter of Prince Lazar of Serbia (see Book 1, Chapter 19, n. 9). Bayezid died in captivity of natural causes (March 1403) at Akşehir in Anatolia (Finkel, *Osman's Dream*, 30), but the jury seems to be out about whether Timur mistreated him or his wife in any way, as Lord Kinross noted that Timur "at first accorded him [Bayezid] the honours due to a sovereign, but later sought to degrade him as a captive," and cites a suspicion that the Sultan committed suicide (*Ottoman Centuries*, 76). There were, in any case, various legends and literary versions of the story; in Christopher Marlowe's *Tamburlane the Great*, part 1 (1587), she appears as Zabina, and Rycaut may also have known a French play entitled *Le grand Tamerlan et Bajazet* (1648) by Jean Magnon (1620–1662), in which the playwright makes much of the tragedy of Bayzeid's son and wife, whom he names Orcazie.

was the principal reason of the murder of Sultan Osman [II], tenth Emperor of the Turks, contrived by the rebellion and toleration of the soldiery, it being objected that he had married a Sultana, whereby he had contracted alliances contrary to the fundamental constitutions of the Empire.[602]

The tie and solemnity of marriage and the nature thereof amongst the Turks is as before related, from which the woman hath no ways to unloose herself while her husband maintains her with bread, butter, rice, wood, and flax to spin for her clothing; the law supposes her so industrious a housewife as with her own labour to supply herself. There are some other points pleadable in law for divorce in behalf of the woman, as impotency or frigidity in the husband and the like, but the man hath divers means to acquit himself and can do it by several allegations, and may upon as easy terms and on as light grounds sue out his divorce, as was permitted to the Jews in cases of dislike or that she found no favour in his eyes.

There are amongst the Turks three degrees of divorce,[603] every one of which is made before the *kadi* or justice, and by him drawn out and registered. The first separates the man and wife only from the same house and bed, the maintenance of the wife being still continued. The second not only divides them in that manner, but the husband is compelled to make good her *kabin*, which is a jointure or dowry promised at her marriage so as to have no interest either in him or his estate and to remain in a free condition to marry another. The third sort of divorce, which is called *uç talák*,[604] is made in a solemn and more serious manner with more rigorous terms of separation, and in this case the husband repenting of his divorce and desirous to retake his wife cannot by law be admitted to her without first consenting and contenting himself to see another man enjoy her before his face, which condition the law requires as a punishment of the husband's lightness and inconstancy and as evidence to show that the Turkish law is very indulgent and open in the free choice and enjoyment of women, yet that it punishes such as unadvisedly frustrate the solem points thereof with remarkable notes of infamy and disgrace. It is a merry story told of one who in this case being put to a great strait, resolved to call the first man he conveniently met to this office, that so as one unknown his reputation might be the less concerned.

---

[602] Osman II's murder in 1622 had nothing to do with his choice of a wife. The Janissaries, Caroline Finkel writes, "were threatened by Osman's radical plan to recruit military manpower from new sources. . .most owed their positions to their links with statesmen and high-ranking bureaucrats, and they argued that Osman had brought his fate upon himself by taking the advice of unscrupulous advisers" (*Osman's Dream*, 201), a verdict which is shared by Lord Kinross (*Ottoman Centuries*, 292–94). Osman II had two wives, Akile and Ayşe, and he was actually the sixteenth Sultan, not the tenth.

[603] The term for divorce is *talák*. The man may pronounce it three times, and the third time is final. Rycaut is essentially correct in his account, although women may petition a *qadi* to grant them a divorce if the husband refused to do so.

[604] Lierally, "extremity divorce."

The man he lighted on, however, happened to be a *kayakçi* or boatman, who, it seems, so well satisfied and pleased the wife that she afterwards renounced all interest in her husband and resolved to adhere to her new lover, of whom she supposed she had sufficient proof and acquaintance with already to esteem a better husband than her former. There are but few amongst the Turks, though some are found, who so heartily repent of their divorce and so fond of their separated wives as to be contented to take them with the foregoing condition, for it it reputed a kind of abomination, and when they would signify any matter far alienated or estranged they call it *uç talak*, something so divided and separated as to be a sin and profabnation so much as to covet or desire it.

# Chapter XXII. *Of the other parts of the Turkish religion.*

### *Of circumcision.*

Circumcision is not reckoned amongst one of the five points which constitute a true Muhammadan believer,[605] but 'tis only, as we have said before, proposed as a trial and proof of man's obedience to the more necessary parts of the law. This rite of circumcision is not received by them as an article or precept derived expressly from the Qur'an, but by tradition and ancient practice and use amongst the Arabians before the time of Muhammad, derived originally from Ishmael or Esau, whose progeny they are and from thence give themselves the name of Ishmaelites.[606] The Arabian doctors affirm that Muhammad himself was born with his navel cut and naturally circumcised, perhaps to equal the same story which the Jews report of Moses[607] and some others of the patriarchs, and it seems in those countries where circumcision is in practice that it is not unusual for children to be so born, who are therefore called "sons of the Moon," on whom the virtue of the Moon hath more than ordinary manner of influence: "*Credebant siquidem Arabes, quod ille qui sub lunae radiis nasceretur, contrahi perinde ac circumcisum praeputium.*"[608]

The Turks never circumcise their children until the age of seven years and upwards, and then they do it by a barber or surgeon, it not being esteemed a matter appropriated to the office of the *imam* or priest. For, as we have said before, they make no such distinction as clergy and laity, I mean as to any spiritual character of priesthood, for a man may cry upon the steeple today and like their pastor be the first to lead his congregation to their prayers and expound the Qur'an, and the next day be expelled his parish and become free to any secular employment or profession. They observe some ceremonies amongst them on this occasion, often differing according to the country and place, but commonly the child is set on horseback in his best clothes, attended with his schoolfellows and companions, who with loud shouts repeat some words in the Qur'an. And, being brought home

---

[605] Rycaut is in direct contradiction to Ottavio Bon, who states that "until which time [they are circumcised] they are not accounted perfect Mussulmen, nor may till then pray in the congregation" (*Seraglio*, 139).

[606] Ishmael was the son of Abraham and Hagar. Muslims regard him as a prophet and patriarch (see, for example, Sura 19:55) and he is revered as the ancestor of northern Arabia. Muhammad was said to have been descended from him through Adnan, Ishmael's great-great-grandson. There is no mention of Esau in the Quran.

[607] For the story of Moses's wife Zipporah circumcising her husband to save his life, see Exodus 4:24–26.

[608] "Indeed, the Arabs believed that he who was born under the rays of the moon in the like manner had the prepuce cut off" (Pococke, *Nota de Arabum moribus*; Rycaut's note). For Edward Pococke, see Book 2, Chapter 11, n. 12.

and the act of circumcision performed, he is carefully attended for his coure, and in the meantime there is a feast or banquet prepared for the guests. Those who of riper years become Muhammadans in some places are carried about the town on horseback with a dart in their left hand pointing to their heart, signifying that they will rather suffer themselves to be passed through with that instrument than renounce the faith they then possess. And this circumcision is an admission and introduction of them into the number of the faithful, as it is amongst the Jews, and baptism with the Christians.

**Chapter XXIII.** *Of the five necessary points which are required to constitute a true Muḥammadan.*

*Of their washings.*

Though Muhammad saith in the Qur'an that his religion is founded in cleanness and that it is half of his law, yet much before Muhammad's time washings were observed according to the same prescriptions by the Arabians, who, descending from Ishmael, maintained by tradition the practice of washings, and he had no other share in this invention than that it was enforced by his authority on the professors of his sect. The Turks are certainly a very cleanly people in their exterior manner of living, as in their washings relating to their holy exercises and duties they are very precise and superstitious, some of them believing that the very water purifies them from the foulness of their sins as well as from the uncleanness of their bodies.

There being three sorts of washings observed by them, the first is called *abdest*,[609] which is a preparation for their prayers. Entering the mosque or reading the Qur'an, they first wash their hands and arms, then their neck and forehead, the crown of their head, their ears, their teeth, the face, under the nose, and last of all their feet, but if the weather be cold and not convenient to uncover them, it is sufficient if they make some evidence thereof by any other outward signification. The second is called *gusül*,[610] which is the cleansing of the bath after copulation or nocturnal pollutions, until which time a man is called *giunuh*, that is, his prayers are accounted abominable before God and his society to be avoided by men. The third is *taharet*,[611] which is a washing after the ease or evacuation of nature. To this homely office they design the three last fingers of the left hand, and upon this account they call Christians *taharatsis*, which is as much as "one defiled and impure" for want of this manner of cleaning. And washing is so usual and frequent amongst them both before and after meat as hath caused a common proverb amongst them that God hath created meat that men may have occasion often to wash their hands.

*Secondly, of their prayers.*

After their washing follow their prayers, which Muhammad, to recommend to his disciples the force and virtue of prayer, calls it in his Qur'an "the Pillar of Religion" and "the Key of Paradise," and enjoyed the performance five times in the space of twenty-four hours, *viz.* between the day-breaking and sun-rising,

---

[609] A Turkish word derived from the Persian *âb* (water) and *dast* (hand). It is the general term for "ablution."

[610] The ritual washing of the entire body.

[611] In modern-day Turkey, the nozzle attached to the tap in a toilet used to clean oneself before taking the toilet paper is still called the *taharet musluğu*.

called *imsak namaz*; secondly, at noon, called *ögle namaz*; thirdly, at the middle hour between the noon and the setting of the sun, *ikindi namaz*; fourthly, at sun-setting, called *aksam namaz*; fifthly, at an hour and a half in the night, *yatsi namaz*.[612] This action they perform with very much reverence and devotion, and hold that they ought to be so intent and fixed in their thoughts on this religious act towards God that no business of the world, though the execution of the Sultan's decree should in the same moment be commanded, or fire should burst forth in the very chamber where they remain, or an armed enemy within their gates or camp, they ought not yet to be diverted or break abruptly off their prayers to extinguish or oppose themselves against their inevitable destruction. Nay, if they do but cough or spit or sneeze, or rub any part of their face or hands where a fly bites during their prayers, they must begin them again, for they are void and esteemed to be of no effect. It is much in my opinion that infidels should be possessed with that awe and sense of the Divine Majesty in the time of their audience with him, and yet that friars and others of the Roman Church, obliged to their office as the Turk to his *namaz*, should perform it so perfunctorily as to mix the discourse of business with the repetition of their breviary[613] and join with their responsals answers and resolutions of questions made them, and so satisfy themselves in the *opus operatum*[614] as if it were more important to comply with his command who imposed the office than with his who primarily enjoined the sacrifice of prayer.

The form of their prayers is not extracted out of the Qur'an; only the collections of sentences, as "in the name of God," "God is great and merciful," and the like are deduced from thence, as Christians do from the fountain of the Holy Scriptures. The rest is compiled by the four doctors we have before mentioned, *viz.* Abu Bakr, Omar, Osman and Ali, whose names are wrote in golden characters on the walls of most mosques. Herein they observe many postures and gestures of their body, as placing their hands one on the other before them, bending the body, kneeling, touching the ground with their forehead, moving the head to each side, and the like, in which it is difficult to make distinction of those merely invented and ordained by Muhammad from those which were primarily in use amongst the ancient Arabians. But, that the orderly ceremonies in their prayers

---

[612] I have given the modern Turkish names for the prayer-times. *Namaz* means "prayer." In modern Turkey there are six prayer-times, the additional one being *günes namaz*, which is to take place at dawn just before the sun comes up. Ottavio Bon also lists the names of the prayers, but adds that "upon the Friday (which is their Sabbath) [they] pray six times, for they pray then at nine of the clock in the forenoon also, and that is called *Selaw*" (*Seraglio*, 133).

[613] The book listing the rites of the Catholic Church, which is usually carried by priests.

[614] Literally "the work wrought," or the spiritual result of carrying out a religious rite. Rycaut refers here to the Catholic idea that the sacraments contain inherent grace.

may be better described, it will be to our purpose to hear what Busbecq relates of the whole Turkish army, whom he had seen drawn up orderly in the field at their devotion. "I saw," said he,

> in that plain, a great multitude of heads folded up in turbans, who, with profound silence, attended to the words of a priest their conductor, all of them being drawn up in rank and file and covering with their extended orders the whole plain, seemed to have framed a wall or bulwark by the regular disposition of their bodies. Their clothings were of light colours and their turbans comparable to the whiteness of the snow, and the variety of the different colours of their garments fed the eyes with a strange pleasure. In this manner so immovable they stood, as if they had grown in the place where their feet were fixed. No coughing, hemming nor voice was heard, nor so much as any motion was perceived of their heads. Everyone, at the name of Muhammad pronounced by the priest, bowed his head to his knees, and at the name of God reverently prostrated himself and kissed the earth. And thus the Turks with devout ceremony and profound attention perform their whole devotions, supposing that prayer to become fruitless which is interrupted by scratching the head, rubbing the hands or any other gesture not essential to their prayer.[615]

But of all nations and religions that I have known, they are the most hypocritical; they are those who love to pray in the market-place and in the corners of the streets to have praise of men, for it is observable with the Turks that where they find the most spectators, especially of Christians, to choose that place, how inconvenient soever, to spread first their handkerchief and then begin their prayers.

The substance of their prayers consists for the most part in praises of the divine power and attributes, mixing therewith petitions for the safety of the Prince and his dominions and for dissentions and wars amongst Christians, which part they conceive God hath greatly gratified them in, and rejoicing upon the rumours of wars and disturbances in Christendom as an effect of the divine facility and concession to their prayers. They know well by experience what Tacitus reports of the Roman policy, that "*Omne scelus externum cum laetitia habendum, semina etiam odiorum iacienda*," and, as the Romans destined Armenia to be a prize held up and the stage also on which the tragedy of the ruin of the eastern nations were to be acted, "*Eandem Armeniam specte largitionis turbandis barbarorum animis praebuerint.*"[616] So the Turk forbore for several years the conquest of the provinces of Transylvania, Moldavia and Wallachia, reserving them

---

[615] This is Rycaut's translation. See Busbecq, *Turkish Letters*, 109–10.

[616] "Every crime in a foreign country should be welcomed with joy and the seeds of strife should actually be sown. . .this same Armenia given away to excite the spirits of the barbarians" (Tacitus, *Annals* 12.48). Rycaut mistakenly gives a marginal citation as "*Lib.* 12. *Hist.*"

for the Cadmean Fields,[617] wherein the Hungarians, Germans, Polonians, and
the people of those countries themselves might destroy one the other and make
his entrance to the possession of them the more facile and less bloody.

### Thirdly, of their Ramazan

The third necessary point of their religion is the observation of the month of
*Ramazan*, or a fast in the whole month in which time they can neither eat, drink,
or take anything in their mouths whilst the sun is above the horizon. Afterwards, upon shuttering in of the evening, the imam lights the lamps, which in
that month are exposed round the steeple of every mosque, they have liberty to
eat.[618] Most part of the night they spend in feasting, reserving commonly their
greatest delicacies and best provisions for the consolation of that fast; their business and employments they attend most to in the night, passing the day as over-
tedious in sleeping, so that their fast is nothing but a changing the day into night.
This month they call holy and the time when the Gates of Paradise are opened
and of Hell are shut, and so strict is the imposition of this fast that it is no less
than death for a Turk to be accused of the breach thereof. In this month to drink
wine is esteemed an inexpiable crime, and such as who give themselves that liberty at other times do yet, not to give scandal, abstain from it fourteen days before the beginning of this month, and women and other of the more superstitious
sort begin fifteen days after their fast before it is enjoined by the precept of their
Prophet. But such as are sick or have any infirmity, or are travellers in their country have a permission to eat, but with that condition as to remain obliged at other
times of their health and convenience to make good those days of the Ramazan
of which they remain indebted to the performance of their law.

The institutions of this month of Ramazan proceeded from Muhammad
himself in the second year of his prophetic office, which he did not assume until
he had fully completed forty years, having before, in imitation of the Jews' fast
of Ashura[619] in memory of the overthrow of Pharaoh and his host in the Red

---

[617] A Cadmean victory is another name for a Pyrrhic victory. When Cadmus was establishing the city of Thebes, he needed a water supply, but the available one was guarded
by a monster. He sent people to kill it, but they were all slain; undeterred, Cadmus kept
on sending people to their deaths until the monster was disposed of, thus winning his
victory, but at a heavy cost.

[618] See also Ottavio Bon, *Seraglio*, 135–36.

[619] There is some confusion here. Ashura is "a voluntary fast day observed on the
tenth of the month of Muharram. . .it was a day respected by Jews and Christians"
(Hughes, *Dictionary*, 25). God is said to have created Adam and Eve, Hell, and a number
of other things on that day. For Shi'a Muslims, it marks the anniversary (and mourning
period) of the battle of Karbala (October 10, 680), where caliph Yazid defeated and killed
Imam Hussain, the grandason of Muhammad. Because of the lunar calendar, Muharram
is a moveable month, as Rycaut correctly observes (see also Busbecq, *Turkish Letters*, 103).
Rycaut also cites Leviticus 16:29, which reads "And this shall be a statute for ever unto

Sea, enjoined to the Arabians the same time of abstinence. But afterwards, apprehending it dishonourable to be beholding to the Jews for the invention of a fast, instituted the Ramazan, the time of which is governed by the course of the moon, and falls out commonly ten days sooner than in the preceding year, so that this fast with time comes to run through all the months, and it is more easy to the Turks when it happens in the short days of the winter rather than in the summer, when the days are long and hot, which become tedious to the ordinary sort of people who are for necessity forced to labour, and yet for the quenching thirst dare not refresh their mouths with a drop of water.

### Fourthly, Of their zakat

Which is another necessary point to the constitution of a Muhammadan, which is the bestowing alms according to certain rules prescribed by four principal doctors of their law. The word *zakat*[620] signifies as much as "increase," because the alms procure the blessing of God and multiply the store of the merciful. According to this command every man is obliged to give one in a hundred of all their estate to the relief of the poor, and though this precept is enjoined as an ingredient to constitute a true Muhammadan, yet covetousness and policy so much prevail with the Turks that the rich are both unwilling to part with so much of their estate and fearful to evidence their wealth by a true calculate according to the *zakat*, so that the poor are the best observers of this injunction, the rich conceiving it superfluous and never intended by God to make the performance of religion a snare to their estates.

### Fifthly, Of their Pilgrimage to Mecca

Which is enjoined to everyone who hath riches and freedom from great offices and charges of government to perform, it being a type or signification of their passage out of this world into the next. The number of those who yearly undertake this pilgrimage is uncertain, though most commonly are registered from divers parts where the Muhammadan religion is professed, above fifty thousand souls. These pilgrims depart about the latter end of May from Constantinople to meet with those from Anatolia, Carmania, and others of that quarter of the world at Damascus. Those from Persia assemble at Babylon, those of the parts of Egypt at Grand Cairo, and all unite upon a mount not far distant from Mecca, where they observe divers ceremonies, as making *korban*[621] or sacrifice, which

---

you: that in the seventh month, on the tenth day of the month, ye shall afflict your souls and do no work at all. . ." The next verse states that, "for on that day the priest shall make an atonement for you." There is no mention of the parting of the Red Sea.

[620] See Book 2, Chapter 1, n. 8.

[621] This is the Hebrew word for "offering." Rycaut should, strictly, have written it *kurban* or *qurban*, which literally means "approaching near. . .A term used in the Quran and in the Traditions for a sacrifice or offering" (Hughes, *Dictionary*, 530).

they do by killing sheep and sending part thereof as presents to their friends and distribution thereof to the poor. They also here strip themselves of their garments, and, being covered only with a blanket, go in procession through the mountain in signification that they must now leave all their sins and affections of the world behind them. Here also they leave their Christian slaves, so that they may not profane the Holy City with the uncircumcised.

The chief commander over the pilgrims, for amongst so considerable a number of people there must be rule and government, is appointed by the Grand Signior and is called *Sur Emini*,[622] by whom he sends 500 sequins, a Qur'an embossed with gold carried on a camel, and as much black cloth as serves for hangings for the mosques at Mecca, and this is yearly presented by the Sultan to that place. When the new hanging is set up, that of the former year is pulled down and is by the pilgrims torn in pieces, some getting more and some less, carry any rag of it home as a relic and token of their pilgrimage, which serves them in place of the *kaaba*[623] to which they turn their faces at the time of their prayers. The camel which carried the Qur'an at his return home is decked with flowers and other ornaments, and, having performed this holy journey, is ever after exempted from all labour and service.

---

[622] The annual treasurer of the pilgrimage. Rycaut is correct in reporting that he is appointed by the Sultan.

[623] The cube-shaped building in Mecca said to have been placed in Mecca by Abraham; it is situated in the centre of the mosque and contains the black stone, which Muhammad said came from Paradise.

## Chapter XXIV. *Of the* Bayram *and ceremonies used at that time by the chief officers to the Grand Signior.*

The *Bayram*[624] is the feast of the Turks of which there are two in the year, one following the fast of Ramazan as our Easter doth the Lent, which is called the Great Bayram. The other is the Little Bayram, which happens about seventy days after the former, at which time the people for three days cease from their labour, present one the other, rejoice, and take greater liberty than at other times, which no question was invented by Muhammad for relaxation of the bodies and minds of his followers as well as in imitation of the Christian feasts.

The Bayram is then conceived to begin at the first appearance of the new moon after the Ramazan, which is sometime deferred a day's time if the weather prove cloudy that the moon is not visible. If longer the sky be obscured according to the course of nature, it is presumed that the moon is begun, and so their feast begins also, which is published at Constantinople by the discharge of the great guns at the point of the Seraglio upon the seashore, at which time the lights or lamps on the steeples of the mosques are extinguished or omitted to be lighted, and drums and trumpets are sounded in all public places of the city and courts of great persons, so that everyone betakes himself to mirth or pastime as his own inclination or convenience leads him.

But that which will be most curious to the observation of the judicious reader is the relation of the ceremonies used in the Seraglio at this feast by the several officers of state to the Grand Signior and to one another, which are so formal, precise and constant to the least motion of every member of the body as will clear the Turks from that opinuion which passes of them in the world of being rude, uncivil, and void of all ceremony or courtship in their comportment or behaviour, which, according to the best information I could procure is for the most part in this manner. The antiport leading to the lodgings of the Kapi Agasi (or chief eunuch who commands the pages) being adorned with rich carpets, cushions, and other furniture after their fashion, on the vigil or eve before the Bayram all the prime officers of state belonging to the Empire then at Constantinople assemble themselves at the Grand Signior's Seraglio three or four hours before day, where as soon as day breaks the Grand Signior, mounted on horseback, passes through the midst of them and goes to the mosque of Santa Sophia, where, having said his morning prayer, he returns again to the Seraglio.

Being returned, he enters the *haz-oda* or royal chamber, and, setting himself in his seat of state, having the Chief Eunuch of the Pages on his left hand, the sons of the Tatar Khan, which remain as hostages in the Turkish court, upon signs made to them are the first to present themselves before him to wish him a happy festival, whom, as I have heard reported, he walks three paces to meet,

---

[624] The Turkish word *bayram* denotes "holiday" or "festival," and does not necessarily carry religious overtones.

and they, prostrating themselves, say *"ayam-i şerif,"* which is "may these days be happy,"[625] and arising, kiss his hand, and so retire. The next who makes his address is the Prime Vizier, who, standing on the right hand of the Grand Signior in the front of all the beylerbeys, pashas and other great officers, compliments the Grand Signior upon one knee, and, nearer approaching, kisses his hand, and then arising, takes the station of the Kapi Agassi or chief eunuch of the pages. The next who follows in this ceremony is the Mufti, who on the left hand fronts the officers and principal heads of the law, as the Kaziaskers or Lords Chief Justices of Anatolia and Greece, the Nakib ül-Eşraf, principal Head or Primate of the Kindred of Muhammad, the mullahs, preachers called şeyhs,[626] and others. Then the Mufti, bowing his head to the ground, holding his hand on his girdle kisses him on the left shoulder, and the Grand Signior steps one pace forward to meet him, and so retires to his place. Then all the others in their several orders take their turns to pass this ceremony, who are treated according to what the Prime Vizier informs the Grand Signior, for some kiss his hand, others the hem of his vest, some his sleeve and others his breast, therafter as their quality and authority is, which is so full of variety and formal niceties that there is a book wrote expressly treating of all the particularities of this ceremony. The last of all who is called to perform his compliment is the Janissar Aga, or the General of the Janissaries.

This part being thus far passed, the Grand Signior enters into a more retired chamber of the Seraglio where the *Arz Ağalar* or the four principal pages of the court do their obeisance as before, then follow the eunuchs and other pages. In the meantime a dinner is provided in the chamber of the divan, where the officers of state, having complied with their obligation, take a plentiful repast at the Grand Signior's charge, after which the Grand Signior makes a present to each of the sixteen principal officers of sable vests, with which the ceremony concludes. Then is way made for the coaches of the Sultanas, who, having been cloistered in the Old Seraglio the whole year before, are glad at the Feast of Bayram to have occasion to make their visits to the Grand Signior, in the first place as being of his kindred and relations, and then to see the Queen or Queen Mother and to the other Sultanas and ladies, with whom they use variety of ceremony according to their condition and quality, and there have liberty to remain for the space of three days in banqueting and other divertissements of music and discourse.

It may well be observed from the premises how generally the world is mistaken in the opinion [that] is conceived of the courtship used amongst the Turks, commonly reputed by travellers to be rude, coming much short of that

---

[625] My thanks to Professor Virginia Aksan for transliterating and translating Rycaut's *eiamischerif.* Rycaut's translation is accurate enough.

[626] More familiar to readers in its Arabic form *sheikh,* the word means "elder," and is used as an honorific title.

quaintness,[627] bowings, cringings and reverent postures used in Christendom. It is true the Turk's deportment, even in the most vile and mechanic vulgar,[628] though never so mean, is carried with a strange kind of barbarity and rudeness towards the best of Christians in those parts, which proceeds rather from a sort of pride and detestation taught them by their religion than from any want of being instructed in their duty of due reverence to their superiors. For in their carriage one towards the other they observe the rules and niceties of compliment with as much variety and exactness as is exercised in Rome or the most civilised courts of Christendom, and amongst their chief ministers there is much preciseness and caution used not to exceed the limits of that ceremony which inferiors owe their superiors, lest they should disparage their own quality ot give occasion to the world to believe their disorderly submission to be a part of adulation. And therefore it is worthy the study of Christian ministers employed in embassies in the Ottoman court to be well-informed in the rules and manner of their carriage in the presence of the chief ministers of state, for uncovering the head, as in Christendom, is amongst them esteemed ridiculous and affrontive, and the manner of little bowings and often inclinations of the body taken as acknolwdegments of the great difference there is between the masters they represent. And therefore a little ceremony at the entrance and the like at departure, with a steady and constant behaviour at the time of the treaty or discourse is the best rule for a Christian minister, which is interpreted amongst Turks as the effect of gravity and estimation of themselves, it being certain that the contrary hath caused many Christian ministers to fall lower in the estimation of the Turks than they had deserved for their wisdom and dexterity in the management of the mores substantial points of affairs.

---

[627] Oddness, with the overtone of being rather charming.
[628] The lowest and commonest of the manual labouring classes.

**Chapter XXV.** *Of the prohibition of swine's flesh and wine.*

The five foregoing principles already treated of are, as we have said before, the essential points required towards the constitution of a true Muhammadan. Other matters are proofs and trials of their obedience, amongst which none is more enjoined than the prohibition of swine's flesh and wine, which are called *haram*, things abominable and forbidden. The first is in reality abhorred by them and as displeasing as the flesh of a man to civilised people or a dog's thigh to such as have been used to delicacies and wholesome viands. But wine, of late years, though forbidden by the law,[629] hath gained a better reputation, and though accursed by them, is yet accounted of so strong a temptation that the sin is the more excusable, and though the Qur'an positively inhibits the use thereof and the expositors of the law have so far removed it from all possibility of becoming lawful that they have determined that if wine be spilt upon the ground and in that place grass grows and with that pasture a sheep or an ox is nourished, those cattle become *haram*, and are as abominable as the flesh of swine.

But notwithstanding the severe prohibition hereof by their religion, wine is so commonly used that it is publicly drunk without cautions or fear of giving scandal; the great men, because in office, are more careful how the world discovers what delight they take in that liquor lest the miscarriages of their office should be attributed to the excess of wine or their knowledge of the use of that which deprives them of their reason render them incapable of their truth and dignity. For the Turks account it impossible to drink wine with moderation,[630] and are ignorant of the benefit of it for concoction of crude humours and indigestions of the stomach, and wonder to see it by English, French, and Italians tempered with water, for unless they may drink it with full bowls and have sufficient thereof to give them their *kaif*[631](as they call it) thereof, that is, to transport them into a dissolute mirth or the ridiculous actions of drunkenness or to a surfeit or a

---

[629] See, for example, "They will ask thee concerning wine and games of chance. Say: In both is great sin, and advantage also, to men; but their sin is greater than their advantage" (Sura 2:216), or "O believers! Surely wine and games of chance, and statues, and the divining arrows, are an abomination of Satan's work? Avoid them,that ye may prosper" (Sura 5:92). Originally, Muslims were simply forbidden from attending the mosque whilst intoxicated (Sura 4), but as new verses were revealed the prohibition became stronger. The story of precisely why Muhammad forbade his followers to drink wine is related in full by Busbecq (*Turkish Letters*, 104–5), and paraphrased below in Rycaut's account..

[630] Sandys reported in 1610 that whilst wine is "prohibited them by their *Alchoran*," nevertheless "they will quaff freely when they come to the house of a Christian: insomuch as I have seen but few go away unled from the Embassadours houses" (*Travels*, 51).

[631] Also rendered as *kif* or *kayf*, this word denotes, as Rycaut implies, a kind of euphoria, and may also refer to a compound derived from cannabis which may be smoked to achieve that euphoria .

vomit, they esteem it not worth the drinking, and a provocation to the appetite and palate to remain with a desire of demanding more.[632]

But such as would appear religious amongst them and are superstitious, morose and haters of Christians abstain wholly from wine and are of a stoical pride, melancholy temper and censorious of the whole world. These men, who drink only water and coffee, enter into discourses of state matters, censure the actions and pass characters on the grandees and great officers, *"Adsumpta Stoicorum adrogantia, sectaque, quae turbidos et negotiorum adpententes faciat [nec ultra mora]."*[633] And this was the reason why the Great Vizier Köprülü put down the coffee-houses in Constantinople and yet privileged the taverns, because the first were melancholy places where seditions were vented, where reflections were made on all occurrences of state and discontents published and aggravated. But wine raised the spirits of men to a gay humour and would never operate those effects to endanger his condition as the counsels which were contrived in the assemblies of those who addicted themselves to a more melancholy liquor.

The drinking wine in young men is esteemed amongst the extravagancies of youth, but in old men is a crime more indecent and scandalous in a higher degree. But why Muhammad should so severely forbid the use of wine to his disciples is recounted in a fable on this occasion, that their Prophet, being once invited by a friend to an entertainment at his house, chanced in his way thither to be detained at a nuptial feast where the guests, raised with the cheerful spirits of the wine, were merry, embracing, and in a kind temper each towards other. Which pleasing humour Muhammad, attributing to the effect of the wine, blessed it as a sacred thing and so departed. But it happened that in the evening returning again and expecting to see the love and caresses he had before blessed, he found the house to the contrary, full of brawls and noise, fightings, and all confusion, which he also having understood to be another effect of the wine, changed his former blessing into a curse and for ever after made it *haram*, or an abomination to his disciples.

---

[632] However, George Sandys observed that "They prefer our beer above all other drinks" (*Travels*, 51).

[633] "Takes on the assumptions of the Stoics along with a philosophy that makes people restless and eager for a busy life" (Tacitus, *Annals* 14.57). Rycaut does not cite the quotation in full.

**Chapter XXVI.** *Of their morality, good works and some certain of their laws worthy of observation.*

Though according to the preceding discourse the character that may thence result from the nature and temperance of the Turks doth not promise any long treatise concerning their deep morality, virtues and elevated graces, yet in the minds of all mankind, though never so barbarous, God having wrought the law of nature and made that impression of doing right to our neighbour, which tends towards conversion of the world, we may well expect to find the same principles in the Turks, especially their victories and spoils abroad. Having procured them conversation with other nations and their wars and treaties with Christians having refined their minds in a good part of that rude temper they brought with them out of Scythia, it will not be strange for us to find amongst them men whom education hath made civil, polished in all points of virtuous deportment and made heroes of their age, though I must confess I cannot applaud the generality of this people with so high encomiums as I have read in the books of some ingenious travellers, and do believe without partiality that they come short of the good nature and virtues [that] are to be found in most parts of Christendom. However, wherein they conceive a great part of charity is placed and meritorious works, it will not be unworthy nor unpleasant to consider.

And in the first place, they esteem it a good work to build houses, though from thence they obtain a rent, because it is a habitation for those who have no lands or estates to have them of their own. But especially such as are princes and great men who build *hans* or inns which are receptacles for traders at night are ranked in the first order of sacred benefactors and are blessed and prayed for by the weary guests who have found repose and refreshment through their munificence. And in these buildings the Turks are extraordinary magnificent in most parts of the Empire, having united to many of them a stately mosque, baths and shops for artisans and tradesmen to supply all the necessities of the travellers, and some of them are so endowed that every night the guests are entertained at free cost with a convenient supper, be their numbers more or less according as the *han* is capable to receive.

The form of these buildings is for the most part according to the model of the highest and stateliest of our halls, covered with lead though not altogether so high-roofed. Yet some I have observed for their breadth and length very magnificent, yet by reason they have been somewhat lower, have only in that come short of the pride of the stateliest fabrics. Though in few of them are apartments for different companies, yet everyone is sufficiently retired, having at a convenient distance different chimneys for all parties of guests to dress their meat and in the winter for their fire. The greatest inconvenience to men of watchful spirits and used to quiet retirements is the want of sleep, which until I have been overtired with labour and accustomed thereto by divers days journeys, hath been always a stranger to my eyes, by reason of the molestation of various companies, some of which are always awake, some mending their carts, others dressing meat, others upon their departure that in public places never want noise to disturb those who sleep but of one ear. These stately *hans* or inns, which with the mosques are the only durable and magnificent buildings of the Empire, are the edifices of certain great men, who, fearing to be deprived of their riches by a hasty death should they endeavour to continue them to their family, choose to perpetuate their names and secure their conditions by these public works.

Those who would appear of a compassionate and tender nature hold it a pious work to buy a bird from a cage to give him his liberty and hold it a merciful action to buy bread and feed the dogs, of which there are a great number of diseased curs[634] in all streets appropriate to no master, but are mangy and foul and no small causes of breeding the plague so frequent in all the cities of the Turks.[635] And this care of dogs is accounted so charitable that there are certain laws made for the protection and maintenance of them, and it is a lighter offence to deny bread to a poor Christian who is famished in his chains than to the dogs of their street, which are fit for nothing but to breed infection. And some bind themselves by a vow to give such a quantity of bread a day to the dogs of such a street; others bequeath it by testament, for they maintain their quarters from other wandering curs and join together in a strange manner to preserve certain limits free from others that are not whelped and bred amongst them.

The camel is another sort of beast to which the Turks bear not only a love but a religious reverence, accounting it a greater sin to overburden and tire them with too much labour than the horse, because it is the beast most common to the holy parts of Arabia and carries the Qur'an in the pilgrimage, so that I have observed those who have the government of the camels, when they have given water to them in a basin, to take off the foam or froth that comes from the mouth of the beast, and with that, as if it were some rare balsam, with a singular devotion to anoint their beards, and thereat with a religious sigh groan out "*Hajji baba, hajji baba*," which is as much as "O father pilgrim, O father pilgrim!"

And thus, having run through the most observable points of the Turkish religion, it will be now time to take a view of their host and militia, being that by which their Empire is more supported than either by their policy or civil government or profession in religion.

---

[634] Mongrels; it is also used to denote any aggressive (stray) dog.

[635] By the sixteenth century, local judges had been made responsible for enforcing sanitary regulations in Ottoman cities and there were many available treatises on the plague. For further details, see J. P. Byrne, *Encyclopedia of Pestilence, Pandemics and Plagues* (Westport, CT: Greenwood Publishing Co., 2008), 576–77.

# THE
# THIRD BOOK
## Wherein is treated of the
# TURKISH MILITIA

**Chapter I.** *Of the present state of the military discipline in general amongst the Turks.*

Whoever is acquainted with the state of the Turkish Empire and hath duly considered the premises of this foregoing treatise will easily judge that the main sinews of the Ottoman kingdom consists in the force of the Sipahis, Janissaries and the other auxiliaries, and that this government, being wholly founded on martial discipline and the law of arms, is most obliged to the constitutions and supported on the props related in this following discourse. For this people, having neither entered into the possession of this Empire as into an uninhabited and desert land as colonies of other nations have done into countries new-found or discovered, nor got admittance precariously from the Grecian princes for the benefit of their neighbourhood and commerce, but have opened their way to possession and government by mere force and power of the sword, whereby their constitutions, laws, customs and manners of living are wholly agreeable to the warlike discipline of a camp and to the quickness and ready execution of martial law. And if it be true in morality as it is in nature that things are conserved by the same cause by which they are produced, it will necessarily follow that this Ottoman Empire, which was begot by arms and had Mars its only father, will never be nourished by softness and the arts and blandishments of peace.

But he that takes a view of the Ottoman armies as described in various histories, renowned for their chivalry and discipline in the times of Sultan Selim [I] or Süleyman the Magnificent, and designs thence to extract a draught or copy for his present speculation, will find himself much at a loss in framing true conjectures of the puissance of the Turks or the rules of their government by comparison of former times with this present age. For the ancient sublimity and comely majesty in the Empire is much abated, the forces by land decayed, and the maritime power by ill success and slothful seamen reduced to an inconsiderable condition. The countries are dispeopled and the royal revenue abated; nothing remains of those plenteous stores and provisions of war nor that regiment and discipline continued in peace, none of that ancient observation of their laws and religion nor that love and respect to the militia, which is now become degenerate, soft and effeminate, nor is the Ottoman court so prone to remunerate the services and exalt the interest of the cavalry or maintain the reputation of the Janissaries. In brief, there are no relics of ancient justice or generosity of discreet government or obedience to it, nor yet of confidence, friendship, or generous fidelity.

But though this Empire hath many of these distempers and begins to grow factious and yet slothful, and yet desirous to avoid the occasions of war, as all governments have been which in their youth and first beginnings were eager, active and provoked through poverty, in their riper years grown rich and luxurious with plenty have declined afterwards as from the meridian of their greatness and power. Yet the Turks maintain still the extent of their dominions, and if they have lost ground in one place like the sea, they have recovered it in another. If in Asia the Persians have taken from them Yerevan, Sirvan, Tabriz, Lorestan, and Ghenge, [636] it is but a recovery of their own dominions. If they are dispossessed in Ethiopia of Aden [637] and other parts of Arabia Felix, [638] they have recompensed themselves in Europe by their footing in Candia [639] and in Hungary by the late conquest of Neuhausel and Novigrad, [640] and in Transylvania by the additions of Janova and Varaždin. [641] But this Empire, as vast and large as it is, is yet dispeopled, the villages abandoned and whole provinces as pleasant and fruitful as Tempe or Thessaly [642] uncultivated and turned into a desert or wilderness, all which desolation and ruin proceeds from the tyranny and rapine of the

---

[636] Yerevan is a province and city in Armenia (now the capital), one of the oldest inhabited places in the world; Sirvan in the eastern Caucasus region is now in modern Azerbaijan; Tabriz is a city in Iran which was captured from the White Sheep Turkmen by Shah Ismail I in 1501 and made the capital of the new Safavid dynasty; Lorestan is in western Iran near the Zagros mountains; Ghenge is in Azerbaijan.

[637] Aden was under Ottoman rule from 1538 to 1645, with a brief interlude in 1547–1548. It was finally taken by the Sultan of Lahej, who was nominally the vassal of the Zaidi imams of Yemen.

[638] The southern part of the Arabian peninsula, comprising modern-day Yemen, literally Happy Arabia, so-called because it is greener and therefore more fertile than the other parts of the peninsula, which are called Arabia Deserta (the interior) and Stony Arabia (Arabia Petraea, now Jordan and parts of Syria), named after a mistranslation of Petraea, referring to the city of Petra, as a Latinised version of the Greek πέτρος, "stony."

[639] Candia is the Italicised version of Χάνδαξ, an old name for both Crete and its capital, Heraklion. The Turks called it *Kandiye*. During the Cretan War (1645–1669), the city was besieged for twenty-two years by Ottoman forces, until Fazil Ahmed Köprülü finally took it in 1669.

[640] See Book 2, Chapter 7, n. 12.

[641] Janova (Hungarian name Jánosgyarmat) is now in central Slovakia; Varaždin is north of Zagreb in modern-day Croatia.

[642] The Vale of Tempe in Thessaly was believed by the Greeks to be the home of Apollo and the Muses.

beylerbeys, who either in their journeys to the possession of their government or return from thence expose the poor inhabitants to violence and injury of their attendants as if they had entered the confines of an enemy or the dominions of a conquered people.

In like manner the insolence of the horse and foot is unsupportable, for in their marches from one country to another parties of 20 or 30 are permitted to make excursions into divers parts of their own dominions, where they not only live upon free quarter but extort money and clothes from the poor vassals, taking their children to sell for slaves, especially the Bulgarians and Serbians and the people of Bosnia and Albania, which, being ignorant of the Turkish tongue, are sold for Russians, Hungarians, or Muscovites, so that rather than be exposed to such misery and license of the soldiery, the poor people choose to abandon their dwellings and seek for refuge in the mountains and woods of the country. In fine, though generally the military offices are in the same form and the soldiery disposed according to the ancient rule and canon, yet licentiousness and negligence have so prevailed in the officers as to introduce that corruption which renders them wholly altered and estranged from their first discipline. For the commanders, upon every slight occasion, are contented to make *otoraks* or stipendiaries,[643] such as enjoy the pay and privileges of a soldier and yet are excused from the wars, which they may easily purchase with a small sum of money for a scratch or a flesh-wound gained in the wars, wholly against the original institution, which designed that benefit only for maimed and disabled soldiers. So now there is so great a number of soldiery lusty and healthy under the title of dead men's pay as disfurnishes the Grand Signior's treasury and weakens his forces.

The Janissaries also, marrying freely and yet dispensed with as to the absence from their duty and chambers, apply themselves to trades and other studies besides the war, by which means, having children and dependencies, they are forced by other arts than their few aspers of daily pay to seek the provision and maintenance of a family, and, their minds growing estranged from the war, are solicitous with the care and anxiety for a wife and children, and in my time have so abhorred the thoughts of war both in Candia and Hungary that many have offered great presents to be excused. And so general hath been the dislike of all kinds of martial action for the reasons before-mentioned that at first the very rumours and discourse of war and afterwards the reality thereof caused so general a discontent as had, if not prudently prevented and timely suppressed, burst into a mutiny of the militia, whose mere inquiry but into the reasons and grounds of the war is little different from a sedition. Another corruption hath the covetousness of the officers produced, for small presents and donatives, in owning many under

---

[643] Someone receiving a stipend, but also "hireling" in a pejorative sense, as here.

the title and name of Spahis and Janissaries which have no place in the rolls or registry of the soldiery, by which means many offenders and outlawed persons are defended by the military privileges, and the ancient honour due to arms is prostituted for the maintenance and protection of the rascalities and scum of the world.

And this shall serve to have spoken in general of the present state of the Turkish soldiery. We shall now proceed to the particulars of the force and numbers of the Turkish militia and from whence and how they are raised.

## Chapter II. *Of the Turkish militia.*

In the twelfth chapter of the first book we made an estimate of the revenue and riches of all the beylerbeys and pashas of the Empire, by which might be collected the number of soldiers which these great men are able out of their own families to furnish unto the wars. It will now be time to make a just computation, in its due place, of the forces in particular, the numbers, the countries from whence they are raised, the several military orders and the true puissance of the Ottoman Empire, which is indeed so incredibly great and numerous that with good reason they have formed it into a proverb, "That no grass grows where the Turkish horse hath once set his foot." This speculation is absolutely necessary to a true description of the regiment of a country, for the martial constitutions are the best part of political science, and civil laws have no rigour unless they receive their authority by the enforcement of the sword. This consideration is also necessary to the art of a statesman, that he ill-studies the geography of his enemies' provinces who knows not the utmost strength it contains by land and sea, and is ill-prepared to gain a perfect knowledge of the prudent arts wherewith a nation or people is conserved in peace, who is ignorant of their force and constitutions appropriated to the time of war. Wherefore we shall discourse as succinctly of this subject as the matter will permit, and with the same certainty that one of the principal muster-masters of the Turkish rolls,[644] long-practiced and accurate in his office, hath deciphered, from whose report itself I profess to derive my authority in this following relation.

The whole Turkish militia then is of two sorts, one that receives maintenance from certain lands or farms bestowed on them by the Grand Signior, others that receive their constant pay in ready money. The great nerve or sinew of the Turkish Empire is that of the first rank, which are of two sorts, *viz. zaims,*[645] which are like barons in some countries, and *timariots,* who may be compared to the *decumani* amongst the Romans.[646] Those of the second sort, paid out of the Grand Signior's treasury, are Sipahis, Janissaries, armourers (*cebeçi*), gunners (*topçi*) and sea-soldiers called *levents,*[647] who have no pay for life or are enrolled

---

[644] A muster-master is responsible for checking the number of soldiers in the army and managing equipment. Rolls are documents that may be rolled up in scroll form, making it easier to file them; also as in "roll call" for the military. In England, the Master of the Rolls was responsible for keeping the records of the Court of Chancery.

[645] People who command mounted soldiers or militia, often recruited by themselves, hence the comparison with European barons.

[646] For *timariots,* see Book 1, Chapter 2, n. 5. *Decumani* refers to Roman farmers whose land paid the provincial tax of one-tenth.

[647] According to David Nicolle, "The revived *Levent* forces of the late sixteenth century were Muslims armed with muskets, swords and, later, pistols. They were supposedly

amongst the military orders, but only make an agreement for five or six thousand aspers for their voyage, which, being ended, they are disbanded.

### Of the *zaims* and *timariots*.

The nature of these two and their institution is the same; the only difference is in their commissions or patents, or rather we may call them the conveyances or evidences for their lands, which they have from the Grand Signior. For the rent of a *zaim* is from 20,000 aspers to 99,999 and no further, for, adding one asper more, it becomes the estate of a *sanjak bey* called a pasha, which is from 100,000 aspers to 199,999, for, adding one asper more, it becomes the revenue of a beylerbey.

The *timariots* are of two sorts, one called *tezkereliv*,[648] who have their evidences for their land from the Grand Signior's court, whose rent is from 5 or 6000 aspers to 19,999, for then with the addition of one asper they enter the number of *zaims*. The other sort is called *tezkeretis*, who hath his patent or writing from the beylerbey of the country, whose rent is from 3000 to 6000 aspers.

The *zaims,* in all expeditions of war, are obliged to serve with their tents, which are to be furnished with kitchens, stables, and other necessary apartments agreeable to their state and quality, and for every 500 aspers of rent received from the Grand Signior they are to bring a horseman into the field which is called *gebelu,* as, for example, one of thirty thousand aspers is to come attended with six, one of ninety thousand with 18 horsemen, and so proportionately. Every *zaim* is entitled *kilic ustaçi* or sword-man, so that when the Turks calculate the strength or numbers that a beylerbey is able to bring into the field for the service of his prince, they make a computation upon so many *zaims* and *timariots* themselves, which they call so many swords, not numbering the people with which they come accompanied.

The *timariots* are expected to serve with lesser tents and to be provided with 3 or 4 baskets for every man that attends them, for their office is, besides fighting, as also of the *zaims* and Sipahis, to carry earth and stones for making batteries and trenches whilst the Janissaries are in skirmish with the enemy. And for every three thousand aspers rent the *timariots* are assessed at a man and a horse as the *zaim* is for every five thousand; both one and the other of these soldiers little differ from those in England which hold their lands in *capite*[649] or the ancient tenure of knights' service.

---

recruited from bandits in Anatolia and seem to have had no connection with earlier *Levent* marines of the fourteenth century" (*Janissaries*, 50).

[648] From *tezkere*, meaning "licence."

[649] Alternative form of *per capita*, "by the head."

Both *zaims* and *timariots* are disposed into regiments under command of
colonels called *alai beys*, who march with colours and the kettle-drum, in Turkish *timbalem*. These colonels are again under the command of the pasha or *sanjak
bey* and he under the beylerbey, which forces being united into one body repair
to the rendezvous appointed by the general (in Turkish *seraskier*), who is either
the Grand Signior in person or the Azem Vizier or some other eminent person
qualified with the title of vizier. The two orders of soldiery are not only appropriated to land service, but some also are destined to the sea, who are called *derya
keleminde* and are under the command of the Captain-Pasha or Admiral. The
*zaims* are most commonly dispensed with as to the sea-service in their own persons upon payment of so much money as they are esteemed at in the Signior's
book, out of which *levents* are raised, and are enrolled in the registers of the arsenal, but the *timariots* can never be excused from their personal duty and service
with their ascendance of soldiery according to the value of their lands. Neither
one nor the other of these can be dispensed with from their service at land; no
excuse in time of the Grand Signior's wars is lawful or pleadable. If sick, they
are carried in horse-litters or beds; if infants, in hampers or baskets and in the
very cradles accustomed to the hardship, hazard, and discipline of war. And thus
much shall serve in brief to have spoken in explication of the nature of the *zaims*
and *timariots*, which come under the general denomination of Sipahis and compose the best part of the Turkish armies, We shall now proceed to declare, as far
as can probably be computed, the number of these horse which fill up the vast
host that hath overspread so large a proportion of the world.

## Chapter III. *A computation of the numbers of the forces arising from the* zaims *and* timariots.

It were a work of too great labour, considering the little satisfaction and
delight it would afford the reader, to proceed accurately in describing the just
numbers of those which follow these *zaims* and *timariots*. It will be sufficient
to denote that the smallest number of a *zaim* is four men, as is the greatest of
a *timariot*, whose lowest condition is obliged to maintain a single man, and the
highest of a *zaim* to serve with nineteen, so that whosoever will survey this Turkish host must make his calculate a little more or less by conjecture and judgment.
And this difficulty is the more augmented when I consider the fraud [that] is used
by the accountants, registers, and muster-masters of the Grand Signior's enrol-
ments, who are as well-acquainted with the arts and sweetness of making false
musters as they are in the most ingenious places of Christendom. And perhaps
policy may afford a connivance to this fraud for the sake of a superlative face of
their armies, which they love to express by this usual similitude, "*Asker reml derya
missal*, as innumerable as the sands of the seashore," but in effect the noise is

greater than the reality, and he that will sum up their number may find arithmetic to make the account, which by the vast extent of tents, confusion of baggage, train of servants and attendants of the camp appears infinite in the popular estimation. Besides, the Turkish army admits of great increase and decrease by many interlopers, as we may call them, which the *zaims* for their own honour introduce to fill up their numbers on a day of muster or appearance, so that one would admire to see in so short time so apparent a decay in the Turkish camp, which abuse the great and famous vizier Mehmed Köprülü with cruelty and extraordinary severity endeavoured to remedy upon his expedition for recovery of Tenedos and Lemnos and conquest of Janova in Transylvania.[650] But it is impossible for one man to know and see and remedy all disorders, and is amongst the Turks called *hain ayun*, "a secret fraud,"[651] as difficult to be totally remedied as it is to be thoroughly discovered.

But that which makes the principal difference and various change herein is the death of *zaims* and *timariots*, some of which, holding an estate only for life, and others dying without heirs of their bodies, their lands revert to the Crown, which estates, being improved by the industry of the possessors above the primary valuation in the records and afterwards falling into the hands of the Prince, are bestowed again on others according to their true estimate, which is oftentimes double of the former. By which means the Grand Signior's soldiery is increased, and it is a point very observable that as other princes lose by the fall and death of their subjects, the Grand Signior is the only gainer, for of the most that are slain on the day of battle, the estates accrue to him, in disposal again of which he observes this rule, to gratify many with that which was before the property of a single person.

But to come now to the express and distinct account of the *ziamets* and *timariots* in every part and government of the Empire, this computation is extracted out of the imperial rolls and registers of the Grand Signior:

## Table

There was further, in past times, allotted to the attendance of this army about 6900 men for mending the ways, bringing provisions and service of the

---

[650] The Greek island of Tenedos was first occupied by the Turks in 1455 when it was uninhabited, but disputed over the next one hundred years by the Venetians. After the battle of the Dardanelles in 1657, the Venetian blockade of the area was broken by Mehmed Köprülü and Tenedos was finally recaptured by the Ottomans. Lemnos was also hotly contested; in 1453, after the capture of Constantinople, it became an Ottoman fief, but the Venetians captured it in 1476, after which it was returned to Turkish control three years later under the Treaty of Constantinople. The Venetians were back in 1656, but Köprülü recaptured the island in 1657. For Janova in Croatia, see Book 3, chapter 1, n. 6.

[651] Literally "wicked trick." My thanks to Dr. Viriginia Aksan of McMaster University for locating the modern Turkish phrase and translating it.

artillery; there was also an allowance for 1280 sutlers[652] or victuallers of the camp and for 128 trumpeters and drummers, which were gypsies. But this was when Anatolia was a frontier country to the Christians, and was therefore better-fortified and accommodated, but since it has become one of the innermost parts of the Empire that rent is converted into the possession of *zaims* and *timariots*, so that there is a farther addition of 330 *ziamets* and 1136 *timariots*.

## Table

In the government of Diyarbakir[653] are reckoned 12 *sanjaks* besides those of Kurdistan[654] and Gurdia,[655] which are computed to make 1800 men, but I find only 9 denoted for the *ziamets* and *timariots*,

## Tables

Besides this militia in Romania, there is another sort called *Jureghian* or *Yörük-ler*, who have their estates in fee from father to son, of which there are accounted about 1294 families. There is also another sort in the province of Dobruja,[656] called *oçaks*,[657] of which there are about 4000 houses; of the same kind in the province of Kirkkilissa are 200 houses, in Chirnomen[658] 351 of çingani, which are the same amongst us as the race of gypsies, in Vize 170, so that the whole sum of *oçaks* may arrive to the number of 4721, or at the most to 5000. These are obliged every year to draw out of every thirty-five persons called *eshkingi* or volunteers, who are to join themselves with the Tatars for making excursions into Rus-

---

[652] Sutlers were usually civilians or merchants who sold supplies to the army from waggons.

[653] A large and important city in southeastern Turkey on the banks of the Tigris.

[654] Kurdistan was an area in the *vilayet* of Diyarbakir which was divided between the Ottomans and Persians from 1514 onwards; the Turkish part extended from Palu on the Euphrates river to Mardin on the plains of Mesopotamia.

[655] Rycaut may mean Gungüs or Çungüš, which was a Kurdish *sanjak* dating from 1520. It is now situated in Diyabakir province.

[656] Dobruja (Turkish *Dobruca*) is located in modern-day Bulgaria and Romania between the Danube and the Black Sea. It was captured from Wallachia in 1420 and designated a border province or *udi*, after which it became a full-fledged *eyalet* of the Ottoman Empire.

[657] The *oçaks* were units of about 30 soldiers, "five of whom served in rotation while the others supported them financially" (Nicolle, *Janissaries,* 45).

[658] Kirkkilissa, now the city and province of Kirklareli, Turkey, was captured by Murad I in 1363 from the Byzantines, who in turn had taken it from the Bulgarians in 1003. Chirnomen, in southern Serbia, was the site of a catastrophic defeat of the Serbs by the Ottomans in 1371. Vize is in the *sanjak* of Rumelia in the Balkans. It came under Ottoman occupation in 1467/68. Now a small town in Kirklareli province, Vize, under the name Bizye, was the capital city of the ancient Thracian kingdom.

sia, Poland, or other parts, and so yearly they interchangeably take their course. The other 25 remaining are called *jamak*,[659] and are not obliged personally to serve when the Grand Signior's wars call them to employment, but then for every 5000 aspers rent they possess of the Grand Signior's lands they are assessed at one man, who is obliged to serve out of those whose turn it was that year to have accompanied the Tatars in their robberies. The principal office of these is to attend the artillery, baggage and provisions, to mend the ways and bridges for passage of the army; to the like service are obliged certain families of Bulgarians, for carriage of hay and cutting grass, according to the season of the year.

The number of the *zaims* and *timariots* in the governments of the beylerbeys of Buda, Temeşvar,[660] and Bosnia I find not particularly described in Ottoman books, but however, according to the best information, that militia on the confines of the Empire called *serhadly* amount to the number of about 70,000 fighting men paid out of the rents of the *sanjaks* of that country. But though the militia of Buda be not set down in the registers of more ancient date at Constantinople because it is, as it were, a principality independent both for its eminency, revenue and large extent of dominions. Yet in that city itself is strict order observed and the rolls of their force most exactly known and computed, to which the Turks have a strict eye, it being a frontier garrison of much importance and the key of Hungary, the militia of which, as I learned from officers of note during my residence in that place, was according to this precise account:

| | |
|---|---|
| Janissaries | 12000 |
| Sipahis | 1500 |
| *Zaims* and *Timariots* | 2200 |
| *Azaps*, which are the meanest sort of soldiery[661] | 1800 |
| Belonging to the castle of Buda | 1200 |
| *Cebeçis* or armourers[662] | 1900 |

[659] A *jamak* was (more accurately) the servant of a Janissary. The *muteferika* looked after the baggage and the *yayas* mended roads and maintained bridges.

[660] A province comprising parts of modern-day Romania, Serbia, and Hungary; its principal city is now known as Timisoara (Romania).

[661] Originally they were Anatolian volunteers who often fought as archers, "by the sixteenth century they had declined to mere ammunition carriers, pioneers and sappers, and had been absorbed into the Janissaries *Cebeci* as porters. Then, however, the *azaps* enjoyed a new lease of life. From the late sixteenth century all Muslim men in frontier regions were liable to be enlisted as *azaps*, armed with matchlocks and sabres, one man from each 20 or 30 households being supported by the rest" (Nicolle, *Janissaries*, 46). The word *azap* means "bachelor."

[662] These men "made, repaired and issued weapons and also formed a fully-organised unit" (Nicolle, *Janissaries*, 31).

| | |
|---|---|
| The guard at the gate called *küçük kapi*[663] | 500 |
| *Topçis* or gunners | 500 |
| *Martalos*, a sort of foot-soldiers[664] | 300 |
| Soldiers belonging to the powder-house | 280 |
| The soldiery who are servants to the Pasha | 3000 |

In all 22180, to which, adding the militia of Bosnia and other parts of Slavonia and all along the frontier countries which extend for above 800 English miles, the number may amount to no less than 70,000 fighting men. But we here discourse only of the number of *zaims* and *timariots*, which whole sum amounts to of *zaims* 10,948 and of *timariots* 72,436, which makes in all 83,380, but this is calculated at the lowest rate. They may very well be reckoned to be one-third more, besides other militias of Cairo or other orders of soldiery to be treated of in the following chapters.

These partitions or divisions were first made by Süleyman the Magnificent as the best rule and method for an orderly disposition of his militia and as the strongest nerve of the Ottoman force. But, as with time in the most exact compositions of discipline corruptions through covetousness and ambition of officers are introduced, so also in the just disposal of these rents according to the ancient institutions, for the beylerbeys, pashas, treasurers, and other officers, instead of following this maintenance to their soldiers, reserve it to prefer and gratify their servants and pages, obliging them in recompense thereof under various services. Some, that live at Constantinople or near the sea, defray the charges of all boats and vessels which carry their household provisions. Others, that live in the inland countries, agreeing with the treasurer of the soldiery without regard to the true heirs or any other consideration, set to sale these rents to them who proffer most, so that in time of harvest the pasha sends abroad his officers to gather his profits from the poor *timariots* with that oppression and violence as causes disturbances, differences and lawsuits amongst them, which, being to be decided by judges partly interested in the quarrel, the sentence is certainly determined on their side who have most power and money.

The aforegoing account of *zaims* and *timariots* is the most reasonable one can be given, and because we have reckoned them at the lowest rate, making some allowance to the 83,380, this militia may amount to an hundred thousand men, which, as I have heard, is the utmost number of this sort of soldiery.

---

[663] Literally, "the small gate."

[664] These were Greeks, "originally Byzantine irregulars," who were eventually "recognised as. . .'proper soldiers' and paid. . .to control *Klepht* Greek mountain bandits" (Nicolle, *Janissaries*, 48).

**Chapter IV.** *Of certain customs and laws observed amongst the* ziamets *and* timariots.

Amongst these forces of *ziamets* and *timariots* are in times of war and action mixed certain volunteers or adventurers called by the Turks *gönüllyan*,[665] who maintain themselves upon their own expense in hopes by some signal actions of valour to obtain the succession into a *zaim's* or *timariot's* lands as places are made void by the slaughter of war. These men are often very hardy and ready to attempt the most desperate exploits, moved by a desire of the reward and by the persuasion that at worst, dying in a war against Christians, they become martyrs for the Muhammadan faith. It is reported that in one day, upon the assults given to Új-Zrínyívar or the new fort of Count Zrínyí,[666] one *timariot's* farm was bestowed eight times; one being slain, it was conferred on another, and so on a third, and so the rest, all of which had the misfortune to fall until it rested on the eighth, the others dying only with the title of *timariots*.

The *zaims* or *timariots* being aged or impotent have in their lifetime power to resign up the right of their estates to their sons or other relations. It is not lawful for a peasant or clown[667] to mount his horse or gird his sword like a Sipahi until first he hath had part of his education in the service or family of some pasha or person of quality unless it be on the confines of the empire, where, having given evident testimonies of his courage, he may then become competitor for the vacant farms of a *zaim* or *timariot*.

It is the custom of Romania that a *zaim* or *timariot* dying in the wars, his *zaim's* rents are divided into as many *timariot* farms as he hath sons, but if a *timariot* hath no more than 3000 aspers rent, it descends entirely to his eldest son, but if it be more, it is proportionately divided amongst the rest of his children. But if they die of a natural death at their own homes, the lands fall to the

---

[665] These were "soldiers formally assigned to the local garrison" (C. L. Wilkins, *Forging Urban Solidarities: Ottoman Aleppo 1640–1700* [Leiden: Brill, 2010], 73).

[666] Count Miklós Zrínyí (1620–1664) was a Hungarian general, poet, and statesman who fought continually against the Turks in 1652–1653 and on and off through the early 1660s. The "new fort" mentioned by Rycaut (and which he calls *Sorinswar*) was built at the count's own expense in 1661; in 1664 he was ordered to lead an invasion across the Drava river in south central Europe, where he had built the fort. His forces were defeated by the Ottoman army after some initial success, and they retreated to the new fort, which was blown up some time later by the Turks. Shortly afterwards the Ottomans were defeated at St. Gothard, as Rycaut has already mentioned. Count Zrínyí was killed in a hunting accident. For details, see O. C., *The Conduct and Character of Count Nicholas Serini, Poet, Protestant Generalissimo of the Auxiliaries in Hungary* (London, 1664), which is probably Rycaut's source.

[667] A low-class rustic.

disposal of the beylerbey of the country either to confer them on the heirs of the deceased or any of his servants or sell them at the best advantage. But in Anatolia there are many *zaims* and *timariots* whose estates are hereditary to them and their heirs, and are not obliged to serve in person in the war but only to send their *gebelus* or number of servants according to the value of their estates, of which duty if they fail in the time of war, the year's rent is confiscated to the Exchequer and this estate descends to the next of kin, whether derived from the male or female line.

## Chapter V. *The state of the militia in Grand Cairo and Egypt.*

The guard and protection of the Kingdom of Egypt is committed to the charge of twelve beys, some of which are of the ancient race of the Mamluks, confirmed by Sultan Selim [I] upon the taking of Cairo. These have the command of the whole militia in their hands, whereby they are grown proud, powerful and ready upon every discontent to rise in rebellion. Every one of these maintains 500 fighting men well-appointed for war and exercised in arms which serve but as their guard and for servants of their court, with which they go attended in journeys, in their huntings and public appearances. Under command of these twelve captains are 20,000 horse paid at the charge of the country, whose office is by turns to convey yearly the pilgrims to Mecca and the annual tribute of 60,000 sequins to the Ottoman court, whether it be judged requisite to send it either by land or sea. These are the standing militia of the country, out of which, unless upon the foregoing occasions they are not obliged to other service, their principal duty being to provent the invasion of the African mountaineers who often make incursion from the barren rocks into the fat and fruitful soils of Egypt. Besides this militia are computed 80,000 *timariots* out of which they yearly transport about 2500 or 3000 men to the wars of Candia, but to more remote countries or the late wars of Hungary I did not hear that this soldiery has usually been called.

These twelve beys of Egypt are noble by blood, enjoying an hereditary estate descending from father to son, which richness, joined with the command of a powerful army, hath rendered them so formidable and insolent that oftentimes they take upon them an authority to imprison and depose the pasha from his office and spoil him of all the riches he hath collected in his three years government, by which means are always great jealousies and enmities between the pasha and these beys, dissentions and rebellions to that high degree that many times it hath been little different from an absolute revolt. Ibrahim Pasha[668] was in the year 1664 imprisoned by them and obtained his liberty for 600 purses of money,[669] after whose departure the brother of the same Ibrahim, upon some certain pretences on the pasha's score falling into their hands, was imprisoned also, but shortly after obtained his releasement by the Grand Signior's Master of Horse, who was sent expressly to compose the disorders of Egypt, which were now proceeded to that degree as without some satisfactory atonement could not be termed otherwise than a total defection, and therefore they resigned up one called Zülfikar Bey[670] to justice, who, being brought to Adrianople, was immediately in the presence of the Grand Signior put to death. But the Turk hath

---

[668] Ibrahim Pasha was *wali* (governor) of Egypt 1661–1664.

[669] About 100,000 dollars at Cairo (Rycaut's note).

[670] In the month of Feb[ruary], 1664 (Rycaut's note).

always, on occasions of these disturbances and insolences, dissembled and connived at the disorders, perceiving the distemper of that kingdom to be such as can with much difficulty be redressed, fearing that were forcible remedies applied, they would cause so violent a commotion of humours as would absolutely rent it from the body of the Empire.

### *The auxiliary forces to the fore-mentioned militia of the Turks.*

[They] are the Tatars, Wallachians, Moldavians, and Transylvanians, under the command of their respective princes, who are obliged to serve in person whensoever called by the Sultan's command. The Tatars, I mean of Crimea, are to furnish one hundred thousand men; the Tatar *ban* or prince in person to lead them when the Grand Signior himself appears in the field, but if the army is commanded by the [Grand] Vizier only, then the son of the Tatar *ban* is to serve, or, having no issue, the army, to the number of forty or fifty thousand fighting men, is to be conducted under the chief minister. But the princes of Wallachia, Moldavia, and Transylvania are never excused from personal attendance in the camp, each of which respectively are to be attended with six or seven thousand men apiece. And though the Prince of Transylvania called Apafi[671] was in the last war against the Emperor not called out of the confines of his own country, it was with design that he should keep that station free from the eruption of the enemy, not that he was disobliged from his personal attendance on the Vizier's camp.

---

[671] Michael III Apafi reigned from 1661 to 1690. See Book 1, Chapter 14, n. 17.

that he ſhould keep that Station free from the irruption of the Enemy not that he was diſobliged from his perſonal attendance on the Viſiers Camp.

## CHAP. VI.

*Of the Spahees.*

*A Spakee.*

## Chapter VI. *Of the Sipahis.*

Hitherto we have treated of the Turkish horse that are maintained by the farms and rents of lands. Now it will be necessary to discourse of those that receive their constant pay from the Grand Signior's treasury, and these are called Sipahis, who may not improperly be termed the gentry of the Ottoman Empire, because they are commonly better educated, courteous and refined than the other Turks, and are in number 12,000. Of those there are two orders, one called *silahtars*,[672] who carry yellow colours, and the other *Sipahi oğlan* or the servants of the Sipahis,[673] and have their colours red. These servants have now obtained the precedency above their masters, for though the *silahtars* are very ancient and deduce their institution from Ali, their first founder, who was one of the four companions of Muhammad, yet Sultan Mehmed III, on a day of battle in Hungary seeing the Sipahis routed and put to flight, with violent passion and earnestness endeavoured to stop their course. And perceiving the servants of these Sipahis to remain still in a body, incited them to revenge the shameful cowardice of their masters, who, immediately encouraged with the worlds of the Sultan, clapping up a red flag gave so bold an onset on the enemy and with that success as wholly recovered the day, in remembrance of which service and notable exploit the Sultan as disposer of all honours and orders gave ever after the pre-eminence to these servants before their masters, since which time this new institution of *Sipahi oğlan* hath always been continued.[674]

These light horsemen are armed with their scimitar and lance, called by them *mizrak*, and some carry in their hands a *gerit*, which is a weapon about two foot long headed with iron, which I conceive to be the same with the *pila*[675] amongst the Romans, which by long exercise and custom they throw with a strange dexterity and violence, and, sometimes darting it before them in the full career of their horse, without any stop recover it again from the ground. They also

---

[672] Literally, "weapon-master" or "weapon-bearer." They were some of the best warriors in the Ottoman army, usually mounted, but also later included infantry. They were long-time rivals of the elite Janissary corps.

[673] The term means "children or boys of the Sipahis," and refers to an extremely elite group of soldiers, as Rycaut points out.

[674] The actual historical account is a little different. At the battle of Mezö-Keresztes or Haçova (1596), Mehmed III engaged an Austrian, Hungarian, and Transylvanian army under Archduke Maximilian of Austria and King Sigismund of Transylvania. The battle raged for two days, and things began to look bad for the Ottomans, the Austrian forces penetrating as far as Mehmed III's tent. However, they were forced back through a desperate and courageous defence carried out by cooks, camel minders, and servants of various kinds using whatever weapons came to hand. The Sultan, who had wished to order a retreat, was persuaded to keep fighting, and after the heroic action of the camp servants the rest of his army rallied and won the battle, "in which more than thirty thousand Germans and Hungarians were killed. . .it was a decisive Turkish victory which at a perilous moment indubitably saved for the Ottoman Empire Bulgaria, Macedonia, half of Hungary, and, with the exception of Transylvania, most of the territories north of the Danube" (Kinross, *Ottoman Centuries*, 289). Shaw states that it was "a major contribution from their artillery" which enabled the Turks to defeat the enemy (*Ottoman Empire* 1, 185), and does not make mention of heroic camp followers or camel minders.

[675] The *pilum* was a heavy javelin which was designed to stick into an enemy's shield and weigh it down.

wear a straight sword named *gaddara*[676] with a broad blade fixed to the side of their saddle, which, or the scimitar, they make use of when they arrive at handy-blows with the enemy. Many of them are armed with bows and arrows and with pistols and carbines,[677] but esteem not much of firearms, having an opinion that in the field they make more noise than execution. Some of them wear jacks of mail and headpieces painted with the colour of their squadron. In fight they begin their onset with "Allah, Allah!" and make three attempts to break within the ranks of the enemy, in which, if they fail, they make their retreat.

The Asian Sipahis are better-mounted than commonly those of Europe, though these, being borderers on the confines of the Christians, having learned much of their discipline by constant skirmishes and combats, are trained in the art of war and become the more valiant and experienced soldiers. But the Asiatic Sipahis were formerly the more rich, many particular men of them bringing into the field thirty of forty men apiece besides their led horses, tents and other accommodations appropriate to their retinue. But these cavaliers seemed too great and proud to the Vizier [Mehmed] Köprülü for the condition of common troopers and infected with the epidemical spirit of faction and mutiny which raged at that time amongst all the grandees of the Empire, which caused him to strike off their heads with as little remorse as one would do to the tops of poppies until he had absolutely made a destruction of them.[678] Those now which remain are poor and inconsiderable, contented to comrade ten or twelve in a company for maintenance of a poor tent and two or three horses and a mule for baggage and provisions. These are more tame, and subject to the cudgel, and can take a beating patiently on the soles of the feet, which is their punishment as the Janissaries' is to receive the blows on the buttocks, that so this chastisement may neither incommode the seat of the horseman nor the marches of the foot. But if the crime be great and capital, they are sent for by çavuses or pursuivants to appear before the Vizier, by whom being condemned and strangled near the walls of the Grand Signior's seraglio, their bodies are afterwards, about two or three hours in the night, thrown into the sea without any other solemnity than the firing of one of those great guns next the sea which are planted under the walls of the Seraglio, which serve for so many warning pieces for others' example.

---

[676] Nicolle describes the *gaddara* as "a broad, straight or slightly-curved 'bowie-knife' of Persian origin" (*Janissaries*, 21).

[677] Carbines are cavalry firearms which are shorter than muskets or rifles, and thus easier for mounted troops to use.

[678] In 1657 the Sipahis in Istanbul had rebelled against the newly-appointed Grand Vizier in order to replace him with their own candidate, but he firmly suppressed them with the help of the Janissary corps and the blessings of the Grand Mufti.

Their pay is divers, but in general it is from twelve to one hundred aspers a day. Those who proceed from the seraglios of Pera, Ibrahim Pasha,[679] and Adrianople, which are so many nurseries and schools as well as of the principles of war as literature, or have been cook's mates (for the cook of these societies is a principal officer of respect) or *baltaçis*, that is, hatchet-men who cut wood for the Grand Signior's seraglio and are licensed to live abroad with the title of Sipahi, have the lowest pay of twelve aspers a day. But those who are extracted from the less or greater chamber of the Grand Signior's own seraglio, called *Seni serai*, have 19 aspers pay, and if they are favoured with the title of an office, they receive two or three aspers augmentation. But such as are elected to the war out of more eminent chambers as the laundry, the turban-office, the dispensary, the treasurer, the falconers' lodge and others which we have mentioned in the description of the Seraglio, have at first thirty aspers daily pay, an increase of which is obtained sometimes by the Vizier's or Register's favour unto two aspers more, sometimes by services in the war by receiving two aspers augmentation for the head of every enemy he brings in, two more for the intelligence of the death of any Sipahi out of the pay of the deceased, as also at the incoronation or instalment of every Grand Signior, five aspers increase is given as a donative general to the whole army of Sipahis. And thus many of them are by art, industry and good success go augmenting until they arrive to an hundred aspers, and here is their *non plus ultra*,[680] and they can rise no higher.

They are paid quarterly from three months to three months, which they may omit to receive for nine months, but if twelve pass they can only demand the nine; the other quarter or more is confiscated to the public exchequer. Their place of payment is now in the Hall of the Vizier, which formerly was in the houses of the paymasters and Treasurer, but changed by the Vizier Köprülü on occasion of the disorders and abuses of the officers, which caused mutinies and disturbances amongst the soldiery. For the rich Sipahis living far distant, to excuse themselves from a long journey to the city, agreed with the paymasters that they, for some certain part of their income, should without farther trouble to themselves take up their dues and make it over quarterly to their countries of abode. These men, thus tasting the benefit of this trade, agreed with others for some little gains to dispatch them before the rest, by which means and their payment only on

---

[679] Originally the palace of Ibrahim Pasha Pargali (c. 1493–1536), who had served Süleyman the Magnificent as Grand Vizier from 1523 to 1536, when he was executed for over-reaching himself. He is the only commoner for whom a palace was ever built; it is situated in Sultanahmet, Istanbul. Afterward the building was "used variously as an extension of the Palace School, the High Court of Justice, barracks for unmarried Janissaries, and a prison" (Taylor, *Imperial Istanbul,* 153). It is now the Museum of Turkish and Islamic Arts.

[680] The utmost point.

Wednesdays and Saturdays those Sipahis that came from remote parts, making so long attendance, had with their excesses in Constantinople spent as much as the principal sum they expected, of which growing sensible, at first they began to murmur and then to threaten the paymasters, and at last proceeded to open mutiny by forcing the doors, breaking the windows of the officers with many other insolencies and disorders until Köprülü, to remedy these abuses, ordered the money to be given out in his presence and the payment to be continued every day until the pay was ended.

The sons of Sipahis, presenting themselves before the Vizier, may claim the privilege of being enrolled in the Grand Signior's books, but their pay, which is the lowest rate [of] twelve aspers a day, is to issue forth from their father's proportion, but then they are in the road of preferment and are capable by their services and merits to make additions upon foundation of their own industry. Besides the foregoing ways by which the Sipahis gain their increase of pay, I am given to understand that formerly they had another benefit called *gulâmiye*[681] or safe-conduct money, which was one percent of all moneys to those whom the collectors of the Grand Signior's revenue summoned to convey the treasure for more security to the capital city, besides the maintenance of themselves and horses in the journey. But this, as too chargeable a deduction from the imperial revenue, was with time taken off, to the great discomfort of the Sipahis in general. The Grand Signior going in person to the wars according to the ancient custom of other Sultans, bestows a largesse on the Sipahis of five thousand aspers a man, which they call *sadak akçiasi*, or a donative for buying bows and arrows, as also to the Janissaries, as we shall hereafter mention.

This army of Sipahis is in the war a mere confused multitude without any government or distribution into troops of regiments, but march in heaps, fight without order, little account kept of their presence or absence from the camp. Only at the pay in the month of November[682] whoever appears not, unless favoured by the officers, hath his name erased from the Grand Signior's register. Their duty in the war is to stand sentinel with a Janissary at the end of every cord at the Grand Signior's pavilion, as also at the Vizier's, armed with his scimitar, bows, arrows, and lance, mounted on horseback, as the Janissary on foot with his sword and musket, and also the charge of the treasure for payment of the militia is committed in the field to their custody.

---

[681] This term usually referred to the salary that tax collectors could take from the money they collected. For details, see Linda T. Darling, *Revenue-Raising and Legitimacy: Tax Collection and Finance Administration in the Ottoman Empire 1560–1660* (Leiden: Brill, 1995), 168–69.

[682] Called in Turkish *kasim ulefast* (Rycaut's note).

This order of soldiers was in ancient times in great esteem and honour in
all parts of the Empire by reason of their accomplishments in learning, refined
education in the imperial court, their nearness to preferments and acquaintance
and interest with the grandees of the Empire. The place of the *silahtari* in their
marches to the war was to flank the Grand Signior on the left hand, and the
*Sipahi oglani* on the right, and were always the ultimate reserve of the battle as
the life-guard to the Sultan. But, like men not knowing how to comport themselves in prosperity, growing mutinous and ambitious to have a hand in the government, became confederates with the Janissaries in conspiracy against the life
of their true sovereign Sultan Osman [II], to which treason adding other insolencies, they justly were deprived of the favour of Sultan Murad [IV] and Sultan
Ibrahim. The terrors also of their late sedition remaining freshly still impressed in
the memory of this present Sultan Mehmed [IV] when they complotted against
his own and his mother's life is the cause they have gone still declining from
the degree of their pristine honour and esteem, for the Prince, as he is the fountain of honour, so is his countenance and favour the spirit and life which gives
a lustre and sparkling to those titles and riches he hath conferred. Other seditions hastened the ruin of their reputation, and in the year 1657, when the Vizier
Mehmed Köprülü, on occasion of his expedition against Janova, summoned the
Asian Sipahis to the rendezvous in Hungary, who instead of yielding obedience
to the command of their general, elected a new captain, a Sipahi of their own
rank called Hasan Aga,[683] preferred to be Pasha of Aleppo, whose name at that
time, I remember, upon the hopes of the dissentions he might create amongst the
Turks, was greatly famed and celebrated all over Christendom.

These combustions in Asia, headed by the chief enemy to the Vizier, caused
Köprülü to leave many of his designs against Transylvania unaffected, and to clap
up a peace on reasonable and moderate terms of honour that so he might hinder
the progress of a dangerous evil which now approached the capital city. For by
this time Hasan Pasha, being arrived near the walls of Scutari, began to treat
by way of petition to the Grand Signior and represent that out of his zeal to the

---

[683] Abaza Hasan Pasha (d. 1659), "a supporter of the former rebel and grand vezir
[*sic*] İpşir Mustafa Pasha. . .could not accept the legitimacy of Köprülü Mehmed's grand
vezirate," and objected to the Vizier's "purge of the Sultan's cavalrymen in Edirne" (Finkel, *Osman's Dream*, 257). Together with some other provincial governors, he started a
revolt, and even set up a provincial administration in Anatolia. "His intention," Finkel
states, "was to create his own state" (259). However, he found it increasingly difficult to
supply his rebel army, although he managed to defeat Murteza Pasha's forces which had
been sent against him in central Anatolia. Hasan was eventually murdered in Aleppo as
he stayed with the same Murteza Pasha, who had extended to him the promise of a truce
and the possibility of a pardon from the Sultan. Rycaut's following account here is quite
accurate.

good of His Majesty and his Empire he had undertaken a long march to inform him of the corruption of his ministers and the miscarriages of government, his tender years[684] as yet not having ripened his judgment to penetrate those evils, which with time his understanding would discover to be too inveterate and incurable. All the oppressions and aggrievances of the soldiery he seemed to object[685] to the cruelty and oppression of Köprülü, and, in appearance, had nothing but thoughts of the honour and safety of the Grand Signior's person. And doubtless this man was unfit to manage such a design, for he entertained scruples of conscience and a remorse and tenderness in spilling Muhammadan blood, considerations which are incompatible with the condition of a rebel, for who hath the impiety to draw his sword against his prince must stop at no bars either of divine or human right to maintain it. This gave advantage to Köprülü to effect his design upon his enemy, for in the interim of his treaty, Murteza Pasha of Babylon was commanded to possess the city of Aleppo, and Hasan, after many fair messages and promises from the Grand Signior and the Vizier, was persuaded to return again to Aleppo to capitulate with Murteza concerning those points and aggrievances he sought to have redressed, it being alleged to him that Murteza had received instructions to treat and a plenipotentiary power to grant and affirm as far as should be reasonable and honourable for the Grand Signior to condescend. Hasan, with this easy answer, returned toward Aleppo, near which place he credulously committed himself into the hands of Murteza, who no sooner had him within his tents but he concluded all controversies and capitulations by the decision[686] of his head from his body. The whole army of Sipahis immediately, with the fall of their general, was scattered and divided themselves, but about three hundred of them being apprehended by Murteza were sent to Constantinople, where, in the presence of the Grand Signior within the walls of the Seraglio at Scutari they were all executed, since which their pride hath ever gone declining and their name become so odious amongst the people that upon the very nominating a Sipahi the vulgar were ready to run upon them with stones or

---

[684] Mehmed IV was born in 1642, and was therefore fifteen in 1657.

[685] Here, "to offer as an accusation."

[686] Here, "outcome." It was Murteza who "gave the instructions that when the cannon was fired from Aleppo fortress on the night of 24 February 1659, the rebels were to be murdered by those in whose houses they were guests. Abaza Hasan Pasha. . .and some others were dining with Murteza Pasha that night" (Finkel, *Osman's Dream*, 261). Her source is Mustafa Na'ima (1655–1716), an eminent Turkish historian who wrote the *Ravzatü 'l-Hüseyn* (1704), a chronicle history of the times. However, Finkel suggests that "There is no direct evidence to suggest that Köprülü Mehmed Pasha was complicit" (*Osman's Dream*, 261–62); Lord Kinross notes that the vizier put down the rising, "causing [Abaza's] head, with that of thirty other rebels, to be dispatched to the capital for public display" (*Ottoman Centuries*, 333).

other weapons that came next to hand, so that now the Sipahis are much eclipsed in their ancient fame and honour.

There are, besides these two foregoing sorts of Sipahis, other four. The first, called *sağ ulfeci*, is appointed to march on the right hand of the *Sipahi oğlani*, and carry red and white colours. The second is *sol ulfeci*, whose place is on the left hand of the *silahtari*, which carry white and yellow colours. The third [is] *sağ garipa*, that is, soldiers of fortune that are to march on the right hand of the *sağ ulfeci* and carry green colours. The fourth is *sol garipa*, whose place is to march on the left hand of the *ulfeci* and carry white banners.[687] But these four sorts of Sipahis are raised and lifted according to necessity and occasions of war, and are obliged to all services and duties; their pay is from 12 aspers to 20 a day, and are capable, according to their merits, of being promoted to one of the superior orders. There is also another sort of more elevated Sipahi called *mütefferrika*,[688] who issue out from the Seraglio with more favour than the ordinary sort of Sipahis and are four or five hundred in number. Their pay is forty aspers a day, and [they] have always the obligation or duty on them to serve and attend the Grand Signior when he goes in progress for pleasure from one village to another.

And this much shall serve to have declared in brief concerning the institution and discipline of the Sipahis as also of all the militia of the Turkish horse; we shall now proceed to declare something of their infantry.

---

[687] The words describe their condition; *ulfeci* means "the salaried ones" and *garip* "the poor ones."
[688] Palace guards.

## CHAP. VII.

*A Janizary*

## Chapter VII. *Of the Janissaries.*

The next main sinew of the Ottoman power is the Order of Janissaries, which is as much to say the new militia, and yet their antiquity may be deduced from Osman, the first king of the Turks, but because they received honours and privileges from Murad [I], their third king, our *Turkish History* accounts that to be the time of the first original.[689] It is certain that in his time they were modelised and

---

[689] According to David Nicolle, "It is difficult to separate truth from legend concerning the real origins of the Janissary *Ocak* or Corps. Most traditional accounts credit Orhan with creating the Corps." Nicolle mentions the important connection with the

certain laws prescribed both for their education and maintenance when by the counsel of [Çandarli Hayreddin Pasha], otherwise called [Kara Halil],[690] Murad's Prime Vizier, it was ordained that for the augmentation of this militia every fifth captive taken from the Christians above the age of fifteen years should be the dues of the Sultan, who at first were to be distributed amongst the Turkish husbandmen in Asia to learn and be instructed in the Turkish language and religion.

Their number at first was not accounted above six or seven thousand; now with time they are increased to the number of twenty thousand effective men. But, were there a list taken of all those who assume the title of Janissary and enjoy their privileges though not their pay, there would be found above 100,000. Six or seven go under the name of one Janissary, for gaining by this means a privilege of being free from all duties and taxes, they bestow a certain sum of money or annual presents on the officers, in consideration of which they are owned and countenanced as Janissaries. Their habit is as the picture represents, wearing always the beard of the chin and under-lip shaven, which some say they learned from the Italians, but certain it is that this cutom is more ancient than since the time of their neighbourhood unto Italy, this manner of their shaving being generally used as a token of their subjection, and so all pages and officers in the seraglio of great men, orders of gardeners, *baltaçis* or hatchet-men, and others are

---

Bektaşi dervishes, "if only in the design of the Janissaries' distinctive *Börk* or white felt hat," but also states that other accounts credit this to Ali Pasha, military adviser to Sultan Orhan, who "may actually have been a *Bektaşi* dervish" (*Janissaries* 7). Caroline Finkel writes that the Janissaries were "first raised during the reign of Sultan Murad I from prisoners of war captured in the Christian lands of the Balkans" (*Osman's Dream*, 28), and Lord Kinross first mentions them in connection with the same Sultan, suggesting that they had already been formed by 1388, when Murad used them against the Bulgarians (*Ottoman Centuries*, 58).

[690] Çandarli Hayreddin Pasha (d. 1387) was Grand Vizier under Murad I from 1364 to 1387, the Ottoman Empire's longest-serving Grand Vizier. "Kara Halil Hayreddin held the post of kadi (judge) in Izník and Bursa," Finkel tells us, "and then became Murad's first chief justice and also his chief minister, in addition to his military command. This joint supervision over army and administration made him, in effect, the first grand vezir [*sic*] of the Ottoman Empire" (*Osman's Dream*, 20). Rycaut renders his name as "*Catradin,* otherwise called *Kara Rusthenes,*" but he may have conflated the vizier's name with that of the fourteenth-century scholar Kara Rustem from Karaman, who is said to have pointed out to Kara Halil that "in accordance with the word of God one-fifth of booty belonged to the sovereign, and this included the prisoners. . .one out of every five of the captives was taken"(Bernard Lewis, *Istanbul and the Civilization of the Ottoman Empire* [Norman: University of Oklahoma Press, 1963], 58). Halil made them into "new soldiers," which is the meaning of the word "Janissary" (*Yeniçeri*). See also Daniel Goffman, *The Ottoman Empire and Early Modern Europe* (Cambridge: Cambridge University Press, 2002), 47–49.

distinguished by this mark to be in service and obliged to the attendance of a master. But when they are either licensed from the war or promoted to office or freed to their own disposal, they immediately suffer their beards to grow as a sign of their liberty and gravity.

In former times this militia consisted only of the sons of Christians, educated in the Muhammadan rites, but of late that politic custom hath been disused, the reason of which some attribute to the abundance of people the Turks have of their own to supply all their occasions. But I am induced rather to another opinion, having not observed the multitude which histories and travellers tell us that the Turks swarm with, and rather assign the neglect of this practice so prejudicial to Christian interest to the corruption of the officers and carelessness in their discipline. And though this election of Janissaries out of the eldest and lustiest sons of Christians that inhabit Europe (for Asia was exempted) is now disused,[691] yet such as enter into this Order, whoseoever they are, unless the necessity of the present state of the war be over-urgent, are obliged to perform their novitiate like *tyrones Romani*[692] before they can be enrolled in the Register of Janissaries and are called *acemi oğlans.*[693] The chief officers of these are called *Constantinople Ağasi,*[694] in whose care and charge it is to enure these men to all labours, pains and fortifications, as to cut wood, carry burdens, endure heats, colds and other sufferings which may render them obedient, temperate, vigilant and patient of all the inconveniences and miseries of war.

The quarters many of these have in the garden-lodges of the Grand Signior's seraglios, whereof there are many in and about Constantinople, to manure and dig the ground, learn the art of plantation and husbandry and practice, as occasion requires, meaner offices of labour and servitude. Others of them are placed in the three seraglios we have before-mentioned in the chapter of Sipahis, *viz.* of Pera, Ibrahim Pasha, and Adrianople, where their principal art is the mystery of plantation and delicious disposal of gardens into the variety of knots, walks, groves and fountains. And though there are many of this profession who have no

---

[691] The recruitment system, more like impressment, known as the *devşirme*, "was roughly based on the recruitment of one child from every 40 households; this was carried out approximately once every five years somewhere in the Balkans. . .[it] forcibly enlisted between 1,000 and 3,000 youths in a year out of a normal total recruitment of up to 8,000 male slaves, until the continuing shortage of military manpower meant that Muslim volunteers were finally allowed into the Janissary corps late in the 16th century" (Nicolle, *Janissaries*, 11). Exemptions included Jews, families with only one son, islands, and large urban centres.

[692] Roman recruits.

[693] Literally, foreign boys.

[694] So called because he was "in charge of trainees and garrison units in Istanbul" (Nicolle, *Janissaries*, 18).

other thoughts to employ their minds, few of them are acquainted with any part of polite husbandry[695] or know more than the season to plant their artichokes or coleworts.[696] As to the rules and symmetry of setting trees, ordering the labyrinth of knots, making pleasing walks, fountains and groves, it is so strange a people that delight so much in flowers, in fields and arbours and have themselves or ancestors ruined many of the delightful paradises of Christians should be so wholly ignorant and dull in the contrivance of what they love as not to be able to borrow one example or model which amongst all the Grand Signior's gardens in Constantinople may deserve a better name than of a wilderness.

Others of these *açem oğlans* are made *baltaçis* or hatchet-men to cut out wood for the Seraglio, others are made cooks and officers in the kitchen, such, I mean, as can already speak the Turkish language, for those that are ignorant in that speech or in the Muhammadan religion are disposed into remoter parts of Anatolia where the Janissaries have possessions and authority. As to Ciotahia, where the Lieutenant-General of the Janissaries[697] hath a revenue, to Karahizar[698] and Angora, where the *Constantinople* Ağasi hath principal power, to Menteşe,[699] Sultan Ughi and Karosi, where the *Turnacibaşi* and *Yayabaşi*,[700] who are chief officers of the Janissaries, have rents and profits belonging to their offices, and here

---

[695] Ornamental and formal gardening; in Rycaut's time (and for a century before) this was all the rage in Europe and England. Most Turkish gardens, unlike European ones, were found in courtyards, and even in Rycaut's time flowers were hung from balconies. Yildiz Park in Istanbul, for example, was not turned into what Rycaut would have called a "polite garden" until the nineteenth century, when Abdul Hamed II had it landscaped and planted in the European style. For details see Taylor, *Imperial Istanbul*, 196–97. On the other hand, Ottavio Bon wrote about "an artificial four square lake. . .proceeding from about thirty fountains" in the grounds of the Seraglio (*The Sultan's Seraglio*, 30).

[696] A colewort is any green vegetable of the *Brassica* family, such as kale.

[697] "Called *Kâhya Bey*" (Rycaut's marginal note). He probably means one of the *Kul Kâhya*, the adjutants to the *Yeniçeri Ağha*, who commanded the Janissary corps. Ciotahia is unidentified.

[698] Karahizar, now known as Afyonkarahizar, is about 250 kilometres south-west of Ankara (Angora). Its name means "opium black castle," and for centuries it was the major centre of opium production in the Ottoman Empire. It is a very ancient city which scholars can trace back as having been inhabited since Hittite times; it was captured by Bayezid I in 1398 from its Gerniyanid rulers, but lost to Timur ten years later. It was recaptured in 1429.

[699] See Book 1, Chapter 12, n. 7.

[700] These officers were, respectively, the commander of one of the "elite hunting *Ortas*" or "crane-keepers" and "commander of the *Yaya* infantry, but later responsible for the Janissary muster-rolls" (Nicolle, *Janissaries*, 16, 18). Sultan Ughi and Karosi are unidentified.

## Diſcipline in War. 193

content they evidence by ſlighting, by kicking down their Plates of Rice, and ſhewing better ſtomacks to be revenged, than to their Entertainment ; which Mutinies the Grand Signior and Principal Miniſters having found oftentimes fatal, endeavour by fair promiſes and ſatisfactory compliance with their deſires to pacifie in their firſt motion. *Mutinies.*

*Janyzar Agaſi or Generall of the Janizaries*
The Generall of this Militia is called

are employed in ploughing and sowing the ground or other laborious exercises until such time as supplies for the wars give them occasion to draw out these men from their several stations. And then, being called to the chambers of Janissaries, they orderly march one after the other according to their seniority, one holding the end of his fellow's garment, [and] appear before the Muster-Master, who, having enrolled their names in the Grand Signior's register, they run as fast as they can by their *Odabaçi*[701] or Master of their Chamber, who gives everyone as

---

[701] Literally, barrack-room chief (Nicolle, *Janissaries*, 18).

he passes a blow under the ear to signify their subjection to him, and this is the ceremony observed in creating Janissaries.

At their first enrolment some have but one asper a day, others four and five, unto seven and a half, and so with time and favour of their officers increase to twelve aspers a day, which is the highest pay of any Janissary, and can have no other advance unless good fortune promote them to the degree of a *Kâhya Bey*, which is as much as Lieutenant-General of the Janissaries, or any other office. Besides this pay they have their daily provision and diet from the bounty of the Grand Signior and their table ordered at constant hours, where they find their rice, fifty drams[702] of flesh and one hundred of bread, their ordinary commons,[703] and eat in their respective refectories like monks in convents or scholars in their colleges. They receive also one soldier's coat yearly of cloth made at Salonica of a coarse thread, but warm and convenient, so that their bellies are full and backs are warm, and in all parts are better-provided than the tattered infantry which are to be seen in most parts of Christendom. And thus this people, being pampered without cares of seeking their bread, grow often querulous and apt to take the fire of sedition with every spark of discontent in their officers, the beginnings of which they commonly make known at their assemblies of the public *divan*, whither four of five hundred of them are obliged four times a week, that is Saturday, Sunday, Monday, and Tuesday, to accompany the *Yeniçeri Ağha* or their general. At that place they have their commons from the Grand Signior's kitchen, which, when they have any subject of discontent they evidence by slighting, kicking down their plates of rice and showing better stomachs to be revenged than to their entertainment, which mutinies the Grand Signior and principal ministers, having found oftentimes fatal, endeavour by fair promises and satisfactory compliance with their desires to pacify in their first motion.

The general of this militia is called the *Yeniçeri Ağha*, and is always elected from the royal chamber of the Seraglio, because it, being an office of great charge, it is thought necessary to be entrusted to one whose education and preferment hath made a creature of the court, which policy hath been the suppression of divers mutinies amongst the Janissaries, the discovery of their combination[704] and an engagement to a stronger dependency on the favour of the Seraglio. When this general either dies by a natural death or the sword of the Grand Signior's justice or authority, his riches, like that of other pashas, is not confiscated to the Sultan's exchequer but the inheritance accrues to the public treasury of the Janissaries, which how dangerous it is to a state to have a militia endowed with revenues appropriated to their officers, as already we have declared they possess

---

[702] A dram is about one-sixteenth of an ounce.
[703] Rations.
[704] Plotting.

194 *Of the Turkish Militia, and*

Officers.

The second Chief Officer is the *Kiahaia Begh*, or Lieutenant-General.

The third is *Segban bajchi*, the Overseer of the Carriage of the Souldiers Baggage.

The fourth is the *Turnagi Bashee*, or Guardian of the Grand Signiors Cranes.

The fifth is the *Samsongi Bashee*, chief Master of the Grand Signiors Mastives.

The sixth is the *Zagargi Bashee*, Master of the Spaniels.

The seventh is the *Solack Bashee*, Captain of the Archers, or of such Janizaries who go armed with Bow and Arrows.

The eighth is *Subashi* and *Assabashi*, who are chief of the Serjeants and Bailiffs, and attend always at the Grand Signiors Stirrop when at any time on solemn occasions he shews himself to the people.

.I Solack or one of the *Grand Signors Footmen* | A *Paick* or another sort of *Footmen*

in some parts of Anatolia, and a bank of wealth united to the maintenance of a licentious sword the Ottoman princes have by sad effects rather felt than able by virtue of their absolute power to remedy.

The second chief officer is the *Kâhya Bey*, Lieutenant-General.

The third is [the] *Sekbanbaşi,*[705] the overseer of the carriage of the soldiers' baggage.

The fourth is the *Turnacibaşi,* or guardian of the Grand Signior's cranes.

The fifth is the *Samsoncubaşi,*[706] Chief Master of the Grand Signior's mastiffs.

The sixth is the *Sarkikbaşi,* Master of the Spaniels.[707]

The seventh is the *Solakbaşi,*[708] Captain of the Archers, or as such of the Janissaries who go armed with bows and arrows.

The eighth is [the] *Subaşi* and *Assaçbaşi,* who are chief of the serjeants and bailiffs, and attend always at the Grand Signior's stirrup when at any time on solemn occasions he shows himself to the people.[709]

The ninth is the *Peykbaşi,* or commander of that sort of pages which are called *peyks,*[710] who wear caps of baten gold, of which there are 60 in number, who march at solemnities together with the *solaks* near the person of the Grand Signior.

The tenth is [the] *Muzhar Ağha,* or the Head Bailiff[711] of the Janissaries.

These eight last arise from the Order of the Janissaries, and have their several commands in the army, though the Grand Signior, to augment their power and honour the more, bestows on them titles and wealth in other offices.

The Janissaries' chambers, of which there no others but in Constantinople, are in number 162, of which 80 are ancient foundations and are called *eski odalar* and 82 called *yeni odalar* or the new chambers, over most of which is a *çorbaşi*[712] or captain. In these chambers those that are not married enjoy their lodgings and

---

[705] A *sekban* is a dog handler. This, and some of the other terms below, is derived from hunting.

[706] "*Sakson* were mastiffs or large hunting dogs;" this official was also the Keeper of the Lions (Ådahl, *Sultan's Procession,* 251). The mastiff-keepers eventually formed the 71st Janissary Battalion (Nicolle, *Janissaries,* 16).

[707] Although *sarkik* means "spaniel," some later writers have translated this word as "bulldog."

[708] The *solaks* were "an elite guard (first mentioned in 1402)," according to Nicolle, and "remained as infantry archers for many centuries" (*Janissaries,* 15).

[709] The Swedish envoy Rålamb noted in 1657 that Mehmed IV was attended by "2 *capuci passaj* in gold brocaded coats," and they are depicted walking by the Sultan's stirrups (Ådahl, *Sultan's Procession,* 78).

[710] See Book 1, Chapter 10, n. 3.

[711] Nicolle translates this term as "the Summoner" (*Janissaries* 16). This official usually orders people to appear in court.

[712] Literally "soup man." As Nicolle points out, "the command structure also reflected the original need to feed slaves who depended on the Sultan." He was the commanding officer or colonel (not captain), "appointed from outside the unit" (Nicolle, *Janissaries,* 15).

habitation and twice a day find their repast, as we have before mentioned. And thus, instead of monasteries of friars, the Turk maintains convents and socities of soldiers who are trained up with all modesty and severity of discipline.

The principal officers of these chambers are:

First, the *Odabaşi* or Master of the Chamber, who in the wars serve as lieutenants of the company.

Second is the *Vekilharç* or Expenditor[713] for maintenance of the chamber.

The third is *Bayraktar* or Ensign-bearer.

Fourth is *Aşçi* or the Cook of the Chamber.

Fifth is *Karakullukçu* or the Under-Cook.[714]

Sixth is the *Saka[başi]* or the Water-Carrier.[715]

The Cook is not only an officer to dress the diet and provision of the Janissaries but is also a monitor or observer of their good behaviour, so that one of them commits a crime the Cook is the officer that executes the punishment. The Under-Cook also serves for an apparitor[716] and is he that summons the married Janissaries at their several dwellings in Constantinople when their officers command their attendance.

The greatest part of the Janissaries consists of bachelors or single men, for though marriage cannot be denied to any of them, yet it is that which determines their preferments and renders their seniority incapable of claiming a right to any offices or military advancement, for being encumbered with wife and other dependencies, they are judged in a condition not capable to attend the discipline of the war or service of the Grand Signior, and therefore as to other duty in the times of peace besides their appearance every Friday in their chambers and presence of their officers, they wholly are dispensed with.

In the wars this militia is considered as the most valiant and best-disciplined soldiery of the Turkish camp, and therefore are either kept as a reserve or march in the main body of the army. In times of peace their quarters are many times changed to keep them in employment from one castle or garrison to another, as to Buda, Canisia, Timişoara, to Rhodes, Chania[717] and other parts. Some of them are appointed to keep courts of guard at all gates and avenues of Constantinople to prevent the insolencies and injuries their companions are

---

[713] "Quartermaster" (Nicolle, *Janissaries*, 18).

[714] Nicolle calls him the "head scullion" (*Janissaries*, 18).

[715] "Head of water-distribution" (Nicolle, *Janissaries*,18).

[716] A constable or sheriff.

[717] A city in western Crete, captured by the Ottomans from the Venetians in 1645. So many Turkish soldiers were killed in the siege that Sultan Ibrahim had the Ottoman commander executed.

apt to offer to Christians, Jews, and others in the streets, who at some times, being heated with wine, have in open market forced women whilst their comrades have, with their daggers[718] drawn, stood over them to defend them from the people. To prevent which disorders, the *Yeniçeri Ağha* accustoms to ride the streets attended with about 40 bailiffs of the Janissaries, where, meeting any guilty of such crimes or other enormities, he seizes them and carries them to his court, where after examination of their fault he orders them to be beaten, or, if their crime be great, to be strangled or sewn in a sack and thrown into the sea. But always their punishment is administered privately, perhaps because they are jealous of mutiny.

In every province the Janissaries have their *serdars*,[719] who are colonel or chief of all the Janissaries within that jurisdiction, who greatly abuse their office by taking into their protection any that present or pay them for this privilege, by which means they have grown so powerful and rich that some time past the command of the whole Ottoman Empire hath reposed in the hands of this militia.

Their arms are muskets and swords; they fight confusedly in the field and with no more order than the Sipahis. Only sometimes they draw themselves up into *cunei*[720] observed amongst the Romans.

And thus much shall serve to have spoken of the institution and discipline of the Janissaries. We shall now proceed to declare how this militia is decayed and upon what grounds it is not maintained in its ancient and flourishing estate.

---

[718] "Called *hançers*" (Rycaut's marginal note).
[719] *Serdars* are generals or commanders-in-chief, not colonels.
[720] Wedge formations (Latin).

**Chapter VIII.** *Whether the maintenance of an army of Janissaries according to the original institution be now agreeable to the rules of polity amongst the Turks.*

This problem I find first moved by Busbecq, once the German Emperor's ambassador to Constantinople, who pretends to speak the Grand Signior's sense in this particular on occasions of difference which the insolent rudenesss of the Janissaries had caused between themselves and his family. For Rustem Pasha,[721] then Prime Vizier, admonished him friendly to condescend to any terms of composition, for that law could not avail where soldiers ruled, and the powerful Süleyman himself, who then reigned, trembled at nothing more than the apprehension of some secret ulcer of perfidiousness which might lie concealed within the retirement of the Janissaries. But as there is no question but a standing army of veteran and well-disciplined soldiers must be always useful and advantageous to the interest of a prince, so on the contrary negligence in the officers and remissness of government produces that licentiousness and restiness in the soldiery as betrays them to all the disorders which are dangerous and of evil consequence to the welfare of a state.

And so it hath fared with the Ottoman Empire, which, rising only by the power of arms and established on the blood of many valiant and daring captains, gave privileges, honours, and riches to the militia and at all times encouraged their prowess and forwardness by rewards and connivance at their crimes, by which indulgence and impunity these men, ill-principled in rules of virtue and unequally bearing prosperity and the favour of the Prince, have for a long time been gathering a stock of ill humours ready to receive any contagion of seditious design and to maintain it with an impudence contrary to the Janissaries for some ages, which may equal the levity of the Roman soldiery until they shamelessly set their empire to sale and forgot both their old obedience to the Senate and reverence to their new emperors.[722] The death of so many grandees and of the Sultan himself by suchlike seditions hath at length by dear experience taught the principal ministers how unsafe it is to permit an army lodged in the bowels

---

[721] Kehle-i-ikbâl Damad Rustem Pasha (1500–1561), born in Albania, served Süleyman I as Grand Vizier 1544–1553 and 1555–1561. Busbecq is ambiguous about Rustem, sometimes praising his tolerance for other religions and at others complaining about rudeness or ill-treatment. The incident from Busbecq to which Rycaut refers here may be found in *Turkish Letters,* 107–8.

[722] Rycaut refers here to what happened immediately after the murder of emperor Pertinax in March 193. The Roman Empire was literally put up for sale and finally purchased by Didius Julianus, who offered 25,000 sesterces to every soldier, outbidding his rival Sulpicianus. Julianus, though not an evil man, lasted only three months as emperor, and was deposed and put to death by his successor Septimius Severus.

of the capital city, of a disposition favourable to itself, envious and impatient of any other, jealous and always at enmity with the court, rich and powerful with possessions and rents pertaining to its commanders in Anatolia and a treasury of unknown sums which have descended to the common bank by the decease of their generals or *Yeniçeri Ağhas*, and therefore have by degrees and as prudently as might be begun to diminish the strength of this militia by the destruction of the veteran soldiers and ruin of their reputation by various arts in the estimation of the world.

The particular means whereby the Janissaries have been studiously destroyed are by many ways evident, for first they are exposed upon every obscure service and drawn forth to encounter every assault of the Empire. As the wars of Candia have exhausted the flower of this militia, the battles at sea buried vast numbers who were formerly reserved for times of eminent exploits and glory. Secondly, destruction of the veteran soldiers hath created mischiefs to this order in point of discipline as prejudicial to the former, for as the *açemi oğlans* were obliged to perform six or seven years novitiate, now by reason of the constant necessity to supply the wars they overskip the ordinary formalities of the first institution and create them Janissaries after a year or half a year's service. And others I have known, educated in mechanic professions and from framing timber and carrying burdens in the arsenal, have at once for the service of Candia been created Janissaries, who neither know how to manage a musket nor are otherwise disciplined to any exercise of arms.

Thirdly, that Europe may not be dispeopled by the triennial seizure of Christian children for the Grand Signior's service, which in Turkish is called *devşirme*, that politic custom and principal conservation of the discipline of Janissaries is, as we have said before, wholly forgotten, and instead thereof election is made of vagabonds that proffer themselves out of Asia and other parts, who, having passed five or six months like novices, are afterwards made Janissaries, and, being ignorant in the use of arms and unaccustomed to labours and sufferings, run from their colours and renounce their order, which has in times past one of the most honourable in the whole Empire.

Fourthly, the old veteran officers, which had by degrees and steps proceeded to honour methodically from inferior soldiers, have either by their own seditious spirits or jealousies of the Prince been dispeeded[723] from this world, and in their places the sons of Constantinopolitan Janissaries succeeded, who have been bred up with softness and effeminacy, and their *çorbaşis* or captains have not obtained their commands by time by valour, but buy their places with money and presents to their prime officers.

---

[723] Dispatched.

Fifthly, and to forward the decay of this militia and to take off their warlike and haughty courages, the confinement to their chambers is not severe, but liberty given upon colour of poverty and impossibility of livelihood on their mean pay to attend other trades and services, whereby the exercise of arms and thoughts of the war is converted to mechanic arts and an intention to ways of maintenance of themselves and families.

Sixthly, hope of reward and fear of punishment, which are the incitements to worthy actions and restrictions from the vilest crimes, are rarely held up to the Janissaries in these times for their encouragement or terror, for without money to the superior officers none of them obtains preferment. Nor can any worn out with age and wounds procure dismission from the war with the enjoyment of the usual stipend, who are called by the Turks *otorak*[724] and by the Latins *exauctorati*,[725] and on the contrary the children of officers born in Constantinople are often made *otoraks* in their cradles, and lusty youths are with favour and money exempted in the flower of age from the labours of war and yet enjoy the benefits given to a toilsome militia.

And yet, as if all the connivance at these various disorders and subversion of the good institutions of this soldiery were not sufficient to impoverish their spirits, to mould them into a more effeminate temper and cause them to lose their interest and reputation, it is the common opinion that the Vizier Köprülü laid the designs for the late war with Germany before his death and enjoined it to his son to prosecute with an intention, amongst other expectations of benefit to the Empire, to complete the final destruction of the ancient Sipahis and Janissaries so as to be able to lay a foundation of new discipline which may more easily for the future restrain the Turkish militia within the compass of better modesty and obedience, which design hath taken so severe effect in the war of Hungary. In the year 1664 the bloodiest part of slaughter in the battles fell on the Janissaries and Sipahis, and by how much more any were more bold and forward in their attempts, by so much more fatal and hasty was their ruin, so that it is reported that the valiantest soldiers of the confines, the veteran and best-disciplined of the Sipahis and Janissaries and the best number of their skilful commanders and expert captains perished promiscuously together, to the great damage and weakening to the Ottoman power. So that now it is not probable that a new militia succeeding, capable of receiving other customs and laws and neither remembering nor concerned in former mutinies, will adventure to follow the seditious practices of their predecessors, for men are commonly modest at their first entrance into any condition, and unless debauched by corruption and government, are easily

---

[724] A person exempted from military service.

[725] Those who have left the service; for the Romans, it could also mean soldiers who had been cashiered.

contained within the bounds of reasonable moderation. And yet, notwithstanding that the pride of the Turkish religion is reduced to follow the abatement of their power and to a condition easily for the future, with good management, to be ruled, yet this present Sultan Mehmed, still retaining the memory and impression of the amazement he suffered in his infancy on occasion of a dangerous combination and conspiracy of the Janissaries, will never confine himself to their guard nor be reconciled to Constantinople, in consideration of the many chambers it contains of that loathed miltia, which have been so many nurseries and seminaries of treasons complotted against himself and his other progenitors.

# CHAP. IX.

## *Of the* Chiaufes.

*The Chaousbashee or Cheife the Pursuivants*

## Chapter IX. *Of the Çavuses.*

These, having both offensive and defensive arms assigned them, may be reckoned in the number of the militia, though their office, being chiefly in relation to civil processes and laws, they may rather deserve the name of pursuivants or serjeants. They are in number about 5 or 600, their pay is from 12 to 40 aspers

a day, and chief officer is called Çavusbaşi, to whose custody prisoners of quality are committed. Their place of attendance is the palace of the Prime Vizier, to
be ready on all occasions to carry letters and commands to any part of the Empire. Such Christian renegados as become Turks they most commonly for their
encouragement and subsistence in the Muhammadan superstition admit to this
rank, because, having commonly an endowment of other languages besides the
Turkish, are most serviceable on messages into foreign countries, and sometimes
are sent with the title of ambassadors, as one was once sent into England, France
and Holland. Their arms are a scimitar, a bow and arrows and a truncheon with
a knob at the end, called in Turkish *topuz*; these officers that are servants to the
Vizier or beylerbeys carry this truncheon covered with silver, but the çavuses of
simple pashas only wood. Their harvest they make upon the occasions of lawsuits
and differences between one party and another, being apparitors or serjeants to
call the guilty person to justice, or, if the business comes to composition, they
commonly are in the midst to persuade both sides to reason, in which action they
want not their fees or acknowledgment of labour from both parties.

# Chapter X. *Of the other parts of the Turkish militia, the* Topçu.[726]

These are gunners, called so from the word *top*, which in Turkish signifies a cannon, and are in number about 1200, distributed in 52 chambers. Their quarters are at Tophana, on the Place of the Guns in the suburbs of Constantinople. Few of these are expert in their art and are ill-practiced in the proportions and mathematical part of the gunner's mystery, for were they as skilful as many engineers in the world, they might doubtless with that train of vast artillery they either march with in their camp or found in their trenches give much more annoyance to the Christian forces. And therefore, knowing their own imperfections in this exercise, when Christian gunners are taken in the war they entertain them with better usage than other captives, quartering them in the chambers appropriated to that profession, allotting them with others pay from 8 to 12 aspers a day, but because this is too considerable a maintenance to allure men who are otherwise principled, most of them, as occasion offers, desert the service of the Turk and fly to their own country. Their officers are:

1. The *topçibaşi* or general of the ordnance.
2. The *dukiçibaşi* or the chief of them that found[727] the great guns.
3. The *odabaşi*, the chief of all the chambers of gunners in the suburbs of Constantinople.
4. The *kiatib* or their muster-master, who is always a Sipahi.

Their guns are the biggest and as well-cast and moulded as any in the world; for the last expedition in Hungary there were 40 pieces of new cannon cast and transported by way of the Black Sea, and thence by the Danube unto Belgrade and Buda. Their gunpowder is made but in small quantities about Constantinople, but comes from divers places in Europe, but that from Damascus is most esteemed. The biggest size of their bullets are from 36 to 40 inches diameter, but these are most commonly of stone, which they make use of in the castles or blockhouses[728] situate on the sea, as at the castles upon the Hellespont called anciently Sestos and Abydos,[729] and at the forts at entrance of the Black Sea.[730] Once and Englishman, gunner of a ship which lay at Constantinople, had the

---

[726] This whole chapter is a slightly expanded and updated version of Knolles, *Turkish History* Volume 2, Chapter 4, 69–70.

[727] Cast.

[728] Small forts built in strategic locations to "block" access to ports and other vital places.

[729] These would be Kilitbahir Castle on Sestos and Canak Castle on Abydos, both built by Mehmed II.

[730] Yoros Castle at the entrance to the Black Sea was fought over for many years by Ottomans and Venetians.

Çebe, or one of the Viziers Guard

curiosity and confidence to measure the dimensions of these bullets, but, being apprehended in the very act, was imprisoned for a spy, but by the intercession of our ambassador then resident with much labour and some expense was at length released.

## Of the Cebeçis

These are armourers, so-called from the word *cebeç*, which signifies in Turkish as much as arms of back or breast. They are in number 630, distributed into 60 chambers and have their quarters near the church of Santa Sophia in Constantinople. Their office is to conserve the arms of ancient times from rust by cleaning and oiling of them so as to remain trophies for ever of the Turkish conquests. Their pay is from 6 to 12 aspers a day; their officers are first the *cebeçibaşi*, who is their commander-in-chief; 2. The *odabaşis*, who are so many masters of the chambers. On all expeditions these armourers are necessary to officers, and oftentimes in days of battle distribute forth the antique arms of which they have a care into the hands of the Janissaries. But of these, men that are indifferently rich and have favour and friends enjoy their pay with ease at their own homes, and, like other *ocaks*[731] are capable of being made *otoraks* or retaining their pension with a dispensation from the war.

## Of the Delis

*Deli* signifies as much as a mad fellow or a hector;[732] these are the Prime Vizier's Lifeguard, and are in number from 100 to 400 more or less, according as the Vizier is more or less rich and splendid in his retinue.[733] Their pay is from 12 to 15 aspers a day; they are by nation of Bosnia or Albania. Their habit is very ridiculous, according to this picture; they are men chosen for their great stature and stomachs, they speak big, talk of nothing but killing and adventurous exploits, but in reality their heart and courage is not esteemed proportionable to their bulk and bodies. In the city they march before the Vizier on foot and make way for him to the *divan*. On journeys they are too heavy and lazy not to be well-mounted; they have a captain over them called the *delibaşi*, their arms are a lance after the Hungarian fashion, a sword and poleaxe, and some of them carry a pistol at their girdle. This sort of people being naturally more faithful than the Turks and more inclinable to the Vizier Köprülü for being of the same country, he maintained 2000 of them for his guard, which was so great a curb to the Janissaries and other militia that they were never able to execute any conspiracy against him. The same course his son the present Vizier follows, and is doubtless, next the Grand Signior, his principal security.

---

[731] "*Ocaks* signifies a family, as also a military family, so *sipahi ocaki*, the order of the Sipahis, so *Yeniçeri ocaki*, the militia of the Janissaries etc." (Rycaut's marginal note). Nicolle translates *ocak* as "corps" which appears to be more accurate. In modern Turkish the word means "local branch."

[732] Not the Trojan hero, but a mere swaggering bully.

[733] *Delis* were originally irregular infantry forces recruited from various parts of the Ottoman Empire, and by the nineteenth century had actually become respectable cavalrymen who often functioned as army scouts.

## Of the Sekbans[734] and Saricas[735]

It is not to be omitted that the beylerbeys and pashas maintain always a militia called *sekbans*, to whose custody the charge of the baggage belonging to the horse is committed, and a select number called *saricas*, to whose care the baggage of the infantry is entrusted. These serve on foot with muskets like Janissaries, and the others on horseback like dragoons in Christendom; their pay, besides their meat, is 3 or 4 dollars a month. The beylerbeys have oftentimes on occasion of their rebellions enrolled many of this sort of militia to encounter the Janissaries, the which was practiced by Ipşir Pasha,[736] [Abaza] Hasan Pasha and Murteza Pasha, who, having lifted great numbers to fight under this denomination, the Vizier Köprülü for terror and more easy destruction of this people proclaimed through all Asia that strict inquisition should be made after the *sekbans* and *saricas*, and that it might be lawful for anyone to kill and destroy them without mercy, by which means many were butchered in several places, and 30,000 of them revolted to the Sophy[737] of Persia.

## The Muhlagi and Beşli

Are the servants of beylerbeys and pashas. The first make profession of a principal art in horsemanship and exercise themselves in throwing the *gerit*, which is a dart much-used amongst the Turks, in the true management of which there is a great dexterity, and because there are considerable rewards bestowed on those who are expert herein, the Turks practice it on horseback as their only exercise and study. Very much delight herein the Grand Signiors have always taken, and to be spectators of the combats between the servants of several pashas born in different countries and nations who, from a principle of honour to their nation and hopes of preferment, contend with that heat and malice one against the other as surpass the cruelty of the ancient gladiators. And not only limbs and eyes are lost in this skirmiush, but oftentimes sacrifice their blood and life for

---

[734] "Early in the seventeenth century," Nicolle writes, "the new *sekbans* were organized on a regular basis in *Bölük* units of between 50 and 100 men, mostly paid as private armies by provincial governors." They were, he states, "an answer to the Ottoman army's acute shortage of musket troops in the face of ever-stronger European enemies" (*Janissaries* 49).

[735] These soldiers, usually called *sarrâj*, were also known as *saricas* (wasps), "and tended to be excellent marksmen, perhaps because so many had been huntsmen or bandits before becoming soldiers" (Nicolle, *Janissaries* 49).

[736] Ipşir Mustafa Pasha (d. 1655), of Abkhazian origin, was respectively governor of Karaman and Sivas provinces and finally Grand Vizier (1653–1654). He was executed after a rebellion.

[737] The standard name in the west for the Shah; it was probably derived from the name of the Persian royal line, the Safavids.

the pastime of their Prince. Such as are observed to be bold, active and dexterous at this game are preferred to the degree and benefit of a *zaim* or *timariot*. The *beşlis*[738] are footmen, who for their great abilities in walking and running attain oftentimes to be made Janissaries.

And thus we have now, with as much brevity as may be, run through the several degrees, numbers, institutions, laws, and discipline of the Turkish militia by land, whose farther progress into Christendom and damage to the Christian cause may the Almighty Providence so disappoint that his Church, corrected and grown more pious by this chastisement, may at length be relieved from the rod and yoke of this great oppressor.

---

[738] So-called because their name means "the five;" one of them was recruited from every five families. Some later authorities state that they were cavalry, not "footmen" as Rycaut states here; Charles Macfarlane, for example, described them as "light cavalry" (*Constantinople in 1828: A Residence of Sixteen Months*, vol. 1 [London: Sanders and Otley, 1829], 282). They were used to defend frontier forts and perform scouting duties.

**Chapter XI.** *Certain observations on the Turkish camp and the success of the last battle against the Christians.*

In the year of Our Lord 1665, the Earl of Winchilsea, our Lord Ambassador, for certain affairs of His Majesty and the Company of Merchants having commanded me to meet the Great Vizier in his return from the wars in Hungary, through ill or rather uncertain information of the Vizier's motion, I was forced to proceed as far as Belgrade in Serbia on the confines of Hungary, 23 days journey from Constantinople, where, finding a good part of the Turkish army encamped near that city, for better convenience and expedition of my business I entered within the quarters of the Sipahis and pitched my tent as near the Vizier and the other principal officres as consisted with due respect. In which place I remained for seven days until the army removed towards Adrianople, and, not having fully completed my business, I marched and remained other 13 days together with the army, in which time I had leisure to make some reflections on the order of the Turkish camp.

In the front of the camp are quartered the Janissaries and all others dedicated to foot-service, whose tents encompass their agha or general. In the body of the camp are erected the stately pavilions of the Vizier, of his *Kâhya* or Chief Steward or councillor, the *Reis Effendi* or Lord Chancellor,[739] the *Defterdar Pasha* or Lord Treasurer and the *Kapujilar Kâhyasi* or Master of the Ceremonies, which five pavilions take up a large extent of ground, leaving a spacious field in the midst in the centre of which is raised a lofty canopy under which offenders are corrected or executed, and serves to shelter from the sun or rain such as attend the *divan* or other business with the officers of state. Within the same space of ground also is the *hazne* or treasury, in small chests one piled on the other in form of a circle, for guard of which 15 Sipahis every night keep watch with their arms in their hands. Near these quarters are the tents of pashas, beys, aghas, and persons of quality, who, with their retinue, make up a considerable part of the Turkish army. In the rear are the quarters of the Sipahis and others that attend the horse service as *sekbans*, *saricas*, and others. On the right hand of the Vizier without the camp are placed the artillery and ammunition, which in the time I was there was inconsiderable, the great cannon remaining in Buda and in the city of Belgrade. Only 40 or 45 small field-pieces of brass (as I reckoned them), each drawn by four horses, marched with the Vizier more at that time for state and ostentation than for real service.

The pavilions of the Great Vizier and other persons of principal office and quality may be rather called palaces than tents, being of a large extent, richly-wrought within, adorned beyond their houses, accommodated with stately

---

[739] The *Reis Effendi* also functioned as a kind of foreign minister. Originally he was little more than a record-taking secretary to the Sultan's *divan*.

furniture with all the conveniences of the city and country, and in my opinion far exceed the magnificence of the best of their buildings, for being but for few years continuance, the maintenance of them is beyond the expense of marble or porphyry[740] or the perpetual edifices of Italy, durable to many olympiads[741] and myriads of years. With these houses and movable habitations, which with the posts that support them are of great weight and bulk, the Turkish army marches daily four, five and sometimes six hours journey, all which baggage is carried on horses, mules and camels. The great persons are furnished with two sets of tents, one of which, as the Vizier rides, is advanced the *konak*[742] or day's journey beyond, so that in the morning leaving one tent, another is found at noon ready-furnished and provided at arrival, which is the reason why the Turkish camp abounds with such multitudes of camels, mules, and horses of burden, with so many thousands of attendants on the baggage, which are of a vast expense, and if duly considered is a matter of the greatest state and magnificence in the Turkish Empire.

Though it is reported by those who are soldiers and have experienced the valour of the Turks in fight that their victories are obtained by multitudes of men rather than by art or military discipline, the conquests they have made on the parts of Christendom is a demonstration undeniable of some supereminent order in their army which recompenses the defect of knowledge in the true mystery of war. And this regulation, in my opinion, proceeds from nothing more than the strict prohibition of wine upon pain of death, (two men being executed during the time of my residence there for bringing a small quantity of it in the field), for hereby men become sober, diligent, watchful and obedient. In the Turkish camp no brawls, quarrels, nor clamours are heard; no abuses are committed on the people by the march of their army. All is bought and paid with money as by travellers that are guests at an inn; there are no complaints by mothers of the rape of their virgin daughters, no violence or robberies offered on the inhabitants, all of which order tends to the success of their armies and enlargement of their empire. As, on the contrary, the sloth of the Germans and other nations in the counsels against the Turks, the liberty is given to the Christian soldiery, or rather the difficulty to correct, proceeds from nothing more than intemperance in wine, which moves in the soldiery a lust and promptitude to all evils and is occasion of the horrid outrages they commit, quarrels among themselves and disobedience to their officers, and betrays oftentimes a whole army to ruin by surprisal.[743] For how can those

---

740 An igneous rock with large crystals, much valued for building stately homes and monuments.

741 Four year periods.

742 Halting place.

743 Busbecq has this to say on the subject: "On our side is public poverty, private luxury, impaired strength, broken spirit, lack of endurance and training; the soldiers are

men be watchful whose heads are charged with the fumes of wine and not yield opportunity of sad advantages to so awakened an enemy as the Turk? Busbecq, who had been ambassador from the Emperor to the Grand Signior in two several embassies and had known and seen the vigilance of the Turkish camp, attributes much of their success against the Germans to the ancient vice of intemperance of his country. And so sensible are the Turks of the abuses and disorders which arise in their camp by the use of wine that they endeavour all that is possible to debar their people from it, and therefore two or three days before the army arrives at any place officers are dispatched before to seal off all taverns and make proclamation against the sale of wine, for though it be against their law to drink wine, yet drunkenness is now become so common a vice amongst them (as we have already declared in the Second Book) that scarce one in ten but is addicted to a brutish intemperance therein.

The camp is always free from ordure[744] and filth, there being holes digged near every tent which are encompassed about with canvas for the more privacy and accommodation in men's necessary occasions, and whenever these places become noisome[745] and full they are covered with earth and the canvas removed, so that the whole camp is clear of all excrements of men as also kept more free from other stench which may cause putrefaction than the most orderly cities of the world. If the march be in the summertime and the weather hot, the beasts of burden and baggage begin to travel about seven o'clock in the evening, and the pashas and Great Vizier presently after midnight, who are accompanied with so many lights as equal almost the brightness of the day. Those that carry these lights are Arabians from the parts of Aleppo and Damascus, men used to travel on foot, who are in Turkish called *meşallâh*, over whom is a superintendent or chief called *meşallâhgibaşi*, whose office it is to govern and to punish these people and is liable for their disorders. The lights they carry are not torches[746] but a bituminous[747] oily sort of wood which they burn in an iron grate, carried in a staff made in the form of our beacons and of the same fashion with those lights we see drawn in ancient hangings and pictures hich represent night-pieces of Roman stories.

And since I have discoursed something of the Turkish camp in this return homewards, it will not be much from my promise to acquaint the reader with what cheerfulness and alacrity the army marched this way after their illsuccess,

---

insubordinate, the officers avaricious; there is contempt for discipline; license, recklessness, drunkenness and debauchery are rife. . ." (*Turkish Letters*, 77).

[744] Excrement.
[745] Smelly.
[746] Nevertheless, *meşale* means "torch" in Turkish.
[747] Bitumen is a heavy, thick kind of petroleum.

and also to declare the occasion that put a hook into the nostrils of this great oppressor and deprived him for the present of the farther spoil of Christendom. After the taking of the castle called [Uj-]Zrínyivar by the Great Vizier,[748] built by Count Zrínyi,[749] the which was the first original and occasion of the war, and the defeat of the Pasha of Buda[750] near Levice[751] by Count Souches,[752] governor of Komàrom;[753] the Vizier made many and various attempts to pass the Raab to make some conquests in parts of Croatia and Styria, but by reason of the forts the Christians had made along the banks of the river in every adventure lost considerable numbers of men. At which loss of men and the ill-success near Levice the Vizier, being greatly moved, made another adventure on the 27th of July, 1664, advancing with the gross of his army as far as Körmend,[754] a place between the river Raab and Terne, endeavouring there to make his passage with better success, but by the valour of the Hungarians and the assistance of the general Montecuculi[755] were repulsed with extraordinary slaughter. On the first of August following the Turk made another considerable attempt, and passed over in one place 6300 Janissaries and Albanians, and in another where the river was fordable and not above ten paces broad, the whole body of the Turkish horse crowded over in vast numbers, which caused the Christians to join forces into one army and retreat farther into the country and put themselves into a posture of giving battle to the enemy.

As soon as the Turkish army had thus waded over the water, the night following fell so much rain and such a deluge came pouring down from the mountains that the river, which was fordable the day before, did now overswell its own banks and [was] not passable without floats and bridges. As soon as the army had thus passed the river, the Great Vizier despatched immediately messengers

---

[748] Now Fazil Ahmed Köprülü, who had succeeded his father in 1661.

[749] See Book 3, Chapter 4, n. 13.

[750] Ali Pasha was sent by the Grand Vizier to halt the advance of the Habsburgs, but was supplied only with irregular troops. He himself was killed in the battle which ensued.

[751] Levice (German Lewenz) is in western Slovakia on the left bank of the Hron river. From 1663 to 1685 it was a Turkish *sanjak*.

[752] Jean-Louis Raduit, comte de Souches (1608–1682), whom Samuel Pepys described as "a soldier of fortune," defeated the Turks twice, first at Žarnovica (16 May, 1664) and then at Levice (16 July). "[He] hath had a great victory against the Turk," Pepys wrote on August 1, "killing 4000 men and taking the most extraordinary spoil" (Samuel Pepys, *Diary*, http://www.pepysdiary.com/diary/1664/08/01/). Souches was named commander-in-chief of Imperial forces on the Slavonian frontier.

[753] Komàrom is a Hungarian city on the banks of the Danube.

[754] A town in western Hungary.

[755] See Book1, Chapter 16, n. 13. This is the battle of St. Gotthard.

to the Grand Signior to acquaint him of his progress and passage, which news he knew would come very grateful, because in all letters from the Grand Signior he was urged by threats and positive commands to proceed forward in his march and not to suffer the impediment of a narrow ditch to be an interruption to the whole Ottoman force, which was never before restrained by the ocean. The Grand Signior, having received this intelligence as if the whole victory and triumph over the world consisted in the passage over the Raab, was transported with such an extraordinary joy and assurance of victory that all Hungary and Germany were already swallowed in his thoughts. And when by a second message he received intelligence that a forlorn hope of the enemy consisting of 1000 men was cut off, the Ottoman court was so transported with the joy and assurance of victory that, to anticipate the good news, the Grand Signior commanded that a solemn festival should be celebrated for the space of seven days and seven nights called by the Turks *dunalma*,[756] in which time the whole nights were spent in fireworks, shooting great guns, volleys of muskets, sound of drums and trumpets, revelling and what other solemnities might testify their joy and triumph. But scarce three nights of this vain dream had passed before the Grand Signior, awakened by intelligence contrary to what was presaged and expected—of the defeat of the best part of his army—shamefully commanded the lights to be extinguished and the remaining four nights appointed for joy to be turned to melancholy and darkness. And indeed this rash joy was the more shameful and ridiculous by how how much more fatal and destructive the loss was to the Turks, for they, being now got over the river and the Christians drawn up in battalia,[757] a most furious fight began, which from nine o'clock in the morning until four in the afternoon continued with variable fortune. At length the Turks, assailed by the straordinary valour of the Christians, which were now of equal number to them,[758] began to give back and put themselves into a shameful flight, leaving

---

[756] A *dunalma* could be proclaimed to celebrate happy or auspicious events, such as the Sultan's visit to a town or, as here, a victory. It was also known as a *ziné* or *eziné*. Typically there was firing of cannons and muskets, street decorations and fireworks, as Rycaut tells us. In his *Letters Written by a Turkish Spy*, Paolo Marana has his fictional spy in the last letter lamenting: "I die in contemplation of the sacred fasts and feast, the nocturnal joys of Ramazan, the revels and cheerful illuminations of Bairam and the imperial *dunalmas*" (6, 261).

[757] Order of battle.

[758] Andrew Wheatcroft states that "Even with allies, [the Habsburgs] were heavily-outnumbered. In total the little Habsburg army numbered fewer than forty thousand and with inadequate artillery" (*The Enemy at the Gate*, 70). He goes on to note, calling any comparison with Lepanto "unrealistic," that Montecuccoli's victory at St. Gotthard was gained "entirely by good fortune," and that he had "trapped a divided Ottoman army in a position where it could neither retreat not manoeuvre" (73).

dead upon the place about 5000 men and the glory of the day to the Christians. The Turks, who always fly disorderly, knowing not the art of a handsome retreat, crowded in heaps to pass the river, the horse trampling over the foot and the foot throwing themselves headlong into the water without consideration of the depth or choice of places fordable after the great rains. Those sinking, catching hold of other that could swim, sunk down and perished together; others, both men and horses, through the rapidness of the stream were carried down the river and swallowed in the deeper places. The water was dyed with blood and the whole face of the river was covered with men, horses, garments all swimming promiscuously together; no difference was here between the valiant and the cowardly, the foolish and the wise, counsel and chance, all being involved in the same violence of calamity: "*Non vox et mutui hortatus iuvabant, adversante unda, nihil strenuous ab ignavo, sapiens a prudenti, consilia a casu differe, cuncta pars violentia involvebantur,*"[759] so that the waters devoured a far greater number than did the sword, whilst the Great Vizier, standing on the other side of the river, was able to afford no kind of help or relief, but as one void of all counsel or reason knew not where to apply a remedy.

This defeat, though in Christendom not greatly boasted by reason that the destruction of the Turks, which was most by water, was partly concealed to them, yet the Turks acknowledge the ruin and slaughter to have been of a far greater number than what the Christian diaries relate, confessing that since the time that the Ottoman Empire arrived at this greatness, no stories make mention of any slaughter or disgrace it hath suffered to be equal to the calamity and dishonour of this. On the Turks' side were slain Ismail Pasha, lately of Buda and *kaymakam* of Constantinople,[760] by a shot from the enemy in his passage over the river, the *Sipahilar Agasi* or general of the Sipahis, and several other persons of quality fell that day. 15 pieces of cannon were taken with the tents and rich spoils; of the Christians were slain near 1000. Those of note were [the] Count of Nassau,[761] Count Charles of Brakensdorff, captain of the guards to Montecucculi, Count [von] Fugger,[762] general of the artillery, with many other

---

[759] Tacitus, *Annals* 1.70. Rycaut has already translated the passage.

[760] A *kaymakam* was a deputy governor or sub-governor of a province or governor of a provincial district. For Ismail Pasha, see Book 1, Chapter 9, n. 5.

[761] The only reference to a "Count of Nassau" dying in 1664 is to William Frederick, count and prince of Nassau-Dietz (1613–1664), who died from a misfiring pistol. Prince Walrad Usingen of Nassau (1635–1702) arrived just too late to participate in the battle, but distinguished himself later in the siege of Vienna.

[762] Count Franz von Fugger (1612–1664), a descendent of the famous merchant family of that name, was from Augsburg. He had served under Wallenstein during the Thirty Years War and was Governor of Ingolstadt.

gentlemen of the French nation who deserve ever to be chronicled for their virtue and valour.

The Turks were with this news greatly ashamed and dejected, having but two days before demonstrated excesses of joy, congratulated the happy news one to the other, sending presents abroad after their manner, derided the Christians living amongst them with the news, expropriated them with a thousand injuried, applauded their own virtue and valour and the righteousness of their cause and religion. But on a sudden, intelligence coming contrary to their expectations, such a dampness fell upon their spirits that for some days there was a deep silence of all news at Constantinople. They that the day before sought for Christians to communicate to them the miracles of their victory now avoided their company, ashamed of their too-forward joy and the liberty they had taken to condemn and deride the low condition of the Christian camp. And now, the ill news not being able to be longer concealed, prayers and humiliation were appointed publicly to be made at all the royal mosques both at Constantinople and Adrianople, where all the imams or parish priests with their young scholars were commanded to resort, singing some doleful chapter of the Qur'an.

The minds of the soldiery after this defeat were very much discomposed, tending more to sedition than obedience; everyone took license to speak loudly and openly his opinion that the war was commenced upon unjust and unlawful grounds, that comets lately seen to fall were prodigious, foretelling the ill-success of the war, that the total eclipse of the Moon, which portends always misfortunes to the Turks, should have caused more caution in the commanders of engaging the army untill the malignity of that influence had been overpassed. And, calling to mind the solemn oath with which the Sultan Süleyman [I] confirmed his capitulations with the Emperor, particularly vowing never to pass the Raab or places where the Turks received their defeat without a solid or reasonable ground of war. All concluded that this invasion was a violation of the vow and an injury to the sacred memory of that fortunate Sultan and that all endeavours and attempts of this war would be fatal and destructive to the Muslims or believers and the end dishonourable to the Empire.

This opinion was rooted with much firmness and superstition in the mind of the vulgar, and the rumours in the camp that the Vizier had been cause of the soldiers' flight by commanding them to retreat after they had been engaged, upon a false alarm that the enemy in great numbers were coming to fall upon the quarters where the Vizier's person remained, and that this error was the first original of the slaughter that ensued, augmented their discontents and animosities against the government. The soldiery, besides, was greatly terrified and possessed with the fear of the Christians and amazed upon every alarm; the Asian Sipahis and other soldiers, having wives and children and possessions to look after, were grown poor and desired nothing than in peace and quietness to return to their home, so that nothing could come more grateful to this camp, no largesses nor hopes could pacify the minds of the soldiery more than the promises and expectations of peace. And this was the true cause that brought on the treaty of peace between the Emperor and the Turk[763] in such an instant, contrary to the opinion of most in the world, and gave occasion to the Vizier to embrace the propositions offered by Reniger,[764] then Resident for the Emperor, who was carried about according to the motions of the Turkish camp to be ready to improve any overtures of peace that might be offered. The Vizier, to show his real intentions, flattered and caressed this Resident with the present of a horse richly-furnished, a vest of sables, and a commodious tent, whilst the propositions and condescensions on the Turkish part were dispeeded[765] to Vienna, which were returned again with an entire assent to most of the articles, and those wherein there might be any differemce were to be referred until the arrival of the Extraordinary Ambassador, who was supposed might reach the Ottoman court by the end of April.

The Asian Sipahis were overjoyed at the news and immediately obtained license to depart, and most of the militia was dispersed, everyone with joy betaking himself to his own home. But this ambassador, missing of his time allotted for his arrival above a month later than he was expected, put all things into a strange combustion. I was then in the camp when it was whispered that the treaty was at an end, that the Christians had deluded them and caused them to disband their army that so they might fall upon them with the greater advantage, the misfortune of which, according to the custom of the commonwealth, was charged on the heads of the governors and the too much credulity of the Vizier. But at length, on the 28 of May 1665, news coming that the ambassador from the Emperor was arrived at Buda, the Vizier the next day departed from Belgrade with his whole army, which I accompanied as far as Niš,[766] about nine days march towards Adrianople. And there, having put an end to my business, and wearied with the slow pace and heats and other inconveniences of an army, I took my leave of the Great Vizier and proceeded further by longer journies to attend the court at Adrianople. And that I may give my reader an account of these countries and the nature of the people that inhabit them, I hope it will not

---

[763] The Treaty of Vasvár (10 August 1663), actually a confirmation of an earlier agreement, was a twenty-year truce "hurriedly concluded. . .to the satisfaction of neither the Hapsburgs nor the Ottomans, and the despairing fury of the Hungarians" (Wheatcroft, *The Enemy at the Gate*, 72).

[764] Baron Simon Reniger von Reningen (d. 1666) was the Imperial Resident in Constantinople 1649–1666.

[765] Quickly sent off.

[766] Niš is an ancient city in southern Serbia, which is often seen as the gateway between the east and the west. It was first captured by the Ottomans in 1375; they held it until 1443, and five years later regained it, bringing it under Turkish rule until 1877.

be judged much besides my purpose if I entertain him a little with a relation of some part of my journey to Belgrade.

On the 29th of April 1665 I departed from Adrianople towards Belgrade, and on the first of May I lodged at a village called Semesge, the first town I came to, inhabited by Bulgarians, who are Christians, that day being a festival. The women, upon the arrivial of guests, come running from their houses with cakes of dough-baked bread which they call *pogacha*,[767] only laid upon the coals between two tiles, which they soon kneaded and prepared for the stomachs of travellers. Others brought milk, eggs, and wine to sell, and what else their homely cottages afforded, which they pressed on us with much importunity, the younger and handsomer challenging a priority in the sale of their provisions before those who were ancient and more homely. These country lasses had that day put on their holy garments, which put me in mind of those dresses I have seen in pictures of the ancient shepherdesses in Arcadia, being a loose gown of various colours with hanging sleeves. Their arms had no sleeve but that of their smock, which though it were of canvas or some very coarse linen, was yet wrought with many various works of divers colours. Their hair was braided, hanging down at length behind, which some had adorned with little shells found upon the seashore, tied at the end with fringes of silk, bobs and tassels of silver. Their heads were covered with pieces of silver coin of different sorts strung upon thread, and their breasts were in the same manner decked, those being most honoured and most rich who were adorned with these strings of coin and bracelets on their wrists, with which every one, according to her ability, had dressed and made herself fine. Amongst these we passed with plenty of provision and a hearty welcome, for these people called Bulgarians inhabit all that country to the confines of Hungary. They till all that ground, pasture vast numbers of cattle and are industrious and able husbandmen, by which means and the liberty they enjoy by the small number of Turks which live amongst them, they pass their time with reasonabkle comfort and are more commodious in wealth than they suffer to appear outwardly to the envious eyes of the Turks. Their language is the old Illyrian or Slavonian tongue, which hath much similitude with the Russians, because this people is said to come originally from beyond the river Volga, and so by corruption are called Bulgarians or Volgarians.

On the third of May we arrived at Philippopolis,[768] where we were civilly entertained at the house or monastery of the Metropolitan or Greek bishop of

---

[767] *Pogacha* is actually a kind of puff-pastry; in Bulgaria it is often served instead of bread and filled with feta cheese.

[768] Now Plovdiv, Bulgaria's second-largest city. Originally named after Philip II of Macedon, this ancient city was in Ottoman hands from 1364 to 1878, and served as the administrative centre for the *sanjak* of Edirne (Adrianople). Recent excavations (December 2011) have uncovered extensive new Roman ruins in the city centre.

that place. By this city runs the river Hebrus,[769] having its original from the mountains Rhodope,[770] in sight of which we travelled towards Sofia, of which Ovid thus speaks: "*Qua patet umbrosum Rhodope glacialis ad Haemum, / Et sacer amissas exigit Hebrus aquas.*"[771] The city of Philippopolis is situate in a large and open plain and level, whereon are great numbers of little round hills which the inhabitants will have to be the graves of the Roman legions slain in those fields. A certain Greek once had the melancholy dream of much treasure buried in one of these hills, and this fancy so troubled him in his sleep that it took a strong impression in his mind when he was waking, and so far troubled him that he could take no rest nor contentment until he had eased his mind to the *Nazir Agha*,[772] who is he who oversees the waterworks and places of pleasure belonging to the Grand Signior in that country. The Turk, though he had a great mind to the treasure, durst not yet open the ground until he had acquainted the Grand Signior with the mind of the Greek, who, upon the first intimation dispatched away officers (so apt are the Turks in matters of profit to catch even at a shadow) to open the hill, to which work the country villagers were summoned. And whilst they digged very deep, not well understanding the art of mining, the earth broke from the top and buried seventy persons, and so the work ended and the Greek awaked from his dream.

This town hath one part of it built on the side of a little hill; two others are also near it,[773] which appear like bulwarks or fortifications on that side the city, all the rest of the country thereabouts being a dead plain or level. At this place remains no other antiquity besides the ruins of two ancient chapels built of brick in the form of a cross, one of which the Greeks hold in great devotion and report to be the place wherein St. Paul preached often to the Philippians, and with that opinion they often resort thither, especially on the days of devotion, to say their prayers.[774] The walls of the city are likewise very ancient, over the gates of which is writ something in the Greek character, but time hath so defaced it that to me it seemed no longer legible. And so ignorant are the Greeks also, even such as were born in that city and are priests and *colories*, which are the strictest sort of religious men amongst them, who have nothing more to do than to attend to their office and studies, that they cannot give any reasonable account of the

---

[769] The longest river in the Balkans, it is known in Bulgaria as the Maritsa.

[770] The Rhodope mountains are in southeastern Europe. Most of the range lies in Bulgaria, with some also in Greece.

[771] "Where icy Rhodope extends to shady Haemus / And sacred Hebrus drives through its lost waters" (Ovid, *Epistles* 2, 113–14).

[772] *Nazir* means "inspector."

[773] The city was also known as Trimontium, "three hills."

[774] St. Paul was in the area around 52 CE; the Philippians were the first people he visited on his missionary journeys.

original of that city, who it was built by or anything else of the history of it, and with much admiration they hearken to us when we tell them anything what our books relate concerning it. [775]

From hence I departed towards Sofia, [776] passing in this journey the *Montes Haemi*, [777] called by the Turks *Kapi Dervent*, [778] which is as much as "the Gate of the Narrow Way." The ascent hereunto is rugged and sharp, commodious for robbers, who there have such caves and places of refuge that they defy very considerable forces that are sent against them. On the top of this hill is a village of Bulgarians, where the women, used to the diversity of travellers, are become free in their discourse, and only entertain strangers whilst their husbands are in the field or with their cattle or fly away for fear of some injurt from the Turks. Descendeing hence is a very narrow enclosure, on both sides being environed with high mountains and woods, which is a shady and melancholy journey for the space of two hours. To this place the *hayduts* or *hayduks* [779] (as that people call them) frequently resort in great numbers out of Transylvania, Moldavia, Hungary, and other parts, which, taking advantage of these close woods, discharge volleys of shot on the strongest caravans and, rolling stones from the mountains in the narrowest passages, do as much execution as with cannon, for as I have understood, in one of those *dervents* (for there are many of this nature in the journey to Belgrade) 18 thieves only killed above 300 merchants who for security united together, and their whole baggage became a prey to the robbers.

In these places thus fortified by nature the inhabitants resisted the force of the Grecian emperors and killed Baldwin, Earl of Flanders, [780] after he had subjected

---

[775] See above, n. 28.

[776] Now, of course, the capital of Bulgaria, Sofia was captured by the Ottomans in 1382 and became the capital of the *beylerbeylik* of Rumelia. In 1443 Władysław III, the King of Poland, launched a crusade to get it back, but he failed, and the Ottomans retaliated by eliminating any influential Christians they could find. This is why Rycaut found, as he says later, that the city was "so wholly Turkish." In 1599 Sofia actually fell into the hands of the Bulgarian *hayduts* for a very short time.

[777] Now known as the Balkan Mountains, they are in the eastern part of the Balkan peninsula.

[778] More accurately "gateway across the valley." The modern Turkish name is *Kodzhalbalkan*, which means "a chain of wooded mountains."

[779] A word commonly used in the Balkans for highwaymen or robbers.

[780] Baldwin IX, count of Flanders (1172–1205), became the first Latin Emperor of Constantinople as Baldwin I in 1204. His army was defeated by the Bulgarians under Tsar Kaloyan at the battle of Adrianople (1205) and the Emperor was captured. Historians are uncertain about the nature of his death; Kaloyan reported that Baldwin had died in prison, but rumours persisted that he had put the Emperor to death after Baldwin had tried to seduce his wife.

the city of Constantinople. Amongst these Blugarians is a sort of people which they call Paulines, who had in former times strange confused notions of Christianity, pretending to follow the doctrine of St. Paul, used fire in the sacrament of baptism, and preferred this apostle before his master Christ. But, there being some Roman priests in those parts that, observing the ignorance of these poor people and their willingness to be instructed, took the advantage and reduced them all to the Roman faith, to which now they are strict and superstitious adherents.

Through these narrow *dervents* before spoken of we arrived after three days of weary journey at Sofia, a place so wholly Turkish that there is nothing in it that appears more antique than the Turks themselves. It is situated in a pleasant plain or broad valley between two high mountains, the highest of them wearing a snowy head in the heat of the summer solstice, which is the reason that that city is cool and wholesome, but of a subtle penetrating air, being supplied with admirable waters of easy digestion which come pouring down in great abundance from the mountains, and supply the town with plentiful streams in all parts of it and are said to be the waters of those fountains which Orpheus delighted in. There are, besides these cool waters, certain baths naturally hot, to which the Turks resort very frequently, being of the same nature and virtue with ours in England.[781] From this place we made nine long days journey to Belgrade, in which passage there is nothing more memorable than the desolation of the country, and, being there arrived we pitched our tent in the camp, where after five or six days we marched back with the army, to whom nothing could come more joyful than their return home and the conclusion of the war, by which may be observed in some manner how far the nature of the Turks is degenerated from the sncient warlike disposition of the Saracens.

---

[781] Sofia is located at the foot of Mount Vitosha, which has four separate parts to it, the highest being the Black Peak, which is probably the one to which Rycaut is referring here. The city is also well-known today for its thermal and mineral springs. The Bulgarians have many legends about Orpheus, who was supposed to have been born in the Rhodope Mountains.

## Chapter XII. *Of the Turks' armada or naval forces.*

Having particularly run over the force of this formidable enemy and scourge of Christianity by land, we are now to take a view, according to the true method of this discourse, of the strength of their fleets and maritime forces, which though to a nation situated on the continent, are not so necessary or prevalent to defend themselves from their neighbours or transport their power and conquests into other dominions as they are to a people whose habitation is encompassed by the sea. Yet certainly, a prince can never be said to be truly puissant who is not master in both elements, for not to expatiate on the common theme of the riches and power which arise from navigation, it is sufficient, considering how often the mighty force of the Ottoman Empire hath been foiled and baffled by the small republic of Venice for want of true knowledge or success or application of their minds to maritime exercise, to demonstrate of what efficacy in most designs is a well-provided and regulated fleet.[782]

The Turks are now very much weakened in their naval forces in their war against Candia, and are so discouraged in their hopes of success at sea that ships and galleasses, called by them *mahons*,[783] are wholly in disuse amongst them. Whether it be that they want able seamen to govern them or that they despair of ever being able to meet the Venetians in open sea, for which those vessels of battery are only in use, they are fallen into a fancy of light galleys, a sign that they intend to trust more of their safety to their oars than their arms, of which, in the year 1661, after the loss of 28 well-provided galleys wrecked with their men in the Black Sea, the Vizier Köprülü built thirty others for reparation of that loss, but of that green and unseasoned timber that the first voyage many of them became unserviceable for the leaks, and the rest, at the return of the fleet in the month of October following, were laid up amongst the old and worn vessels.

It may seem a difficult manner to assign the true reason and by what means the Turks come to be so decayed in their naval forces, who abound with so many conveniences for it and with all sorts of materials fit for navigation as cordage,[784] pitch, tar, and timber, which arise and grow in their own dominions and are easily brought to the imperial city with little or no danger of their enemies. For timber, the vast woods along the coast of the Black Sea and parts of Asia at the bottom of

---

[782] Compare Sandys, who noted that "As for their forces at sea, they are but small in comparison of what they have been, and compared to those of particular Christian princes, but contemptible" (*Travels*, 40). An attempt at naval reform was finally made during the reign of Selim III (1789–1807), for which see Shaw, *History of the Ottoman Empire and Modern Turkey* 1, 263–64).

[783] A galleass is a ship powered by oars as well as sails.

[784] Rope.

the Gulf of Nicomedia[785] supply them; pitch, tar, and tallow are brought to them from Albania and Wallachia, canvas and hemp from Grand Cairo, and biscuit[786] is plenty in all parts of the Turk's dominion. Their ports are several of them convenient for building both ships and galleys; the Arsenal at Constantinople hath no less than one hundred thirty-seven *voltas* or chambers for building, and so many vessels may be upon the stocks at the same time. At Sinopolis[787] near Trebizond is another arsenal; at Midia[788] and Anchiale,[789] cities on the Black Sea, are the like, and many parts of the Propontis,[790] the Hellespont and the Bosphorus are such ports and conveniences for shipping, as if all things had conspired to render Constantinople happy and not only capable of being mistress of the earth but formidable in all parts of the ocean, and yet the Turk for several years, especially since the war with Candia and their defeats at sea, have not been able at most to equip a fleet of above 100 sail of galleys, of which 14 are maintained and provided at the charge of the beys of the archipelago, for which they have certain isles in the sea assigned them.

The Turks do neither want slaves to bogue[791] at the oars of the galleys, for Tatary supplies them with great numbers. Besides, divers persons in Constantinople make it a trade to hire out their slaves for the summer's voyage for 6000 aspers, running the hazard of the slave's life, who, returning home safe, is consigned to the possession of his patron, And if want still be of the *kürek*, as the Turks call it, or "slaves for the oar,"[792] a collection is made in several provinces of the lustiest and stoutest clowns, called by the Turks *azabs*[793] but by other slaves çakal.[794] These are chosen out of several villages, one being elected out of every 20 houses, the hire of which is 6000 aspers, for payment whereof the other 19 families make a proportionable contribution. Upon receipt of their pay they give in security not to fly but to serve faithfully for that year's expedition, but these men, unused to the service

---

[785] Now known as the Gulf of Izmit in the Sea of Marmara.

[786] Usually known as sea biscuit, sometimes called "hardtack" in the United States; it is made of flour, water and salt, rather like a "cracker."

[787] Now Sinop, a port city on the northern edge of the Black Sea. It was formerly part of the Empire of Trebizond, and fell into Ottoman hands in 1458.

[788] Probably the ancient city of Tomis, it later became the Black Sea port of Constanţa in modern-day Romania, which now has a satellite port named Midia.

[789] Now known as Akiali, this city was founded during Assyrian times and is on the west coast of the Black Sea.

[790] The Sea of Marmara.

[791] Bogue means "to fall off from the wind or to leeward." Rycaut appears to have some other meaning in mind.

[792] The Turkish phrase for "galley-slave" is *kürek mahkümu*. An oarsman is *kürekciler*.

[793] Irregular infantry.

[794] Rascals. Possibly so called because some of them had engaged in criminal activities.

of the sea, unskilful at the oar and seasick, are of little validity, and the success of their voyage may be compared to the fable of the shepherd who sold his possessions on the land to buy merchandise for sea-negotiations. The soldiers which are destined to sea-service are called *levents*, who come voluntarily and enter themselves in the regiments of the arsenal, obliging themselves to serve that summer's expedition for 6000 aspers and biscuit for the voyage. The stoutest and most resolute of these fellows are those called *cazdagli*, who are a certain sort of moutaineers in the country of Anatolia near Troy, whose country I once passed through with some apprehension and more than ordinary vigilance and caution to preserve my life, for being all robbers and freebooters[795] we admitted no treatise or discourses with them but with our arms in our hands. Others there are also obliged to sea-service who are *zaims* and *timariots* and hold their land in sea-tenure, but being not bound to go in person themselves they bring or send their servants, called in Turkish *bedel*,[796] to supply their place, everyone providing one, two or more according to the value of his lands, as we have before declared in the chapter of the *zaims* and *timariots*. Some Janissaries are also drawn out for sea-service and some Sipahis of the four inferior banners, and, not to make too bold with the veteran soldiers, command only such to sea as are new and green soldiers lately registered in the rolls of the Sipahis.

The auxiliary of the Turks' forces by sea are the pirates of Barbary from those three towns of Tripoli, Tunis, and Algiers, but these of late years have disused the custom of coming into the Turks' assistance. Yet oftentimes they ply towards the Archipelago and to the Levant, but it is to supply themselves with soldiers and recruits of people for increase of their colonies. The other part of the auxiliary forces is from the beys of [the] Archipelago, being 14 in number, every one of which commands a galley and for their maintenance have the contribution of certain islands in that sea allotted to them, the which are better-manned and armed than these of Constantinople. But these, neither, are not willing to expose their vessels to fight or danger, in regard that being built and maintained at their own charges and their whole substance they are the more cautious how they venture all their fortunes in the success of a battle. These beys also give themselves up much to their delights and pleasure, and employ more thoughts how to please their appetites than to acquire glory and fame by war. What they gain in summer when joined with the gross of the Turkish fleet is the prize of the Grand Signior, but what chance throws upon them in the winter is their own proper and peculiar fortune.

The gunners of the Turkish fleet are wholly ignorant of that art, for any person who is either English, French, Dutch, or of any other Christian nation they design

---

[795] An adventurer (as opposed to a mere pirate) who simply makes war by land and sea for pillage and profit.

[796] Substitute.

to this office, whether he be skilful or unskilful in the management of artillery, having an opinion that those people are naturally addicted to a certain proneness and aptitude in gunnery, in which they find their error as often as they come to skirmish with the enemy.

The Chief Admiral or generalissimo of the Turkish armada is called the *Kapudan Pasha*; his Lieutenant-general is called the *Tersane Kiabaşi*; the next officer is *Tersane Emin* or Steward of the Arsenal,[797] who hath the care of providing all necessaries for the navy, but this place, being bought, occasions a necessity in these persons to rob mails, anchors, cables, and other provisions of the fleet to satisfy the debts they contracted for the purchase of their places. In the like manner doth every *reis* or captain of a galley keep his hand in exercise as often as convenience offers; these are all, for the most part, Italian renegadoes or the race of them born and educated near the Arsenal. The officers command their slaves in corrupted Italian, which they call *Franke*, and afford them a better allowance of biscuit than is given to the slaves in the Venetian armada.

The Turks, now despairing of being equal to the Christian forces by sea and to be able to stand with them the shock of a battle, build light vessels for robbing, burning and destroying the Christian coast, and afterwards to secure themselves by flight and also to transport soldiers, ammunition, and provisions for succour of Candia and other places of their new conquests near the seashore. The arsenal at Venice is so greatly esteemed by the Turks that they seem not to desire the conquest of that place for any other reason more than the benefit of the Arsenal. As a person of great quality amongst them said once, that had they made a conquest of Venice they would not inhabit there but leave it to the Venetians, in regard that the city affords not fresh water, which is necessary for the use of their mosques and their washing before prayer, but that the arsenal and a tribute would satisfy the desires of the Grand Signior. But the Turks are not likely to be masters of this seat of Neptune whilst they so unwillingly apply their minds to maritime affairs, who, being conscious of their former ill-success at sea and how little use they make of those advantages they have for shipping, acknowledge their inabilities in sea affairs and say that God hath given the sea to the Christians but the land to them. And no doubt but the large possessions and riches they enjoy on the staple element of the earth is that which takes off their minds the deep attention to matters of the sea, which is almost solely managed by renegadoes amongst them who hath abandoned their faith and their country. And it is happy for Christendom that this faintness remains on the spirits of the Turks, an aversion from all naval employment, whose numbers and power the great God of Hosts hath restrained by the bounds of the ocean as he hath limited the ocean by the sands of the seashore.

---

[797] *Tersane* means "arsenal." *Emine* means "intendant."

## The Conclusion

By the discourse made in the three foregoing books it will evidently appear what sort of government is exercised amongst the Turks, what their religion is and how formidable their force, which ought to make the Christian world tremble to see so great a part of it subjected to the Muhammadan power, and yet no mean thought of to unite our interests and compose our dissentions, which lay us open to the inundation of this flowing Empire. To which I shall add this one thing very observable, that the Grand Signior wages his war by land without any charge to himself, an advantage not to be paralleled by the policy of any government I ever heard or read of before, for his Sipahis and Janissaries are always in pay both in war and peace. His zaims and timariots have their lands to maintain them and other militias enjoy the fixed revenue from their respective countries. And yet, notwithstanding, through the expense of the naval forces, the building galleys and the like matters not provided for [by] those who laid the first foundation of this government, the revenue of the Empire hath been bankrupted, and by the corruption of the officers or ill-management, been sold for 3 years to come, until all was redeemed and restored again by the wisdom of that famous vizier Köprülü, whom we have occasion so often to mention in the foregoing treatise.

We cannot now but pity those poor borderers in Hungary, Styria, Croatia, and other parts subject to the incursions of this cruel enemy, since we know that in the last war, not three English miles from Vienna, many poor people have been surprised and fallen into the hands of the Tatar and Turk and sold afterwards into perpetual slavery. This consideration ought to move us, who are barricaded and fortified by the seas from the violence of our enemies, to bless God we are born in so happy and so secure a country, subject to no dangers but from ourselves, nor other miseries but what arise from our own freedom and too much felicity. We ought to consider it is a blessing that we never have felt any smart of the rod of this great oppressor of Christianity, and yet have tasted of the good and benefit which hath proceeded from a free and open trade and amicable correspondence and friendship with this people, which have been maintained for the space of above eighty years, begun in the reign of Queen Elizabeth of blessed memory, preserved by the prudence and admirable discretion of a series of worthy ambassadors, and daily improved both in business and reputation by the excellent conduct and direction of that Right Worshipful Company of the Levant, hath brought a most considerable benefit to this kingdom and gives livelihood and employment to many thousands of people in England, by which His Majesty, without any expense, gains a considerable increase of his customs.

The sense of this benefit and advantage to my own country, without any private considerations I have as a servant to that embassy or to the obligations

I have to that worthy Company, cause me to move with the greatest sedulity[798] and devotion possible to promote and advance the interest of that trade. And, as some study several ways and prescribe rules by which a war might be most advantageously managed against the Turk, I, on the contrary, am more inclinable to give my judgment in what manner our peace and trade may best be secured and maintained, knowing that so considerable a welfare of our nation depends upon it that a few years of trade's interruption in Turkey will make all sorts of people sensible of the want of so great a vent[799] of the commodities of our country. And therefore, as I am obliged to pray for the glory and prosperity of His Majesty our gracious Sovereign, so likewise as that which conduces to it for the continuance of the honour of this embassy in Turkey and the profitable returns of the Levant Company.

    *FINIS.*

---

[798] Assiduousness.

[799] Outlet.

# BIBLIOGRAPHY

Abbott, G. F. *Turkey, Greece and the Great Powers: A Study in Friendship and Hate*. New York: McBride and Co., 1917.

———. *Under the Turk in Constantinople: Sir John Finch's Embassy 1674–81*. London: Macmillan, 1920.

Ådahl, Karin, ed. *The Sultan's Procession: The Swedish Embassy to Sultan Mehmed IV in 1657–1658 and the Rålamb Paintings*. Constantinople: Swedish Research Institute, 2006.

*Adventures of Mr. T. S., An English Merchant Taken Prisoner by the Turks of Algiers*. London, 1670.

Aksan, Virginia. "Locating the Ottomans Among Early Modern Empires," *Journal of Early Modern History* (1999): 103–34.

———, and Daniel Goffman, eds. *The Early Modern Ottomans: Remapping the Empire*. Cambridge: Cambridge University Press, 2007.

Alderson, A. D. *The Structure of the Ottoman Dynasty*. Oxford: Oxford University Press, 1956.

Allen, Joseph. *Battles of the British Navy, from A. D. 1000 to 1840*. Volume I. London: A. H. Baily, 1852.

Ambrose, Gwilym. "English Traders at Aleppo, 1658–1756," *Economic History Review* (1931–1932): 246–67.

Anderson, Sonia P. *An English Consul in Turkey: Paul Rycaut at Smyrna 1667–1678*. Oxford: Oxford: Oxford University Press, 1989.

———. "Sir Paul Rycaut, F. R. S (1629–1700): His Family and Writings." *Huguenot Society Proceedings* 21, no. 5 (1970): 464–91.

Andrea, Bernadette, ed. *English Women Staging Islam, 1696–1707: Delarivier Manley and Mary Pix*. Toronto: University of Toronto Press, 2012.

———. *Women and Islam in Early Modern English Literature*. Cambridge: Cambridge: Cambridge University Press, 2009.

App, Urs. *The Birth of Orientalism*. Philadelphia: University of Pennsylvania Press, 2010.

Ashton, Peter. *A shorte treatise upon the Turkes Chronicles*. London, 1546.

Bacon, Francis. *The Major Works*. Edited by Brian Vickers. Oxford: Oxford University Press, 2002.

Baer, David. *Honored by the Glory of Islam: Conversion and Conquest in the Ottoman Empire*. Oxford: Oxford University Press, 2007.

Bakay, Gönül. "The Turk in English Renaissance Literature," *Open Democracy* (February 2003), http://www.opendemocracy.net/arts-europe_islam/article_982.jsp.

Ballaster, Ros. *Fabulous Orients: Fictions of the East in England 1662–1785.* Oxford: Oxford University Press, 2005.

Balzac, Jean-Louis Guez de. *Aristippe, ou De la cour.* Paris: Etienne de la Place, 1704.

Barber, Noel. *Lords of the Golden Horn.* London: Macmillan, 1973.

Bashan, Eliezer. "Contacts between Jews in Smyrna and the Levant Company of London in the Seventeenth and Eighteenth Centuries," *Jewish Historical Review* 29 (1983–1986): 53–73.

Baudier, Michel. *The History of the Imperiall Estate of the Grand Seigneurs: Their Habitations, Lives, Titles, Qualities, Workes, Revenues, Judgements, Officers, Favourites, Religion, Power, Government and Tyranny.* Translated by Edward Grimeston. London: William Stansby, 1635.

Baumer, Franklin L. "England, the Turk, and the Common Corps of Christendom," *The American Historical Review.* 50.1 (October, 1944): 26–48.

Bayouli, Tahar. "Elizabethan Orientalism and its Contexts: The Representation of the Orient in Early Modern English Drama," *International Journal of Euro-Mediterranean Studies* 1 (2008): 109–28.

Bell, Gary M. *A Handlist of British Diplomatic Representatives 1509–1688.* London: Royal Historical Society, 1990.

Bendysh, Sir Thomas. *News from Turkie, Or a True Relation of the Passages of the Right Honourable Sir Tho. Bendish, Baronet, Lord Ambassador, with the Grand Signieur at Constantinople,* (London, 1648). Reprint, London: EEBO Editions, 2011.

Bent, J. T., ed. *Early Voyages and Travels in the Levant.* Vol. 1. London: Hakluyt Society, 1893.

Berridge, G. R. *British Diplomacy in Turkey, 1583 to the Present: A Study in the Evolution of the Resident Embassy.* The Hague: Martinus Nijhoff, 2009.

Betts, C. J. *Early Deism in France.* The Hague: Martinus Nijhoff, 1984.

Biddulph, William, *The Travels of Certaine Englishmen.* London, 1609. *See* Purchas.

*Biographica Britannica.* Vol. 5. London: W. Innys, 1760.

Birch, Thomas, ed. *A Collection of the State Papers of John Thurloe, Esq., Secretary, First to the Council of State, And afterwards to the Two Protectors, Oliver and Richard Cromwell.* London: Printed for the Executors of F. Gyles, 1742.

Birken, Andreas. *Die Provinzen des Osmanisches Reiches.* Wiesbaden: Ludwig Reichert, 1976.

Bisaha, Nancy. *Creating East and West: Renaissance Humanists and Ottoman Turks.* Philadelphia: University of Pennsylvania Press, 2006.

Blount, Sir Henry. *A Voyage into the Levant* (1634) New York: General Books Reprints, 2010.

Bodin, Jean. *On Sovereignty.* Edited and translated by Julian H. Franklin. Cambridge: Cambridge University Press, 1996.

Boissard, Jean-Jacques. *Vitae et icones sultanarum Turcicorum, principum Persarum aliorumque illustrium heroum heroiarumque ab Osmanem usq[ue] ad Mahometem II.* Frankfurt, 1597.

Bon, Ottaviano. *The Sultan's Seraglio: An Intimate Portrait of Life at the Ottoman Court.* Translated by John Withers and Godfrey Goodwin. London: Saqi Books, 2001.

Bosworth, Clifford. *An Intrepid Scot: William Lithgow of Lanark's Travels in the Ottoman Lands, North Africa and Central Europe 1609–1621.* Farnham, UK: Ashgate, 2006.

Boyar, Ebru / Fleet, Kate. *A Social History of Ottoman Constantinople.* Cambridge: Cambridge University Press, 2009.

Brentjes, Sonja. "The Interest of the Republic of Letters in the Middle East, 1580–1700," *Science in Context* 12 (1999): 435–68.

———. *Travellers from Europe in the Ottoman and Safavid Empires, 16th-17th Centuries.* Farnham, UK: Ashgate, 2010.

Brown, John Pair. *The Darvishes, or Oriental Spiritualism.* London: Frank Cass (1868), 1968.

Burian, Orhan, ed. "A Dramatist of Turkish History and his Source: Goffe in the Light of Knolles." *Journal of the Royal Central Asian Society* (1953): 266–71.

———. "The Interest of the English in Turkey as Reflected in the Literature of the Renaissance." *Oriens* (1952): 209–29.

———. *The Report of Lello, third English Ambassador to the Sublime Porte.* Ankara: Türk Tarih Kurumu Basimevi, 1952.

Burke, Sir John Bernard. *A Genealogical and Heraldic History of the Extinct and Dormant Baronetcies of England.* London: Scott Webster and Geary, 1838.

Burke, Peter. *Lost (and Found) in Translation: A Cultural History of Translators and Translating in Early Modern Europe.* Wassenaar: Netherlands Institute for Advanced Study, 2006.

Burton, Jonathan. *Traffic and Turning: Islam and English Drama, 1579–1624.* Newark: University of Delaware Press, 2005.

Busbecq, Ogier Ghislen de. *Turkish Letters.* Translated by E. S. Forster (1927). London: Eland Books, 2005.

Çalişir, M. Fatih, "Decline of a 'Myth:' Perspectives on the Ottoman 'Decline,'" *The History School* (2011): 37–60.

Carr, Ralph. *The Mahumetaine or Turkish historie.* London, 1600.

Charry, Brinda, and Gitanjali Shahani. *Emissaries in Early Modern Literature and Culture: Mediation, Transmission, Traffic, 1550–1700.* Farnham, UK: Ashgate, 2008.

Chew, Samuel C. *The Crescent and the Rose: Islam and England during the Renaissance.* New York: Oxford: Oxford University Press, 1937.

Çirakman, Asli. *From the "Terror of the World" to the "Sick Man of Europe:" European Images of the Ottoman Empire and Society from the Sixteenth Century to the Nineteenth Century.* Bern: Peter Lang, 2005.

Clarendon, Henry Hyde, Earl of. *The State Letters of Henry, Earl of Clarendon, Lord Lieutenant of Ireland.* Vol 2. Edited by John Douglas. Oxford: Oxford University Press, 1763.

Cole, Richard G. "Sixteenth-Century Travel Books as a Source of European Attitudes towards Non-White and Non-Western Culture." *Proceedings of the American Philosophical Society* 116 (1972): 59–67.

Coles, Paul. *The Ottoman Impact on Europe*. New York: Harcourt, Brace and World, 1968.

Colyer, Justinus. *Journal du voyage de Mr. Collier, Résident à la Porte*. Translated by Vincent Minutoli. Paris: Gervais Clouzier, 1672.

Creagh, James. *Armenians, Koords and Turks*. London: Samuel Tinsley, 1880.

Creasy, Sir Edward. *History of the Ottoman Turks*. London: Bentley, 1877.

Dallam, Thomas. *See* Bent.

Darling, Linda T. "Ottoman Politics through British Eyes: Paul Rycaut's *Present State of the Ottoman Empire*." *Journal of World History* Vol. 5 (1994): 71–97.

———. *Revenue Raising and Legitimacy: Tax Collection and Financial Administration in the Ottoman Empire 1560–1660*. Leiden: Brill, 1995.

Dew, Nicholas. *Orientalism in Louis XIV's France*. Oxford: Oxford University Press, 2009.

Di Biase, Carmine, ed. *Travel and Translation in the Early Modern Period*. Amsterdam: Editions Rodopi, 2006.

Durnsteter, Eric R. *Venetians in Constantinople: Nation, Identity and Coexistence in the Early Modern Mediterranean*. Baltimore: Johns Hopkins University Press, 2006.

Ergene, Boğaç A. "On Ottoman Justice: Interpretations in Conflict (1600–1800)," *Islamic Law and Society*, 8.1 (2001): 52–87.

Eton, Sir William. *A Survey of the Turkish Empire*. London, 1799.

Evliya Çelebi. *An Ottoman Traveller: Selections from The Book of Travels*. Edited and translated by Robert Dankoff and Sooyong Kim. London: Eland Books, 2007.

Faroqhi, Suraiya. *The Ottoman Empire and the World Around It*. London: I. B. Tauris, 2008.

———, Bruce McGowan, Donald Quataert, and Sevket Pamuk. *An Economic and Social History of the Ottoman Empire. Vol. 2, 1600–1914*. Cambridge: Cambridge University Press, 1997.

Filmer, Sir Robert. *Patriarcha and Other Writings*. Edited by Johann P. Somerville. Cambridge: Cambridge University Press, 1996.

Finkel, Caroline. *Osman's Dream: The History of the Ottoman Empire*. New York: Basic Books, 2005.

Fissel, Mark Charles, "Early Stuart Absolutism and the Strangers' Consulage," in T. G. Barnes, B. Sharp, and M. C. Fissel, eds. *Law and Authority in Early Modern England: Essays Presented to Thomas Garden Barnes*. Cranberry: Associated University Presses, 2007.

———, and Daniel Goffman. "Viewing the Scaffold from Constantinople: The Bendysh-Hyde Affair, 1647–51." *Albion* 22.3 (1990): 421–48.

Fraser, Antonia. *King Charles II*. London: Weidenfeld and Nicolson, 1980.

Freely, J. *Constantinople, the Imperial City*. New York: Viking, 1992.

Games, Alison. *The Web of Empire: English Cosmopolitanism in an Age of Expansion, 1560–1660*. Oxford: Oxford University Press, 2009.

Garcia, Humberto. *Islam and the English Enlightenment*. Baltimore: Johns Hopkins University Press, 2012.

Gatenby, E. V. *Material for a Study of Turkish Words in English*. Ankara: Tarih-Coğrafya Fakültes Dergisi, 1954. http://www.dergiler.ankara.ed.tr/dergiler26/1246/14245.pdf.

Gilles, Pierre. *The Antiquities of Constantinople.* Translated by John Ball and edited by Ronald G. Musto. New York: Italica Press, 1988.

Goffman, Daniel. *Britons in the Ottoman Empire 1642–1660.* Seattle: University of Washington Press, 1998.

———. *The Ottoman Empire and Early Modern Europe.* Cambridge: Cambridge University Press, 2002.

Gök, Nedjet. "An Introduction to the *beràt* in Ottoman Diplomatics." *Bulgarian Historical Review* (2001): 141–50.

Goldstone, Jack A. "East and West in the Seventeenth Century: Political Crises in Stuart England, Ottoman Turkey, and Ming China," *Comparative Studies in Society and History* 31 (1988): 103–42.

Goodwin, Jason. *Lords of the Horizons: A History of the Ottoman Empire.* New York: Henry Holt, 1999.

Greaves, John. *See* Withers.

Grotius, Hugo. *De jure belli ac pacis.* Translated by Francis Kelsey (1925). http://www.lonang.com.

Habesci, Elias. *The Present State of the Ottoman Empire, Containing a more Accurate and Interesting Account of the Religion, Government, Military Establishment, Manners, Customs and Amusements of the Turks. . . ..* London, 1794.

Hadfield, Andrew, ed. *Amazons, Savages and Machiavels: Travel and Colonial Writing in English 1550–1630.* Oxford: Oxford University Press, 2001.

———. *Literature, Travel, and Colonial Writing in the English Renaissance 1545–1625.* Oxford: Oxford University Press, 1998.

Hagen, Gottfried. "Ottoman Understandings of the World in the Seventeenth Century." In *An Ottoman Mentality: the World of Evliya Çelebi,* edited by Robert Dankoff, 215–56. Leiden: Brill, 2004.

Hamilton, A., M. van den Boogert, and Bart Westerveel, eds. *The Republic of Letters and the Levant.* Leiden: Brill, 2005.

Haynes, Jonathan. *The Humanist as Traveller: George Sandys's Relation of a Journey Begun An. Dom. 1610.* Rutherford: Fairleigh Dickinson University Press, 1986.

Henriques, H. S. Q. *The Jews and the English Law.* Clark, NJ: Law Book Exchange Reprints, 2006.

Heyd, Uriel. "The Jewish Community of Istanbul in the Seventeenth Century," *Oriens* 6 (1953): 299–314.

Heywood, Colin, ed. *Writing Ottoman History: Documents and Interpretations.* Farnham, UK: Ashgate, 2002.

Hill, Aaron. *A Full and Just Account of the Present State of the Ottoman Empire in all its Branches: With the Government, and Policy, Religion, Customs, and Way of Living of the Turks, in General Faithfully Related from Serious Observations taken in many Years Travels thro' those Countries.* London, 1709.

Horniker, Arthur. "Anglo-French Rivalry in the Levant from 1583 to 1612." *Journal of Modern History* 18.4 (December 1946): 289–305.

———. "The Corps of the Janizaries." *Gorget and Sash* 3, 1–2 http://www.xenophon-mil. org/milhist/modern/janizar.htm.

———. "William Harborne and the Beginning of Anglo-Turkish Diplomatic and Commercial Relations." *Journal of Modern History* 14.3 (September 1942): 289–316.

Hughes, Thomas Patrick. *A Dictionary of Islam, being a Cyclopaedia of the Doctrines, Rites, Ceremonies and Customs, together with the Technical and Theological Terms of the Muslim Religion* (London, 1886). Reprint, Chicago: Kazi Publications, 1994.

Hunter, Michael, ed. *Printed Images in Early Modern Britain: Essays in Interpretation.* Farnham, UK: Ashgate, 2010.

Imber, Colin. *The Ottoman Empire: The Structure of Power.* New York: Palgrave Macmillan, 2009.

Inalcik, Hali. *History of the Ottoman Empire Classical Age 1300–1600.* London: Phoenix Books, 1988.

Ingram, Anders. "English Literature on the Ottoman Turks in the Sixteenth and Seventeenth Centuries." PhD thesis, Durham University, 2009.

Jacobsen, G. J. *William Blathwayt, a Late Seventeenth Century English Administrator.* New Haven: Yale University Press, 1932.

Jardine, Lisa. "The Original Artful Dodger," BBC Series "A Point of View," http://news. bbc.co.uk/go/pr/fr (2007).

Jeffery, George. "The Levant Company in Smyrna." *Notes and Queries* 11, Ser. 12 (July 1915): 61–63.

*Journals of the House of Commons, March 15, 1642 to December 24, 1644.* Vol. 3. London: House of Commons, 1803.

Kafadar, Cemal. "The Ottomans and Europe, 1450–1600." In *Handbook of European History 1400–1600,* edited By T. Brady, H. Oberman, and J. Tracy, 589–636. Leiden: Brill, 1995.

———. "The Question of Ottoman Decline," *Harvard Middle Eastern and Islamic Review* (1997–1998): 30–75.

Kaplan, Yosef. "Thomas Coenen in Smyrna: Reflections of a Dutch Calvinist on the Sabbatean Awakening of the Levantine Jews," Introduction to *Vain Expectations of the Jews as Revealed in the Figure of Sabbatai Zevi,* by Thomas Coenen, 22–108. Jerusalem: Ben-Zion Dinur Institute for Research in Jewish History, 1998): 22–108.

Kinross, Lord Patrick. *The Ottoman Centuries: The Rise and Fall of the Turkish Empire.* New York: Harper Perennial, 2002

Kirk, Thomas Allison. *Genoa and the Sea: Policy and Power in an Early Modern Maritime Republic 1559–1684.* Baltimore: Johns Hopkins University Press, 2005.

Knolles, Richard. *General History of the Turks.* London, 1603.

———. *The Turkish History, Comprehending the Origin of that Nation and the Growth of the Othoman Empire, with the Lives and Conquests of their several Kings and Emperors. Written by Mr. Knolles, and Continu'd by the Honourable Sir Paul Rycaut, to the Peace at Carlowitz, in the Year 1699. And abridg'd by Mr. Savage. Revised and Approv'd by the late Sir Paul Rycaut, and adorn'd with nine and twenty copper-plates, of the Effigies of the several Princes, &c.* 2 vols. London: Isaac Cleave, 1701.

Knoppers, Laura Lunger, ed. *Puritanism and its Discontents*. Newark: University of Delaware Press, 2003.

Konrad, Felix. "From the 'Turkish Menace' to Exoticism and Orientalism: Islam as Antithesis of Europe (1453–1914)?" In *European History Online* (EGO). Mainz: Institute of European History, 2011, http://www.ieg.ego.eu/konradf-2010-en

Kornrumpf, Hans-Jürgen. *Turkish Universal Dictionary*. Berlin: Langenscheidt, 1979.

Krstić, Tijana. *Contested Conversions to Islam: Narratives of Religious Change in the Early Modern Ottoman Empire*. Stanford, CA: Stanford University Press, 2011.

Lachs, Phyllis E. *The Diplomatic Corps under Charles II and James II*. Piscataway: Rutgers University Press, 1966.

Levine, Lynn. *Frommer's Constantinople*. Hoboken, NJ: Wiley Publishing Company, 2008.

Lewis, Bernard. *Constantinople and the Civilization of the Ottoman Empire*. Norman: University of Oklahoma Press, 1963.

———. *Cultures in Conflict: Christians, Muslims and Jews in the Age of Discovery*. Oxford: Oxford University Press, 1995.

———. *Islam and the West*. New York: Oxford: Oxford University Press, 1994.

———. *A Middle East Mosaic: Fragments of Life, Letters and History*. New York: Random House, 2000.

———. *The Muslim Discovery of Europe*. New York: W. W. Norton, 2001.

Longino, Michèle L. "Imagining the Turk in Seventeeth Century France: Grelot's Version," http://www.duke.edu/~michelel/projects/visions.

Lucinge, René, sieur des Alymes. *The beginning, continuance and decay of estates, wherein are handled many notable questions concerning the establishment of empires and monarchies*. Translated by Sir John Finnett. London, 1606.

MacLean, Gerald. *The Rise of Oriental Travel: English Visitors to the Ottoman Empire 1580–1720*. Basingstoke, UK: Palgrave, 2004.

———. "Strolling in Syria with William Biddulph," *Criticism* (Summer 2004): 1–20.

———, and Nabil Matar. *Britain and the Islamic World 1558–1712*. New York: Oxford University Press, 2011.

Mansel, Philip. *Constantinople, City of the World's Desire 1453–1924*. Harmondsworth, UK: Penguin Books, 1997.

Marana, Giovanni Paolo. *Letters Writ by a Turkish Spy who lived for five and forty years undiscovered at Paris: giving an impartial account to the Divan at Constantinople, of the most remarkable transactions of Europe: and discovering several intrigues and secrets of the Christian courts (especially that of France)*. Translated by William Bradshaw. London, 1687.

Marcell, Robert. "Kara Mustafa: The Ottoman Architect of the 1683 Siege of Vienna," http://www.suite101.com/content/kara-mustafa-a125082.

Marcus, Abraham. *The Middle East on the Eve of Modernity*. New York: Columbia University Press, 1989.

Marsh, Henry. *A new survey of the Turkish Empire and government in a brief history deduced to the present time, and to the reign of the new Grand Signior, Mahomet the IV, the present and XIV emperor: with their laws, religion, and customs: as also an account of the siege of Newhausel*. London, 1633.

Marshall, John. *John Locke: Toleration and Early Enlightenment Culture*. Cambridge: Cambridge University Press, 2006.

Masters, Bruce, and Gábor Ágoston. *Encyclopedia of the Ottoman Empire*. New York: Facts on File, 2009.

Matar, Nabil. *Europe through Arab Eyes 1578–1727*. New York: Columbia University Press, 2008.

———. *Turks, Moors and Englishmen in the Age of Discovery*. New York: Columbia University Press, 1999.

Mather, James. *Pashas: Traders and Travellers in the Islamic World*. New Haven: Yale University Press, 2011.

McJannet, Linda. *The Sultan Speaks: Dialogue in English Plays and Histories about the Ottoman Empire*. New York: Palgrave Macmillan, 2006.

Melvin, Patrick. "Sir Paul Rycaut's Memoranda and Letters from Ireland 1686–87," *Analecta Hibernica* 27 (1972): 125–99.

Meserve, Margaret. *Empires of Islam in Renaissance Thought*. Cambridge, MA: Harvard University Press, 2008.

Mignot, Vincent. *The History of the Turkish or Ottoman Empire from its Foundation in 1300 to the Peace of Belgrade in 1740*. Volume 3. Translated by A. Hawkins. London, 1747.

Moczar, Diane. *Islam at the Gates: How Christendom Defeated the Ottoman Turks*. Manchester, NH: Sophia Institute Press, 2008.

Montague, Lady Mary Wortley. *Turkish Embassy Letters*. Edited by Malcolm Jack, Introduction by Anita Desai. London: Pickering, 1993.

Moody, Jim, and Ellen Moody. "'I on myself can live:' An Unfinished Study of Ann Finch," http://www.jimandellen.org/finch.

Moran, Berna. *A Bibliography of English Publications about the Turks from the 15th Century to the 18th Century*. Istanbul: Istanbul University Press, 1964.

Moryson, Fynes. *Itinerary, Containing his Ten Years Travel through the Twelve Dominions of Germany, Bohemia, Switzerland, Netherland, Denmark, Poland, Italy, Turkey, France, Scotland and Ireland*. Vol. 3. London, 1617.

Na'ima, Mustafa. *Annals of the Turkish Empire from 1591 to 1659*. Translated by Charles Fraser. 2 vols. London: Oriental Translations Fund, 1832.

Neudecker, H. "Wojciech Bobowski and his *Turkish Grammar* (1666)." *Dutch Studies in Near Eastern Languages and Literatures* 2 (1996): 167–92.

Nicolay, Nicholas. *The Navigations, peregrinations and voyages made into Turkie by Nicholas Nicholay*. Translated by Thomas Washington. London, 1585.

Nicolle, David. *The Janissaries*. Botley, UK: Osprey Publishing, 1995.

Norman, Daniel. *Islam and the West: The Making of an Image*. Edinburgh: Edinburgh University Press, 1960.

Orr, Bridget. *Empire on the English Stage 1660–1714*. Cambridge: Cambridge University Press, 2001.

Osborne, Toby. *Dynasty and Diplomacy in the Court of Savoy: Political Culture and the Thirty Years War.* Cambridge: Cambridge University Press, 2002.

Ousterhout, Robert G., ed. *Studies in Constantinople and Beyond: the Freely Papers.* Volume I. Philadelphia: University of Pennsylvania Museum of Archaeology, 2007.

Pamuk, Orhan. *Istanbul: Memories and the City.* Translated by Maureen Freely. New York: Vintage, 2006.

Parry, V. J. *Richard Knolles' History of the Turks.* Edited by Salih Özharan. Istanbul: The Economic and Social History Foundation of Turkey, 2003.

Patrides, C. A. "'The Bloody and Cruell Turke:' the Background of a Renaissance Commonplace." *Studies in the Renaissance* 10 (1963): 126–35.

Peck, Linda Levy. *Consuming Splendor: Society and Culture in the Seventeenth Century.* Cambridge: Cambridge University Press, 2005.

Peirce, Leslie P. *The Imperial Harem: Women and Sovereignty in the Ottoman Empire.* Oxford: Oxford University Press, 1995.

Penzer, N. M. *The Harem: Inside the Grand Seraglio of the Turkish Sultans* (London, 1900). New York: Dover Books, 2005.

Pepys, Samuel. *Diary,* 21 April 1669. http://www.pepysdiary.com/encyclopedia/766.

———. *The Shorter Pepys.* Edited by Robert Latham. Berkeley: University of California, 1985.

Picarsic, Jonathan. "T. B., a Levant Company Factor on Pilgrimage, 1669," www. faculty. colostate-pueblo.edu.

Piccirillo, Anthony. "'A Vile, Infamous, Diabolical Treaty:' The Franco-Ottoman Alliance of Francis I and the Eclipse of the Christendom Ideal." Senior honors thesis, Georgetown University, 2009. http://hdl.handle.net/10822/55/65/.

Pignot, Hélène. "A Trip to the Origins of Christianity: Sir Paul Rycaut's and Thomas Smith's accounts of the Greek Church in the seventeenth century." *Studies in Travel Writing* 13 (2009): 193–205.

Pippidi, Andrei. *Visions of the Ottoman World in Renaissance Europe.* New York: Columbia University Press, 2013.

Pitcher, Donald. *An Historical Atlas of the Ottoman Empire.* Leiden: Brill, 1972.

Piterberg, Gabriel. *An Ottoman Tragedy: History and Historiography at Play.* Berkeley: University of California Press, 2003.

Plomer, Henry. *A Dictionary of the Printers and Booksellers who were at work in England, Scotland and Ireland 1668–1725.* Oxford: Oxford University Press, 1922.

Postel, Guillaume. *De la république des Turcs et là au l'occasion s'offrera, de moeurs et loy des tous Muhamedistes.* Paris, 1560.

Purver, Margery. *The Royal Society: Concept and Creation.* London: Routledge, 1967.

*Quran.* Translated by Ustadh Abdullah Yusuf Ali. Medina: King Fahd Holy Quran Publishing Company, 1987.

Rasmussen, William Middendorf. *Reinterpreting Richard Knolles's* Generall Historie of the Turkes *as a Political Treatise.* Cambridge, MA: Harvard University Press, 2004.

Rawashdeh, Mohammed Ahmed. "A Confined Amorous Being: the Eastern Woman between Travel Literature and English Drama." *Damascus University Journal* 28 (2012): 91–114.

Roe, Sir Thomas. *Negotiations in his Embassy to the Ottoman Porte from 1621 to 1628.* London: Samuel Richardson, 1740.

Rogerson, Barnaby. *The Prophet Muhammad: A Biography.* London: Abacus Books, 2006.

Rosedale, Honyel Gough. *Queen Elizabeth and the Levant Company.* London: H. Frowde, 1904.

Ross, Alexander. *The Alcoran of Mahomet, Translated out of Arabique into French: By the Sieur Du Ryer, Lord of Malezair, and Resident for the King of France, at Alexandria.* London, 1649.

Ross, Ian Campbell. "Ottomans, Incas, and Irish Literature: Reading Rycaut." *Eighteenth Century Ireland* 22 (2007): 11–27.

Rothman, E. Natalie. *Brokering Empire: Trans-Imperial Subjects between Venice and Constantinople.* Ithaca, NY: Cornell University Press, 2012.

Rouillard, C. D. *The Turk in French History, Thought and Literature.* 1940 Reprint, New York: AMS Reprints, 1973.

Rubiés, Joan-Pau. "New Worlds and Renaissance Ethnology." *History and Anthropology* 6 (1993): 157–97.

Rycaut, Sir Paul. *The History of the Present State of the Ottoman Empire, Containing the Maxims of the Turkish Polity, the most Material Points of the Mahometan Religion, their Sects and Heresies, their Convents and Religious Votaries. Their Military Discipline, with an Exact Computation of their Forces both by Sea and Land.* The 6th ed. Corrected. London: Charles Brome, 1686. Reprint, London: EEBO, 2011.

———. *The Present State of the Greek and Armenian Churches, Anno Christi 1678.* London: John Starkey, 1679.

———. "A Relation of the Small Creatures Called Sable-Mice, which Have Lately Come in Troops into Lapland, about Thorne, and Other Places Adjacent to the Mountains, in Innumerable Multitudes. Communicated from Sir Paul Rycaut, F. R. S. to Mr. Ellis, and from him to the R[oyal] S[ociety]." *Philosophical Transactions of the Royal Society* 21 (1699): 110–12.

———. *The Turkish History* (see Knolles).

Said, Edward. *Orientalism.* New York: Vintage Books, 1994.

Salahi, M. A. *Muhammad, Man and Prophet.* Shaftesbury, UK: Element Books, 1995.

Sanderson, John. *The Travels of John Sanderson in the Levant, 1584–1602.* Edited by Sir William Foster. London: Hakluyt Society, 1921.

Sandys, George. *Sandys Travels: Containing an History of the Original and Present State of the Turkish Empire, The Mahometan Religion and Ceremonies, A Description of Constantinople, also, of Greece, with the Religion and Custom of the Grecians…of Aegypt, A Description of the Holy-Land, Lastly, Italy* (1621). Seventh Edition (1673). La Vergne, TN: Nabu Public Domain Reprints, 2011.

Sayer, John. *Jean Racine, Life and Legend.* Bern: Peter Lang, 2006.

Schmuck, Stephan. *Politics of Anxiety: The* imago Turci *in Early Modern English Prose, c. 1550–1620.* PhD thesis, University of Wales, Aberystswyth, 2007.

Schwoebel, Robert. *The Shadow of the Crescent: The Renaissance Image of the Turk 1453–1517.* New York: St. Martin's Press, 1967.

Şenlen, Sila. "Ottoman Sultans in English Drama between 1580 and 1660," http://www.dergiler.ankara.edu.tr.

——. "Richard Knolles' *The Generall Historie of the Turkes* as a Reflection of Christian Historiography," http://www.dergiler.ankara.edu.tr.

Setton, Kenneth M. *Venice, Austria and the Turks in the Seventeenth Century.* Philadelphia: American Philosophical Society, 1991.

Shapiro, Barbara J. *Political Communication and Political Culture in England 1558–1688.* Stanford, CA: Stanford University Press, 2012.

Shaw, E. Kural, and C. E. Heywood, eds. *English and Continental Views of the Ottoman Empire.* Los Angeles: William Andrews Clark Memorial Library, 1972.

Shaw, Stanford J. *History of the Ottoman Empire and Modern Turkey.* Volume I: *The Empire of the Gazis / The Rise and Decline of the Ottoman Empire 1280–1808.* Cambridge: Cambridge: Cambridge University Press, 1988.

Singh, N. K. and A. Samiuddin, eds. *Encyclopaedic Historiography of the Muslim World.* 3 volumes. Delhi: Global Vision Publishing House, 2004.

Sisneros, Katie S. "Fearing the 'Turban'd Turk:' Socio-Economic Access to Genre and the 'Turke' of Early Modern English Dramas and Broadside Ballads." MA Thesis, University of Nebraska, 2010.

Skilliter, Susan. *William Harborne and the Trade with Turkey, 1578–1582.* London: British Academy, 1977.

Stephen, Sir Leslie, ed. "Sir Paul Rycaut," *Dictionary of National Biography.* Vol. 50. London: Macmillan 1897, 39–40.

Subrahmanyam, Sanjay. "On World Historians in the Sixteenth Century," *Representations* 91 (Summer 2005): 26–57.

Suranyi, Anna. *The Genius of the English Nation: Travel Writing and National Identity in Early Modern England.* Cranbury, NJ: Associated Universities Press, 2008.

Swinhoe, Gilbert. *The Unhappy Fair Irene.* London: EEBO Reprints, 2011.

Tavernier, Jean-Baptiste. *Nouvelle relation de l'interieur du serrail du Grand Seigneur.* Paris, 1675.

Taylor, Jane. *Imperial Constantinople: A Traveller's Guide.* London: I. B. Tauris, 1998.

Temple, Sir William. *The Works of Sir William Temple, Bart.* Vol. 3. London: T. C. and J. Rivington, 1814.

Tezcan, Baki. *The Second Ottoman Empire: Politics and Social Transformation in the Early Modern World.* Cambridge: Cambridge University Press, 2010.

——. "The 1622 Military Rebellion in Constantinople: A Historiographical Journey," *International Journal of Turkish Studies* (2002): 25–43.

Thornton, Thomas. *The Present State of Turkey.* London: Mawman, 1807.

Toomer, G. J. *Eastern Wisedome and Learning: The Study of Arabic in Seventeenth Century England.* Oxford: Oxford University Press, 1996.